A
MARGINAL
JEW

THE ANCHOR BIBLE REFERENCE LIBRARY is designed to be a third major component of the Anchor Bible group, which includes the Anchor Bible commentaries on the books of the Old Testament, the New Testament, and the Apocrypha, and the Anchor Bible Dictionary. While the Anchor Bible commentaries and the Anchor Bible Dictionary are structurally defined by their subject matter, the Anchor Bible Reference Library will serve as a supplement on the cutting edge of the most recent scholarship. The new series will be open-ended; its scope and reach are nothing less than the biblical world in its totality, and its methods and techniques the most up-to-date available or devisable. Separate volumes will deal with one or more of the following topics relating to the Bible: anthropology, archaeology, ecology, economy, geography, history, languages and literatures, philosophy, religion(s), theology.

As with the Anchor Bible commentaries and the Anchor Bible Dictionary, the philosophy underlying the Anchor Bible Reference Library finds expression in the following: the approach is scholarly, the perspective is balanced and fair-minded, the methods are scientific, and the goal is to inform and enlighten. Contributors are chosen on the basis of their scholarly skills and achievements, and they come from a variety of religious backgrounds and communities. The books in the Anchor Bible Reference Library are intended for the broadest possible readership, ranging from world-class scholars, whose qualifications match those of the authors, to general readers, who may not have special training or skill in studying the Bible but are as enthusiastic as any dedicated professional in expanding their knowledge of the Bible and its world.

David Noel Freedman
GENERAL EDITOR

THE ANCHOR BIBLE REFERENCE LIBRARY

A MARGINAL JEW

RETHINKING THE HISTORICAL JESUS

VOLUME ONE:
THE ROOTS OF THE PROBLEM AND THE PERSON

JOHN P. MEIER

ABRL

Doubleday

NEW YORK   LONDON   TORONTO   SYDNEY   AUCKLAND

THE ANCHOR BIBLE REFERENCE LIBRARY

Published by Doubleday
a division of Bantam Doubleday Dell Publishing Group, Inc.
666 Fifth Avenue, New York, New York 10103

The Anchor Bible Reference Library, Doubleday, and the portrayal of an anchor with the
letters ABRL are trademarks of Doubleday, a division of Bantam Doubleday Dell
Publishing Group, Inc.

Excerpts from *The Gnostic Scriptures* by Bentley Layton, copyright © 1987 by Bentley
Layton, reprinted by permission of Doubleday, a division of Bantam Doubleday Dell
Publishing Group, Inc.

Book design by Patrice Fodero

Library of Congress Cataloging-in-Publication Data
Meier, John P.
    A marginal Jew : rethinking the historical Jesus / John P. Meier. — 1st ed.
        p.   cm. — (The Anchor Bible reference library)
    Includes bibliographical references and index.
    Contents: v. 1. Origins of the problem and the person
    ISBN 0-385-26425-9 (v. 1) : $25.00
    1. Jesus Christ—Historicity. 2. Jesus Christ—Jewishness. I. Title. II. Series.
BT303.2.M465 1991
232.9—dc20   91-10538
                                                  CIP

Imprimatur — New York, June 25, 1991 — The Most Rev. Patrick J. Sheridan, V.G.

First Edition

10 9 8 7 6 5 4 3 2 1

November 1991

Elizabeth O'Reilly Meier

אשת־חיל מי ימצא

Prov 31:10

Contents

ACKNOWLEDGMENTS   ix

INTRODUCTION   1

PART ONE
Roots of the Problem

CHAPTER 1
Basic Concepts: The Real Jesus and the Historical Jesus   21

CHAPTER 2
Sources: The Canonical Books of the New Testament   41

CHAPTER 3
Sources: Josephus   56

CHAPTER 4
Sources: Other Pagan and Jewish Writings   89

CHAPTER 5
Sources: The *Agrapha* and the Apocryphal Gospels   112

CHAPTER 6
Criteria: How Do We Decide What Comes from Jesus?   167

CHAPTER 7
Conclusion to Part One: Why Bother?   196

PART TWO
Roots of the Person

CHAPTER 8
In the Beginning . . . The Origins of Jesus of Nazareth   205

CHAPTER 9
In the Interim . . . Part I: Language, Education, and
Socioeconomic Status   253

CHAPTER 10
In the Interim . . . Part II: Family, Marital Status,
and Status as a Layman   316

CHAPTER 11
"In the Fifteenth Year" . . . A Chronology of Jesus' Life   372

MAP OF PALESTINE IN THE TIME OF JESUS   434

MAP OF THE GALILEE OF JESUS' MINISTRY   435

CHART OF THE FAMILY OF HEROD THE GREAT   436

CHART OF THE REGNAL YEARS OF THE ROMAN
PRINCIPES (EMPERORS)   437

LIST OF ABBREVIATIONS   439

INDEX OF SCRIPTURE

AUTHOR INDEX

INDEX OF SUBJECTS

Acknowledgments

Many people have helped me complete the first volume of this work; only a few can be mentioned here. Various colleagues at the Catholic University of America were kind enough to read portions of the manuscript; chief among them are Professors John P. Galvin, Francis T. Gignac, William P. Loewe, Frank J. Matera, and Carl J. Peter. I have also been blessed by the generous assistance of scholars at other institutions: Professors Myles M. Bourke of Fordham University, N.Y., Harold W. Attridge and John J. Collins of the University of Notre Dame, John P. Reumann of Lutheran Theological Seminary, and Raymond E. Brown, Professor Emeritus of Union Theological Seminary, N.Y. I wish to extend a special word of recognition to Professors Louis H. Feldman of Yeshiva University, N.Y., and Shaye J. D. Cohen of Jewish Theological Seminary, N.Y., for their wise counsel on my treatment of Josephus. No amount of thanks could repay my debt to Professor David Noel Freedman, the editor of the Anchor Bible series, for his invaluable suggestions and corrections along every step of my path.

I also wish to thank the staff members of the libraries at the Catholic University of America, the Woodstock Theological Library at Georgetown University, the Berkeley Theological Union, the Dominican House of Studies, Washington, D.C., Union Theological Seminary, N.Y., St. Joseph's Seminary, Yonkers, N.Y., and Harvard Divinity School. Finally, I owe a word of gratitude to Teresa D'Orsogna, Thomas Cahill, and Michael Iannazzi, my editors at Doubleday, for their patience and understanding, and to Professors Christopher T. Begg and Kathleen Weber for their help in proofreading and indexing.

Portions of Chapters 1 and 7 appeared as "The Historical Jesus: Rethinking Some Concepts," *TS* 51 (1990) 3–24; portions of Chapter 3 appeared as "Jesus in Josephus: A Modest Proposal," *CBQ* 52 (1990) 76–103. I am grateful to both journals for permission to use the material in this book.

A
MARGINAL
JEW

INTRODUCTION

1. THE NATURE AND ORIGIN OF THIS BOOK

This book grapples with one of the greatest puzzles of modern religious scholarship, the historical Jesus. As I will explain at length in Chapter 1, by the "historical Jesus" I mean the Jesus whom we can recover, recapture, or reconstruct by using the scientific tools of modern historical research. Granted the fragmentary state of our sources and the often indirect nature of the arguments we must use, this "historical Jesus" will always remain a scientific construct, a theoretical abstraction that does not and cannot coincide with the full reality of Jesus of Nazareth as he actually lived and worked in Palestine during the 1st century of our era. Properly understood, such an approach seeks neither to prove any faith stance nor to attack it. My method follows a simple rule: it prescinds from what Christian faith or later Church teaching says about Jesus, without either affirming or denying such claims.

To explain to my academic colleagues what I propose to do in this book, I often use the fantasy of the "unpapal conclave." Suppose that a Catholic, a Protestant, a Jew, and an agnostic—all honest historians cognizant of 1st-century religious movements—were locked up in the bowels of the Harvard Divinity School library, put on a spartan diet, and not allowed to emerge until they had hammered out a consensus document on who Jesus of Nazareth was and what he intended in his own time and place. An essential requirement of this document would be that it be based on purely historical sources and arguments. The resulting unreligious "formula of concord" would suffer from all the ills endemic to ecumenical statements drawn up by committees. At times ambiguous language would be carefully chosen to paper over differences, at times points of divergence on which no agreement could be reached would have to be openly admitted. Probably this white paper on Jesus would reflect fully the opinions of no one member of the famished conclave. Certainly it would not contain affirmations that the Catholic or Protestant member would firmly hold by faith. The basic requirement that the consensus document be open to verification by any and all persons using the means of modern historical research would produce a narrow focus, a fragmentary vision, perhaps even distortions.

Nevertheless, something would be gained. We would have a rough draft of what that will-o'-the-wisp, "all reasonable people," could say about the historical Jesus. The document could serve as common ground, a starting point for dialogue between Christians and Jews, between various Christian confessions, and between believers and nonbelievers, as well as an invitation to further research by both historians and theologians. Such a limited consensus statement, which does not claim to act as a substitute for the Christ of faith, is the modest goal of the present work.

This book on the Jesus of history has a long history of its own. In 1984 I was asked by Professor Raymond E. Brown of Union Theological Seminary in New York to write an article on the Jesus of history for the new edition of the *Jerome Biblical Commentary*, which was published in 1990.[1] It was perhaps symptomatic of the state of American Catholic biblical studies in the sixties that no extended treatment of the historical Jesus was included in the original edition of the *Jerome Biblical Commentary*, published in 1968.[2] Hence I had to start from scratch; the ensuing research proved to be much more intriguing and engaging than I had first expected.

During the time of my research and writing, I was requested by a number of organizations to supply popular lectures and articles that would distill the results of my more technical work. These attempts at popularization included an article in the "Outlook" section of the Washington *Post* in December 1984[3] and a much longer essay in the *New York Times Book Review* in December 1986.[4] A still lengthier study was later published in my collected essays, *The Mission of Christ and His Church*.[5]

Around this time, early in 1987, a number of colleagues at Catholic University and in the Catholic Biblical Association urged me to write a book-length treatment of the historical Jesus for use with students in the classroom as well as for the educated lay reader. At first I was hesitant to attempt a project so often launched with such mixed results. But Professor Joseph A. Komonchak of Catholic University pointed out to me that there was at the present time a real lacuna in solid presentations of the historical Jesus aimed at both doctoral-level students and the more general audience of clergy, seminarians, and educated laity. The well-known *Jesus of Nazareth* by Günther Bornkamm,[6] originally published in 1956, is now somewhat dated; and recent work on early Judaism leads one to detect in Bornkamm's portrait of Jesus of Nazareth some of the features of those two great Martins of Germany, Luther and Heidegger.[7] The more recent and extensive *Jesus and Judaism* by E. P. Sanders (1985)[8] avoids many of the pitfalls of Bornkamm's *Jesus,* yet some of Sanders' positions on Jesus have proved highly controversial. As in the 1st century, so today: no one's Jesus—and no one Jesus—suits everyone.

By a happy coincidence, it was around this time that Professor David Noel Freedman approached me with a request to write a Jesus book for the Anchor Bible Reference Library series. It was with much misgiving that I agreed. Despite all the encouragement I have received, the scattered rubble left by two centuries of questing for Jesus has often made me ask: Why even try where so many have failed? Why join the legion of scholars who have peered narcissistically into the pool of the historical Jesus only to see themselves? No other line of research seems so geared to making skeptics out of scholars. From Jesus the violent revolutionary to Jesus the gay magician, from Jesus the apocalyptic fanatic to Jesus the wisdom teacher or Cynic philosopher unconcerned about eschatology, every conceivable scenario, every extreme theory imaginable, has long since been proposed, with opposite positions canceling each other out and eager new writers repeating the mistakes of the past. In one sense, there are enough "Jesus books" to last three lifetimes, and a sinful Buddhist might well be condemned to spend his next three incarnations wading through them.

2. REASONS FOR TRYING

Yet, in another sense, each biblical scholar—indeed, any educated person interested in Christian origins—cannot avoid the challenge of facing and answering key questions for himself or herself. I often remember a philosophy professor who taught me years ago asking my class why anyone should struggle with the question of whether or how we can know truth, when the greatest minds down through the centuries have come up with contradictory answers to that question. Why bother to try when the best and the brightest have floundered? One thoughtful student replied that no one thinks that we should stop the quest for and the practice of love, just because our forebears have made a mess of that subject. There are certain great questions that each human being has to work out for himself or herself. We learn from past quests, to be sure, but we cannot substitute the lessons of others for our own personal wrestling with the central problems of life, problems that each person must face squarely alone. In effect, my fellow student was quoting Plato back to the professor: the unexamined life is not worth living—and it is an examination we cannot pay someone else to take for us.

If this be true of every person's need to search for answers about the nature of truth, the reality of God, the meaning of life and death and what may lie beyond, it is also true of every educated Christian's need to search for answers about the reality and meaning of the man named Jesus. To be sure, a student first learns from studies done by others—but only to decide how best to grapple with the problem firsthand; that is what education is all about. Indeed, in view of Jesus' impact on all of Western civilization, no person of any religious persuasion can be considered truly educated today if he or she has not investigated to some degree what historical research can tell us about this enigmatic figure who unleashed one of the major religious and cultural forces of the world. The unexamined religious life—or even antireligious life—is not worth living.

3. THE QUEST FOR OBJECTIVITY

Still, the very nature of this intense personal grappling with an emotionally charged question makes one doubt whether any objective perspective is possible. Even the most careful contemporary scholars have left their own lineaments on the portraits of Jesus they painted. How could it be otherwise? Nevertheless, this inevitable influence of one's personal stance does not justify junking all objectivity in favor of a Jesus manufactured by new journalism. Objectivity in the quest for the historical Jesus is, to borrow a phrase from the theologian Karl Rahner, an "asymptotic goal." It is a goal we have to keep pressing toward, even though we never fully reach it. Pressing toward the goal is what keeps us on track. Concretely, that means knowing one's sources, having clear criteria for making historical judgments about them, learning from other questers past and present, and inviting the criticism of one's peers. All this will be attempted in the chapters that follow.

In a sense, though, the most important hedge against rampant subjectivism is an honest admission of one's own personal stance, one's own point of view and background. I say "most important" because I never cease to be amazed at how present-day writers will first censure past critics for not being sufficiently self-critical and then proceed to engage in an uncritical projection of their own ideas and agendas onto a portrait of the historical Jesus, hardly suppressing a gasp at how relevant he turns out to be. The late Norman Perrin's various approaches to Jesus all reflected the intellectual mentor he admired at a given moment: first Joachim Jeremias, then Rudolf Bultmann, and finally Paul Ricoeur and Mircea Eliade. Bultmann, of course, reflecting the intellectual currents in Germany after World War I, created Jesus the Heideggerian rabbi who issued the existential call to decision. The postliberal Protestant E. P. Sanders seems pleased that the Jesus he reconstructs is not the preacher of the social gospel beloved of classic liberal Protestants. If I may paint with a very broad brush: in general, Catholics worship a Catholic Chalcedonian Jesus, Protestants find their hearts strangely warmed by a Protestant Jesus, while Jews, quite naturally, seek to reclaim the Jewishness of Jesus.

All this is said not to drive us into academic agnosticism but to remind us that whatever is written is written from some point of view. There is no neutral Switzerland of the mind in the world of Jesus research. The rejection of a traditional faith stance does not mean neutrality, it simply means a different philosophical view that is itself a "faith stance" in the wide sense of the phrase. For example, Paul Hollenbach, who is interested in sociological analysis and liberation theology, openly admits that he pursues the Jesus of history "in order to overthrow, not simply correct 'the mistake called Christianity.' "[9] The mistake, says Hollenbach, was the "divinization of Jesus as Son of David, Christ, Son of God, Second Person in the Trinity, etc."[10] Rejecting any "incipient christology" prior to Jesus' crucifixion, Hollenbach logically denies that there is any continuity between the man Jesus of Nazareth and the Jesus Christ proclaimed by the Church. Obviously, Hollenbach is as firmly committed to a particular worldview as is a Roman Catholic or an orthodox Protestant. Whether we call it a bias, a *Tendenz*, a worldview, or a faith stance, everyone who writes on the historical Jesus writes from some ideological vantage point; no critic is exempt.[11] The solution to this dilemma is neither to pretend to an absolute objectivity that is not to be had nor to wallow in total relativism. The solution is to admit honestly one's own standpoint, to try to exclude its influence in making scholarly judgments by adhering to certain commonly held criteria, and to invite the correction of other scholars when one's vigilance inevitably slips.

In my own case, I must candidly confess that I work out of a Catholic context. My greatest temptation, therefore, will be to read back anachronistically the expanded universe of later Church teaching into the "big bang" moment of Jesus' earthly ministry. In what follows I will try my best to bracket what I hold by faith and examine only what can be shown to be certain or probable by historical research and logical argumentation. I hope non-Catholic scholars in particular will point out where I may fail to observe my own rules by reading Catholic theology into the quest. At the same time, Catholic readers of this book should not be upset by my holding to a strict distinction between what I know about Jesus by research and reason and what I hold by faith. Such a distinction is firmly within the Catholic tradition; for example, Thomas Aquinas distinguishes carefully between what we know by reason and what we affirm by faith. This book remains in the prior realm, while of course not denying the relevance of investigations into the historical Jesus for faith and theology. It is simply a matter of asking one question at a time. I would be delighted if systematic theologians would pick up where this book leaves off and pursue the line of thought further. But one book can do only so much.

4. A MARGINAL NOTE ON MARGINALITY

When David Noel Freedman, the editor of the Anchor Bible Reference Library series, first heard that I intended to entitle this book *A Marginal Jew*, he remarked that the title was "intriguing and a little mysterious."[12] It was meant to be exactly that, both a "come-on" and a riddle, something of a Hebrew *māšāl* (parable) in the sense of an engaging mind-teaser. Rather than being a pat answer or a rigid grid, the word "marginal" is meant to open up a set of questions and point out some possible ways of answering those questions. The category of the "marginal" is defined in different ways by different authors and is thus suited to reflect the puzzling, many-faceted reality of Jesus as well as provide some approaches to it.

The basic spatial image behind the word "marginal" is simple enough. A piece of paper, a group of people assembled in one place, and a geographical territory all have their margins, their borders, their extremities, their outer limits. This spatial image lends itself easily to metaphorical applications. The ordinary, the usual, the clear, the stable, the safe, the well-off all tend to operate in or gravitate toward the center or main part of the space available; the strange, the unusual, the ambiguous, the unstable, the dangerous, the impoverished all appear on or are pushed to the borders or margins of that space. Often the marginal reality, precisely because it is fixed on a border, finds itself straddling two different concrete areas, sharing something of both but belonging entirely to neither.

As employed by sociologists, anthropologists, and economists, however, the metaphorical use of the spatial image has generated a bewildering variety of more specific meanings. To take but one example, Janice E. Perlman, in her study of urban poverty and politics in Rio de Janeiro, distills five different ways of identifying marginal groups in urban society.[13] The marginal may be seen as (1) those located in substandard squatter settlements at the periphery of the city; (2) the jobless or underemployed; (3) migrants from a rural to an urban culture who are caught in the transition; (4) racial or ethnic minorities who have trouble integrating into the dominant ethnic group; or (5) deviants, be they pathological, gifted, or nonconformist.

Some of these definitions of "marginal" have intriguing possibilities for Jesus research,[14] but my point here is simply to emphasize how varied the use of the word can be even in sophisticated scholarly analysis of a single sociological problem. In this Jesus book, the word likewise has a multiplicity of meanings—hopefully not because of sloppy thinking or a desire to be obscure. Rather, as a *māšāl*, as a tease-word, "marginal" is used to conjure up and connect a number of allied aspects of Jesus' life and ministry. By way of examples, it may help to list just six of these aspects:

(1) From the viewpoint of the Jewish and pagan literature of the century following Jesus, the Nazarene was at most a "blip" on the radar screen. As we shall see in Chapter 3, it is remarkable that the 1st-century Jewish historian Josephus mentions Jesus at all, but hardly remarkable that Josephus gives more space and praise to John the Baptist. In his side glance at Christ, the Roman historian Tacitus is briefer still. As hard as

it is for the devout Christian to accept, the fact is that Jesus was simply insignificant to national and world history as seen through the eyes of Jewish and pagan historians of the 1st and early 2d centuries A.D. If he was seen at all, it was at the periphery of their vision.

(2) Any person declared a criminal by the highest authority of his or her society and accordingly put to death in a most shameful and brutal way at a public execution has obviously been pushed to the margins of that society. The ultimate impoverishment, the ultimate margin, is death, especially death by torture as a punishment meted out by the state for gross criminality. In Roman eyes, Jesus died the ghastly death of slaves and rebels; in Jewish eyes, he fell under the stricture of Deut 21:23: "The one hanged [on a tree] is accursed by God." To both groups Jesus' trial and execution made him marginal in a terrifying and disgusting way. Jesus was a Jew living in a Jewish Palestine directly or indirectly controlled by Romans. In one sense, he belonged to both worlds; in the end, he was ejected from both.

(3) Yet it was not only historians and politicians who marginalized Jesus. To a certain degree, Jesus first marginalized himself. At the age of roughly thirty, Jesus was an ordinary carpenter in an ordinary hill town of lower Galilee, enjoying at least the minimum of economic necessities and social respectability required for a decent life. For whatever reason, he abandoned his livelihood and hometown, became "jobless" and itinerant in order to undertake a prophetic ministry, and not surprisingly met with disbelief and rejection when he returned to his hometown to teach in the synagogue. In place of the "honor" he once enjoyed he was now exposed to "shame" in an honor/shame society, where the esteem of others determined one's existence much more than it does today. Relying basically on the goodwill, support, and economic contributions of his followers, Jesus intentionally became marginal in the eyes of ordinary working Jews in Palestine, while remaining very much a Palestinian Jew himself.

(4) Some of Jesus' teachings and practices (e.g., his total prohibition of divorce, his rejection of voluntary fasting, his voluntary celibacy) were marginal in the sense that they did not jibe with the views and practices of the major Jewish religious groups of his day. His marginality as a teacher was only increased by the fact that, as a poor rural Galilean, he had never attended any scribal school or studied under a noted teacher. Yet he dared to challenge teachings and practices accepted by many Jews of his day; he proclaimed his own teachings with a sovereign authority whose basis was by no means clear to his opponents.

(5) Jesus' style of teaching and living was thus offensive to many Jews. It pushed them away from him, and so pushed him to the margin of Palestinian Judaism. By the time he died, he had managed to make himself appear obnoxious, dangerous, or suspicious to everyone from pious Pharisees through political high priests to an ever vigilant Pilate. One reason Jesus met a swift and brutal end is simple: he alienated so many individuals and groups in Palestine that, when the final clash came in Jerusalem in A.D. 30, he had very few people, especially people of influence, on his side.

(6) In modern sociological studies, the word "marginal" is often applied to poor people from a rural culture who migrate to cities but do not integrate well into the dominant urban culture. They are lost on the border between two worlds. I may be stretching an analogy, but Jesus may have been marginal in a similar sense. Jesus, the poor layman turned prophet and teacher, the religious figure from rural Galilee without credentials, met his death in Jerusalem at least in part because of his clash with the rich aristocratic urban priesthood. To the latter, a poor layman from the Galilean countryside with disturbing doctrines and claims was marginal both in the sense of being dangerously antiestablishment and in the sense of lacking a power base in the capital. He could be easily brushed aside into the dustbin of death.

These facets of Jesus' life, teaching, and death do not exhaust the ways in which he might be considered marginal, but at least they open up some paths for exploration. They also raise the question of whether or to what extent various aspects of Jesus' marginality (voluntary joblessness, itinerant prophetic ministry, voluntary celibacy, rejection of divorce and fasting) tie together and explain one another. We will have to pursue these elusive leads throughout the book, but at least the key word "marginal" gives us some leads to pursue.

5. A NOTE ON SOCIOLOGY, LITERARY CRITICISM, AND NT EXEGESIS

Some of the most exciting and controversial advances in NT exegesis during the past two decades have come from the application of sociological analysis and modern literary criticism to NT texts. I owe the reader a brief explanation of how this book relates to these new exegetical methods.

For anyone engaged in the quest for the historical Jesus, scholarly work on social, political, and economic realities at the time of Jesus can only be welcome. To take into consideration the social environment in which Jesus moved is simply to take history seriously in all its human dimensions. All too often highly theological treatments of the historical Jesus have prescinded from the concrete circumstances of his own time and place, only to produce a disembodied and usually un-Jewish Jesus.

To deal with the concrete circumstances of Jesus' milieu, I had originally intended to have a separate chapter in this book covering the political, social, and economic environment of his day. But upon consideration, this approach seemed only to guarantee that these concrete circumstances would remain detached from the treatment of Jesus himself. Besides, this book is not intended to be a "Background to the NT" book or "World of the NT" book; other volumes in the Anchor Bible Reference Library series will serve that purpose. Instead, I opted for an approach that sought to blend various social, political, economic, and cultural data into the appropriate places within the wider discussion of Jesus' life and ministry. For example, the "blank" period of Jesus' "hidden years" (Chapters 9 and 10) offers an opportunity to sketch in some cultural, linguistic, social, and economic aspects of life in Galilee as the young Jesus would have experienced them. Likewise, the lengthy treatment of the chronology of Jesus' life in Chapter 11 permits the introduction of various rulers and historical events that will affect the outcome of his life. A similar procedure of "blending" will be employed throughout the book.

To forestall misconceptions, though, I should emphasize from the start two important distinctions. First, there is a significant distinction between a consideration of the social realities at the time of Jesus on the one hand and formal sociological analysis (or the cross-cultural analysis of anthropology) on the other. Formal sociological analysis goes beyond mere description of social data; it proposes a model or models to explain the data within an overarching theory. I should make plain from the start that such sociological analysis is not the aim of this book.[15]

Rather, this book operates on a very fundamental level as it asks what, within the Gospels and other sources available, really goes back to the historical Jesus. The primary goal of this book is the detection of reliable data. Inevitably, interpretation will accompany the assemblage of data, if for no other reason than that the selection and compiling of such data already involve a certain degree of interpretation. But every attempt will be made to keep interpretation to an absolute minimum. Our goal will be primarily the ascertaining of reliable data, not sophisticated sociological interpretation of the data via models. As Jerome H. Neyrey wisely remarks when applying the models of Mary Douglas to NT exegesis: "Because Douglas aims at cross-cultural analysis, her models necessarily work at a rather high level of abstraction. . . . Douglas's modeling, moreover, cannot reconstruct history, for it is a static photograph of a society and does not yield the particularity of experience that constitutes data for the writing of history."[16]

In contrast, what we seek in this book are precisely the particular data needed for the historical reconstruction of individual persons and events in a very narrow time frame. Thus, while concerned about the social dimensions of the available data, I am not engaged in the "modeling" Neyrey describes. This is not meant to deny that such sociological analysis might be applied to the material assembled in this book; it is merely to insist on one step at a time.

A second important distinction that needs to be made is the difference between being attentive to the social conditions within which Jesus' life and ministry took place and a wholesale reduction of the religious dimension of his work to social, economic, and political forces. This reductionism, which is usually rejected by the most prominent practitioners of the sociology of the NT, does creep into some popular presentations. In these, religion and religious concerns are not simply understood within the social context of the time; religion becomes *nothing but* a mask for social and political agendas, a tool by which various socioeconomic groups advance their power plays. Not only is such reductionism usually the result of imposing a particular ideology (often Marxist) on the data; more to the point, it is unscientific and unhistorical because it cannot come to grips with all the data, e.g., the acceptance by an individual or group of deprivation or martyrdom for the sake of their religious convictions and contrary to their own best economic and political interests. Such unscientific reductionism will have no place in this work. This is not to deny that, unlike our own experience of the separation of church and state in a secularized society, religion, social life, and politics were very much intertwined in the ancient world in general and Palestine in particular. For pious Jews, religion permeated the whole of life. But to recognize this fact is not to reduce religion to simply one dimension or aspect of social and political forces.

Another welcome addition to the tools of NT exegesis is the contribution made in recent years by contemporary literary criticism. As applied to the Gospels, literary criticism—also referred to at times as narrative criticism, rhetorical criticism, or reader-response criticism—insists on the autonomy of each Gospel as an aesthetic whole, a piece of literary art that must be appreciated on its own terms, without the distraction of inquiring after hypothetical sources, historical background, or the intention of the historical author. The focus is rather on the literary "world" projected by or contained in the text, not the real, historical world standing behind the text as background and source. In its most stringent form, narrative criticism demands that we imagine an "implied reader" who knows nothing of the Gospel story beyond what the "implied author" tells him or her at any given moment in the narrative. While of course quite artificial (even the first Christian audiences of the written Gospels already knew the basic story), this method focuses our attention on the literary techniques used by individual authors to shape and develop the story, as well as the many signals backward and forward in the text that tie the various parts of the narrative together.

Literary criticism is thus a useful way of focusing on what otherwise could get lost in our zealous quest for sources and historical background. It helps us listen to the literary whole and understand how individual parts of the narrative function within that whole. Obviously, though, such an ahistorical approach to 1st-century documents of Christian propaganda that advanced truth claims about Jesus of Nazareth, truth claims for which some 1st-century Christians were willing to die, cannot be the main method employed in a quest for the historical Jesus.[17] Nevertheless, contemporary literary criticism provides a salutary caveat by reminding us to ask what is the literary function of a verse or pericope in the larger work before we glibly declare it a reliable source of historical information.[18] Along with the emphasis on social context, it is a useful addition to the toolbox of the working exegete.

6. THE STRUCTURE OF THIS BOOK

Finally, a word should be said about the arrangement of the material in this book and the rationale thereof. In addressing its audience, this book seeks to work on two levels. The basic text is cast in language intelligible (hopefully) to a university student on the master's level, or perhaps even to a well-read undergraduate, as well as to the general educated reader. As far as possible, more technical questions and detailed discussions of literature are relegated to the notes, where doctoral students and scholars can pursue particular problems at greater length and find references for further reading. My hope is that this two-tier approach will make this volume accessible and useful to a wide range of readers. Neither completely original nor in any sense definitive, it simply seeks to introduce new students to the scholarly conversation about Jesus and to make a modest contribution to those already engaged in the dialogue.

This book is divided into four major parts, with Parts One and Two forming Volume One. Part One, "Roots of the Problem," deals with all those messy issues of definitions, method, and sources that most people —even scholars—would prefer to bypass to get to "the good stuff." All too many popular presentations of the historical Jesus show the confusion and superficiality that result when one goes questing for Jesus without first checking one's flashlight and road map. A careful weighing of what exactly we are looking for and how we are to look for it will prevent many false steps later on.

Part Two, "Roots of the Person," then begins the quest at its most intractable point: the birth, the years of development, and the cultural background of Jesus. Making a virtue of necessity, I use these relatively blank years to fill in some of the linguistic, educational, political, and social background needed to understand the stage onto which Jesus steps as he begins his ministry.

Part Three, which will begin Volume Two, will be occupied with the public ministry proper. Since, as will be clear from Chapter 11 (on chronology), we do not for the most part know the order of events between Jesus' baptism and the final week of his life, the major actions and sayings of the Nazarene will be ordered topically: proclamation of the kingdom of God, table fellowship with sinners, miracles, etc.

Part Four will bring us to the momentous and tragic final days of Jesus' life, ending with his crucifixion and burial. As will become clear in Part One, a treatment of the resurrection is omitted not because it is denied but simply because the restrictive definition of the historical Jesus I will be using does not allow us to proceed into matters that can be affirmed only by faith.

An Epilogue will then attempt some initial reflection, both historical and theological, on all that we will have seen. As I will make clear at that point, this entire work is, in a sense, a prolegomenon and an invitation to theologians to appropriate from this particular quest what may be useful to the larger task of a present-day christology—something this book pointedly does not undertake. If this invitation is accepted, then this book will have done its work and achieved its ultimate purpose.

NOTES TO THE INTRODUCTION

[1] "Jesus," *The New Jerome Biblical Commentary*, ed. Raymond E. Brown, Joseph A. Fitzmyer, and Roland E. Murphy (Englewood Cliffs, NJ: Prentice Hall, 1990) 1316–28.

[2] *The Jerome Biblical Commentary*, ed. Raymond E. Brown, Joseph A. Fitzmyer, and Roland E. Murphy (Englewood Cliffs, NJ: Prentice Hall, 1968).

[3] "Who, Really, Was Jesus of Nazareth?" "Outlook" section of the Sunday Washington *Post*, December 23, 1984, pp. 1 and 5.

[4] "Jesus Among the Historians," *New York Times Book Review*, December 21, 1986, pp. 1, 16–19.

[5] "Jesus Among the Historians," *The Mission of Christ and His Church* (Good News Studies 30; Wilmington, DE: Glazier, 1991) 7–32. In the same volume, see also the two studies on the use of the Jesus of history by contemporary Roman Catholic systematic theologians (pp. 33–48, 49–69).

[6] Günther Bornkamm, *Jesus of Nazareth* (New York: Harper & Row, 1960 [German original, 1956]).

[7] It is the tendency of Bornkamm to read German Lutheran polemics about legalism into the situation of Jesus that especially calls for correction. The great challenge to a simplistic (and indeed polemical) view of Judaism at the time of Jesus was given from the Christian side by E. P. Sanders in his controversial work, *Paul and Palestinian Judaism* (Philadelphia: Fortress, 1977), updated by his *Paul, the Law, and the Jewish People* (Philadelphia: Fortress, 1983). In many ways, Sanders represents to this generation what George Foot Moore (*Judaism in the First Centuries of the Christian Era* [2 vols.; New York: Schocken, 1971; original copyright 1927, 1930]) represented to the first decades of this century: a more sympathetic, less polemical view of Judaism, one less distorted by Protestant-Catholic controversies read back into the first centuries A.D. As is to be expected, Jewish scholars have been in the forefront of championing a more balanced view of early Judaism vis-à-vis Christian origins. Notable in this regard have been Jacob Neusner and Geza Vermes. An easy first step into the monumental works of Neusner would be his *First Century Judaism in Crisis* (Nashville/New York: Abingdon, 1975) and his *Judaism in the Beginning of Christianity* (Philadelphia: Fortress, 1984). Vermes' works include *Jesus the Jew* (Philadelphia: Fortress, 1973) and *Jesus and the World of Judaism* (Philadelphia: Fortress, 1984). To be sure, the opinions of Sanders, Neusner, and Vermes hardly coincide, and their various positions are very much debated today. For example, Sanders conducts something of a running debate with Neusner about the latter's views on the Pharisees and the Mishna in *Jewish Law from Jesus to the Mishnah. Five Studies* (London: SCM; Philadelphia: Trinity, 1990); see esp. pp. 309–31. For Vermes' thoughts on the debate, see his review of Sanders' *Jewish Law* in the *London Times Literary Supplement* for Jan. 11, 1991, p. 19. Another critique of Sanders' ideas on "Pharisees" and "sinners" can be found in James D. G. Dunn, "Pharisees, Sinners and Jesus," *The Social World of Formative Christianity and Judaism* (Howard Clark Kee

Festschrift; ed. Jacob Neusner et al.; Philadelphia: Fortress, 1988) 264–89. Yet, for all their differences, these scholars represent a turning point in research: simplistic generalizations about "late Judaism" (a dreadful misnomer!) being a religion of legalism and fear will no longer be taken seriously by most scholars. Likewise, much greater care must be taken in quoting chronologically later rabbinic sources to explain 1st-century NT texts. Unfortunately, not all scholars —especially those who are not professional exegetes—have learned the lesson. For example, Thomas Sheehan's *The First Coming* (New York: Random House, 1986) still uses the pejorative term "late Judaism" to describe a religion that saw God as a distant and almost impersonal Sovereign, a religion of fear (see, e.g., p. 59).

[8] E. P. Sanders, *Jesus and Judaism* (Philadelphia: Fortress, 1985).

[9] Paul Hollenbach, "The Historical Jesus Question in North America Today," *BTB* 19 (1989) 11–22, p. 20, borrowing a phrase from the liberation theologian José Porfirio Miranda. The directly opposite approach, stressing the continuity between Jesus of Nazareth and the Christ proclaimed by the Church, is taken by Marinus de Jonge, *Jesus, the Servant-Messiah* (New Haven/London: Yale University, 1991).

[10] Hollenbach, "The Historical Jesus Question," 19.

[11] One must still take seriously the warnings of Henry J. Cadbury, *The Peril of Modernizing Jesus* (London: SPCK, 1962; 1st published in London: Macmillan, 1937); see esp. pp. 1–27.

[12] Letter to me, dated Oct. 15, 1990.

[13] Janice E. Perlman, *The Myth of Marginality. Urban Poverty and Politics in Rio de Janeiro* (Berkeley/Los Angeles/London: University of California, 1976) 93–96. She goes on to list seven schools of thought in sociology that seek to explain marginality and to propose ways of dealing with it. She herself takes a critical stance toward all seven approaches.

It is interesting to note that a number of dictionaries and encyclopedias of the social sciences do not supply definitions of "marginal" or "marginality." Those that give definitions do not always agree in their approaches; compare, e.g., Perlman's explanation with the definitions offered by Thomas Ford Hoult, "marginality," "marginal man," *Dictionary of Modern Sociology* (Totowa, NJ: Littlefield, Adams & Co., 1972) 192; and Arthur W. Frank III, "Marginal Man," *Encyclopedia of Sociology* (Guilford, CT: Dushkin, 1974) 165.

[14] See, e.g., Perlman's observation about the "deviant": "In the case of an artist, criminal, prophet, or revolutionary, marginality implies a lack of participation in the occupational, religious, or political mainstream" *(The Myth of Marginality,* 96). See also Schuyler Brown, "Jesus, History, and the Kerygma," *Vom Urchristentum zu Jesus* (Joachim Gnilka Festschrift; ed. Hubert Frankemölle and Karl Kertelge; Freiburg/Basel/Vienna: Herder, 1989) 487–96.

[15] For a brief sketch of the promise, problems, and limitations of a sociological approach to the NT, see Bengt Holmberg, *Sociology and the New Testament. An Appraisal* (Minneapolis: Fortress, 1990), esp. pp. 145–57.

[16] Jerome H. Neyrey, *An Ideology of Revolt. John's Christology in Social-Science Perspective* (Philadelphia: Fortress, 1988) 210; cf. Holmberg, *Sociology and the New Testament*, 153–54.

[17] A fortiori this holds true of the still more abstract and ahistorical methods of structuralism and semiotics.

[18] See, e.g., the discussion of the function of Luke 1:80 in the Baptist's "Infancy Narrative" in Chapter 12.

PART ONE

ROOTS OF
THE PROBLEM

CHAPTER 1

BASIC CONCEPTS:

The Real Jesus and the Historical Jesus

The historical Jesus is not the real Jesus. The real Jesus is not the historical Jesus. I stress this paradox from the start because endless confusion in the "quest for the historical Jesus"[1] arises from the failure to distinguish these two concepts clearly.

THE REAL JESUS

What do we mean when we say we want to investigate the "real" Jesus or the "real" Nero or the real anybody in ancient history? The notion of "real" is a tricky one that needs careful distinction, whether we are dealing with ancient or modern history. In historical research there are different gradations in the sense of "real."

(1) Obviously we cannot mean the *total* reality of that person, everything he or she ever thought, felt, experienced, did, and said. Even today, despite all the printed government records, TV news tapes, and biographies available, one could not know the *total* reality of, say, Richard Nixon or Ronald Reagan. Indeed, how could these individuals themselves—let alone anyone else—ever know their *total* reality, defined in such sweeping, all-encompassing terms?

(2) Still, when it comes to modern public figures, the historian or biographer can usually assemble a "reasonably complete" picture. We

will probably debate from now to doomsday the great talent and tragic flaws of Richard Nixon, but there is no debating the mountain of empirical data that public archives, military records, nightly newscasts, election tallies, presidential press conferences, Watergate tapes, congressional hearings, and presidential libraries supply *ad nauseam.* Wading through and interpreting the facts is a monumental task, but at least the facts are there. The "total reality" of Richard Nixon will continue to elude us as it eluded him. But we have and can hope to refine a "reasonably complete" portrait and record of the "real" Richard Nixon. Passionate and biased interpretations are inevitable, but the vast fund of verifiable facts does exercise some control over wild hypotheses. In this limited, sober sense, the "real" Richard Nixon—and any recent public figure—is in principle available to the historian. The real and the historical do not coincide, but there is considerable overlap.

(3) Not so with Jesus of Nazareth. Jesus lived for roughly thirty-five years in 1st-century Palestine. Each of those years was filled with physical and psychological changes. Even before he began his public ministry, many of his words and deeds would have been witnessed by his family and friends, his neighbors and customers. In principle, these events were available at the time to the interested inquirer. Then, for the last three years or so of his life, much of what Jesus said and did occurred in public or at least before his disciples, especially those who traveled with him. Again, in principle, these events were recoverable at the time to a zealous inquirer.

And yet the vast majority of these deeds and words, the "reasonably complete" record of the "real" Jesus, is irrevocably lost to us today. This is no new insight of modern agnostic scholars. Traditionally Christianity has spoken of "the hidden years" of Jesus' life—which amounted to all but three or four of them! The apocryphal gospels of the patristic period, mystical visions of medieval times, and modern speculation have sought to fill in the gap, but to no avail. The "real Jesus," even in the Richard Nixon sense of a reasonably complete record of public words and deeds, is unknown and unknowable. The reader who wants to know the real Jesus should close this book right now, because the historical Jesus is neither the real Jesus nor the easy way to him. The real Jesus is not available and never will be. This is true not because Jesus did not exist—he certainly did—but rather because the sources that have survived do not and never intended to record all or even most of the words and deeds of his public ministry—to say nothing of the rest of his life.

(4) I emphasize this insight about the real Jesus not simply to revel in

subtle scholastic distinctions or to set up a theological shell game I can then win on my own terms. The point I am making is true of most figures of ancient history. The life and ideas of Socrates or Pythagoras amounted to much more than we can know today. Indeed, the further back we go, usually the more meager the sources become and the less we can say. Many rulers of Babylonia and Egypt are only names to us, although in their own day they loomed like giants and their impact was immense. An expert in Greco-Roman history once remarked to me that what we know with certitude about Alexander the Great can be fitted onto a few pages of print.[2] This simply reminds us that what really occurs in history is much broader than the history recoverable by a historian.[3]

(5) Granted, some of the great figures of ancient history, such as Julius Caesar or Cicero, have left us a store of autobiographical writings and public records that allow some access to the "real" person. Hence we must distinguish from the mass of human beings in ancient history the special case of certain well-known public figures.[4] To take a clear example: in Marcus Aurelius (reigned A.D. 161–80) we have the rare case of a Roman emperor who wrote down his innermost musings in a book called *The Meditations*. This, plus large amounts of correspondence, official records, ancient histories, coins, and archaeology, allow the noted historian Anthony Birley to write a fairly full biography. Yet even here there are certain years in which it is unclear where Marcus was or what he was doing.[5]

Sir Moses Finley constantly warned us about the severe limitations historians face in studying Greco-Roman history, including even the long and glorious reign of Augustus.[6] Indeed, Finley felt so strongly the lack of "hard" data, including reliable statistics, that he concluded that the study of ancient history is in no significant sense a science.[7] Perhaps it is wiser to distinguish between the "hard" sciences like chemistry and physics and the "soft" sciences, including the humanities, especially ancient history (softer, surely, than modern history). Ancient history is much less quantifiable, much more dependent on inference based on such rough rules of thumb as the best explanation available, the more or most probable explanation, particular criteria for judging historicity, and analogy.[8] At any rate, Finley's basic caution is well advised. With the exception of a relatively few great public figures, the "real" persons of ancient history—be they Hillel and Shammai or Jesus and Simon Peter—are simply not accessible to us today by historical research and never will be.[9]

I stress this point because scholars pursuing the Jesus of history often begin their treatments with the difficulties posed by the four canonical Gospels and—especially if they are spiritual descendants of Rudolf Bultmann—with the danger of trying to legitimize faith by historical research. All that may be true, but it is necessary to begin one step further back: the difficulty of knowing anything about Jesus must be placed in the larger context of the difficulty of knowing anything about Thales, Apollonius of Tyana, or anyone else in the ancient world. David Noel Freedman has rightly pointed out that the same problem holds true for those engaged in OT studies. He observes: "While no one questions that people like David and Solomon actually lived and reigned, there is not, to my knowledge, a single piece of evidence outside of the Bible to attest to their existence, much less anything about their noteworthy achievements. Neither one is mentioned in any record of any nation known to us."[10] Thus, the problem is not unique to Jesus or the sources that narrate his story. Indeed, in comparison to the many shadowy figures of ancient history, it is surprising how much we can know about Jesus.

To summarize the upshot of these various distinctions about "real" figures in history: (1) The total reality of a person is in principle unknowable—despite the fact that no one would deny that such a total reality did exist. This simply reminds us that all historical knowledge about human persons is limited by the very nature of the case. We may take some comfort from the thought that a good deal of the total reality of a person would be irrelevant and positively boring to historians even if it could be known. (2) For many public figures of modern history, the mounds of empirical data available make possible a "reasonably complete" portrait of the "real" person, while varying interpretations of the data naturally remain. (3) While the amount of source material is much less extensive, students of ancient history can sometimes reconstruct a reasonably complete portrait of a few great figures (e.g., Cicero, Caesar). (4) However, we lack sufficient sources to reconstruct a reasonably complete portrait for the vast majority of persons in ancient history; the "real" Thales or Apollonius of Tyana is simply beyond our grasp. It is in this last category that Jesus of Nazareth falls. We cannot know the "real" Jesus through historical research, whether we mean his total reality or just a reasonably complete biographical portrait. We can, however, know the "historical Jesus."

THE HISTORICAL JESUS

Having abandoned the naive hope of knowing the "real" Jesus by means of historical criticism, what do we mean when we say that we are pursuing the "historical Jesus" or the "Jesus of history"?[11] In brief, the Jesus of history is a modern abstraction and construct. By the Jesus of history I mean the Jesus whom we can "recover" and examine by using the scientific tools of modern historical research.[12] Since such research arose only with the Enlightenment in the 18th century (Hermann Reimarus [1694–1768] being the first famous example of a "quester"), the quest for the historical Jesus is a peculiarly modern endeavor and has its own tangled history, from Reimarus to E. P. Sanders and lesser lights.[13] Of its very nature, this quest can reconstruct only fragments of a mosaic, the faint outline of a faded fresco that allows of many interpretations. We constantly have to be reminded that not only are there no VCR videotapes or Sony cassette recordings of what Jesus said or did. For better or for worse, there are no Watergate tapes of Jesus' trial before Pilate. Worse still, this marginal Jew in a marginal province at the eastern end of the Roman Empire left no writings of his own (as Cicero did), no archaeological monuments or artifacts (as Augustus did), nothing that comes directly from him without mediators. A moment's reflection on these stark facts makes clear why my initial paradox has to be true: the historical Jesus is not the real Jesus, and vice versa. The historical Jesus may give us fragments of the "real" person, but nothing more.[14] Thus, the two terms, "real Jesus" and "historical Jesus," are relatively clear-cut, even though some theologians like Hans Küng tend to confuse them.[15]

More ambiguous is the phrase "the earthly Jesus" or "Jesus during his life on earth." While the Four Gospels do not and do not claim to portray the real Jesus with the full range of everything he ever said or did in public or before his disciples in private (see John 20:30; 21:25), and while they obviously do not provide a modern hypothetical reconstruction (the historical Jesus), they do present us with "the earthly Jesus," i.e., a picture—however partial and theologically colored—of Jesus during his life on earth. The ambiguity of this term "earthly Jesus" lies in the fact that it can also be used, with different nuances, of the real Jesus and the historical Jesus: they too refer to Jesus on earth. The ambiguity is compounded by the fact that, to a theologian, the very phrase "earthly Jesus" may imply existence in heaven either before the incarnation or after the resurrection.[16] Because of this lack of clarity in the concept, I will not use "earthly Jesus" as a major category in this book.

One important ramification of these distinctions is that scholars should not write glibly that, in a given story, the Gospels depict or fail to depict "the historical Jesus." That is a hopeless anachronism. During most of their narrative (excluding John 1:1–18 and most resurrection appearances), the Gospels portray Jesus on earth (in the sense I have just explained), not the historical Jesus.[17] To be sure, the Gospels serve as the chief *sources* for our reconstruction of the historical Jesus; but to speak of the Gospel writers as presenting or intending to present the historical Jesus transports them in an exegetical time machine to the Enlightenment.

HISTORICAL AND HISTORIC

Real, historical, earthly—these are the distinctions I shall use in an attempt to bring some terminological clarity into the murky debate about the historical Jesus. In doing this, I purposely choose not to lean on the classic distinction found in many German authors, who distinguish the "historical" *(historisch)* from the "historic" *(geschichtlich)*.[18] The "historical" refers to the dry bare bones of knowledge about the past, with the researcher prescinding from any possible relevance to or influence on our present-day life and quest for meaning. Imagine, for instance, an expert in ancient Babylonian history, driven by nothing except a thirst for exactitude, trying to draw up a precise chronology of the reigning kings of Babylon in a given century. Such a "historical" study aims at the past as dead past, viewed with the cold eye of objective research, interested in pure, verifiable data for their own sake. The "historic," in contrast, refers to the past as it is meaningful and challenging, engaging and thought-provoking for present-day men and women. Imagine, for instance, a black college student writing a thesis on Dr. Martin Luther King, Jr. The young scholar might be quite careful in researching the facts; but the figure of King could never be for that student simply a datum embalmed in the past. Inevitably, the student would select, arrange, and underscore certain data insofar as they seemed to speak to the problems and promises of today.

In principle, this distinction of historical and historic can be applied to Jesus just as much as to any other great personage of the past. *In theory,* he can be made the object of a coolly distant scientific investigation, or he can be approached as the highly significant source and center of Christian thought and life down through the ages, a figure still worshiped by millions today.

Although this distinction of historical *(historisch)* and historic *(geschichtlich)* is often repeated in Jesus research (especially among those strongly influenced by the Bultmannian tradition), I remain doubtful of its usefulness for English-speaking scholars today, for four reasons. (1) After close to a century of use, the distinction remains ambiguous and varies in meaning or function from author to author, with even some Germans not observing it. (2) The distinction, while supposedly employed to facilitate objective research, often carries with it the extra baggage of theological or ideological agendas. (3) The twofold distinction does not do justice to the complexity of the situation. (4) While defensible in theory, it is useless in the real world—even the "real" world of scholars.

First of all, the distinction does not always mean the same thing or function in the same way even among the various writers who use it. Martin Kähler (1835–1912), who applied the distinction to Jesus in the last century, did so in defense of a particular kind of "critical pietism" in late 19th-century German Protestantism—and even he did not always observe his own distinction with strict rigor.[19] His ultimate goal seems to have been the protection of basic traditional Christian teachings about Jesus Christ (e.g., true divinity and true sinless humanity) from the inroads of historical criticism.[20]

This was not exactly the driving concern of Rudolf Bultmann (1884–1976) when he took over the distinction in his 20th-century synthesis of Christianity and Martin Heidegger's brand of existentialism.[21] Bultmann is one with Kähler in emphasizing the central Christian proclamation *(kerygma)* of Jesus' death and resurrection and in rejecting the historical Jesus as the basis or the content of Christian faith. Bultmann, however, pushes the distinction in a direction that Kähler would hardly have followed. For Bultmann, it makes no difference whether Jesus actually broke down and despaired on the cross;[22] the mere fact *that* Jesus died on the cross is sufficient for Christian faith, i.e., for the encounter between the believer and God.[23] While something can be known of

Jesus' teaching, "we can now know almost nothing concerning the life and personality of Jesus, since the early Christian sources show no interest in either, are moreover fragmentary and often legendary. . . ."[24] At this point, the reader may get the uneasy feeling that the historic Christ, the kerygmatic Christ, the Christ of faith exalted by Bultmann, looks suspiciously like a timeless gnostic myth or a Jungian archetype, no matter how much Bultmann stresses historicity and the identity of the crucified Jesus with the *kerygma* that is preached.[25]

Hence it is not surprising that some German theologians, notably Paul Althaus (1888–1966), sought to reclaim Kähler's historical/historic distinction for a more conservative school of thought.[26] Yet, as Heraclitus observed, no one can put his foot into the same stream twice. Faced with the historical skepticism of Bultmann, and appropriating the "new quest" of Bultmann's pupils (e.g., Günther Bornkamm),[27] Althaus looks to historical research for the guarantee that the Christ of faith is not just another great myth of world religions.[28] So, while rejecting Bultmann's approach, Althaus takes a basically positive stance toward the new quest of post-Bultmannians like Bornkamm since, "by its very nature, Christian faith has a burning interest in what scientific history can know about Jesus."[29] One cannot imagine Kähler saying this about the German "liberal lives of Jesus" in the 19th century. Thus, although Althaus, in his opposition to Bultmann, seeks to remain the faithful interpreter of Kähler, the distinction between historical and historic receives a new twist.[30]

What makes the historical/historic distinction even more problematic is that some key scholars within 20th-century German Lutheranism (and German Lutheranism was the source of the distinction) reject its validity or simply ignore it. Most curious is the treatment given the distinction by Albert Schweitzer (1875–1965), the great chronicler and critic of the "liberal lives." On the one hand, Schweitzer shows no knowledge of Kähler or his work and does not utilize Kähler's distinction in his own presentation.[31] On the other hand, while treating early 20th-century disputes over the historicity of Jesus, Schweitzer notes in passing the position of G. Wobbermin, a professor at Breslau, who "goes off on a dangerous path."[32] Wobbermin's dangerous path is his "attempt" to distinguish between the historical (*historisch*) and the historic (*geschichtlich*) Jesus. The distinction is understood roughly in the sense Kähler proposed, but Schweitzer will have none of it. With sarcastic indignation he points out that the historic Jesus has been responsible for untold evils down through the ages, from the destruction of ancient culture to the very fact of the Middle Ages to Catholicism's attempt to destroy "the many progressive achievements of the modern state." Who would want to give up the historical Jesus for this historic figure?[33]

Closer to our own day, Joachim Jeremias (1900–79), one of the 20th century's greatest experts on the historical Jesus, simply refused to operate with the historical/historic distinction.[34] Thus, we are left asking ourselves: With such a variety of uses or nonuses among German scholars, is the distinction all that vital or useful among English-speaking scholars?

A second problem with the distinction is that, almost inevitably, it leads to a "good guy/bad guy" presentation. Either the historical Jesus is exalted in order to dethrone a Christ of faith that was merely a fraudulent creation of the Church (so many from Reimarus to Hollenbach), or the historic Christ is extolled over the oscillating and contradictory reconstructions of the historical Jesus (so Kähler and followers, including many "dialectical" theologians like Barth and Bultmann after World War I). Granted, the distinction need not be accompanied by value judgments and theological programs, but such has been the case for about a century. All that seems to happen is that new agendas (e.g., liberation theology) replace the old ones; the game of good guy/bad guy continues.

A third problem is that the dichotomy of historical/historic, while applicable to most well-known figures of the past, does not do justice to the complexity of the case of Jesus. Norman Perrin[35] pointed out that a three-part distinction fits the special situation of Jesus better. (1) One can collect descriptive historical knowledge ("hard" knowledge) about a person of the ancient past called Jesus of Nazareth; this is the level of the "historical." (2) One can then proceed to highlight and appropriate those aspects of this historical knowledge that would be significant for us today. This is the level of the "historic." However, one could do the same thing in the case of Socrates, St. Augustine, or Sigmund Freud. Any great thinker and actor of the past can be studied on the level of cold disconnected facts and bare chronology or on the level of a meaningful synthesis of his or her thought and action, seen as relevant and challenging for people today. In that sense, one could be committed to the "program" of Socrates or Freud, one could be entranced and gripped by the person of Thomas More or Thomas Jefferson; in the same way one can be personally fascinated by the historic Jesus, whether one is a Jew, a Buddhist, or an agnostic. (3) Hence the second level must be carefully distinguished from a third level, namely faith-knowledge of Jesus as Lord and Christ, the faith-stance that prompts me to call Jesus my Lord and my Savior. This level, in the eyes of the believer, is the unique and exclusive territory of Jesus; unlike the first and second levels, it cannot be applied to other figures of ancient history.

Perrin's three-part model seems to fit the complex situation better than the simple dichotomy of historical/historic,[36] but unfortunately it introduces further muddle into the already muddled terminology. As Perrin himself admits,[37] Kähler uses the term "historic" for what Perrin calls faith-knowledge, while Perrin restricts "historic" to the second-level knowledge of any past figure that is relevant to our existence to-day.[38] Complicating the picture even further is the fact that, actually, Kähler's discussion starts out with an existential meaning of "historic" similar to Perrin's second level, only to slide quickly into the use of "historic" for faith-knowledge of Jesus as the Lord (Perrin's third level).[39] The ambiguity inherent in the terminology thus stems from Kähler himself; indeed, it aroused strong objections in his own day.[40] Perrin's refinement, while justified in theory, only increases the confusion in practice.

Apart from these difficulties caused by the usage of Kähler and Perrin, there is a final problem in the distinction between "historical" and "historic" that makes its application to Jesus not very serviceable. The distinction presupposes that some scholars do or at least could study Jesus' life and teaching in detail without any interest in its impact on subsequent history or on thoughtful people today. While that may be theoretically possible in the University of Phnom Penh or for a visiting professor from Mars, is it really conceivable that a scholar in the Western world—Christian, Jew, or agnostic—could approach a detailed study of the historical Jesus without a philosophical or religious interest in—or antipathy toward—the material under the microscope? Jesus continues to be studied in all parts of the world because Marxists, Buddhists, and agnostics are all intrigued—for very different reasons—by this enigmatic Jew. As Bultmann never tired of saying, all of us come to the exegesis of Scripture with our own presuppositions, biases, and interests. This amounts to admitting that our quest for the historical Jesus contains from the beginning something of an interest in the historic Jesus as well. Perrin's first and second levels are hopelessly intertwined in the flesh-and-blood world of human scholars.

What can and must be bracketed in this book for the time being, for the sake of the scientific method employed, is the third level, i.e., faith-knowledge. Bracketed, I say, not betrayed. We abstract from Christian faith because we are involved in the hypothetical reconstruction of a

past figure by purely scientific means: empirical data from ancient documents, sifted by human minds operating by inference, analogy, and certain specific criteria. Both method and goal are extremely narrow and
limited; the results do not claim to provide either a substitute for or the
object of faith. For the moment, we are prescinding from faith, not
denying it. Later on a correlation between our historical quest and the
stance of faith may be possible, but that lies beyond the main and modest goal of this book. For the time being, we will be focusing on the
theoretical construct I have called "the historical Jesus," with the realization that in practice one cannot adequately disentangle him from the
"historic Jesus." In reality, the one flows too much into the other. While
the scholar may try to prescind from a specifically Christian or ecclesiastical commitment, a more general "existential commitment," a concern
about what Jesus may mean for human life today, necessarily energizes
the historical quest.

We come back to where we started: the historical Jesus is not the real
Jesus, but only a fragmentary hypothetical reconstruction of him by
modern means of research. All this pushes us to the next logical question: Whence do we derive the fragments to be fitted together? What are
the primary sources of our knowledge of the historical Jesus?

NOTES TO CHAPTER 1

[1] More traditionally, one spoke of the quest "of" the historical Jesus; a major influence here is the title of the English translation of Albert Schweitzer's classic *Geschichte der Leben-Jesu-Forschung*, *The Quest of the Historical Jesus*, trans. W. Montgomery (New York: Macmillan, 1910; repr. 1968; the original title of Schweitzer's work, first published in German in 1906, was *Von Reimarus zu Wrede* [Tübingen: Mohr]; since 1913 it has borne the title *Geschichte der Leben-Jesu-Forschung*). But the wording "The Quest *of* the Historical Jesus" can lead to a misunderstanding among the uninitiated (who is questing for whom? subjective or objective genitive?); hence the unambiguous "for." James H. Charlesworth (*Jesus within Judaism* [Anchor Bible Reference Library; New York: Doubleday, 1988]) thinks the words "quest" and "search" are loaded, as though in a dark room we had lost something we might or might not find by fumbling around; he prefers the neutral term "Jesus research." I agree with his point but despair of changing the speech habits of close to a century of scholars. In this work "quest," "search," and "Jesus research" will be used interchangeably.

[2] Some of the ancient biographers of Alexander the Great were themselves aware of the difficulty of conflicting sources and of the selectivity of their own presentations. For a sample of the ancient lives, see Diodorus Siculus, Book 17 of his *Historical Library* (LCL, vol. 8; London: Heinemann; Cambridge: Harvard University, 1963); Quintus Curtius Rufus, *The History of Alexander* (Harmondsworth: Penguin, 1984); Plutarch, "Alexander," *The Age of Alexander* (Harmondsworth: Penguin, 1973) 252–334; and Arrian's *The Campaigns of Alexander* (Harmondsworth: Penguin, 1971). On the problem of historiography in the case of Alexander, see N. G. L. Hammond, *Three Historians of Alexander the Great* (Cambridge: Cambridge University, 1983); earlier fragmentary evidence is surveyed in L. Pearson, *The Lost Histories of Alexander the Great* (Philological Monographs 20; New York: American Philological Association, 1960). For a recent biography, see A. B. Bosworth, *Conquest and Empire. The Reign of Alexander the Great* (Cambridge: Cambridge University, 1988); note the bibliography of both ancient sources and modern authors, pp. 295–314.

[3] On the application of this principle to the quest for the historical Jesus, see Edward Schillebeeckx, *Jesus. An Experiment in Christology* (New York: Seabury, 1979) 67–71.

[4] To this extent, I must disagree with Marcus J. Borg's assertion that "we can in fact know as much about Jesus as we can about any figure in the ancient world," including Caesar (see his *Jesus: A New Vision* [San Francisco: Harper & Row, 1987] 15 and 21 n. 29).

[5] Anthony Birley, *Marcus Aurelius. A Biography* (rev. ed.; New Haven/London: Yale University, 1987). Complaints about the scarcity and ambiguity of sources are a common thread in most biographies of Roman emperors; see, e.g., Michael Grant, *Nero* (New York: Dorset, 1970) 14–15, 209–14; Anthony A. Barrett, *Caligula. The Corruption of Power* (New Haven/London: Yale University, 1989) xv–xxiii, 244. Reading through Michael Grant's *The Roman Emperors* (New York:

Scribner's, 1985) reminds us how little we know about many of the men who ruled the ancient Mediterranean world in the first Christian centuries.

[6] Moses I. Finley, *Ancient History. Evidence and Models* (New York: Viking, 1985) 10–11.

[7] Ibid., 27, 104.

[8] On this point, with reference to Jesus research, see the methodological discussion of Ben F. Meyer, *The Aims of Jesus* (London: SCM, 1979) 23–110. For more general methodological considerations on the justification of historical judgments, see C. Behan McCullagh, *Justifying Historical Descriptions* (Cambridge: Cambridge University, 1984). In Chapter 3, "Justifying singular descriptions: II Statistical inferences" (pp. 45–73), McCullagh considers various mathematical formulas for quantifying historical probabilities—and the grave difficulty of applying such an approach thoroughly becomes obvious for ancient history in general and the fragmentary data on the historical Jesus in particular. Hence in this work I will content myself with such general judgments as "very probable," "more probable," "less probable," "unlikely," etc. To try to assign exact percentages to my assertions (e.g., very probable = 95–80 percent) and then to add, subtract, multiply, and divide percentages to arrive at the overall percentage of probability for a given judgment is to pretend to a mathematical accuracy that is not to be had when the data base is so meager.

I feel a similar unease with regard to the procedures of the Jesus Seminar sponsored by the Westar Institute of Sonoma, California (founded in 1985 by Robert Funk). A group of scholars meets regularly to vote on whether Jesus actually said certain things contained in the Gospels. Four categories are used: Jesus certainly said this, Jesus probably said this, Jesus probably did not say this, Jesus definitely did not say this. The aim of the project is an edition of the "five gospels" (including the Coptic *Gospel of Thomas* from Nag Hammadi) which will print the sayings of Jesus in four colors (red, pink, gray, and black) to represent the four categories, ranging from certainly historical to certainly not. While these procedures both appeal to our democratic sympathies and give an air of scientific accuracy, I do not think they really add anything new to our knowledge. For over a century scholars have been exchanging opinions and papers as they debated the historicity of individual sayings of Jesus, formed various schools of thought, and then left some schools to form others. Gathering a particular group in one place to express their opinion by a vote and then printing the majority opinion in colors does not generate a fundamentally new method or new data. For the rationale of the method, with some preliminary results, see Robert W. Funk, Bernard Brandon Scott, and James R. Butts, *The Parables of Jesus. Red Letter Edition* (Sonoma, CA: Polebridge, 1988) esp. xiii–xv.

[9] In one sense, the situations of Paul of Tarsus or Ignatius of Antioch come closer to those of Caesar or Marcus Aurelius in that Paul and Ignatius have both left us a number of letters written by themselves and containing autobiographical information. Needless to say, such information contains personal biases, but it nevertheless constitutes a uniquely privileged source of historical knowledge. In each case, we are aided further by biographical information (of varying qual-

ity) from later writers (Luke for Paul, Eusebius for Ignatius)—hence the paradox that the "real" Paul or "real" Ignatius is more accessible to the modern historian than is Jesus or Simon Peter.

[10] In a written communication to the author (letter dated Oct. 15, 1990).

[11] At times, a distinction between the two phrases, "the Jesus of history" and "the historical Jesus," has been suggested. But in an area where many esoteric distinctions are already in play, I prefer to use the two terms interchangeably.

[12] This definition is not some arbitrary invention of mine; it is the commonly accepted one in present Jesus-of-history research. The same definition or its equivalent can be found in scholars who otherwise differ widely in their views, e.g., Schillebeeckx, *Jesus. An Experiment in Christology*, 67; and James M. Robinson, *A New Quest of the Historical Jesus* (SBT 25; London: SCM, 1959) 26. While Robinson (pp. 28–29) emphasizes—quite rightly—that "objective" historical research cannot grasp the peculiarly existential, human aspect of history (e.g., the stance and outlook from which a person acts, the understanding of existence "behind" what a person does), I am rather focusing on the frequent absence of even objective data when we try to investigate figures of ancient history. This difficulty is not one of principle but of fact: data that might once have been available are not so today. Simon Peter knew a great deal more about the daily habits, sayings, and thoughts of Jesus than has been preserved in written documents. And what has not been preserved has been—in all probability—irretrievably lost.

[13] In the past it was almost *de rigueur* to begin any book on the historical Jesus with a history of modern research. Indeed, whole books have been dedicated to such a review. Besides Schweitzer's *Geschichte der Leben-Jesu-Forschung*, which summed up the entire history from the late 18th century (Reimarus) to the beginning of the 20th (William Wrede), see the handy summary (from a conservative point of view) in Charles C. Anderson, *Critical Quests of Jesus* (Grand Rapids: Eerdmans, 1969); or still more schematically, John S. Kselman, "Modern New Testament Criticism," *JBC* 2. 7–20. A 116-page bibliography, introduced by a 111-page sketch of the chief questers, can be found in Warren S. Kissinger, *The Lives of Jesus* (New York/London: Garland, 1985). A more general bibliography on christology, including sections on the historical Jesus, is available in Leland Jennings White, *Jesus the Christ. A Bibliography* (Wilmington, DE: Glazier, 1988). The most recent full review of literature since 1950 can be found in W. G. Kümmel's *Dreissig Jahre Jesusforschung (1950–1980)* (BBB 60; Bonn: Hanstein, 1985). This great scholar of Jesus research continues his work in recent volumes of *Theologische Rundschau* (see, e.g., "Jesusforschung seit 1981. I. Forschungsgeschichte, Methodenfragen," *TR* 53 [1988] 229–49). A useful annotated bibliography is supplied by Craig A. Evans, *Life of Jesus Research* (NTTS 13; Leiden/New York/Copenhagen/Cologne: Brill, 1989). Some trenchant critiques of the unexamined presuppositions of many "questers" can be found in Meyer's *The Aims of Jesus* and in James P. Mackey's *Jesus the Man and the Myth* (New York/Ramsey: Paulist, 1979), esp. 10–51. Further methodological considerations and caveats can be found in Joachim Gnilka, *Jesus von Nazaret. Botschaft und Geschichte* (HTKNT,

Supplementband 3; Freiburg/Basel/Vienna: Herder, 1990) 11–34; and Ben Witherington III, *The Christology of Jesus* (Minneapolis: Fortress, 1990) 1–31.

It is perhaps symptomatic of a newer, different approach that E. P. Sanders does not begin his work *Jesus and Judaism* (Philadelphia: Fortress, 1985) with a lengthy history of all research on the subject. Rather, in a "State of the Question" (pp. 23–58), he reviews and criticizes positions of major 20th-century scholars. Given all this material already in print, I think it unnecessary to drag the reader on another stroll down quest-for-Jesus lane. The present book will be in dialogue with recent literature as each topic is dealt with; there is no need to parrot the many histories of the quest already published. For those who would like to read the key works of major questers, these are available in English thanks to the *Lives of Jesus Series*, ed. Leander E. Keck (Philadelphia: Fortress Press).

[14] Hence the appropriateness of the title of John Dominic Crossan's book, *In Fragments: The Aphorisms of Jesus* (San Francisco: Harper & Row, 1983).

[15] Of course, one must allow for the fact that Küng's famous work *Christ sein (On Being a Christian)* was written for a wide audience. Nevertheless, in describing the Jesus we can know through historical-critical research, Küng interchanges "real" *(wirklich)*, "true," "original," and "historical" (both *historisch* and *geschichtlich*) with abandon. This does not make for clear expression of thought, either in German or in English. For a striking example of this interchange of terms, see his *Christ sein* (6th ed.; Munich: Piper, 1975) 148–53 (English trans.: *On Being a Christian* [Garden City, NY: Doubleday, 1976] 156–61). (The reader should be warned that the English translation is not entirely reliable: e.g., the German phrase *Rückfrage nach Jesus*—roughly the equivalent of our "quest for the historical Jesus"—is regularly translated by the strange "counterquestion about Jesus.")

[16] One could pursue this point further: some of the resurrection appearances present the risen Jesus as living and acting "on earth," e.g., the Emmaus story (Luke 24:13–35; cf. Acts 1:1–5). In the Emmaus story, is the risen Jesus at the same time "earthly" insofar as he is interacting and conversing with others on earth?

[17] Curiously, Schillebeeckx uses "earthly" as a synonym for "real" after censuring its use as a synonym for "historical"; see *Jesus,* 67–68 (cf. the Dutch original, *Jezus, het verhaal van een levende* [3d ed.; Bloemendaal: Nelissen, 1975] 54–55). (The reader is warned that the English translation of *Jesus* is often unreliable; hence the recourse to the Dutch original here.)

[18] Of course, in doing this German exegetes continue a learned word game played by many German theologians, namely, taking two words, one from a Teutonic root and the other from a Latin root—both of which are used more or less interchangeably in common speech—and creating a fine philosophical distinction between them.

[19] A good critical edition of Kähler's pivotal work (first published in 1892), with annotations giving reactions by other scholars as well as Kähler's responses

and additions, can be found in Martin Kähler, *Der sogenannte historische Jesus und der geschichtliche, biblische Christus* (Theologische Bücherei 2; 4th ed.; ed. E. Wolf; Munich: Kaiser, 1969). A translation, with a foreword by Paul Tillich and a helpful introduction by the translator, Carl E. Braaten, can be found in *The So-Called Historical Jesus and the Historic Biblical Christ* (Philadelphia: Fortress, 1964). For further reflections on Kähler's relation to more recent quests, see Carl E. Braaten, "Martin Kähler on the Historic Biblical Christ," *The Historical Jesus and the Kerygmatic Christ*, ed. Carl E. Braaten and Roy A. Harrisville (New York/ Nashville: Abingdon, 1964) 79–105. On p. 84 of *Der sogenannte historische Jesus*, Kähler affirms the divinity of Jesus—although elsewhere he makes clear that theologians are not bound to the wording and concepts of conciliar dogmas and later systematic theology. As Otto Michel observes, Kähler thought his position on Jesus as "true God and true man" was "pre-dogmatic"; see Michel's "Der 'historische Jesus' und das theologische Gewissensproblem [*sic*, probably for Gewissheitsproblem]," *EvT* 15 (1955) 349–63, esp. 352–53. For varying views on Kähler's key categories of *geschichtlich* and *übergeschichtlich*, see Heinrich Leipold, *Offenbarung und Geschichte als Problem des Verstehens. Eine Untersuchung zur Theologie Martin Kählers* (Gütersloh: Mohn, 1962); and Johannes Wirsching, *Gott in der Geschichte. Studien zur theologiegeschichtlichen Stellung und systematischen Grundlegung der Theologie Martin Kählers* (Forschungen zur Geschichte und Lehre des Protestantismus 10/26; Munich: Kaiser, 1963). In general, Leipold is more positive on Kähler's use of the terms than is Wirsching. For further criticism of Kähler's approach, see N. A. Dahl, "Der gekreuzigte Messias," *Der historische Jesus und der kergymatische Christus*, ed. Helmut Ristow and Karl Matthiae (2d ed.; Berlin: Evangelische Verlagsanstalt, 1962) 149–69, esp. 150. For a full bibliography of Kähler's works, see Martin Kähler, *Geschichte der protestantischen Dogmatik im 19. Jahrhundert* (Theologische Bücherei 16; Munich: Kaiser, 1962) 290–307. For Kähler's treatment of the historicity of Jesus within the wider framework of the various systematic presentations of the historicity and personhood of Jesus by 19th-century German theologians, see Reinhard Slenczka, *Geschichtlichkeit und Personsein Jesu Christi. Studien zur christologischen Problematik der historischen Jesusfrage* (Forschungen zur systematischen und ökumenischen Theologie 18; Göttingen: Vandenhoeck & Ruprecht, 1967) 259–302. For the historical influences on Kähler's thought, see, besides the monographs of Leipold and Wirsching, Arij de Willigen, *Martin Kähler* (Assen: van Gorcum, n.d.; dissertation defended in 1945); and Christoph Seiler, *Die theologische Entwicklung Martin Kählers bis 1869* (Beiträge zur Förderung christlicher Theologie 51; Gütersloh: Mohn, 1966).

[20] It is often claimed that Kähler invented the historical/historic distinction. But, at least by way of negative reaction, he owes something to Wilhelm Herrmann's distinction between the basis of faith (everything about the earthly Jesus that is accessible to natural knowledge) and the content of faith (the exalted Christ); see Braaten, *The So-Called Historical Jesus*, 14. Slenczka (*Geschichtlichkeit*, 281–95) points out that Herrmann's distinction is not to be equated with the distinction between the Jesus of history and the Christ of faith (p. 275). On p. 259, Slenczka notes how surprising it is that the overviews of Jesus-of-history research by Albert Schweitzer and James M. Robinson ignore the importance of

the Herrmann-Kähler debate. Beyond the influence of Herrmann, however, one must recognize that talk of *historisch* and *geschichtlich* was very much in the academic air at the time, especially under the impact of the historical-critical method and the seminar system developed by the great German historian Leopold von Ranke (1795–1886). Another significant influence on Kähler's views was probably the Erlangen school of theology (not as well known outside Germany as the Tübingen school), which stressed *Heilsgeschichte* and the nature of Christianity as a historical religion.

[21] See his *Theology of the New Testament* (2 vols.; London: SCM, 1952), especially Chapter 1, "The Message of Jesus," pp. 3–32. A famous lecture on the subject became the monograph *Das Verhältnis der urchristlichen Christusbotschaft zum historischen Jesus* (3d ed.; Heidelberg: Winter/Universitätsverlag, 1962); a brief synopsis of the monograph appeared as "Das Verhältnis des urchristlichen Christuskerygmas zum historischen Jesus," *Der historische Jesus und der kerygmatische Christus*, 233–35; an English translation of the lecture can be found in "The Primitive Christian Kerygma and the Historical Jesus," *The Historical Jesus and the Kerygmatic Christ*, ed. Carl E. Braaten and Roy A. Harrisville (New York/Nashville: Abingdon, 1964) 15–42. An earlier form (first published in 1926) of Bultmann's thought on Jesus' teaching (with heavy existentialist overtones) is *Jesus and the Word* (London/Glasgow: Fontana [Collins], 1958). In general, note that at times Bultmann will use "kerygmatic" in place of "historic," an echo of his "kerygmatic" theology.

[22] "The greatest embarrassment to the attempt to reconstruct a portrait of Jesus is the fact that we cannot know how Jesus understood his end, his death. . . . We cannot tell whether or how Jesus found meaning in it. We may not veil from ourselves the possibility that he suffered a collapse" ("The Primitive Christian Kerygma and the Historical Jesus," 23–24).

[23] As Braaten points out ("Martin Kähler on the Historic Biblical Christ," 101), Kähler would not have agreed with Bultmann that the NT *kerygma* needs only the bare fact of Jesus and his cross. "For Kähler the kerygma contains a larger historical section than Bultmann deems necessary. The meaning of the kerygma is nullified if the redemptive events attested—including incarnation, life and teachings, cross and resurrection—never happened. Faith cannot appropriate the meaning of events if there are no events in the first place. . . . There is no necessity to eliminate everything but the cross of Jesus" (ibid.). As R. Hermann points out in the article on Martin Kähler in the 3d ed. of *RGG* (Vol. 3, cols. 1082–84), "a tendency to 'demythologize' was far from the mind of Kähler" (col. 1082).

[24] Bultmann, *Jesus and the Word*, 14. In fairness to Bultmann, two points should be noted. First, in the text quoted, Bultmann is reacting against the excesses of the heavily psychologizing 19th-century "liberal lives" of Jesus. Second, Robinson (*A New Quest*, 19–22) detects a shift in Bultmann's position in a later article ("Allgemeine Wahrheit und christliche Verkündigung," *ZTK* 54 [1957] 244–54): Bultmann sees some continuity between Jesus and the Christian *kerygma* on the question of law and grace (pp. 251–54). Be that as it may, the

article in no way changes his basic position on the *historisch/geschichtlich* distinction.

²⁵ Bultmann himself rejects the claim that he destroys the continuity between the historical Jesus and the *kerygma*. Nevertheless, one is not encouraged when in a key essay he specifies that he will treat only the continuity between the historical Jesus and the primitive Christian proclamation "and not, between the historical Jesus and the Christ. The Christ of the kerygma is not a historical figure which could enjoy continuity with the historical Jesus" ("The Primitive Christian Kerygma and the Historical Jesus," 18). At the same time, even Bultmann's great opponent Paul Althaus admits that Bultmann never went to the extreme of some theologians who, deeply influenced by German idealism, distinguished between the historical person of Jesus and the concept or ideal of a symbolic Christ: the former is not unconditionally tied to the latter and can ultimately be dispensed with. For Althaus' criticism of Martin Werner, Fritz Buri, and like-minded theologians, see his *The So-Called Kerygma and the Historical Jesus* (Edinburgh/London: Oliver and Boyd, 1959) 13–18.

²⁶ See Paul Althaus, *Der gegenwärtige Stand der Frage nach dem historischen Jesus* (Bayerische Akademie der Wissenschaften, Philosophisch-Historische Klasse, Sitzungsberichte, Heft 6; Munich: Verlag der Bayerischen Akademie der Wissenschaften, 1960) 3–19; idem, *The So-Called Kerygma and the Historical Jesus*, esp. 38–42, where he criticizes what he considers the undue narrowing of the meaning of *geschichtlich* in the Bultmannian camp.

²⁷ There is no reason to go into the precise positions of the various post-Bultmannians like Bornkamm and Conzelmann, since that would not alter my basic point, namely, the wide variation in meaning and use of the historical/ historic distinction. For a representative sample of the post-Bultmannians, see Günther Bornkamm, *Jesus of Nazareth* (New York: Harper & Row, 1960); Hans Conzelmann, "The Method of the Life-of-Jesus Research," *The Historical Jesus and the Kerygmatic Christ*, 54–68; idem, *Jesus* (Philadelphia: Fortress, 1973); Ernst Fuchs, *Studies of the Historical Jesus* (SBT 42; Naperville, IL: Allenson, 1964); Herbert Braun, "The Significance of Qumran for the Problem of the Historical Jesus," *The Historical Jesus and the Kerygmatic Christ*, 69–78; idem, *Jesus of Nazareth. The Man and His Time* (Philadelphia: Fortress, 1979). Ernst Käsemann is widely acknowledged to be the "father" of the new quest among post-Bultmannians; his two most important essays on the topic are "The Problem of the Historical Jesus," *Essays on New Testament Themes* (SBT 41; London: SCM, 1964) 15–47; and "Blind Alleys in the 'Jesus of History' Controversy," *New Testament Questions of Today* (London: SCM, 1969) 23–65. See also his *Der Ruf der Freiheit* (4th ed.; Tübingen: Mohr [Siebeck], 1968). The standard survey of the "new quest" of the post-Bultmannians is James M. Robinson's *A New Quest of the Historical Jesus;* note especially the section on "the ambiguous term 'historical Jesus' " on pp. 26–32.

²⁸ Note the telling use of *Gewähr* (guarantee, surety, warrant) on p. 14 of *Der gegenwärtige Stand.*

[29] Ibid, 19. Althaus hastens to add, in the spirit of Kähler, that such historical knowledge cannot be the basis of faith.

[30] Althaus implicitly admits his shift and the reasons for it in *The So-Called Kerygma*, 25.

[31] However, the great scholar of Jesus research, John Reumann, has suggested to me in an oral communication that Schweitzer may well have known of Kähler's distinction but purposely suppressed Kähler's work on the subject, so as not to disturb the pattern and development Schweitzer wanted to see in the history of Jesus research.

[32] The translations of the quotations about Wobbermin are my own and rest upon the text of Schweitzer's *Geschichte der Leben-Jesu-Forschung* published in 1966 (Vols. 77/78, 79/80; Munich/Hamburg: Siebenstern Taschenbuch) 520–21.

[33] In light of Schweitzer's voluminous knowledge of the 19th-century literature on the historical Jesus, it is astounding that he was ignorant of Kähler's contribution. One might speculate that, if it had not been for Bultmann's recycling of Kähler's distinction, the latter's work might have been lost to large sectors of the theological world.

[34] Joachim Jeremias, "Der gegenwärtige Stand der Debatte um das Problem des historischen Jesus," *Der historische Jesus und der kerygmatische Christus*, 12–25 (English translation: *The Problem of the Historical Jesus* [FBBS 13; Philadelphia: Fortress, 1964]). At one point, the English translation misses a nuance when Jeremias implicitly equates *Historie* and *Geschichte*, instead of engaging in the Kähler/Bultmann distinction: "For the kerygma—God was in Christ and reconciled the world with himself—refers to a historical *(historisches)* event. God was revealing himself in a happening in history *(Geschichte)*" ("Der gegenwärtige Stand," 19). (This way of putting things may also reflect the fact that, in ordinary German, *Historie* would not be used all that often, being largely an academic loanword from Latin.)

It is characteristic that Jeremias did not regularly employ the adjective *geschichtlich* of Jesus when he described his own theological program; he rather spoke of the historical Jesus and the faith-witness of the early Church. John Reumann has pointed out to me that this usage mirrors Jeremias' own theological agenda: revelation is to be found in the historical Jesus, not in the later, post-Easter response of the Christian Church.

For a full presentation of what Jeremias thought could be said about the historical Jesus, see his *New Testament Theology. Part One. The Proclamation of Jesus* (London: SCM, 1971). Interestingly, Küng has shown a similar distaste for a firm distinction between *historisch* and *geschichtlich*; see his *Christ sein*, 148–53.

[35] Norman Perrin, *Rediscovering the Teaching of Jesus* (London: SCM, 1967) 234–38.

[36] For further comments on Perrin's approach, see Amos N. Wilder, "Norman Perrin and the Relation of Historical Knowledge to Faith," *HTR* 82 (1989) 201–11, with the literature cited there.

[37] Ibid., 238.

[38] It is intriguing that, while Perrin claims that his position is that of Bultmann, he admits that Bultmann was prepared "to describe almost all of the faith-knowledge in terms of historic knowledge" (ibid., 240 n. 1). In effect, does this not grant that Bultmann's distinction was basically the twofold one of Kähler, not the threefold one Perrin is urging?

[39] It is remarkable how quickly Kähler leaps from the general sense of "historic," applicable to any person who has been influential in molding posterity, to the exclusivistic sense in which he applies the term to Jesus as Lord, whose influence in molding posterity consists precisely in the creation of the Easter faith in his disciples; see Kähler, *The So-Called Historical Jesus*, 63–64. In a sense, Kähler is operating by way of theological analogy: from the use of "historic" for any influential figure of the past, relevant to us today, he moves to the uniquely influential figure of Jesus, relevant to Christianity as its only Lord. The linchpin of the analogy is that, in Jesus' case, his influence is the creation of a unique, exclusivistic faith. No doubt it is this "slide" which both opens up the possibility of a three-part distinction for Perrin but also creates difficulties for him.

[40] It is significant that Willibald Beyschlag, Otto Ritschl, and Ferdinand Kattenbusch all found Kähler's concept of the historic Christ objectionable because it seemed to put Jesus on the same level as, e.g., Francis of Assisi vis-à-vis later Franciscans. Kähler replied that Jesus' unique historic impact flows from the revelation of him as the Risen One; hence the historic Jesus is not to be compared with Francis of Assisi or Ignatius of Loyola as the founding fathers of the Franciscans or the Jesuits respectively. See the excerpts of the arguments in the footnotes in the German edition of Kähler's essay, *Der sogenannte historische Jesus*, 38–39 n. a.

CHAPTER 2

SOURCES:

The Canonical Books of the New Testament

The major source of our knowledge about the historical Jesus[1] is also the major problem: the four canonical Gospels (Mark, Matthew, Luke, and John) that Christians accept as part of the New Testament. The Gospels are not primarily works of history in the modern sense of the word. They aim first of all at proclaiming and strengthening faith in Jesus as Son of God, Lord, and Messiah. Their presentation from start to finish is formed by their faith that the crucified Jesus was raised from the dead and will come in glory to judge the world. Moreover, the Gospels do not intend or claim to give anything like a complete narrative or even summary of Jesus' life. Mark and John present the adult Jesus beginning his ministry, a ministry that lasts at most for a few years. Both Matthew and Luke prefix to the public ministry two chapters of infancy narratives, the historicity of which is very much debated. Immediately, we recognize the impossibility of writing a biography (in the modern sense) of a man who died in his thirties when we know at best selected events from three or four years of his life.

Still worse, we know next to nothing about the true historical sequence of the events that are preserved for us. The form critics of the 1920s rightly pointed out that behind Mark, our earliest Gospel, lie collections of oral or written traditions tied together by common forms, themes, and key words.[2] Such collections are still visible in Mark: e.g., the controversy stories placed early in the Galilean ministry (2:1–3:6), balanced by Mark with another collection of controversy stories placed in Jerusalem at the end of the ministry (11:27–12:34); a central section of miracle stories and sayings of Jesus tied together by the key word "bread" (6:6b–8:21); and a collection of parables (4:1–34). There is no reason for us to take these collections as preserving the inviolable chronological order of events, especially since Matthew and Luke did not. Matthew, for instance, freely reorders Mark's miracle stories to create a neat collection of nine miracle stories divided into three groups of stories divided by "buffer" material (Matthew 8–9). Matthew's grand Sermon on the Mount is found partly in Luke's smaller Sermon on the Plain (both sermons being placed in Galilee) and partly in material scattered throughout Luke's lengthy account of Jesus' final journey up to Jerusalem (Luke 9:51–19:27).

In short, each Synoptist has rearranged the rosary beads (= the pericopes) on the rosary chain (= the structure of his Gospel) to suit his own theological vision. Since even the pre-Gospel collections of pericopes were already artificially arranged, in most cases there is no way in which we can determine which order of events might be historical—if, indeed, any is. We can be fairly sure that Jesus' ministry began after his baptism by John in the Jordan and ended with a final, fateful journey to Jerusalem for the feast of Passover. The exact length of the intervening time and the exact order of the events of the public ministry cannot be known. Without a sense of "before and after," any biography in the modern sense—and indeed any sketch of the psychological or religious development of Jesus—is impossible.

To compound the confusion, in the Fourth Gospel John largely goes his own way, concentrating Jesus' ministry not in Galilee, like the Synoptists, but rather in Judea and Jerusalem. Apart from the "epilogue" of Chapter 21 (probably added by a final redactor),[3] only one chapter in John focuses solely on the Galilean ministry (Chapter 6). In the Fourth Gospel, the adult Jesus journeys to Judea and Jerusalem at least four times, as opposed to one journey at the end of the public ministry in the Synoptics. From the patristic period onward, Christians have sought to dovetail the Synoptic and Johannine chronologies to create a "harmony of the Gospels,"[4] but any such conflation remains highly speculative and ignores the nature of the sources.[5] For, if each Gospel contains not a historically accurate chronological order but an artificial theological schema, putting all Four Gospels together will produce only a confused heap of theological schemas, not the chronological order that none of them has anyway.

Chronological order is not the only thing that the Gospels do not yield. There is a basic question of whether the Gospels preserve for us the exact words of Jesus, or only—at best—the substance of what he said. Perhaps the 20th-century scholar who was most confident about our ability to extract the very voice of Jesus from the Gospels was Joachim Jeremias, who labored to reconstruct the original Aramaic of various authentic sayings of Jesus.[6] Yet there is real reason to wonder whether the Gospel tradition and the evangelists were all that concerned about the precise wording of what Jesus said. Granted, some variations in the same saying or parable can be explained away by supposing that Jesus the peripatetic teacher regularly repeated his material in various forms. Even here, though, we are led to the logical conclusion that no one form of a saying can be designated *the* original form.

However, Jesus' repetition of the same teaching on many different occasions cannot explain all the variations in wording in the NT. For example, we have four reports of what Jesus said over the bread and wine at the Last Supper (Mark 14:22–25; Matt 26:26–29; Luke 22:19–20; 1 Cor 11:23–26), and all four versions differ among themselves. Obviously, Jesus was able to say these words only once before his life abruptly ended; hence we cannot appeal to supposed repetitions in various forms. We have here a telling datum: the "eucharistic words" were clearly important to the early Church—witness their four formulations! Yet importance to the early Church guaranteed agreement in substance, not in exact wording. If this is true for these vital "words of institution" at the Last Supper, do we have any reason to think that other words of Jesus were preserved with greater zeal for word-for-word accuracy? Decades of liturgical adaptation, homiletic expansion, and creative activity on the part of Christian prophets[7] have all left their mark on the words of Jesus in the Four Gospels. The different versions of such important material as the Lord's Prayer (Matt 6:9–13; Luke 11:2–4) and the beatitudes (Matt 5:3–12; Luke 6:20b–23) only reinforce the impression that, in seeking the teaching of the historical Jesus, we must often be satisfied with basic content and hypothetical reconstructions of "the earliest form available" —whether or not that actually goes back to Jesus.

All these observations raise the question of the dating of the canonical Gospels and of their sources. I accept the standard view in NT research today:[8] Mark, using various collections of oral and possibly written traditions, composed his Gospel somewhere around A.D. 70. Both Matthew and Luke, working independently of each other, composed larger Gospels in the 70–100 period (most likely between 80 and 90) by combining and editing Mark, a collection of Jesus' sayings that scholars arbitrarily label Q,[9] and special traditions peculiar to Matthew and Luke. This is known as the two-source hypothesis. Though it is the most commonly used today, it is not universally accepted. For example, some critics like William Farmer and C. S. Mann maintain the Griesbach hypothesis: Matthew wrote first, then Luke wrote, depending on Matthew, and finally Mark composed a digest or conflation of Matthew and Luke.[10] Other scholars accept Mark's priority but doubt the existence of the hypothetical Q document, which must be reconstructed from the material common to Matthew and Luke but not found in Mark.[11] My previous work in redaction criticism of Matthew has convinced me that the two-source hypothesis, while not without its problems, is the most viable theory.[12] It is also the one most used by the international community of scholars; hence it will be the hypothesis employed here. The important upshot of this position is that Mark and Q provide two different sources for comparison and verification.

Whether the Gospel of John likewise offers an independent source of knowledge about Jesus alongside of Mark and Q is still hotly debated. Early in this century it was largely taken for granted that John knew and used the Synoptic Gospels. P. Gardner-Smith challenged that view in 1938,[13] claiming that John represented an independent tradition. This position was worked out in detail by C. H. Dodd[14] and was accepted by such major commentators as Raymond Brown, Rudolf Schnackenburg, and Ernst Haenchen.[15] It is probably the majority opinion today, but by no means the unanimous one.[16] For instance, the great Louvain exegete Frans Neirynck holds that John is dependent on Mark, Matthew, and Luke.[17] In my opinion, however, scholars like Dodd and Brown have the better part of the argument. The Johannine presentation of Jesus' ministry is just too massively different to be derived from the Synoptics; and even where John does parallel the Synoptics, the strange mixture and erratic pattern of agreements and disagreements are best explained by a stream of tradition similar to, but independent of, the Synoptics.[18] In short, our survey of the Four Gospels gives us three separate major sources to work with: Mark, Q, and John.

I call these sources "major" to contrast them with two minor and problematic sources, namely, M and L. By M and L, I mean the traditions that are unique to the Gospels of Matthew (M) and Luke (L) respectively.[19] One isolates these traditions by subtracting from the given Gospel all that is judged to come from Mark, Q, and the redactional activity of the evangelist. Precisely because these M and L traditions were formed and/or handed down by the local churches that also helped form the theological outlooks of Matthew and Luke themselves, it is at times extremely difficult to distinguish M tradition from Matthew's redaction and L tradition from Luke's redaction. Not surprisingly, the vocabulary, style, and theological content of these traditions can frequently coincide with those of Matthew and Luke. Hence the source critic is left in something of a quandary. Only when the vocabulary, style, and theological vision of the material unique to Matthew or Luke diverge from that of the evangelist can we feel fairly secure in declaring the material M or L tradition and not a redactional creation.[20] Even then, we cannot automatically move from M or L tradition to an authentic saying of Jesus. Because the M or L material, by definition, lacks any parallel, decisions on historicity are not easy to reach and must be made on a case-to-case basis. Granted all these caveats—as well as the fragmentary nature of the M and L traditions[21]—I think one must rank them as minor rather than major sources.

The question of historical value plagues the material from the Fourth Gospel even more, and some critics simply ignore John. Nevertheless, contrary to the tendency of Bultmann and his followers, John's Gospel, in my opinion, is not to be rejected en masse and a priori as a source for the historical Jesus. To be sure, the rewriting of narratives for symbolic purposes and the reformulation of sayings for theological programs reach their high point in John. Yet such tendencies are not totally absent from the Synoptics, and at times (e.g., in such questions as the nature of the Last Supper and the date of Jesus' death) John rather than the Synoptics may be historically correct.[22] Each case must be judged on its own merits; the "tyranny of the Synoptic Jesus"[23] should be consigned to the dustbin of the post-Bultmannians.

Outside of the Four Gospels, the NT yields precious little about Jesus. By sheer bulk the most likely source of information is Paul, the only writer of NT material who without a doubt comes from the first Christian generation.[24] Since the center of Paul's theology is the death and resurrection of Jesus, the events and sayings of the earthly Jesus simply do not play a large role in his letters. More to the point, his letters did not aim generally at imparting initial knowledge about Jesus, which was rather presupposed—and recalled only when necessary. It is usually in the few cases where pressing problems (notably in the church at Corinth) force Paul to repeat basic doctrine that he had imparted when he first preached the gospel to a given congregation that he has recourse to the words of Jesus and the events of his life. For example, the problem of divorce among the Corinthians leads Paul—in a most unusual move for him—to appeal to the teaching of Jesus forbidding divorce (1 Cor 7:10–11); yet even here it is paraphrased rather than given verbatim (cf., e.g., Mark 10:11–12; Matt 5:32; Luke 16:18). Paul's defense of his independent way of supporting himself financially causes him to allude to Jesus' sayings on the support of missionaries (1 Cor 9:14; cf. Matt 10:10; Luke 10:7). The lack of Christian charity displayed at Corinthian eucharists moves Paul to recall the actions and words of Jesus at the Last Supper (1 Cor 11:23–26). Difficulties over the doctrine that Christians will rise on the last day occasion the recitation of a very ancient Christian creed that includes the basic fact of Jesus' death and burial (1 Cor 15:3).

Yet in most of these cases we should not speak of Paul "quoting" the words of Jesus. They are allusions rather than citations, since, except in the case of the eucharistic words of Jesus, Paul gives simply the gist of Jesus' teaching, always with an eye to the application Paul wishes to make as he argues with the Corinthians. The very fact, though, that Paul (1) can allude in passing to sayings of Jesus, (2) can expect the Corinthians to recognize them and accept them as normative, and (3) can appeal at times to precise teaching about Jesus that Paul received after his conversion and imparted to the Corinthians after their conversion (1 Cor 11:23; 15:3) argues for a certain fund of teachings from and about Jesus circulating among first-generation Pauline churches. It is surely significant that, in each case in 1 Corinthians where Paul appeals to teachings from or about Jesus, we find parallel material in the Synoptics. It is likewise noteworthy that Paul carefully distinguishes (1 Cor 7:10–13) between Jesus' saying on divorce and Paul's own application of that saying to a new situation (marriages between Christians and pagans). For all his claims to apostolic authority, Paul does not feel free to create teachings and put them into the mouth of Jesus. We might ask: Who in the first generation did?

While these few clear cases in 1 Corinthians are helpful in giving us an independent source for checking the Synoptics (especially in the sayings on divorce and on the eucharist), one must admit that they nearly exhaust the usefulness of the Pauline epistles in the quest for the historical Jesus. One can find a few pieces of further data scattered throughout the epistles (e.g., Jesus was of Davidic descent, Rom 1:3; his mission was oriented to Israel, not to the Gentiles, Rom 15:8). But, again, these at best simply confirm what the Gospels tell us anyway. At most, these Pauline texts inform us that such facts about Jesus were taught even in far-flung churches not founded by Paul (Rome!) during the first Christian generation.

Some critics point to another possible Pauline source of information: the large sections of Paul's parenesis (= moral exhortation) that find parallels in the teaching of Jesus. The data, however, allow of many explanations. Was Paul consciously using teaching that both he and his converts knew came from Jesus—Paul not bothering to advert to the well-known source of his exhortation? Or was Paul using material that de facto came from Jesus without Paul's knowing its origin? Or did Jesus and Paul both use similar Jewish ethical and wisdom traditions in their exhortations? Or did Paul and other first-generation Christians develop parenesis that then passed into the Synoptic tradition and was attributed to Jesus? All of these options are possible, and all may be true to some degree. At times, close similarity in both form and content, as well as dissimilarity from the wider religious environment of the 1st century, may make dependence of Paul on Jesus likely. Such may be the case in the exhortation to love one's enemies or persecutors, as it is preserved in Matt 5:38–48; Luke 6:27–36 on the one hand and in Rom 12:14, 17–20; 1 Thess 5:15; 1 Cor 4:12 (cf. 1 Pet 3:9) on the other.[25]

Outside of such special cases, though, one remains uncertain as to how much Paul knew. At any rate, our knowledge of the historical Jesus would not be enhanced even if these parenetic passages were shown to be derived from Jesus. After all, the very reason they are candidates for consideration is that they parallel material present also in the Synoptics. At best, therefore, they could only serve as checks on the Synoptic tradition, not sources of new information.

Beyond Paul, the rest of the NT yields an even more meager harvest. The Epistle of James, like the Pauline and other NT epistles, may contain some reworked sayings of Jesus. The clearest candidate is the prohibition of oaths in James 5:12 (cf. Matt 5:34–37). The First Epistle of Peter is another possible source, though the question whether the author knew other documents now found in the NT complicates the issue.[26] The Epistle to the Hebrews does mention—as an apparent obstacle to its thesis that Jesus is *the* high priest of the new covenant—that he was of the tribe of Judah, not Levi (Heb 7:14). It also knows a tradition akin to Jesus' agonized prayer in Gethsemane (Heb 5:7–8; cf. Mark 14:32–42 parrs.; also John 12:27–36a). The Revelation of John knows apocalyptic language and metaphors found also in Jesus' eschatological discourse. For example, the daring image of the thief applied to Jesus coming at the end of time is found both in Q (Matt 24:43; Luke 12:39) and Rev 3:3; 16:15 (cf. the softened version in 1 Thess 5:2,4; 2 Pet 3:10, where the "day of the Lord" comes like a thief).[27] In all four texts the words are spoken directly by Jesus—in the Gospels, the earthly Jesus; in Revelation, the risen and exalted Jesus. Here, of course, is the problem: Has a saying of the historical Jesus been put into the mouth of the risen Christ, seen in a vision by the seer of Revelation? Or have Christian prophets, having heard these words in their visions of the risen Lord, put them into the mouth of the earthly Jesus? In the larger picture, a decision makes little difference to our project, since once again the material adds nothing of substance to the fund of data available from the Four Gospels. Within the NT, we are basically thrown back on the Gospels. Hence, in subsequent chapters we must inquire whether we can find any independent source of information about the historical Jesus outside of the NT.

[1] From now on, unless explicitly specified, the noun "Jesus" will be understood to mean "the historical Jesus" as defined in Chapter 1. This will save needless repetition of modifying phrases.

[2] We owe this insight in particular to the three "greats" of form criticism: Rudolf Bultmann, Martin Dibelius, and Karl Ludwig Schmidt. The key works of Bultmann and Dibelius will be cited according to the German originals, since the English translations of both works are unreliable: Rudolf Bultmann, *Die Geschichte der synoptischen Tradition* (FRLANT 29; 8th ed.; Göttingen: Vandenhoeck & Ruprecht, 1970; 1st ed. 1921), with *Ergänzungsheft* (4th ed.; ed. Gerd Theissen and Philipp Vielhauer; Göttingen: Vandenhoeck & Ruprecht, 1971); ET: *History of the Synoptic Tradition* (2d ed.; New York/Evanston: Harper & Row, 1968); Martin Dibelius, *Die Formgeschichte des Evangeliums* (6th ed.; ed. Günther Bornkamm; Tübingen: Mohr [Siebeck], 1971; 1st ed. 1919); ET: *From Tradition to Gospel* (New York: Charles Scribner's Sons, n.d.). It is unfortunate that the work of the third giant has not been translated into English, since more than anyone else he established that the narrative framework of Mark (and, a fortiori, the other evangelists) should not be taken as historical: Karl Ludwig Schmidt, *Der Rahmen der Geschichte Jesu* (Darmstadt: Wissenschaftliche Buchgesellschaft, 1969; 1st ed., 1919).—As is clear from what I say in the text, I do not agree with those Marcan critics who think that Mark created most of his material, with at best fragments of tradition existing before his composition. Needless to say, even such a view allows of degrees of creativity. See, e.g., the various views of the authors in Werner H. Kelber, ed., *The Passion in Mark* (Philadelphia: Fortress, 1976); cf. Werner H. Kelber, *The Oral and the Written Gospel* (Philadelphia: Fortress, 1983); also Burton L. Mack, *A Myth of Innocence. Mark and Christian Origins* (Philadelphia: Fortress, 1988).

[3] The basic arguments for seeing a different hand in Chapter 21 can be found in Raymond E. Brown, *The Gospel According to John (xiii–xxi)* (AB 29A; Garden City, NY: Doubleday, 1970) 1077–82. I do not think that they are effectively overcome by Paul S. Minear, "The Original Functions of John 21," *JBL* 102 (1983) 35–98.

[4] For the grand example in the patristic period, see Augustine of Hippo's *De consensu Evangelistarum libri IV*, available in PL 34, 1041–1230; and F. Weihrich, ed., CSEL 43 (1904). A scholarly treatment of the patristic approach to the problem can be found in Helmut Merkel, *Die Widersprüche zwischen den Evangelien. Ihre polemische und apologetische Behandlung in der Alten Kirche bis zu Augustin* (WUNT 13; Tübingen: Mohr [Siebeck], 1971).

[5] For a learned but highly imaginative attempt to conflate John and the Synoptics in the matter of Jesus' many crossings of the Sea of Galilee, see Heinz Kruse, "Jesu Seefahrten und die Stellung von Joh. 6," *NTS* 30 (1984) 508–30. The grand example of this sort of harmonization of all Four Gospels, with John providing the framework, is J. A. T. Robinson's posthumous *The Priority of John,*

ed. J. F. Coakley (Oak Park, IL: Meyer-Stone, 1985). Both works demonstrate how the project at times takes on the appearance of writing a novel.

[6] A typical example of his work is "Kennzeichen der ipsissima vox Jesu," *Abba* (Göttingen: Vandenhoeck & Ruprecht, 1966 [original article, 1954]) 145–52. The great final summary of his work is his *New Testament Theology. Part One. The Proclamation of Jesus* (London: SCM, 1971).

[7] The exact function and the extent of the creative activity of early Christian prophets are much debated among NT scholars. For a range of opinions, see, e.g., D. Hill, "On the Evidence for the Creative Role of Christian Prophets," *NTS* 20 (1973–74) 262–74; idem, *New Testament Prophecy* (Atlanta: John Knox, 1979) 160–85; James D. G. Dunn, "Prophetic 'I' Sayings and the Jesus Tradition," *NTS* 24 (1977–78) 175–98; M. E. Boring, "Christian Prophecy and the Sayings of Jesus: The State of the Question," *NTS* 29 (1983) 104–12; idem, *Sayings of the Risen Jesus* (SNTSMS 46; Cambridge: Cambridge University, 1982); D. Aune, *Prophecy in Early Christianity* (Grand Rapids: Eerdmans, 1983) 233–45. Boring thinks that Christian prophets influenced the Synoptic tradition of Jesus' words in a variety of ways, in addition to coining new sayings of the risen Jesus; such influence can frequently be detected with a reasonable degree of probability. Hill and Aune are more negative toward the idea that Christian prophets created oracles of the risen Lord that were then assimilated to sayings of the earthly Jesus.

[8] The most thorough challenge to the commonly accepted dating of the Gospels is that of J. A. T. Robinson, *Redating the New Testament* (Philadelphia: Westminster, 1976). Robinson wishes to place *all* the writings of the NT before A.D. 70. While he does not even attempt a serious argument for the hopeless case of 2 Peter, he does strain to mount such a defense for Matthew, Luke, and John. The result is a dazzling tour de force that fails to convince. The thesis has been largely rejected by NT scholars; for a telling review, see Robert M. Grant in *JBL* 97 (1978) 294–96.

[9] Recent scholarship indicates that the letter Q was not chosen originally to signify the German word *Quelle* ("source"); see Frans Neirynck, "The Symbol Q (= Quelle)," *ETL* 54 (1978) 119–25; L. Silberman, "Whence *Siglum* Q? A Conjecture," *JBL* 98 (1979) 287–88; for a different view, see H. K. McArthur, "The Origin of the 'Q' Symbol," *ExpTim* 88 (1976–77) 119–20. For reviews of scholarship on Q, see Frans Neirynck, "Recent Developments in the Study of Q," *Logia. Les paroles de Jésus—The Sayings of Jesus* (BETL 59; Joseph Coppens Memorial; ed. J. Delobel; Leuven: Peeters/ Leuven University, 1982) 29–75; a lengthy bibliography on Q compiled by Frans Neirynck and Frans Van Segbroeck, can be found in the same volume on pp. 561–86; Dieter Lührmann, "The Gospel of Mark and the Sayings Collection Q," *JBL* 108 (1989) 51–71. For various presentations and discussions of Q's content, arrangement, theology, tradition history, and community, see Dieter Lührmann, *Die Redaktion der Logienquelle* (WMANT 33; Neukirchen-Vluyn: Neukirchener Verlag, 1969); Siegfried Schulz, *Q. Die Spruchquelle der Evangelisten* (Zurich: Theologischer Verlag, 1972); Paul Hoffmann, *Studien zur Theologie der Logienquelle* (NTAbh 8; 2d ed.; Münster: As-

chendorff, 1975); Richard A. Edwards, *A Theology of Q. Eschatology, Prophecy, and Wisdom* (Philadelphia: Fortress, 1976); Athanasius Polag, *Die Christologie der Logienquelle* (WMANT 45; Neukirchen-Vluyn: Neukirchener Verlag, 1977); Petros Vassiliadis, "The Nature and Extent of the Q Document," *NovT* 20 (1978) 49–73; Rudolf Laufen, *Die Doppelüberlieferungen der Logienquelle und des Markusevangeliums* (BBB 54; Königstein: Hanstein, 1980); John S. Kloppenborg, "Tradition and Redaction in the Synoptic Sayings Source," *CBQ* 46 (1984) 34–62; Ivan Havener, *Q. The Sayings of Jesus* (Good News Studies 19; Wilmington, DE: Glazier, 1987); John S. Kloppenborg, *The Formation of Q. Trajectories in Ancient Wisdom Collections* (Philadelphia: Fortress, 1987); idem, *Q Parallels* (Sonoma, CA: Polebridge, 1988); Migaku Sato, *Q und Prophetie. Studien zur Gattungs- und Traditionsgeschichte der Quelle Q* (WUNT 2/29; Tübingen: Mohr [Siebeck], 1988). See also the report by James M. Robinson, "The International Q Project. Work Session 17 November 1989," *JBL* 109 (1990) 499–501.

[10] William Farmer, *The Synoptic Problem* (New York: Macmillan, 1964); C. S. Mann, *Mark* (AB 27; Garden City, NY: Doubleday, 1986). Paradoxically, Mann winds up refuting the Griesbach hypothesis by being forced to suppose that, in many pericopes that are supposed to be conflations of Matthew and Luke, Mark also used early oral traditions that came from Peter or other first-generation witnesses. This is simply to reintroduce Marcan priority through the back door. Hans-Herbert Stoldt (*Geschichte und Kritik der Markushypothese* [Göttingen: Vandenhoeck & Ruprecht, 1977]) likewise attempts a critique of the two-source hypothesis (implicitly in favor of the Griesbach hypothesis), but the sweeping generalizations of the book, plus its lack of detailed analysis and argumentation, fail to prove anything. Of the making of Synoptic theories there is no end. Another well-known hypothesis is that of P. Benoit and M.-E. Boismard, *Synopse des quatre évangiles en français* (2 vols.; Paris: Cerf, 1966, 1972); the very complexity of this hypothesis tells against it. John M. Rist, on the other hand, has attempted to show that there is no direct literary dependence of one Synoptic on another; see his *On the Independence of Matthew and Mark* (SNTSMS 32; New York: Cambridge University, 1978). But the massive amount of verbal agreements among the Synoptics makes this thesis untenable, even from a purely statistical point of view. On statistics and Synoptic theory, see Robert Morgenthaler, *Statistische Synopse* (Zurich/Stuttgart: Gotthelf, 1971).

[11] For one attempt to dispense with Q in Matthean studies, see M. D. Goulder, *Midrash and Lection in Matthew* (London: SPCK, 1974); for a defense of both the priority of Mark and Q in Lucan studies, see Joseph A. Fitzmyer, "The Priority of Mark and the 'Q' Source in Luke," *To Advance the Gospel* (New York: Crossroad, 1981) 3–40. For a thorough study of the two-source theory from the vantage point of Luke's Gospel, see Joseph A. Fitzmyer, *The Gospel According to Luke (I–IX)* (AB 28; Garden City, NY: Doubleday, 1981) 63–106. A useful collection of essays both for and against the two-source theory can be found in Arthur J. Bellinzoni, Jr., ed., *The Two-Source Hypothesis. A Critical Appraisal* (Macon, GA: Mercer University, 1985).

[12] I became especially convinced of the two-source hypothesis during the

writing of a commentary on Matthew *(Matthew* [NT Message 3; rev. ed.; Wilmington, DE: Glazier, 1981]). It is significant that, when Robert H. Gundry approached the writing of his large commentary on Matthew *(Matthew* [Grand Rapids: Eerdmans, 1982]), he was disposed against the two-source hypothesis. It was precisely his detailed work with the Greek texts of Matthew and Mark that convinced him of the two-source hypothesis (though with his own modifications: Q is much expanded and Luke used Matthew as a secondary source). Perhaps the staunchest defender of the two-source theory in the latter part of the 20th century has been Frans Neirynck; his collected essays, which form something of a *Summa apologetica* for the two-source theory, can be found in *Evangelica. Gospel Studies—Etudes d' évangile,* ed. Frans Van Segbroeck (Leuven: Peeters/Leuven University, 1982). For further bibliography on the Synoptic problem, see Thomas R. W. Longstaff and Page A. Thomas, *The Synoptic Problem. A Bibliography, 1716–1988* (Macon, GA: Mercer University, 1989).

[13] P. Gardner-Smith, *Saint John and the Synoptic Gospels* (Cambridge: Cambridge University, 1938).

[14] C. H. Dodd, *Historical Tradition in the Fourth Gospel* (Cambridge: Cambridge University, 1963).

[15] Raymond E. Brown, *The Gospel According to John (i–xii)* (AB 29; Garden City, NY: Doubleday, 1966) XLIV–XLVII; Rudolf Schnackenburg, *The Gospel According to St John* (3 vols.; London: Burns & Oates, Vol. 1: 1968) 1. 26–43; Ernst Haenchen, *John 1. A Commentary on the Gospel of John, Chapters 1–6* (Hermeneia; Philadelphia: Fortress, 1984) 74–78.

[16] One of the few recent critical commentators on John's Gospel to defend John's dependence on Mark is C. K. Barrett, *The Gospel According to St. John* (2d ed.; Philadelphia: Westminster, 1978). It is symptomatic, though, that in the 2d ed. of his commentary Barrett begs the question by saying that John depends on Mark or Mark-like traditions; that distinction is the very point at issue. The followers of the late Norman Perrin tend to defend John's dependence on Mark; see, e.g., the various essays in Kelber, ed., *The Passion in Mark.* However, the authors' position seems to proceed from the a priori desire to see Mark as the sole creator of an extended Passion Narrative; an independent but similar Passion Narrative from John would destroy their neat thesis (as, indeed, in my opinion, it does). Against John's dependence on Mark in the Passion Narrative is Robert T. Fortna, "Jesus and Peter at the High Priests' House: A Test for the Question of the Relation Between Mark's and John's Gospels," *NTS* 24 (1977–78) 371–83; see also his *The Fourth Gospel and Its Predecessor* (Philadelphia: Fortress, 1988). Also in favor of John's independence of Mark is Barnabas Lindars, "John and the Synoptic Gospels: A Test Case," *NTS* 27 (1981) 287–94. Still in favor of the basic independence of John, but stressing the complexity of the problem, is D. Moody Smith, "John and the Synoptics: Some Dimensions of the Problem," *NTS* 26 (1980) 425–44.

[17] From among his voluminous writings, see in particular "John and the Synoptics," *L'évangile de Jean: Sources, rédaction, théologie* (BETL 44; ed. M. de

Jonge; Leuven: Leuven University, 1977) 73–106; "John and the Synoptics: the Empty Tomb Stories," *NTS* 30 (1984) 161–87; and *Jean et les Synoptiques* (Leuven: Leuven University, 1979). Other scholars in favor of John's dependence include W. Klaiber, "Die Aufgabe einer theologischen Interpretation des 4. Evangeliums," *ZTK* 82 (1985) 300–24; and K. Kleinknecht, "Johannes 13," *ZTK* 82 (1985) 361–88. Neirynck's approach to the empty tomb story is correctly (in my opinion) criticized by J. Becker, "Das Johannesevangelium im Streit der Methoden (1980–84)," *TRu* 51 (1986) 1–78, esp. pp. 22–23: one has to imagine John at his writing desk with the three Synoptics spread out before him, taking one line from one Gospel, another from the second, etc. A similar critique of the view that John knew all the Synoptics is found in Haenchen, *John 1*, 75.

[18] A prime example of this phenomenon is the relation of the narrative of the multiplication of loaves in John to the parallel narratives in the Synoptics; see the comparative chart drawn up by Brown, *John (i–xii)*, 240–43. Especially striking in this comparison is the fact that Mark *thrice* mentions the site of the miracle as wilderness or desert *(erēmos,* 6:31,32,35), while John has no such specification in the parallel verses; yet it is John who makes so much of the manna-in-the-desert theme in the discourse that follows (John 6:31,49). We would have to suppose that John deleted from Mark the very point that would have fit John's redactional theology perfectly—a strange way to edit!

[19] For the M tradition, see W. D. Davies and Dale C. Allison, *The Gospel According to Saint Matthew* (ICC; Edinburgh: Clark, 1988) 121–27. For an attempt to describe Matthew's community from the evidence of his special sayings material, see Stephenson H. Brooks, *Matthew's Community. The Evidence of His Special Sayings Material* (JSNTSup 16; Sheffield: JSOT, 1987). On the special material in Luke, see J. A. Fitzmyer, *The Gospel According to Luke* (AB 28, 28A; Garden City, NY: Doubleday, 1981, 1985) 1. 82–91.

[20] For an example of this delicate procedure, see John P. Meier, "Two Disputed Questions in Matt 28:16–20," *JBL* 96 (1977) 407–24.

[21] The question whether there was a primitive Lucan Gospel (proto-Luke) that existed prior to the incorporation of Marcan material is a special problem. Some aspects of it will be treated in Chapter 11, on chronology.

[22] It is not by accident that these two examples are from the narrative part of the Fourth Gospel rather than from the sayings tradition. In the quest for the historical Jesus, the former is much more useful than the latter, which has undergone massive reformulation from the Johannine perspective.

[23] To this extent, the battle cry of Charles W. Hedrick is well taken; see his "The Tyranny of the Synoptic Jesus," *The Historical Jesus and the Rejected Gospels* (Semeia 44; Atlanta: Scholars, 1988) 1–8. However, I do not share his view that material from Nag Hammadi notably increases our fund of data on the historical Jesus.

[24] For an introduction to the whole problem, a survey of major texts and positions, and a judicious weighing of the evidence, see Frans Neirynck, "Paul

and the Sayings of Jesus," *L'Apôtre Paul* (BETL 73; ed. A. Vanhoye; Leuven: Leuven University/Peeters, 1986) 265–321; Neirynck thinks that, outside of 1 Cor 7:10–11 and 9:14, "there is no certain trace of a conscious use of sayings of Jesus. Possible allusions to gospel sayings can be noted on the basis of similarity of form and context but a direct use of a gospel saying in the form it has been preserved in the synoptic gospels is hardly provable" (p. 320). For a similar though less detailed survey of the data, see N. Walter, "Paulus und die urchristliche Tradition," *NTS* 31 (1985) 498–522; cf. Helmut Koester, *Ancient Christian Gospels. Their History and Development* (London: SCM; Philadelphia: Trinity, 1990) 52–62 (with some debatable views about the problems at Corinth). More positive than Walter on Paul's knowledge of collections of Synoptic sayings is Dale C. Allison, Jr., "The Pauline Epistles and the Synoptic Gospels: The Pattern of the Parallels," *NTS* 28 (1982) 1–32. For detailed studies that concentrate on particular test cases, see David Wenham, "Paul's Use of the Jesus Tradition: Three Samples," and Peter Richardson and Peter Gooch, "Logia of Jesus in 1 Corinthians," both in David Wenham, ed., *Gospel Perspectives. The Jesus Tradition Outside the Gospels. Vol. 5* (Sheffield: JSOT, 1984) 7–37 and 39–62 respectively.

For an older survey that concentrates on the two clear cases mentioned by Neirynck, see David L. Dungan, *The Sayings of Jesus in the Church of Paul* (Philadelphia: Fortress, 1971). Dungan, on the whole, holds a more positive view than Neirynck of the connection between Jesus' teaching and Paul's doctrine and exhortations. Similar positive positions are held, e.g., by W. D. Davies, *Paul and Rabbinic Judaism* (New York/Evanston: Harper & Row, 1948; rev. ed. 1955; Harper Torchbook ed. 1967) 136–46, with a lengthy list of possible texts of Paul that might be dependent on Jesus; David M. Stanley, "Pauline Allusions to the Sayings of Jesus," *CBQ* 23 (1961) 26–39; F. F. Bruce, "Paul and the Historical Jesus," *Paul: Apostle of the Heart Set Free* (Grand Rapids: Eerdmans, 1977) 95–112. Quite negative on any direct relation is Bultmann, *Geschichte der synoptischen Tradition*, 330; similarly in his *Theology of the New Testament* (2 vols.; London: SCM, 1952) 1. 35.

[25] For this special case, see John Piper, *"Love Your Enemies." Jesus' Love Command in the Synoptic Gospels and the Early Christian Paraenesis* (SNTSMS 38; Cambridge: Cambridge University, 1979). Contrary to Piper, Jürgen Sauer ("Traditionsgeschichtliche Erwägungen zu den synoptischen und paulinischen Aussagen über Feindesliebe und Wiedervergeltungsverzicht," *ZNW* 76 [1985] 1–28) does not think the command to love one's enemies and waive retaliation comes from Jesus; rather, Paul represents the oldest Christian literary stage of the tradition, which entered Christianity from OT wisdom, Hellenistic popular philosophy, and Hellenistic Judaism. The bearers of the Q tradition attributed the teaching to Jesus to give it authority. Whatever one thinks of the thesis, Sauer's article is a mine of bibliographical information.

[26] For James, see Koester, *Ancient Christian Gospels*, 71–75; of the eight cases Koester considers, James 5:12 (the prohibition of oaths) seems the best candidate. As Koester points out, we cannot be sure whether James knew any of these sayings as sayings of Jesus, but "it is quite possible" that he did so (p. 75). Peter H. Davids ("James and Jesus," David Wenham, ed., *Gospel Perspectives. The Jesus*

Tradition Outside the Gospels [Sheffield: JSOT, 1984] 63–84) inclines to the view that the Epistle of James presupposes the Jesus tradition as the rule of life for the community; see also his "The Epistle of James in Modern Discussion," *Aufstieg und Niedergang der römischen Welt* II/25.5, 3621–45.

Dependence on the Jesus tradition is also supported for 1 Peter by Gerhard Maier, "Jesustradition im 1. Petrusbrief," David Wenham, ed., *Gospel Perspectives. The Jesus Tradition Outside the Gospels* (Sheffield: JSOT, 1984) 85–128. Maier stresses that his conclusions must remain speculative. Indeed, his claim that 1 Peter was probably written by the Apostle Peter and his assigning of quite early dates to various NT documents make his whole position problematic. Also complicating the question of 1 Peter is the claim made by some scholars that the author of 1 Peter used Romans or Ephesians; this position is considered but rejected by Edouard Cothenet, "La Première de Pierre: bilan de 35 ans de recherches," *Aufstieg und Niedergang der römischen Welt* II/25.5, 3685–3712, esp. 3693–94.

[27] For the possibility that Paul as well as the author of Revelation knew a pre-Synoptic form of Jesus' eschatological discourse and used it, see David Wenham, *The Rediscovery of Jesus' Eschatological Discourse* (Gospel Perspectives 4; Sheffield: JSOT, 1984) 366–67, 372. Wenham stresses that the examination of the eschatological material indicates that Paul was not unfamiliar with or uninterested in the Jesus tradition. Unfortunately, Wenham's unusual views on the Synoptic problem (all three Synoptists used a primitive Gospel, and Matthew and Luke used Mark as well) and on Pauline authorship (both Ephesians and the Pastorals are attributed to Paul) weaken his conclusions somewhat.

CHAPTER 3

SOURCES:

Josephus

When we look for statements about Jesus from noncanonical writings of the 1st or 2d century A.D., we are at first disappointed by the lack of references. We have to remember that Jews and pagans of this period, if they were at all aware of a new religious phenomenon on the horizon, would be more aware of the nascent group called Christianity than of its putative founder Jesus. Some of these writers, at least, had had direct or indirect contact with Christians; none of them had had contact with the Christ Christians worshiped. This simply reminds us that Jesus was a marginal Jew leading a marginal movement in a marginal province of a vast Roman Empire. The wonder is that any learned Jew or pagan would have known or referred to him at all in the 1st or early 2d century. Surprisingly, there are a number of possible references to Jesus, though most are riddled with problems of authenticity and interpretation.

The first and most important potential "witness" to Jesus' life and activity is the Jewish aristocrat, politician, soldier, turncoat, and historian, Joseph ben Matthias (A.D. 37/38–sometime after 100).[1] Known as Flavius Josephus from his patrons the Flavian emperors (Vespasian and his sons Titus and Domitian), he wrote two great works: *The Jewish War*, begun in the years immediately following the fall of Jerusalem in A.D. 70, and the much longer *Jewish Antiquities*, written ca. 93–94.[2] Both books, at least in some versions, contain passages mentioning Jesus. The problem is that at least one passage is certainly a later Christian product. The question is: Are the other passages spurious as well?[3]

The clearly unauthentic text is a long interpolation found only in the Old Russian (popularly known as the "Slavonic") version of *The Jewish War*, surviving in Russian and Rumanian manuscripts.[4] This passage is a wildly garbled condensation of various Gospel events, seasoned with the sort of bizarre legendary expansions found in apocryphal gospels and acts of the 2d and 3d centuries. Despite the spirited and ingenious attempt of Robert Eisler to defend the authenticity of much of the Jesus material in the Slavonic *Jewish War*, almost all critics today discount his theory. In more recent decades, G. A. Williamson stood in a hopeless minority when he tried to maintain the authenticity of this and similar interpolations, which obviously come from a Christian hand (though not necessarily an orthodox one).[5]

More difficult to judge are the two references to Jesus in *The Jewish Antiquities*. The shorter passage—and the one less disputed—occurs in a context where Josephus has just described the death of the procurator Festus and the appointment of Albinus as his successor (A.D. 62). While Albinus is still on his way to Palestine, the high priest Ananus the Younger convenes the Sanhedrin without the procurator's consent and has certain enemies put to death. The key passage *(Ant.* 20.9.1 §200) reads: "Being therefore this kind of person [i.e., a heartless Sadducee], Ananus, thinking that he had a favorable opportunity because Festus had died and Albinus was still on his way, called a meeting [literally, "sanhedrin"] of judges and brought into it the brother of Jesus-who-is-called-Messiah [*ton adelphon Iēsou tou legomenou Christou*], James by name, and some others. He made the accusation that they had transgressed the law, and he handed them over to be stoned."[6]

There are a number of intriguing points about this short passage. First of all, unlike the text about Jesus from the Slavonic Josephus, this narrative is found in the main Greek-manuscript tradition of *The Antiquities* without any notable variation. The early 4th-century Church historian Eusebius also quotes this passage from Josephus in his *Ecclesiastical History* (2.23.22).

Second, unlike the extensive review of Jesus' ministry in the Slavonic Josephus, we have here only a passing, almost blasé reference to someone called James, whom Josephus obviously considers a minor character. He is mentioned only because his illegal execution causes Ananus to be deposed. But since "James" (actually, the Greek form of the English name James is *Iakōbos*, Jacob) is so common in Jewish usage and in Josephus' writings, Josephus needs some designation to specify which Jacob/James he is talking about.[7] Josephus apparently knows of no pedigree (e.g., "James the son of Joseph") he can use to identify this James; hence he is forced to identify him by his better-known brother, Jesus, who in turn is specified as that particular Jesus "who-is-called-Messiah."

This leads to a third significant point: the way the text identifies James is not likely to have come from a Christian hand or even a Christian source. Neither the NT nor early Christian writers spoke of James of Jerusalem in a matter-of-fact way as "the brother of Jesus" *(ho adelphos Iēsou)*, but rather—with the reverence we would expect—"the brother of the Lord" *(ho adelphos tou kyriou)* or "the brother of the Savior" *(ho adelphos tou sōtēros)*. Paul, who was not overly fond of James, calls him "the brother of the Lord" in Gal 1:19 and no doubt is thinking especially of him when he speaks of "the brothers of the Lord" in 1 Cor 9:5. Hegesippus, the 2d-century Church historian who was a Jewish convert and probably hailed from Palestine, likewise speaks of "James, the brother of the Lord" (in Eusebius' *Ecclesiastical History* 2.23.4);[8] indeed, Hegesippus also speaks of certain other well-known Palestinian Christians as "a cousin of the Lord" (4.22.4), "the brothers of the Savior" (3.32.5), and "his [the Lord's] brother according to the flesh" (3.20.1). The point of all this is that Josephus' designation of James as "the brother of Jesus" squares neither with NT nor with early patristic usage, and so does not likely come from the hand of a Christian interpolator.[9]

Fourth, the likelihood of the text coming from Josephus and not an early Christian is increased by the fact that Josephus' account of James's martyrdom differs in time and manner from that of Hegesippus. Josephus has James stoned to death by order of the high priest Ananus before the Jewish War actually breaks out (therefore, early in A.D. 62). According to Hegesippus, the scribes and Pharisees cast James down from the battlement of the Jerusalem temple. They begin to stone him but are constrained by a priest; finally a laundryman clubs James to death (2.23.12–18). James's martyrdom, says Hegesippus, was followed immediately by Vespasian's siege of Jerusalem (A.D. 70). Eusebius stresses that Hegesippus' account agrees basically with that of the Church Father Clement of Alexandria (2.23.3,19); hence it was apparently the standard Christian story. Once again, it is highly unlikely that Josephus' version is the result of Christian editing of *The Jewish Antiquities*.

Fifth, there is also the glaring difference between the long, legendary, and edifying (for Christians) account from Hegesippus and the short, matter-of-fact statement of Josephus, who is interested in the illegal behavior of Ananus, not the faith and virtue of James. In fact,

Josephus never tells us why James was the object of Ananus' wrath, unless being the "brother of Jesus-who-is-called-Messiah" is thought to be enough of a crime. Praise of James is notably lacking; he is one victim among several, not a glorious martyr dying alone in the spotlight.[10] Also telling is the swipe at the "heartless" or "ruthless" Sadducees by the pro-Pharisaic Josephus; indeed, Josephus' more negative view of the Sadducees is one of the notable shifts from *The Jewish War* that characterize *The Antiquities*.[11] In short, it is not surprising that the great Josephus scholar Louis H. Feldman notes: ". . . few have doubted the genuineness of this passage on James."[12]

If we judge this short passage about James to be authentic, we are already aided in the much more difficult judgment about the second, longer, and more disputed text in *Ant.* 18.3.3 §63–64. This is the so-called *Testimonium Flavianum* (i.e., the "testimony of Flavius Josephus"). Almost every opinion imaginable has been voiced on the authenticity or inauthenticity of this passage. Four basic positions can be distilled.[13] (1) The entire account about Jesus is a Christian interpolation; Josephus simply did not mention Jesus in this section of *The Antiquities*. (2) While there are signs of heavy Christian redaction, some mention of Jesus at this point in *The Antiquities*—perhaps a pejorative one—caused a Christian scribe to substitute his own positive account. The original wording as a whole has been lost, though some traces of what Josephus wrote may still be found. (3) The text before us is basically what Josephus wrote; the two or three insertions by a Christian scribe are easily isolated from the clearly non-Christian core. Often, however, scholars will proceed to make some modifications in the text after the insertions are omitted. (4) The *Testimonium* is entirely by Josephus.

With a few exceptions, this last position has been given up today by the scholarly community.[14] The first opinion has its respectable defenders but does not seem to be the majority view.[15] Most recent opinions move somewhere within the spectrum of the second and third positions.[16] It is perhaps symptomatic that among sustainers of some authentic substratum (plus Christian additions, changes, and deletions) are the Jewish scholars Paul Winter and Louis H. Feldman, the hardly orthodox Christian scholars S. G. F. Brandon and Morton Smith, main-line Protestant scholars like James H. Charlesworth, and Catholic scholars like Carlo M. Martini, Wolfgang Trilling, and A.-M. Dubarle.[17]

As it stands in the Greek text of *The Antiquities* (the so-called "Vulgate" text), the *Testimonium* reads thus:

At this time there appeared[18] Jesus, a wise man, if indeed one should call him a man. For he was a doer of startling deeds, a teacher of people who receive the truth with pleasure.[19] And he gained a following both among many Jews and among many of Greek origin. He was the Messiah. And when Pilate, because of an accusation made by the leading men among us, condemned him to the cross, those who had loved him previously did not cease to do so.[20] For he appeared to them on the third day, living again, just as the divine prophets had spoken of these and countless other wondrous things about him. And up until this very day the tribe of Christians, named after him, has not died out.[21]

At first glance, three passages within the *Testimonium* strike one as obviously Christian:

(1) The proviso "if indeed one should call him a man" seeks to modify the previous designation of Jesus as simply a wise man. A Christian scribe would not deny that Jesus was a wise man, but would feel that label insufficient for one who was believed to be God as well as man.[22] Granted, as Dubarle points out,[23] Josephus elsewhere uses hyperbole (including words like "divine" and "divinity") to describe great religious men of the past; and so Dubarle prefers to retain this clause in the original text. However, I do not think the context of the *Testimonium* as a whole exudes the lavish laudatory tone that would cohere with such a reverent conditional clause here.[24]

(2) "He was the Messiah" is clearly a Christian profession of faith (cf. Luke 23:35; John 7:26; Acts 9:22—each time with the *houtos* used here in Josephus, and each time in a context of Jewish unbelief). This is something Josephus the Jew would never affirm. Moreover, the statement "He was the Messiah" seems out of place in its present position and disturbs the flow of thought. If it were present at all, one would expect it to occur immediately after either "Jesus" or "wise man," where the further identification would make sense.[25] Hence, contrary to Dubarle, I consider all attempts to save the statement by expanding it to something like "he was thought to be the Messiah" to be ill advised. Such expansions, though witnessed in some of the Church fathers (notably Jerome), are simply later developments in the tradition.[26]

Other critics have tried to retain a reference to *Christos,* "the Messiah," at this point on the grounds that the title seems to be presupposed by the last part of the *Testimonium,* where Christians are said to be "named after him" (i.e., Jesus who is called Christ). This explanation of the name Christian, it is claimed, seems to require some previous reference in the passage to the title Christ. But as André Pelletier points out, a study of the style of Josephus and other writers of his time shows that the presence of "Christ" is not demanded by the final statement about Christians being "named after him." At times both Josephus and other Greco-Roman writers (e.g., Cassius Dio) consider it pedantry to mention explicitly the person after whom some other person or place is named; it would be considered an insult to the knowledge and culture of the reader to spell out a connection that is rather taken for granted.[27] Moreover, a glancing reference to the name Christ or Christians, without any detailed explanation, is exactly what we would expect from Josephus, who has no desire to highlight messianic figures or expectations among the Jews.[28]

(3) The affirmation of an appearance after death ("For he appeared to them on the third day, living again, just as the divine prophets had spoken of these and countless other wondrous things about him") is also clearly a Christian profession of faith, including a creedal "according to the Scriptures" (cf. 1 Cor 15:5).[29] Dubarle seeks to save the post-mortem appearance for Josephus by rewriting the text to make this statement the object of the disciples' preaching.[30] In my view, Dubarle's reconstruction rests on a shaky foundation: he follows the "majority vote" among the various indirect witnesses to the *Testimonium* in the Church fathers.[31]

In short, the first impression of what is Christian interpolation may well be the correct impression.[32] A second glance confirms this first impression. Precisely these three Christian passages are the clauses that interrupt the flow of what is otherwise a concise text carefully written in a fairly neutral—or even purposely ambiguous—tone:

> At this time there appeared Jesus, a wise man. For he was a doer of startling deeds, a teacher of people who receive the truth with pleasure. And he gained a following both among many Jews and among many of Greek origin. And when Pilate, because of an accusation made by the leading men among us, condemned him to the cross, those who had loved him previously did not cease to do so. And up until this very day the tribe of Christians (named after him) has not died out.

The flow of thought is clear. Josephus calls Jesus by the generic title "wise man" (*sophos anēr*, perhaps the Hebrew *ḥākām*). He then proceeds to "unpack" that generic designation with two of its main components in the Greco-Roman world: miracle working and effective teaching.[33] This double display of "wisdom" wins him a large following among both Jews and Gentiles, and presumably—though no explicit reason is given—it is this huge success that moves the leading men to accuse him before Pilate.[34] Despite his shameful death on the cross,[35] his earlier adherents do not give up their loyalty to him, and so (note the transition that is much better without the reference to the resurrection)[36] the tribe of Christians has not yet died out.

But even if these deletions do uncover an earlier text, is there sufficient reason to claim that it comes from Josephus? The answer is yes; our initial, intuitive hypothesis can be confirmed by further considerations drawn from the text's history, context, language, and thought.

First of all, unlike the passage about Jesus in the Slavonic *Jewish War*, the *Testimonium* is present in all the Greek manuscripts and in all the numerous manuscripts of the Latin translation, made by the school of Cassiodorus in the 6th century; variant versions in Arabic and Syriac have recently been added to the large inventory of indirect witnesses.[37] These facts must be balanced, however, by the sobering realization that we have only three Greek manuscripts of Book 18 of *The Antiquities*, the earliest of which dates from the 11th century. One must also come to terms with the strange silence about the *Testimonium* in the Church Fathers before Eusebius.[38] I will return to this point at the end of the treatment of Josephus.

Second, once we have decided that the reference to "the brother of Jesus-who-is-called-Messiah, James by name" is an authentic part of the text in Book 20, some earlier reference to Jesus becomes a priori likely. Significantly, in *Ant.* 20.9.1 Josephus thinks that, to explain who James is, it is sufficient to relate him to "Jesus-who-is-called-Messiah." Josephus does not feel that he must stop to explain who this Jesus is; he is presumed to be the known fixed point that helps locate James on the map. None of this would make any sense to Josephus' audience, which is basically Gentile, unless Josephus had previously introduced Jesus and explained something about him.[39]

Of course, this does not prove that the text we have isolated in *Ant.* 18.3.3 is the original one, but it does make probable that some reference to Jesus stood here in the authentic text of *The Antiquities*.

Third, the vocabulary and grammar of the passage (after the clearly Christian material is removed) cohere well with Josephus' style and language; the same cannot be said when the text's vocabulary and grammar are compared with that of the NT.[40] Indeed, many key words and phrases in the *Testimonium* are either absent from the NT or are used there in an entirely different sense; in contrast, almost every word in the core of the *Testimonium* is found elsewhere in Josephus—in fact, most of the vocabulary turns out to be characteristic of Josephus.[41] As for what I identify as the Christian insertions, all the words in those three passages occur at least once in the NT.[42] One must beware of claiming too much, though. Some of the words in the interpolations occur in the NT only once, and some occur more often in Josephus. Still, the main point stands: in that part of the *Testimonium* which—on other grounds—seems to come from Josephus and not from a Christian, the vocabulary and style jibe well with that of Josephus,[43] and not quite so well with that of the NT. This distinction between the vocabulary of Josephus and the vocabulary of the NT does not hold in the three passages I identify as Christian interpolations. There, the text shows more of an affinity to NT vocabulary than does the rest of the *Testimonium*.

This comparison of vocabulary between Josephus and the NT does not provide a neat solution to the problem of authenticity, but it does force us to ask which of two possible scenarios is more probable. Did a Christian of some unknown century so immerse himself in the vocabulary and style of Josephus that, without the aid of any modern dictionaries and concordances, he was able to (1) strip himself of the NT vocabulary with which he would naturally speak of Jesus and (2) reproduce perfectly the Greek of Josephus for most of the *Testimonium*—no doubt to create painstakingly an air of verisimilitude—while at the same time destroying that air with a few patently Christian affirmations? Or is it more likely that the core statement, (1) which we first isolated simply by extracting what would strike anyone at first glance as Christian affirmations, and (2) which we then found to be written in typically Josephan vocabulary that diverged from the usage of the NT, was in fact written by Josephus himself? Of the two scenarios, I find the second much more probable.

These observations are bolstered by a fourth consideration, which dwells more on the content of what is said, especially its implied theological views.

(1) If we bracket the three clearly Christian passages, the "christology" of the core statement is extremely low: a wise man like Solomon or Daniel who performed startling deeds like Elisha, a teacher of people who gladly receive the truth,[44] a man who winds up crucified, and whose only vindication is the continued love of his devoted followers

after his death. Without the three Christian passages, this summary description of Jesus is conceivable in the mouth of a Jew who is not openly hostile to him, but not in the mouth of an ancient or medieval Christian. Indeed, even if we were to include the three passages I designate as Christian, the christology would still be jejune for any Christian of the patristic or medieval period, especially if, as many suppose, the Christian interpolation would have to come from the late 3d or early 4th century.[45] By this time, whether one was an Arian or an "orthodox" Catholic, whether one had incipient Nestorian or Monophysite tendencies, this summary about Jesus' person and work would seem hopelessly inadequate.[46] What would be the point of a *Christian* interpolation that would make Josephus *the Jew* affirm such an imperfect estimation of the God-man? What would a Christian scribe intend to gain by such an insertion?[47]

(2) The implied "christology" aside, the author of the core of the *Testimonium* seems ignorant of certain basic material and statements in the four canonical Gospels.

(a) The statement that Jesus "won over" or "gained a following among" *both (men)* many Jews *and (de kai) many* of those of Gentile origin flies in the face of the overall description of Jesus' ministry in the Four Gospels and of some individual affirmations that say just the opposite.

In the whole of John's Gospel, no one clearly designated a Gentile ever interacts directly with Jesus;[48] the very fact that Gentiles seek to speak to Jesus is a sign to him that the hour of his passion, which alone makes a universal mission possible, is at hand (John 12:20–26). In Matthew's Gospel, where a few exceptions to the rule are allowed (the centurion [Matt 8:5–13]; the Canaanite woman [15:21–28]), we find a pointedly programmatic saying in Jesus' mission charge to the Twelve: "Go not to the Gentiles, and do not enter a Samaritan city; rather, go only to the lost sheep of the house of Israel" (Matt 10:5–6). The few Gentiles who do come into contact with Jesus are not objects of Jesus' missionary outreach; they rather come to him unbidden and humble, realizing they are out of place. For Matthew, they point forward to the universal mission, which begins only after Jesus' death and resurrection (28:16–20). While Mark and Luke are not as explicit as Matthew on this point, they basically follow the same pattern: during his public ministry, Jesus does not undertake any formal mission to the Gentiles; the few who come to him do so by way of exception.

Hence the implication of the *Testimonium* that Jesus equally *(pollous men . . . pollous de kai)* won a large following among both Jews and

Gentiles simply contradicts the clear statements of the Gospels. Unless we want to fantasize about a Christian interpolator who is intent on inserting a summary of Jesus' ministry into Josephus and who nevertheless wishes to contradict what the Gospels say about Jesus' ministry, the obvious conclusion to draw is that the core of the *Testimonium* comes from a non-Christian hand, namely, Josephus'. Understandably, Josephus simply retrojected the situation of his own day, when the original "Jews for Jesus" had gained many Gentile converts, into the time of Jesus. Naive retrojection is a common trait of Greco-Roman historians.[49]

(b) The description of the trial and condemnation of Jesus is also curious when compared to the Four Gospels. All Four Gospels state explicit reasons why first the Jewish authorities and then Pilate (under pressure) decide that Jesus should be put to death. For the Jewish rulers, the grounds are theological: Jesus claims to be the Messiah and Son of God. For Pilate, the question is basically political: Does Jesus claim to be the king of the Jews? The grounds are explicated differently in different Gospel texts, but grounds there are. The *Testimonium* is strangely silent on *why* Jesus is put to death. It could be that Josephus simply did not know. It could be that, in keeping with his general tendency, he suppressed references to *a* or *the* Jewish Messiah. It could be that Josephus understood Jesus' huge success to be sufficient grounds. Whatever the reason, the *Testimonium* does not reflect a Christian way of treating the question of why Jesus was condemned to death; indeed, the question simply is not raised.

(c) Moreover, the treatment of the part played by the Jewish authorities does not jibe with the picture in the Gospels. Whether or not it be true that the Gospels show an increasing tendency to blame the Jews and exonerate the Romans, the Jewish authorities in the Four Gospels carry a great deal of responsibility—either by way of the formal trial(s) by the Sanhedrin in the Synoptics or by way of the *Realpolitik* plotting of Caiaphas and the Jerusalem authorities in John's Gospel even before the hearings before Annas and Caiaphas. Of course, a later Christian believer, reading the Four Gospels, would tend to conflate all four accounts, which would only heighten Jewish participation—something the rabid anti-Jewish polemic of many patristic writers only too gladly indulged in. All the stranger, therefore, is the quick, laconic reference in the *Testimonium* to the "denunciation" or "accusation" that the Jewish leaders make before Pilate; Pilate alone, however, is said to condemn Jesus to the cross. Not a word is said about the Jewish authorities passing any sort of sentence. Unless we are to think that some patristic or medieval Christian undertook a historical-critical investigation of the Passion Narratives of the Four Gospels and decided à la Paul Winter that behind John's narrative lay the historical truth of a brief hearing by some Jewish official before Jesus was handed over to Pilate, this description of Jesus' condemnation cannot stem from the Four Gospels—and certainly not from early Christian expansions on them, which were fiercely anti-Jewish.

(3) Another curiosity in the core of the *Testimonium* is the concluding statement that "to this day the tribe of Christians . . . has not died out." The use of *phylon* (tribe, nation, people) for Christians is not necessarily demeaning or pejorative. On the one hand, Josephus uses *phylon* elsewhere of the Jews (*J.W.* 7.8.6 §327); on the other hand, Eusebius also uses *phylon* of Christians.[50] But the phrase does not stand in isolation; it is the subject of the statement that this tribe has not died out or disappeared down to Josephus' day. The implication seems to be one of surprise: granted Jesus' shameful end (with no new life mentioned in the core text), one is amazed to note, says Josephus, that this group of post-mortem lovers is still at it and has not disappeared even in our own day (does Josephus have in the back of his mind Nero's attempt to get it to disappear?). I detect in the sentence as a whole something dismissive if not hostile (though any hostility here is aimed at Christians, not Jesus): one would have thought by now that this "tribe" of lovers of a crucified man might have disappeared. This does not sound like an interpolation by a Christian of any stripe.

(4) A final curiosity encompasses not the *Testimonium* taken by itself but the relation of the *Testimonium* to the longer narrative about John the Baptist in *Ant.* 18.5.2 §116–19, a text accepted as authentic by almost all scholars. The two passages are in no way related to each other in Josephus. The earlier, shorter passage about Jesus is placed in the context of Pontius Pilate's governorship of Judea; the later, longer passage about John is placed in a context dealing with Herod Antipas, tetrarch of Galilee-Perea.[51] Separated by time, space, and placement in Book 18, Jesus and the Baptist (in that order!) have absolutely nothing to do with each other in the mind and narrative of Josephus. Such a presentation totally contradicts—indeed, it is the direct opposite of—the NT portrait of the Baptist, who is always treated briefly as the forerunner of the main character, Jesus. Viewed as a whole, the treatment of Jesus and John in Book 18 of *The Antiquities* is simply inconceivable as the work of a Christian of any period.[52]

Finally, a definite advantage of the position I propose is its relative simplicity. Too many of the other proposals we have reviewed indulge in rewriting the Greek text, sometimes on flimsy grounds. This holds all the more for those who would rewrite Josephus to turn his statement into a hostile attack on Jesus.[53] In contrast, I have simply bracketed the clearly Christian statements. What is remarkable is that the text that remains—without the slightest alteration—flows smoothly,[54] coheres with Josephus' vocabulary and style, and makes perfect sense in his mouth. A basic rule of method is that, all things being equal, the simplest explanation that also covers the largest amount of data is to be preferred.[55] Hence I submit that the most probable explanation of the *Testimonium* is that, shorn of the three obviously Christian affirmations, it is what Josephus wrote.

An intriguing allied question is whence Josephus drew his information. Thackeray leaves open the possibility that in Rome Josephus had met Luke or read his work.[56] But, as we have seen, the language of the *Testimonium* is not markedly that of the NT. Of course, it is possible that Josephus had known some Christian Jews in Palestine before the Jewish War; it is even more likely that he had met or heard about Christians after taking up residence in Rome. Yet there is a problem with supposing that Josephus used the oral reports of Christians as a direct source. Strange to say, the *Testimonium* is much vaguer about the Christians than it is about Jesus. If my reconstruction is correct, while the *Testimonium* gives a fairly objective, brief account of Jesus' career, nothing is said about the Christians' belief that Jesus rose from the dead—and that, after all, was the central affirmation of faith that held the various Christian groups together during the 1st century (cf. 1 Cor 15:11). That Josephus drew directly on oral statements of Christians and yet failed to mention the one belief that differentiated them markedly from the wide range of Jewish beliefs at the time seems difficult to accept. My sense is that, paradoxically, Josephus seems to have known more about Jesus than he did about the Christians who came after him. Hence I remain doubtful about any direct oral Christian source for the *Testimonium*.

Feldman notes that, as a ward of the Flavians, with residence and pension provided for his work, Josephus would have had easy access to the archives of provincial administrators that were kept in the imperial court at Rome.[57] Granted the obsessively suspicious nature of Tiberius in his later years, a desire for detailed reports from provincial governors on any trial that smacked of possible treason or revolt would not be surprising. Was there an account of Jesus' trial among the records? An interesting surmise, but impossible to verify. Martin prefers to think that Josephus recounts the common opinion he heard among the educated, "enlightened" Jews of the partially Romanized world he inhabited.[58] Finally, one cannot exclude—no more than one can prove—that, even apart from direct contact with Christian Jews, Josephus learned some basic facts about Jesus in Palestine before the outbreak of the Jewish War. In short, all opinions on the question of Josephus' source remain equally possible because they remain equally unverifiable.

We seem to have given much space to a relatively small passage; but it is a passage of monumental importance. In my conversations with newspaper writers and book editors who have asked me at various times to write about the historical Jesus, almost invariably the first question that arises is: But can you prove he existed? If I may reformulate that sweeping question into a more focused one, "Is there extrabiblical evidence in the first century A.D. for Jesus' existence?" then I believe, thanks to Josephus, that the answer is yes.[59] The mere existence of Jesus is already demonstrated from the neutral, passing reference in the report on James's death in Book 20.[60] The more extensive *Testimonium* in Book 18 shows us that Josephus was acquainted with at least a few salient facts of Jesus' life.[61] Independent of the Four Gospels, yet confirming their basic presentation, a Jew writing in the year 93–94 tells us that during the rule of Pontius Pilate (the larger context of "during this time")—therefore between A.D. 26 and 36—there appeared on the religious scene of Palestine a man named Jesus. He had the reputation for wisdom that displayed itself in miracle working and teaching. He won a large following, but (or therefore?) the Jewish leaders accused him before Pilate. Pilate had him crucified, but his ardent followers refused to abandon their devotion to him, despite his shameful death. Named Christians after this Jesus (who is called Christ), they continued in existence down to Josephus' day. The neutral, or ambiguous, or perhaps somewhat dismissive tone of the *Testimonium* is probably the reason why early Christian writers (especially the apologists of the 2d century) passed over it in silence, why Origen complained that Josephus did not believe that Jesus was the Christ, and why some interpolator(s) in the late 3d century added Christian affirmations.[62]

When we remember that we are hunting for a marginal Jew in a marginal province of the Roman Empire, it is amazing that a more prominent Jew of the 1st century, in no way connected with this marginal Jew's followers, should have preserved a thumbnail sketch of "Jesus-who-is-called-Messiah." Yet practically no one is astounded or refuses to believe that in the same Book 18 of *The Jewish Antiquities*

Josephus also chose to write a longer sketch of another marginal Jew, another peculiar religious leader in Palestine, "John surnamed the Baptist" (*Ant.* 18.5.2 §116–19). Fortunately for us, Josephus had more than a passing interest in marginal Jews.[63]

NOTES TO CHAPTER 3

¹ For initial orientation in the vast literature on Josephus, see Emil Schürer, *The History of the Jewish People in the Age of Jesus Christ (175 B.C.–A.D. 135)*, rev. and ed. Geza Vermes and Fergus Millar (Edinburgh: Clark, 1973) 1. 61–63. The fullest bibliographies and reviews of literature on Josephus available today have been drawn up by Louis H. Feldman; see his "Flavius Josephus Revisited: The Man, His Writings, and His Significance," *Aufstieg und Niedergang der römischen Welt*, ed. W. Haase and H. Temporini (Berlin/New York: de Gruyter, 1984) II/ 21.2, esp. 822–35; idem, *Josephus and Modern Scholarship 1937–1980* (Berlin/New York: de Gruyter, 1984), esp. 679–703 for the *Testimonium Flavianum*; idem, *Josephus. A Supplementary Bibliography* (New York/London: Garland, 1986). See also the older bibliography by Heinz Schreckenberg, *Bibliographie zu Flavius Josephus* (ALGHJ 1; Leiden: Brill, 1968); by following the marginal indication of number 17, one can trace the development of the argument over the authenticity of the *Testimonium Flavianum* from 1655 (T. Faber) down to 1965 (A. Pelletier). Major studies in Josephus that are also sources of bibliography include Harold Attridge, *The Interpretation of Biblical History in the Antiquitates Judaicae of Flavius Josephus* (HDR 7; Missoula, MT: Scholars, 1976); Shaye J. D. Cohen, *Josephus in Galilee and Rome. His Vita and Development as a Historian* (Columbia Studies in the Classical Tradition 8; Leiden: Brill, 1979); Tessa Rajak, *Josephus. The Historian and His Society* (Philadelphia: Fortress, 1984); Louis H. Feldman and Gohei Hata, eds., *Josephus, Judaism, and Christianity* (Detroit: Wayne State University, 1987); Per Bilde, *Flavius Josephus Between Jerusalem and Rome. His Life, His Works, and Their Importance* (Journal for the Study of the Pseudepigrapha, Supplement Series 2; Sheffield: JSOT, 1988).

² The standard Greek-English edition used in the United States today is that of the Loeb Classical Library (Cambridge, MA: Harvard University; London: Heinemann, 1926–65), encompassing 10 vols. (Nos. 186, 203, 210, 242, 281, 326, 365, 410, 433, and 456); the editors through the years have been H. St. J. Thackeray, Ralph Marcus, and Louis H. Feldman. For the key passages in Books 18 and 20 of *The Antiquities*, I have also consulted the critical edition of Benedict Niese, *Flavii Josephi Opera* (7 vols.; 2d ed.; Berlin: Weidmann, 1955; originally 1885–95) 4. 150–53 and 308–11. English translations of *The Jewish War* include the Penguin edition by G. A. Williamson (rev. ed.; Harmondsworth: Penguin, 1970); and the beautifully laid-out edition with commentary, illustrations, and photographs presenting the archaeological background: *Josephus. The Jewish War*, ed. G. Cornfeld, B. Mazar, and P. Maier (Grand Rapids: Zondervan, 1982).

³ On the question of Christian interpolations into Josephus in particular and Jewish writings in general, see Eva Matthews Sanford, "Propaganda and Censorship in the Transmission of Josephus," *TAPA* 66 (1935) 127–45; James H. Charlesworth, "Christian and Jewish Self-Definition in Light of the Christian Additions to the Apocryphal Writings," *Jewish and Christian Self-Definition. Volume Two. Aspects of Judaism in the Graeco-Roman Period*, ed. E. P. Sanders et al. (Philadelphia: Fortress, 1981) 27–55. Charlesworth (p. 28) notes that Christian interpolations into Jewish writings range from very minor insertions through

blocks of material to massive rewriting of the whole document. As will become clear, I hold that the Christian interpolations into the *Testimonium Flavianum* are of the first, relatively minor, type; Charlesworth, however, thinks that the *Testimonium* is "full of Christian additions" (p. 27).

⁴ The point of insertion of the Jesus interpolation is *J. W.* 2.9.2 §169, where Pontius Pilate is introduced into the narrative.

⁵ For G. A. Williamson's opinion on the Slavonic version, see his *The World of Josephus* (Boston/Toronto: Little, Brown, and Company, 1964) 308–9. His position, though not well defended, has had an influence beyond its merits because it was enshrined in an appendix of the Penguin edition of *Josephus. The Jewish War* (rev. ed.; Harmondsworth: Penguin, 1970). The text of the main "Jesus interpolation" (though Jesus is never mentioned in it by name), along with other pertinent insertions, can conveniently be found in the appendix of Williamson's translation, pp. 397–401. (In fairness, it should be noted that more recent Penguin editions have omitted Williamson's defense of the Slavonic version; see the 1981 version edited by E. M. Smallwood, pp. 470–71.) Another convenient compendium, which supplies the text of all the principal additional passages in the Slavonic *Jewish War*, can be found in Vol. 3 (No. 210) of the Loeb Library edition of Josephus' works. But for a full exposition and defense of the Slavonic version one must have recourse to the once famous, now largely forgotten volumes of Robert Eisler, *IĒSOUS BASILEUS OU BASILEUSAS* (2 vols.; Heidelberg: Winter, 1929, 1930); the English translation by Alexander Krappe *(The Messiah Jesus and John the Baptist* [London: Methuen & Co., 1931]) contains only parts of the German original. On Eisler, see Schürer, *The History of the Jewish People*, 1. 60–61; E. Bammel, "The Revolution Theory from Reimarus to Brandon," *Jesus and the Politics of His Day*, ed. E. Bammel and C. F. D. Moule (Cambridge: Cambridge University, 1984) 11–68, esp. 32–37. Bammel thinks that underlying the text in the Slavonic Josephus is a Jewish account redacted by a Christian; the basis of the reference to Jesus is *Sanh.* 43a in the Talmud; similar developments can be seen in the apocryphal Acts of Pilate and the Jewish life of Jesus, the *Toledoth Yeshu.* Bammel reaches this conclusion about the Slavonic Josephus account of Jesus: "Its evaluation is only possible if its *Sitz im Leben* in the Jewish-Christian controversy is recognised and the direct link with Josephus and the first centuries abandoned" (p. 33). Paul Winter, in his excursus on Jesus in Josephus in the revised Schürer *(The History of the Jewish People*, 1. 440), argues that the Slavonic statement on Jesus must have been composed after the *Testimonium Flavianum* (on which, see below) reached its present form. A survey of recent thought on the Slavonic version can be found in Feldman, "Flavius Josephus Revisited," 771–74.

An attempt to salvage something about the original, political Jesus from the Slavonic Josephus was made by J. Spencer Kennard, "Gleanings from the Slavonic Josephus Controversy," *JQR* 39 (1948–49) 161–70. It was rightly rejected by Solomon Zeitlin ("The Hoax of the 'Slavonic Josephus,' " *JQR* 39 [1948–49] 171–80), who concludes: "All the Jesus passages are interpolations based on Christian literature." Indeed, Kennard himself admits that portions of the Slavonic text are based on the Church Fathers and the pseudo-Acts of Pilate. The appeal to supposed oral Jewish traditions reflected in the writings of Augustine simply lacks evidentiary support; worse still, Kennard, according to Zeitlin, depends on false translations of the Slavonic text. Kennard himself later admitted his error and recanted his position that the arrest of Jesus in the Slavonic Josephus might contain an element of genuine historical tradition; see his "Slavonic Josephus: A Retraction," *JQR* 39 (1948–49) 281–83. Zeitlin continued his critique of the use of Slavonic Josephus in "The Slavonic Josephus and the Dead Sea Scrolls: An Exposé of Recent Fairy Tales," *JQR* 58 (1967–68) 173–203. He shows that both external and internal criticism points to the Slavonic Josephus being a compilation of the 11th century. A 10th- or 11th-century date is also accepted by J. Strugnell, "Josephus, Flavius," *NCE* 7 (1967) 1120–23.

On the other hand, Zeitlin, in my view, dismisses the two Jesus passages in the Greek text of *The Antiquities* without sufficient reasons (pp. 172–74). Zeitlin's disciple, Ellis Rivkin, accepts the reference to Jesus in *Ant.* 20 but rejects it in *Ant.* 18; see his *What Crucified Jesus?* (Nashville: Abingdon, 1984) 64–67.

⁶ The translations from Josephus are my own.

⁷ Abraham Schalit *(Namenwörterbuch zu Flavius Josephus* [Leiden: Brill, 1968] s.v.) counts five different people named *Iakōbos* who are mentioned by Josephus in his various works.

⁸ This is also the form Eusebius himself uses (see 2.23.1), but we need not suspect that Eusebius has foisted his reverential form onto the quotation of Hegesippus. When Eusebius claims to be citing Josephus, he is faithful to Josephus' un-Christian form, "the brother of Jesus" *(Ecclesiastical History* 2.23.20,22—the latter passage being a direct citation of *Ant.* 20.9.1).

⁹ Paul Winter, in his excursus on the disputed Josephus passages in the revised Schürer *(The History of the Jewish People,* 1. 428–41), also argues that "if a Christian forger had inserted a reference to Jesus, he would scarcely have been content to mention Jesus in such non-committal fashion" (p. 431).

¹⁰ Douglas R. A. Hare *(The Theme of Jewish Persecution of Christians in the Gospel According to St Matthew* [SNTSMS 6; Cambridge: Cambridge University, 1967] 34) notes the vagueness of the accusation in Josephus. He suggests that Ananus was acting out of personal animosity and that the "certain others" killed at the same time were not Christians but other personal enemies of Ananus.

¹¹ On this, see Cohen, *Josephus in Galilee and Rome,* 237–38.

¹² In Vol. 10 (No. 456) of the Loeb Library edition, p. 108 n. a; cf. his treatment in *Josephus and Modern Scholarship,* 704–7, where the vast majority of scholars affirm authenticity; see the similar judgment of Winter in Schürer's *The History of the Jewish People,* 430. Even Hans Conzelmann, who doubts the authenticity of the *Testimonium Flavianum,* accepts *Ant.* 20.9.1 *(Jesus* [Philadelphia: Fortress, 1973] 13–14); similarly, Bilde, *Flavius Josephus Between Jerusalem and Rome,* 223. H. St. J. Thackeray states flatly ("Lecture VI. Josephus and Christianity," *Josephus. The Man and the Historian* [The Hilda Stich Stroock Lectures; New York: Jewish Institute of Religion, 1929] 131) that, in his opinion, the authenticity of the two

passages in *The Antiquities* on John the Baptist and on James is "beyond question." One of the few authors to doubt the authenticity of the James passage in recent years is Rajak, *Josephus*, 131 n. 73. Even she admits that "it has been unfashionable, of late, to doubt the James passage. . . ." Her main reason for rejecting the passage is that Josephus presents a positive picture of Ananus in *J.W.* 4.5.2 §319–25, as opposed to the negative picture in the *Antiquities*. Yet, as we have noted above, a shift to a more negative view of the ruling Sadducees is typical of the *Antiquities* compared to the *Jewish War*. Rajak's supplementary reason for rejection, namely, that the James passage presupposes some previous mention of Jesus and therefore the basic authenticity of the *Testimonium Flavianum*, will be challenged at length below. Feldman rightly questions Rajak's position in his Introduction to *Josephus, Judaism and Christianity*, 56.

¹³ As Ernst Bammel shrewdly notes ("Zum Testimonium Flavianum [Jos Ant 18, 63–64]," *Josephus-Studien. Untersuchungen zu Josephus, dem antiken Judentum und dem Neuen Testament* [Otto Michel Festschrift; ed. Otto Betz, Klaus Haacker, and Martin Hengel; Göttingen: Vandenhoeck & Ruprecht, 1974] 9–22, on p. 10 n. 17), it is not always clear whether a particular scholar judges the *Testimonium* spurious or whether he simply thinks that it is impossible to reconstruct the original form of what Josephus said about Jesus.

¹⁴ But see the (mostly uncritical) position of Franz Dornseiff, "Lukas der Schriftsteller. Mit einem Anhang: Josephus und Tacitus," *ZNW* 35 (1936) 129–55; idem, "Zum Testimonium Flavianum," *ZNW* 46 (1955) 245–50. Dornseiff maintains that the received *Testimonium Flavianum* in the Greek manuscripts of Josephus is entirely authentic, yet Josephus remained a Jew, not a Christian. The second article is written against Felix Scheidweiler ("Das Testimonium Flavianum," *ZNW* 45 [1954] 230–43), who accepts a basic core as original, while suggesting that the received form may come from the circle of Paul of Samosata. A. Feuillet ("Les anciens historiens profanes et la connaissance de Jésus," *Esprit et Vie* 87 [1977] 145–53) states that at least the greater part of the *Testimonium* is authentic; however, his comments on the individual "Christian interpolations" seem to favor authenticity of the entire text.

More recently, the authenticity of the full *Testimonium* has been defended by Etienne Nodet, "Jésus et Jean-Baptiste selon Josèphe," *RB* 92 (1985) 320–48, 497–524. His thesis labors under two difficulties: (1) *ho christos houtos ēn* must be read as "he was Christ [taken purely as a proper name, not as a set title of the Messiah]." The main problem with this interpretation is the definite article *ho*, which makes the titular sense ("the Messiah") the more likely interpretation, especially with the predicate nominative thrown before the copulative verb. (2) All the other phrases that many interpreters judge to be "too Christian" are said to be simply ambiguous, and intentionally so in the mind of Josephus. The neutral tone of Josephus may indeed be purposely ambiguous or guarded; but some of the Christian phrases, especially those referring to the appearance of the living Jesus after his death and the testimony of the divine prophets, are too straightforward to be explained in this way. The thesis is not helped by the further claim (p. 524) that Josephus carefully arranged the material in Book 18 of *The Antiquities* for a polemical purpose: to separate John the Baptist from Jesus and thus to deprive the Baptist of his status as the forerunner of Jesus. In Nodet's view, Luke responded to Josephus' polemic in the Third Gospel and the Acts. A great deal is made to hang from very thin threads.

For a precritical defense of total authenticity, see William Whiston, "The Testimonies of Josephus Concerning Jesus Christ, John the Baptist, and James the Just, Vindicated," *Josephus. Complete Works* (Grand Rapids: Kregel, 1960; 1st ed. 1737) 639–47.

[15] Representative of total rejection—in the line of A. von Harnack, F. C. Burkitt, and E. Norden—is Conzelmann *(Jesus,* 13–14), who claims that the passage "is constructed in accord with a pattern of the Christian kerygma (and indeed the Lukan one)" (p. 14). Unfortunately, he does not go on to substantiate his claim. One is left wondering what a short summary of Jesus' life by a Jew at the end of the 1st century would look like instead. Walter Pötscher rejects Conzelmann's claim in "Josephus Flavius, Antiquitates 18, 63f. (Sprachliche Form und thematischer Inhalt)," *Eranos* 73 (1975) 26–42, esp. 27–28. Pötscher points out the similarities between the *Testimonium* and "paradoxographic" authors like Apollonius, who wrote similar summaries of the careers of Epimenides and Hermotimus. The whole *Testimonium* is also rejected as an interpolation by Léon Herrmann, *Chrestos. Témoignages païens et juifs sur le christianisme du premier siècle* (Collection Latomus 109; Brussels: Latomus, 1970) 97–98; one is not reassured, however, when one discovers that both the passage on John the Baptist and the mention of James in *The Antiquities* are likewise declared to be interpolations (pp. 99–104). Also in favor of a complete interpolation, though somewhat tentative in his judgment, is J. Neville Birdsall, "The Continuing Enigma of Josephus's Testimony about Jesus," *BJRL* 67 (1984–85) 609–22. Similarly, Bilde *(Flavius Josephus Between Jerusalem and Rome,* 223) claims that, "at best, the text is partly genuine and most likely a thoroughly secondary Christian fabrication. . . ." It is wise to remember that Catholic as well as Protestant scholars were once given to total rejection of the *Testimonium;* Carlo M. Martini ("Il silenzio dei testimoni non cristiani su Gesù," *La Civiltà Cattolica* 113/2 [1962] 341–49) reminds us that both P. Battifol and M.-J. Lagrange judged the whole inauthentic (p. 347).

Perhaps symbolic of the shift from the total skepticism of the 19th century to the yes-but approach of the 20th century was the change of opinion by the former "prince" of Josephan scholars, Thackeray. He had earlier held that the *Testimonium* was a complete forgery; he later came to believe that a core of authentic material could be reconstructed by removing or reformulating Christian interpolations. For the expression of his later view, see his "Josephus and Christianity," 125–53. One regrets that, under the heady influence of the contemporary work of Eisler, Thackeray adopted some emendations on the basis of the Slavonic Josephus, leaning in the direction of Eisler's Jesus the Political Rebel. Nevertheless, Thackeray does not accept Eisler's views in toto, and Feldman indicates that Thackeray recanted his pro-Eisler views before his death *(Josephus and Modern Scholarship,* 52). For another expression of the shift from complete skepticism to partial acceptance, see F. J. Foakes Jackson, *Josephus and the Jews* (Grand Rapids: Baker, 1977; 1st ed., 1930) 279; see p. 278 for Jackson's curious view on why Josephus might have inserted the *Testimonium* into *The*

Antiquities. Granted the notable swing away from total skepticism, it is surprising to read the claim of Michael J. Cook: "The overwhelming consensus among scholars today . . . is that Josephus' celebrated testimony about Jesus is spurious" ("Jesus and the Pharisees—The Problem as It Stands Today," *JES* 15 [1978] 441–60, p. 451). But n. 45 on p. 451 indicates that Cook may be including judgments of partial inauthenticity in his sweeping statement.

[16] In his review of the literature, Feldman ("Flavius Josephus Revisited," 822) says flatly: ". . . the great majority of modern scholars have regarded it [the *Testimonium*] as partly interpolated, and this is my conclusion as well." C. Martin ("Le 'Testimonium Flavianum.' Vers une solution définitive?" *Revue belge de philologie et d'histoire* 20 [1941] 409–65) is likewise of the opinion that scholars increasingly favor the judgment of partial interpolation (p. 415). Some critics hold to the view that some parts of the *Testimonium* come from Josephus and other parts from an interpolator, but consider any attempt to reconstruct the genuine text as sheer speculation; so Zvi Baras, "The *Testimonium Flavianum* and the Martyrdom of James," *Josephus, Judaism, and Christianity,* 338–48, esp. 339; see also his earlier "*Testimonium Flavianum:* The State of Recent Scholarship," *Society and Religion in the Second Temple Period* (The World History of the Jewish People 1/8; ed. Michael Avi-Yonah and Zvi Baras; Jerusalem: Massada, 1977) 303–13, esp. 308. For the view that originally the *Testimonium* contained a hostile reference to Jesus that can no longer be reconstructed, see Clyde Pharr, "The Testimony of Josephus to Christianity," *AJP* 48 (1927) 137–47. For the view that the *Testimonium* originally made some unfavorable mention of Jesus at this point in *The Antiquities,* and that we can at least attempt a reconstruction, see Bammel, "Zum Testimonium Flavianum," 9–22.

[17] See Winter in the revised Schürer, *The History of the Jewish People,* 432–41; Feldman, "Josephus Revisited," 822–35; S. G. F. Brandon, *The Trial of Jesus of Nazareth* (Historical Trials Series; New York: Stein and Day, 1968) 151–52; Morton Smith, *Jesus the Magician* (New York: Harper & Row, 1978) 45–46; Charlesworth, *Jesus Within Judaism,* 90–98. In addition to Winter's excursus, a cogent defense of an authentic core going back to Josephus can be found in Louis H. Feldman, "The *Testimonium Flavianum:* The State of the Question," *Christological Perspectives. Essays in Honor of Harvey K. McArthur,* ed. R. F. Berkey and S. A. Edwards (New York: Pilgrim, 1982) 179–99. See also Martini, "Il silenzio," 347; Wolfgang Trilling, *Fragen zur Geschichtlichkeit Jesu* (Düsseldorf: Patmos, 1966) 51–56; A.-M. Dubarle, "Le témoignage de Josèphe sur Jésus d'après la tradition indirecte," *RB* 80 (1973) 481–513, and his update, "Le témoignage de Josèphe sur Jésus d'après des publications récentes," *RB* 84 (1977) 38–55.

[18] I take the sense of the much-disputed *ginetai* to be "come, appear on the scene, arise," not unlike the sense of *egeneto anthrōpos* in John 1:6 (perhaps echoing the Hebrew *wayhî,* used to begin a narrative; cf. 1 Sam 1:1). A number of translations prefer "there lived," which is possible; but the translation "was born" seems out of place here. Karl H. Rengstorf (*A Complete Concordance to Flavius Josephus* [4 vols.; Leiden: Brill, 1973–83] s.v.) illustrates the vast range of

meanings *ginomai* can have in Josephus, including "to be born, to arise, to be, to live, to have lived, to have existed."

[19] The Greek phrase *tōn hēdonę talēthē dechomenōn* could imply simple-minded enthusiasm, even self-delusion. Yet, while possible, that is not necessarily the sense. We may have here one example of what Josephus is doing throughout the *Testimonium:* carefully writing an ambiguous text that different audiences could take in different ways.

[20] This is probably the meaning of *epausanto;* other possibilities are "did not give him up" (i.e., desert him) or "did not cease" (i.e., to exist). The last option would make the final sentence of the *Testimonium* redundant; and since, in Josephus as in the rest of ancient Greek, *pauomai* is often completed by a supplementary participle, it is most natural to understand *agapēsantes* (or *agapōntes*) from *hoi to prōton agapēsantes;* see William Goodwin and Charles Gulick, *Greek Grammar* (Boston: Ginn & Co., 1958) 333; also Bammel, "Zum Testimonium Flavianum," 9–22, on p. 14.

[21] The Greek text, with brackets supplied for those sections I consider Christian additions (see below), is as follows: *ginetai de kata touton ton chronon Iēsous sophos anēr, [eige andra auton legein chrē;] ēn gar paradoxōn ergōn poiētēs, didaskalos anthrōpōn tōn hēdonę talēthē dechomenōn, kai pollous men Ioudaious, pollous de kai tou Hellēnikou epēgageto;* [*ho christos houtos ēn.*] *kai auton endeixei tōn prōtōn andrōn par' hēmin staurǭ epitetimēkotos Pilatou ouk epausanto hoi to prōton agapēsantes; [ephanē gar autois tritēn echōn hēmeran palin zōn tōn theiōn prophētōn tauta te kai alla myria peri autou thaumasia eirekotōn.] eis eti te nyn tōn Christianōn apo toude ōnomasmenon ouk epelipe to phylon.* Consult Feldman's notes in the Loeb Library edition (pp. 48–50) for the major emendations suggested by editors. The translations in the text are my own.

[22] See André Pelletier, "Ce que Josèphe a dit de Jésus (Ant. XVIII 63–64)," *REJ* 124 (1965) 9–21, esp. 14.

[23] Dubarle, "Le témoignage de Josèphe sur Jésus d'après la tradition indirecte," 481–513.

[24] It is curious that Martin, though preferring to view *eige andra auton legein chrē* as an interpolation, remains hesitant ("Le 'Testimonium Flavianum,' " 450–52), especially since he interprets Josephus as saying that Jesus seduced both Jews and Gentiles and thus brought upon himself the condemnation due an agitator (pp. 445–46).

[25] See Pelletier, "Ce que Josèphe a dit," 14.

[26] See Dubarle, "Le témoignage de Josèphe sur Jésus d'après la tradition indirecte," esp. p. 495. Among the many others who favor some reading like *legomenos* with *ho Christos* is G. C. Richards, "The *Testimonium* of Josephus," *JTS* 42 (1941) 70–71. Williamson *(The World of Josephus,* 308) tries to save the authenticity of the sentence by claiming that the definite article before *Christos* is just the untranslatable article before a proper name; hence the sense is not "This man was the Messiah," but rather "the man I have called Jesus was the man com-

monly called Christ." This explanation ignores the three precise NT parallels, where the sense of *houtos estin ho Christos* is obviously "this man is the Messiah." If Josephus had wanted to say what Williamson wants to make him say, there were much clearer ways of doing so.

²⁷ Pelletier, "Ce que Josèphe a dit," 9–21; a variant of this article can be found in "L'originalité de témoignage de Flavius Josèphe sur Jésus," *RSR* 52 (1964) 177–203; his position is accepted by Henri Cazelles, *Naissance de l'église. Secte juive rejetée?* (Paris: Cerf, 1968) 106. Pelletier points to *Ant.* 17.5.1 §87, where Josephus explains the name of the port Sebastos by saying that "Herod, having constructed it at great expense, named it Sebastos in honor of Caesar." Josephus leaves out the logically necessary explanation that Caesar's honorific name is in Latin *Augustus*, which was translated into Greek as *Sebastos*. Similarly, it may be argued, Josephus presupposes in *Ant.* 18.3.3 that the cultured reader knows that Jesus' "second name" was *Christos.* That cultured Roman readers would indeed have known this equivalence is made likely by the statement of the pagan Tacitus in his *Annales* (15.44) some two decades later, when he simply uses *Christus* as the name of the man Pilate put to death, without ever mentioning the proper name Jesus.

²⁸ On this point, see Martin, "Le 'Testimonium Flavianum,'" 452–55.

²⁹ The use of the phrase "according to the Scriptures" precisely at the mention of the resurrection is employed (probably under the influence of 1 Cor 15:5) in the so-called "Shorter Epiphanian Creed" (ca. A.D. 374) and the official creed of the first ecumenical council of Constantinople (A.D. 381).

³⁰ Curiously, a similar view is found in the theories of Eisler and Thackeray, who read *ephanē gar autois*, etc., as indirect discourse in the original text (Thackeray, "Josephus and Christianity," 147).

³¹ Dubarle, "Le témoignage de Josèphe sur Jésus d'après la tradition indirecte," esp. p. 499. I do not mean to disparage the great contribution Dubarle makes in providing easy access to so many patristic citations of the *Testimonium.* He himself admits the variety of the indirect tradition and the liberty the patristic writers take with the text (p. 502). I do not share his confidence that taking a majority vote among the diverging patristic witnesses gives us a good chance of restoring the original text. Despite his protests at the analogy, one would never think of going about NT text criticism in this way; I do not think the method is more valid when applied to the *Testimonium.*

³² Here I am in basic agreement with Joseph Klausner, *Jesus of Nazareth. His Life, Times, and Teaching* (New York: Macmillan, 1925) 55–60. But, while Klausner hesitates over whether something else originally stood in the place of the three interpolations, I am convinced that the deletion of these three passages restores the *Testimonium* to its original form. Perhaps the scholar who comes closest to my own view is Martin ("Le 'Testimonium Flavianum,'" 409–65), whose work was not available to me during the writing of the bulk of this chapter. I am encouraged by finding independent support for my own stance. At the same

time, I find a number of Martin's positions curious or improbable; I will note my disagreements at the appropriate places.

[33] Martin ("Le 'Testimonium Flavianum,' " 440) misses this point by making *ēn gar paradoxōn ergōn poiētēs* merely a parenthetical explanation of *sophos anēr*, instead of seeing it as coequal with *didaskalos anthrōpōn* as the two-part definition of *sophos anēr*. He is quite correct, however, in emphasizing that in Josephus, as in many other Greek authors, *sophos* could convey the idea of a possessor of supernatural knowledge and power (pp. 442–44).

[34] The causal link would be clearer if we could be sure that *epēgageto* meant "seduced, led astray." That is a possible, though not necessary, meaning of the verb. Once again, Josephus may be engaging in a studied ambiguity.

[35] As Martin points out ("Le 'Testimonium Flavianum,' " 446), the genitive absolute *epitetimēkotos Pilatou* has the force of a concessive clause: "Although Pilate condemned him to the cross, nevertheless those who had loved him previously did not cease to do so."

[36] Indeed, one could argue that the *te* in *eis eti te nyn* demands *ouk epausanto hoi to prōton agapēsantes* just before it. It is almost impossible to make sense of the telltale *te* following upon the reference to the resurrection appearance and the OT prophecies; cf. Martin, "Le 'Testimonium Flavianum,' " 441.

[37] For a discussion of the manuscript tradition and the confusing references in the Church Fathers, see Feldman, "The *Testimonium Flavianum,* " 181–85; also David Flusser, "Der lateinische Josephus und der hebräische Josippon," *Josephus-Studien,* 122–32. On the Latin translation Feldman makes an intriguing observation: "Despite the obvious importance of the Latin version, since it antedates by half a millennium the earliest extant Greek manuscript, it has not been edited. . . . The main manuscript of the Latin version, the *Ambrosianus papyraceus,* dates from the ninth century, two centuries before the earliest of the Greek manuscripts" (p. 289 n. 12). For the history of the tradition of the Latin translation, see Franz Blatt, *The Latin Josephus. I. Introduction and Text. The Antiquities: Books I–V* (Acta Jutlandica 30/1, Humanities Series 44; Aarhus: Universitetsforlaget, 1958) 9–116.

On the Arabic and Syriac texts, see Shlomo Pines, *An Arabic Version of the Testimonium Flavianum and Its Implications* (Publications of the Israel Academy of Sciences and Humanities, Section of Humanities; Jerusalem: The Israel Academy of Sciences and Humanities, 1971); Dubarle, "Le témoignage de Josèphe sur Jésus d'après la tradition indirecte," 485–86. An English translation of the Arabic text of Agapius, with a brief discussion, is readily available in the Cornfeld edition of *Josephus. The Jewish War,* 510. Feldman (*Josephus and Modern Scholarship,* 701) believes that Agapius used both Josephus and other sources and combined them: "We may . . . conclude that Agapius' excerpt is hardly decisive, since it contains several elements, notably changes in order, that indicate that it is a paraphrase rather than a translation." Nodet ("Jésus et Jean-Baptiste selon Josèphe") thinks that Agapius represents a deformed tradition of the Eusebius text found in the *Ecclesiastical History* (pp. 335–36). Personally, I am doubtful that this 10th-century Arabic manuscript preserves the original form of the *Testimonium*, especially since it contains sentences that, as I have just argued, are probably later expansions or variants of the text. Indeed, Bammel ("Zum Testimonium Flavianum," 21) thinks that the text of the *Testimonium* was much more subject to summaries and expansions in the East than in the West. But, at the very least, the text from Agapius does expand our knowledge of the indirect witnesses to the text. Zvi Baras ("The *Testimonium Flavianum* and the Martyrdom of James," *Josephus, Judaism, and Christianity*, 338–48) judges (p. 340): "Although it is not considered the genuine text of Josephus, it provides us with an example of another more moderate attempt at the Christianization of the original text, probably unfavorable to Christians, and one which may have been known to Origen and Jerome." As will become clear, I do not share the latter part of this judgment.

[38] One possible explanation of this silence would jibe well with my reconstruction of the *Testimonium* and my isolation of the Christian interpolations. If until shortly before the time of Eusebius the *Testimonium* lacked the three Christian interpolations I have bracketed, the Church Fathers would not have been overly eager to cite it; for it hardly supports mainline Christian belief in Jesus as the Son of God who rose from the dead. This would explain why Origen in the 3d century affirmed that Josephus did not believe Jesus to be the Messiah *(Commentary on Matthew* 10.17; *Contra Celsum* 1.47). Origen's text of the *Testimonium* lacked the interpolations; and, without them, the *Testimonium* simply testified, in Christian eyes, to Josephus' unbelief—not exactly a useful apologetic tool in addressing pagans or a useful polemical tool in christological controversies among Christians. Indeed, if something like the text I reconstruct was *not* in Origen's copy of Josephus, one is left asking the question: What was it in the text that caused Origen to state apodictically that Josephus did not believe Jesus to be the Christ? The James passage in Book 20 is not a sufficient reason.

[39] So, e.g., Richards, "The *Testimonium* of Josephus." Some translators even take *Iēsou tou legomenou Christou (Ant.* 20.9.1) to mean "Jesus, the aforementioned Messiah"—not a necessary meaning, though a possible one in this context (see Feldman, "The *Testimonium Flavianum,*" 192). If this were the correct translation, it would help argue for some reference to messiahship in the original form of the *Testimonium;* hence, some hold that Jerome's reading, *credebatur esse Christus* ("he was believed to be the Messiah"), reflects part of the original text. However, since by the time of Josephus Christians had made *Christos* practically a second proper name of Jesus, Josephus may be presupposing in Book 20 that the Jesus mentioned in Book 18 is generally known as *Christos*. Of course, none of this speculation is necessary. Josephus may be introducing the title for the first (and only) time in *The Antiquities* in Book 20. In this case, the phrase does mean "Jesus, who is called the Messiah," perhaps intimating why James (whose activity is otherwise not described) is a source of aggravation to the high priest.

[40] Here we face a basic methodological problem. Since we do not know who the Christian interpolator(s) were, or whether indeed the interpolations are anything more than random marginal notes that entered the text at different times,

it is impossible to compare Josephus' vocabulary and style with any one Christian author. The NT is chosen for the sake of providing some fixed point of contrast; it is one corpus of 1st-century Christian works, most of which were written within the span of five decades, just as Josephus supplies us with a corpus of 1st-century Jewish works, all written within the span of three decades. The choice of the NT is not totally arbitrary, since presumably a Christian theologian or scribe of the first few centuries would be steeped in NT thought and vocabulary and would naturally narrate the story of Jesus out of his NT background.

⁴¹ As Thackeray states, ". . . practically the whole of the language [of the *Testimonium*] can be illustrated from Josephus" ("Josephus and Christianity," 141). For Thackeray, it is the criterion of style that turns the scale in favor of authenticity: "If the text has been mutilated and modified, there is at least a Josephan basis" (ibid.). For an examination of Josephus' vocabulary, the indispensable tool is Rengstorf, *A Complete Concordance to Flavius Josephus*, along with Schalit, *Namenwörterbuch zu Flavius Josephus*.

Before we begin a comparison of vocabulary and stylistic usage between the NT and Josephus' *Testimonium*, a few caveats are in order. Word statistics are used here simply to indicate whether a word occurs fairly frequently in Josephus or in the NT. The statistics should not be used simplistically to contrast the two bodies of material; Josephus represents a much larger corpus of works than does the NT, and he is one well-known author as opposed to numerous NT authors, many of whom are anonymous. The differences in subject matter and literary genre must also be borne in mind.

To take only the most obvious examples of the differences between the usage of the NT and that of the core of the *Testimonium: poiētēs* is never used of Jesus in the NT; *bellēnikos* is used only 1×, of the Greek language, in Rev 9:11; *bēdonē* is used only 5× in the NT, and always in a pejorative sense of sensual or illicit pleasure; *epagō* occurs 3×, but never in the middle voice with the sense of "win over" or "gain a following"; the crasis form *tālēthē* is never used in the NT; nothing even vaguely like the phrase *anthrōpōn tōn bēdonę tālēthē dechomenōn* is ever used in the NT to describe the disciples of Jesus or those who decide to follow Jesus; *endeixis* occurs 4×, always in Paul, and always with the general sense of showing, manifesting, demonstrating, proving, never with the formal judicial sense of accusation, charge, denunciation, indictment; *prōtoi andres* never occurs in the NT (the closest analogue is Luke 19:47, *hoi prōtoi tou laou*, designating not all the Jewish leaders but only the elders as distinct from the high priests and the scribes; even here the phrase occurs outside the Passion Narrative; cf. Acts 13:50; 17:4; 25:2; 28:7); *epitimaō* is always used in the NT of verbal rebukes (most often in the mouth of Jesus), never of any physical punishment, and certainly not of crucifixion; *onomazō* is never used in the NT in the form of the perfect passive participle and never in reference to the naming of Christians (cf. the statement of Luke in Acts 11:26); *epileipō* is used in the NT only once, in the transitive sense of "fail," never in the intransitive sense of "disappear, die out"; *phylon* is never used in the NT; the NT instead uses *phylē* 31×, in the sense of either (1) a tribe or the twelve tribes of Israel or (2) all the nations or peoples of the earth; the first sense is sometimes used symbolically of Christians (the clearest case is Jas 1:1), but *phylē* is never used directly with *Christianōn* or any equivalent (the disciples, the brethren, etc.). No one of these differences means all that much; but the accumulated evidence of all these differences may point to an author who is not taking his material from the NT.

The usage of Josephus presents a totally different picture. With regard to "wise man" *(sophos anēr)*, Josephus calls Solomon *(Ant.* 8.2.7 §53) and likewise Daniel *(Ant.*10.11.2 §237) a "wise man," while no NT writing ever predicates the adjective "wise" *(sophos)* directly of Jesus. *kata touton ton chronon* and similar time references with *kata* + *chronon* are frequent in Josephus (see, e.g., *Ant.* 13.2.3 §46; 18.2.4 §39), but the NT never uses *kata* + *chronon* in any connection; *paradoxos* occurs 50× in Josephus (1× in NT), including two cases where it modifies *erga,* as here *(Ant.* 9.7.6 §182: *thaumasta gar kai paradoxa . . . epedeixato erga* [of Elisha the prophet]; *Ant.* 12.2.8 §63: *ergōn kainōn kai paradoxōn); paradoxon touto poiōn (Ant.* 12.2.11 §87) also occurs. *poiētēs* is used elsewhere in Josephus only in the sense of "poet"; but Josephus (or his secretary, according to Thackeray) has a fondness for resolving a simple verb into two words: a noun expressing the agent and the auxiliary verb (e.g., *kritēs einai* for the simple *krinein).* Moreover, Josephus uses such cognates as *poiēteos,* "that which is to be done," *poiēsis,* "doing, causing" (as well as "poetry, poem"), and *poiētikos,* "that which causes something" (as well as "poetic"). *didaskalos* occurs 16× in Josephus (59× in NT); *anthrōpos,* needless to say, is extremely common in Josephus. *hēdonē* is used 128× by Josephus (5× in NT), who uses it in both positive and negative senses; *hēdonę* in the dative is used in the sense of "with pleasure," "gladly," as here. (Thackeray sees in this "receive with pleasure" locution the hand of a particular secretary of Josephus, "the Thucydidean hack" ["Josephus and Christianity," 141, 144]; I prescind from theories of secretaries, since my only concern is to show that the language is Josephan. Moreover, Thackeray's position about helpers in the composition of *The Antiquities* has not been universally accepted. Heinz Schreckenberg *[Rezeptionsgeschichtliche und textkritische Untersuchungen zu Flavius Josephus* (ALGHJ 10; Leiden: Brill, 1977) 173–74] stresses Josephus' command of Greek and the unity of his style in *The Antiquities.* The differences in style that exist in *The Antiquities* are to be attributed to Josephus himself, who over many years wrote *The Antiquities,* using various sources and being influenced by various classical authors he was reading.) *alēthēs* occurs 150× in Josephus (26× in NT); more importantly, Josephus frequently uses the crasis forms *tålēthēs* and *tålēthē,* which never occur in the NT (note the phrase *tålēthē kai ta dikaia labōn* in *Ant.* 8.2.1. §23). *dechomai* is used 221× in Josephus (56× in NT). Indeed, language very similar to the *Testimonium* is found in *Ant.* 17.12.1 §329: *tōn anthrōpōn to hēdonę dechomenon tous logous;* moreover, *hēdonē* is used remarkably often with *dechomai* in Josephus (never in NT). *hellēnikos* occurs in Josephus 25× (NT 1×). *epagō* is used 106× in Josephus (3× in NT); unlike the NT, Josephus does use it in the middle voice to mean "attract, persuade, motivate, induce"; see especially *J.W.* 7.6.1 §164: *pollous eis apostasian epagagetai* (said of the fortress Machaerus, whose strength might lead many to revolt); and *Ant.* 17.12.1 §327: *Ioudaiōn hoposois eis homilian aphiketo epēgageto eis pistin* (said of a Jew who falsely claims to be Alexander, the son of Herod, and who wins the confidence of the Jews on Crete. *endeixis* is used once in Josephus in the sense of "denunciation, charge, accusation" *(Ant.* 19.9.16 §133); but the NT never uses it in this sense. *hoi prōtoi andres* occurs some 6× just in *The Antiquities* (allowing for different word order); slightly variant forms of the same phrase occur three more times in the same work. Especially interesting is the fact that there is a high concentration of this phrase or very similar phrases in Book 18: 18.1.1 §7; 18.4.4 §98, 99; 18.5.3 §121; 18.9.9 §376. While there is no exact equivalent to the full phrase *tōn prōtōn andrōn par' hēmin, Ant.* 18.9.9 reads: *tōn prōtōn par' hekaterois andrōn,* "the leading men on both sides"; closer still are *Ant.* 20.1.1 §2: *chōris gnōmēs tēs tōn prōtōn par' autois,* "without the consent of their leaders"; *Ant.* 20.9.1 §198: *hoper oudeni synebē tōn par' hēmin archiereōn,* "which happened to none of our high priests"; and *Ag. Ap.* 2.12 §136: *peri de tōn par' hēmin andrōn gegonotōn,* "but concerning our own men of past history." (For further examples, see Eisler, *IĒSOUS BASILEUS,* 73.) *epitimaō* is used 13× in Josephus (29× in NT), including a number of instances where it means "to sentence" or "to fix (a punishment)," a sense never found in the NT; note the perfect active forms in *Ant.* 18.5.6 §183; *Ap.* 2.32 §239. The one difference from the other texts is the unusual accusative of the person and dative of the punishment, but such a construction would be unusual in any Greek author; and amid so many examples of typical Josephan style some minor variations are to be expected. Eisler (ibid., 74), noting the similarity to Tacitus' reference to Jesus' death *(Annales* 15.44), suggests a literal translation of a technical Latin juridical phrase. *agapaō* in Josephus can mean "to like, love, value, welcome; to content oneself; to tolerate, accept." Passages dealing with God, parents, children, justice, etc., make it clear that Josephus does use the word in the sense of affective love; vaguely reminiscent of our passage is *J.W.* 1.1.12 §30: *tois ge tēn alētheian agapōsin, alla mē pros hēdonēn anegrapsa.* Hence it is hardly justified to claim that *agapēsantes* is "specifically and technically Christian" (so A. von Gutschmid, quoted by Bammel, "Zum Testimonium Flavianum," 11 n. 22). Thackeray ("Josephus and Christianity," 147) prefers here the sense of "to be content with," but only because he insists on seeing an originally hostile sense in the *Testimonium. pauō* occurs 170× in Josephus, in both active and middle, the meanings of the middle including the sense witnessed here, "to stop (doing something), to give up"; the NT has only one example of the active and 14 of the middle, the middle regularly meaning "to stop (doing something)." The words *eis, eti, te,* and *nyn* are all very common in Josephus, but their conjunction here is unusual. The *Testimonium* is the only passage in Josephus where *Christianoi* appears; but then, it occurs only 3× in the NT. *onomazō* occurs in Josephus 62× (10× in NT). Josephus often uses the phrase *onomazō apo tinos* in the sense of "to name something after someone," which occurs in the passive as well as the active voice; see, e.g., *Ant.* 1.15 §241; 1.6.1 §123; note the exact form of the perfect passive participle in *Ag. Ap.* 1.26 §245. The *onomazō apo tinos* construction does not occur in the NT. *hode* is used frequently by Josephus. While *epileipō* occurs only 1× in the NT, in the sense of "time will fail me" (Heb 11:32), it occurs 40× in Josephus, including the sense of "stop, cease, become extinct, die out"; note *Ant.* 2.9.3 §210: *dediōs hyper tou pantos ethnous, mē spanei tēs epitraphēsomenēs neotētos epileipē.* While Josephus uses *phylē* more often than *phylon,* he does use the latter

11×, usually in the sense of "tribe, people, nation"; note *J.W.* 2.15.4 §397: *anairēsein de pan hymōn to phylon.*

The upshot of all this is that, apart from *Christianōn,* not one word of what I identify as the original text of the *Testimonium* fails to occur elsewhere in Josephus, usually with the same meaning and/or construction. As indicated in the first part of this note, the same cannot be said of the NT.

⁴² In what I identify as the three Christian interpolations, the occurrence of the words in the NT is as follows: (1) In the first interpolation, *eige* 5×; *anēr* 216×; *chrē* 1×. (2) In the second interpolation, *christos* 531× (versus the one occurrence in Josephus outside the *Testimonium);* indeed, the whole second interpolation seems lifted directly from the NT. (3) In the third interpolation, *phainō* 31×, mostly in passive deponent forms, and often in the aorist passive; *ephanē* is used of angelic appearances in Matt 1:10; 2:13, 19; of Elijah in Luke 9:8; and of the risen Jesus in Mark 16:9 (added later to the original Marcan text). *tē tritē hēmerą* is the common NT way of referring to the resurrection on the third day. What is unusual is the construction *tritēn echōn hēmeran,* which lacks a precise parallel in Josephus as well. Both the NT and Josephus do use *echō* with cardinal numerals to express duration of time and age. Two NT texts that partially parallel the usage here are Luke 24:21, *tritēn tautēn hēmeran agei;* and John 11:17, *heuren auton tessaras ēdē hēmeras echonta en tǭ mnēmeiǭ.* The rest of the vocabulary in the third interpolation offers no problem: *zaō,* 140×, often as a present participle; *palin,* 141×; *theios,* 3×; *prophētēs,* 144×; *myrias,* 8×, *myrioi* (though not the form *myria),* 3×; *thaumasios,* 1×. When we consider the number of words and constructions in the core of the *Testimonium* that are not found in the NT, the total agreement of the interpolations with the vocabulary of the NT is striking. Of course, there are some stylistic quirks (e.g., the *tritēn echōn hēmeran),* pointing to a Christian interpolator or interpolators who naturally drew upon NT vocabulary as he (they) wrote about Jesus in his (their) own style. It must also be admitted that Josephus likewise uses all the words found in the three interpolations. In a few cases, the usage is more Josephan than that of the NT (e.g, *theios* used 206×, including occurrences with *prophētēs* [though not in the plural]; *thaumasios* 31×). Hence, in the case of the three interpolations, the major argument against their authenticity is from content. Still, the difference from the core text is clear: in the core, not only are the vocabulary and style overwhelmingly Josephan, but at least some of the vocabulary is absent from the NT and some of the content is at variance with what the NT says.

⁴³ For an opposing view of the argument from "Josephan" vocabulary, see Birdsall, "The Continuing Enigma," 619–21. In my view, Birdsall applies the measuring rod of Josephan vocabulary and style a little too mechanically. The undisputed epistles of Paul have their share not only of *hapax legomena* but also of Pauline words and phrases that Paul uses in a given passage with an unusual meaning or construction. Especially since Josephus is dealing in the *Testimonium* with peculiar material, drawn perhaps from a special source, we need not be surprised if his usage differs slightly at a few points.

More specifically, I do not think all of Birdsall's claims concerning divergent style or meaning stand up to close scrutiny. For example, Birdsall claims that *tálēthē* only once elsewhere in Josephus carries the abstract sense of truth; the sense usually is the objective truth of a statement or report about a man's character. Actually, this is a fine distinction that does not always work well in practice. More to the point, there are a number of cases in Josephus where *tálēthē* means truth in some global or general sense: e.g., *J.W.* 1.1.15 §16; *Ant.* 8.2.1 §23; 14.1.1 §3. In another usage as well ("receive with gladness"), Birdsall has to admit that there is at least one other example in Josephus of the phrase being used in the same sense as in the *Testimonium*. I fail to see how this warrants a judgment of inauthenticity.

Furthermore, Birdsall presumes that he knows the precise tenor or nuance of all of the phrases in the *Testimonium*. But that is far from certain. It is quite possible that the old fox Josephus purposely wrote a neutral or ambiguous state-ment about Jesus that could be read in more than one way. Simply as a matter of fact, the Christian interpolator(s) read it one way, while Eisler and his followers read it in a totally different way.

Finally, if Birdsall wishes to attribute the whole of the *Testimonium* to the pre-Nicene patristic period, then he must explain why some notable phrases from the core do not appear in any of the Church Fathers before Eusebius—e.g., (1) *sophos anēr* used to describe Jesus; and (2) *phylon* used to describe Christians. Indeed, while G. W. H. Lampe lists applications of *sophos* to God, OT heroes such as Daniel, Esther, and Judith, the authors of the wisdom books, St. Paul, and others possessed of Christian wisdom, he catalogues no application to Jesus; see his *A Patristic Lexicon* (Oxford: Clarendon Press, 1961).

[44] Notice that Josephus does not say outright that Jesus was a teacher of the truth; rather, he was a teacher of *people who receive the truth with pleasure*. As Pelletier points out from similar passages in Josephus ("Ce que Josèphe a dit," 18), the phrase "receive the truth with pleasure" refers to the subjective "good faith" of those listening, not necessarily the objective truth of what the speaker propounds.

[45] Some critics suggest that Eusebius, or at least a source only a few decades earlier than Eusebius, is the author of the *Testimonium;* see Zeitlin, "The Hoax of the 'Slavonic Josephus,'" 171–80; and Kennard, "Gleanings," 161–63, who thinks that the received text of the *Testimonium* dates from a few decades before Eusebius. Pelletier, citing Martin, mentions Origen as a possible author of the Christian interpolations ("Ce que Josèphe a dit," 14–15); Pelletier also suggests the possibility of a Christian polemicist of the 4th century.

[46] In light of the *Testimonium*'s diffusion among the "mainstream" Fathers of the Church from the 4th century onward, it seems highly unlikely that it would have been composed by some remnant of an Ebionite or other suspect group.

[47] The question, of course, may be put the other way round: If the three statements I have bracketed are later Christian interpolations, what were the intention and the theology of the later interpolator? Actually, I think it more likely that we are dealing with random Christian glosses that secondarily crept into the text; they need not all be from the same hand or the same time. Hence

to ask about *the* one purpose or theology of the three interpolations may be a mistake from the start. For the many marginal glosses in the manuscripts of Josephus, see Sanford, "Propaganda and Censorship," 132: "The process of interpolation [into the text of Josephus] was furthered by the intrusions into the text of glosses and *adversaria* by Christian students studying and copying Josephus. No existing manuscript of his work is free from such interpolation."

[48] One should not make of the royal official in John 4:46–53 a pagan centurion (*contra* John Marsh, *The Gospel of St John* [Harmondsworth: Penguin, 1968] 235–41); that is to read into John what only the Synoptics say in a notably different version of the miracle story. The Samaritans of Chapter 4 serve as a halfway house between the Jewish and pagan worlds.

[49] Shaye J. D. Cohen, of Jewish Theological Seminary in New York, was kind enough to read my views on Josephus and make some comments. He saved me from more than one embarrassing slip. Dr. Cohen felt that the particular argument I make in point (a) is weak because later Christians had no hesitation in projecting back on Jesus the theology and ideology of Paul: of course Jesus had come to bring salvation to the Gentiles—and this is what the *Testimonium* says. How many premodern (and preecumenical) Christians would have said otherwise? Cohen shrewdly pointed out to me that what would have been unusual for an ancient Christian author was the statement that Jesus won over *many* Jews as well as many Gentiles. Cohen's point is well taken, but I think there is a difference between an anachronistic attribution to Jesus of an intention to save both Jew and Gentile and a statement about what Jesus de facto did during his public ministry, i.e., a description of his public activity (and its results) that simply flies in the face of what the four canonical Gospels say.

[50] Hence, Thackeray's claim ("Josephus and Christianity," 148) that *phylon* is distinctly disparaging and cannot have come from a Christian hand is not correct. See instead Solomon Zeitlin, "The Christ Passage in Josephus," *JQR* 18 (1927–28) 231–53, esp. 238–39, 253; Zeitlin points to Eusebius' *Ecclesiastical History*, 3.33: *to tōn Christianōn phylon*.

[51] This point is stressed especially by Nodet, "Jésus et Jean-Baptiste," 320–48, 497–524.

[52] This difficulty must be faced especially by those critics who are enthusiastic about the authenticity and importance of the passage about the Baptist, while dismissing the *Testimonium* as a complete fabrication; so, e.g., Bilde, *Flavius Josephus Between Jerusalem and Rome*, 223, 225.

[53] For example, by changing *sophos anēr* to *sophistēs* (used of leaders of factions Josephus dislikes) or *talēthē* to *taethē* (the unusual, the abnormal, the bizarre); so Eisler, *IĒSOUS BASILEUS*, 1. 46–88; S. G. F. Brandon, *Jesus and the Zealots* (Manchester: Manchester University, 1967) 359–68; similarly, Smith, *Jesus the Magician*, 45–46; Pötscher, "Josephus Flavius, Antiquitates 18, 63f.," 26–42. The changes Eisler introduces can be found in Vol. 9 (No. 433) of the Loeb Library edition of Josephus' works, p. 48 n. a.

Baras ("The *Testimonium Flavianum* and the Martyrdom of James," 340) correctly observes that if the original text of the *Testimonium* had been derogatory or ironic, it would have called forth a strong denunciation from Origen. Hence I am also very skeptical of the theory that originally the *Testimonium* had a derogatory reference to Jesus' virginal conception; for such a position, which in my view fails for lack of any direct evidence, see Pharr, "The Testimony of Josephus to Christianity," 137–47. For an attempt to bolster Pharr's suggestion by appealing to the 4th-century pseudo-Hegesippus (and even this demands reading into the evidence), see Albert A. Bell, Jr., "Josephus the Satirist. A Clue to the Original Form of the *Testimonium Flavianum?*" *JQR* 67 (1966–67) 16–22.

Bammel ("Zum Testimonium Flavianum," 20–22) thinks that the *Testimonium* originally expressed a negative view of Christians (less so of Christ), but that good method demands that the modern scholar keep conjectural emendations to a minimum. However, his own corrections *(apatēthentes* or *autous apatōntes* for *agapēsantes, apēgageto* for *epēgageto*, the omission of *ēn* after *ho christos houtos*, and the insertion of *phaskontes hoti)* are based on tenuous arguments, and even they are much more complicated than the simple procedure of bracketing the three obviously Christian statements.

[54] I have purposely not spent any time on the objection that the *Testimonium* breaks the thread of the narrative in Book 18; if one is interested in such a line of argumentation, one should see Thackeray, "Josephus and Christianity," 140–41 (where, in my view, he is much too dependent on Eisler). Perhaps the best insight in Thackeray's whole explanation is the simple observation: "Josephus was a patchwork writer" (p. 141). Cohen is blunter: "We have emphasized another aspect of Josephus' work: his inveterate sloppiness. Texts suitable for tendentious revision as well as passages which contradict his motives are sometimes left untouched. The narrative is frequently confused, obscure, and contradictory" (*Josephus in Galilee and Rome,* 233). In the present case, one wonders whether any greater link need exist for Josephus than the fact that the account of Jesus (who is crucified by Pilate) is preceded by a story about Pilate in which many Jews are killed *(Ant.* 18.3.2 §60–62) and is followed by a story in which tricksters are punished by crucifixion *(Ant.* 18.3.4 §65–80). Hence I think the lengthy attempt of Bammel ("Zum Testimonium Flavianum," 15–18) to explain the connections with what precedes and follows the *Testimonium* is beside the point. For a detailed refutation of Norden's claim that the *Testimonium* supposedly disrupts the narrative flow and thematic unity of the larger context, see Martin, "Le 'Testimonium Flavianum,' " 422–31).

[55] As Thackeray observes, in view of the pervasive Josephan vocabulary and style, "alterations should be reduced to a minimum" ("Josephus and Christianity," 143). In my view, Thackeray himself undertook too many alterations.

[56] Ibid., 127–28; Thackeray, however, says no more than that there is "nothing improbable" in this. He also notes that Mark's Gospel would probably have been in circulation in Rome when Josephus wrote *The Antiquities.*

[57] Feldman, "The *Testimonium Flavianum,* " 194–95.

[58] Martin, "Le 'Testimonium Flavianum,' " 450.

[59] Needless to say, such an answer cannot claim absolute certitude, but only that high degree of probability which is commonly called moral certitude. Yet the passages of Josephus do supply us with that. It is significant that the *Testimonium Flavianum* is quickly and facilely dismissed without detailed examination by G. A. Wells in his popular and somewhat sensationalistic *Did Jesus Exist?* (Buffalo, NY: Prometheus Books, 1975). Obviously, Wells's desire to maintain the thesis that Jesus never existed (pp. 205–7) demands such a treatment of Josephus, who would otherwise destroy Wells's whole argument before it could really get started. Wells's presentation descends to simple affirmation, supported not by argumentation but by citation of generally antiquated authorities, in the case of the James passage, which is declared to be a brief marginal gloss from a Christian, which was later incorporated into the text (p. 11). Wells's book, which builds its arguments on these and similar unsubstantiated claims, may be allowed to stand as a representative of a whole type of popular Jesus book that I do not bother to consider in detail.

[60] Although one might debate the exact source of Josephus' knowledge expressed in the *Testimonium*, the passing reference to James in Book 20 of *The Antiquities* is of a different order when it comes to the question of sources. For the reasons I have indicated, it is unlikely that Josephus derives his account of James's death from Christians. Both in its narrative and in its way of referring to James, Josephus' account is at variance with the accepted Christian version of James's death. The natural source for an event happening in Jerusalem in A.D. 62 would be the Jews who had taken part in that event and whom Josephus would have known personally. Indeed, Josephus himself could well have been present in Jerusalem during these events. From his *Life* (3 §12–13) it appears that he returned to Jerusalem from his desert experience ca. A.D. 56–57 and went to Rome ca. 64. Hence it is very likely that he was in Jerusalem during James's trial and death in 62. At any rate, it is from either firsthand knowledge or from other Jews involved in the events that Josephus writes about the death of James, "the brother of Jesus-who-is-called-Messiah." The idea that Josephus needed to be informed about events in Jerusalem in the early sixties by Christians is a gratuitous and unnecessary hypothesis.

[61] It is important to stress here that the basic fact of Jesus' existence and at least some stray facts about him remain unquestioned whether one accepts my reconstruction or any of the many others offered across the spectrum of scholarship in the 20th century. If one prefers the position of the later Thackeray, Dornseiff, Dubarle, Pelletier, or Feldman, the basic point I make in the text remains the same.

[62] Hence I do not find the silence of Christian writers in the first three centuries as powerful an objection to authenticity as does Feldman ("Flavius Josephus Revisited," 822). In my opinion, it is unfortunate that Martin, in his otherwise fine article, tries to launch the hypothesis that Origen himself was the author of the interpolations ("Le 'Testimonium Flavianum,' " 458–65). Any attempt to name *the* author of the three interpolations seems futile since we must take

seriously the possibility that each of the three interpolations was scribbled into the margin by a different Christian at a different time.

[63] I must acknowledge a debt of gratitude to Professors Shaye J. D. Cohen, Harold W. Attridge, Jr., and Myles M. Bourke for their generous help in evaluating the material from Josephus.

CHAPTER 4

SOURCES:

Other Pagan and Jewish Writings

1. TACITUS AND OTHER PAGAN AUTHORS OF THE SECOND CENTURY A.D.[1]

The statement of Tacitus is shorter and simpler to treat than that of Josephus. The Roman historian Tacitus (ca. 56/7–ca. 118) wrote as the last great work of his life the *Annals*, in which he intended to cover the history of Rome from A.D. 14 to 68. Some books of the *Annals* have been lost, and Book 16 breaks off in A.D. 66. Unfortunately for us, one of the gaps in the *Annals* occurs during the treatment of A.D. 29, with the narrative resuming in A.D. 32. Hence the most likely year for the trial and death of Jesus (A.D. 30) is not covered in our present manuscripts of the *Annals*. Barring the discovery of a fuller manuscript, we will never know whether Tacitus mentioned Jesus in his treatment of the years 30–31.

There is, however, a short retrospective reference to Jesus when Tacitus treats the great fire of Rome under Nero and Nero's subsequent use of the Christians of Rome as scapegoats *(Annals* 15.44). Nero, says Tacitus, fastened on the Christians because popular opinion suspected that he was responsible for the fire:

Therefore, to squelch the rumor, Nero created scapegoats and subjected to the most refined tortures those whom the common people called "Christians," [a group] hated for their abominable crimes. Their name comes from Christ,[2] who, during the reign of Tiberius, had been executed by the procurator Pontius Pilate.[3] Suppressed for the moment, the deadly superstition broke out again, not only in Judea, the land which originated this evil, but also in the city of Rome, where all sorts of horrendous and shameful practices from every part of the world converge and are fervently cultivated.

This passage is important primarily for the history of early Christianity in Rome,[4] but here I will focus only on what it contributes to our quest —which is not much.[5]

Despite some feeble attempts to show that this text is a Christian interpolation in Tacitus, the passage is obviously genuine. Not only is it witnessed in all the manuscripts of the *Annals*,[6] the very anti-Christian tone of the text makes Christian origin almost impossible. True, Tacitus can manage a modicum of sympathy for people unjustly saddled with the guilt of the hated Nero. But Christians, seen in themselves, are clearly despised for their abominable crimes or vices (*flagitia*); they constitute a deadly or dangerous superstition. That is to say, they are a recently invented and rapidly spreading oriental cult that spurns the Roman gods, practices secret and probably nefarious rites, and therefore is subversive of the good order of the Roman state. In Tacitus' pessimistic view of Roman history, Christians are just another sign of Rome's decline from integrity and virtue into corruption and decadence.

To the mind of this Roman senator and former proconsul, nothing worse could be charged against this cult than that it started with and took its name from some Jew in Judea named Christ,[7] who was executed by Pontius Pilate.[8] The mention of Christ and his fate plays a key part in Tacitus' negative portrait of the Christians; such a short and dismissive description of Jesus hardly comes from a Christian hand.[9]

Although Tacitus' main concern is to describe the brutal execution of Christians in Rome by Nero, he does in passing make three key statements about Jesus.[10] (1) He fixes the time of Christ's death as being during the reign of the Emperor Tiberius (A.D. 14–37) and the governorship of Pontius Pilate (A.D. 26–36). (2) He affirms that Christ's death was a matter of execution by the Roman governor of Judea; while nothing is said explicitly of crucifixion, that would be the natural implication of a Jew being executed in Judea by a Roman governor. Indeed, the phrase referring to Christ's execution (*supplicio adfectus*) may be intentionally placed between two references to the torture and execution of Christians. The second reference, which occurs in *Annals* 15.44 soon after the mention of Christ's execution, explicitly refers to their crucifixion: *aut crucibus adfixi* ("or fastened to crosses").[11] (3) In Tacitus' view, the execution of this Christ suppressed the dangerous religious movement of Christians for a brief time; but it quickly broke out again, first in Judea, but then spreading rapidly as far as Rome. What should be noted here is that Tacitus implies by his phraseology that the Christian movement was already in existence before Christ's execution; otherwise, it could not have been "suppressed" for a brief period by his death. This could, of course, be just another example of naive retrojection by a Greco-Roman historian; we have already seen an example in Josephus. But it is worth noting that Tacitus has no sense that Christians, as a movement named for Christ, arose only after his death. By implication, the same hateful vices of the movement that caused their execution under Nero caused the execution of Christ under Tiberius.

An important question is the source of Tacitus' information. Some scholars, highlighting similarities to the *Testimonium*, suggest that Tacitus had read Josephus.[12] While that is possible, one must recognize the many differences as well as similarities in the two texts.[13] It could be, instead, that Tacitus is simply repeating what was common knowledge about Christians at the beginning of the 2d century. Tacitus had been the governor of the province of Asia (i.e., the western third of Asia Minor) ca. A.D. 112, and might have had judicial contacts with Christians similar to those reported by Pliny the Younger. In addition, Pliny was a close friend of Tacitus and might have conveyed to him the knowledge he had gained about Christians. Nor can we exclude the possibility that Tacitus used Roman archives. However, if he did so, his mistake in calling Pilate a procurator instead of a prefect shows that he is not directly citing any official record. In any case, while Tacitus at best supplies us with another early non-Christian witness to the existence, temporal and geographical location, death, and continued historical impact of Jesus, he tells nothing that Josephus had not already said.

With Josephus and Tacitus we exhaust the early independent witnesses to Jesus' existence, ministry, death, and ongoing influence. Suetonius, Pliny the Younger, and Lucian are often quoted in this regard, but in effect they are simply reporting something about what early Christians say or do; they cannot be said to supply us with independent witness to Jesus himself.

Suetonius,[14] in his life of the Emperor Claudius *(Claudius* 25.4), tells of an expulsion of Jews from Rome: "Since the Jews were constantly causing disturbances at the instigation of Chrestus, he [Claudius] expelled them from Rome."[15] It is often suggested by scholars that the Chrestus referred to here is actually Christ *(Christus,* pronounced in the same way at this time as *Chrestus).* Possibly the source Suetonius used understood "Chrestus" to be Jesus, while Suetonius misunderstood the name to be that of some Jewish slave or freedman causing upset in the Roman synagogues during the reign of Claudius.[16] Even if this is so, the text simply tells us about Christian Jews spreading their faith in Roman synagogues ca. A.D. 40–50. No new knowledge is gained about the historical Jesus.

Pliny the Younger,[17] proconsul in the province of Bithynia (in Asia Minor) during A.D. 111–13, describes for the Emperor Trajan his method of handling Christians who are denounced to him *(Letter* 10.96). Among the practices of Christians, Pliny mentions their custom of meeting regularly before dawn on a fixed day to chant verses "to Christ as to a god" *(Christo quasi deo).*[18] That Christ is being treated by Christians as a god is something new in our sparse non-Christian sources. But, again, it adds nothing to our knowledge of the historical Jesus.

Finally, the satirist Lucian of Samosata (ca. 115–ca. 200) wrote a mocking life of a convert to and then apostate from Christianity, *The Passing of Peregrinus.*[19] The Christians are said to be so enamored of Peregrinus that they revered him as a god ". . . next after that other, to be sure, whom they still worship, the man who was crucified in Palestine because he introduced this new cult into the world."[20] Lucian goes on to describe the Christians as "worshiping that crucified sophist himself and living under his laws."[21] Thus, like Josephus and Tacitus, Lucian knows that the "sophist" revered by the Christians—Lucian never uses the names Jesus or Christ—was executed in Palestine; and, like Josephus, he specifies the mode: crucifixion. Like Tacitus, he presumes that this crucified man himself introduced the new religion called Christianity. Like Pliny, he reports that Christians worship their crucified founder. Once more, we learn what an educated pagan of the second century might know about Jesus, but no doubt Lucian is reflecting the common knowledge "in the air" at that time, not an independent source of historical data.

In short, Josephus is our only independent non-Christian source of information about the historical Jesus in the first century. There is just the bare possibility that Tacitus may represent another independent source at the beginning of the second century; but if so, he adds nothing really new.

2. JEWISH SOURCES BESIDES JOSEPHUS

Judaism around the time of Jesus was a rich tapestry of many different religious tendencies. Recent research on Qumran,[22] the Pseudepigrapha (including a good deal of Jewish apocalyptic literature),[23] Jewish Hellenistic writers (especially Philo and Josephus),[24] and the sources of later rabbinic literature has taught us to avoid thinking of Judaism as one neat, definable entity called "orthodox Judaism."[25] The consolidation of the various streams of Judaism into one "rabbinic" or "orthodox" Judaism did not take place until after A.D. 70, and even then underground or secondary movements such as *Merkabah* mysticism,[26] magical texts,[27] and the later Karaite resistance to rabbinic teaching were not totally suppressed.[28] Some scholars today even prefer to speak of "Judaisms" rather than "Judaism," so vast and variegated, in their view, was the phenomenon we call ancient Judaism.[29]

All of this literature must be kept in mind when one seeks to grasp the religious, cultural, social, and political background of Jesus' day. And that precisely is the literature's contribution to Jesus research: appreciation of the background out of which Jesus comes. In my opinion, apart from the texts of Josephus we have already seen, this vast literature contains no independent[30] reference to or information about Jesus of Nazareth. For most of the works in question, this statement is a truism that need not be documented in detail. No serious scholar claims that there are references to Jesus in Philo or in Jewish apocalyptic writings that have not suffered later Christian interpolations. The question becomes more complicated, though, when we turn to two large bodies of Jewish literature: Qumran and the rabbis.

The discovery of the first Qumran scrolls in 1947 unleashed a flood of theories and speculation about the connection of this quasi-monastic Jewish sect with Jesus and/or early Christianity. Actually, the Qumran finds were much more important for their impact on the study of the Hebrew text of the Bible[31] and of sectarian groups in Second-Temple Judaism,[32] and of the development of apocalyptic and gnosticizing thought in ancient Palestine.[33] To be sure, fascinating parallels with the Synoptic Gospels, the Pauline epistles, the Epistle to the Hebrews, and the Revelation of John were detected[34]—although the exaggerations of some popularizers led scholars to denounce a certain "parallelomania." An ascetic Jewish group practicing purification rites in the Judean wilderness near the southern end of the Jordan River naturally conjured up thoughts of John the Baptist, and some scholars suggest that John was for at least a while a member of Qumran.[35]

Be that as it may (and there is no way of verifying such a claim), there is no indication that Jesus was ever directly connected with the Qumran community. He is never mentioned in the documents found at or near Qumran, and his freewheeling attitude toward the stricter interpretation of the Mosaic Law is the very antithesis of the superobservant Qumranites, who considered even the Pharisees too lax. All this has not kept some imaginative scholars from seeing Jesus and John the Baptist in certain Qumran texts.[36] This simply proves that learned fantasy knows no limits. The same can be said of attempts to find fragments of NT documents among the smaller scraps from Qumran.[37]

More complicated and, at first glance, promising is the vast corpus of rabbinic literature, which includes the Mishna (the first extant large collection of the so-called "oral" traditions of the rabbis), the Palestinian (or Jerusalem) and Babylonian Talmuds (containing the Mishna with further commentary on the Mishna, called the Gemara), the Tosefta (early rabbinic traditions left out of the Mishna and written down later), the targums (Aramaic translations and paraphrases of the Hebrew Scriptures), and the midrashim (rabbinic commentaries on the Scriptures). These huge collections of centuries-old traditions are treasure houses of Jewish laws, customs, homilies, legends, anecdotes, and axioms. Their primary value is as witnesses to the ongoing life of ancient and early medieval Judaism, and to ask them about Jesus of Nazareth is, in almost all cases, to ask the wrong question of a body of literature with its own valid concerns. The proper context for these documents is first of all the history of Judaism, not the Jesus of history.[38]

Nevertheless, a few passages out of this sprawling labyrinth of literature have been cited by scholars as referring to Jesus. Immediately, we run into two distinct but intertwined problems: (1) Is there really a reference to Jesus in a given rabbinic text? (2) If there is, is the knowledge of Jesus displayed in the text independent of all Christian influence and sources, or is it a garbled version of or a polemical reply to Christian claims? This second question raises the major problem of dating. Our earliest collection of rabbinic material, the Mishna, comes from the end of the 2d or the beginning of the 3d century A.D.; all other collections are still later.[39] It would never occur to most Christian commentators to

claim that early 3d-century Fathers of the Church had direct, historically reliable knowledge of Jesus that was independent of the NT. Likewise, one must be wary a priori of claims that a late 2d- or early 3d-
century Jewish document contains such independent traditions. It was
not a biased Christian apologist but the great Jewish scholar Joseph
Klausner who wrote earlier in this century that the very few references
to Jesus in the Talmud are of little historical worth, "since they partake
rather of the nature of vituperation and polemic against the founder of a
hated party, than of objective accounts of historical value."[40] Moreover,
as Klausner notes, the Talmud on the whole speaks only rarely of historical events of the Second-Temple period, and usually then only when
they are connected with some legal debate or homiletic application.

To return to our first question, scholars of rabbinic literature do not
agree among themselves on whether even a single text from the Mishna,
Tosefta, or Talmud really refers to Jesus of Nazareth. For instance, a
radical position is represented by Johann Maier, who maintains that not
only the Mishna but also both Talmuds lack any authentic, direct mention of Jesus of Nazareth.[41] To uphold this view, Maier engages in a
detailed form- and redaction-critical study of all the passages in rabbinic
literature that supposedly contain references to Jesus. His conclusion is
that even the original text of the two Talmuds never mentioned Jesus of
Nazareth; all such references to Jesus are later interpolations inserted in
the Middle Ages.

In my opinion, Maier's arguments are especially convincing for the
Mishna and other early rabbinic material: no text cited from that period
really refers to Jesus. He thus confirms the view I defend in this section.
However, while I admire Maier's careful study of all the forms of a
given rabbinic tradition, his position that all references to Jesus of Nazareth in the two Talmuds are interpolations rests on lengthy and sometimes tenuous hypothetical arguments, and here and there it seems to
function as a *deus ex machina.* Even if Maier pushes a good thesis too far,
at least one of his basic points is well taken. Jesus of Nazareth is simply
absent from the Mishna and other early rabbinic traditions.

Indeed, while not too many scholars would be willing to take as
radical a stance as Maier's, a good number of experts in rabbinics remain
skeptical about using rabbinic writings as a source for the historical
Jesus. For example, Jacob Z. Lauterbach holds that "not even one single
statement preserved to us in the talmudic-midrashic literature can be
regarded as authentic in the sense that it originated in the time of Jesus
or even in the first half century of the Christian era."[42] The Talmud

does not record even one talmudic teacher who lived at the time of Jesus or in the first half century of the Christian era as mentioning Jesus by name. As for the rabbis of the 2d century A.D., they were reacting to the Christ proclaimed by Christianity, not the historical Jesus. Samuel Sandmel basically agrees with Lauterbach. He also points out that, even if one were to allow that the few texts championed by scholars like Joseph Klausner or Morris Goldstein actually spoke about Jesus and possibly represented independent tradition, the net result would be so meager as to be useless, except for proving Jesus' existence.[43] From what has been said so far, it is obvious that one must be leery of inflated claims about what rabbinic literature can tell us concerning the "Jewish Jesus."

Even critics who do see some authentic references to Jesus in rabbinic texts reject a number of the claimants. For instance, Klausner excludes from consideration the texts that speak of a "Ben Stada," a dangerous beguiler of the people who was supposedly stoned to death by Jewish scholars in the town of Lod. Only in later talmudic traditions was Ben Stada related to Jesus; no early rabbinic traditions support the identification of the two.[44]

On the other hand, Klausner does connect Jesus with early rabbinic references to a person called "Ben Pandera" or "Ben Pantere."[45] The name occurs in connection with a story about a Jewish maiden who had illicit relations with a Roman soldier named Panthera. According to the Church Father Origen (ca. A.D. 185–254), the 2d-century pagan polemicist Celsus, writing about A.D. 178, reported that he heard a Jew tell such a story of Mary, the mother of Jesus.[46] It is therefore likely, says Klausner, that such a story circulated among the Jews in the 2d century A.D. and is reflected in some rabbinic sayings of the period.[47] The story about Panthera seems to be a garbled or mocking, polemical reference to the Infancy Narratives of Matthew and Luke, where Mary the virgin (Greek: *parthenos*) conceives Jesus by the power of the Holy Spirit apart from her husband Joseph.[48]

Among the very few texts that Klausner accepts as referring to Jesus of Nazareth is one found in the Babylonian Talmud's tractate *Sanhedrin* 43a.[49] It contains a reference to Yeshu (= Jesus) who was hanged on the eve of Passover (which would agree with the Fourth Gospel's chronology of the passion), but the correct information is mixed in with a confused statement about a herald calling for defense witnesses for forty days before Yeshu is to be stoned to death. The text describes Yeshu as a magician who beguiled Israel and led it astray. This agrees with the whole tendency of ancient Jewish sources, which do not deny the existence and execution of Jesus. Indeed, not even the miracles of Jesus are denied, but are rather interpreted as acts of sorcery.[50] The reference to the herald seeking out defense witnesses for forty days may be an apologetic thrust against the canonical Gospels' depiction of arrest, trial, and execution, all in one twenty-four-hour period. All in all, there is nothing here that we do not know from the Gospels, and most likely the talmudic text is simply reacting to the gospel tradition.[51]

Even the few passages Klausner judges as genuine early references to Jesus are not without their problems. It is significant that he can find only one passage in the Mishna that, in his view, refers to Jesus. The passage occurs in a discussion of who is to be considered a bastard (mamzer) in law. The Mishna tractate Yebamot 4:13 records a number of opinions, among which is the statement of Rabbi Simeon ben Azzai: "I found a family register in Jerusalem and in it was written, 'Such-a-one is a bastard through [a transgression of the law of] thy neighbor's wife [i.e., through adultery of a married woman with a man not her husband].' "[52] Klausner sees an allusion here to the Jewish tradition of Jesus' illegitimate birth, but Gustaf Dalman (rightly, in my view) objects that the whole context is simply a debate over the correct definition of "bastard," with various opinions appealing to various passages in the OT.[53] In any case, Klausner stresses that this Jewish tradition of Jesus' illegitimate birth lacks historical foundation and arises from opposition to the Christian teaching of the virginal conception. Hence, the text, whatever its meaning, does not represent independent knowledge about Jesus.[54] In my view, even Klausner's cautious position is too optimistic. Personally, I tend to the view of Morris Goldstein, who finds no certain reference to Jesus in this passage, and indeed in the Mishna and the tannaitic midrashim in general.[55]

I am similarly skeptical about a tradition in which Eliezer ben Hyrcanus hears about Jesus' teaching that the wages of a prostitute should be used to buy the high priest a latrine (in the Babylonian Talmud's tractate 'Aboda Zara 16b–17a; cf. Tosefta Ḥullin 2.24).[56] To establish the reliability of this passage, Klausner must engage in a contorted argument that includes an appeal to Hegesippus' account of the martyrdom of James—something that would not inspire confidence in many scholars today.[57] Joachim Jeremias weighs the pros and cons of the argument about authenticity and decides in the negative—rightly, in my view. The saying is a polemical invention meant to make Jesus look ridiculous.[58]

Klausner's final example is an anecdote mocking Jewish Christians

and their "gospel," found in the Babylonian Talmud's tractate *Šabbat*
116a and b. The fact that it is recorded in Aramaic, occurs nowhere else
in Talmud or midrash, and has the Jewish Christian quoting a garbled
version of Matt 5:17 from "a gospel scroll"[59] makes it highly unlikely
that we have here any independent tradition.[60]

In short, I remain doubtful as to whether any of Klausner's texts
convey to us knowledge independent of Christian writings.[61] More to
the point, even if we were to accept all of his claims, they would not add
anything new to the information we already have from the NT.[62] While
not accepting the full, radical approach of Maier, I think we can agree
with him on one basic point: in the earliest rabbinic sources, there is no
clear or even probable reference to Jesus of Nazareth. Furthermore, I
favor the view that, when we do finally find such references in later
rabbinic literature, they are most probably reactions to Christian claims,
oral or written. Hence, apart from Josephus, Jewish literature of the
early Christian period offers no independent source for inquiry into the
historical Jesus.[63] Indeed, why should it? Engaged in a fierce struggle for
its own survival and definition, early rabbinic Judaism had other matters on its mind—matters that, from its own perspective, were much
more important.

[1] On the whole question, see Murray J. Harris, "References to Jesus in Early Classical Authors," *Gospel Perspectives. The Jesus Tradition Outside the Gospels*, 343–68.

[2] Literally, "the author of this name, Christ." The translation is my own. The Latin text reads: *ergo abolendo rumori Nero subdidit reos et quaesitissimis poenis adfecit quos per flagitia invisos vulgus Christianos appellabat. auctor nominis eius Christus Tiberio imperitante per procuratorem Pontium Pilatum supplicio adfectus erat; repressaque in praesens exitiabilis superstitio rursum erumpebat, non modo per Iudaeam, originem eius mali, sed per urbem etiam quo cuncta undique atrocia aut pudenda confluunt celebranturque.* The text is taken from John Jackson, ed., *Tacitus* (LCL; 4 vols.; Cambridge, MA: Harvard University; London: Heinemann, 1937) 4. 282; the traditional citation is Book 15, Chap. 44.

[3] Léon Herrmann *(Chrestos. Témoignages païens et juifs sur le christianisme du premier siècle* [Collection Latomus 109; Brussels: Latomus, 1970] 8) prefers to read the phrase *per procuratorem Pontium Pilatum* as modifying *Tiberio imperitante*. The sense in this case would be "while Tiberius was governing [Judea] through Pontius Pilate his procurator"—the emphasis being on the firm control of Tiberius. While possible, this leaves *adfectus erat* without any agent; hence I prefer to take *per procuratorem* with *adfectus erat.*

The phrase *supplicio adfectus erat* is remarkably vague. It certainly indicates inflicting a grave penalty (legally imposed by some Roman authority); it is usually connected with fierce physical suffering and/or the shedding of blood. Quite often—but not always—it refers to execution. That execution is meant here is suggested not so much from the phrase taken alone as from the larger context: Christ is not mentioned after the inflicting of the punishment, Tacitus immediately speaks of Christ's movement being suppressed for the moment in Judea, and the followers of Christ, the Christians, are put to death by Nero. Would a lesser penalty be inflicted on their founder? (One wonders whether *crucibus adfixi*, the phrase Tacitus uses later in *Annals* 15.44 for Nero's crucifixion of Christians, may be a vague verbal echo of *supplicio adfectus erat*, the description of Christ's own punishment.)

There is a great historical irony in this text of Tacitus; it is the only time in ancient pagan literature that Pontius Pilate is mentioned by name—as a way of specifying who Christ is. Pilate's fate in the Christian creeds is already foreshadowed in a pagan historian.

[4] For this, see Wolfgang Wiefel, "The Jewish Community in Ancient Rome and the Origins of Roman Christianity," *The Romans Debate*, ed. Karl P. Donfried (Minneapolis: Augsburg, 1977) 100–19; Raymond E. Brown, "The Beginnings of Christianity at Rome," in Raymond E. Brown and John P. Meier, *Antioch and Rome* (New York/Ramsey: Paulist, 1983) 92–104, esp. 98–99.

[5] Joseph Klausner *(Jesus of Nazareth. His Life, Times and Teaching* [New York: Macmillan, 1925] 60) is to the point: "These words [of Tacitus] would have had considerable value as the spontaneous evidence of a Gentile if they had been

written earlier than seventy-five years after the event." Nevertheless, as we shall
see, they do raise some intriguing points.

⁶ As with Josephus, so with Tacitus our observation must be tempered by the
fact that the earliest manuscript of the *Annals* comes from the 11th century.

⁷ The mention of the common people makes possible that Tacitus originally
wrote "Chrestianos" and "Chrestus," a common confusion among pagans of the
first centuries, since *e* and *i* vowels in Greek at this time had come to sound
identical ("itacism"). However, like his friend Pliny the Younger, Tacitus had
probably come to know Christians firsthand when he was proconsul of Asia (i.e.,
western Asia Minor) in A.D. 112–13. Hence he would probably have known the
correct form of the name and its spelling. However, Harald Fuchs ("Tacitus
über die Christen," *VC* 4 [1950] 65–93) suggests that Tacitus is consciously re-
marking that the common people *(vulgus)* use the pronunciation "Chrēstianos";
he is also playing on the root meaning of the Greek word *chrēstos* ("good, kindly,
benevolent") by ironically juxtaposing "Chrestianos" with the description
"hated because of their vices." This suggestion is accepted by Carlo M. Martini,
"Il silenzio dei testimoni non cristiani su Gesù," *La Civiltà Cattolica* 113/2 (1962)
341–49, esp. 344 n.10.

⁸ As we now know from the Caesarea Maritima inscription discovered in
1961, Pontius Pilate bore the title of "prefect," not "procurator," during his
governorship of Judea. During the reigns of Augustus and Tiberius, governors
of Egypt and Judea were of equestrian (not senatorial) rank and were usually
entitled "prefect." This title stressed military functions, while "procurator" carried more of the idea of being a financial administrator and (increasingly) the
emperor's personal agent. In practice, however, the difference between prefect
and procurator probably did not mean all that much in a backwater province
like Judea; and it is not impossible that, when speaking of the official, people
spoke loosely and interchangeably of either "the prefect" or "the procurator." It
is therefore not surprising that neither Tacitus nor Philo nor Josephus is completely consistent in his usage. Technically, though, the Caesarea Maritima inscription shows that the official title of Pilate was prefect. On all this, see Emil
Schürer, *The History of the Jewish People in the Age of Jesus Christ (175 B.C.–A.D. 135),*
rev. and ed. Geza Vermes and Fergus Millar (Edinburgh: Clark, 1973), 1. 358–60;
also Jerry Vardaman, "A New Inscription Which Mentions Pilate as 'Prefect,'"
JBL 81 (1962) 70–71. Unless we gratuitously suppose that Pilate's title was
changed during his tenure in office, we must conclude that Tacitus is, strictly
speaking, mistaken when he calls Pilate a procurator; once again, the state of
affairs at a later period (the governorship was elevated to the status of procurator
probably during the reign of the Emperor Claudius) was retrojected naively into
an earlier period. The reason why Claudius changed the title of the governor of
Judea is not entirely clear. Some authors speak of "upgrading" the office in the
face of increasingly difficult relations with the Jewish population. Actually, the
change of title in Judea may rather have been part of a wider change Claudius
undertook. By transforming "prefects" into "procurators," he may have been
seeking to bring the office more directly under the personal control of the em-

peror as opposed to the Senate. On this interpretation, see Barbara Levick, *Claudius* (New Haven/London: Yale University, 1990) 48–49.

[9] For the attempt to dispute the authenticity of this text by L. A. Yelnitsky and for its refutation, see Feldman, *Josephus and Modern Scholarship*, 319. See also Herrmann, *Chrestos*, 161–62. Trilling, citing Johannes Weiss, claims that our passage is a masterpiece of Tacitus' genuine style and thought *(Fragen zur Geschichtlichkeit Jesu*, 57).

Nodet ("Jésus et Jean-Baptiste," 342–45) defends the authenticity of the passage, but tries to show that the sentence narrating the death of Jesus comes from another context, possibly the lost sixth book of Tacitus' *Histories*. This procedure strikes one as not only unnecessary but also strange, since Nodet strenuously resists any surgery or amputation in the case of the *Testimonium*. He then attempts to show that Tacitus drew his statement about Christ from Book 18 of *The Antiquities;* he also points to parallels between the *Testimonium* and Paul's sermon at Pisidian Antioch in Acts 13. All this seems forced. For others who hold a theory of displacement, see Jean-Pierre Lémonon, *Pilate et le gouvernement de la Judée. Textes et monuments* (EBib; Paris: Gabalda, 1981) 173. As Lémonon notes (p. 174 n. 5), all that need concern us is authenticity. That Christ shares in the negative judgment Tacitus passes on Christians in this passage is stressed by Martini, "Il silenzio," 345.

[10] Of course, the name Jesus does not appear; for Tacitus, "Christ" is a proper name. Note the difference from Josephus, who speaks (in the original form of the text) only of Jesus. Even the Christian interpolation seems to use *ho christos* as a title: "He was the Messiah," not "He was Christ."

[11] Note the order of the statements and the choice of similar verbs and grammatical constructions in *Annals* 15.44: *Nero subdidit reos et quaesitissimis poenis AD-FECIT. . . . Christus . . . supplicio ADFECTUS ERAT. . . . aut crucibus AD-FIXI. . . .*

[12] See Franz Dornseiff, "Lukas der Schriftsteller. Mit einem Anhang: Josephus und Tacitus," *ZNW* 35 (1936) 148–55. Appealing to the view of von Harnack, Dornseiff stresses the parallel between the *Testimonium* and *Annals* 15.44. If Dornseiff were shown to be correct in his position, it would in effect prove the core of the *Testimonium* to be authentic. But, as Martini notes ("Il silenzio," 344–45), the view that Tacitus is dependent here on Josephus is generally rejected by scholars.

[13] To name only some of the differences: (1) Josephus (in the core of the *Testimonium)* speaks only of "Jesus"; Tacitus, only of "Christ," understood as a proper name. (2) The reign of Tiberius is mentioned in the larger context of *Ant.* 18.2.4 and 3.4, but not in the *Testimonium;* Tacitus mentions Tiberius alongside of Pilate. (3) Josephus first describes the ministry of Jesus (miracles, teaching, great success among both Jews and Greeks); Tacitus mentions only his being the origin of the Christians and his execution. (4) Josephus speaks of the accusation of the Jewish leaders before Pilate; Tacitus speaks only of Pilate's role in the execution. (5) Josephus explicitly mentions death by crucifixion; Tacitus speaks

vaguely of the infliction of extreme punishment. All this is not to deny a number of strong similarities: In a brief passage, (1) Jesus/Christ is named, (2) his execution in Judea by Pilate (hence during the reign of Tiberius) is mentioned, (3) the derivation of the name "Christian" from him is noted, and (4) the Christian group that stems from him is said to have continued after his death. Granted the perspectives of two non-Christian historians writing in Rome at the end of the 1st or the beginning of the 2d century, such similarities are not so startling as to prove the literary dependence of Tacitus on Josephus.

[14] The dates of Suetonius' birth and death cannot be fixed with any precision. He was born ca. A.D. 69–70 and certainly was alive in A.D. 121–22. How long he lived after that is not clear; some think he survived into the early part of the reign of the Emperor Antoninus Pius (reigned 138–61). His best-known work is his *Lives of the Twelve Caesars* (published in 120), of which the life of Claudius is the fifth.

[15] The Latin text reads: *Iudaeos impulsore Chresto assidue tumultuantis Roma expulit;* see J. C. Rolfe, ed., *Suetonius* (LCL; 2 vols.; Cambridge, MA: Harvard University; London: Heinemann, 1914) 2. 52 n. a.

[16] Two arguments favor a reference to Christ rather than to some Roman Jew named Chrestus: (1) Good Latin style would seem to demand a *quodam* after *Chresto* if some new and otherwise unknown figure were being introduced into the narrative. (2) Raymond E. Brown reports that "among the several hundred names of Roman Jews known from the Jewish catacombs and other sources, no instance of 'Chrestus' appears" *(Antioch and Rome, 100)*.

[17] Pliny the Younger (ca. A.D. 61–ca. 112) was the nephew and adopted son of Pliny the Elder (ca. A.D. 23–79), who died during the eruption of Vesuvius. As we shall see in Chapter 10, Pliny the Elder is of great importance to the history of 1st-century Judaism because of his description of the Essenes.

[18] See Betty Radice, ed., *Pliny. Letters and Panegyricus* (LCL; 2 vols.; Cambridge, MA: Harvard University; London: Heinemann, 1969) 2. 288; the traditional citation is Book 10, letter 96.

[19] On Lucian and *The Passing of Peregrinus*, see Robert L. Wilken, *The Christians as the Romans Saw Them* (New Haven/London: Yale University, 1984) 96–97.

[20] For *The Passing of Peregrinus*, see A. Harmon, ed., *Lucian* (LCL; 8 vols.; Cambridge, MA: Harvard University; London: Heinemann, 1936) 5. 1–51; quotation taken from Chapter 11 (p. 12). The Greek literally speaks not of a crucified man but rather a man who has been impaled *(anaskolopisthenta)*. Actually, Lucian has a historical basis for his use of the word, since crucifixion probably developed from impalement; but the word is most likely used here in a mocking tone.

[21] Ibid., Chapter 13.

[22] In each of the areas mentioned here, it is impossible to give even a survey of the flood of literature in recent years. All I will attempt to do is to mention a few works (mostly in English) that can serve as an introduction to the texts and

their meaning. For the Qumran texts in English, see G. Vermes, *The Dead Sea Scrolls in English* (3d ed.; London: Penguin, 1987); idem, *The Dead Sea Scrolls. Qumran in Perspective* (Philadelphia: Fortress, 1977; rev. ed., 1982); John Allegro, *The Dead Sea Scrolls. A Reappraisal* (2d ed.; London: Penguin, 1964); the chapter on Qumran in the revised Schürer, *The History of the Jewish People*, 3/1. 380–469; Joseph A. Fitzmyer, *The Dead Sea Scrolls: Major Publications and Tools for Study. With an Addendum (January 1977)* (SBLSBS 8; Missoula, MT: Scholars, 1977); H. Bietenhard, "Die Handschriftenfund vom Toten Meer (Ḥirbet Qumran) und die Essenerfrage. Die Funde in der Wüste Juda," *Aufstieg und Niedergang der römischen Welt 2/19.1*, ed. H. Temporini and W. Haase (Berlin/New York: de Gruyter, 1979) 704–78; D. Dimant, "Qumran Sectarian Literature," *Jewish Writings of the Second Temple Period* (CRINT 2/2; ed. M. E. Stone; Assen: Van Gorcum; Philadelphia: Fortress, 1984) 483–550. For the *editio princeps* of the various published manuscripts, see the series *Discoveries in the Judaean Desert* (Oxford: Clarendon, 1955–). A convenient manual edition of the earlier published texts with Hebrew vowel pointing, German translation, and short notes is Eduard Lohse, ed., *Die Texte aus Qumran* (2d ed.; Munich: Kösel, 1971), which must, however, be used with care.

[23] The standard text of the Pseudepigrapha in English used to be R. H. Charles, *The Apocrypha and Pseudepigrapha of the Old Testament in English. Volume II. Pseudepigrapha* (Oxford: Clarendon, 1913). More recently we have the much larger compendium edited by James H. Charlesworth, *The Old Testament Pseudepigrapha* (2 vols.; Garden City, NY: Doubleday, 1983, 1985). For an overview of research, see idem, *The Pseudepigrapha and Modern Research. With a Supplement* (SBLSCS 7S; Ann Arbor, MI: Scholars, 1981). A survey of Pseudepigrapha and other "intertestamental" Jewish literature can be found in Vols. 3/1 and 3/2 of the revised Schürer, *The History of the Jewish People;* George Nickelsburg, *Jewish Literature Between the Bible and the Mishnah* (Philadelphia: Fortress, 1981); also (arranged by topics) George Nickelsburg and Michael E. Stone, *Faith and Piety in Early Judaism. Texts and Documents* (Philadelphia: Fortress, 1983). On Jewish apocalyptic literature, see D. S. Russell, *The Method and Message of Jewish Apocalyptic* (London: SCM, 1964); John J. Collins, ed., *Apocalypse: The Morphology of a Genre* (Semeia 14; no place given: SBL, 1979); John J. Collins, *The Apocalyptic Imagination* (New York: Crossroad, 1987); Paul D. Hanson, *The Dawn of Apocalyptic* (rev. ed.; Philadelphia: Fortress, 1979); M. E. Stone, "Apocalyptic Literature," *Jewish Writings of the Second Temple Period* (CRINT 2/2), 383–441. The first volume of Charlesworth's compendium is given over mostly to Jewish and Jewish-Christian apocalypses.

[24] For Jewish Hellenistic literature apart from Philo and Josephus, see John J. Collins, *Between Athens and Jerusalem* (New York: Crossroad, 1983); see also the essays in *Aufstieg und Niedergang der römischen Welt 2/20.1 and 2*, ed. H. Temporini and W. Haase (Berlin/New York: de Gruyter, 1986, 1987). For an introduction to Philo, with further bibliography, see the lengthy essay of Jenny Morris in Vol. 3/2 of the revised Schürer, *The History of the Jewish People*, 809–89; also P. Borgen, "Philo of Alexandria. A Critical and Synthetical Survey of Research since World War II," *Aufstieg und Niedergang der römischen Welt 2/21.1* (1983), 98–154; idem,

"Philo of Alexandria," *Jewish Writings of the Second Temple Period* (CRINT 2/2), 233–82. Among older works, see E. R. Goodenough, *An Introduction to Philo Judaeus* (New Haven: Yale University; London: Oxford University, 1940; 2d ed., 1962); S. Sandmel, *Philo of Alexandria. An Introduction* (New York: Oxford University, 1979). On Philo and the NT, see Ronald Williamson, *Philo and the Epistle to the Hebrews* (ALGHJ 4; Leiden: Brill, 1970). For Josephus, see above, p. 70.

[25] For an older but sympathetic portrayal of ancient Judaism that leans in the "orthodox, normative" direction, see George Foot Moore, *Judaism in the First Centuries of the Christian Era* (2 vols.; New York: Schocken, 1971; originally, 1927, 1930). For one attempt to carry forward Moore's sympathetic program in a more sophisticated way, see E. P. Sanders, *Paul and Palestinian Judaism* (Philadelphia: Fortress, 1977).

[26] The old classic in this field is Gershom G. Scholem, *Major Trends in Jewish Mysticism* (3d ed.; New York: Schocken, 1961; originally, 1941).

[27] On Jewish incantations and magical texts, see the revised Schürer, *The History of the Jewish People*, 3/1. 342–79.

[28] Essays on Judaism's struggle to define itself in the early centuries B.C. and A.D. can be found in E. P. Sanders, A. I. Baumgarten, and Alan Mendelson, eds., *Jewish and Christian Self-Definition. Volume Two. Aspects of Judaism in the Greco-Roman Period* (Philadelphia: Fortress, 1981).

[29] See, e.g., Jacob Neusner, William S. Green, and Ernest Frerichs, *Judaisms and Their Messiahs at the Turn of the Christian Era* (Cambridge: Cambridge University, 1987).

[30] By "independent" I mean information about Jesus of Nazareth that is not drawing on or reacting to Christian documents, known directly or indirectly.

[31] See, e.g., the essays in F. M. Cross and S. Talmon, eds., *Qumran and the History of the Biblical Text* (Cambridge, MA: Harvard University, 1975); Eugene Ulrich, "Horizons of Old Testament Textual Research at the Thirtieth Anniversary of Qumran Cave 4," *CBQ* 46 (1984) 613–36; K. A. Mathews, "The Leviticus Scroll (11QpaleoLev) and the Text of the Hebrew Bible," *CBQ* 48 (1986) 171–207.

[32] See, e.g., Shaye J. D. Cohen, *From the Maccabees to the Mishnah* (Library of Early Christianity 7; Philadelphia: Westminster, 1987) 123–73; Lawrence H. Schiffman, *Sectarian Law in the Dead Sea Scrolls* (Brown Judaic Studies 33; Chico, CA: Scholars, 1983); Philip R. Davies, *Behind the Essenes. History and Ideology in the Dead Sea Scrolls* (Brown Judaic Studies 94; Atlanta: Scholars, 1987).

[33] See, e.g., Jean Duhaime, "Dualistic Reworking in the Scrolls from Qumran," *CBQ* 49 (1987) 57–73.

[34] Among the many studies documenting or suggesting parallels between Qumran and Jesus or Christianity, see Krister Stendahl, ed., *The Scrolls and the New Testament* (Westport, CT: Greenwood, 1957); Matthew Black, *The Scrolls and Christian Origins. Studies in the Jewish Background of the New Testament* (Brown Judaic Studies 48; Chico, CA: Scholars, 1961, reprint 1983); H. Braun, *Qumran und*

das Neue Testament (2 vols.; Tübingen: Mohr [Siebeck], 1966); Jerome Murphy-O'Connor, ed., *Paul and Qumran* (London: Chapman, 1968); James H. Charlesworth, ed., *John and Qumran* (London: Chapman, 1972); W. S. LaSor, *The Dead Sea Scrolls and the New Testament* (Grand Rapids: Eerdmans, 1972); R. Alan Culpepper, *The Johannine School* (SBLDS 26; Missoula, MT: Scholars, 1975) 145–70; many of the essays in Joseph A. Fitzmyer, *Essays on the Semitic Background of the New Testament* (SBLSBS 5; Missoula, MT: Scholars, 1974) and *A Wandering Aramean. Collected Aramaic Essays* (Missoula, MT: Scholars, 1979); Paul J. Kobelski, *Melchizedek and Melchireša'* (CBQMS 10; Washington, DC: CBA, 1981); Jerome Murphy-O'Connor, "The Judean Desert," *Early Judaism and Its Modern Interpreters*, ed. R. A. Kraft and G. Nickelsburg (Atlanta: Scholars, 1986) 119–56. See the short but helpful summary by Joseph A. Fitzmyer, "The Qumran Scrolls and the New Testament after Forty Years," *RevQ* 13 (1988) 609–20.

[35] So, e.g., J. A. T. Robinson, "The Baptism of John and the Qumran Community," *HTR* 50 (1957) 175–91; he is supported in his view by Joseph A. Fitzmyer, *The Gospel According to Luke* (AB 28, 28A; Garden City, NY: Doubleday, 1981, 1985) 1. 453–54, plus the bibliography on p. 462. See also Jean Danielou, *The Dead Sea Scrolls and Primitive Christianity* (A Mentor Omega Book; New York: New American Library, 1962; originally 1958) 16–24.

[36] See, e.g., Barbara E. Thiering, *Redating the Teacher of Righteousness* (Australian and New Zealand Studies in Theology and Religion 1; Sydney: Theological Explorations, 1979) 213–14. Thiering suggests that John the Baptist is the Teacher of Righteousness and Jesus the Wicked Priest.

[37] José O'Callaghan created a sensation when he claimed that various papyrus fragments from Qumran contained parts of the NT; see his article "Papiros neotestamentarios en la cueva 7 de Qumran?" *Bib* 53 (1972) 91–100; translation by W. L. Holladay, "New Testament Papyri in Qumran Cave 7?" *Supplement to the Journal of Biblical Literature* 91 (1972) 1–14; see also O'Callaghan's book, *Los papiros griegos de la cueva 7 de Qumran* (Madrid: Biblioteca de autores cristianos, 1974). O'Callaghan has had his defenders; see C. P. Thiede, "7Q—Eine Rückkehr zu den neutestamentlichen Papyrusfragmenten in der siebten Höhle von Qumran," *Bib* 65 (1984) 538–59; idem, *Die älteste Evangelien-Handschrift? Das Markus-Fragment von Qumran und die Anfänge der schriftlichen Überlieferung des Neuen Testaments* (Wuppertal: Brockhaus, 1986). In general, though, scholars have rejected the claim; see M. Baillet, "Les manuscrits de la grotte 7 de Qumran et le Nouveau Testament," *Bib* 53 (1972) 508–16; 54 (1973) 340–50; P. Benoit, "Note sur les fragments grecs de la grotte 7 de Qumran," *RB* 79 (1972) 321–24; 80 (1973) 5–12.

[38] Especially prolific in authoring books on the origins and interpretation of rabbinic literature is Jacob Neusner, who has pioneered an approach to rabbinics that incorporates form and redaction criticism. Among his many publications, the following are especially accessible: *The Pharisees. Rabbinic Perspectives* (Hoboken, NJ: Ktav, 1973); *First-Century Judaism in Crisis* (Nashville/New York: Abingdon, 1975); *Midrash in Context* (Philadelphia: Fortress, 1983); *Messiah in Context* (Philadelphia: Fortress, 1984); *Torah* (Philadelphia: Fortress, 1985); *Judaism in*

the Beginning of Christianity (Philadelphia: Fortress, 1984); *The Mishnah Before 70* (Brown Judaic Studies 70; Atlanta: Scholars, 1987); *What Is Midrash?* (Philadelphia: Fortress, 1987); *Why No Gospels in Talmudic Judaism?* (Brown Judaic Studies 135; Atlanta: Scholars, 1988). See also the essays in *Aufstieg und Niedergang der römischen Welt 2/19.2* (1979); and S. Safrai, ed., *The Literature of the Sages. First Part* (Assen/Maastricht: Van Gorcum; Philadelphia: Fortress, 1987).

[39] Hence Klausner *(Jesus of Nazareth,* 20) refuses to consider statements handed down by the "Amoraim," i.e., rabbinic teachers dating from A.D. 200 to 500.

[40] Klausner, *Jesus of Nazareth,* 18–19.

[41] See Johann Maier, *Jesus von Nazareth in der talmudischen Überlieferung* (Erträge der Forschung 82; Darmstadt: Wissenschaftliche Buchgesellschaft, 1978). His position, which is argued in minute detail throughout the volume, is summarized on pp. 263–75.

[42] Jacob Z. Lauterbach, "Jesus in the Talmud," *Rabbinic Essays* (Cincinnati: Hebrew Union College, 1951) 473–570, esp. p. 477.

[43] Samuel Sandmel, *We Jews and Jesus* (New York: Oxford University, 1965) 28.

[44] Klausner, *Jesus of Nazareth,* 20–23. That the Ben Stada tradition originally had nothing to do with Jesus of Nazareth is a common opinion today; see, e.g., Morris Goldstein, *Jesus in the Jewish Tradition* (New York: Macmillan, 1950) 57–81, where he also rejects allusions to Jesus supposedly masked as other figures (e.g., Balaam, "a certain person"). See also Maier *(Jesus von Nazareth,* 237), who further suggests that the traits of two different persons had already been conflated in the "Ben-Stada" texts, long before Ben Stada was identified with Jesus of Nazareth (according to Maier, after the completion of the Babylonian Talmud).

[45] These texts will be taken up again when the question of the possible illegitimacy of Jesus is discussed in Chapter 8 of this book. Here I am considering not the larger question of the illegitimacy tradition but simply whether particular rabbinic texts refer to Jesus and whether they may reflect independent tradition. If Maier is correct, the earliest Palestinian tradition about Ben Pandera contained no charge of illegitimacy; that first arose in Diaspora Judaism, and the two forms of the tradition must be distinguished. Indeed, Maier goes so far as to claim that not only Ben Stada but even Ben Pandera originally had nothing to do with Jesus of Nazareth *(Jesus von Nazareth,* 243–55).

[46] Origen, *Contra Celsum* 1.32; see the Greek text, French translation, and notes in Marcel Borret, *Origène. Contre Celse. Tome I* (SC 132; Paris: Cerf, 1967) 162–63.

[47] Klausner *(Jesus of Nazareth,* 23) mentions several baraitas from the time of Rabbi Eliezer ben Hyrcanus and Rabbi Yishmael (at the end of the first and the beginning of the second century A.D.). Baraitas are early rabbinic teachings that were not taken up into the Mishna but which were preserved in later documents (the Tosefta, the Talmuds). Naturally, the question of the reliability of the attri-

butions becomes pressing in such cases. If a baraita attributes a certain saying to one of the tannaitic rabbis, are we ipso facto justified in accepting the attribution as historically reliable? Contrary to many authors today, Maier (*Jesus von Nazareth*, 255) strenuously distinguishes between the tradition of Diaspora Jews related by Celsus and the traditions of Palestinian and Babylonian Jews, who in the 2d century A.D. knew nothing of the story. Maier even suggests that the story circulating among Diaspora Jews ultimately arose from a Christian gloss on Jesus' genealogy (pp. 263, 267).

[48] Klausner (*Jesus of Nazareth*, 24) hypothesizes that the Greek *huios tēs parthenou* ("son of the virgin") became in mockery "Ben ha-Panthera" ("son of the leopard"). In due time the Jewish tradition forgot that the reference was originally to Jesus' mother. "Pantere" or "Pandera" was taken to be the name of Jesus' father. Since this was not a Jewish name, the idea arose that Jesus' biological father must have been a foreigner; in occupied Judea, the most likely candidate was a Roman soldier. In fact, Panthera was a common name in the first two centuries of the Christian era, notably as a surname of Roman soldiers; see L. Patterson, "Origin of the Name Panthera," *JTS* 19 (1917–18) 79–80. The attempt by Morton Smith (*Jesus the Magician* [New York: Harper & Row, 1978] 47) to take the Ben Pandera story literally, to the point of suggesting that the tombstone of a Sidonian archer in Germany, one Tiberius Julius Abdes Pantera, might be the gravesite of Jesus' father, is more curious than convincing (note Smith's own qualification: "possible, though not likely"). Smith, along with a number of other scholars today, discounts Klausner's derivation of the name Panthera from *parthenos;* there is no proof that Jesus was referred to by the title *ho huios tēs parthenou* this early on. It is possible, though, that the accidental similarity of the Infancy Narratives' *parthenos* to "Panthera," a common name among soldiers, caused "Panthera" to be picked as the name of the adulterer, once the theme of an adulterous soldier arose in the tradition. Other attempts at explaining the name "Panthera" can be found in R. Travers Herford, *Christianity in Talmud and Midrash* (New York: Ktav, reprint of 1903 ed.) 39–40. Herford despairs of discovering the original meaning of the name; see also Maier, *Jesus von Nazareth*, 263, 267.

[49] For an English translation of the text, see I. Epstein, ed., *The Babylonian Talmud. Seder Nezikin in Four Volumes. III. Sanhedrin*, trans. Jacob Shachter (London: Soncino, 1935) 281–82.

[50] Cf. the Jewish portrayal of Jesus as a magician in Justin Martyr's *Dialogue with Trypho*, Chapter 69: *magon einai auton etolmōn legein* (PG 6. 640).

[51] Klausner (*Jesus of Nazareth*, 28–30) proceeds to consider another baraita immediately following in *San.* 43a, but at best it is a later garbled tradition, playing on the double meanings of the names of five of Jesus' supposed disciples (possibly Matthew, Luke[!], Andrew, John, and Thaddeus). Again, even if the core of the tradition represented independent knowledge, it would add nothing new. Maier, as might be expected, denies that the reference in *San.* 43a had anything to do originally with Jesus of Nazareth (*Jesus von Nazareth*, 229).

⁵² Texts of the Mishna are taken from the standard English translation by Herbert Danby, *The Mishnah* (Oxford: Oxford University, 1933); I have checked them against the newer translation by Jacob Neusner, *The Mishnah. A New Translation* (New Haven/London: Yale University, 1988).

⁵³ Klausner, *Jesus of Nazareth*, 35–36, rejecting the opinion of Gustaf Dalman, *Die Worte Jesu. Band I. Einleitung und wichtige Begriffe* (Leipzig: Hinrichs, 1898) 4 n. 2. R. Travers Herford, in his article "Jesus in Rabbinical Literature" *(The Universal Jewish Encyclopedia*, ed. Isaac Landman [10 vols.; New York: Universal Jewish Encyclopedia, 1942] 6. 87–88) states on p. 88 that the reference to Jesus in *Yeb.* 4:13 is "doubtful and probably unfounded." Maier *(Jesus von Nazareth*, 50) likewise rejects any reference to Jesus in *m. Yebam.* 4:13, calling it "odd speculation," despite the fact that even Klausner engages in it. Similarly, T. W. Manson ("The Life of Jesus: A Study of the Available Materials," *BJRL* 27 [1942–43] 323–37) affirms that there are no direct references to Jesus in the Mishna (p. 327). He allows that there are a few possible allusions *(Yebam.* 4:13; *ʾAbot* 5:19; *Sanh.* 10:1–2), "but nothing that can be regarded as an absolutely certain reference to Jesus" (p. 327 n. 2).

⁵⁴ Since I do not think that the *m. Yebam.* 4:13 text refers to Jesus, I will not go into the baraita from the Tosefta cited by Klausner *(Jesus of Nazareth*, 36–37), which might possibly refer to Jesus, but only if one first accepted a reference to Jesus in the Mishna text. On the whole question of the supposed illegitimacy of Jesus in Jewish tradition, see Chapter 8 of this book.

⁵⁵ See Goldstein, *Jesus in the Jewish Tradition*, 22–56, esp. 22. However, Goldstein comes close to Klausner's views in that he allows for five allusions to Jesus in baraitas and the Tosefta. Goldstein's conclusion on the whole of the tannaitic corpus is striking: "The findings in the vast realm of this literature are amazingly scant and restricted. There are remarkably few passages that prove to be genuine" (p. 94). Another basically skeptical view is that of Gösta Lindeskog, *Die Jesusfrage im neuzeitlichen Judentum. Ein Beitrag zur Geschichte der Leben-Jesu-Forschung. Mit einem Nachwort zum Nachdruck* (Darmstadt: Wissenschaftliche Buchgesellschaft, 1973; original, 1938). While admitting that one cannot speak of absolute agreement among Jewish scholars, Lindeskog states: "Jewish researchers are therefore one with Christian researchers in holding that the Talmud is not serviceable as a source for the life of Jesus; it offers nothing positive beyond what we already know from the Gospels. What it does offer is an intentionally polemical caricature" (p. 187).

⁵⁶ Klausner, *Jesus of Nazareth*, 37–44. For the talmudic text, see I. Epstein, ed., *The Babylonian Talmud. Seder Nezikin. ʿAbodah Zarah*, trans. A. Mischon (London: Soncino, 1935) 84–85.

⁵⁷ See my treatment of the martyrdom of James above, in Chapter 3.

⁵⁸ See Joachim Jeremias, *Unknown Sayings of Jesus* (2d ed.; London: SPCK, 1964) 28–30. In Jeremias' view, the earliest version of the story (in the Tosefta) spoke simply of a heretical saying which Jacob of Kephar-Sikhnin spoke in the name of Jesus "ben Pantere," without specifying the content of the saying; the

later, more developed form of the story (in the Babylonian Talmud) satisfied natural curiosity by inventing a saying. Maier (*Jesus von Nazareth*, 159–74) also rejects any reference to Jesus of Nazareth in the original form of the story.

[59] Actually, the mocking form *'awen gillayon* ("falsehood of the [blank] parchment" or "falsehood of the blank margin of the scroll") is used as a play on the Greek *euaggelion* ("gospel"). See the English translation, with notes, in I. Epstein, ed., *The Babylonian Talmud. Seder Mo'ed. Shabbath* (2 vols.; trans. H. Freedman; London: Soncino, 1938) 2. 571.

[60] Klausner (*Jesus of Nazareth*, 44–46) maintains that Matthew misunderstood the original Aramaic form of the saying—which we know, thanks to tractate *Šabbat*—when he wrote his Greek text. Joachim Jeremias does not try to maintain the historicity of the anecdote, which, depending on K. G. Kuhn, he assigns to the 3d century A.D. However, going against the opinion of Kuhn, Jeremias claims that the core logion of the anecdote ("I did not come to take away from the law of Moses, rather, I came to add to the law of Moses") preserves the original sense of *plērōsai* in Matt 5:17. On all this, see Joachim Jeremias, *New Testament Theology. Part One. The Proclamation of Jesus* (London: SCM, 1971) 83–84; and K. G. Kuhn, "Giljonim und sifre minim," *Judentum, Urchristentum, Kirche* (Joachim Jeremias Festschrift; BZNW 26; ed. Walther Eltester; Berlin: Töpelmann, 1960) 24–61, especially p. 54 n. 110, where Kuhn points out that the rabbinic anecdote presupposes the Greek NT. Indeed, it seems that the wider context of Matt 5:14–17 is being parodied; see Burton L. Visotzky, "Overturning the Lamp," *JJS* 38 (1987) 72–80, esp. pp. 78–79. The article on "Jesus" in *EncJud* 10 (1971) col. 17 also considers *Šabbat* 116 a and b to be a parody on Matthew's text and therefore not authentic. It should be noted that both the exact reading and the translation of the text of *Šabbat* 116 a and b are disputed. The text is judged to be late by W. D. Davies (*The Setting of the Sermon on the Mount* [Cambridge: Cambridge University, 1963] 419 n. 5); see also John P. Meier, *Law and History in Matthew's Gospel* (AnBib 71; Rome: Biblical Institute, 1976) 73 n. 76.

Since, in my view, *plērōsai* in Matt 5:17 is a result of Matthew's redaction, and since many redaction critics would hold today that Matt 5:17 is largely or totally the creation of Matthew the evangelist, all this speculation about the original Aramaic form that Matthew misunderstood seems very tenuous.

[61] I am hardly alone in this view. The article on "Jesus of Nazareth" in the *Universal Jewish Encyclopedia*, Vol. 6, states that ". . . in Jewish writings there is no report about Jesus that has historical value" (p. 83) and that ". . . the Talmudic statements about him [Jesus] are not about the real Jesus, but about an imagined originator of a hateful persecutor" (pp. 86–87). R. Travers Herford continues in this vein in his article on "Jesus in Rabbinical Literature" in the same volume (p. 88): "In itself, the tradition [of the rabbis about Jesus] is only of value as independent evidence that Jesus really lived, and as showing that his influence on the Judaism of his own and succeeding times was practically nil. It does not supplement the tradition recorded in the Synoptic Gospels. . . ." See also his evaluation of the rabbis on Jesus in his book, *Christianity in Talmud and Midrash*, especially pp. 344–60. Similarly, the article on "Jesus" in the *EncJud* 10

(1971) col. 14 judges: "Even those statements [by rabbis about Jesus] dating from the second century are to be regarded as reflecting the knowledge and views of Jews of that time about Christians and Jesus, which derived in part from contemporary Christian sources."

Like Klausner, Morton Smith (*Jesus the Magician*, 46–50) is willing to accept a historical core in certain stories found in the Tosefta and the Babylonian Talmud. Personally, I remain doubtful about such claims. Scholars who exercise great care in judging which traditions about Jesus are really historical must show the same care in judging rabbinic stories. Two main sources for our knowledge of Jesus (the Gospel of Mark and the Q_document) were written down in fairly definitive form about A.D. 70, some forty years after the events and sayings they recount. Yet we must agonize over what in their store of information is historical. A fortiori, one must be concerned about declaring information historical when it has been written down in final form only centuries after the original events or sayings. That is not to say that all rabbinic material is a priori excluded; it is to say that weighty reasons must be brought forward if such material is to be judged historical. Similar objections might be raised against Smith's eclectic and arbitrary use of Celsus, in tandem with various rabbis, Fathers of the Church, and pagan authors, to create the picture of the historical Jesus as the libertine magician (pp. 45–67).

[62] Klausner (*Jesus of Nazareth*, 46) summarizes the reliable statements of the rabbinic tradition as follows: (1) Yeshu of Nazareth practiced sorcery (i.e., he performed miracles) and led Israel astray. (2) He mocked the words of the Wise (i.e., the revered teachers of Israel). (3) He expounded Scripture the same way the Pharisees did. (4) He had five disciples. (5) He said that he had not come to take away anything from the Law or to add anything to it. (6) He was hanged (i.e., crucified) as a false teacher and beguiler on the eve of a Passover that fell on a Sabbath. (7) His disciples healed the sick in his name. As can readily be seen, we have here simply a polemical reverse-mirror image of various statements in the Four Gospels.

[63] Needless to say, there is no point in going into the Jewish polemical biography of Jesus, the Hebrew *Toledot Yeshu*, which probably did not reach its full form until the Middle Ages. Klausner thinks that it was not composed earlier than the 10th century A.D. His summary judgment is shared by many scholars: ". . . it [the *Toledot Yeshu*] cannot possibly possess any historical value nor in any way be used as material for the life of Jesus" (*Jesus of Nazareth*, 53). For the wide variety of views on dating the *Toledot* (from the 1st century [Voltaire] to the 10th century [Klausner]), see Günter Schlichting, *Ein jüdisches Leben Jesu. Die verschollene Toledot-Jeschu-Fassung Tam ū-mū'ād* (WUNT 24; Tübingen: Mohr [Siebeck], 1982) 2. Schlichting's monograph provides an annotated Hebrew text plus a German translation of one form of the *Toledot*.

Pinchas E. Lapide (*Der Rabbi von Nazaret. Wandlungen der jüdischen Jesusbilder* [Trier: Spee, 1974] 79) holds that, while the earliest manuscript of the *Toledot* is from the 9th century, its contents go back to a book already known in the 5th century. Sandmel (*We Jews and Jesus*, 12) thinks that the *Toledot* is "possibly as old as the sixth century." For Lindeskog *(Die Jesusfrage,* 16), the *Toledot* lacks any historical worth; it simply shows how Jews in the Middle Ages thought of Jesus.

In the face of such varying opinions among experts, what can be said with fair certainty? That the roots of some of the stories in the *Toledot* go back as far as the Jewish "Infancy Narrative" recorded by Celsus is clear. But the *Toledot* itself must not be confused with such roots; the work as a whole was composed centuries later. This point is well made by Goldstein *(Jesus in the Jewish Tradition,* 160–61), who thinks that the *Toledot,* in more or less its present form, does not reach back before the beginning of the 9th century; an earlier form of the work might go back to the 6th century.

SOURCES:

The Agrapha *and the Apocryphal Gospels*

1. THE *AGRAPHA*

Alongside the major sources I have already mentioned, there is a wide-ranging mass of scattered material known to scholars as the *agrapha*, literally, the "unwritten [sayings and deeds]" of Jesus. Of course, we know of them only because they *were* written down at a later date; the point is that these scattered sayings are not recorded in any of the four canonical Gospels.

Much broader than the term *agrapha* is the general rubric, "extra-canonical sayings of Jesus." This very broad category is the object of William D. Stoker's book, *Extracanonical Sayings of Jesus*, which includes not only what has been traditionally called the *agrapha* but also a large number of parallels to or variants of the canonical sayings—parallels that are found in Christian literature.[1] In his desire to be as complete as possible, Stoker renounces any attempt to discern "authentic" sayings of Jesus from later creations. Rather, his wide-ranging collection endeavors to illumine the process of tradition and growth in the Jesus material during the first five centuries A.D.

More focused on the question of recovering material that might come from Jesus himself, and therefore more selective than Stoker's collection, is Joachim Jeremias' *Unknown Sayings of Jesus*,[2] which includes material reaching down to medieval Islamic writings. In his quest for possibly authentic sayings of Jesus, Jeremias draws on every conceivable source, from the NT through additions and variants in Gospel manuscripts, apocryphal Christian writings of the early centuries A.D., the Church Fathers to A.D. 500, liturgies and church orders, gnostic revelation discourses and hymns, the Talmud (an area we have already covered), and finally a 17th-century Arabic inscription from a mosque in North India![3] No doubt a Catholic author might have included sayings of Jesus in the writings of great mystics down through the ages.

The reader needs no great expertise in Arabic or apocryphal gospels to sense that most of this material, while having historical interest for a study of the picture of Jesus down through the centuries, probably has nothing to do with the quest for the historical Jesus[4]—and in this judgment Jeremias concurs. "The bulk of it [the corpus of *agrapha*] is legendary, and bears the clear mark of forgery. . . . The range of material which is of any use to the historian is remarkably small."[5] Most of the candidates can be quickly rejected as being tendentious inventions or tendentious modifications of Jesus' words, legendary inventions marked by fairy-tale-type fantasies, accidental or deliberate transference to Jesus of sayings that really come from other persons or sources,[6] secondary adaptations of real sayings of Jesus, transformations of narrative passages in the canonical Gospels into sayings of Jesus, or links artificially constructed to connect real sayings of Jesus.[7]

After all this winnowing, Jeremias feels that there are only eighteen candidates that he would accept as genuine words[8] of the historical Jesus. It may seem mean-spirited of me to deny Jeremias his holy remnant, but I think in every case his argument does not result in anything more than a vague "Jesus *could* have said this" or simply a *non liquet*, i.e., it is not clear one way or the other. In the next chapter we will be looking at the various criteria for assessing the historicity of sayings and deeds attributed to Jesus. What is noticeable in Jeremias' treatment is a lack of clearly enunciated and rigorously applied criteria. What criteria are mentioned do not really bring us all that far.[9]

For instance, to say that a saying has "Palestinian" color or flavor, to say that the saying can be retroverted into Aramaic, or to point out the saying's rhythm, assonance, and parallel structure does not necessarily prove origin from the historical Jesus. Presumably, between A.D. 30 and 70 there were any number of competent Christian teachers and preachers in Palestine—speaking the same Aramaic Jesus did—who knew and could imitate the style of their revered Rabbi and Lord. Jesus did not have a monopoly on poetry, rhythm, and parallelism in 1st-century Aramaic. Moreover, the teaching and preaching of Jewish Christians in Aramaic certainly did not come to a complete halt after A.D. 70. And to say that certain rhythms and parallel structures are typical of Jesus' sayings can easily involve us in a vicious circle. After all, where does one get the initial data base that tells us that authentic sayings of Jesus are marked by particular poetic qualities?

There are other problems as well. Many of the eighteen candidates are readily understood as homiletic expansions on and conflations of various passages in the NT. In other cases, Jeremias strives mightily to overcome the many objections raised to a dubious anecdote (e.g., Jesus' encounter with "a certain Pharisaic high priest" in the temple precincts). One can only admire Jeremias' erudition as he calls on data from all quarters to rescue his candidate. But, in the end, one gets the impression of a tour de force, not a convincing argument. Hypothesis is piled on hypothesis, and the obvious meaning of some embarrassing phrases is dodged.

In the end, one wonders what would be gained even if all eighteen examples were accepted as authentic. One of Jeremias' major arguments throughout is that each candidate echoes some aspect of Jesus' message in the canonical Gospels. As a result, even when all eighteen are accepted, nothing new is added to our picture. A great deal of effort over dubious material produces absolutely no significant new data.[10] To be on the safe side, we will be keeping an eye on these extracanonical *agrapha* as we move through the material in the Four Gospels. But, judging from this initial sounding, not much is to be expected from this quarter.

2. THE APOCRYPHAL GOSPELS

By "apocryphal gospels" I mean those early Christian documents which related the words and/or deeds of Jesus,[11] which called themselves gospels or received such a designation from later generations, but which were not received into the Christian "canon," i.e., the normative list of books considered inspired Scripture.[12] The category of the apocryphal gospels overlaps that of the *agrapha*, since the apocryphal gospels are one of the main sources of extracanonical sayings of Jesus. But the extent and significance of apocryphal gospels in the early Church, as well as their high estimation by some scholars today, demand separate consideration.[13]

Like the *agrapha* that they contain, many of the apocryphal gospels are mixed bags of scattered fragments. We need only read through the standard collection of Edgar Hennecke and Wilhelm Schneemelcher[14] to see that, in many cases, we are faced with a field of rubble, largely produced by the pious or wild imaginations of certain 2d-century Christians.

Prime examples of such fantasy are the "infancy gospels,"[15] especially the *Protevangelium Jacobi* and the *Infancy Gospel of Thomas*. The former is a hilarious mishmash of the infancy stories of Matthew and Luke,[16] with a heavy dose of novelistic folklore that betrays ignorance of the very Jewish institutions being described. For example, Zechariah, the father of John the Baptist, is slain by officers of King Herod, his blood congeals on the altar of the temple, and the other priests are told of the murder by a heavenly voice. Then the aged Simeon of Luke 2:25 is elected by lot to take his place. This book is one of the major sources of later infancy gospels and of subsequent legends about the Virgin Mary —but certainly not of knowledge about the historical Jesus. Yet it is a prophetic book in that it foreshadows what would happen to the Infancy Narratives of Matthew and Luke when they became conflated in the memories and imaginations of Christians. Such conflation and confusion continue to mark the way most Christians would spontaneously narrate the Infancy Narratives even today—catechetical instruction, liturgical reading, and scholarly monographs not withstanding.

The same can be said of the *Infancy Gospel of Thomas*,[17] which presents the child Jesus as a self-willed little brat who, throwing a tantrum, makes a child who runs up against him drop dead. The portrait of this sinister superboy belongs more in a horror movie than a gospel. If nothing else, it is a healthy reminder that much apocryphal material stems from "pop" rather than learned Christian circles and reflects neither early reliable traditions nor elevated theology, but instead curiosity, fascination with the bizarre and miraculous (not to say magical), and sheer desire for "religious" entertainment.

The one thing these two infancy gospels have in their favor is that they have come down to us relatively intact. Unfortunately, the same cannot be said of many other early gospels that are known only through fragments or quotations in the Church Fathers. The problem is especially difficult in the case of the so-called "Jewish-Christian gospels," e.g., the *Gospel of the Nazarenes*, the *Gospel of the Ebionites*, and the *Gospel of the Hebrews*.[18] Except for a few scattered fragments, we are entirely dependent on the statements and quotations of the Church Fathers, which are often contradictory. To compound the confusion, the Church Fathers had no uniform way of referring to the different gospels, and so we are not even sure how many Jewish-Christian gospels existed and to which gospel a given fragment properly belongs. Worse still, although these gospels were written in the 2d century, most of the fragments we have come from Church Fathers of the 4th century (Eusebius, Jerome, Epiphanius) or later.[19]

The largest amount of material comes from the *Gospel of the Nazarenes,* which closely follows in outline the Gospel of Matthew and may indeed be a secondary, "creative" translation of Matthew into Aramaic.[20] The expansions on Matthew's text often engage in moralizing or legend-building. We have only seven fragments from the *Gospel of the Ebionites,* which was written in Greek, apparently with a knowledge of all three Synoptic Gospels, and reflects the particular theological views of the Jewish-Christian sect known as the Ebionites.[21] Seven fragments also are all we retain of the *Gospel of the Hebrews,* a Greek gospel that highlights James, the brother of the Lord, to the point of contradicting what the NT has to say about him. Meant for Greek-speaking Jews, the gospel develops mythological motifs already present in the Synoptics and at times speaks with a gnostic accent.[22]

At this point, one might wonder why we are bothering with such unpromising material. One reason is that, in recent years, some scholars have claimed that they have found in certain apocryphal gospels traditions that are as early as or even earlier than the traditions enshrined in the four canonical Gospels. Perhaps the most impressive full-scale attempt to establish such a position is John Dominic Crossan's treatment of the 2d-century apocryphal *Gospel of Peter.*[23] Crossan proposes that behind the present *Gospel of Peter* there stood what he labels a *Cross Gospel.* So early is this *Cross Gospel* that it is the sole source for the Passion Narrative in all four canonical Gospels. According to Crossan, the *Gospel of Peter* developed in three stages: (1) the *Cross Gospel* was written sometime in the middle of the 1st century. (2) The *Cross Gospel* was used by Mark as the only source of his Passion Narrative. The other canonical Gospels, besides using Mark, also knew the *Cross Gospel.* (3) A later redactor expanded the *Cross Gospel* to adapt it to the canonical views concerning the honorable burial of Jesus, the discovery of the empty tomb, and the resurrection appearance to the apostles.

Crossan himself affirms, at the start of his project, that, all things being equal, the simplest theory that explains the most data is to be preferred. It is at this basic level that his theory fails. Crossan has to spin

a complicated and sometimes self-contradictory web as he assigns documents questionably early dates or unlikely lines of dependence.[24] The
baroque construct is less convincing than the simple position established
independently by two other authors using different approaches. Both
Léon Vaganay and Jerry W. McCant demonstrate that the *Gospel of Peter*
is dependent on the canonical Gospels.[25] Vaganay's painstaking analysis
of individual phrases, overall structure, and developed Christian tendencies shows that the *Gospel of Peter* betrays a knowledge of, at the very
least, Matthew, probably Mark and Luke, and possibly John.[26] It was
perhaps to escape some of this probative material that Crossan extracted
his *Cross Gospel,* which is supposedly immune from signs of Synoptic
influence.[27]

However, even the hypothetical *Cross Gospel* bears telltale marks of
dependence on the Synoptics. This is especially true of the story of the
setting of the guard at the tomb of Jesus, as Joel B. Green has shown.[28]
To take a single example: one small but damaging piece of evidence can
be found in the precise wording of the fear that leads to the setting of
the guard at the tomb. Both *Gospel of Peter* 30 (included in Crossan's *Cross
Gospel)* and Matthew 27:64b read exactly the same phrase: ". . . lest his
disciples, coming, steal him and . . ." When it comes to who is dependent on whom, all the signs point to Matthew's priority. "His disciples"
(referring to Jesus' disciples) is a common phrase in Matthew, and of
course the word "disciple" itself is extremely common in Matthew (73x,
more than in any other NT book). In contrast, the word "disciple"
never occurs elsewhere in Crossan's *Cross Gospel;* even when we look at
the full *Gospel of Peter,* all we can find is the un-Matthean "female disciple" *(mathētria,* v 50) and "we the twelve disciples of the Lord" *(hēmeis de
hoi dōdeka mathētai tou kyriou,* v 59). Similarly, the verb "to steal" *(kleptō)*
occurs four other times in Matthew, but nowhere else in the *Gospel of
Peter.* Also, the conjunction "lest" *(mēpote)* occurs seven other times in
Matthew; it occurs once again in *Gospel of Peter* 15, but in a somewhat
different construction (object clause of a verb of fearing). The use of the
participle "coming" *(elthontes)* as an accompaniment to a principal verb
of action occurs twenty-seven times elsewhere in Matthew,[29] but nowhere else in the *Gospel of Peter.* In short, the clause is a tissue of
Matthean vocabulary and style, a vocabulary and style almost totally
absent from the rest of the *Gospel of Peter.*[30]

What this one clause shows in miniature, the comprehensive analy-
ses of Vaganay and McCant show throughout the *Gospel of Peter:* it is a
2d-century pastiche of traditions from the canonical Gospels, recycled

through the memory and lively imagination of Christians who have heard the Gospels read and preached upon many a time.[31] It provides no special access to early independent tradition about the historical Jesus.[32]

I have spent so much time on Crossan's claim of independent, early tradition in the *Gospel of Peter* because it is perhaps the best-argued case for a large piece of pre-Synoptic tradition in an apocryphal gospel. If the claim fails, as I think it does, not much should be expected from the other apocryphal gospels. This is not to say that all these gospels are alike. But, as Raymond E. Brown has pointed out, extravagant assertions about very early traditions in apocryphal gospels often share three dubious tendencies:[33]

(1) The assertions about some apocryphal gospel, while bold and accompanied by a great show of learning, turn out, on close analysis, to be based on rather slim evidence and questionable reasoning. Often the initial claims cause a sensation in the popular media, while the thoughtful refutations are ignored.

(2) The radical claims usually overlook the fact that, for all the differences and even conflicts among first-generation Christian leaders, there was a common gospel message on which all of them agreed (cf. Paul's affirmation of a common proclamation by all Christian preachers in 1 Cor 15:11). Unlike the picture painted by those who want to make some form of gnostic Christianity an equally valid manifestation of first-generation Christian experience, the mainstream picture of Christianity presented by documents and traditions that definitely do come from the first and second generations are different from some of the wilder developments among certain Christians in the 2d century.

(3) The exaltation of a gnosticizing form of Christianity ignores the fact that, from the very beginning of Christian preaching about Jesus, there was a certain "biographical" thrust that formed the Jesus tradition in a direction that ultimately produced the canonical Gospels. There was no period when individual bits of tradition about Jesus floated about in a Church bereft of the larger grid that the life, death, and resurrection of Jesus provided.

These general considerations, plus the failure of Crossan's case for the *Gospel of Peter*, make one very dubious about Crossan's claim of priority for three other apocryphal gospels or gospel fragments: the Coptic *Gospel of Thomas*, *Egerton Papyrus 2*, and the *Secret Gospel of Mark*.[34] We shall consider the Coptic *Gospel of Thomas* below, when we take up the material from Nag Hammadi. As for *Egerton Papyrus 2* (four small fragments of papyrus first published in 1935),[35] the fragmentary nature of the material makes a clear judgment difficult, especially since the question of sources does not seem to admit of a uniform answer for all the fragments.[36]

The first two "sections" of Fragment One (according to C. H. Dodd's mode of division) weave together various verses from the Fourth Gospel (John 5:39,45; 9:29; John 7:30,32,44; 8:20,59; 10:31,33,39), with some possible Lucan touches. Dodd thinks it probable that the author of the papyrus was dependent on the Fourth Gospel.[37]

Section Three from Fragment One is a variant version of Jesus' healing of the leper, which in Dodd's estimation is best explained as an independent version of the story found in Mark 1:40–44 parr., with no direct literary connection in either direction.[38] My own view is that we have a retelling of the Synoptic story—most likely from Luke—with a legendary expansion (the afflicted man caught the leprosy while eating at an inn with lepers).[39] Dodd rightly stresses the importance of living oral tradition in the formation of the version in *Egerton 2.* That is correct; but living oral tradition continued in Christian communities after the canonical Gospels were written, read, and assimilated in the memories of Christians, some of whom continued to rework creatively what they had heard.[40] I think this is the more likely explanation of Section Three, though I admit that Dodd's explanation is also possible.[41]

Dodd uses a similar explanation in dealing with Section Four from Fragment Two, the question about paying tribute (cf. Mark 12:13–17; there are also possible echoes from John and Q). Here, while there is something of a similar structure in both the papyrus and the Marcan version (although the "punch-line" conclusion is not present in *Egerton 2*, confusing the situation even more),[42] the language of the papyrus follows no one Synoptic Gospel. What makes me suspicious that *Egerton 2* may represent a later reworking of the Synoptic version is the use of the vague and generalizing question: "Is it licit to pay *to the kings* what *pertains to the government?*" In my view this sounds secondary to the concrete Synoptic form, "to pay the *poll tax* to *Caesar.*" One wonders whether the plural *kings*[43] reflects the increasingly common custom of the Roman emperor associating his prospective heir with his throne. But Dodd makes a strong case for mutually independent traditions, and the judgment could easily go either way. In any case, the use of the curious address "teacher Jesus" (= Rabbi Jesus) in *Egerton 2* does not reflect, as far as we know, actual Jewish usage in the 1st century. Dodd thinks that the attaching of the title Rabbi to particular teachers' names began with the disciples of Johanan ben Zakkai after the fall of the temple in A.D.

70.[44] Hence the composition of *Egerton 2* would belong to a period in which this usage of referring to "Rabbi X" had already been established and become known in Christian circles—obviously a time after the composition of Mark's Gospel. Once again, Crossan's claim that the Marcan version is "directly dependent on the papyrus text" seems without foundation.[45]

Section Five from Fragment Two is woefully incomplete. At best, one can divine that it recounts some sort of nature miracle by Jesus as he walks along the shore of the Jordan River. The story is not paralleled anywhere in the Synoptics. Dodd quickly moves to the judgment that it comes from a non-Synoptic *source*. That, of course, is possible; but granted the creativity we have seen in other apocryphal gospels, one cannot exclude the alternative of a free creation by the author of *Egerton 2*. Not every pericope unique to Matthew or Luke comes from some special source; some are simply creations of the evangelists. Since we have no idea of the style, scope, or complete content of the larger document to which *Egerton 2* belonged, a firm decision is impossible. Finally, Section Six from Fragment Three is so fragmentary that nothing certain can be said about it; just possibly it may reflect a version of John 10:30–31.[46]

In sum, we have two texts that are conflations of passages in Mark's Gospel: an alternate version of the healing of the leper, and an alternate version of the coin-of-tribute story. Even if the latter two are independent versions of stories also found in the Synoptics, they give us no new knowledge about the historical Jesus—only, at best, independent confirmation of these stories' existence in the oral tradition. The attempt of Crossan to make the texts of John and Mark literarily dependent on the version in *Egerton 2* simply will not stand up to the detailed analysis of the Greek done by Dodd.[47]

Crossan also presses the claim of the dependence of the Synoptics and John on a fragmentary apocryphal gospel in the case of the so-called *Secret Gospel of Mark*. This fragment was discovered by Morton Smith in 1958, but not published by him until 1973.[48] The text of the *Secret Gospel* is contained in a document that purports to be a letter of Clement of Alexandria (ca. 150–ca. 215). The authenticity of the letter has been challenged, but is accepted by many experts today. Since, however, the possibility of a modern forgery has not been put to rest once and for all,[49] and since detailed examination of the original document has not yet been carried out by independent scholars, a definitive judgment in the matter is not possible.

Worse still, Clement of Alexandria, like Epiphanius and Jerome, is not always the most reliable witness to the nature and source of ancient documents, especially when polemics with heretics are involved. Clement tells us how Mark wrote a "public" gospel, selecting basic material from Peter's preaching while Peter was still active in Rome. After Peter was martyred, Mark came to Alexandria, where, using his own notes and those of Peter, he expanded his Roman gospel to create a "more spiritual gospel" for those on the way to perfection. This "secret gospel," carefully guarded by the church of Alexandria, was subsequently reinterpreted (with interpolations?) in a libertine direction by the heretical Carpocratians. Those who are acquainted with the legend-building that goes on in the Church Fathers (e.g., Mark's ministry in Alexandria), and those who know something of Clement's not entirely critical approach to his sources, will remain hesitant about accepting this story at face value.[50] The authenticity of Clement's letter (i.e., that the letter really does come from the pen of Clement) in no way guarantees the authenticity of the *Secret Gospel* (i.e., that it really comes from the pen of Mark).

Complicating the matter further is that the entire text of the *Secret Gospel,* insofar as it has been preserved in the letter of Clement, comprises only twenty lines of Greek in Smith's edition.[51] It contains three short additions to Mark: (1) (after Mark 10:34) Jesus raises a young man from the dead (the story is reminiscent of the raising of Lazarus in John 11); (2) the young man, with only a linen cloth over his naked body, comes by night to be taught by Jesus about the mystery of the kingdom of God; and (3) (after Mark 10:46a) Jesus refuses to receive three women at Jericho. To use such a small fragment of dubious origins to rewrite the history of Jesus and the Gospel tradition is to lean on a reed.

Significantly, the different revisionists of Christian origins do not agree on what depends on what. Smith himself holds that the latter part of the Gospels of John and Mark had as their source an Aramaic document, known to them in different Greek translations. The earliest form of Mark, while using this source, did not incorporate the resurrection and initiation stories contained in the *Secret Gospel* (at least the resurrection story was in the source, and probably both stories were). A later editor put these stories into Marcan style and added them to the Marcan text. Matthew probably used this expanded text. Smith leaves open whether the expanded text was cut down again to form our canonical Mark or whether canonical Mark is the older form.[52]

Things get more complicated in Crossan's theory of relationships.[53]

In the beginning, there was a common source for the resurrection story in the *Secret Gospel* and the Lazarus story in John 11. Then came the Marcan traditions, in a number of stages. Within these Marcan traditions, the *Secret Gospel* came first, then the new interpretation and possible interpolation of the *Secret Gospel* that produced the Carpocratian version of Mark. To counteract this heretical version, some editor dismembered the three stories we possess in the fragment of the *Secret Gospel*, scattered parts of them throughout his revised Marcan Gospel, which becomes the public or canonical Mark. Matthew worked with this public version.

Complicating things still more, Helmut Koester has suggested that instead Matthew and Luke used an early "Proto-Mark," which was later developed into *Secret Mark*, which in turn was used by the Carpocratians to create the *Carpocratian Mark*. *Secret Mark* was then purified to create the public or canonical Mark.[54] Building on Koester's theory, Hans-Martin Schenke unconsciously offers a *reductio ad absurdum* by suggesting that in the beginning was Carpocratian Mark, which was purified and shortened to create first *Secret Mark* and then, in a second stage, canonical Mark.[55] The wide variety of these wild theories only demonstrates how hypotheses expand in diverse ways to fill the vacuum left by a paucity of data—in this case, dubious data to boot. Obviously, no serious sketch of the Jesus of history can use such material—which has not kept Smith from doing just that.[56]

Common to all these approaches is the position that in one way or another both canonical Mark and John 11 are dependent on the *Secret Gospel* or its source. That is by no means a necessary conclusion from the data. The great Marcan scholar Frans Neirynck has shown by careful analysis that the *Secret Gospel* presupposes the Synoptics,[57] and Raymond E. Brown demonstrates that, contrary to Smith's claims, the author of the *Secret Gospel* may well have drawn upon the Gospel of John, at least from memory.[58] In the view of Robert M. Grant, *Secret Mark* is a combination of elements from John and the two later Synoptics with elements derived from canonical Mark.[59] After a detailed study of key Greek phrases in *Secret Mark*, Helmut Merkel comes to a similar conclusion: it presupposes all four canonical Gospels.[60]

One could go on with further surveys of other apocryphal gospels like the *Gospel of the Egyptians*[61] or the *Acts of Pilate*.[62] No doubt someone somewhere will claim that these are prior to the canonical Gospels as well. But I think we have probed enough representatives of the over-heated imaginations of various 2d-century Christians to show that critics like Crossan, Koester, and James M. Robinson[63] are simply on the wrong track. These apocryphal gospels are very important, but they belong in a study of the patristic Church from the 2d to the 4th century. Unfortunately, the public and the press, not to mention publishers and universities, are much more interested in sensational studies about the NT than in "dull" studies of the patristic Church. In recent years we have been witnessing the "selling" of the apocrypha to these audiences under the guise of NT research and the quest for the historical Jesus. This is a misuse of useful material. There is nothing here that can serve as a source in our quest for the historical Jesus. To use these texts on what is from the start a precarious venture would render the venture completely incredible.

3. THE NAG HAMMADI MATERIAL

In 1945,[64] a peasant from the village of Nag Hammadi in Upper Egypt (near ancient Chenoboskia or Chenoboskion) discovered the remains of an ancient Coptic library.[65] The find comprised twelve codices (= books) plus eight leaves from a thirteenth codex, all written in the 4th century A.D. The codices, in turn, contained fifty-two tractates; with the elimination of duplicate copies, this number is reduced to forty-five separate titles. The find was truly a "library," since the codices embrace everything from a fragment of Plato's *Republic* through pagan moral works like the *Sentences of Sextus*, as well as pagan or Jewish works with varying degrees of gnostic influence, to Christian works that also reflect a range of gnostic views.

The vast majority of the material has nothing to do with our concerns. Indeed, even such a key work of Christian gnosticism as the *Gospel of Truth* turns out to be a theological tract or homily, completely different from the narrative form of the four canonical Gospels.[66] Some of these tracts-called-gospels (e.g., the *Gospel of Philip*) do contain words or deeds of Jesus, some paralleled in the canonical Gospels, some not. In the case of the *Gospel of Philip*, these words and deeds are scattered throughout a rambling document that seems to have as its main object instruction on Christian gnostic sacraments. The material about Jesus is sometimes on the level of the fanciful apocryphal gospels seen above. For example, Jesus goes into the dye works of Levi, takes 72 different colors, and throws them into the vat; they all come out white *(Gos. Phil.* 63, 25–30). Still more bizarre, Joseph the carpenter grows a tree from which he makes the cross on which Jesus is later hanged *(Gos. Phil.* 73, 8–15). This is the stuff of *The Last Temptation of Christ,* not the historical Jesus.

Fortunately for us, we do not have to agonize our way through every Christian document in the Nag Hammadi library to see whether it contains sayings or deeds of Jesus independent of the Synoptic tradition. The British NT scholar Christopher Tuckett has already performed that service. His conclusion in a book-long study is that, apart from the special case of the Coptic *Gospel of Thomas,* there is no evidence for the use of pre-Synoptic sources (including the Q document) in the Christian Nag Hammadi material.[67] The Christian texts at Nag Hammadi that do reflect Synoptic tradition presuppose one or more of the Synoptic Gospels in their final form. Instead of helping us see the development of the Synoptic tradition *before* the composition of the Synoptic Gospels, these texts witness to the development of the Synoptic tradition *after* the redaction of the Gospels. The use of the Synoptic Gospels at Nag Hammadi is roughly in proportion to what we find elsewhere in the early patristic period: Matthew is used most often, Luke somewhat less, and Mark rarely.[68] Working independently of Tuckett and concerned only with the Gospel of Matthew, Wolf-Dietrich Köhler has found probable or possible traces of Matthew in a goodly number of the clearly Christian texts.[69]

Tuckett wisely reserved the *Gospel of Thomas* for a separate study, since scholars have been fiercely divided on the nature and sources of this work almost from the time of its publication in 1959.[70] The *Gospel of Thomas* is a collection of 114 sayings of Jesus, with usually no or minimal narrative framework or accompanying dialogue.[71] The string of sayings shows no overarching compositional structure, most of the material being tied together by the repetition of key words or motifs or by clusters of similar material (proverbs, parables, prophecies, and community rules). Nevertheless, various clusters of sayings and parables, along with the repetition of dominant themes, do give some indication of the redactor's intention.

The phenomenon of a document made up solely of sayings of Jesus, without an overall narrative structure, naturally conjures up the idea of the Q document, which supposedly was just such a work. The question of sources and dependence thus arises from the shape as well as the content of the material. Complicating the source question further, a number of the sayings in the *Gospel of Thomas* were discovered earlier in this century in a more original Greek version—though, of course, at the time, they were not known to be part of what we now call the *Gospel of Thomas*. These Greek fragments are written on three scraps of papyri recovered from a garbage heap at the site of the ancient Egyptian town of Oxyrhynchus (hence the name of the collection: the Oxyrhynchus papyri). Oxyrhynchus Papyrus 1 contains what we now know as sayings 26–30, 77, and 31–33 from the *Gospel of Thomas*. The papyrus's different way of ordering the sayings from the full Coptic text, plus some difference in wording between the Greek and the Coptic, shows us that the *Gospel of Thomas* may have circulated in more than one form and passed through various stages of redaction. The Coptic version we possess is probably not identical to whatever was the original Greek form of the work—if, indeed, one can speak of *the* original Greek form. The other two Oxyrhynchus papyri contain their sayings in the same order as that found in the *Gospel of Thomas:* Oxyrhynchus Papyrus 654 contains sayings 1–7, and Oxyrhynchus Papyrus 655 contains sayings 36–40.[72]

An evaluation of the *Gospel of Thomas* is made still more difficult by the disagreement among scholars as to whether the work can be considered gnostic in its theology. Such a decision would of course have some ramifications on the further question of whether the gospel tells us anything about the historical Jesus. On the one hand, the gospel does contain sayings that are the same as or very similar to sayings in the Synoptic Gospels. Taken by themselves, or, a fortiori, taken in their Synoptic context, such sayings would never strike one as gnostic. Yet in the *Gospel of Thomas* such Synoptic-like sayings are juxtaposed to sayings with a definite gnostic tinge and seem at times to have been reworked to convey a gnostic message.[73] Hence, while not including the *Gospel of Thomas* in what he calls "classic gnostic Scripture," which embodies the full-blown gnostic myth (as in, e.g., the *Apocryphon of John*), Bentley Layton does include it as one of the "related writings" within the larger corpus of "the gnostic Scriptures."[74] As he points out, the "secret" or "hidden" meaning of the 114 sayings can be found, in the mind of the redactor of the gospel, only by those who understand the interpretive key to all of Jesus' words: the gnostic myth implied in many of the sayings of the *Gospel of Thomas*, but a myth that can be fully understood only by looking at other gnostic writings from the "School of St. Thomas," such as the *Hymn of the Pearl*.

In the gnostic myth implied in the *Gospel of Thomas*, the individual spirits originally dwelt in the kingdom of light, the kingdom of the

Father, who is the first principle of "the All" (= the spiritual universe of divine beings). By their very nature, these spirits were all united with and of one substance with the divine. Through some sort of primeval catastrophe, some of the spirits entered into the poverty of this material world and are imprisoned in the fleshly garments of human bodies.[75] This fall and imprisonment have caused them to fall asleep spiritually, have caused them to forget their true origin in the kingdom of light; they are like drunkards and blind men in the realm of darkness.[76] The "living" Jesus (basically, the timeless, eternal Son, without any true incarnation in matter, lengthy earthly ministry to the Jewish people in general, real death, or true bodily resurrection) comes into this world to wake these spirits up, to remind them of their true origin and destiny, to free them from the illusion that they belong to this material world of death.

One in divine substance with those he seeks, Jesus saves them simply by revealing to them the truth of who they are, i.e., divine beings who belong to another world. This knowledge, pure and simple, saves these spiritual persons right now. As soon as they realize who they are, they are immediately free from the "garments" of their material bodies, which they can trample underfoot.[77] Even now they can find the treasure of true knowledge that means eternal life; even now they can enter into the "place" or "rest" of the Father. Fully integrated with the divine source from which they came, there is no salvation to be awaited in the future; the *Gospel of Thomas* thus represents "realized eschatology" in its most radical form.

Indeed, it is perhaps more accurate to speak of a return to the primordial paradise than an anticipation of a future consummation.[78] There is no kingdom to be awaited from above or in the future; the spiritual kingdom is already within them and surrounding them, if only they open their inner eyes to see it.[79] The material world and physical body are rejected as evil, and one abstains as far as possible from things material. Sex is seen as an evil, and the female role in bearing new spirits imprisoned in bodies is especially deprecated.[80] By asceticism the spirits already triumph in principle over the body, which will be totally left behind at physical death. Physical death does not spell destruction for the initiated who have "found the interpretation" of Jesus' sayings and who therefore do not experience death.[81] Physical death is simply final release from the evil material world.[82]

It is only in the light of this strange mixture of mysticism, asceticism, pantheism, and polytheism that many of the sayings of the "living"

Jesus can be understood:[83] "If you do not abstain from the world, you will not find the kingdom" (27). "I am amazed at how this great wealth has come to dwell in this poverty" (29). "Where there are three divine beings they are divine. Where there are two or one, I myself dwell with that person" (30). "If they say to you, 'Where are you from?' say to them, 'It is from the light that we have come' " (50). "Jesus said, 'It is I who am the All; it is from me that the All has come, and to me that the All goes. Split a piece of wood: I am there. Lift a stone, and you will find me there' " (77). "Jesus said, 'Whoever drinks from my mouth will become like me; I, too, will become that person' " (108). "Simon Peter said to them, 'Mary should leave us, for females are not worthy of life.' Jesus said, 'See, I am going to lead her to make her a male so that she too might become a living spirit that resembles you males. For every woman that makes herself male will enter the kingdom of heaven' " (114).

With this summary before us, it is clear that the overarching intention of the redactor of the *Gospel of Thomas* is a gnostic one and that the Synoptic-like sayings are meant to be (re-)interpreted according to their "genuine," secret, gnostic meaning.[84] Since a gnostic world view of this sort was not employed to "reinterpret" Christianity in such a thoroughgoing way before sometime in the 2d century A.D.,[85] there can be no question of the *Gospel of Thomas* as a whole, as it stands in the Coptic text, being a reliable reflection of the historical Jesus or of the earliest sources of 1st-century Christianity.[86] Indeed, it is symptomatic that the earliest of the Oxyrhynchus papyri, the first witnesses (in Greek) to the *Gospel of Thomas*, is usually dated ca. A.D. 200; it is somewhere in the 2d century that the composition we know as the *Gospel of Thomas* took shape as one expression of 2d-century gnostic Christianity.[87]

However, this 2d-century date and the gnostic character of the final document do not answer the question of whether some early source of authentic sayings of Jesus, perhaps even earlier and more original than what we find in the Synoptics, might be preserved in the *Gospel of Thomas*. The debate on this point has been lively and varied, and it is not likely to come to rest soon.

From the time of the first publication of the *Gospel of Thomas*, a sizable number of specialists have held that the gospel represents an independent tradition as early as, if not earlier than, that of the Synoptics. One of the earliest and most persistent was Gilles Quispel, who pointed out that none of the Synoptic-like sayings agreed exactly with the wording of the canonical Gospels; he suggested that some of these sayings might have come from the *Gospel of the Hebrews*.[88] There was in his approach, however, a strong apologetic motif: the *Gospel of Thomas*, in his mind, gave the lie to the skepticism of some form critics, for it supplied independent evidence that the Jesus tradition was not a myth produced by a later community's theology. Jacques E. Ménard likewise feels that many of the sayings in the *Gospel of Thomas* do not have a gnostic "allure" and may represent an ancient stratum independent of and older than the canonical texts.[89] The great quester for the historical Jesus, Joachim Jeremias, welcomed the idea of the independence of the *Gospel of Thomas* because it thus offered a separate source that aided the attempt to reconstruct the original form and meaning of Jesus' sayings, especially the parables.[90]

On this side of the Atlantic, recent decades have seen a veritable flood of publications promoting the independence of the Synoptic-like sayings in the *Gospel of Thomas*. Yet even in this country the impetus has come especially from a distinguished German scholar who has taught for many years at Harvard University, Helmut Koester. Koester maintains that the *Gospel of Thomas* was written possibly as early as the second half of the 1st century A.D., shows no influence from the canonical Gospels, and contains some sayings of Jesus in a more primitive form than the form witnessed in our Gospels.[91] Koester's influence is reflected in the views of many of his American colleagues and students, including Ron Cameron,[92] Stevan Davies,[93] James M. Robinson,[94] and John Dominic Crossan.[95] So convinced of their position are some of these scholars that they do not even bother to argue for their stance; it is simply taken for granted.[96]

When arguments are enunciated, this "pro-independence" school usually stresses the fact that the sayings and parables in the *Gospel of Thomas* are generally shorter and more streamlined, and lack the allegory, theological concerns, narrative framework, and other redactional "fingerprints" of the four evangelists.[97] The redactor of the *Gospel of Thomas*, it is claimed, would have had no reason to reduce a given saying or parable of the Synoptics so drastically.[98] The parables in the *Gospel of Thomas* often coincide remarkably with the hypothetical original forms reconstructed from the Synoptics by 20th-century form critics. Many of the sayings are easily retroverted into Aramaic and show the rhythm and rhetoric scholars associate with the authentic sayings of Jesus.[99] Crossan also points out that one would expect the order of the sayings in at least one of the Synoptics to peek through, since Thomas has no overarching redactional order of his own; yet, says Crossan, the Synoptic order is not apparent.[100]

These arguments are weighty, but they have not convinced everyone.[101] From the beginning, some scholars have favored the view that the *Gospel of Thomas* did depend, directly or indirectly, on some if not all of the canonical Gospels. Early on in the debate, H. E. W. Turner expressed his hesitations about Quispel's claim of independence; Turner pointed out that the different versions of the sayings in the *Gospel of Thomas* could be due to gnostic methods of exegesis and particular gnostic patterns of doctrine and spirituality.[102] Robert M. Grant thinks that most of the material in the gospel parallel to the Synoptics comes from Matthew and Luke.[103] He holds that one can understand why Thomas rearranged the order of sayings in the Synoptics to suit his own purposes, and that traces of the Synoptic order can still be found in the *Gospel of Thomas*.[104]

Jean-Marie Sevrin demonstrates in detail why Thomas regrouped certain Synoptic parables (sayings 63, 64, and 65) to make a characteristically gnostic point: ties to this material world lead to death, while the laborious quest for self-knowledge leads to life.[105] Bertil Gärtner, criticizing Quispel for building on too many questionable hypotheses, points to the relatively free way in which the early Church quoted the canonical Gospels, often citing from memory, often combining sayings of Jesus or adding to the text, often tending toward the creation of a type of Gospel harmony or "diatessaron."[106] Gärtner claims that the Synoptic-like sayings in the *Gospel of Thomas* regularly follow the text of Luke rather than Matthew, though a few are closer to Matthew. Kurt Rudolph sees traces of Mark, Matthew, and Luke.[107] Rejecting the customary comparison of the *Gospel of Thomas* with the Q document, Boudewijn Dehandschutter points out that the gospel attributes to Jesus sayings that earlier in the Christian tradition were not attributed to Jesus; in other words, the *Gospel of Thomas* represents a relatively late, rather than early, stage in the tradition of Jesus' words.[108]

The problem with many of these arguments, of course, is that they remain on a general plane or use only a few sayings to support a thesis. The value of the work of Wolfgang Schrage is that he has examined in detail all the sayings in the *Gospel of Thomas* that have Synoptic parallels. Although there are always some cases that do not allow of a firm decision, most of the parallels, in his judgment, are best explained by dependence of the *Gospel of Thomas* on the Synoptics.[109] Even when occasionally a saying in the *Gospel of Thomas* does seem to be more original, the saying still seems to be "filtered through" a knowledge of the Synoptics. Usually, instead, it is a question of the Synoptic tradition being "filtered through" gnostic thought—though the dependence on the Synoptics may at times be an indirect one of ongoing oral tradition or a Gospel harmony rather than direct copying from the manuscript of a Synoptic Gospel.[110] Schrage's study remains useful, even though his reliance on comparisons with later (and varied) Coptic versions of the canonical Gospels and his failure to focus upon redactional passages of the Synoptics have left him open to criticism.[111]

The possibility that the Synoptics were known to Thomas through a single harmonized text is taken seriously by Tuckett, who holds that at least some of the Synoptic-like sayings in the *Gospel of Thomas* show dependence on redactional material in the Synoptic Gospels.[112]

The fact that great scholars can be so divided on this issue shows how the data allow of more than one interpretation. It is a question of weighing all the arguments and trying to decide which position is more probable; absolute certainty is not to be had. With all due hesitation, I incline to the view that the *Gospel of Thomas* is dependent on the Synoptic tradition. A number of arguments weigh heavily with me.

(1) First of all, there is a preliminary consideration that influences my judgment: the general impression created by all the Christian material we have seen in this chapter prior to our overview of the Nag Hammadi documents. In the case of both the *agrapha* and the apocryphal gospels, some scholars claimed to find authentic sayings of Jesus independent of the canonical Gospels. Many of the examples could be dismissed quickly as bizarre examples of lively Christian imagination run riot. Other cases demanded more sober consideration. But in each of those instances (especially the *Gospel of Peter, Egerton Papyrus 2*, and the *Secret Gospel of Mark*), a closer examination showed it more likely that the 2d-century material was dependent on the canonical Gospels.

More importantly, certain patterns began to appear. Under the powerful impact of the Four Gospels, written in the 1st century but gradually recognized as canonical only later on, 2d-century Christianity exploded with feverish attempts to imitate, conflate, and harmonize these four "lives" of Jesus—as well as to create new lives and new Jesuses. Sometimes the driving motive was just the pious imagination and curiosity of "popular" Christianity, verging on the novelistic (e.g., the *Protevangelium Jacobi*). Other times, more of a theological agenda, often of a gnostic stripe, peeped through the fragments (e.g., the *Gospel of the Egyptians*). But in no case prior to our investigation of the *Gospel of Thomas* did we find any document likely to contain authentic sayings of Jesus that were independent of the canonical Gospels. Thus, if the *Gospel of Thomas* does contain such independent sayings, it is practically unique in 2d-century Christian literature. If, instead, it is dependent on the canonical Gospels, it fits perfectly into the larger picture of 2d-century Christianity. I stress that this point is merely a preliminary or a priori consideration. But it does flow from all we have seen so far, and it does pose the pointed question of how we are to imagine the *Gospel of Thomas* within the development of 2d-century Christian literature.

(2) A second preliminary consideration is the fact that our canonical Gospels not only come from ongoing oral tradition but also generate ongoing oral tradition. It is often affirmed, quite rightly, that oral traditions did not die out the day after a canonical Gospel was published. But the writing of the canonical Gospels did change the situation. The canonical Gospels—long before they were definitively recognized as "canonical"—were regularly preached on at worship, studied in catechetical schools, and cited strictly and loosely by patristic authors; and so increasingly they lodged themselves in the memory of individual Christians and whole communities. Inevitably they "contaminated" and modified the oral tradition that existed before and alongside themselves.[113]

Thus, as one passes through the 2d century, it becomes increasingly difficult to identify sayings of Jesus that one could reasonably hope would be totally free of Synoptic and Johannine influence.[114] The differences between sayings of Jesus in 2d-century documents and his sayings in the canonical Gospels are likely due to citation from memory (2d-century Christians having none of our 20th-century academic zeal for exact citation of a written text), inadvertent errors, conscious or unconscious harmonizing,[115] and at times a clear desire to rework a given saying to score a theological point. The Jewish tendency to produce "targums" and "midrashim" finds its correlative in the reception and use of the Four Gospels in 2d-century Christianity.

Hence, when we ask whether the *Gospel of Thomas* is dependent on the Synoptics and/or John, that dependence has to be understood in more than one way. Given the lengthy process by which the *Gospel of Thomas* was formed, both direct dependence on the written forms of the Gospels and indirect dependence on them through preaching and catechesis, citation from memory, Gospel harmonies, and creative reworking must be taken seriously. In light of all this, Crossan's objection that, if the *Gospel of Thomas* were dependent on the canonical Gospels, we would see much more of the Synoptic order of the sayings loses much of its force.[116] Moreover, as Tuckett points out, thanks to the Oxyrhynchus papyri, we know of at least one case where the Coptic redactor of the

Gospel of Thomas rearranged the order of the Greek text in order to create a link between catchwords.[117] It may well be that such links create a "logic" that was clear to the redactor, if not to us, and that this "logic" is the reason for the reordering of the Synoptic sayings.

(3) Thirdly, from these preliminary considerations we can now turn to the data in the *Gospel of Thomas*. When scholars argue for independence from the canonical Gospels, one of the most frequently used arguments is that the *Gospel of Thomas* presents us with a shorter, more concise version of a given saying or parable, without the allegory and redactional theology added on by the four evangelists. At first glance, this argument is straightforward and attractive; but further reflection shows that it is not as probative as might first appear.

(a) It is by no means invariably true in the Gospel tradition that the shorter text is earlier than and independent of the longer text containing the same material. Matthew usually shortens and streamlines Mark's miracle stories, but he is no less dependent on Mark for all the brevity.[118] In fact, it is quite possible that a tradition may not develop along a straight line of shorter to longer or longer to shorter, but may meander back and forth.[119]

For example, the earliest form of Jesus' prohibition of divorce may have looked something like the Q form behind Luke 16:18/Matt 5:32, which views divorce completely from the husband's vantage point, since in Jewish law of the time (with rare exceptions) only the husband could effect a divorce.[120] Working in a Greco-Roman legal setting, where women could divorce their husbands, Mark expanded the tradition he received to make the prohibition apply to women as well as men (see his two-part statement in vv 11–12 within his controversy-dialogue on divorce, Mark 10:1–12). Matthew took over that controversy-dialogue from Mark; but, reflecting the Jewish-Christian background of his church, Matthew dropped the second half of the two-part statement in Mark 10:11–12, thus creating a statement on divorce which reverts to the husband's point of view alone (Matt 19:9).

Notice what has happened: in the history of the tradition, Matthew's version is actually twice removed from the most primitive form. Yet, because of his redactional pruning of Mark's two-part version, Matthew, by coincidence, produces a form close to the primitive one. Matthew does this not because he has studied form criticism or has direct access to the most primitive tradition, but simply because his redactional concerns lead him to abbreviate Mark in a way that just happens to produce a version similar to the primitive version. It would never occur to any critic who otherwise held the two-source theory to claim that, in this one case, Matthew is independent of and prior to Mark. Instead, the critic would simply take note of another tendency of the Synoptic tradition: at times, later redactional editing may produce abbreviated forms of a saying that, by coincidence, approximate a primitive form of the saying.

(b) It may be that something analogous is happening in the *Gospel of Thomas'* use of the canonical Gospels. When comparing the Synoptics and the *Gospel of Thomas,* we should always remember the controlling hermeneutical principle stated at the beginning of the latter work: "These are the obscure [or 'hidden' or 'secret'] sayings that the living Jesus uttered. . . . Whoever finds the meaning [or 'interpretation'] of these sayings will not taste death" (saying 1). The redactor of the gospel does not intend that the sayings of Jesus be readily intelligible to any reader who happens along. Instead, they are presented as esoteric teaching, intelligible only to the initiate who, equipped with the "flashlight" of the gnostic worldview, searches in the dark to find the hidden, gnostic significance of Jesus' words. The upshot of this hermeneutic is that the redactor of the *Gospel of Thomas* will purposely drop from the tradition anything that makes Jesus' sayings too clear or univocal, or anything that employs the general saying to highlight one specific (often moral or ecclesial) application. Thus, the redactor naturally undoes what the four canonical evangelists have struggled so hard to do: for, by allegory or other redactional additions and reformulations, the four evangelists often explain the meaning of Jesus' statements or apply them to concrete issues in the Church.

It is these clarifying additions that Thomas systematically drops, thus creating a shorter, tighter version of a saying or a parable. The whole gnostic approach of Thomas makes him favor a laconic, "collapsed," streamlined form of the tradition. This form may indeed, at times, approximate by coincidence what form critics imagine the primitive tradition to have looked like. But, as with Matthew vis-à-vis Mark, this coincidence is not to be confused with priority and independence. Indeed, since such a procedure may easily remove material that comes from Jesus himself, it by no means guarantees a return to the original form of the saying.

(c) It is not simply a general preference for the short, mysterious, laconic formulation that moves Thomas to reduce canonical sayings radically. Thomas also has a complex theological stance that causes him to remove from the canonical material a great deal of both traditional and redactional theology. Thomas' gnostic vision has no room for a multi-stage history of salvation, with its early phase in the OT (replete with prophecies), its midpoint in Jesus' earthly ministry, death, and resurrection, its continuation in a Church settling down in the world and proclaiming the gospel equally to all men and women, and its climax in a glorious coming of Jesus the Son of Man to close out the old world and create a new one—in other words, so much of what the Four Gospels teach as they relate the words and deeds of Jesus. Thomas' rejection of the material world as evil also means a rejection of salvation history, of a privileged place in that history for Israel, of the significance of OT prophecies, of any real importance given to the "enfleshed" earthly ministry of Jesus leading to his saving death and bodily resurrection, of a universal mission of the Church to all people (instead of only to a spiritual elite), and of a future coming of Jesus to inaugurate a new heaven and a new earth.

In other words, Thomas' view of salvation is ahistorical, atemporal, amaterial, and so he regularly removes from the Four Gospels anything that contradicts his view. Sevrin, for instance, demonstrates convincingly how Thomas pulls together three diverse parables in sayings 63, 64, and 65 (the parables of the rich man who dies suddenly, of the great supper, and of the murderous tenants of the vineyard) to develop his own gnostic polemic against "capitalism," while rigorously censoring out of the parables any allegory, any reference to salvation history, and any eschatological perspective.[121] The result is a dehistoricized, timeless message of self-salvation through self-knowledge and ascetic detachment from this material world. At times, Thomas will introduce amplifications into the tradition, but they always serve his theological program.[122]

(4) A further consideration focuses on the broad "spread" of the Synoptic parallels that we find in the *Gospel of Thomas*. Critics often emphasize the parallels between the *Gospel of Thomas* and the Q material, sometimes all but ignoring parallels to other types of material within the canonical tradition. To be sure, the parallels to Q are especially plentiful. But attention to the broad "spread" of parallel material, which extends to special Matthean material, special Lucan material, possible redactional traits from each of the three Synoptics, the "triple tradition," and possible Johannine material, leads to some intriguing conclusions.[123]

Especially noteworthy is the amount of material in Thomas that finds a parallel only in Matthew among the canonical Gospels: e.g., the triple instruction on almsgiving, prayer, and fasting in Matt 6:1–18 (cf.

sayings 6 and 14); the parables of the fisherman with the net (Matt 13:47–50; saying 8), the treasure in the field (Matt 13:44; saying 109), and the merchant buying the single pearl (Matt 13:45–46; saying 76); Jesus' presence promised to a small number of believers (Matt 18:20; saying 30); the metaphor of the city on a hill (Matt 5:14; saying 32); and the saying on being shrewd as snakes and innocent as doves (Matt 10:16; saying 39, where the Coptic text takes over the Greek adjectives that appear in Matthew's text, *phronimos* and *akeraios*).

These and other examples of uniquely Matthean material (the "M" material) are especially intriguing since some of the M passages may be Matthew's own redactional creations.[124] For example, in Chapter 15, Matthew inserts into Mark's dispute story on clean and unclean (Mark 7:1–23) what is apparently Matthew's own redactional observation on the Pharisees: "Every plant that my heavenly Father has not planted will be rooted out" (Matt 15:13).[125] Saying 40 therefore sounds suspiciously Matthean when, after a warning about Pharisees and scribes (paralleled in Matt 23:13/Luke 11:52) and after the uniquely Matthean aphorism about snakes and doves, it has Jesus say: "A grapevine has been planted outside the Father. And because it is not sound, it will be plucked up by its roots and destroyed." Also specifically Matthean—and possibly redactional—is the parable of the wheat and the weeds (Matt 13:24–30; saying 57),[126] the invitation to come to Jesus and bear his yoke (Matt 11:28–30; saying 90),[127] and the warning not to give one's valuables to dogs and swine (Matt 7:6; saying 93). To these examples may be added those sayings from the Marcan or Q traditions that appear in the *Gospel of Thomas* with the precise form or wording found only in Matthew's Gospel. For example, sayings 33 (on preaching from the housetops), 34 (on the blind leading the blind), and 99 (on doing "the will of my Father") reflect the Matthean redactional form of sayings from the double and triple tradition. In sum, only one of the passages I have listed would have to be Matthew's own creation or reflect Matthew's redaction to prove beyond a doubt that Thomas knows and uses Matthew's Gospel to compose his own. I think that at least Matt 15:13 and 13:24–30 do exactly that.[128]

At the same time, there is a fair amount of material in the *Gospel of Thomas* that is specific to Luke among the canonical Gospels (the "L" material): e.g., the saying about Jesus' casting fire on the earth (Luke 12:49; saying 10);[129] the parable of the rich man who dies suddenly (Luke 12:16–21; saying 63); the refusal of Jesus to act as the arbitrator of an inheritance (Luke 12:13–15; saying 72); the two Lucan sayings concerning the blessing of a womb and breasts (Luke 11:27–28 and 23:29; saying 79); [130] the saying on the kingdom of God being within you (Luke 17:20, reflected in parts of saying 113 and saying 3).[131]

As for Lucan redactional traits, Tuckett locates them by turning to sayings in Thomas that come from both Q and the triple tradition. Lucan redactional elements are especially clear in saying 5, for which we have the Greek text from Oxyrhynchus Papyrus 654.[132] The Greek text of the papyrus agrees with Luke's redactional form in Luke 8:17 rather than with the basic Marcan form in Mark 4:22.[133] The author of the papyrus obviously knew Luke's redactional form and therefore Luke's Gospel. Tuckett suggests that other examples of sayings in Thomas that reflect in part redactional elements from Luke include sayings 16 and 55.[134]

Besides Q, special M material, special L material, and likely traces of Matthean and Lucan redaction, the "spread" of material extends to pericopes from the "triple tradition" (i.e., pericopes of Mark that Matthew and Luke also have): e.g., the parable of the sower (Mark 4:1–8; saying 9), the parable of the mustard seed (Mark 4:30–32; saying 20),[135] and the parable of the murderous tenants of the vineyard (Mark 12:1–8; saying 65).[136] Of its very nature, Marcan redaction is harder to establish (even in Mark's Gospel itself!), but Tuckett thinks that some redactional traits from Mark can be found in sayings 9 and 20.

References or allusions to Johannine material are not so clear.[137] The opening promise in saying 1 that "whoever finds the meaning of these sayings will not taste death" is reminiscent of John 8:52 ("if anyone keeps my word, he will not taste death for all eternity"). The promise of the bubbling spring that Jesus gives his disciples to drink (saying 13) may echo John 4:14 and 7:37–38. Jesus proclaims, "I am the light," in both saying 77 and John 8:12. Grant lists a number of other parallels, but it must be admitted that, while the language in his examples is vaguely Johannine, often the echo is weak.[138]

Raymond E. Brown moves painstakingly through the whole of the *Gospel of Thomas*, carefully noting every possible allusion to the Gospel of John.[139] He grants that many of the suggested allusions are extremely tenuous. But he feels that some dependence of Thomas on John is suggested by material in Thomas that reflects John's Last Supper discourses and the discourse at the end of the feast of tabernacles (John 7:37–8:59). These parts of the Fourth Gospel were probably among the last to take their present shape. Since the parallels in the *Gospel of Thomas* are to various sections of these discourses, it is most unlikely that the *Gospel of*

Thomas is dependent on just one of the strands of Johannine tradition that have gone into the discourses. It seems probable, therefore, that Thomas is dependent—though perhaps indirectly, through some intermediary document or oral tradition—on the Gospel of John itself rather than on some hypothetical source of John.[140]

We arrive, then, at an intriguing picture: the sayings in the *Gospel of Thomas* that resemble sayings found in the canonical Gospels are not simply parallels to the Q material. Besides many Q sayings, there is a good deal of special M material, a fair representation of special L material, indications of Matthean and Lucan redactional traits, some pericopes from the triple tradition (though not necessarily in the specific Marcan form), some possible redactional traits from Mark, and a few parallels to statements in John's Gospel. This broad "spread" of Jesus' sayings over so many different streams of canonical Gospel tradition (and redaction!) forces us to face a fundamental question: Is it likely that the very early source of Jesus' sayings that the *Gospel of Thomas* supposedly drew upon contained within itself material belonging to such diverse branches of 1st-century Christian tradition as Q, special M, special L, Matthean and Lucan redaction, the triple tradition, and possibly the Johannine tradition? What were the source, locus, and composition of this incredibly broad yet very early tradition? Who were its bearers? Is it really conceivable that there was some early Christian source that embraced within itself all these different strands of what became the canonical Gospels? Or is it more likely that the *Gospel of Thomas* has conflated material from the Gospels of Matthew and Luke, with possible use of Mark and John as well? Of the two hypotheses I find the second much more probable, especially given all we have seen of such conflating tendencies in other 2d-century Christian documents. Indeed, it may even be that the *Gospel of Thomas* is directly dependent not on the four canonical Gospels, but on some conflation of them that had already been composed in Greek.[141]

(5) This hypothesis becomes all the more likely when we notice that, while the *Gospel of Thomas* regularly censors out elements of Synoptic redaction, now and then a trace of the order or theological tendencies of the Synoptic Gospels survives.

The survival of the Synoptic order in a few places is especially striking since—as we have seen—Thomas reorders the Synoptic sayings around clusters of similar motifs and catchwords. For example, the order of Luke 10:8–9 peeks through in part of saying 14: "If you fast you will acquire sin. . . . And when you go into any land, when they receive you, eat whatever they will set before you (= Luke 10:8). Heal those among them who are sick (= Luke 10:9). For nothing that enters your mouth will defile you. . . ." Thomas has gathered these diverse sayings around the leitmotif of eating (fasting, eating what is set before you, what enters your mouth). The reference to healing is completely intrusive in Thomas' context; it plays no function, comes from nowhere, and goes nowhere. Or rather, it comes clearly from Luke 10:9, where it makes sense within Luke's missionary discourse, following Luke 10:8 and introducing the proclamation of the coming of the kingdom in Luke 10:9b. Indeed, so closely does Luke 10:9 follow upon Luke 10:8 that it has followed it straight into the *Gospel of Thomas*, even though it makes no sense there, given the leitmotif Thomas has chosen for his cluster.[142]

The Synoptic order also seems to surface at the end of the parable of the murderous tenants of the vineyard. It is quite probable that the parable originally ended with the death of the son in Mark 12:8. Mark, followed by Matthew and Luke, adds the destruction of the tenants by the owner of the vineyard and then a reference to Psalm 118:22: "The stone the builders rejected has become the cornerstone."[143] Correspondingly, in the *Gospel of Thomas*, after the death of the son in saying 65, saying 66 follows with a paraphrase of Ps 118:22: "Show me the stone that the builders rejected. That one is the cornerstone."[144] The order of sayings 65 and 66 seems to presuppose the Marcan composition.

Two possible traces of the "theological atmosphere" of the Synoptic Gospels may be present in sayings 55 and 57. Saying 55 ends with the warning: ". . . those who do not . . . take up their cross like me [or "in my way," or "as I have"] will not become worthy of me" (cf. Luke 14:26–27; Matt 10:37–38). The *Gospel of Thomas* does not elsewhere make such an explicit reference to the crucifixion of Jesus and the disciple's imitation of it; the idea of Jesus' real death on the cross is understandably absent from this gnostic gospel.[145] Saying 57 (the parable of the wheat and the weeds) is an obvious condensation of the Matthean version of the parable, and accordingly it ends in the same way: "For on the day of the harvest the weeds will be plainly visible, and they will be pulled up and burned." The idea of a future day of judgment (= the harvest) and the punishment of the wicked on the last day by fire (= "they will be . . . burned") is perfectly at home in the eschatology of the Synoptics in general and Matthew in particular, but it does not fit the gnostic perspective of the *Gospel of Thomas*, which ordinarily avoids references to Jesus' final coming and the last judgment.

In view of all this, I conclude that the more probable hypothesis is that the *Gospel of Thomas* knew and used at least some of the canonical Gospels, notably Matthew and Luke. Indeed, if the *Gospel of Thomas* used all Four Gospels, the frequency with which each Gospel is used would roughly mirror what we see throughout the rest of 2d-century Christian literature: of the Synoptics, Matthew is used most often, then Luke, and least of all Mark. Before the time of Irenaeus, John stands to one side, and in some writings we have at best weak echoes rather than clear citations or allusions. The tendency to conflate, reorder, and paraphrase Gospel sayings is likewise common in the 2d century. Thus, rather than diverging from the common pattern of 2d-century Christian literature, Thomas by and large conforms to it.

Since I think that the Synoptic-like sayings of the *Gospel of Thomas* are in fact dependent on the Synoptic Gospels and that the other sayings stem from 2d-century Christian gnosticism, the *Gospel of Thomas* will not be used in our quest as an independent source for the historical Jesus.[146] Nevertheless, I realize that not all scholars will agree with my evaluation of the *Gospel of Thomas*. To give due consideration to their views, I will always keep one eye on the sayings in this gospel as a check and control on my own interpretation of the data in the canonical Gospels. Even if the *Gospel of Thomas* represents only a gnostic reworking of the Synoptic tradition, what Thomas does to that tradition may highlight certain aspects of it that otherwise might be overlooked. The same holds true for the rabbinic material, the *agrapha*, and the other apocryphal gospels. I will not drag the reader through all this material again, but I will be consulting it as I go about my own work of sifting and evaluating the canonical tradition.

4. SUMMARY ON THE SOURCES

In one sense, the results of our survey have been negative and disappointing. The four canonical Gospels turn out to be the only large documents containing significant blocks of material relevant to a quest for the historical Jesus. The rest of the NT offers only bits and pieces, mostly in the Pauline corpus. Outside the NT, the only independent, non-Christian witness to Jesus in the 1st century A.D. is Josephus, but his famous *Testimonium Flavianum* demands some critical pruning to remove later Christian interpolations. Even then, Josephus gives independent verification of the main lineaments of the Gospels' portrait of Jesus—but nothing really new or different. If Tacitus represents an independent source—which is doubtful—all he gives us is an added confirmation of Jesus' execution by Pontius Pilate in Judea during the reign of Tiberius. The rest of the pagan Greco-Roman authors (Suetonius, Pliny the Younger, Lucian of Samosata) offer no early, independent information about Jesus. For all practical purposes, then, our early, independent sources for the historical Jesus boil down to the Four Gospels, a few scattered data elsewhere in the NT, and Josephus.

Contrary to some scholars, I do not think that the rabbinic material, the *agrapha*, the apocryphal gospels, and the Nag Hammadi codices (in particular the *Gospel of Thomas*) offer us reliable new information or authentic sayings that are independent of the NT. What we see in these later documents is rather the reaction to or reworking of NT writings by Jewish rabbis engaged in polemics, imaginative Christians reflecting popular piety and legend, and gnostic Christians developing a mystic speculative system. Their versions of Jesus' words and deeds can be included in a "corpus of Jesus material" if that corpus is understood to contain simply everything and anything that any ancient source ever identified as material coming from Jesus. But such a corpus is the Matthean dragnet (Matt 13:47–48) from which the good fish of early tradition must be selected for the containers of serious historical research, while the bad fish of later conflation and invention are tossed back into the murky sea of the uncritical mind. In Part One of this book, we have been sitting on the beach, sorting the dragnet and throwing the *agrapha*, apocryphal gospels, and the *Gospel of Thomas* back into the sea.[147]

It is not surprising that scholars have wanted to see reliable early traditions in some of these documents. Indeed, it is quite understandable. Once these documents are declared to be dependent, directly or indirectly, on the NT for their reliable information about Jesus, we are left alone—some would say forlorn—with the Four Gospels, plus scattered tidbits. It is only natural for scholars—to say nothing of popularizers—to want more, to want other access roads to the historical Jesus. This understandable but not always critical desire is, I think, what has recently led to the high evaluation, in some quarters, of the apocryphal gospels and the Nag Hammadi codices as sources for the quest. It is a case of the wish being father to the thought, but the wish is a pipe dream. For better or for worse, in our quest for the historical Jesus, we are largely confined to the canonical Gospels; the genuine "corpus" is infuriating in its restrictions. For the historian it is a galling limitation. But to call upon the *Gospel of Peter* or the *Gospel of Thomas* to supplement our Four Gospels is to broaden out our pool of sources from the difficult to the incredible.

The Four Gospels are indeed difficult sources; their initial selection from the dragnet does not mean that they are guaranteed to represent the historical words and deeds of Jesus. Shot through and through with the Easter faith of the early Church, highly selective, and ordered according to various theological programs, the canonical Gospels demand careful, critical sifting if they are to yield reliable information for the quest. In a backhanded way, this is the positive upshot of our fifth chapter. The more our focus is narrowed to the "corpus" of the canonical Gospels and the more we appreciate the special and highly theological nature of these limited sources, the more we realize the pressing need to hammer out clear criteria for discerning what within the Gospels can be judged historical. Therefore, in the next chapter we will take up the task of articulating criteria of historicity, criteria we can then apply to the words and deeds of Jesus as presented in the Four Gospels.

NOTES TO CHAPTER 5

[1] William D. Stoker, *Extracanonical Sayings of Jesus* (SBLSBS 18; Atlanta: Scholars, 1989). Although he is not interested in questions of authenticity, Stoker shares Koester's view that some noncanonical collections of Jesus material are independent of the canonical Gospels; he also thinks that the sayings preserved in the *Gospel of Thomas* are best viewed as stemming from a collection earlier than the canonical Gospels (p. 1 n. 2).

[2] Joachim Jeremias, *Unknown Sayings of Jesus* (2d English ed. [from the 3d German ed.]; London: SPCK, 1964). Another collection, categorized differently, can be found in Edgar Hennecke and Wilhelm Schneemelcher, *Neutestamentliche Apokryphen in deutscher Übersetzung. I Band. Evangelien* (Tübingen: Mohr [Siebeck], 1968) 52–74.

[3] For the Oxyrhynchus papyri that parallel material in the Coptic *Gospel of Thomas*, see Section 3.

[4] Needless to say, our concern here is with sayings that have a good chance of coming from the historical Jesus; words ascribed to the risen Jesus do not come under the limited scope of this investigation.

[5] *Unknown Sayings of Jesus*, 120.

[6] Here Jeremias places the only *agraphon* in the Acts of the Apostles, recorded in Paul's farewell speech at Miletus to the elders of Ephesus: ". . . one must remember the words of the Lord Jesus, that he himself said, 'It is more blessed to give than to receive.' " Jeremias *(Unknown Sayings of Jesus*, 33 n. 1) agrees with the judgment of Ernst Haenchen that Luke is putting into the mouth of Jesus a proverb well known in the Greco-Roman world *(Die Apostelgeschichte* [MeyerK 3; 6th ed.; Göttingen: Vandenhoeck & Ruprecht, 1968] 526–27 n. 5); similarly, Hans Conzelmann, *Acts of the Apostles* (Hermeneia; Philadelphia: Fortress, 1987) 176.

[7] *Unknown Sayings of Jesus*, 26–42; Jeremias gives examples of each type of development of the sayings tradition.

[8] The first three candidates (the rich young man, Jesus' encounter with a Pharisaic chief priest, Jesus' evaluation of the man who worked on the Sabbath) have a narrative framework and are therefore classified by Jeremias as "stories about Jesus." Yet what is at stake in Jeremias' treatment of each story is the saying or sayings of Jesus at the heart of the story. The other examples are classified as apocalyptic sayings dealing with the imminent eschatological denouement.

[9] See the discussion of the criteria of historicity in Chapter 6 of this book.

[10] It is ultimately for this reason that I do not spend more time on these individual pieces of *agrapha;* offering no significantly different information about Jesus, they are simply not worth the effort.

[11] This definition therefore excludes from consideration those "gospels" from Nag Hammadi and elsewhere which are really philosophical-theological tracts

and in which the words and deeds of the earthly Jesus figure marginally, if at all. Obviously, such material has no bearing on a quest for the historical Jesus. The Coptic *Gospel of Thomas* could properly be treated in this present section. But, for convenience' sake, I delay a consideration of the *Gospel of Thomas* until Section 3, which treats the Nag Hammadi material. Even with these restrictions, "apocryphal gospels" must remain a useful catchall rubric rather than the designation of a single literary genre. For a brief survey of recent research on apocryphal gospels (sympathetic to the approach of Koester), see Stephen Gero, "Apocryphal Gospels: A Survey of Textual and Literary Problems," *Aufstieg und Niedergang der römischen Welt* II/25.5, 3969–96.

[12] The word "apocryphal" is therefore being defined here in a sober, empirical way, without the prejudice of which Helmut Koester complains in his article, "Apocryphal and Canonical Gospels," *HTR* 73 (1980) 105–30. If we decide that a given apocryphal gospel contains bizarre material or does not represent independent historical tradition about Jesus, that judgment will flow from a reading of the text, not from the adjective "apocryphal."

[13] Significant proponents of the importance of at least some apocryphal gospels for the history of Jesus and the earliest Christian tradition include Koester, "Apocryphal and Canonical Gospels," 104–12, 130; and John Dominic Crossan, *Four Other Gospels. Shadows on the Contours of Canon* (Minneapolis: Winston, 1985).

[14] Edgar Hennecke and Wilhelm Schneemelcher, *Neutestamentliche Apokryphen in deutscher Übersetzung. I Band. Evangelien. II Band. Apostolisches, Apokalypsen und Verwandtes* (4th ed.; Tübingen: Mohr [Siebeck], 1968, 1971). The English translation is *New Testament Apocrypha*, trans. and ed. R. M. Wilson (2 vols.; London: Lutterworth, 1963, 1965). The references here are to the German edition.

[15] Like a number of the other so-called "gospels" in the NT apocrypha, the "infancy gospels" do not really belong to the same literary genre as do the four canonical Gospels. Here we enter into the vexed question of the definition of "gospel" as a literary genre; see Charles H. Talbert, *What Is a Gospel?* (Philadelphia: Fortress, 1977); Philip L. Shuler, *A Genre for the Gospels* (Philadelphia: Fortress, 1982); David E. Aune, *The New Testament in Its Literary Environment* (Library of Early Christianity 8; Philadelphia: Westminster, 1987); idem, ed., *Greco-Roman Literature and the New Testament* (SBLSBS 21; Atlanta: Scholars, 1988) 107–26; Detlev Dormeyer and Hubert Frankemölle, "Evangelium als literarische Gattung und als theologischer Begriff," *Aufstieg und Niedergang der römischen Welt* II/25.2, 1543–1704. All these works—though with different emphases—favor the view that the canonical Gospels are a special form of ancient biography.

In my view, while the four canonical Gospels certainly show similarities to both Greco-Roman biographies (along with other types of contemporary literature, e.g., the "romance" or novel) and the biographical material present in the OT and developed in subsequent Jewish literature (e.g., Philo's *Life of Moses, The Lives of the Prophets*), they have enough special traits to qualify as a distinct genre. Following Aune's dictum that genre is constituted by content, form, and function *(The New Testament and Its Literary Environment,* 32–36), I define the genre of the Christian gospel as follows: a gospel is a narrative of the words and deeds of

Jesus of Nazareth, necessarily culminating in his death and resurrection, which narrative is meant to communicate to the believing audience the saving effects of the events narrated. The reader will notice that this definition attempts to include considerations of content, form, and function: constitutive of this gospel genre is a focus on Jesus of Nazareth, some treatment of both his words and his deeds during his public ministry in an overarching narrative form, the necessary and organic connection of that ministry with his death and resurrection as the ministry's climax, and the function of the narrative as mediating salvation to the later believing community.

It is here that I disagree strongly with the approach to defining "gospel" that Helmut Koester takes in his book *Ancient Christian Gospels. Their History and Development* (London: SCM; Philadelphia: Trinity, 1990) 44–47. Although Koester's book is a mine of information, his definition of gospel is vague and lacking in methodological rigor. For Koester, a gospel seems to include every major source that is taken into an acknowledged gospel as well as "all those writings which are constituted by the transmission, use, and interpretation of materials and traditions from and about Jesus of Nazareth" (p. 46). This is to cast the net exceedingly wide, as Koester himself immediately admits: "Obviously, such writings belong to different literary genres." But that is precisely the point at issue: gospel as a literary genre. Not every source (e.g., a chain of miracle stories or logia) that enters into the overarching genre of gospel is itself a gospel, nor is every document connected with or bearing the "Jesus tradition" ipso facto brought into the literary genre of gospel. The fact is that, for all their differences, the four canonical Gospels do fit into one literary genre (as I have defined it above), while most of the material Koester is interested in does not. Koester does not like that fact, so he dismisses the category of literary genre in favor of a vague approach more amenable to his purposes. From this basic disagreement over the definition of gospel stem many of my other disagreements with Koester's positions in his *Ancient Christian Gospels*.

If one accepts my definition, then certain documents that are called "gospels" today by critics such as Koester (e.g., the Q document and the *Gospel of Thomas*) do not really qualify because they contain very little or nothing of the deeds of Jesus during his public ministry and do not have a narrative culminating in the death and resurrection. Likewise, gnostic works like the *Gospel of Truth* are more philosophical tracts than gospels, despite their titles. Not every work that has the word "gospel" at the beginning or end of its manuscript qualifies as a gospel when it comes to literary genre. Other works, such as the *Gospel of Peter* or *Egerton Papyrus 2* might have been gospels in their original forms; but, since we have only fragments of these works, we cannot say whether or not they fit the definition given above.

A practical result of all this is that, when Koester ("Apocryphal and Canonical Gospels," 105–12) compares the attestation of "canonical" and "apocryphal" gospels in the 2d century, the evidence is skewed by the fact that on the one side stand the four complete canonical Gospels, while on the other side stand such works as the *Gospel of Thomas* and the *Protevangelium Jacobi*, which are not gospels as regards literary genre. For further problems with Koester's presentation of the question of attestation in the 2d century, see David F. Wright, "Apocryphal

Gospels: The 'Unknown Gospel' (Pap. Egerton 2) and the *Gospel of Peter,* "David Wenham, ed., *Gospel Perspectives. The Jesus Tradition Outside the Gospels* (Sheffield: JSOT, 1984) 207–32, esp. 208–10.

[16] Wolf-Dietrich Köhler *(Die Rezeption des Matthäusevangeliums in der Zeit vor Irenäus* [WUNT 2/24; Tübingen: Mohr (Siebeck) 1987] 429–36) documents the clear use of Matthew's Infancy Narrative; Köhler considers the use of Luke's Infancy Narrative to be even more frequent.

[17] Not to be confused with the Coptic *Gospel of Thomas* from Nag Hammadi; the former is a narrative about Jesus' childhood years, the latter a collection of sayings spoken by the risen Jesus. The *Infancy Gospel of Thomas* has a confusing and tangled tradition history, witnessed to by a number of versions in a number of languages. Since there is no real possibility of its containing any historical information of use to our quest, these matters of text criticism and tradition history may be ignored here. Köhler *(Rezeption,* 449–50) notes that the more recent Latin version has clear references to Matthew's Infancy Narrative, but references to Matthew in the longer Greek version are fewer and less clear.

[18] While this is the way Hennecke and Schneemelcher divide up and categorize the fragments *(Neutestamentliche Apokryphen,* 1. 76), it should be noted that agreement on precisely three Jewish-Christian gospels is by no means universal; some scholars, for instance, identify *The Gospel of the Hebrews* with *The Gospel of the Ebionites.* Johannes Quasten, on the other hand, apparently identifies the *Gospel of the Hebrews* with the *Gospel of the Nazarenes;* see his *Patrology. Vol. I. The Beginnings of Patristic Literature* (Westminster, MD: Christian Classics, 1950) 111–12.

[19] One regrets to report that Jerome and Epiphanius are not always reliable witnesses when reporting on these gospels. See, e.g., J. N. D. Kelly, *Jerome. His Life, Writings, and Controversies* (Westminster, MD: Christian Classics, 1975) 65: ". . . at Antioch . . . Jerome had those dealings with the Nazaraeans . . . which, if they ever took place at all, form one of the most obscure episodes of his career . . . . while we need not doubt that Jerome had some knowledge of the *Gospel of the Nazaraeans,* the trustworthiness of his more precise statements is open to the gravest suspicion . . . . as so often, his tendency to exaggerate his learning in his eagerness to impress has led him to transform into actual achievements what were at best plans or wistful hopes."

[20] Indeed, one might call it an Aramaic targum of our Greek Matthew. The Jewish phenomenon of "targumizing," i.e., translating paraphrastically the sacred Hebrew books into Aramaic, often with homiletic expansions and legendary accretions, may be mirrored to a certain degree in the explosion of apocryphal gospels in the 2d century A.D. One might ask whether such an explosion would have been possible without our Four Gospels, which during the 2d century were moving toward "sacred" and "canonical" status. It should be noted that Köhler *(Rezeption,* 298–300) does not accept the view of the *Gospel of the Nazarenes* as a paraphrase of Matthew; nevertheless, he states that Matthew is more important to the author of the *Gospel of the Nazarenes* than the other two Synoptics, if indeed he knew them.

[21] Köhler *(Rezeption,* 287) judges that the author of the *Gospel of the Ebionites* clearly knew both Matthew and Luke in their present form.

[22] It should be noted, however, that Köhler *(Rezeption,* 270) does not think that any parallel with Matthew's Gospel is probable.

[23] John Dominic Crossan, *The Cross That Spoke. The Origins of the Passion Narrative* (San Francisco: Harper & Row, 1988). Besides Crossan's account of the finding of the main manuscript, see also Koester *(Ancient Christian Gospels,* 216–40) and Wright, "Apocryphal Gospels," 207–32, esp. 221–27. Wright emphasizes the increased uncertainty inherent in all arguments about dependence or independence since the discovery of P. Oxy. 41. 2949 (two small papyrus fragments from Oxyrhynchus, dated ca. A.D. 200). In Wright's view, the two fragments are at some points closer to the Synoptics. But the overall impact of the new find is to remind us how fragmentary our evidence is for any position and how shaky any grand hypothesis must be. A detailed study of the two fragments that affirms their identity as part of the *Gospel of Peter* can be found in Dieter Lührmann, "POx 2949: EvPt 3–5 in einer Handschrift des 2./3. Jahrhunderts," *ZNW* 72 (1981) 216–26; see the summary of his position on p. 224.

[24] Interestingly, even Koester *(Ancient Christian Gospels,* 219–20), who supports Crossan's basic thesis of the independence of the *Gospel of Peter* from the canonical Gospels, has difficulties with aspects of Crossan's theory.

[25] Léon Vaganay, *L'évangile de Pierre* (EBib; Paris: Gabalda, 1930); Jerry W. McCant, *The Gospel of Peter: The Docetic Question Re-examined* (Unpublished doctoral dissertation; Atlanta: Emory University, 1978). It is curious that Crossan appeals to McCant's separate article on the *Gospel of Peter* when he denies docetic theology in the gospel, yet he never adverts to McCant's affirmation that the *Gospel of Peter* is dependent on the Synoptics; see Jerry W. McCant, "The Gospel of Peter: Docetism Reconsidered," *NTS* 30 (1984) 258–73, esp. 271 n. 15.

[26] Vaganay's minute examination of every possible parallel between the *Gospel of Peter* and the canonical Gospels contrasts favorably with the less thorough investigation of Jürgen Denker, *Die theologiegeschichtliche Stellung des Petrusevangeliums* (Europäische Hochschulschriften; Series 23, Theology; vol. 36; Bern: Herbert Lang; Frankfurt: Peter Lang, 1975). Köhler *(Rezeption,* 437–48) is not impressed by arguments from similar vocabulary but is convinced by McCant's argument from structure that the *Gospel of Peter* is dependent on Matthew.

[27] Koester *(Ancient Christian Gospels,* 220–40) takes a somewhat different approach. When examples of Matthean redactional reworking of Mark seem likely in the *Gospel of Peter* (e.g., Pilate's washing of his hands during the trial), Koester takes the view that both Matthew and the *Gospel of Peter* represent independent expressions of the same exegetical tradition that expanded the core narrative of Jesus' death by reflecting on various OT texts. When this type of explanation has to be employed repeatedly to save us from the embarrassment that the *Gospel of Peter* echoes redactional passages from the canonical Gospels, credulity is strained to the breaking point. Koester's position is weakened by a convoluted theory of the tradition-history of OT allusions that relies heavily on the *Epistle of*

Barnabas. The latest possible date of *Barnabas* is still disputed among scholars and makes its use for writing the prehistory of the Passion Narratives questionable; see Quasten, *Patrology. Vol. I,* 90–91.

[28] Joel B. Green ("The Gospel of Peter: Source for a Pre-Canonical Passion Narrative?" *ZNW* [1987] 293–301) gives a convenient list of the parallels in this story and in other similar instances (see especially pp. 298–301). Summing up his treatment of the story of the setting of the guard, Green affirms that, "given the large measure of verbal agreement between the two stories, it is difficult to avoid the conclusion that, in this story, underlying the Gospel of Peter is the Gospel of Matthew" (p. 301). Similar parallels with other Gospels lead Green to the conclusion that the *Gospel of Peter* "is dependent on the canonical Gospels" (p. 294).

[29] It should be emphasized that I am counting here only those cases where the singular or plural nominative of the present participle of *erchomai* (simple form of verb) is used in the predicate position as an accompaniment to the principal verb of action in a clause. Thus, I am not counting genitive absolutes, participles with accusatives after verbs of seeing, or *erchomenos* in the attributive position *(ho erchomenos).* This Matthean stylistic trait occurs with many other verbs as well.

[30] It is symptomatic of Denker's argument that he passes over this evidence for dependence with hardly a comment; see, e.g., *Die theologiegeschichtliche Stellung,* 74.

[31] Vaganay and McCant document this at great length, but again perhaps one small trait is especially telling: Jesus is never called "Jesus" throughout the whole of the *Gospel of Peter* (N.B.: in this, the supposed *Cross Gospel* differs not one wit from the rest of the document). The preferred nomenclature is the very Lucan "the Lord" *(ho kyrios),* with a number of other honorifics also used. The air and vocabulary of 2d-century Christian piety permeate the document just as "the Lord" does. It is not surprising that C. H. Dodd judges summarily: "The Gospel according to Peter, so far as it is preserved, contains a Passion-narrative which depends on all four canonical Gospels, and probably not on any independent tradition" ("A New Gospel," *New Testament Studies* [Manchester: Manchester University, 1953; repr. with corrections, 1967] 46). Koester, who argues for the *Gospel of Peter*'s independence ("Apocryphal and Canonical Gospels"), nevertheless admits: "Until recently, the almost universal judgment of scholars saw in this gospel [of Peter] secondary compilation on the basis of the canonical gospels" (p. 126). That consensus is reflected in C. Maurer's treatment of the gospel in *Neutestamentliche Apokryphen,* 1. 118–20; and in Quasten's judgment in *Patrology,* 114; see also Wright, "Apocryphal Gospels," 227.

[32] See the trenchant judgment of T. W. Manson, "The Life of Jesus: A Study of the Available Materials," *BJRL* 27 (1942–43) 323–37: "There is all the difference in the world between . . . the *[Infancy] Gospel of Thomas* and . . . the *Gospel of Peter. . . .* But they have one thing in common: They are fiction." In his study on criteria of authenticity, Francesco Lambiasi *(L'autenticità storica dei vangeli* [Studi biblici 4; 2d ed.; Bologna: EDB, 1986]) devotes a whole chapter to

the *Gospel of Peter* (pp. 171–84). He cautions against a wholesale rejection of the gospel as fantasy (p. 184), but only because he judges that in its narrative it follows the Synoptics and in its theology it follows John (p. 172).

[33] Raymond E. Brown, "The *Gospel of Peter* and Canonical Gospel Priority," *NTS* 33 (1987) 321–43. While Brown is especially addressing Crossan's treatment of the *Gospel of Peter*, he also refers to claims about the priority of the Coptic *Gospel of Thomas, Egerton Papyrus 2,* and the *Secret Gospel of Mark.* For a similar skeptical approach to the apocryphal gospels (presented in a more popular form), see Johannes B. Bauer, "Jesusüberlieferungen in den Apokryphen," *BK* 47 (1987) 158–61.

[34] John Dominic Crossan, *Four Other Gospels.* The book also contains a précis of Crossan's treatment of the *Gospel of Peter,* which was then fully developed in *The Cross That Spoke.*

[35] The four fragments come from three leaves of a codex and are often dated ca. the middle of the 2d century A.D. However, Koester *(Ancient Christian Gospels,* 206) reports the discovery of another small fragment, *Pap. Köln Nr. 255,* containing five lines, which its editor, Michael Gronewald, identifies as part of *Egerton Papyrus 2* and dates ca. 200.

[36] For the Greek text with translations and careful analysis, see Dodd, "A New Gospel," 12–52; also Wright, "Apocryphal Gospels," 207–32, esp. 210–21.

[37] C. H. Dodd, *The Interpretation of the Fourth Gospel* (Cambridge: Cambridge University, 1953). Others who hold dependence of this passage on John include F.-M. Braun, *Jean le théologien. I. Jean le théologien et son évangile dans l'église ancienne* (Paris: Gabalda, 1959) 87–94; C. K. Barrett, *The Gospel According to St John* (London: SPCK, 1955) 92; Raymond E. Brown, *The Gospel According to John* (AB 29 and 29A; Garden City, NY: Doubleday, 1966, 1970) 1. 229–30; Barnabas Lindars, *The Gospel of John* (NCB; London: Marshall, Morgan & Scott, 1972) 230; Ernst Haenchen, *John 1* (Hermeneia; Philadelphia: Fortress, 1980) 264; J. A. T. Robinson, *The Priority of John* (Oak Park, IL: Meyer-Stone, 1985) 317–18. It is interesting to note Koester's arguments for early, independent traditions in this section ("Apocryphal and Canonical Gospels," 120–21). As often in these cases, there is an appeal to a "carefully constructed unit" that flows well. Logically, that tells us that whoever wrote the unit is a good writer; if he had John's Gospel in front of him or in his memory, he is a good digester and compiler. One wonders where such an argument would get us in treating Matthew vis-à-vis Mark or Ephesians vis-à-vis Colossians. Moreover, sometimes the smooth flow and pellucid logic can be largely in the eye of the critic. Curiously, Koester seeks to bolster his case by pointing out that some elements are more Synoptic than Johannine (p. 121); this may merely indicate that the author knew at least one of the Synoptics (not necessarily all three!) as well as John. In the end, the judgment that a verse fits one context better than another is often very subjective; after a detailed study of *Egerton 2* and John, Braun *(Jean le théologien. I.,* 91) comes to a conclusion directly opposed to that of Koester: the material fits the context of the Fourth Gospel better than that of the papyrus. Braun's view is supported

by the careful analysis of Wright ("Apocryphal Gospels," 210–21), who points out that the order of verses in *Papyrus Egerton 2* is sometimes incoherent, especially in comparison to the parallels in the canonical Gospels.

[38] Note that this is different from the judgment of Crossan *(Four Other Gospels,* 75), who holds that, if there is any direct dependence at all, it may well be that Mark is literarily dependent on the form in *Egerton 2.* Koester *(Ancient Christian Gospels,* 215 n. 4) judges that Crossan "is possibly right."

[39] Even Koester, who is dedicated to finding early independent traditions in apocryphal gospels, admits that the source of the leprosy is "a later feature and reveals that the author had no knowledge of the Palestinian milieu" ("Apocryphal and Canonical Gospels," 122 n. 57). Lucien Cerfaux ("Parallèles canoniques et extra-canoniques de 'l'Evangile inconnu,' " *Recueil Lucien Cerfaux* [BETL 6–7; Gembloux: Duculot, 1954] 279–99) states that "everyone" recognizes that the pericope of the healing of the leper is inspired by the Synoptic Gospels. A detailed treatment of the healing of the leper pericope is given by Frans Neirynck, "Papyrus Egerton 2 and the Healing of the Leper," *ETL* 61 (1985) 153–60. Rejecting a complicated theory of M.-E. Boismard that would involve a proto-Luke, Neirynck reaffirms what he claims is the generally accepted opinion: dependence on the canonical Gospels, especially Luke (with possible echoes from the parable of the good Samaritan and the healing of the ten lepers); knowledge of Mark and Matthew is possible, though less certain. (At the end of this article, Neirynck pointedly rejects the approach of Koester and Crossan.) A similar view is held by Joseph A. Fitzmyer, *The Gospel According to Luke* (AB 28 and 28A; Garden City, NY: Doubleday, 1981, 1985) 1. 573. But Ernst Haenchen *(Der Weg Jesu* [2d ed.; Berlin: de Gruyter, 1968] 97) considers the pericope in the papyrus a "simplified Mark-text."

[40] For an approach that stresses what the author of *Egerton 2* might have *remembered* from the canonical Gospels, see Wright, "Apocryphal Gospels," 210–21.

[41] Joachim Jeremias's approach to *Egerton 2* is similar to mine, but he prefers to affirm that the author of the papyrus knew all four canonical Gospels and used them from memory for all the material except the nature miracle by the Jordan *(Neutestamentliche Apokryphen,* 1. 59). It seems to me that all that is absolutely demanded by a position that holds dependence on the canonical Gospels is knowledge of John and Luke, with knowledge of either Mark or Matthew as a further possibility. Crossan *(Four Other Gospels,* 74) sharply rejects Jeremias's view, noting that "Helmut Koester has rejoined sarcastically [to Jeremias's position] that Eger P 2 should then 'be treated as a spectacularly early witness for the four gospel canon' of the New Testament . . ." (see Koester, "Apocryphal and Canonical Gospels," 120). One must be careful about terminology here. Even if all four of what *we* call the canonical Gospels were known to the author of *Egerton 2,* that would not prove that there was a four-gospel *canon* recognized as such in the early 2d century. If we place the composition of *Egerton 2* close to what Crossan considers its latest possible date (ca. A.D. 120; so Crossan, *Four Other Gospels,* 69), there is nothing terribly surprising about its author knowing both

the Fourth Gospel and at least one of the Synoptics—especially since a papyrus fragment of the Fourth Gospel (Papyrus 52) dating from the first half of the 2d century has been discovered in Egypt (see Bruce M. Metzger, *Manuscripts of the Greek Bible* [New York/Oxford: Oxford University, 1981] 62). If *Egerton 2* should be placed closer to A.D. 200, the problem of its author knowing a number of the canonical Gospels totally disappears. Whether *Egerton 2* was actually written in Egypt is another question; the discovery of Papyrus 52 in Egypt certainly does not prove that the Fourth Gospel was written there. All it proves is that the Egyptian climate was more conducive to the preservation of papyri than was the climate of many other parts of the Roman Empire. A sober conclusion from the papyri finds is that John's Gospel received wide acceptance in Egypt earlier than did at least some of the Synoptics, and that Egypt was a hotbed for the composition of apocryphal gospels in the 2d century.

[42] A prime example of how the fragmentary nature of some apocryphal gospels can lead to opposite conclusions on the part of scholars, even when they are closely aligned on many points, is the disagreement between Koester and Crossan on this section. Koester ("Apocryphal and Canonical Gospels," 122–23) seems to suppose that this apophthegm is complete and is an instance of those apophthegmata in which Jesus rejects a question and refuses to give an appropriate answer (cf. Luke 12:13–14). Jesus refuses to deal with such secular matters, which is not the case in the Synoptic version of the coin-of-tribute story. Taking the opposite view, Crossan *(Four Other Gospels,* 80) complains that such authors as Joachim Jeremias and Ron Cameron (Koester is not mentioned) take for granted that the pericope comes to an end, while in fact it is not clear that originally Jesus' reply did not follow, but is now lost in the lacuna. All this points up a major problem in building such monumental hypotheses on such a slim basis: the paucity of material allows for much theorizing and little verification.

[43] The Greek *basileus* was the regular title for the Roman emperor in the eastern part of the empire.

[44] Dodd, "A New Gospel," 21. After these observations, Dodd concludes that *Egerton 2* is probably later than Luke-Acts and not earlier than the period when the form "Rabbi X" as a set title became common use among the Jews.

[45] See Crossan, *Four Other Gospels,* 77–87, esp. 86. Curiously, he never addresses Dodd's position in favor of a dating of the story after Luke-Acts.

[46] The other fragments are so small and the text on them so limited that no conclusion can be drawn from them.

[47] As noted already, one drawback of Crossan's whole approach in dealing with the apocryphal material is that he tends to spin unnecessarily complex hypotheses, when simpler ones can explain the data quite adequately. Köhler *(Rezeption,* 451–52) restricts himself to a consideration of Matthean influence on the story of the leper. He notes that the introductory phrase is closer to Matthew than to Mark or Luke, but admits that one cannot place too much weight on that observation. While he leaves open the question of *Egerton 2*'s dependence on the canonical Gospels, he does think that, from the viewpoint of tradition

history, the papyrus represents a more recent stage of the gospel tradition than do the canonical Gospels.

[48] The scholarly form of publication was *Clement of Alexandria and a Secret Gospel of Mark* (Cambridge, MA: Harvard University, 1973); the popular form is *The Secret Gospel* (New York: Harper & Row, 1973).

[49] See, e.g., Quentin Quesnell, "The Mar Saba Clementine: A Question of Evidence," *CBQ* 37 (1975) 48–67. Morton Smith replied vigorously in his "On the Authenticity of the Mar Saba Letter of Clement," *CBQ* 38 (1976) 196–99, to which Quesnell responded in "A Reply to Morton Smith," *CBQ* 38 (1976) 200–3. That the letter of Clement is actually a pious forgery is maintained by Eric Osborn, "Clement of Alexandria: A Review of Research, 1958–1982," *The Second Century* 3 (1983) 219–44, esp. 223–25. While Osborn notes some Greek words that do not appear elsewhere in Clement, his major argument is from the ideas in the letter that are contrary to Clement's usual positions. Writing ten years after the original publication of Clement's letter, Smith summed up the situation thus: ". . . most scholars would attribute the letter to Clement, though a substantial minority are still in doubt" ("Clement of Alexandria and Secret Mark: The Score at the End of the First Decade," *HTR* 75 [1982] 449–61).

[50] See the review of Smith's *Clement of Alexandria* by Patrick W. Skehan, *CHR* 60 (1974) 451–53; Skehan notes that Smith himself (p. 78) quotes Theodor Zahn on Clement's gullibility: "His amazingly uncritical attitude to apocryphal literature exceeds anything to be found in other Church fathers."

[51] Smith, *Clement of Alexandria*, 450–52, with photographs of the manuscript on opposite sides of the pages.

[52] See the summary of Smith's conclusions in *Clement of Alexandria*, 194.

[53] Crossan, *Four Other Gospels*, 119–20.

[54] Helmut Koester, "History and Development of Mark's Gospel (From Mark to *Secret Mark* and 'Canonical' Mark)," *Colloquy on New Testament Studies. A Time for Reappraisal and Fresh Approaches*, ed. Bruce Corley (Macon, GA: Mercer University, 1983) 35–57, esp. 54–57. See also his earlier reflections, "Apocryphal and Canonical Gospels," 105–30. More recently, Koester has presented an updated and slightly altered version of his theory in his *Ancient Christian Gospels*, 295–303.

[55] Hans-Martin Schenke, "The Mystery of the Gospel of Mark," *The Second Century* 4 (1984) 65–82, esp. 75–76.

[56] See his presentation in *Clement of Alexandria*, 195–278, which acts as a preliminary sketch for his book *Jesus the Magician*.

[57] Frans Neirynck, "La fuite du jeune homme en Mc 14, 51–52," *ETL* 55 (1979) 43–66. Neirynck calls attention to the intriguing point that the author of *Secret Mark* seems to have brought together all the occurrences of the noun *neaniskos* ("young man") in the Synoptic Gospels: Mark 14:51; 16:5; Luke 7:14; Matt 19:20, 22. Neirynck goes on to show many other contacts with the Synop-

tics. Curiously, though Crossan *(Four Other Gospels,* 193) lists a number of Neirynck's articles on Mark, he does not note this one.

⁵⁸ Raymond E. Brown, "The Relation of 'The Secret Gospel of Mark' to the Fourth Gospel," *CBQ* 36 (1974) 466–85. Brown wisely speaks in terms of possibilities; the extremely limited nature of the data in the fragment of the *Secret Gospel* we possess hardly allows for absolute certitude. Nevertheless, Skehan (in his review of Smith, *CHR* 60 [1974] 452) states firmly: ". . . a dependence on the canonical John is, in the reviewer's judgment, unmistakable. . . ."

⁵⁹ Robert M. Grant, "Morton Smith's Two Books," *ATR* 56 (1974) 58–64. On pp. 60–61, Grant shows how the whole of *Secret Mark* could easily be put together by a 2d-century Christian who searched the canonical Gospels in order to correlate what he thought were the same persons in all Four Gospels. Grant then puts this within the larger context of the tendency of 2d-century Christians to create gospel parallels and composite gospels. In my view, this may be the true *Sitz im Leben* for many of our apocryphal gospels.

⁶⁰ Helmut Merkel, "Auf den Spuren des Urmarkus?" *ZTK* 71 (1974) 123–44, esp. 130–36. To his sharp critique Smith responded with an equally sharp rejoinder, "Merkel on the Longer Text of Mark," *ZTK* 72 (1975) 133–50.

⁶¹ A gospel that circulated in Egypt in the 2d century. We have only a few fragments, culled from citations in the Church Fathers. The tone seems to have been severely ascetic ("encratite") and/or gnostic. Negative views are expressed concerning sexuality, especially the woman's role in childbearing. Quasten summarizes the situation when he says *(Patrology,* 113): "The *Gospel of the Egyptians* belongs to that class of apocrypha which were written for the support of certain heresies. It is most probably of Gnostic origin."

⁶² In its present form, *The Acts of Pilate* (later joined to the *Descent of Christ into Hades* to form *The Gospel of Nicodemus)* comes from the 4th or 5th century. An earlier form of the *Acts* may go back to the 2d century, but scholars are not agreed on whether Justin Martyr's references to an *Acts of Pilate* have anything to do with the document we know. It is possible, instead, that our *Acts of Pilate* were written at the beginning of the 4th century to counteract a pagan *Acts of Pilate* that slandered Christ (Quasten, *Patrology,* 116).

⁶³ James M. Robinson, "Jesus: From Easter to Valentinus (or to the Apostles' Creed)," *JBL* 101 (1982) 5–37.

⁶⁴ The date of the discovery has been variously given as 1945 or 1946—indeed, at times 1947 has even been mentioned. That the real date was about December 1945 is affirmed in a careful study of the events surrounding and subsequent to the find; see James M. Robinson, "From the Cliff to Cairo," *Colloque international sur les textes de Nag Hammadi (Québec, 22–25 août 1978)* (Bibliothèque Copte de Nag Hammadi, Section Etudes 1; ed. Bernard Barc; Quebec: Les presses de l'université Laval; Louvain: Peeters, 1981) 21–58, esp. 29.

⁶⁵ Coptic is the latest form of the ancient Egyptian language. In the early Christian era it began to be written in the Greek alphabet, augmented by seven

characters taken from the popular form of Egyptian known as demotic. It came into use in the 2d century A.D. and developed as an almost exclusively Christian language with numerous Greek loanwords. The *Gospel of Thomas*, for instance, is studded with various Greek words, from technical religious terms *(mathētēs*, disciple; *aggelos*, angel) to ordinary nouns *(thalassa*, sea; *petra*, rock), conjunctions *(hina*, so that), and particles (the Greek *de*, often best left untranslated).

⁶⁶ When the term "gospel" is used of such works as the *Gospel of Truth*, the word is being used to designate the content, the "good news" the document claims to contain, and *not* the literary genre.

⁶⁷ Christopher Tuckett, *Nag Hammadi and the Gospel Tradition* (Studies of the New Testament and Its World; Edinburgh: Clark, 1986) 149. In n. 553 on p. 149, Tuckett adds that this judgment "should not exclude the possibility of the existence of tradition lying on trajectories which are independent of those leading to and from the synoptic gospels. . . ." He suggests that such traditions might be present, e.g., in the *Apocryphon of James* and the *Second Apocalypse of James*. Since both of these works present discourses of the risen Jesus that have a clearly gnostic coloration, I do not think that they have anything to contribute to a quest for the historical Jesus.

Especially to be noted is Tuckett's rejection (pp. 128–35) of Koester's claim that the *Dialogue of the Savior* contains pre-Synoptic forms of the Jesus tradition. Tuckett finds the influence of Matthew's Gospel (with cases of Matthean redaction being used in the *Dialogue)* and probably influence from Luke as well. These results are of special interest in light of their similarity to what we shall see in the case of the *Gospel of Thomas* below. For Koester's article, see Helmut Köster [note the German spelling of the name], "Dialog und Spruchüberlieferung in den gnostischen Texten von Nag Hammadi," *EvT* 39 (1979) 532–56.

⁶⁸ Tuckett, *Nag Hammadi*, 150.

⁶⁹ Köhler, *Rezeption*. Köhler divides the cases into three categories: (1) Dependence on Matthew seems quite possible, but not positively provable in *Treatise on Resurrection, Tripartite Tractate, Book of Thomas the Contender, Dialogue of the Savior, First Apocalypse of James, Second Apocalypse of James*, and *The Concept of Our Great Power*. (2) Dependence seems quite possible or even probable in *Gospel of Truth, Exegesis on the Soul, Second Treatise of the Great Seth, Teachings of Silvanus, Letter of Peter to Philip*, and *Testimony of Truth*. (3) Dependence seems very probable in *Apocryphon of James, Gospel of Thomas, Gospel of Philip, Sophia of Jesus Christ, Acts of Peter and the Twelve Apostles, Apocalypse of Peter*, and *Interpretation of Knowledge*. Köhler's general conclusion is striking *(Rezeption*, 425): The overall picture of Matthew's Gospel in the Christian writings at Nag Hammadi is the same as that of the reception of Matthew elsewhere in the 2d century A.D. These writings clearly presuppose Matthew as an important, indeed in some cases the most important, in any case the widely accepted "ecclesial" Gospel. Thus they are witnesses to a development whose most important stage is Justin Martyr—a development whereby Matthew became the "chief gospel."

⁷⁰ See Christopher Tuckett's article, "Thomas and the Synoptics," *NovT* 30

(1988) 132–57. Tuckett wryly notes (p. 132) how either side in the debate has declared that the majority of scholars favor its view. For the original published form of the *Gospel of Thomas* in Coptic with an English translation, see A. Guillaumont et al., eds., *The Gospel According to Thomas. Coptic Text Established and Translated* (Leiden: Brill; New York/Evanston: Harper & Row, 1959). The critical edition is *Nag Hammadi Codex II, 2–7. Vol. One. Gospel According to Thomas, Gospel According to Philip, Hypostasis of the Archons, and Indexes* (NHS 20; ed. Bentley Layton; Leiden: Brill, 1989). The introduction to the *Gospel of Thomas,* by Helmut Koester, is found on pp. 38–49. A convenient list of Synoptic parallels to the *Gospel of Thomas* is found on pp. 46–47. The volume also contains the Greek fragments of the Oxyrhynchus papyri 1, 654, and 655, edited by Harold W. Attridge; see pp. 96–128. For a detailed bibliographical survey of the debate over the *Gospel of Thomas,* see Francis T. Fallon and Ron Cameron, "The Gospel of Thomas: A Forschungsbericht and Analysis," *Aufstieg und Niedergang der römischen Welt* II/25.6, 4195–251; the treatment of the relationship of *Thomas* to the canonical Gospels is found on pp. 4213–24, with a list of authors favoring dependence or independence. Fallon and Cameron rightly observe (p. 4213): "On this issue [the relation of *Thomas* to the Synoptics] scholars remain sharply divided and have not yet reached a conclusion that would solve the problem to everyone's satisfaction."

For a defense of the position that the material in the *Gospel of Thomas* parallel to material in the canonical Gospels is basically independent of the canonical Gospels, see Koester, *Ancient Christian Gospels,* 84–124. Koester must strain to assign special M and L material to Q in order to preserve his theory that the parallel material in *Thomas* reflects the supposedly earlier stage of the redaction of Q. The strain becomes severe when *Thomas* at times apparently parallels phrasing that probably comes from the redactional activity of Matthew or Luke and when Koester must breathe new life into the old theory of a more primitive version of Mark's Gospel, supposedly reflected in *Thomas.* Koester's explanations become so convoluted that the view that *Thomas* does reflect knowledge of the written canonical Gospels must be judged the more likely hypothesis. Nevertheless, Koester's treatment is useful for its review of the material and of recent bibliography. For an approach that is more cautious than Koester's, but still open to finding some authentic, independent Jesus traditions in *Thomas,* see Bruce Chilton, "The Gospel According to Thomas as a Source of Jesus' Teaching," *Gospel Perspectives. The Jesus Tradition Outside the Gospels,* 155–75. More skeptical, especially with reference to the parable material, is Craig L. Blomberg, "Tradition and Redaction in the Parables of the Gospel of Thomas," ibid., 177–205. On the whole question, see Michael Fieger, *Das Thomasevangelium* (NTAbh 22; Münster: Aschendorff, 1991).

[71] The enumeration of 114 sayings is not in the Coptic manuscript but has become traditional among editors and commentators. At times, though, the division into 114 sayings may be misleading; some material intended to be read as a unit by the final editor may now be unhappily divided. On this point, and on the danger of supposing that the *Gospel of Thomas* is a simple, primitive collection of sayings, see Boudewijn Dehandschutter, "L'évangile de Thomas comme collec-

tion de paroles de Jésus," *Logia.—Les Paroles de Jésus.—The Sayings of Jesus* (BETL 59; ed. Joël Delobel; Leuven: Peeters/Leuven University, 1982) 507–15, esp. 511–13.

[72] For a comparison of the texts of the papyri and the *Gospel of Thomas*, see Joseph A. Fitzmyer, "The Oxyrhynchus Logoi of Jesus and the Coptic Gospel according to Thomas," *Essays on the Semitic Background of the New Testament* (SBLSBS 5; Missoula, MT: Scholars, 1974) 355–433, with abundant bibliography on both the papyri and the gospel; and the critical edition by Attridge in the Brill volume, *Nag Hammadi Codex II, 2–7. Vol. One*, 96–128. Attridge (pp. 97–99) dates P. Oxy. 1 shortly after A.D. 200, P. Oxy. 654 in the middle of the 3d century, and P. Oxy. 655 between 200 and 250. Hence the three papyri are not parts of the same manuscript. Attridge thinks that it is unclear whether the Oxyrhynchus papyri represent a different recension of the sayings from that of the Coptic *Gospel of Thomas;* it remains possible that they are the same recension.

[73] The reworking of typical Synoptic parables (the foolish rich man who suddenly dies, the great supper, the murderous tenants of the vineyard) to convey gnostic theology is made clear by Jean-Marie Sevrin in his essay, "Un groupement de trois paraboles contre les richesses dans l'Evangile selon Thomas. EvTh 63, 64, 65," *Les paraboles évangéliques. Perspectives nouvelles*, ed. Jean Delorme (Paris: Cerf, 1989) 425–39.

[74] Bentley Layton, *The Gnostic Scriptures* (Garden City, NY: Doubleday, 1987); his introduction to the *Gospel of Thomas* is on pp. 376–79, the text of the gospel on pp. 380–99. A different introduction and translation may be found in James M. Robinson, ed., *The Nag Hammadi Library in English* (3d ed.; San Francisco: Harper & Row, 1988) 124–38.

[75] See saying 29.

[76] See saying 28.

[77] See saying 37.

[78] See Crossan, *Four Other Gospels*, 32: ". . . [in the *Gospel of Thomas* we find] a vision where the first things have returned rather than the last things are present."

[79] See sayings 3 and 113.

[80] See sayings 79 and 114. Alternately, the duality of male and female sex is to be overcome in favor of the original unity and integration of the kingdom of light (see saying 22). Crossan tries to maintain that the gospel is ascetic rather than gnostic *(Four Other Gospels,* 31), but that is to ignore other elements of the gnostic myth implied in various sayings.

[81] See saying 1.

[82] See saying 111.

[83] The translation is basically that of Layton, but I have also consulted and sometimes used the English translations in the original 1959 edition of the *Gospel*

of Thomas, in Robinson's *Nag Hammadi Library in English,* trans. Thomas O. Lambdin, and the translation by Bruce M. Metzger in the appendixes of Kurt Aland, ed., *Synopsis quattuor evangeliorum* (Stuttgart: Württembergische Bibelanstalt, 1964) 517–30. I place the number of the saying in parentheses immediately after the saying.

[84] The most significant attempt to deny this is found in Stevan L. Davies, *The Gospel of Thomas and Christian Wisdom* (New York: Seabury, 1983). Davies argues that in no meaningful sense is Thomas gnostic. The ideas of the gospel come from Jewish wisdom and apocalyptic traditions, with the wisdom stream dominant (pp. 3, 79). Davies's book is a learned tour de force, but he must constantly argue against the obvious sense of the data. As we have seen, the gnostic meaning is supposed to be hidden in the sayings, to be discovered like a treasure by those who have the hermeneutical key of the gnostic myth, which is explicated in other works of Layton's "school of St. Thomas." Davies never comes to grips with the elements of pantheism/polytheism, self-salvation through self-knowledge, radical dualism, and the rejection of matter, body, and sex found in some of the sayings. I find it incredible that Davies would claim that "Thomas has something of the dualism of John, but it has a far more positive view of the world than does John. Thomas has something of the antagonism toward the flesh we find in Paul, but this is less emphatic than in Paul" (p. 146).

Similarly, I cannot accept Gilles Quispel's distinction, according to which the *Gospel of Thomas* is encratite, but not gnostic ("The *Gospel of Thomas* Revisited," 254–55); the encratite element is there, but it is part of a larger mythic worldview, which I think is rightly designated gnostic. I would also disagree with the evaluation of Crossan *(Four Other Gospels,* 31), who claims that the gospel "still stands on the borders between Catholic and Gnostic Christianity." I think the material we have reviewed shows that the border into gnosticism has been crossed, at least in the final form of the gospel. Contrast with the views of Davies and Crossan the position of Robert M. Grant (with David N. Freedman), *The Secret Sayings of Jesus* (Garden City, NY: Doubleday, 1960) 113: "It [the *Gospel of Thomas]* goes far beyond John, however, because its contents have been immersed in Gnosticism. . . ." Also in favor of seeing the *Gospel of Thomas* as gnostic is Jacques E. Ménard, "Thomas, Gospel of," *IDBSup,* 904–5.

[85] I do not deny that, to varying degrees, NT books like Colossians, Ephesians, the Epistle to the Hebrews, and especially the Gospel of John reflect a "gnosticizing tendency" present in various streams of 1st-century Christianity. But this is not the same thing as the gnosticism of the final form of the *Gospel of Thomas,* where the spirits of the saved are actually preexistent particles of the divine that unfortunately have become divided from their divine source, have tragically entered the evil world of matter and the human body, and are now called back to a knowledge of their divine origin and essence by a Jesus who is really consubstantial with the very people he saves. All this, plus the fierce asceticism that rejects all sexuality and the implication that humans who are not made up of the divine essence are excluded a priori from salvation, is simply not the Christianity represented by any of the admittedly varied views of the canonical books of the NT. One wonders whether even the adversaries of Paul at

Corinth, of the author of the Epistle to the Ephesians, or of the author of the First Epistle of John went as far as the redactor of the *Gospel of Thomas.*

[86] Hence, Davies's startling claim that the *Gospel of Thomas* should be dated ca. A.D. 50–70 falls to the ground. It is not surprising that most scholars have not rallied to his position.

[87] Ménard states in his article on "Thomas, Gospel of," in *IDBSup,* 902: "The Greek original [of the *Gospel of Thomas*] . . . has always been dated about A.D. 140, and there are so far no reasons to modify that conclusion." He places the Coptic version at the end of the 2d century in his *L'Evangile selon Thomas* (NHS 5; ed. Martin Krause; Leiden: Brill, 1975) 3.

[88] Gilles Quispel, "The Gospel of Thomas and the New Testament," *Gnostic Studies* (Publication de l'Institut historique et archéologique néerlandais de Stamboul 34, 2; 2 vols.; Leiden: Nederlands Historisch-Archaeologisch Institut te Istanbul, 1975) 2. 3–16 (reprinted from *VC* 11 [1957] 189–207). Vol. 2 of *Gnostic Studies* contains many of Quispel's earlier articles on the *Gospel of Thomas* and on Jewish Christianity. Many of his subsequent articles on this topic are listed by Tuckett, "Thomas and the Synoptics," p. 137 n. 21. Quispel's suggestion concerning the *Gospel of the Hebrews* has not received general support, since this merely seeks to explain the obscure by the more obscure. It is therefore not surprising that in his later writings Quispel prefers to leave unnamed the Jewish-Christian gospel on which Thomas depends; see his "The *Gospel of Thomas* Revisited," *Colloque international sur les textes de Nag Hammadi (Québec, 22–25 août 1978)* (Bibliothèque Copte de Nag Hammadi, Section Etudes 1; ed. Bernard Barc; Quebec: Les presses de l'université Laval; Louvain: Peeters, 1981) 218–66.

[89] Jacques E. Ménard, "Les problèmes de l'Evangile selon Thomas," *Essays on the Nag Hammadi Texts in Honour of Alexander Böhlig* (NHS 3; ed. M. Krause; Brill: Leiden, 1972) 59–73, esp. 59–62.

[90] Joachim Jeremias, *The Parables of Jesus* (rev. ed.; London: SCM, 1963).

[91] Helmut Koester, *Introduction to the New Testament. Vol. Two. History and Literature of Early Christianity* (Berlin/New York: de Gruyter, 1982) 152; see also his article, "Apocryphal and Canonical Gospels," esp. 112–19; his introduction to the *Gospel of Thomas* in *The Nag Hammadi Library in English,* 124–26; his introduction to the *Gospel of Thomas* in the Brill critical edition, *Nag Hammadi Codex II, 2–7. Vol. One,* 38–49.

[92] Ron Cameron, *The Other Gospels. Non-Canonical Gospel Texts* (Philadelphia: Westminster, 1982) 24–25.

[93] Davies, *The Gospel of Thomas and Christian Wisdom,* 4–5 (appealing to Quispel and Koester); he thinks that the independent nature of the sayings is one of the strongest indications that the *Gospel of Thomas* comes from the 1st century.

[94] James M. Robinson, "On Bridging the Gulf from Q to the Gospel of Thomas (or Vice Versa)," *Nag Hammadi, Gnosticism and Early Christianity,* ed. C. Hedrick and R. Hodgson (Peabody, MA: Hendrickson, 1986) 127–75, esp. 162–

63: at least the parables in the *Gospel of Thomas* are as old as or older than the composition of Q.

[95] Crossan, *Four Other Gospels*, 35: the sayings in the *Gospel of Thomas* are completely independent of the canonical tradition; but Crossan wisely emphasizes that independent does not necessarily mean earlier and earlier does not necessarily mean better. Unlike his treatment of other documents in the *Four Other Gospels* (*Gospel of Peter, Papyrus Egerton 2, Secret Gospel of Mark*), Crossan's view of the *Gospel of Thomas* does not suggest that the four canonical Gospels are in any way dependent on the tradition in the *Gospel of Thomas*. The two traditions are mutually independent.

[96] So Davies, *The Gospel of Thomas and Christian Wisdom*, 5. Needless to say, there is a danger here of a certain *ipse dixitism*.

[97] So, e.g., Quispel, "The Gospel of Thomas and the New Testament," 6, 15; Ménard, "Les problèmes de l'Evangile selon Thomas," 59–60; Cameron, *The Other Gospels*, 24.

[98] Crossan, who is more careful than many in his articulation of this argument, emphasizes that this argument has force only when one can show that the redactor of the *Gospel of Thomas* had no reason to remove the redactional traits of the canonical Gospels (*Four Other Gospels*, 36–37). Crossan thinks that such an argument has been constructed by John H. Sieber in a 1966 dissertation done at the Claremont Graduate School in California (*A Redactional Analysis of the Synoptic Gospels with Regard to the Question of the Sources of the Gospel according to Thomas* (available from Ann Arbor, MI: Microfilms International).

[99] Ménard, "Les problèmes de l'Evangile selon Thomas," 60. But since many authors hold that the *Gospel of Thomas* comes from a Syrian milieu, an Aramaic background to some of the sayings does not tell us very much.

[100] Crossan, *Four Other Gospels*, 35–36. The authors mentioned here are meant to be only representative of those holding the position of independence; the list could easily be extended to include, e.g., H. Montefiore, W. D. Davies, W. C. Van Unnik, C. H. Hunzinger, and J. Leipoldt.

[101] It should be emphasized that not everyone who shares Koester's view of Thomas' independence vis-à-vis the Synoptics also accepts his further theories about the nature and dating of the gospel and of its tradition. Quispel, e.g., speaks of Koester's "radical and extreme views" ("The *Gospel of Thomas* Revisited," 227).

[102] H. E. W. Turner, "The Gospel of Thomas: Its History, Transmission and Sources," in Hugh Montefiore and H. E. W. Turner, *Thomas and the Evangelists* (SBT 35; London: SCM, 1962) 11–39, esp. 39.

[103] Grant, *The Secret Sayings of Jesus*, 113.

[104] Robert M. Grant, *Gnosticism and Early Christianity* (rev. ed.; New York: Harper & Row, 1966) 185–86.

[105] Sevrin, "Un groupement de trois paraboles," 425–39, esp. 438–39.

[106] Bertil Gärtner, *The Theology of the Gospel according to Thomas* (New York: Harper & Brothers, 1961).

[107] Kurt Rudolph, *Gnosis. The Nature and History of Gnosticism* (San Francisco: Harper & Row, 1987) 263.

[108] Dehandschutter, "L'évangile de Thomas," 513–15. As will become clear in what follows, Dehandschutter is a strong opponent of those who see independent tradition in Thomas; he attributes all Synoptic-like sayings to the Synoptic Gospels. For a sample of his approach, see "Les paraboles de l'Evangile selon Thomas. La Parabole du Trésor caché (log. 109)," *ETL* 47 (1971) 199–219; idem, "La parabole de la perle (Mt 13, 45–46) et l'Evangile selon Thomas," *ETL* 55 (1979) 243–65.

[109] Wolfgang Schrage, *Das Verhältnis des Thomas-Evangeliums zur synoptischen Tradition und zu den koptischen Evangelienübersetzungen* (BZNW 29; Berlin: Töpelmann, 1964); see the summary of his views on pp. 1–11. It is surprising to see how infrequently Schrage is cited, let alone discussed, by proponents of the independence of the *Gospel of Thomas*. His findings show that there is less of a solid consensus than is sometimes claimed.

[110] As with those defending independence, the list of authors defending the dependence of the *Gospel of Thomas* on the canonical Gospels is only representative of a much larger group including, among others, E. Haenchen, R. Kasser, R. Schippers, and H. K. McArthur.

[111] See Tuckett, "Thomas and the Synoptics," 134–35. Tuckett observes that one must allow for the possibility that, when the Greek *Gospel of Thomas* was translated into Coptic, the language of the *Gospel of Thomas* was assimilated to that of the Coptic NT. Moreover, there is the problem that the Oxyrhynchus papyri show us that the Coptic *Gospel of Thomas* was probably not always an exact translation of its Greek source, either in wording or in the order of the sayings. Finally, in the course of the history of the transmission of the text, the Coptic *Gospel of Thomas* could have been assimilated secondarily to the Coptic versions of the canonical Gospels.

[112] Tuckett, "Thomas and the Synoptics," 157. Tuckett is careful about what conclusions the fact of Thomas' dependence on redactional material in the Synoptics allows us to draw. Such examples, he points out, indicate that *in some cases* Thomas is dependent on the Synoptics; there could be Synoptic-like sayings that reached Thomas by another route. Tuckett suggests that, methodologically, it may be impossible to prove dependence or independence in cases where the Synoptic-like sayings in Thomas contain only traditional material, without redactional traits.

While Tuckett's cautions are well taken, I think that one must add to his analysis of redactional traits an investigation of the broad sweep of material parallel to the Synoptics and John that is contained in Thomas (see my treatment below). When these two data (redactional traits in individual sayings and a broad range of sayings representing all the strands of the Gospel tradition) are put together, I think the burden of proof must lie with anyone wishing to assert that, even in just some parallel sayings, Thomas is independent of the canonical Gospels.

[113] For a consideration of the differences between an orally proclaimed gospel and the written Gospels, see Werner H. Kelber, *The Oral and the Written Gospel* (Philadelphia: Fortress, 1983). In my opinion, while Kelber makes a valid point, he tends to exaggerate the differences into a gaping abyss.

[114] I think this is true even for most of the Apostolic Fathers, in particular Ignatius of Antioch and probably the author (at least the final author) of the *Didache*, who seem to know and use Matthew's Gospel; see my discussion in Raymond E. Brown and John P. Meier, *Antioch and Rome* (New York/Ramsey, NJ: Paulist, 1983) 24–25, 81–82. Accordingly, I am skeptical of Helmut Koester's attempt to show that many of the Apostolic Fathers are dependent on oral tradition and not the written Synoptic Gospels when they use material parallel to Synoptic sayings. For Koester's position, see Helmut Köster [note the German spelling], *Synoptische Überlieferung bei den apostolischen Vätern* (TU 65; Berlin: Akademie, 1957). For views that stress much more the influence of the Gospel of Matthew on patristic writers before the time of Irenaeus, see Edouard Massaux, *Influence de l'évangile de saint Matthieu sur la littérature chrétienne avant saint Irénée* (Universitas catholica Lovanensis 2/42; Louvain: Publications universitaires, 1950; repr. with supplements, Louvain: University Press, 1986) esp. 94–135 for Ignatius; in a more careful, critical vein, Köhler, *Rezeption*, 73–96 for Ignatius.

I think Koester has an arguable case with regard to *1 Clement*—which is not surprising, since *1 Clement* is the only Apostolic Father clearly from the 1st century, being written not too long after Matthew and possibly even before John and Luke-Acts. It is significant that while Köhler usually decides in favor of probable knowledge of Matthew on the part of the Apostolic Fathers, he states that the question of *1 Clement* must remain open *(Rezeption,* 72). For a number of the other Apostolic Fathers, Köhler thinks that knowledge of Matthew's Gospel is very probable or nearly certain; this is his judgment on the *Didache (Rezeption,* 55), Polycarp *(Rezeption,* 109–10), and *2 Clement (Rezeption,* 147–49). In the case of the *Letter of Barnabas,* the *Shepherd of Hermas,* and the *Letter to Diognetus,* Köhler gives a rating of "quite possible," but not "probable" *(Rezeption,* 122–23, 125–28, 159). However, I would not want to create the impression that almost all scholars would agree with my view or that of Köhler. For example, Donald A. Hagner ("The Sayings of Jesus in the Apostolic Fathers and Justin Martyr," *Gospel Perspectives. The Jesus Tradition Outside the Gospels,* 233–68) not only favors independent oral tradition in *1 Clement* but also argues in favor of independent oral tradition and against dependence on the canonical Gospels for almost all of the patristic writers before Justin. Also in favor of independent oral tradition rather than dependence on Matthew and Luke in the case of the *Didache* is Jonathan Draper, "The Jesus Tradition in the Didache," ibid., 269–87.

In my view, while Koester may have a good case in the one instance of *1 Clement*, once he arrives at Ignatius of Antioch (and beyond), he is arguing against the most natural reading of the data. This is especially true of a famous passage in Ignatius, *Smyrneans* 1:1, which alludes to Matt 3:15, a redactional verse that inserts typically Matthean language into a Marcan context. The best Koester can do in this case is to argue that Ignatius' dependence on Matthew is indirect, by way of some otherwise unknowable kerygmatic or creedal formula. (I argue this point at greater length in a collection of essays by various scholars entitled *Social History of the Matthean Community: Cross-Disciplinary Approaches to an Open Question* [Minneapolis: Fortress, 1991] 176–84.) It is perhaps not by accident that, in his *Ancient Christian Gospels,* Koester treats other Ignatian passages in his main text while relegating *Smyrneans* 1:1 to a brief footnote (p. 8 n. 1).

It is basically because I disagree with Koester's whole approach to the Fathers that I do not consider a separate treatment of patristic material to be required by the goals of my book. While I will keep an eye on the patristic citations of Jesus' words as I move through the Jesus tradition, I do not think that, on the whole—with the exception of *1 Clement* and possibly the *Didache*—they offer any independent access to the historical Jesus. Moreover, even if a good deal of the material investigated by Hagner and Draper does represent independent variants of the gospel tradition, nothing substantially new about the historical Jesus is added to our data base.

[115] It is quite possible that some of the Church Fathers cite the Synoptics from Gospel harmonies or catechetical collections of sayings of the Lord that in turn depend on the Synoptic Gospels.

[116] Crossan, *Four Other Gospels,* 35–36. Grant *(Gnosticism and Early Christianity,* 185) notes that one of the striking features of the *Gospel of Thomas* is its tendency to combine sayings found separately in the Synoptic Gospels and to change the order of the sayings: "Such combinations and alterations were common among Christian writers of the second century, but they were especially characteristic of Gnostics." Grant observes that the gnostic group known as the Naassenes (who used the *Gospel of Thomas)* gives a perfect example of this kind of conflation and reordering of sayings: in a single saying the Naassenes bring together John 6:53–56; Matt 5:20; 18:3; John 3:5; Mark 10:38; John 8:21; 13:33.

[117] Tuckett, "Thomas and the Synoptics," 139. The saying on "splitting the wood," which appears in Oxyrhynchus Papyrus 1 as the end of saying 30, is part of the second half of saying 77 in the Coptic *Gospel of Thomas.* The reason for the regrouping seems to be the link word in *Gospel of Thomas* saying 77a+b; both halves of the spliced verse contain the Coptic verb meaning "attain" or "split." See the comments by Fitzmyer, "The Oxyrhynchus Logoi," 397–401.

[118] See H. J. Held, "Matthew as Interpreter of the Miracle Stories," in G. Bornkamm, G. Barth, and H. J. Held, *Tradition and Interpretation in Matthew* (New Testament Library; Philadelphia: Westminster, 1963) 165–299.

[119] For a salutary warning against a simplistic view of how the Synoptic traditions developed, see E. P. Sanders, *The Tendencies of the Synoptic Tradition* (SNTSMS 9; Cambridge: Cambridge University, 1969).

[120] See H. Baltensweiler, "Die Ehebruchsklauseln bei Matthäus. Zu Matth. 5,

32; 19, 9," *TZ* 15 (1959) 340–56. For possible exceptions, see E. Bammel, "Markus 10,11f. und das jüdische Eherecht," *ZNW* 61 (1970) 95–101.

[121] Sevrin, "Un groupement de trois paraboles," 438–39.

[122] There is nothing unusual about a redactor who usually abbreviates his material suddenly expanding it when it suits his purposes. Matthew, who usually shortens Mark's miracle stories, will at times expand them in order to insert verses that serve his theological program; see, e.g., Matthew's special material about Peter walking on the water, inserted into the Marcan story of Jesus walking on the water (Mark 6:45–52; Matt 14:22–33, esp. vv 28–31).

[123] I construct my argument on the basis of this broad "spread" of material, with a secondary consideration of possible redactional elements, especially from Matthew. Independently, Tuckett ("Thomas and the Synoptics," 145–56) constructs his argument from redactional elements, mostly from Luke and Mark. I think that the convergence and complementarity of the two approaches reinforce an important conclusion: at least in some sayings, the dependence of Thomas on the canonical Gospels is fairly clear.

[124] Although Köhler remains very reserved in his judgment, allowing that in some places the *Gospel of Thomas* may have preserved a form of the tradition earlier than the Synoptics' form, he nevertheless decides, on the basis of Synoptic redactional traits, that in its present form the *Gospel of Thomas* (notably in the parables) presupposes the Synoptics in general and Matthew's Gospel in particular *(Rezeption,* 385–86). In Köhler's view, very probable cases of dependence on Matthew include sayings 33, 34, and 99 (pp. 386–88).

[125] Commenting on Matt 15:13–14, Francis W. Beare *(The Gospel According to Matthew* [Peabody, MA: Hendrickson, 1981] 339) remarks: "Matthew's insertion is partly of his own composition, but the saying about the blind leading the blind [i.e., v 14] is found as a separate 'parable' in Luke. . . ." Presumably, then, it is v 13 that Beare considers to be Matthew's "own composition." Georg Strecker mentions Matt 15:12–14 among the passages that convey Matthew's redactional polemic against the Pharisees; he refers to 15:12–14 as "a redactionally inserted apophthegm" *(Der Weg der Gerechtigkeit* [FRLANT 82; 3d ed.; Göttingen: Vandenhoeck & Ruprecht, 1971] 139). Reinhart Hummel likewise refers to 15:13–14 as the "Matthean insertion into the controversy dialogue on levitical purity" *(Die Auseinandersetzung zwischen Kirche und Judentum im Matthäusevangelium* [BEvT 33; 2d ed.; Munich: Kaiser, 1966] 152). Supporting this view is the fact that the phrase "my heavenly Father" (with the adjectival form *ouranios)* occurs only in Matthew within the NT; *phyteia* (plant) occurs nowhere else in the NT.

Tuckett ("Thomas and the Synoptics," 143–44) prefers to argue for redactional elements in Matt 15:11 (saying 14 in Thomas), though he notes possible objections to seeing 15:11 as Matthew's own work rather than as the result of a Mark-Q overlap.

[126] Schrage *(Verhältnis,* 124–25) shows that Thomas' form of the parable pre-

supposes Matthew's and would not make sense without Matthew's version in the background. Ménard *(L'Evangile selon Thomas,* 158) is of the same opinion. It is striking that the Coptic text of the parable uses the Greek word for "weed" *(zizanion)* four times; the word occurs in the NT only in Matthew's parable of the wheat and the weeds and in its subsequent explanation (eight times in all). Schrage observes that it is difficult to decide what Thomas understood by the parable. Perhaps the (good) seed is the soul and the weed is the body; alternately, the seed could be the gnostic and the weed the nongnostic.

[127] Schrage *(Verhältnis,* 173) concludes that dependence on Matthew is the most probable solution. Ménard *(L'Evangile selon Thomas,* 191) thinks Thomas has edited the Matthean text here.

[128] I concentrate here on the special material in Matthew because it is especially abundant in the *Gospel of Thomas* and offers some of the best candidates for redactional traits of a canonical evangelist being taken over by Thomas. Tuckett ("Thomas and the Synoptics," 156) holds that Thomas "shows links with material that is due to the redactional activity of all three synoptic evangelists." He thinks examples of redactional elements from Mark and Luke are more "significant" because it may well be that Matthew was the most widely used Gospel at the time and that therefore assimilation of the wording of Thomas to a Coptic version of Matthew "would not be unexpected" (p. 137).

[129] Fitzmyer *(The Gospel According to Luke,* 2. 994) comments on Luke 12:49 vis-à-vis saying 10 in the *Gospel of Thomas:* "Logion 10 is almost certainly a derivative of the Lucan v. 49. . . ."

[130] This is a prime example of what Grant has highlighted elsewhere in the *Gospel of Thomas,* namely, the tendency of Thomas to tear apart the order of sayings in any Synoptic Gospel to create his own clusters of material, ordered according to leitmotifs and catchwords. Schrage *(Verhältnis,* 165–66) sees this logion as a combination of two pieces of Luke's special tradition and decides that Thomas is here dependent on Luke's Gospel.

[131] Schrage *(Verhältnis,* 30–31) thinks that saying 113 is dependent on Luke 17:20–21 and that therefore dependence on Luke in saying 3 is also possible. While commenting on saying 3, Ménard *(L'Evangile selon Thomas,* 81) states that, "in any case, the compiler knew Luke 17:20–21, cf. logion 113."

[132] By a slip of the pen, Tuckett cites this as Oxyrhynchus Papyrus 1.

[133] The point becomes very clear when the three texts are compared:

ou gar estin ti krypton, ean mē hina phanerōthē	(Mark 4:22a)
ou gar estin krypton ho ou phaneron genēsetai	(Luke 8:17)
[ou gar est]in krypton ho ou phane[ron genēsetai]	(POxy 654)

The papyrus is unfortunately fragmentary, but the basic agreements of the papyrus with Luke's redactional form over against Mark are clear: no *ti* as in

Mark, *ho ou* instead of Mark's *ean mē hina.* As Tuckett points out ("Thomas and the Synoptics," 146), the Greek papyrus is especially important because it proves that the agreement with Luke instead of Mark predates the translation of Thomas into Coptic; thus, assimilation of the saying to the Lucan text by the Coptic translator is excluded. What is even more intriguing about this papyrus fragment is that the words just before the Lucan parallel may correspond to Matthew's redactional form of the Marcan saying, if Fitzmyer's reconstruction is correct (Fitzmyer, "The Oxyrhynchus Logoi," 381):

ouden gar estin kekalymmenon ho ouk apokalyphthēsetai (Matt 10:26)

[to kekalymmenon] apo sou apokalyph< th > ēsetai soi (POxy 654)

If we accept Fitzmyer's reconstruction, it appears that the author of the papyrus has meshed a redactional form from Matthew with a redactional form from Luke. Schrage *(Verhältnis,* 35) also holds for Thomas' dependence on the Lucan redaction of Mark.

[134] Saying 55 borrows redactional elements from both Luke 14:26 ("cannot be my disciple") and Matthew 10:37 ("is not worthy of me"); so Ménard *(L'Evangile selon Thomas,* 157). Schrage *(Verhältnis,* 58–59) holds that saying 16 is dependent on both Matthew and Luke, but primarily Luke; Ménard (p. 103) concurs.

[135] This seems to be a Mark-Q overlap, which offers a special opportunity to the redaction critic; see Tuckett, "Thomas and the Synoptics," 148–53. Schrage *(Verhältnis,* 62–63) holds for dependence on Matthew, Mark, and Luke; similarly, Ménard, *L'Evangile selon Thomas,* 109.

[136] It should be noted that material from the triple tradition will at times be closer to the Matthean or Lucan version and therefore does not automatically prove knowledge of Mark's Gospel. Sevrin ("Un groupement de trois paraboles," 433–34) holds that the parable of the murderous tenants (saying 65) basically follows the Lucan form, with traces of Matthew and Mark; this eclecticism seems typical of Thomas' treatment of the Synoptic material. At times, though, specifically Marcan elements seem to peep through the version in Thomas; this is Tuckett's view of sayings 9 and 20 ("Thomas and the Synoptics," 148–56). Schrage *(Verhältnis,* 139) speaks of a mixed form, a mosaic made up of elements from all three Synoptics.

Michel Hubaut *(La parabole des vignerons homicides* [Cahiers de la Revue Biblique 16; Paris: Gabalda, 1976]) suggests that Thomas' version shows definite dependence on Luke and very probably dependence on either Mark or a primitive version of the parable. Against any possibility of a primitive non-Synoptic source is B. Dehandschutter ("La parabole des vignerons homicides (Mc., XII, 1–12) et l'Evangile selon Thomas," *L'Evangile selon Marc. Tradition et rédaction* [BETL 34; ed. M. Sabbe; Leuven: Leuven University; Gembloux: Duculot, 1974] 203–19), who emphasizes the influence of the Lucan version. Dehandschutter also rejects the idea that, in the parable of the tenants, Luke used a special source that was also known to Thomas; see his "L'Evangile selon Thomas: témoin d'une tradition prélucanienne?" *L'Evangile de Luc. Problèmes littéraires et théo-*

logigues. Mémorial Lucien Cerfaux (BETL 32; ed. F. Neirynck; Gembloux: Duculot, 1973) 287–97. Also skeptical of a non-Synoptic source in Thomas' version is K. R. Snodgrass, "The Parable of the Wicked Husbandmen: Is the Gospel of Thomas Version the Original?" *NTS* 21 (1974–75) 142–44.

¹³⁷ See Raymond E. Brown, "The Gospel of Thomas and St John's Gospel," *NTS* 9 (1962–63) 155–77. He states on p. 174: "Obviously, the affinity of John in *GTh* [the *Gospel of Thomas*] is not nearly so clear or so strong as the affinity to the Synoptic Gospels."

¹³⁸ Grant, *The Secret Sayings of Jesus*, 107.

¹³⁹ See Brown, "The Gospel of Thomas," esp. 158–74.

¹⁴⁰ Ibid., 175–76.

¹⁴¹ In correspondence dated Oct. 15, 1990, David Noel Freedman suggested to me that such an otherwise unknown Greek conflation of the Four Gospels probably preceded the famous Diatessaron of Tatian, which was simply the culmination of a much larger tendency toward conflated texts. Such a process of conflation might help explain the present order of the sayings in the *Gospel of Thomas*.

¹⁴² Yet, as Ménard suggests *(L'Evangile selon Thomas,* 101), the end of the saying probably reflects Matt 15:11, which, unlike Mark 7:15, uses the word "mouth" in the saying, as does Thomas' saying 14. Note the similarity and differences among the three versions:

[There] is nothing outside a man which, going into him, can defile him. But those things coming out of a man are what defile a man.   (Mark 7:15)

Not what goes into the mouth defiles a man, but what comes out of the mouth, that defiles a man.   (Matt 15:11)

For what goes into your mouth will not defile you, but what comes out of your mouth, that is what will defile you.   *(Thomas,* 14)

Thus, once again, we see Thomas' tendency to mesh different sayings from different places in different Gospels to create his own verbal and theological "collage."

¹⁴³ R. Bultmann *(Die Geschichte der synoptischen Tradition* [FRLANT 29; 8th ed.; Göttingen: Vandenhoeck & Ruprecht, 1971] 191) thinks that Mark himself has added the "polemical citation" to the parable. See also D. E. Nineham, *The Gospel of St Mark* (Pelican NT Commentaries; Harmondsworth: Penguin, 1963) 313; Haenchen, *Der Weg Jesu*, 399–402.

¹⁴⁴ "Cornerstone" might also be translated as "building stone," "foundation stone," or "keystone." Significantly, Thomas does not speak of the Psalm verse as a text of Scripture *(graphē)* as does Mark (and, with slightly different wording, Matthew and Luke); there is no place in Thomas' vision for OT prophecy being fulfilled in the death and resurrection of Jesus. Schrage *(Verhältnis,* 143) observes that Matthew and Luke have already begun the process of detaching the citation

from the parable by using a fresh introductory formula for the citation (Matt 21:42; Luke 20:17).—Sevrin ("Un groupement de trois paraboles," 433–36) suggests that it is the tenants, not the owner, of the vineyard who are the positive figures in Thomas' version of the story. This would certainly fit in both with Thomas' silence about any punishment of the tenants and with the general tendency of gnostic exegesis to subvert and reverse the usual sense of Scripture.

[145] Schrage *(Verhältnis,* 123) suggests that a gnostic would understand the phrase to mean "crucify the world" or "strip oneself of the world."

[146] It always remains theoretically possible that some individual stray saying in the *Gospel of Thomas* (or many other 2d-century documents) might actually come from Jesus. For example, many scholars like Jeremias *(Unknown Sayings of Jesus,* 66–73) are fond of saying 82: "He that is near me is near the fire; he that is far from me is far from the kingdom." As I have already indicated, I do not think Jeremias's reasoning persuasive. But one thing should be readily admitted: no method can control the haphazard or random occurrence in history that runs counter to the general impression the data give. But such an isolated, random datum would make no difference in the overall picture we draw of Jesus.

[147] This remark is made *only* with reference to the quest for the historical Jesus. All these documents have great value for the history of early Christianity in the patristic period. Unfortunately, 20th-century American culture is not terribly interested in patristics and Church history, and so some scholars feel constrained to justify their research by creating links with the historical Jesus. It is this "selling" of research to the American public and academies on specious grounds that I find objectionable. On the question of the apocryphal gospels, see also Howard Clark Kee, *What Can We Know about Jesus?* (Cambridge: Cambridge University, 1990) 28–39.

CHAPTER 6

CRITERIA:

How Do We Decide What Comes from Jesus?

In the previous chapters we have seen that, in our quest for the historical Jesus, we are dependent, for the most part, on the four canonical
Gospels. Since these Gospels are suffused with the Easter faith of the
early Church and were written from forty to seventy years after the
events narrated, we are left asking: How can we distinguish what comes
from Jesus (Stage I, roughly A.D. 28–30) from what was created by the
oral tradition of the early Church (Stage II, roughly A.D. 30–70) and what
was produced by the editorial work (redaction) of the evangelists (Stage
III, roughly A.D. 70–100)?[1] All too often, popular books on Jesus pick and
choose among the Gospel stories in a haphazard way, the authors deciding at any given moment that what strikes them as reasonable or plausible is therefore historical.[2] More technical books usually enunciate rules
for judging the Gospel material ("criteria of historicity"), but the rules
sometimes seem to be forgotten when the Gospel pericopes are treated
in detail.[3] In this chapter, I will spell out which rules of judgment (i.e.,
"criteria") are helpful in reaching a decision about what material comes
from the historical Jesus.[4]

Granted the nature of ancient history in general and the nature of
the Gospels in particular, the criteria of historicity will usually produce
judgments that are only more or less probable; certainty is rarely to be
had.[5] Indeed, since in the quest for the historical Jesus almost anything
is possible, the function of the criteria is to pass from the merely possible to the really probable, to inspect various probabilities, and to decide

which candidate is most probable. Ordinarily, the criteria cannot hope to do more.[6]

Scholars seem to vie with one another to see who can compile the longest list of criteria.[7] Sometimes a subtle apologetic motive may be at work: so many criteria surely guarantee the results of our quest! More sober scholars, instead, are no doubt seeking as many controls as possible over the difficult material. Often, however, what is naturally a single criterion is "chopped up" to create a number of criteria; and what are at best secondary, if not dubious, criteria are mixed in with truly useful ones. I agree with Occam that categories are not to be multiplied without necessity. Hence I prefer to distill five "primary" criteria from the many suggested. After we have looked at these five, we will consider four "secondary" (some would say "dubious") criteria; some of these secondary criteria may at times offer post-factum confirmation of decisions we have already reached on the basis of the five primary critera.

PRIMARY CRITERIA

1. The Criterion of Embarrassment

The criterion of "embarrassment" (so Schillebeeckx) or "contradiction" (so Meyer) focuses on actions or sayings[8] of Jesus that would have embarrassed or created difficulty for the early Church. The point of the criterion is that the early Church would hardly have gone out of its way to create material that only embarrassed its creator or weakened its position in arguments with opponents. Rather, embarrassing material coming from Jesus would naturally be either suppressed or softened in later stages of the Gospel tradition, and often such progressive suppression or softening can be traced through the Four Gospels.[9]

A prime example is the baptism of the supposedly superior and sinless Jesus by his supposed inferior, John the Baptist, who proclaimed "a baptism of repentance for the forgiveness of sins."[10] Mysterious, laconic, stark Mark recounts the event with no theological explanation as to why the superior sinless one submits to a baptism meant for sinners (Mark 1:4–11). Matthew introduces a dialogue between the Baptist and Jesus prior to the baptism; the Baptist openly confesses his unworthiness to baptize his superior and gives way only when Jesus commands him to do so in order that God's saving plan may be fulfilled (Matt 3:13–17, a passage marked by language typical of the evangelist). Luke finds a striking solution to the problem by narrating the Baptist's imprisonment by Herod before relating the baptism of Jesus; Luke's version never tells us who baptized Jesus (Luke 3:19–22). The radical Fourth Evangelist, John, locked as he is in a struggle with latter-day disciples of the Baptist who refuse to recognize Jesus as the Messiah, takes the radical expedient of suppressing the baptism of Jesus by the Baptist altogether; the event simply never occurs in John's Gospel. We still hear of the Father's witness to Jesus and the Spirit's descent upon Jesus, but we are never told when this theophany occurs (John 1:29–34). Quite plainly, the early Church was "stuck with" an event in Jesus' life that it found increasingly embarrassing, that it tried to explain away by various means, and that John the Evangelist finally erased from his Gospel. It is highly unlikely that the Church went out of its way to create the cause of its own embarrassment.

A similar case is the affirmation by Jesus that, despite the Gospels' claim that he is the Son who can predict the events at the end of time, including his own coming on the clouds of heaven, he does not know the exact day or hour of the end. Almost at the conclusion of the eschatological discourse in Mark 13, Jesus says: "But concerning that day or hour no one knows, neither the angels in heaven, nor the Son, but only the Father" (Mark 13:32). It is not surprising that a few later Greek manuscripts simply dropped the words "nor the Son" from the saying in Mark.[11] A significantly larger number of manuscripts omit "nor the Son" in the parallel verse in Matthew (Matt 24:36), which was more widely used in the patristic Church than Mark—hence the desire to suppress the embarrassing phrase especially in Matthew.[12] The saying is simply not taken over by Luke. In John, not only is there nothing similar, but the Fourth Evangelist goes out of his way to stress that Jesus knows all things present and future and is never taken by surprise (see, e.g., John 5:6; 6:6; 8:14; 9:3; 11:11–15; 13:1–3,11). Once again, it is highly unlikely that the Church would have taken pains to invent a saying that emphasized the ignorance of its risen Lord, only to turn around and seek to suppress it.

An intriguing corollary arises from these cases of "embarrassment." All too often the oral tradition of the early Church is depicted as a game of "anything goes," with charismatic prophets uttering anything or everything as the words of the Lord Jesus and storytellers creating accounts of miracles and exorcisms according to Jewish and pagan models. The evangelists would simply have crowned this wildly creative process by molding the oral tradition according to their own redactional theology. One would get the impression that throughout the first Christian generation there were no eyewitnesses to act as a check on fertile imaginations, no original-disciples-now-become-leaders who might exercise some control over the developing tradition, and no striking deeds and sayings of Jesus that stuck willy-nilly in people's memories. The fact that embarrassing material is found as late as the redaction of the Gospels reminds us that beside a creative thrust there was also a conservative force in the Gospel tradition.[13] Indeed, so conservative was this force that a string of embarrassing events (e.g., baptism by John, betrayal by Judas, denial by Peter, crucifixion by the Romans) called forth agonized and varied theological reflection, but not, in most cases, convenient amnesia.[14] In this sense, the criterion of embarrassment has an importance for the historian far beyond the individual data it may help verify.

Like all the criteria we will examine, however, the criterion of embarrassment has its limitations and must always be used in concert with the other criteria. One built-in limitation to the criterion of embarrassment is that clear-cut cases of such embarrassment are not numerous in the Gospel tradition; and a full portrait of Jesus could never be drawn with so few strokes. Another limitation stems from the fact that what we today might consider an embarrassment to the early Church was not necessarily an embarrassment in its own eyes. A prime example is Jesus' "cry of dereliction" from the cross: "My God, my God, why have you forsaken me?" (Mark 15:34; Matt 27:46; the words are a citation of Ps 22:1). At first glance, this seems a clear case of embarrassment; the unedifying groan is replaced in Luke by Christ's trustful commendation of his spirit to the Father (Luke 23:46) and in John by a cry of triumph, "It is accomplished!" (John 19:30).

But the matter is not so simple. True, the cry of dereliction does not fit the later theological agendas of Luke or John. But form-critical studies of the Passion Narrative show that the earliest stages of the passion tradition used the OT psalms of lamentation, especially the psalms of the suffering just man, as a primary tool for theological interpretation of the narrative.[15] By telling the story of Jesus' passion in the words of these psalms, the narrative presented Jesus as the one who fulfilled the OT pattern of the just man afflicted and put to death by evildoers, but vindicated and raised up by God. Allusions to, rather than direct quotations of, these psalms are woven throughout the Passion Narrative. A good example is the dividing of Jesus' garments. The words of Psalm 22:19 are made part of the narrative in Mark 15:24, Matt 27:35, and Luke 23:34; only John marks off the words as a citation of Scripture (John 19:24).

Therefore, it is not very surprising, from a form-critical point of view, that the dramatic first words of Psalm 22 supply the climax of the crucifixion and Jesus' last words in Mark's Gospel. The cry is by no means so unedifying or even scandalous as moderns might think. The OT psalms of lamentation regularly direct forceful complaints to God; their strong—to our ears, irreverent—address to God expresses neither doubt nor despair, but the pain of one who fully trusts that a strangely silent God can act to save if he so chooses. The very bitterness of the complaint paradoxically reaffirms the closeness the petitioner feels to this God he dares confront with such boldness. From the Babylonian exile to Auschwitz, pious Jews have used the words of Psalm 22 and other laments without being accused by their fellow religionists of impiety or despair.

Granted the roots of the Passion Narrative in the psalms of lamentation, as well as the bold address to God in those psalms—well understood by early Christian Jews but often misunderstood since—there is no reason for thinking that the earliest Christians (Jews who knew their Scriptures well) would have found the "cry of dereliction" at all embarrassing. Whether or not Jesus actually spoke Ps 22:1 on the cross, the criterion of embarrassment, taken in isolation, cannot establish the historicity of those words. It is not impossible that all of the "seven last words"—including the "cry of dereliction"—represent the theological interpretation of the early Church and the evangelists. But that is a question we will have to face later. The point here is that the criterion of embarrassment—like any other criterion—must not be invoked facilely or in isolation.

2. THE CRITERION OF DISCONTINUITY

Closely allied to the criterion of embarrassment,[16] the criterion of discontinuity (also labeled dissimilarity, originality, or dual irreducibility) focuses on words or deeds of Jesus that cannot be derived either from Judaism at the time of Jesus or from the early Church after him.[17] Examples often given are his sweeping prohibition of all oaths (Matt

5:34,37; but cf. Jas 5:12), his rejection of voluntary fasting for his disciples (Mark 2:18–22 parr.), and possibly his total prohibition of divorce (Mark 10:2–12 par.; Luke 16:18 par.).

This criterion is at once the most promising and the most troublesome. Norman Perrin hails it as the fundamental criterion, the basis of all reconstructions, since it gives us an assured minimum of material to work with.[18] But the criterion is not without its detractors. Morna Hooker complains that the criterion presupposes what we do not possess: a sure and full knowledge of what Judaism at the time of Jesus and Christianity right after him were like, and what they could or would not say.[19]

Her objection does remind us of the healthy modesty required of any historian delving into the religious scene of 1st-century Palestine. Yet historical-critical work of the last two centuries has made notable advances in our understanding of 1st-century Judaism and Christianity. Moreover, one cannot overlook the glaring difference between knowledge about Jesus on the one hand and knowledge about 1st-century Judaism and Christianity on the other. We do have 1st-century documents coming directly from the latter movements—Qumran, Josephus, and Philo for Judaism, most of the NT for Christianity—to say nothing of important archaeological finds. We have no such documents coming directly from Jesus. Indeed, Professor Hooker's own work on the Son of Man title presupposes that we know something about early Judaism and Christianity and can apply such knowledge to outstanding problems. No doubt our present-day judgments will need correction by future generations of scholars. But if we were to wait until we possessed a fullness of knowledge that excluded later revision, we would postpone all NT scholarship until the parousia.[20]

A more serious objection is that the criterion of discontinuity, instead of giving us an assured minimum about Jesus, winds up giving us a caricature by divorcing Jesus from the Judaism that influenced him and from the Church that he influenced. Jesus was a 1st-century Jew whose deeds and sayings the early Church revered and handed on.[21] A complete rupture with religious history just before or just after him is a priori unlikely. Indeed, if he had been so "discontinuous," unique, cut off from the flow of history before and after him, he would have been unintelligible to practically everyone. To be an effective teacher (which Jesus seems to have been by almost every scholar's admission) means adapting oneself to the concepts and positions of one's audience, even if one's purpose is to change those concepts and positions. No matter how original Jesus was, to be a successful teacher and communicator he would have had to submit himself to the constraints of communication, the constraints of his historical situation.[22] To paint a portrait of Jesus completely divorced from or opposed to 1st-century Judaism and Christianity is simply to place him outside of history.

Imagine, for the sake of argument, that in the 16th century Martin Luther had delivered all his teachings orally and that they had been written down only later on by his disciples. If we excluded from the record of Luther's words and deeds everything that could be paralleled in late medieval Catholic authors before him or in 17th-century Lutheran theologians after him, how much would remain—and would it give anything like a representative portrait of Luther?

Hence, while the criterion of discontinuity is useful, we must guard against the presupposition that it will automatically give us what was central to or at least fairly representative of Jesus' teaching. By focusing narrowly upon what may have been Jesus' "idiosyncrasies," it is always in danger of highlighting what was striking but possibly peripheral in his message.[23] Especially with this criterion, complementary and balancing insights from other criteria are vital.

Of course, the same need for balance and correction holds true for the emphasis on Jesus' historical continuity with Judaism and early Christianity. In the case of Judaism in particular, we always have to pose the question: With what sort or branch or tendency of Judaism was Jesus "continuous" in a given saying or action? Moreover, just as we are not to decide that Jesus *must* have been discontinuous with the Judaism of his day in this or that matter, so we cannot decide a priori that he *must* have been in agreement with Judaism in all things. History does have its Luthers and Spinozas. One is surprised, for instance, to read E. P. Sanders's summary judgment on the historicity of Jesus' statement that all foods are clean (Mark 7:15). Without going into detailed arguments, Sanders simply declares: "In this case the saying attributed to Jesus . . . appears to me to be too revolutionary to have been said by Jesus himself."[24] In a sense, Sanders simply takes Perrin's view of the primacy of the criterion of discontinuity and stands it on its head. Instead of "if it is discontinuous, it must be from Jesus," we now have "if it is discontinuous, it cannot be from Jesus." Obviously, dogmatism in either direction must give way to a careful testing of claims in each case.

A further problem that often bedevils the criterion of discontinuity is a terminological one. Scholars will claim that this criterion isolates what is "unique" to Jesus. "Uniqueness" is a slippery concept in historical investigation. In some sense, Beethoven may be hailed as a "unique genius" in music, but that hardly means that individual aspects of his music cannot be found in composers like Bach before him or Mahler after him. Indeed, while it is hard enough for an individual like Beethoven to be "uniquely" different from anyone who has preceded him, it is asking far too much to require as well that he be "uniquely" different from all who follow. The gifted individual could hardly control that, and the more outstanding he was, the more likely he would be to have imitators.[25] Perhaps Beethoven's uniqueness is to be located instead in the special configuration of his personality, talent, production, and career, seen as a whole in a particular historical context, rather than in any one aspect of his work, seen in isolation.

Something similar might be said of the uniqueness of Jesus. When dealing with an individual saying or deed of Jesus, perhaps it is better to speak of what is "strikingly characteristic" or "unusual" in Jesus' style of speaking or acting, instead of claiming uniqueness at every turn. This distinction is especially important when we treat such characteristic phrases as "Amen, I say to you" or "Abba" addressed to God in prayer. Since we are not terribly well informed about popular Jewish-Aramaic religious practices and vocabulary in early 1st-century Galilee, modesty in advancing claims is advisable. Similarly, when we deal with the public actions of Jesus, it may be wiser to speak of "the sort of things Jesus did" (e.g., exorcisms, faith healings) instead of asserting that a particular story tells us precisely what Jesus did on one particular occasion. The same distinction can be applied to the sayings tradition taken as a whole. We can have some hope of learning the basic message of Jesus, the "kind of thing" he usually or typically said (the *ipsissima vox*).[26] Rarely if ever can we claim to recover his exact words (the *ipsissima verba*).

3. The Criterion of Multiple Attestation

The criterion of multiple attestation (or "the cross section") focuses on those sayings or deeds of Jesus that are attested in more than one independent literary source (e.g., Mark, Q, Paul, John) and/or in more than one literary form or genre (e.g., parable, dispute story, miracle story, prophecy, aphorism).[27] The force of this criterion is increased if a given motif or theme is found in both different literary sources and different literary forms.[28] One reason that critics so readily affirm that Jesus did speak in some sense of the kingdom of God (or kingdom of heaven) is that the phrase is found in Mark, Q, special Matthean tradition, special Lucan tradition, and John,[29] with echoes in Paul, despite the fact that "kingdom of God" is not Paul's preferred way of speaking.[30] At the same time, the phrase is found in various literary genres (e.g., parable, beatitude, prayer, aphorism, miracle story). Granted this wide sweep of witnesses in different sources and genres, coming largely from the first Christian generation, it becomes extremely difficult to claim that such material is simply the creation of the Church.[31]

When one moves from general motifs and phrases to precise sayings and deeds, one cannot usually expect such a broad range of attestation. Still, such key sayings as Jesus' words over the bread and wine at the Last Supper (Mark 14:22–25; 1 Cor 11:23–26; cf. John 6:51–58) and his prohibition of divorce (Mark 10:11–12; Luke 16:18 [= Q]; 1 Cor 7:10–11) are found in two or three independent sources.[32] Then, too, we may find "cross-referencing" between sayings dealing with a particular topic and actions of Jesus that also touch on that topic—e.g., sayings about the destruction of the Jerusalem temple and Jesus' prophetic "cleansing" of the temple. The example of the destruction of the temple is all the more forceful when we notice that both sayings and dramatic action are witnessed in more than one source and context (e.g., Mark 13:2; 14:58; John 2:14–22, esp. v 19).

Harvey K. McArthur was so taken with the force of the criterion of multiple attestation that he asserted that it was "the most objective" criterion and should be given first place.[33] Yet even McArthur admitted that multiple attestation was not an infallible indicator of historicity. In an individual case it is not a priori impossible that a saying invented early on by a Christian community or prophet met the needs of the Church so perfectly that it rapidly entered into a number of different strands of tradition.[34] Then, too, the mere fact that a saying occurs only in one source is no proof that it was not spoken by Jesus.[35] For example, the Aramaic invocation *Abba* ("my own dear Father") occurs on the lips of Jesus only once in all four Gospels (Mark 14:36), yet many critics ascribe it on other grounds to the historical Jesus. Once again, we are reminded that no criterion can be used mechanically and in isolation; a convergence of different criteria is the best indicator of historicity.

4. THE CRITERION OF COHERENCE

The criterion of coherence (or consistency or conformity) can be brought into play only after a certain amount of historical material has been isolated by the previous criteria. The criterion of coherence holds that other sayings and deeds of Jesus that fit in well with the preliminary "data base" established by using our first three criteria have a good chance of being historical (e.g., sayings concerning the coming of the kingdom of God or disputes with adversaries over legal observance). As can be readily seen, this criterion, by its very nature, is less probative than the three on which it depends.[36] Since we should not conceive of the earliest Christians as totally cut off or different from Jesus himself, there is no reason why they could not have created sayings that echoed faithfully his own "authentic" words. In a loose sense such derived sayings could be considered "authentic" insofar as they convey the message of the historical Jesus;[37] but they cannot be considered "authentic" in the technical sense, i.e., actually coming from Jesus himself.[38]

Despite this limitation, the criterion of coherence has a certain positive use, namely, broadening an already established data base. One must, however, be wary of using it negatively, i.e., declaring a saying or action inauthentic because it does not seem to be consistent with words or deeds of Jesus already declared authentic on other grounds. Jesus would hardly be unique among the great thinkers or leaders of world history if his sayings and actions did not always seem totally consistent to us.[39] Moreover, we must remember that ancient Semitic thought, much more than our Western tradition of Aristotelian logic, delighted in paradoxical statements that held opposites in tension. (Even in our own day, American and European professors are often befuddled when they find out that students from Asia, while fiercely intelligent, may not subscribe to the Western philosophical principle of noncontradiction.) Then, too, Jesus was a popular preacher addressing a wide range of audiences on particular occasions with great oral skill; we should hardly seek in the various expressions of his teaching the type of systematic presentation expected of a written treatise.[40] Hence the debate between those scholars who stress the eschatological nature of Jesus' core message and those who portray Jesus teaching a wisdom tradition bereft of any eschatological slant may be misplaced. There is no reason why the preaching of Jesus may not have contained elements of both apocalyptic eschatology and traditional Israelite wisdom. Both Jesus and his contemporaries might have been surprised by the charge (a very modern academic one) that such a message would be inconsistent or incoherent. In short, the criterion of coherence has a certain positive value; but its negative use, to exclude material as inauthentic, must be approached very cautiously.

5. THE CRITERION OF REJECTION AND EXECUTION

The criterion of Jesus' rejection and execution is notably different from the first four criteria.[41] It does not directly indicate whether an individual saying or deed of Jesus is authentic. Rather, it directs our attention to the historical fact that Jesus met a violent end at the hands of Jewish and Roman officials and then asks us what historical words and deeds of Jesus can explain his trial and crucifixion as "King of the Jews."[42] While I do not agree with those who turn Jesus into a violent revolutionary or political agitator, scholars who favor a revolutionary Jesus do have a point. A tweedy poetaster who spent his time spinning out parables and Japanese koans, a literary aesthete who toyed with 1st-century deconstructionism, or a bland Jesus who simply told people to look at the lilies of the field—such a Jesus would threaten no one, just as the university professors who create him threaten no one. The historical Jesus did threaten, disturb, and infuriate people—from interpreters of the Law through the Jerusalem priestly aristocracy to the Roman prefect who finally tried and crucified him. This emphasis on Jesus' violent end is not simply a focus imposed on the data by Christian theology. To outsiders like Josephus, Tacitus, and Lucian of Samosata,[43] one of the most striking things about Jesus was his crucifixion or execution by Rome. A Jesus whose words and deeds would not alienate people, especially powerful people, is not the historical Jesus.

SECONDARY (OR DUBIOUS) CRITERIA

6. THE CRITERION OF TRACES OF ARAMAIC

Joachim Jeremias and many of his disciples point to traces of Aramaic vocabulary, grammar, syntax, rhythm, and rhyme in the Greek version of the sayings of Jesus as signs of an authentic saying. Used negatively, this criterion would cast doubt on a saying that could not be easily retroverted from Greek into Aramaic.[44] At first glance, this criterion seems scientific, since it rests on a vast fund of philological data developed in the 20th century by such experts in Aramaic as Jeremias, Matthew Black, Geza Vermes, and Joseph Fitzmyer.

Yet this criterion is not without serious problems. First of all, a good number of the earliest Christians were Palestinian Jews whose native tongue was the same Aramaic Jesus spoke. These Aramaic-speaking Christian Jews continued to exist in Palestine throughout the 1st century. Presumably, if Christians elsewhere in the Mediterranean world developed and sometimes created words of Jesus, Aramaic-speaking Jews in Palestine did the same.[45] Suppose, then, that some scholars are trying to discover an Aramaic substratum beneath a particular Greek saying in our Gospels. Even if they succeed, how—simply on the grounds of the Aramaic—are they to distinguish a saying first spoken in Aramaic by Jesus in A.D. 29 from a saying first spoken in Aramaic by a Christian Jew in A.D. 33? The mere fact that the saying has an Aramaic substratum gives no criterion for making such a distinction. The problem is complicated still further by the fact that the Jerusalem church was both Aramaic- and Greek-speaking from its beginning (cf. the Hellenists in Acts 6). The translation of Jesus' sayings into Greek is therefore not something that happened only at a later stage of the tradition.[46]

Secondly, the mere fact that a particular Greek saying can be retroverted into Aramaic with ease—or, on the other hand, only with great difficulty—does not give us a sure indication that the saying existed originally in Aramaic or originally in Greek. One Aramaic saying might be translated with great skill into elegant Greek, the translator aiming at sense-equivalence rather than a word-for-word rendering.[47]

Another Aramaic saying might be translated by another translator in a very literalistic, wooden fashion. The ease with which the two sayings could be retroverted into Aramaic might lead the unwary critic to judge quite wrongly that the first saying did not exist in Aramaic while the second did. Compounding the problem is that many Greek-speaking Christians knew very well the Greek translation of the Old Testament, the Septuagint, and could imitate the biblical Greek of the Septuagint, thus giving their original Greek composition a Semitic tone. This may have been the case with the Gospel of Luke.[48] Confusing the situation still further is the fact that scholars have become increasingly aware in recent decades that usages in the NT that we once considered "Semitisms" (i.e., vocabulary or grammar showing Hebrew or Aramaic influence) may actually reflect the normal koine Greek of the less educated level of the population.[49]

Jeremias tries to mount a particular form of the "Aramaic argument" by pointing out that Jesus tended to deliver his teaching in Aramaic sayings that had a distinctive rhythm, that employed rhetorical tools like antithetic parallelism, alliteration, assonance, and paronomasia, and that employed the passive voice to avoid the frequent mention of God's name ("the divine passive").[50] While all this may be true, we again run into methodological problems. First, Jeremias' argument cannot entirely avoid being circular. He can tell us what is characteristic of Jesus' sayings only if from the start he can presume that a certain amount of sayings are authentic and then proceed to abstract from them the characteristics he lists. To be sure, such a list could legitimately arise from a lengthy process of isolating, collating, and examining authentic sayings of Jesus from a stylistic viewpoint. But such a list cannot be the starting point for deciding which sayings are authentic, for it would be presuming what is to be proven.[51] Second, if the list does reflect striking characteristics of Jesus' speech, would it be all that unusual if early Christian Jewish teachers and preachers in Palestine imitated the style of their master? Or did Jesus have a monopoly on rhythmic speech and antithetic parallelism in 1st-century Palestine? Was Jesus the only gifted and imaginative teacher among Jews and Christian Jews during this period? The same sort of questions may be asked about the supposed "poetic" quality of Jesus' Aramaic, all the more so since we are poorly informed about what 1st-century Palestinian Aramaic poetry looked like.[52]

At best, then, this criterion of Aramaic traces can provide additional support for an argument for historicity—but only when the material in question has already given indications of being authentic on the grounds of other criteria.

7. THE CRITERION OF PALESTINIAN ENVIRONMENT

A criterion much like the Aramaic one, this criterion of Palestinian environment affirms that sayings of Jesus that reflect concrete customs, beliefs, judicial procedures, commercial and agricultural practices, or social and political conditions in 1st-century Palestine have a good chance of being authentic. Put negatively, a saying that reflects social, political, economic, or religious conditions that existed only outside Palestine or only after the death of Jesus is to be considered inauthentic. This criterion is much more useful in its negative guise. To take a well-known example that applies the criterion theologically rather than socially: parables that reflect concern about the delay of Jesus' parousia, the mission of the Church to the Gentiles, or rules for Church leadership and discipline are post-Easter creations, at least in their final, Gospel form.[53]

The positive use of this criterion is more problematic, for the same reasons mentioned under the Aramaic criterion. The Palestine inhabited by Christian Jews in A.D. 33 was not all that different from the Palestine inhabited by Jesus in A.D. 29. Pilate remained prefect in Judea until A.D. 36, Herod remained tetrarch in Galilee until A.D. 39, and Caiaphas remained high priest until A.D. 36 or 37. Basic commercial, social, and religious conditions naturally remained much longer. Hence, the Palestine reflected in sayings created by Christian Jews in A.D. 33 would hardly differ from the Palestine reflected in the sayings of Jesus in A.D. 29.[54]

8. THE CRITERION OF VIVIDNESS OF NARRATION

In the narratives of the Gospels, liveliness and concrete details—especially when the details are not relevant to the main point of the story—are sometimes taken to be indicators of an eyewitness report. Although he was not as uncritical in using this criterion as some of his followers, Vincent Taylor inclined to accept vivid, concrete details in Mark's Gospel as signs of high historical value.[55] Faithful to the early oral tradition, Mark had the special advantage of hearing Peter's preaching.[56] Taylor himself is aware of the basic objection to this criterion: any skilled narrator can confer vividness on any story, however unhistorical. If liveliness and concrete details were in themselves proofs of historicity, many great novels would have to be declared history books.[57]

In reply to this objection, Taylor first admits that some concrete details may indeed be the result of Marcan redaction. But Taylor goes on to make two points: (1) Some of the details seem to serve no point in the narrative and apparently are included by Mark simply because they were in the tradition. (2) More importantly, a number of key episodes in the Gospel, episodes ripe for dramatic exploitation, are surprisingly jejune and bereft of concrete details: e.g., the choice of the Twelve (3:13–19b), the suspicion held by Jesus' family that he has gone insane (3:21), the plot by the priests (14:1–2), and the treachery of Judas (14:10–11). Taylor argues that the presence of these terse though important narratives shows that Mark did not indulge in massive creative rewriting; on the whole, some narratives are laconic and others detailed because that is the way they were in the early oral tradition that Mark has faithfully followed.[58]

Taylor's arguments do not seem as strong today as they might have appeared in the early fifties. Redaction criticism and contemporary narrative criticism have taught us to appreciate Mark as a talented author who may have his own theological and artistic reasons for alternating sparse and detailed narratives.[59] Moreover, not all critics would concede Mark's direct dependence on the preaching of Peter. If instead Mark is simply passing on oral traditions that come to him from many sources, can we not attribute the liveliness of some pericopes to the skill of certain early Christian preachers or storytellers, with the irrelevant details being explained by the untidy nature of oral as opposed to written composition? *Perhaps* the vividness of narration gets us behind Mark to his oral tradition. But does it get us back to Jesus himself?

A further problem arises from the succinct narratives that Taylor also finds in Mark. The terse, streamlined nature of particular dispute stories, miracle stories, and pronouncement stories may result, not from their unhistorical nature, but from the very fact that they fit well into a particular form or genre. This neat "fit" may have caused some historical events to have been "slimmed down" to the "bare bones" of a particular genre in the oral tradition. In short, just as vividness in itself does not prove historicity, so too a pale skeletal narrative is not necessarily unhistorical.

Thus, as with the other secondary criteria we have seen so far, this criterion can never serve as the main argument for historicity. At best, it may support the impression already created by one or more of the primary criteria.

9. THE CRITERION OF THE TENDENCIES OF THE DEVELOPING SYNOPTIC TRADITION

At this point we begin to consider criteria that, in my view, are highly questionable. The form critics like Bultmann thought they could isolate the laws of development within the Synoptic tradition. For instance, as the Synoptic tradition developed from Mark to Matthew and Luke, there supposedly was a tendency to make details more concrete, to add proper names to the narrative, to turn indirect discourse into direct quotation, and to eliminate Aramaic words and constructions. Bultmann suggested that, once these laws governing the transmission of tradition were discovered by analyzing changes in the Synoptic Gospels, they could be applied to the development of the tradition redacted by Mark and Q.[60] By extension, some critics have suggested, these laws might help us reconstruct original events or sayings coming from Jesus.

However, the whole attempt to formulate laws of the developing Synoptic tradition and then to apply them to the earlier oral tradition is dubious. First of all, one cannot establish that such firm laws exist. As E. P. Sanders has pointed out, we can find examples of the tradition becoming longer and shorter, of discourse becoming both direct and indirect, and of proper names being dropped as well as added. The tendencies run in both directions.[61] Moreover, even if we could discover firm laws among the Synoptic Gospels, we would still be dealing with redaction of the written Gospel of Mark by two other writers, Matthew and Luke. Whether and to what degree such laws would apply to the pre-Marcan oral stage of the gospel tradition is by no means clear.[62] In my opinion, the one negative use that can be made of a criterion based on "tendencies" is to discern the redactional tendency of each evangelist and to exclude from consideration those sayings or narratives which are massively suffused with the characteristic vocabulary and theology of the evangelist.

10. The Criterion of Historical Presumption

This criterion brings us squarely into the debate about where the "burden of proof" lies: on the side of the critic who denies historicity or on the side of the critic who affirms it? Critics who stress the decades between the original events and the writing of our Gospels, as well as the obvious cases of modifications or creations by the oral tradition or the evangelists, conclude that anyone claiming to isolate an authentic saying or action of Jesus must bear the burden of proof.[63] On the opposite side, critics who stress that eyewitnesses of Jesus' ministry were the leaders in the early Church and that in any historical investigation credence is given to early historical reports until the opposite is proven conclude that the burden of proof is on those who wish to discredit a particular saying or event as inauthentic ("in dubio pro tradito"). This is called by Neil J. McEleney the criterion of historical presumption.[64] If accepted, it could cut the Gordian knot in cases where the arguments are finely balanced and the final result seems to be permanent doubt.

However, common sense and the rules of logical argument seem to be on the side of critics like Willi Marxsen and Ben Meyer, who state the obvious: the burden of proof is simply on anyone who tries to prove anything.[65] In effect, this means that critics must allow a galling but realistic third column for a vote of "not clear" *(non liquet)*. There will always be some difficult cases in which no criterion applies or in which different criteria apply but point in opposite directions. Such conundrums cannot be resolved by the *deus ex machina* of the criterion of historical presumption. In the convoluted case of the canonical Gospels, such a criterion simply does not exist.[66]

CONCLUSION

Our survey indicates that five suggested criteria of historicity or authenticity are really valuable and deserve to be ranked as primary criteria: embarrassment, discontinuity, multiple attestation in sources or forms, coherence, and Jesus' rejection and execution. I have stressed the limitations and problems inherent in each criterion lest any single criterion seem a magic key unlocking all doors. Only a careful use of a number of criteria in tandem, with allowances for mutual correction, can produce convincing results.[67]

Despite their exaltation in some quarters, the criteria of Aramaic traces, Palestinian environment, and vividness of narrative cannot yield probative arguments on their own, even when all three are taken together. They can act as secondary, supportive criteria, reinforcing the impressions gained from one or more of the primary criteria. Finally, the criteria of the tendencies of the Synoptic tradition and historical presumption are, for all practical purposes, useless.[68]

As many a weary quester has remarked before, the use of the valid criteria is more an art than a science, requiring sensitivity to the individual case rather than mechanical implementation.[69] It can never be said too many times that such an art usually yields only varying degrees of probability, not absolute certitude. But, as we have already seen, such judgments of probability are common in any investigation of ancient history, and the quest for the historical Jesus cannot apply for a special exemption. Since moral certitude is nothing but a very high degree of probability, and since we run most of our lives and make many of our theoretical and practical judgments on the basis of moral certitude, we need not feel that the results of our quest will be unusually fragile or uncertain. They are no more fragile or uncertain than many other parts of our lives.[70]

NOTES TO CHAPTER 6

[1] This is a schematic statement of the problem. The actual situation was naturally much more complex: e.g., some disciples of Jesus may have begun to collect and arrange sayings of Jesus even before his death (Stage I), and the oral tradition continued to develop during the period of the redaction of the Gospels (Stage III).

[2] Even the fine book by the historian Michael Grant does not entirely escape this tendency; see his *Jesus. An Historian's Review of the Gospels* (New York: Scribner's, 1977); the appendix outlining his approach to criteria (pp. 197–204) is disappointing. Still weaker in the area of criteria is James Breech's *The Silence of Jesus. The Authentic Voice of the Historical Man* (Philadelphia: Fortress, 1983). While the book does at times use familiar criteria (embarrassment, discontinuity), the argument largely depends on scholarly consensus combined with aesthetic intuition about literature. The results cannot help but be highly subjective.

[3] This is even the case with the judicious work of Meyer, *The Aims of Jesus*. The first part of the book (pp. 23–113) spells out method and "indices" of judgment with great care; but, as the book proceeds, more and more of the redactional theology of the evangelists is declared to come from the historical Jesus, leaving one wondering how useful the indices really are.

[4] René Latourelle ("Critères d'authenticité historique des Evangiles," *Greg* 55 [1974] 609-37, esp. 618) rightly warns against confusing criteria with proof. Criteria are rules or norms that are applied to the Gospel material to arrive at a judgment.

[5] In the quest for the historical Jesus, sometimes certainty is more easily had about "secondary" circumstances than about the words and deeds of Jesus himself. For example, the converging evidence of the Four Gospels and the Acts of the Apostles, Josephus, Philo, Tacitus, and the Caesarea Maritima inscription (found in 1961) makes it at least morally, if not physically, certain that Pontius Pilate was the Roman governor of Judea in A.D. 28–30. Even here, though, moral certitude is really just a very high degree of probability. The fact of Pilate's governorship is not absolutely or metaphysically certain, for it is not theoretically or metaphysically impossible that Josephus is mistaken or that the references to Pilate in Philo are Christian interpolations or that the Caesarea Maritima inscription is a fraud. But since any of these possibilities (not to mention all of them together) is so extremely unlikely, we are justified in considering our conclusion morally certain, especially since, in daily life, we constantly make firm theoretical judgments and practical decisions on the basis of high probability. Any talk about "proof" of authentic Jesus material must be understood within this context of a range of probabilities.

[6] Sometimes scholars seek to distinguish between "criteria" and "indices" or even to substitute the word "index" for "criterion"; see, e.g., Latourelle, "Critères d'authenticité historique des Evangiles"; Meyer, *The Aims of Jesus*, 86; and Rainer Riesner, *Jesus als Lehrer* (WUNT, 2d series, 7; Tübingen: Mohr

[Siebeck], 1981) 86–96, esp. 86–87; Francesco Lambiasi, *L'autenticità storica dei vangeli* (Studi biblici 4; 2d ed.; Bologna: EDB, 1986) 189–90. However, scholars favoring some sort of distinction do not always agree among themselves as to what constitutes the distinction. Sometimes "criterion" indicates what allows a fairly certain judgment, while "index" suggests a lower level of probability (so Latourelle; Lambiasi adds a third category, namely "motive," an argument that indicates verisimilitude). Others use indices for individual observations relevant to the question of authenticity, while criteria refer to more general rules (so Riesner). Meyer prefers to drop the language of "criteria" in favor of "indices." Personally, I see no great value in the various distinctions or changes in terminology. My own view is that our judgments about authenticity deal for the most part with a range of probabilities; I do not claim that the use of the criteria I propose will generate absolute certitude. Hence, I see no need to distinguish "criteria" from "indices"; the former term will be used throughout what follows.

⁷ The reader who follows up the bibliographical references will soon discover a wearisome repetition in much of the literature. I have therefore restricted the bibliography to a few contributions that say all that need be said on the issue. In addition to the works of Latourelle, Riesner, and Meyer, see Charles E. Carlston, "A *Positive* Criterion of Authenticity," *BR* 7 (1962) 33–44; Harvey K. McArthur, "A Survey of Recent Gospel Research," *Int* 18 (1964) 39–55, esp. 47–51; idem, "The Burden of Proof in Historical Jesus Research," *ExpTim* 82 (1970–71) 116–19; William O. Walker, "The Quest for the Historical Jesus: A Discussion of Methodology," *ATR* 51 (1969) 38–56; Morna D. Hooker, "Christology and Methodology," *NTS* 17 (1970–71) 480–87; idem, "On Using the Wrong Tool," *Theology* 75 (1972) 570–81; Rudolf Pesch, *Jesu Ureigene Taten?* (QD 52; Freiburg/Basel/Vienna: Herder, 1970) esp. pp. 135–58; D. G. A. Calvert, "An Examination of the Criteria for Distinguishing the Authentic Words of Jesus," *NTS* 18 (1971–72) 209–19; Fritzleo Lentzen-Deis, "Kriterien für die historische Beurteilung der Jesusüberlieferung in den Evangelien," *Rückfrage nach Jesus* (QD 63; Freiburg/Basel/Vienna: Herder, 1974) 78–117; Neil J. McEleney, "Authenticating Criteria and Mark 7:1–23," *CBQ* 34 (1972) 431–60; Francesco Lambiasi, *Criteri di autenticità storica dei Vangeli sinottici. Rassegna storica e tentativo di sistematizzazione dei contributi di criteriologia degli ultimi venti anni (1954–1974)* (dissertation; Rome: Gregorian University, 1974); idem, *L'autenticità storica dei vangeli. Studio di criteriologia* (Studi biblici; 2d ed.; Bologna: EDB, 1986); idem, *Gesù di Nazaret. Una verifica storica* (Fame della Parola; Monferrato: Marietti, 1983) 63–68; Schillebeeckx, *Jesus*, 81–100; Joseph A. Fitzmyer, "Methodology in the Study of the Aramaic Substratum of Jesus' Sayings in the New Testament," *Jésus aux origines de la christologie* (BETL 40; ed. J. Dupont; Leuven: Leuven University; Gembloux: Duculot, 1975) 73–102; Ernst Käsemann, "Die neue Jesus-Frage," *Jésus aux origines de la christologie* (BETL 40; ed. J. Dupont; Leuven: Leuven University; Gembloux: Duculot, 1975) 47–57; D. Lührmann, "Die Frage nach Kriterien für ursprüngliche Jesusworte—eine Problemskizze," *Jésus aux origines de la christologie* (BETL 50; ed. J. Dupont; Leuven: Leuven University; Gembloux: Duculot, 1975) 59–72; David L. Mealand, "The Dissimilarity Test," *SJT* 31

(1978) 41–50; Helge Kjaer Nielsen, "Kriterien zur Bestimmung authentischer Jesusworte," *Studien zum Neuen Testament und seiner Umwelt* 4 (1979) 5–26; Robert H. Stein, "The 'Criteria' for Authenticity," *Gospel Perspectives. Vol. I*, ed. R. France and D. Wenham (Sheffield: JSOT, 1980) 225–63; Reginald Fuller, "The Criterion of Dissimilarity: The Wrong Tool?" *Christological Perspectives* (H. K. McArthur Festschrift; ed. R. Berkey and S. Edwards; New York: Pilgrim, 1982) 42–48; Giuseppe Ghiberti, "Überlegungen zum neueren Stand der Leben-Jesu-Forschung," *MTZ* 33 (1982) 99–115; E. Earle Ellis, "Gospels Criticism: A Perspective on the State of the Art," *Das Evangelium und die Evangelien* (WUNT 28; ed. P. Stuhlmacher; Tübingen: Mohr [Siebeck], 1983) 27–54; Breech, *The Silence of Jesus*, 9, 22–26, 66–85; Dennis Polkow, "Method and Criteria for Historical Jesus Research," *Society of Biblical Literature Seminar Papers* 26 (1987) 336–56; M. Eugene Boring, "The Historical-Critical Method's 'Criteria of Authenticity': The Beatitudes in Q and Thomas as a Test Case," *The Historical Jesus and the Rejected Gospels* (Semeia 44; ed. Charles W. Hedrick; Atlanta: Scholars, 1988) 9–44. For a history of the development of thought about the criteria, see Lambiasi, *L'autenticità storica dei vangeli*, 19–110.

[8] While the criteria are usually aimed at the sayings of Jesus in particular, it must be remembered that they can also be applied to the actions of Jesus. In some forms of the quest, the actions of Jesus and their relation to his sayings are almost ignored. Morton Smith (*Jesus the Magician*), E. P. Sanders (*Jesus and Judaism*), and Joseph A. Fitzmyer ("Methodology," 73) rightly protest against this one-sided emphasis. As Nielsen ("Kriterien," 21) notes, the tradition of words and the tradition of works can act as a reciprocal check. For one reason why the sayings tradition tends to be emphasized, see D. Lührmann, "Die Frage," 64–65.

[9] This phenomenon is sometimes listed as the separate criterion of either "modification" or "tendencies of the developing Synoptic tradition." What I think valid in these two suggested criteria I have subsumed under the criterion of embarrassment. For the criterion of modification, see Walker, "The Quest for the Historical Jesus," 48; Boring, "The Historical-Critical Method's 'Criteria of Authenticity,' " 21. The criterion is usually attributed to Ernst Käsemann, "The Problem of the Historical Jesus," *Essays on New Testament Themes* (SBT 41; London: SCM, 1964) 15–47, esp. 37.

[10] On the baptism of Jesus as a test case for the criterion of embarrassment, see Breech, *The Silence of Jesus*, 22–24.

[11] The few manuscripts that omit "nor the Son" in Mark include codex X (10th century).

[12] The manuscripts that drop "nor the Son" in the Matthean version of the saying include the codices K, L, W, and the vast majority of later texts; the first scribe who sought to correct this text in codex Sinaiticus also omitted the phrase.

[13] As Stein ("The 'Criteria' for Authenticity," 227) notes, another indication of the conservative force of the Jesus tradition is that several of the major problems that the early Church encountered never show up in the sayings of Jesus; a

glaring case is the absence of any explicit pronouncement of Jesus on the question of circumcision for Gentiles. In a letter to me dated Oct. 13, 1990, David Noel Freedman points out an OT analogy. From the viewpoint of the Deuteronomistic Historian(s), Hezekiah and Josiah were the two best kings of Judah after David. Their military defeats, which raise questions about Yahweh's rewarding of the just, are not denied but rather explained theologically in somewhat contorted fashion.

[14] My proviso "in most cases" takes cognizance of the Fourth Gospel's suppression of the baptism of Jesus.

[15] See, e.g., C. H. Dodd, *According to the Scriptures* (London: Collins, Fontana, 1965) 96–103. Eduard Schweizer *(Lordship and Discipleship* [SBT 28; Naperville, IL: Allenson, 1960] 34) holds that "to the early Church the first book of the Passion of Jesus was formed by the Psalms of the suffering of the Righteous One. This is even true of the Gospel according to John. . . ." While Lothar Ruppert criticizes Schweizer for an undifferentiated, homogenized treatment of OT, pseudepigraphic, and rabbinic texts, his own thesis supports the basic point I am making. See Ruppert's *Jesus als der leidende Gerechte?* (SBS 59; Stuttgart: KBW, 1972) 58: ". . . the motif of the suffering just man is dominant in the older form of the Passion Narrative. . . . The motif points us . . . to the tradition of the primitive community." This monograph is in turn an expanded form of the last chapter of another work by Ruppert, *Der leidende Gerechte* (FB 5; Würzburg: Echter/KBW, 1972). Rudolf Pesch has accepted this theory in his treatment of the Passion Narrative in Mark; see his *Das Markusevangelium. II. Teil* (HTKNT II/2; Freiburg/Basel/Vienna: Herder, 1977) 25.

[16] Allied, but not reducible to discontinuity; in this I disagree with Polkow, "Method and Criteria," 341.

[17] In his masterful essay ("The Historical-Critical Method's 'Criteria of Authenticity,'" 17–21), Boring highlights the methodological problem of whether we should speak of material that *can* be derived from Judaism or Christianity or material that *must* be so derived. I think it is preferable to speak in terms of "can."

[18] Perrin, *Rediscovering the Teaching of Jesus,* 39–43.

[19] Hooker, "Christology and Methodology," 480–87; idem, "On Using the Wrong Tool," 570–81. Ellis ("Gospels Criticism," 31) complains that the criterion of discontinuity assumes "that a Gospel traditioner or a Christian prophetic oracle could not have used a unique idea or expression. . . ."

[20] For critiques of Hooker's position, see Mealand, "The Dissimilarity Test," 41–50; Nielsen, "Kriterien," 10–11.

[21] The emphasis on Jesus' connections with the Judaism of his time is common in scholarship today and is well documented by Daniel J. Harrington, "The Jewishness of Jesus: Facing Some Problems," *CBQ* 49 (1987) 1–13.—It is curious that even skeptical scholars use the language of "handing on the Jesus tradition" and engage in tradition criticism. Yet if there really was a complete

rupture in history between Jesus and the earliest Christians, there can be no talk of handing on tradition. However one defines the exact relationship between Jesus and the early Church, it is a fact of history, disputed by almost no scholar, that shortly after the death of Jesus some Jews, including people who had been his closest followers during his public ministry, gathered together to revere and celebrate him as Messiah and Lord, to recall and hand on his teachings, and to spread his teachings among other Jews.

[22] This point is argued at length by A. E. Harvey, *Jesus and the Constraints of History* (Philadelphia: Westminster, 1982); see in particular pp. 1–10. The failure to appreciate this point is one of the weaknesses of Breech's *The Silence of Jesus* (see, e.g., p. 10).

[23] So rightly Walker, "The Quest for the Historical Jesus," 48: "Unique features are not necessarily the most characteristic features . . ."; cf. Boring, "The Historical-Critical Method's 'Criteria of Authenticity,' " 21. We might add that even what was strikingly characteristic about Jesus' message may not have been at the very heart of his message.

[24] E. P. Sanders, *Jewish Law from Jesus to the Mishnah. Five Studies* (London: SCM; Philadelphia: Trinity, 1990) 28.

[25] This problem was pointed out to me in a letter by David Noel Freedman, dated Oct. 15, 1990. For Freedman, to be unique, "it would be enough to be markedly different from those who preceded. What happened afterwards would not affect that status."

[26] See Stein, "The 'Criteria' for Authenticity," 228–29.

[27] The qualification "independent" is important. The mere fact that Peter's confession that Jesus is the Messiah is recorded in Mark, Matthew, and Luke does not satisfy the criterion of multiple attestation, since both Matthew and Luke are dependent on Mark for the basic narrative (though Matthew may be relying on a separate tradition for Jesus' praise and commission of Peter in 16:17–19). There is only one *independent* source for the core of the story. If the focus were broadened to "some sort of confession that Peter addresses to Jesus at a critical moment in the public ministry," then John 6:66–71 could be used; but we could no longer speak of Peter's confession of faith in Jesus precisely as the Messiah; both the location and the content of the confession in John's Gospel are different.

[28] Some count multiple attestation in sources and multiple attestation in forms as two different criteria. Like Polkow ("Method and Criteria," 341), I think that they are better dealt with together under one criterion.

[29] Once again I must stress that I do not accept the a priori exclusion of John from consideration as a possible source for knowledge of the historical Jesus; see Walker, "The Quest for the Historical Jesus," 54.

[30] Those who accept the Coptic *Gospel of Thomas* as another independent source would naturally add it to this list (so Boring, "The Historical-Critical

Method's 'Criteria of Authenticity,'" 13, 25–28; more cautiously, McArthur, "The Burden of Proof," 118). For my skepticism on this subject, see my remarks on the *Gospel of Thomas* under my treatment of the Nag Hammadi material as a source of knowledge of the historical Jesus (chap. 5, section 3).

[31] McArthur ("The Burden of Proof," 118) claims that the following motifs are witnessed to by all four strands of the Synoptic tradition (i.e., Mark, Q, M, and L): Jesus' proclamation of the kingdom of God, the presence of disciples around Jesus, healing miracles, a link with John the Baptist, use of parables, concern for outcasts, especially tax collectors and sinners, a radical ethic, emphasis on the love commandment, a demand that the disciples practice forgiveness, clashes with his contemporaries over Sabbath observance, sayings about the Son of Man, and the Hebrew word "Amen" used to introduce Jesus' sayings.

[32] I do not bother to list the "peeling away" of additions and modifications made by the oral tradition and the final redactor, since I consider such judgments a necessary part of the use of the criterion of multiple attestation. One would like to say that such judgments are simply "preliminary criteria" that precede the use of the "primary criteria" (so Polkow, "Method and Criteria," 342–45). But actual practice of the historical-critical method shows that all the way through the process one is constantly testing and revising one's judgments about modifications made by the oral tradition and the redactor.

[33] McArthur, "A Survey of Recent Gospel Research," 48; idem, "The Burden of Proof," 118. He makes the statement about giving it first place in conscious opposition to Perrin's emphasis on the criterion of discontinuity. In agreement with McArthur's view is Stein, "Criteria," 230.

[34] G. Petzke puts it quite bluntly in his article, "Die historische Frage nach den Wundertaten Jesu," *NTS* 22 (1975–76) 180–204, esp. 183: there is no reason to think that something is more reliable historically because it is reported "a number of times" *(mehrfach)*. Petzke's use of phrases like "a number of times" and "multiple appearances in early Christian tradition" points to a weakness in his argument. Petzke does not seem to take seriously enough the weight of a plurality of early *independent* literary sources and a plurality of literary genres, all acting as vehicles of a single given tradition. At one point, with a rhetorical wave of the hand, he dismisses the question of attestation in a number of independent traditions by observing that we cannot be certain about which early Christian sources were independent. Yet he himself proceeds to analyze the story of the cure of the "lunatic boy" (Mark 9:14–29 parr.) with the tool of the two-source theory.

[35] So rightly Polkow, "Method and Criteria," 351.

[36] Obviously, the conclusions drawn by the criterion of coherence are as good as the data base on which they depend. Carlston, a great proponent of the positive use of this criterion, uses it to discern authentic parables of Jesus: they will fit reasonably well into the eschatologically based demand for repentance that was characteristic of Jesus' message ("A *Positive* Criterion," 33–34). That is fine, provided one does not agree with revisionist exegetes who claim that Jesus' basic

message was not essentially eschatological (e.g., Marcus J. Borg) or that repentance did not play a large role in Jesus' preaching (e.g., E. P. Sanders). Thus, one sees the vital importance of being as certain as possible about the data base created by the first three criteria before one proceeds to the criterion of coherence.

[37] Nielsen, "Kriterien," 14.

[38] I should make clear that it is in this technical and restricted sense that I use the word "authentic" when discussing criteria of historicity; cf. Stein, "The 'Criteria' for Authenticity," 228. The word must not be taken to mean that, from the viewpoint of faith, what the oral tradition or final redaction contributed to our Gospels is any less inspired, normative, or true.

[39] Cf. Hooker, "Christology and Methodology," 483; Stein, "The 'Criteria' for Authenticity," 250.

[40] These considerations should make one wary about declaring a priori that Jesus could not possibly have spoken of the kingdom of God as both present and future or that he could not possibly have prophesied both a coming kingdom and a coming Son of Man. It is a matter of fact that the evangelists, and probably the gospel traditions before them, did just that. Nor are Paul's authentic letters totally devoid of paradoxes that strike some as blatant contradictions.

[41] Hence I would not say that it is simply "the resultant historical data shown by Dissimilarity . . . , Modification . . . , Embarrassment . . . , Incongruity . . . , and Hermeneutical Potential . . ." (Polkow, "Method and Criteria," 340). On p. 341, Polkow finally lists execution as merely a variation of discontinuity (or dissimilarity); cf. Lührmann, "Die Frage," 68.

[42] On this criterion, see Schillebeeckx, *Jesus,* 97; cf. Walker, "The Quest for the Historical Jesus," 55.

[43] See the treatment of their statements in Chapters 3 and 4.

[44] While Jesus may have known and even used some Greek (e.g., during his trial before Pilate), there is no indication that the sayings tradition in our Gospels was rooted, even in part, in sayings spoken by Jesus in Greek (so rightly Fitzmyer, "Methodology," 87). For a general overview of languages used in Palestine at the time of Jesus, see Joseph A. Fitzmyer, "The Languages of Palestine in the First Century A.D.," *A Wandering Aramean. Collected Aramaic Essays* (SBLMS 25; Missoula, MT: Scholars, 1979) 29–56; cf. below, pp. 255–68.

[45] For a similar observation, see Walker, "The Quest for the Historical Jesus," 43.

[46] Riesner, *Jesus als Lehrer,* 93.

[47] One must be especially sensitive to this possibility in the case of a saying that occurs only in Matthew or Luke. It is not impossible that an Aramaic saying was first translated into rough, Semitic Greek during the oral stage of the

special Lucan tradition and then was given a more elegant Greek form when Luke incorporated it into his Gospel; cf. Riesner, *Jesus als Lehrer*, 93.

[48] While not claiming to decide all instances once and for all, Fitzmyer seems to lean in the direction of explaining Luke's "Semitisms," especially his "Hebraisms," by reckoning "with a great deal of influence from the LXX" (Joseph A. Fitzmyer, *The Gospel According to Luke (I–IX)* [AB 28; Garden City, NY: Doubleday, 1981] 125).

[49] So Walker, "The Quest for the Historical Jesus," 44; cf. Fitzmyer, "Methodology," 95 (citing R. M. Grant, *A Historical Introduction to the New Testament* [New York: Harper & Row, 1963] 41); idem, "The Study of the Aramaic Background of the New Testament," *A Wandering Aramean* (SBLMS 25; Missoula, MT: Scholars, 1979) 1–27, esp. 10–15. The question of the existence and extent of Semitisms (both Hebrew and Aramaic) in the NT is hotly debated today. For a short history of the debate, see Elliott C. Maloney, *Semitic Interference in Marcan Syntax* (SBLDS 51; Chico, CA: Scholars, 1981) 1–25. Maloney's conclusions, summarized on pp. 244–45, show how complex and varied Semitic influence may be. In particular, he notes "that much grammatical usage in Marcan Greek which various authors have claimed to be the result of Semitic interference is, in fact, quite possible in Hellenistic Greek. . . . On the other hand, certain constructions which various authors have argued are acceptable in Greek have been shown to be quite abnormal, or even totally unattested in Hellenistic Greek, whereas their appearance in Semitic is normal (sometimes only possible). These are true Semitisms" (pp. 244–45).

[50] Joachim Jeremias, *New Testament Theology. Part One. The Proclamation of Jesus* (London: SCM, 1971) 3–29.

[51] If these linguistic characteristics were first abstracted from sayings that had been declared authentic on other grounds, and if these characteristics were then applied to a new group of sayings to judge their authenticity, we would have a form of the criterion of coherence. Even then, however, the second methodological problem I indicate in the text would remain.

[52] Fitzmyer, "Methodology," 97–98.

[53] See, e.g., the treatment of Joachim Jeremias, *The Parables of Jesus* (rev. ed.; London: SCM, 1969) 48–66. Of course, it is possible that behind the final form of such Gospel parables a scholar might discover, by means of form criticism, an earlier form without these ecclesiastical interests.

[54] See also the observations of Walker ("The Quest for the Historical Jesus," 44), who adds: "Many apparent reflections of Palestinian life, however, may be derived from the Old Testament or other Jewish literature or reflect merely an acquaintance of sorts with the area on the part of a writer or transmitter of the tradition."

[55] Vincent Taylor, *The Gospel According to St. Mark* (2d ed.; London: Macmillan; New York: St. Martin's, 1966) 135–49.

[56] Ibid., 148. Other conservative commentators take a similar tack; see, e.g., William L. Lane, *The Gospel According to Mark* (NICNT; Grand Rapids: Eerdmans, 1974) 10–12. Mark's dependence on Peter is also defended by Martin Hengel, *Studies in the Gospel of Mark* (Philadelphia: Fortress, 1985) 50–53.

[57] What makes the question even more complex is that what we consider a key sign of a historical novel—the creation of dialogue or the use of nonhistorical characters—was permissible in ancient historical writings. Hence the lines between what we would consider history and the historical novel are blurred in ancient literature.

[58] This image of Mark as a conservative redactor of large amounts of early tradition has been revivified and pushed to the extreme by Rudolf Pesch, *Das Markusevangelium* (HTKNT II/1–2; Freiburg/Basel/Vienna: Herder, 1976, 1977); see, e.g., 1. 63–67; 2. 1–25.

[59] In sharp opposition to the picture of Mark as a conservative redactor are the redaction-critical approaches represented by most of the authors in Werner H. Kelber, ed., *The Passion in Mark* (Philadelphia: Fortress, 1976), and the rhetorical, narrative, and structural approaches represented by, e.g., Joanna Dewey, *Markan Public Debate* (SBLDS 48; Chico, CA: Scholars, 1980); Robert M. Fowler, *Loaves and Fishes* (SBLDS 54; Chico, CA: Scholars, 1981); Jack Dean Kingsbury, *The Christology of Mark's Gospel* (Philadelphia: Fortress, 1983); Vernon K. Robbins, *Jesus the Teacher* (Philadelphia: Fortress, 1984); and Elizabeth Struthers Malbon, *Narrative Space and Mythic Meaning in Mark* (San Francisco: Harper & Row, 1986).

[60] Rudolf Bultmann, "The New Approach to the Synoptic Problem," *Existence and Faith* (Meridian Books; Cleveland/New York: World, 1960) 34–54, esp. 41–42 (= *JR* 6 [1926] 337–62); similarly in his "The Study of the Synoptic Gospels," Rudolf Bultmann and Karl Kundsin, *Form Criticism* (New York: Harper & Row, 1962) 32–35; and in his *The History of the Synoptic Tradition*, 307–17 (= *Die Geschichte der synoptischen Tradition*, 335–46).

[61] E. P. Sanders, *The Tendencies of the Synoptic Tradition* (SNTSMS 9; Cambridge: Cambridge University, 1969).

[62] On the whole problem of the difference between oral and written tradition, see Werner H. Kelber, *The Oral and the Written Gospel* (Philadelphia: Fortress, 1983). I think, however, that Kelber exaggerates the gap between the oral and written forms of the Gospel.

[63] So Perrin, *Rediscovering the Teaching of Jesus*, 39: ". . . the nature of the synoptic tradition is such that the burden of proof will be upon the claim to authenticity" (this statement is set entirely in italics in Perrin's book). McArthur ("The Burden of Proof," 118–19) attempts a compromise stance: Initially the burden is on the person affirming historicity; but if a particular motif is supported by three or four Synoptic sources (multiple attestation), then the burden shifts to the person denying historicity.

[64] McEleney, "Authenticating Criteria," 445–48; cf. Ellis, "Gospels Criticism," 32. McEleney's easy and undifferentiated use of the terms "reporter" and

"history" (pp. 446–47) while discussing the Gospels does not inspire confidence. As Latourelle correctly observes ("Critères d'authenticité," 618), this "criterion" actually expresses an attitude of the exegete vis-à-vis the text rather than a criterion; similarly, Lambiasi, *L'autenticità storica dei vangeli*, 101, 137–38.

[65] See Meyer, *The Aims of Jesus*, 83 and 277 n. 8, where he quotes Willi Marxsen, *The Beginnings of Christology: A Study of Its Problems* (Philadelphia: Fortress, 1969) 8. Hooker ("Christology," 485) expresses herself in a similar fashion, though she tends to dismiss the whole problem as not very profitable. This commonsense approach seems preferable to the subtle distinction Lambiasi tries to make between skeptical-systematic doubt and methodological-dynamic doubt *(L'autenticità storica dei vangeli*, 229).

[66] Latourelle ("Critères d'authenticité," 628) claims that the most important of the fundamental criteria, though often ignored, is the criterion of "necessary explanation" *(explication nécessaire)*. Actually, instead of being a precise criterion for judging the special material of the Four Gospels, this "criterion" is more like the "argument to the best explanation," which is one of the basic forms of all historical argumentation (McCullagh, *Justifying Historical Descriptions*, 15–44). In a similar vein, Lambiasi *(L'autenticità storica dei vangeli*, 140) considers the criterion of necessary explanation to be basically the principle of the sufficient reason, a transcendent philosophical principle. But even if one accepts Latourelle's conception of this criterion of necessary explanation, the criterion is not of much use for the project that lies immediately ahead of us in this book: (1) The criterion of necessary explanation seeks to give a coherent and sufficient explanation of a considerable ensemble of facts or data. But most of this book will consist of sifting bit by bit through individual sayings, deeds, and motifs contained in the Gospels. One hopes that a moderate amount of fairly certain data will emerge; but the criterion, if useful at all, will be useful only at the end of this process. (2) The criterion seeks to group all the facts into a harmonious whole. This goal, however, presumes a coherence among the data that may be verified at the end of the process, but methodologically cannot be presumed at the beginning. (3) A review of a representative sample of books on the historical Jesus shows that exegetes of every stripe claim that they have found the true coherent explanation that illuminates all the facts about Jesus: he was an apocalyptic fanatic (Albert Schweitzer), a rabbi and prophet who issued the call to existential decision (Rudolf Bultmann), a gay antinomian magician (Morton Smith), a catalyst of nonviolent social revolution (Richard A. Horsely), or a charismatic man of the Spirit who founded a revitalization movement (Marcus J. Borg)—to name but a few "necessary explanations." Every author just named would claim that he has provided a coherent explanation to cover all the data he considers historical. If one is to argue with the varied explanations of these authors, one must first move back to their judgments about the historicity of individual pieces of the Jesus tradition, about the interpretation of the individual pieces, and only then move on to debate the meaning of the whole. (4) When Latourelle applies the criterion of necessary explanation, he seems to be already operating as a theologian in the area of fundamental theology or apologetics. That is a legitimate undertaking, but it must follow upon, not precede, the

tedious work of the historian and exegete. We are all attracted by calls to a "holistic" approach (so Walker, "The Quest for the Historical Jesus," 54–56). But until we have at least a vague idea of what parts might qualify as belonging to the historical whole, a "holistic" approach remains a distant ideal.

[67] I have omitted from consideration two further criteria suggested by Boring ("The Historical-Critical Method's 'Criteria of Authenticity,' " 23–24): (1) plausible *Traditionsgeschichte* and (2) hermeneutical potential. (1) The criterion of plausible *Traditionsgeschichte* seeks to draw up a genealogy of the various forms of a saying. While this is a laudable goal, I do not think it a practical one for many of the sayings in the Jesus tradition. Even when attempted, the reconstruction of the tradition history must remain very hypothetical. (2) The criterion of hermeneutical potential looks at the variety of forms generated by the original form and asks what this original must have been in order to generate such variety. Again, the quest is a valid and laudable one; but, granted the paucity of data, I feel that the results must be highly subjective and hardly probative.

[68] The one exception here is the negative use of the criterion of an evangelist's redactional tendencies.

[69] So, e.g., McArthur, "A Survey," 47; Walker, "The Quest for the Historical Jesus," 53 (who extends the observation to historiography in general); and Boring, "The Historical-Critical Method's 'Criteria of Authenticity,' " 35–36.

[70] I might add here that, naturally, any scholar must be in dialogue with his or her peers and be respectfully attentive to their consensus on the authenticity of various Gospel material. However, I would not be willing, as Polkow is ("Method and Criteria," 355), to elevate scholarly consensus to another criterion. It should be noted in fairness to Polkow that he stresses that scholarly consensus can only be a corroborative criterion and can be used only when all else is said and done. I wonder, though, whether it is properly a criterion at all. A scholar must be prepared at any moment, because of the force of data and arguments, to go against a scholarly consensus on any issue. The heavy reliance on scholarly consensus from the very start weakens the whole approach of Breech *(The Silence of Jesus,* 9).

CHAPTER 7

CONCLUSION TO PART ONE: WHY BOTHER?

The Relevance of the Quest for the Historical Jesus

In Part One of this book we have struggled with complex terminology (the real, historical, historic, or earthly Jesus), intractable sources (the canonical Gospels, Josephus, Tacitus, the Talmud, the apocryphal gospels), and cumbersome criteria of authenticity. Exhausted at the end of what is only an introduction, an exasperated reader might ask: Why bother? Since we have seen how difficult the quest is and how tenuous its results seem, why spend so much time and effort on a hypothetical Jesus whose outline remains so blurred?

Strange to say, such resistance to the quest comes much more often from committed Christians than from agnostics or Christian "drop-outs." The latter groups regularly have the intellectual curiosity of "out-siders" to spur them on—if for no other reason than to justify their remaining outside. The agnostic or secular humanist is quite used to examining claims from all quarters, however strange, and so has no qualms about examining data about and interpretations of Jesus.

It is rather the staunch believer who often feels that the quest is at best a waste of time and at worst a threat to faith. In this camp one finds strange bedfellows: strict followers of Rudolf Bultmann and dyed-in-the-wool fundamentalists. For opposite reasons they come to the same conclusion: the quest for the historical Jesus is irrelevant or even harmful to true Christian faith. For the strict disciple of Bultmann, the quest is both theologically illegitimate and historically impossible. Theologically, the quest tempts the Christians to prove their faith by human scholarship, a new form of justification by works. Historically, the sources are simply too meager, fragmentary, and theologically colored to allow any full portrait. Fundamentalists[1] object to the quest for the exact opposite reason: the historical Jesus is naively equated with the Jesus presented in all Four Gospels. All tensions and contradictions in the four narratives are harmonized by hilarious mental acrobatics.

Obviously, I do not agree with either group of objectors. My problem is that an adequate reply to them involves a momentary change in method. Both Bultmann and fundamentalists speak from definite theological viewpoints. Therefore, replying to their objections demands that I doff for a moment the hat of an exegete using purely historical-critical methods and put on the hat of a theologian. This shift, adopted for tactical reasons, will last only for this concluding chapter of Part One; but we should be clear on what this shift involves. Once I seek to reply to either Bultmannians or fundamentalists, I necessarily move from a purely empirical, historical-critical framework, which prescinds from what the believer knows or holds by faith, into a larger context in which faith, self-consciously reflecting on itself, seeks understanding. In other words, I move into an explicitly theological context.

This shift makes a great difference in concepts and terminology. For instance, in the historical-critical framework, the "real" has been defined—and has to be defined—in terms of what exists within this world of time and space, what can be experienced in principle by any observer, and what can be reasonably deduced or inferred from such experience. Faith and Christian theology, however, affirm ultimate realities beyond what is merely empirical or provable by reason: e.g., the triune God and the risen Jesus.[2] Thus, to ask about the relation between the historical Jesus, reconstructed from modern historical research, and the risen Jesus is to pass from the realm of the merely empirical or rational into the larger framework of faith and theology, as it seeks to relate itself to the historical-critical project.

Having disagreed so much with Kähler and Bultmann in an earlier chapter, I should start my theological exposition by stressing where I do agree with them: the Jesus of history is not and cannot be the object of Christian faith. A moment's reflection will make clear why that must be so. More than a millennium and a half of Christians believed firmly in Jesus Christ without having any clear idea of or access to the historical Jesus as understood today, yet no one will deny the validity and strength of their faith. The same can be said of many pious Christians in developed as well as developing countries today.[3] But, even if all Christians were acquainted with the concepts and research connected with the historical Jesus, the Church could still not make the historical Jesus the object of its preaching and faith. The reason is obvious: *Whose* historical Jesus would be the object of faith? Albert Schweitzer's or Eduard Schweizer's? Herbert Braun's or Joachim Jeremias's ? Günther Bornkamm's or E. P. Sanders's ? Jesus the violent revolutionary or Jesus the gay magician? Jesus the apocalyptic seer or Jesus the wisdom teacher unconcerned with eschatology? The constantly changing, often contradictory portraits of the historical Jesus served up by scholars, however useful in academia, cannot be the object of Christian faith for the universal Church.

Moreover, and more importantly, the proper object of Christian faith is not and cannot be an idea or scholarly reconstruction, however reliable. For the believer, the object of Christian faith is a living person, Jesus Christ, who fully entered into a true human existence on earth in the 1st century A.D., but who now lives, risen and glorified, forever in the Father's presence. Primarily, Christian faith affirms and adheres to this person—indeed, incarnate, crucified, and risen—and only secondarily to ideas and affirmations about him. In the realm of faith and theology, the "real Jesus," the only Jesus existing and living now, is this risen Lord, to whom access is given only through faith.

What, then—ask the objectors—is the usefulness of the historical Jesus to people of faith? My reply is: none, if one is asking solely about the direct object of Christian faith: Jesus Christ, crucified, risen, and presently reigning in his Church. This presently reigning Lord is accessible to all believers, including all those who will never study history or theology for even a single day in their lives. Yet I maintain that the quest for the historical Jesus can be very useful if one is asking about faith seeking understanding, i.e., theology, in a contemporary context. The theology of the patristic and medieval periods was blissfully ignorant of the problem of the historical Jesus, since it operated in a cultural context bereft of the historical-critical understanding that marks the modern Western mind. Theology is a cultural artifact; therefore, once a culture becomes permeated with a historical-critical approach, as has Western culture from the Enlightenment onward, theology can operate in and speak to that culture with credibility only if it absorbs into its methodology a historical approach.

For contemporary christology, this means that faith in Christ today must be able to reflect on itself systematically in a way that will allow an appropriation of the quest for the historical Jesus into theology. The historical Jesus, while not the object or essence of *faith*, must be an

integral part of modern *theology*. This appropriation of the quest by
theology is not idolatry to passing fads: rather, it serves the interests of
faith in at least four ways:[4]

(1) Against any attempt to reduce faith in Christ to a content-less
cipher, a mythic symbol, or a timeless archetype, the quest for the historical Jesus reminds Christians that faith in Christ is not just a vague
existential attitude or a way of being in the world. Christian faith is the
affirmation of and adherence to a particular person who said and did
particular things in a particular time and place in human history.[5] The
quest underlines the fact that there is specific content to Christian faith,
content connected with specific persons and events in past history.
While the quest cannot supply the essential content of faith, it can help
theology give greater concrete depth and color to that content.

(2) Against any attempt by pious Christians of a mystical or docetic
bent to swallow up the real humanity of Jesus into an "orthodox" emphasis on his divinity (actually, a crypto-monophysitism), the quest affirms that the risen Jesus is the same person who lived and died as a Jew
in 1st-century Palestine, a person as truly and fully human—with all the
galling limitations that involves—as any other human being.

(3) Against any attempt to "domesticate" Jesus for a comfortable,
respectable, bourgeois Christianity, the quest for the historical Jesus,
almost from its inception, has tended to emphasize the embarrassing,
nonconformist aspects of Jesus: e.g., his association with the religious
and social "lowlife" of Palestine, his prophetic critique of external religious observances that ignore or strangle the inner spirit of religion, his
opposition to certain religious authorities, especially the Jerusalem
priesthood.

(4) But lest the "uses of the historical Jesus" all seem to run in one
direction, it should be pointed out that, despite the claims of Reimarus
and many others since, the historical Jesus is not easily coopted for
programs of political revolution either. Compared with the classical
prophets of Israel, the historical Jesus is remarkably silent on many of
the burning social and political issues of his day. He can be turned into a
this-worldly political revolutionary only by contorted exegesis and special pleading.[6] Like good sociology, the historical Jesus subverts not just
some ideologies but all ideologies, including liberation theology.

Indeed, the usefulness of the historical Jesus to theology is that he
ultimately eludes all our neat theological programs; he brings all of them
into question by refusing to fit into the boxes we create for him. Paradoxically, although the quest for the historical Jesus is often linked in

the popular secular mind with "relevance," his importance lies precisely in his strange, off-putting, embarrassing contours, equally offensive to right and left wings. To this extent, at least, Albert Schweitzer was correct.[7] The more we appreciate what Jesus meant in his own time and place, the more "alien" he will seem to us.

Properly understood, the historical Jesus is a bulwark against the reduction of Christian faith in general and christology in particular to "relevant" ideology of any stripe. His refusal to be held fast by any given school of thought is what drives theologians onward into new paths; hence the historical Jesus remains a constant stimulus to theological renewal.[8] For this reason alone, the Jesus of history is worth the pains of the pursuit, including the initial pains of getting one's categories, sources, and criteria straight—the modest goal of Part One.

NOTES TO CHAPTER 7

[1] As is obvious from recent Church history in the United States, fundamentalism is by no means restricted to Protestants. American Catholics have developed their own varieties.

[2] On this point, cf. G. G. O'Collins, "Is the Resurrection an 'Historical' Event?" *HeyJ* 8 (1967) 381–87. O'Collins argues (rightly, in my view) that, although the "resurrection is a real, bodily event involving the person of Jesus of Nazareth" (p. 381), the resurrection of Jesus "is not an event *in* space and time and hence should not be called historical" (p. 384), since "we should require an historical occurrence to be something significant that is known to have happened in our space-time continuum" (p. 384).

[3] As distinct from ordinary pious Christians, some liberation theologians from the third world have attempted critical reflection on the historical Jesus— not always with the happiest of results; see John P. Meier, "The Bible as a Source for Theology," *The Catholic Theological Society of America. Proceedings of the Forty-third Annual Convention* 43 (1988) 1–14.

[4] Cf. the remarks of Rudolf Schnackenburg, "Der geschichtliche Jesus in seiner ständigen Bedeutung für Theologie und Kirche," *Rückfrage nach Jesus* (QD 63; ed. Karl Kertelge; Freiburg/Basel/Vienna: Herder, 1974) 194–220.

[5] Ernst Käsemann expresses the point this way: "Such research [into the historical Jesus] is theologically meaningful insofar as it struggles to grasp the unmistakable individuality of this earthly Jesus. The King of heaven has no countenance, unless it is that of the Nazarene" ("Die neue Jesus-Frage," *Jésus aux origines de la christologie* [BETL 40; ed. J. Dupont; Leuven: Leuven University; Gembloux: Duculot, 1975] 47–57).

[6] Unfortunately, this holds true of the otherwise intriguing book of Richard A. Horsley, *Jesus and the Spiral of Violence. Popular Jewish Resistance in Roman Palestine* (San Francisco: Harper & Row, 1987); see, e.g., his forced interpretation of the pericope on paying the coin of tribute to Caesar (Mark 12:13–17) on pp. 306–17. More satisfying is the book he coauthored with John S. Hanson, *Bandits, Prophets, and Messiahs. Popular Movements at the Time of Jesus* (Minneapolis/Chicago/New York: Winston, 1985).

[7] Schweitzer, *Geschichte der Leben-Jesu-Forschung*, 2. 620: "Recognized by the peculiar, special character of his ideas and action, he [the historical Jesus] will always embody [literally, 'retain'] for our age something strange and puzzling" (translation mine).

[8] For an attempt to write a present-day christology that takes seriously both Christian sources and modern historical consciousness, see John Macquarrie, *Jesus Christ in Modern Thought* (London: SCM; Philadelphia: Trinity, 1990).

PART TWO

ROOTS OF
THE PERSON

CHAPTER 8

IN THE BEGINNING . . .

The Origins of Jesus of Nazareth

Many books concerned with the historical Jesus begin their treatment with the adult Jesus of the public ministry, and understandably so. As we shall see, the sources that might allow us to say anything about Jesus' birth, family, and upbringing are meager at best. Yet I do not think total skepticism is in order. By carefully sifting the Infancy Narratives of the Gospels and reviewing what we know about Palestine in general and Galilee in particular at the time of Jesus, we can sketch a rough picture of Jesus' origins and background.

1. WHAT'S IN A NAME?

Preachers often urge us to imitate the "simple Jesus"—a creature who exists only in preachers' imaginations. Everything about Jesus was complicated, including his name.

Our English form of Jesus' name is derived from the Hebrew name *Yēšû*, the shortened form of the earlier and "more correct" form *Yēšûaʿ*, found in the late books of the Hebrew Bible.[1] The name *Yēšûaʿ* is in turn a shortened form of the name of the great biblical hero Joshua son of Nun, in Hebrew *Yĕhôšûaʿ*,[2] the successor of Moses and leader of the people Israel into the promised land. "Joshua" was the ordinary form of the name used before the Babylonian exile. Among Jews after the Babylonian exile, however, "Jesus" *(Yešûaᶜ* and then later the shorter *Yēšû)* became the common form of the name, though "Joshua" did not die out entirely.[3] "Jesus" remained a popular name among Jews until the beginning of the 2d century A.D., when perhaps Christian veneration of Jesus Christ led Jews to stop using *Yešûaᶜ* and *Yēšû* as a personal name. They instead revived "Joshua" as the common form of the name, the form borne by a good number of notable rabbis.[4] Thus, "Jesus" became a rare name among Jews after the 2d century.[5]

It is hard for Christians today to appreciate that Jesus of Nazareth did not stand out in his contemporaries' minds simply because of his name "Jesus." Out of reverence, Christians in general (except for those of the Spanish and Latin American traditions) have not used "Jesus" for naming their own children; hence the name strikes them as rare and sacred.[6] Such was not the case in the 1st century A.D. So current was the name Jesus that some descriptive phrase like "of Nazareth" or "the Christ (Messiah)" had to be added to distinguish him from the many other bearers of that name.

Josephus mentions some twenty or so men[7] called "Joshua" or "Jesus" in his writings (Greek uses the same form, *Iēsous,* for both "Joshua" and "Jesus"),[8] no less than ten belonging to the time of Jesus of Nazareth. The Joshuas listed by Josephus include not only Joshua the successor of Moses but also Joshua a high priest after the exile and Joshua (Jesus) ben Ananias, a peasant who prophesied against the temple, was delivered up by the Jerusalem priests to the procurator, and was scourged by him before being released *(J.W.* 6.5.3 §300–3). Neither the name nor the fate of the Nazarene was all that unique.

Hence it is no wonder that, when mentioning Jesus of Nazareth in order to identify Jesus' brother James, Josephus adds to "Jesus" the phrase "who is called Christ (Messiah)" in order to distinguish this Jesus from all the others. With an instinct for the essential, Josephus seizes upon the one thing that separated this Jesus from all other bearers of that name: from the time of this Jesus down to Josephus' day, some people hailed him as the Messiah. So important was it to use "Christ" as a distinguishing name for Jesus that, by the time of Paul in the mid-fifties of the 1st century A.D., "Christ" was well on its way to becoming Jesus' second name. It is not surprising, therefore, that when the pagan historians Tacitus and (probably) Suetonius write of Jesus in the early 2d century they use not the name "Jesus" but rather the title "Christ" as though it were his proper name.[9]

Ancient Hebrew names usually were an abbreviated form of a sentence, often proclaiming something about God ("theophoric names"). The name Joshua/*Yĕbôšûaʿ* originally meant "Yahweh helps" or "May Yahweh help."[10] As often happened in the Bible, the original or scientific etymology was forgotten and a popular etymology was invented. In the case of *Yĕbôšûaʿ*, the name was interpreted to mean "Yahweh saves" or "May Yahweh save."[11] It is this popular explanation of the name that is reflected in the angel's remark to the dreaming Joseph in Matt 1:21: "You shall call his name Jesus, for he shall save his people from their sins." Such puns on the popular explanation of a name are common in the OT, especially in stories about the births of famous people. The popular explanation of Jesus/Joshua was not, however, restricted to Christians. Philo, the 1st-century Jewish philosopher, reflects the same tradition: "Jesus is interpreted to mean 'salvation of the Lord.' . . ."[12]

The name of Jesus of Nazareth may signify something else within the context of 1st-century Galilee. It is probably not by accident that, like himself, all of Jesus' relatives bear names that hark back to the patriarchs, the exodus from Egypt, and the entrance into the promised land. His putative father was Joseph, the name of one of the twelve sons of Jacob/Israel and the progenitor, through Ephraim and Manasseh, of two of the twelve tribes. His mother was Mary, in Hebrew Miriam, the name of the sister of Moses. His four brothers, James, Joses, Simon, and Jude, were named after the patriarchs who begot the twelve sons/tribes of Israel (James=Jacob) and after three of those twelve sons (Joses= Joseph, Simon=Simeon, and Jude=Judah).

This may not seem strange to us, but for most of the OT period Israelites were not named for the great patriarchs mentioned in the books of Genesis and Exodus. A change seems to have begun after the exile and accelerated around the time of the Maccabean revolt against the Seleucid monarch Antiochus IV Epiphanes (reigned 175–164/163 B.C.), who tried to impose Hellenistic culture on Jews in Palestine and suppress traditional Jewish religious and ethnic customs. Antiochus' policies proved counterproductive. While certain urban groups already sympathetic to Hellenistic ways supported Antiochus' "reform," many Jews in Palestine—especially in small towns and rural areas—reacted to the Seleucid persecution with an upsurge of native-religious feeling. It may be around this time that the custom of naming children after the great heroes of the past became increasingly common.

The custom may have struck an especially responsive chord in Galilee, where Judaism for centuries had had to live side by side with strong pagan influence; it was only after the victories of the Maccabees that a vigorous Jewish presence could again assert itself in "Galilee of the Gentiles." Most likely, therefore, the fact that all of Jesus' immediate family bear "patriarchal" and "matriarchal" names betokens the family's participation in this reawakening of Jewish national and religious identity, an identity that looked to the idyllic past of the patriarchs for definition. It may not be too farfetched to suggest that we hear an echo of this theme of national restoration years later when the adult Jesus chooses precisely twelve men to be his inner group of disciples. The number twelve was probably meant to conjure up the idea of the twelve patriarchs, the twelve tribes, and hence the restoration of all Israel by Joshua/Jesus of Nazareth.[13] What's in a name? Perhaps a great deal—and not just musings over imaginary etymologies.

2. BIRTH AND LINEAGE

A. THE PROBLEM OF SOURCES

Little or nothing can be said with certitude or high probability about the birth, infancy, and early years of the vast majority of historical figures in the ancient Mediterranean world. In the exceptional cases of towering figures like Alexander the Great or the Emperor Octavian Augustus, some facts were preserved, though even these were often interwoven with mythical and legendary motifs.[14] The same pattern can be found in the OT, where again a large number of heroes and villains lack detailed narratives of their conception, birth, and infancy. Still, some great figures, like Isaac, Jacob, the twelve patriarchs, Samson, Samuel, David, and most notably Moses are favored with stories about their birth or youth. These narratives often display common themes: e.g., annunciation of the birth by an angel and/or a dream, the sterility of the wife before divine intervention, prophecies or portents of the child's future, and precocious words or deeds of the youth. The drive to expand these "midrashic" elements continues beyond the canonical Scriptures into various "retellings" of the OT narratives, e.g., in Josephus' *The Jewish Antiquities*[15] and Philo's *Life of Moses*,[16] as well as in the later midrashim of the rabbis.

Granted this phenomenon of stories of wondrous birth or childhood, composed to celebrate ancient heroes, pagan and Jewish alike, one must approach with caution the Infancy Narratives found in Chapters 1–2 of both Matthew and Luke. Such caution need not betoken an anti-supernatural bias that rejects a priori any extraordinary action of God in human history. One can maintain the theoretical possibility of miracles while being wary of individual claims,[17] especially when such claims occur in a type of literature (i.e., infancy narratives of the ancient Mediterranean world) where angelic annunciations and miraculous births were stock motifs. One can take such motifs seriously—inquiring after their religious message—without necessarily taking them literally. All this simply reminds us that the truth-claims of any literature must be judged according to the specific genre or form of the literature in question.[18]

This kind of general wariness is reinforced by the specific nature of the Infancy Narratives in the canonical Gospels.[19] First of all, these narratives occur in only two places in the whole of the NT, the first two chapters of both Matthew and Luke. Even in these two Gospels, events in the Infancy Narratives are almost never referred to once Chapter 3 of each Gospel is reached. Thus, within Matthew and Luke themselves, the Infancy Narratives stand in relative isolation; they are distinct compositions stemming from traditions different from those found elsewhere in the Four Gospels—and indeed in the rest of the NT. The outline of early Christian preaching reflected in the Gospels of Mark and John, the sermons of Acts, and the early creeds and hymns in the NT epistles know nothing of the events in the Infancy Narratives.[20] Even when preexistence and incarnation are affirmed (as in John 1:1–18 or Phil 2:6–11), the text instantly jumps to the adult—and usually crucified—Jesus.

Second, unlike the public ministry of Jesus, where certain eyewitnesses were also prominent leaders in the early Church, almost all the witnesses to the events surrounding Jesus' birth were dead or otherwise unavailable to the early Church when it formulated the infancy traditions that lie behind Matthew 1–2 and Luke 1–2. Zechariah, Elizabeth, John the Baptist, Joseph, Simeon, Anna, Herod, the Magi, and the Bethlehem shepherds were all presumably deceased or otherwise "unavailable for comment" as the infancy traditions were developed in the first two Christian generations. As a result, some commentators have singled out as *the* source of the Infancy Narratives the one person who did survive into the days of the early Church, Mary the mother of Jesus (see John 19:25–27 for Mary at Jesus' cross; Acts 1:14 for Mary with the twelve apostles and the brothers of Jesus in Jerusalem before Pentecost).[21]

While Mary might theoretically be the ultimate source for some traditions in the Infancy Narratives, grave problems beset the claim that she is the direct source of any narrative as it now stands. To begin with, Mary cannot be the source for all the infancy traditions in both Matthew and Luke; for, as we shall see, Matthew and Luke diverge from or even contradict each other on certain key points. Since Mary is much more prominent in Luke 1–2 (Matthew 1–2 being largely given over to Joseph), she is often claimed as a source for Luke's version.[22] This more limited claim is likewise not without its difficulties, since Luke appears to make some glaring errors in "things Jewish,"[23] especially with regard to Mary's "purification" in the Jerusalem temple, an event for which Mary would presumably have to be the source. After all, if she is not the source for the story of her own purification, where else in the Infancy Narratives would she be the source?

Yet the story of Mary's purification in the temple confuses a number of distinct Jewish rituals.[24] For example, the best Greek texts begin the story with a reference to "*their* purification" (Luke 2:22), where the only natural meaning in the context is "the purification of Mary and Joseph," since the immediately following verb states that "*they* [Joseph and Mary] brought" the child to Jerusalem.[25] Yet in the 1st century A.D. the Jewish husband did not undergo any purification along with his wife; it was the physical birth that rendered the mother, and only the mother, ritually unclean. Furthermore, Luke conflates two distinct rituals, as the two halves of 2:22 show: the purification of the mother (which, according to Lev 12:1–8 and later rabbinic statements, did require a visit to the tent/temple) and the redemption of the firstborn male child (which required the payment of five shekels to the temple, but not a temple visit). Luke is thus inaccurate when he describes the bringing of the child to the temple as "according to" the Mosaic Law (2:23+27). He is likewise incorrect when he connects the redemption or "presentation" of Jesus with the sacrifice of doves or pigeons (actually a part of the purification ritual), while he says nothing about the payment of the shekels, a necessary part of the redemption ritual.

To be blunt: either Mary was not the source of this story of her purification or else she had a remarkably poor memory about important events involving Jesus and herself. Either way, the case for the historical reliability of the Infancy Narratives is not enhanced. The simplest conclusion is that what is operative in Luke 2:22–38, as elsewhere in Chapters 1–2, is the theological program of Luke, not the reminiscences of Mary.[26] Obviously, these same difficulties prevent us from appealing, in desperation, to Jesus himself as the source of the narrative—apart from the fact that neither orthodox nor gnostic writings of the early patristic period present the adult or risen Jesus dispensing detailed revelations about his infancy. We are left, then, with a clear conclusion: the traditions behind the Infancy Narratives differ essentially from those of the public ministry and passion. In the case of the Infancy Narratives, we cannot identify any eyewitnesses of the original events who could have acted as reliable sources in the early Church. Such is not the case with the public ministry or the passion.

A third major problem with the Infancy Narratives is that there are tensions, not to say contradictions, between Matthew's and Luke's versions of Jesus' infancy. Granted, some of the tensions could be harmonized with a little ingenuity. In Matthew, Joseph alone receives from an angel the annunciation of Jesus' virginal conception; in Luke, of course, Mary alone receives such a revelation. Strictly speaking, neither account contradicts the other and the two might be conflated—as indeed they were in later Christian retelling.

More difficult to harmonize are the differing accounts of the journeys of Joseph and Mary in the two Infancy Narratives and the two "geographical" plots at the basis of the two stories. In the case of Matthew, the first place name that occurs in his narrative proper (1:18–2:23) is Bethlehem of Judea (2:1). Since no indication of a change of place is given at this point, the reader who knows only Matthew's story would naturally take the preceding story of "the annunciation to Joseph" (1:18–25) as located in Bethlehem too. This fits in perfectly with details in the Magi story. The Magi find Mary and Jesus when they enter "into the *house*" (2:11), not into a stable or cave. Presumably this is the house Joseph and Mary dwell in permanently in Bethlehem. This in turn fits well with the fact that Herod, having ascertained from the Magi the time of the star's appearance (in order to calculate the child's age), orders the slaughter of all boys in Bethlehem and the surrounding region "*two years* of age and younger." Matthew emphasizes the point by adding the explanation "according to the time he [Herod] had carefully ascertained from the Magi" (2:16). In other words, Matthew's story does not presume that Jesus has just been born when the Magi arrive.[27] To ensure Jesus' murder, Herod must have boys even as old as two years slaughtered. Obviously, we are not dealing in Matthew as in Luke with a birth during a quick trip to Bethlehem from Nazareth, to be followed by a fairly swift return to Nazareth after a visit to Jerusalem.

Matthew thinks of Bethlehem as Joseph's permanent home—so much so that he must strain to explain how Jesus wound up living permanently in Nazareth and so was called "the Nazorean." Matthew's plot takes a long detour to get to Nazareth from Bethlehem. First, the flight into Egypt (Matt 2:16–18), for which there is no time in Luke's plot, conveniently removes Jesus from Bethlehem. On returning from Egypt, Joseph is afraid to return to Judea (and therefore Bethlehem) because Archelaus, Herod's son, is reigning in the old tyrant's place. Curiously, Joseph's solution to the danger posed by a ruler who is a son of Herod the Great is to go into Galilee—where another son of Herod the Great, Herod Antipas, the future slayer of John the Baptist, is ruling! Out of the frying pan into the fire. Joseph has a strange sense of security measures.

More to the point, Matthew brings Joseph's peregrinations to a close by narrating: ". . . and coming he [Joseph] settled down in a city called Nazareth" (2:23). This hardly sounds like a return to the old homestead; Nazareth is formally introduced[28] in a way that intimates that it was not on the mental horizon of author or audience before Joseph's "strategic retreat." Significantly, Matthew uses exactly the same Greek wording to describe the adult Jesus' transferral of his home from Nazareth to Capernaum: "And leaving Nazareth, *coming he* [Jesus] *settled down* in Capernaum" (4:13).[29] This is Jesus' first trip to Capernaum, undertaken to set up a new home there; and so the natural sense of the parallel text in 2:23 is that this is Joseph's first trip to Nazareth, undertaken to set up a new home there, after Bethlehem has proved too dangerous. In short, the whole geographical pattern of Matthew's Infancy Narrative rests upon the basic movement from Bethlehem, Joseph's original home, to Nazareth, his new home, sought out as a refuge.

Luke presents the exact opposite pattern. At the time of the annunciation to Mary, both Mary (explicitly) and Joseph (implicitly) are located in Nazareth of Galilee (1:26–27). The news of Elizabeth's conception of the future Baptist moves Mary to visit her relative in the hill country of Judea, but after the visit Mary naturally returns "to her house" (1:56), i.e., to Nazareth. Another reason must therefore be found for Mary's presence in Bethlehem when Jesus is born. Luke's solution is a worldwide census decreed by Caesar Augustus when Quirinius was governor of Syria (2:1)—unfortunately, such a census (which would have had to occur ca. 5 B.C.) cannot be documented in any other ancient source.

According to ancient records, Quirinius, who became governor of Syria in A.D. 6, conducted a census of Judea, but not of Galilee, in A.D. 6–7. Attempts to reconcile Luke 2:1 with the facts of ancient history are hopelessly contrived.[30] Moreover, Mary would not have had to accompany Joseph to register, and her advanced pregnancy would have positively argued against accompanying him when there was no obligation to do so.

Once Jesus is born in Bethlehem, Luke goes out of his way to insist that Jesus quickly becomes known not only in Bethlehem's environs but also in Jerusalem. Indeed, he is publicly pointed out as the prophesied redeemer (2:25–38)[31] in the temple, "just across town" from the palace of Herod, who (according to Matthew) is doing everything possible to find out where the upstart king of the Jews is located. After the purification/redemption/presentation in the temple, the holy family *returns* peacefully "to *their own* city Nazareth" (contrast Matthew!), with neither time nor thought nor need for a flight into Egypt. In other words, while Matthew's basic geographical plot in his Infancy Narrative moves from original home in Bethlehem to adopted home in Nazareth (necessary for political reasons), Luke's plot moves in the opposite direction: from original home in Nazareth to temporary stay—hardly a home—in Bethlehem (necessary for political reasons), and then back to "their own home" in Nazareth.

Other striking differences between Matthew's and Luke's Infancy Narratives could be explored, but these suffice to show why the historian must be wary about using the Infancy Narratives as sources for historical information about Jesus. Both narratives seem to be largely products of early Christian reflection on the salvific meaning of Jesus Christ in the light of OT prophecies.[32] To a great degree, major Christian themes of the death-resurrection traditions in the Gospels and early creedal formulas have been retrojected into stories of Jesus' conception and birth (e.g., cf. Rom 1:3–4 with Luke 1:31–35).[33] A major theological point made by the Infancy Narratives thus becomes clear: what Jesus Christ was fully revealed to be at the resurrection (Son of David, Son of God by the power of the Holy Spirit) he really was from his conception onward.[34]

In view of all that we have seen, do the Infancy Narratives have anything to contribute to our knowledge of the historical Jesus? Some exegetes would answer: practically nothing.[35] However, a totally negative judgment may be too sweeping. According to the two-source theory, Matthew and Luke did not know each other's Gospels; moreover, as we have just seen, Matthew's and Luke's Infancy Narratives largely diverge from and even contradict each other. Hence, any agreements between Matthew and Luke in their Infancy Narratives become historically significant, insofar as the criterion of multiple attestation comes into play. Such agreements in two independent and sharply contrasting narratives would, at the very least, go back to earlier tradition and not be the creation of the evangelists.

As a matter of fact, some of the points of agreement are generally accepted by scholars as historical. For instance, despite all their differences, Matthew and Luke both place Jesus' birth during the reign of Herod the Great (37–4 B.C.; cf. Matt 2:1 and Luke 1:5). Further, Matthew intimates that it took place toward the end of Herod's reign,[36] a point that coheres well with other ascertainable data concerning the chronology of Jesus' life.[37] Both Infancy Narratives agree that Jesus' putative father was named Joseph and his mother Mary, facts supported by a few scattered references in different streams of Gospel tradition (for Joseph: Luke 3:23; 4:22; John 1:45; 6:42;[38] for Mary: Mark 6:3 [par. Matt 13:55]; Acts 1:14[39]).

B. Birth at Bethlehem

The place of Jesus' birth is more problematic. Both Matthew and Luke affirm that it is Bethlehem, but Matthew 2 and Luke 2 are the only two chapters of the NT that clearly make this claim. It finds no echo elsewhere in the Infancy Narratives or in the rest of Matthew and Luke— or, indeed, in the rest of the NT. Elsewhere even in Matthew and Luke Jesus is simply Jesus of Nazareth, Jesus the Nazarene, or Jesus the Nazorean.

In fact, the only place in the whole of the NT where the word "Bethlehem" appears outside the Infancy Narratives is John 7:42; and that passage is ambiguous in its intent.[40] The concluding section of John 7 deals with the various reactions of Jewish groups and individuals to Jesus' self-revelation. Verses 40–44 focus on the division of opinion in the "crowd" that has listened to his teaching in the temple. Some think that he is the eschatological prophet (v 40), while others say that he is the Messiah. To this some object in vv 41–42: "The Messiah isn't going to come from Galilee, is he? Doesn't the Scripture say that the Messiah will be descended from David and will come from Bethlehem, the town David came from?"

Given the frequent use of ambiguity and irony in John's Gospel, this objection to Jesus' claims can be read in two different ways. If one supposes that the evangelist and his readers knew the Infancy Narrative tradition of Jesus' birth in Bethlehem, then the irony is that those in the crowd objecting to Jesus confidently claim knowledge of Jesus' origins, knowledge that rules him out of consideration as Messiah, while all along their supposed knowledge is actually ignorance of Jesus' true hometown.

The problem with this line of interpretation is that the Fourth Evangelist insists from Chapter 1 onward that Jesus does come from Nazareth (1:45–56), with all the scandal that causes even future believers (e.g., Nathanael in 1:46). John's insistence on Nazareth as the place of Jesus' earthly origins, a code word for the "flesh" that the Word becomes, returns with theological force in his Passion Narrative (18:5,7; 19:19). Moreover, the evangelist never communicates any other tradition about Jesus' hometown to his readers, despite John's tendency to deliver informative asides to his audience while the drama is in progress. There is no clear indication anywhere in the Johannine writings of the NT that readers in the Johannine communities would have known the special Infancy Narrative tradition about Bethlehem. In effect, an interpretation that claims that John's readers obviously know all about Bethlehem as Jesus' birthplace is involved in a vicious circle. It presumes what is to be proved.

It is probable, therefore, that John's irony in 7:42 should be read in a different way. Often in Johannine irony, what the objector says to rule Jesus out of court is perfectly true on the earthly, fleshly level, yet totally fails to grasp the heavenly origin and reality of Jesus Christ, the Word made flesh. What the objector says is perfectly true and totally irrelevant. Thus, in 7:42, the objectors, in John's mind, are correct in saying that Jesus comes from Nazareth, not Bethlehem. This is not surprising, since John's Gospel as a whole does not show great interest in a Son-of-David christology.

But the point of the irony is that the earthly origin of Jesus, be it Nazareth or Bethlehem, is not of ultimate consequence. Jesus comes ultimately from above, from heaven, from the Father, while these blind objectors are fixated on the "below," the "flesh" of this world. Jesus makes this very point later on in the same temple discourse: "You are from below, I am from above" (8:23); hence they cannot understand him. Granted, at the very least, the ambiguity of the reference to Bethlehem in 7:42, the verse is of questionable value for proving a Gospel tradition of Jesus' birth in Bethlehem outside the Infancy Narratives. While Jesus' birth in Bethlehem cannot be positively ruled out (one can rarely "prove a negative" in ancient history), we must accept the fact that the predominant view in the Gospels and Acts is that Jesus came from Nazareth and—apart from Chapters 1–2 of Matthew and Luke—only from Nazareth. The somewhat contorted or suspect ways in which Matthew and Luke reconcile the dominant Nazareth tradition with the special Bethlehem tradition of their Infancy Narratives may indicate that Jesus' birth at Bethlehem is to be taken not as a historical fact but as a *theologoumenon*, i.e., as a theological affirmation (e.g., Jesus is the true Son of David, the prophesied royal Messiah) put into the form of an apparently historical narrative.[41] One must admit, though, that on this point certitude is not to be had.[42]

C. DESCENT FROM DAVID

If birth at Bethlehem is simply a theological symbol of Jesus' Davidic messiahship, is the same true of the explicit affirmations in the Infancy Narratives that Jesus, through Joseph, was legally of the house of David? To answer that question, we must first be clear about what the Infancy Narratives say. Contrary to a common idea held by later Christian theology, an idea that has its beginnings in Ignatius of Antioch and Justin Martyr in the 2d century A.D.,[43] the NT never states that Mary was of the tribe of Judah or of the house of David. The only indication of Mary's lineage is given in Luke 1, where Elizabeth is said to be both "of the daughters of Aaron" (v 5, hence of an elite priestly line within the tribe of Levi) and a "kinswoman" of Mary (v 36, *syggenis*, a vague term). If we take Luke at his word, Mary would be of levitical, and perhaps Aaronic, descent.[44] However, it is questionable whether this implication of Luke 1 yields any historical information. In his Infancy Narrative, Luke is dealing with two cycles of annunciation-and-birth stories, one of the Baptist and the other of Jesus. The two cycles, for the most part, run parallel, without making contact with each other. The one point of direct narrative contact is the kinship between Mary and Elizabeth, which prompts the "visitation" (1:39–56), the only time that the two cycles intersect. This bringing together of otherwise independent cycles by way of Mary's relationship to Elizabeth may well be the work of Luke.[45] Hence it is wise not to put any weight on texts that imply Mary's levitical lineage.[46] In the end, we must admit ignorance of Mary's genealogy.[47]

Actually, from the NT point of view, any consideration of Mary's lineage is beside the point. The Jewish milieu out of which the Infancy Narratives came regularly traced a child's genealogy through his or her father, whether or not the "father" was actually the biological parent. This is quite different from our way of looking at parenthood. To modern Americans, the biological father, not the adoptive father, is the real father; in the eyes of the OT, the legal father is the real father, whether or not he physically procreated the child. Hence the lineage of Joseph is what determines the lineage of Jesus—a point that is stressed not only in the Infancy Narratives in general but more importantly in the very passages that inculcate the idea of Mary's virginal conception.[48]

This affirmation of Jesus' descent from David might easily be placed alongside his birth at Bethlehem as a *theologoumenon*[49] (a theological insight narrated as a historical event) if it were not for the fact that numerous and diverse streams of NT tradition also affirm Jesus' Davidic lineage. Of special interest is the early creedal formula Paul cites in Rom 1:3–4, which states in part that Jesus "was born of the seed of David according to the flesh."[50] What is startling here is that Paul, writing in the late fifties to a church he had never visited or taught, can presume that the Roman Christians will recognize this creedal formula as an expression of their shared faith and as a basis for further discussion.[51] The very reason Paul starts his epistle with this formulation of faith is that it is common ground that he shares with the Romans, a way he can show them that he is a "true believer" who holds the same faith they do. The Roman Christians seem to have been a heterogeneous lot riven by tensions, and at least some of them would have found Paul's version of the Gospel suspect.[52] Yet, by the late fifties, some twenty-eight years after Christ's crucifixion, both he and they can agree without further ado on Jesus' descent from David as a key object of belief. This is all the more striking because Jesus' Davidic descent is of no great interest to Paul himself and never appears in Paul's own statements of his theological views.[53] That this belief in Jesus' Davidic lineage was entrenched early in some Christian creedal formulas is confirmed by the formulation cited in 2 Tim 2:8: "Remember Jesus Christ, raised from the dead, of the seed of David." While 2 Timothy was not written by Paul himself but rather by a disciple of Paul toward the end of the 1st century, critics generally agree that 2 Tim 2:8 represents a primitive Christian profession of faith that circulated well before the writing of the Pastoral Epistles.[54]

Beyond the Pauline epistles, the belief that Jesus was of Davidic stock is also diffused in other streams of early Christianity. It is affirmed by Mark (10:47; 12:35–37),[55] Matthew (9:27; 12:23; 15:22; 20:30; 21:9,15; 22:42–45),[56] and Luke (3:31; 18:38–39; 20:41–44; Acts 2:25–31; 13:22–23).[57] The Epistle to the Hebrews does not directly call Jesus "son of David," but the strong emphasis on Jesus as King-Priest-Messiah in the likeness of Melchizedek, priest-king of Jerusalem (Chapter 7), plus the author's explicit statement that Jesus was born not of the tribe of Levi but of the tribe of Judah (7:14), makes it likely that the author knew the tradition of Davidic descent.[58] That this tradition was also valued in more fiery apocalyptic streams of early Christianity is clear from Rev 3:7; 5:5; 22:16.

In short, there was an early and widely attested belief in Jesus' Davidic descent within 1st-century Christianity. It was affirmed in the first Christian generation, especially in the context of his resurrection. If we look at the confessional formulas in Rom 1:3–4 and 2 Tim 2:8 as well as the sermons of Peter and Paul in Acts 2:24–36 and 13:22–37, the point of affirming Jesus to be "of the seed of David" seems to be that, in Jesus, and especially at his resurrection, God fulfilled the promise he made to David in 2 Sam 7:12–14: "I will *raise up* your *seed* after you . . . and I shall establish his kingly rule . . . and I shall make firm his throne forever. I will be his father and he shall be my son."[59] Perhaps, then, the earliest connection that Christian faith made between Jesus and Davidic descent was in the context of his resurrection and in the light of the OT promise to David.

But does this theological use prove that Davidic sonship is therefore purely a *theologoumenon?* Perhaps it might indicate just the opposite. After all, we are still left asking: What prompted early Christians to see Jesus' resurrection as the enthronement of the royal Davidic Messiah, the seed of David who fulfilled the promise of 2 Sam 7:12–14? As we shall see, the designation "Messiah" in 1st-century Judaism was vague, ill defined, and open to many interpretations, including a priestly Messiah from the tribe of Levi (so at Qumran) or a prophet anointed with God's Spirit (as described in Isa 61:1).[60] Hence, believing that Jesus was the Messiah did not necessitate seeing him as a Son of David. Indeed, such an interpretation of Jesus' messiahship might expose early Christian Jews to easy rebuttal if it were known that Jesus was not of Davidic lineage.

Moreover, there was nothing in the OT or Jewish belief in the 1st century that tied together the resurrection of an individual within ongoing history—certainly a novel concept at any rate—with Davidic messiahship. That the individual should have been a crucified criminal makes the royal title all the stranger. In fact, seeing the resurrection of the crucified Jesus as the enthronement of the royal Davidic Messiah seems totally unmotivated *unless* some of Jesus' disciples during his earthly life thought he was of Davidic stock and fixed their hopes on him partly because of his lineage—hopes that they then considered fulfilled by his resurrection. If certain followers during the public ministry already spoke of Jesus as a son of David, then their interpretation of the resurrection as the royal enthronement of the seed of David in keeping with the promise made in 2 Sam 7:12–14 makes sense. Viewed from this angle, the resurrection was not the catalyst for the idea of Davidic descent; Davidic descent was the catalyst for a particular interpretation of the resurrection.

In sum, Jesus' Davidic sonship should not be so quickly dismissed as a *theologoumenon* of the Infancy Narrative alongside his birth at Bethlehem. Attestation of Jesus' Davidic descent is early and widespread in many diverse strands of NT tradition; and only some idea of Jesus' Davidic lineage, held by disciples during the public ministry, explains the very early interpretation of the resurrection of a crucified criminal as the royal enthronement of the Son of David.[61]

Does all this prove that Jesus of Nazareth was *literally, biologically* of Davidic stock? Of course not. The Infancy Narratives could be taken to say just the opposite. They trace Jesus' Davidic genealogy through Joseph, his legal, not physical, father. All the evidence allows us to suggest is that, during his public ministry, Jesus was already thought by some of his followers to be of Davidic descent. This popular view may or may not have been literally, biologically true. We certainly cannot verify this claim today; and, apart from Jewish priests and aristocrats, such genealogical claims were probably not verifiable at the time either. The one positive point gained by this discussion is that, when we come to treat the ministry, claims, and titles of the adult Jesus, we must remember that, even prior to Easter, some disciples probably esteemed him as "Son of David."

D. Virginal Conception

A final theological theme of the Infancy Narratives that is often called a *theologoumenon* is Mary's virginal conception of Jesus.[62] A number of problems intersect here. First, there is the general problem of miracles in the Gospels. That question will be treated later on, in the context of Jesus' public ministry. For the moment, suffice it to say that, when dealing with ancient history, the historian or exegete can try to discern whether a claim that some miracle occurred goes back to the original figure who supposedly performed (or experienced) the miracle or whether the claim is a later accretion on the oral tradition or even possibly the invention of a later author. Source, form, and redaction criticism all need to be applied to such a question. If, as a result of critical study, it seems that the claim does go back to the supposed performer (or recipient) of the miracle, one can raise further questions, such as the person's integrity, sincerity, mental stability, religious message and practice, as well as the dispositions of his audience. The historian may then try to reach some conclusion as to whether anything really happened and whether it was in some sense startling, extraordinary, or inexplicable. What the historian or exegete cannot hope to do by historical research is to resolve what are really philosophical questions (e.g., whether miracles do take place) or theological questions (e.g., whether God has indeed acted in this particular "miracle," thus calling people to faith). Such questions, while important, simply go beyond the realm of history proper.

Second, while these observations apply to all accounts of the miraculous in the Gospels, the case of the virginal conception poses a special problem and is in a category by itself. That Jesus was *thought* by his contemporaries, foes as well as friends, to have worked miracles is attested by all the various streams of Gospel tradition as well as by Josephus. We thus have the criterion of multiple attestation satisfied abundantly. Even various types of miracles (e.g., exorcisms, healings at a distance) are attested by more than one source. Whether what people *thought* happened actually did happen is obviously another question.

Clearly, our basis for judgment is much narrower in the case of the Infancy Narratives. Strictly speaking, in the whole of the NT the virginal conception is affirmed only in Matt 1:18–25 and Luke 1:26–38;[63] even other parts of the Infancy Narratives do not refer to the tradition explicitly.[64] On the other hand, granted the mutual independence of Matthew and Luke and the divergent or even contradictory forms of their Infancy Narratives, the tradition of the virginal conception, attested by both (though in different ways),[65] certainly goes back earlier than the two Gospels that now contain it. It is thus not a "late legend" created at the end of the 1st century.

How far back the tradition of the virginal conception goes and what its precise origin was is no longer ascertainable by the historian.[66] Exegetes will sometimes speak vaguely of "family traditions" that became known to the early Church. Yet we have already seen that Mary cannot be invoked as the direct source of events that concern her most in the Lucan Infancy Narrative; and a number of Gospel passages[67] indicate that Jesus' brothers did not believe in him during the public ministry—which hardly seems likely if they had known about his miraculous conception.

What of a direct origin from pagan myths of the offspring of divine fathers and human mothers?[68] To begin with, the references to various pagan myths found in some commentaries are not as relevant as they might at first seem. In such stories there is always explicitly or implicitly some sexual union between male and female; the divine male takes the place of the human male in impregnating the woman. That is not the idea in Matt 1:18–25 or Luke 1:26–38. In both texts the virginal conception is referred specifically to God's *Spirit (pneuma,* a neuter word in Greek, representing *rûaḥ,* a word that is usually feminine in biblical Hebrew). Matthew in particular (1:20) says that Jesus is begotten in Mary *ek pneumatos . . . hagiou, "of* the Holy Spirit"; the preposition used to express the Spirit's action *(ek)* occurs in the preceding genealogy (1:1–17) not of the male but of the female role in conception (1:3,5 [*bis*], 6). The idea of the virginal conception, whatever its origins, is not rooted in pagan ideas of impregnation by a god. Rather, the theological affirmation being made by the evangelists—whatever its historical basis—is that the Holy Spirit, who in early Christian tradition was associated with the power that raised Jesus from the dead (cf. Rom 1:3–4; 8:11), is likewise the eschatological power that brought about Jesus' virginal conception. Both events are seen by the NT authors as signs of the end time.[69]

Trying to find the roots of the idea of the virginal conception in speculation supposedly rife among Hellenistic Jews in the Diaspora is not productive either. We have no clear evidence that the famous passage of Isa 7:14 cited by Matthew ("behold, a virgin shall conceive") was ever taken to refer to a virginal conception before NT authors used it.[70] The Hebrew text refers simply to a woman called an *'almâ*, a young woman of marriageable age.[71] Even the Septuagint translation of Isa 7:14 need not refer to a virginal conception. While *parthenos*, the word the Septuagint uses to translate *'almâ*, does often mean "virgin," it can also carry the more general meaning of a young girl of marriageable age and is so used at times in the Septuagint.[72] The most glaring example of this wider meaning is its use of Dinah after she has been raped (Gen 34:3).[73] Hence the Greek form of Isa 7:14 may have carried exactly the same sense as did the Hebrew original. We have no firm proof that Hellenistic Jews before the time of Jesus understood the Septuagint text in terms of a virginal conception. In desperation, scholars sometimes appeal to Philo's allegorical interpretation of stories of the birth of the patriarchs in Genesis; Philo uses the stories as symbols of virtues begotten in the soul by God.[74] Any link between such allegories about the origin of virtues and the story of the virginal conception of Jesus is less than tenuous.

The end result of this survey must remain meager and disappointing to both defenders and opponents of the doctrine of the virginal conception. Taken by itself, historical-critical research simply does not have the sources and tools available to reach a final decision on the historicity of the virginal conception as narrated by Matthew and Luke.[75] One's acceptance or rejection of the doctrine will be largely influenced by one's own philosophical and theological presuppositions, as well as the weight one gives Church teaching.[76] Once again, we are reminded of the built-in limitations of historical criticism. It is a useful tool, provided we do not expect too much of it.

E. The Question of Illegitimacy

One possible source of the virginal conception tradition is usually not mentioned in polite company or in polite books: the possibility that Jesus was at the very least conceived or even born out of wedlock.[77] This idea, which causes shock in the pious and glee in the impious, might be passed over in silence if it were not for the fact that the illegitimacy of Jesus has been proposed as a viable thesis by a few recent scholars.[78] Some Christians might object to any consideration of this theory as an insult to Christian faith. Other Christians might object in return that Christian faith proclaims the shocking scandal of the utter "emptying" (cf. Phil 2:7) of the Son of God into our mortal flesh, even to the depths of condemnation as a criminal, mockery and torture, and finally death on a cross. In the light of all the horrors Jesus experienced in his passion and death, illegitimacy could be considered a minor aspect of the "emptying" *(kenōsis)*. More to the point, though, the method adopted by the quest for the historical Jesus demands that a scholar prescind from, though not deny, what is held by faith. If some researchers seriously propose that Jesus' birth was illegitimate, the proposal must be examined seriously.[79]

Actually, the charge of illegitimacy is not new to our investigation in this book. We have already touched on it in Chapter 4, when we examined rabbinic and other Jewish material as a possible source for the quest. As we saw there, the Jewish traditions about a person named "Ben Pendera" or "Ben Pantere"[80] are often connected by scholars with a claim of the 2d-century pagan author Celsus, who wrote a polemic against Christianity called the *True Discourse (Alēthēs logos)* about A.D. 178. Although Celsus' work has been lost, we have extensive citations of it in the ecclesiastical writer Origen, who wrote a famous counterblast, the *Contra Celsum (Against Celsus)* about A.D. 248. In 1.28, 32 of the *Contra Celsum*, Origen reports that Celsus had heard from a Jew a story about Jesus' illegitimate birth. According to the story, Jesus fabricated the account of his birth from a virgin. In reality, Jesus' mother was driven out by the carpenter husband to whom she was betrothed because she had committed adultery with a soldier named *Panthera* (cf. the Ben *Pantere* of Jewish sources). Left poor and homeless, she gave birth to Jesus in secret. Jesus later spent time in Egypt, where he hired himself out as a laborer, learned magic, and so came to claim the title of God.[81]

Celsus' account is important because it is the first *clear* and *clearly datable* report of such accusations among the Jews.[82] Every other suggested source is either later in time, unclear in its reference, or clearly dependent on and reacting to the Gospel Infancy Narratives.[83] Since Celsus is reporting what a Jew told him sometime before 178,[84] we may presume that such a story was already circulating among certain Hellenistic Jews of the Diaspora around the middle of the 2d century. Most likely such a story does not date earlier than this, since Justin Martyr argues with Trypho the Jew at great length over the virginal conception, without Trypho ever being represented as replying with the charge of illegitimacy.[85] However, the fact that the story is first attested among Diaspora and not Palestinian Jews,[86] and not until around the middle of the 2d century, raises the possibility that the story is a polemical Jewish parody of the Christian account of the virginal conception, especially as presented in Matthew's Gospel.

That Matthew's version should be the major target of the parody is hardly surprising. Matthew—the supposedly "Jewish Gospel"—is much clearer in its affirmation of the virginal conception than is Luke, and by the middle of the 2d century Matthew was fast becoming the most popular Gospel in mainstream Christianity. In fact, when we put Matthew's Infancy Narrative alongside Celsus' story, it becomes highly likely that the former is in some way the source of the latter, since Celsus' account reflects traits unique to Matthew in the entire NT. Matthew, not Luke, intimates the consternation of Joseph when Mary is found to be pregnant and his plan to divorce her (Matt 1:18–20). Matthew alone recounts the flight into Egypt (2:13–15), which comes on the heels of the story of the Magi *(magoi;* cf. Celsus' connection of Jesus' stay in Egypt with *magic).* Matthew also joins the story of the flight into Egypt with his first affirmation that Jesus is the Son of God (2:15; cf. Celsus' connection of Egypt, magic, and the claim to be God).[87] Moreover, within the whole of the NT, Matthew alone refers to Joseph as a carpenter (Matt 13:55). This last point is especially worthy of note, since the designation of Joseph, rather than Jesus, as the carpenter seems to come from Matthew's redactional alteration of Mark 6:3.[88] Hence it is likely that the Jewish story reported by Celsus is reacting, directly or indirectly, to Matthew's Infancy Narrative.[89]

All that the story in Celsus really tells us, therefore, is that by the middle of the 2d century A.D. some Diaspora Jews had become aware of the claims Matthew made in 1:18–25 and had tried to refute them by parody—precisely the sort of development one would naturally expect. We are not all that far away from the Jewish-Christian debates overheard in Justin's *Dialogue with Trypho*—except for the charge of illegitimacy. The Diaspora rather than Palestinian origin of the parody makes it very unlikely that we have here in Celsus a scrap of historical information preserved intact among Jews "underground" for a century and a half. Indeed, if one were to take the account as historical, one would have to press some basic questions of tradition history: How did (presumably hostile) Jews learn of the circumstances surrounding the birth of Jesus, when Jesus would not have come to the attention of the Jewish public until he was around thirty years old, long after the supposed events had transpired in an obscure Galilean village called Nazareth? How was such knowledge preserved over many decades in Palestinian Judaism, only to be transferred at some point to Diaspora Judaism? The whole scenario strains belief.[90] Polemical reaction to the Matthean Infancy Narrative is a much more likely explanation of the data.

Apart from Matthew's Infancy Narrative, are there any indications in the NT that the charge of illegitimacy was raised against Jesus— indications that would push back the "illegitimacy tradition" to a 1st-century A.D. date? Two NT texts have at times been suggested as candidates: Mark 6:3 and John 8:41.

In Mark 6:1–6a,[91] Jesus comes to Nazareth to preach in his hometown synagogue. His former neighbors are struck by the wisdom of his teaching and (presumably) the news about the miracles he has performed. But familiarity breeds contempt; and their amazement quickly turns sour. Disparaging remarks are passed: "Isn't this fellow the carpenter, the son of Mary, and the brother of James [=Jacob] and Joses and Jude [=Judah] and Simon? Aren't his sisters here with us?" Some scholars have suggested that behind the unusual description, "the son of Mary," stands a denial of Jesus' legitimacy. The key text, however, is plagued with a number of problems.

(1) Scholars must contend with variant readings in the Greek text of Mark 6:3. While most Greek manuscripts read the question in the way indicated above, some manuscripts of Mark[92] read instead: "Isn't this fellow the son of the carpenter [and of Mary]?"[93] The parallel texts in Matt 13:55 and Luke 4:22 read respectively: "Isn't this fellow the son of the carpenter? Isn't his mother called Mary . . . ?" and "Isn't this fellow the son of Joseph?" John 6:42 likewise reads: "Isn't this fellow the son of Joseph?" These parallels prompt some scholars to prefer "Isn't this fellow the son of the carpenter [and of Mary]?"[94] as the original reading in Mark. If so, the whole basis for using this text in reference to illegitimacy disappears.

More likely, though, "Isn't this fellow the son of the carpenter?" represents a later assimilation of the text of Mark to the other Gospels, especially Matthew. In fact, Mark is often "corrected" in the later Greek manuscript tradition to bring it into line with Matthew and/or Luke, especially when Mark's wording might be offensive to a Christian scribe or audience. Indeed, it was the derogatory tone of the Nazarenes' remarks that probably led Matthew and Luke, independently of each other, to change "the carpenter, the son of Mary" to "son of the carpenter" or "son of Joseph."[95] Hence, despite the variety of readings in the Greek manuscripts, we may feel fairly sure that "son of Mary" was what Mark originally wrote.[96] Of course, one must beware of naively supposing that Mark 6:3 gives us a word-for-word report via tape recorder of what people in Nazareth were saying about Jesus in A.D. 28. Mark 6:3 is valuable because, at the very least, it tells us what sort of disparaging remarks about Jesus first-generation Christianity might have heard from adversaries.

(2) Does Mark 6:3 imply a slur on Jesus' birth? To be sure, to refer to a man as the son of his mother, instead of as the son of his father, was unusual in the OT and in Judaism at the time of Jesus. Some have pounced on this fact and interpreted "son of Mary" as referring to a charge that Jesus was illegitimate.[97] However, to call a man the son of his mother was not a regular way of indicating either the son's illegitimacy or the mother's widowhood in the OT or at the time of Jesus.[98] Such a usage comes only from later Samaritan, Mandean, and rabbinic writings.[99]

(3) Moreover, a phrase like "son of Mary," while unusual, is not absolutely impossible in biblical usage. In the OT, there is the curious case of Zeruiah, the mother of Joab, Abishai, and Asahel, three leaders of King David's troops. These three notables—individually or together— are always identified in the Bible as the "son[s] of Zeruiah" their mother, never as the sons of their father (see, e.g., 1 Sam 26:6; 2 Sam 2:13; and so without exception throughout 1–2 Samuel, 1 Kings, and 1 Chronicles, for a total of 24 occurrences). The usage continues in Josephus and the rabbinic literature.[100] The reason for the usage is not clear, and various explanations have been offered: e.g., Zeruiah was famous in her own right (perhaps as the sister of David),[101] or the phraseology in these texts preserves an archaic custom that traced descent through the female line. In any case, there is absolutely no indication that the usage stems from a view that the sons (all three of them!) were illegitimate. Thus, the various occurrences of "son[s] of Zeruiah" shows us that the phrase "son of Mary," while unusual, is neither unheard of nor indicative of a charge of illegitimacy.[102] The phrase indicates illegitimacy no more than it indicates virginal conception—another interpretation to which this battered text has at times been subjected![103]

(4) What then is one to make of Mark 6:3? To understand the text correctly, one must read it in context, i.e., in the dramatic scene of conflict Mark sets.[104] The other descriptions thrown in Jesus' face by the townspeople refer not to any great moral turpitude or scandal, but simply to the pedestrian, all too well known nature of Jesus' background. The point of the Nazarenes' objections to Jesus' implicit claims is: "We've known you all your life. You were the town carpenter. We're well acquainted with your mother, brothers, and sisters, who still live

here with us—yes, who are right here with us in this synagogue today. How dare you claim to be somebody special! You're no better than the rest of us." This small-town resentment and envy are the reasons for mentioning Jesus' trade as a carpenter and his relatives;[105] there is no indication that this information conveys moral stain or scandal—just ordinariness. The same thing is probably true of "son of Mary." It is most likely a "flip" comment occasioned dramatically by Mary's (imagined) presence in the synagogue congregation, along with Jesus' brothers and sisters: "Why, he's only Mary's son!" Since Mary was presumably the only surviving parent, the raucous, ad hoc attack on Jesus in the synagogue would naturally point to her standing right there, rather than to a dead and therefore absent father.[106]

The second text that is sometimes cited as an indication of an "illegitimacy tradition" within the NT is John 8:41. This verse is found within the meandering and confusing account of Jesus' disputes with the Jews in Jerusalem during the feast of tabernacles (Chapters 7–8). The interpretation of our key text is not helped by the fact that Chapters 7–8 in John are not among John's most orderly and clearly developed discourses.[107] The general line of development in these two chapters is Jesus' gradual revealing of who he is (=what are his origins? where is he from? what is his relation to God?) and a corresponding, ever increasing hostility on the part of the Jerusalemite Jews. Fittingly, both themes culminate in 8:57–58: Jesus claims eternal, divine existence ("before Abraham came to be, I am"), and the Jews respond by seeking to stone him.

In the proximate context of 8:31–59, the increasing attack and counterattack focus on Abraham, the claim to be the legitimate (spiritual) children of Abraham, the consequent status of being free people instead of slaves, and finally the status of being children of God. Early on in this section, it is Jesus, rather than the Jews, who is on the attack. In v 33, the Jews proudly claim: "*We* are seed of Abraham and have never been slaves to anyone." Jesus, however, intimates that they are spiritually slaves of sin (v 34). He acknowledges that physically they are "seed of Abraham" (v 37); but physical descent is not the point at issue. Spiritually they are acting contrary to the will of *Jesus'* Father.

At this point, therefore, Jesus introduces a split or opposition between a physical relation to "father" Abraham and a spiritual relation to Jesus' Father. But Jesus pushes the point still further: Jesus imitates his Father, they imitate their father (v 38). This last remark of Jesus introduces a new, ominous idea: there is another father whom they do imitate by their actions, and this other father does not seem to be Abraham. And so it is at this point that the Jews stubbornly insist: *"Our father is Abraham"* (v 39).[108] Jesus implicitly denies this by declaring that, if they were spiritual children of Abraham, they would be performing the works Abraham performed.[109] Instead, they are seeking to kill Jesus; ominously Jesus says that this murderous tendency imitates not Abraham but their true spiritual father (vv 40–41a), who will be identified a little later on (v 44) as the devil.

In the face of Jesus' charge that they have as their true spiritual father not Abraham but some murderer, the Jews emphatically reply: *"We* have not been born from fornication; we have only one Father, God" (v 41b). The switch from Abraham to God as their father is a bit abrupt, but the basic sense is clear. Jesus, in effect, has accused them of disobedience or infidelity toward God. They reply: We are not guilty of spiritual infidelity to or apostasy from God, sins described in the OT in terms of fornication.[110]

What is most noteworthy in this rambling development of the main themes is that from v 31 to v 47 it is basically Jesus, not the Jews, who is on the attack, with the Jews defending themselves as best they can. Only when we reach v 48 do they reply with their own attack against Jesus. During his attack, Jesus twice pushes the Jews to defend their legitimacy, first as children of Abraham (v 39) and then as children of God (v 41). The emphatic *"our* father" (v 39) and *"we* have not been born from fornication" (v 41) are uttered as part of an angry and exasperated defense of their own *spiritual* legitimacy, which Jesus has questioned with an emphatic *"you* are doing what you heard from [your] father" (v 38) and *"you* are doing the works of *your* father" (v 41a).[111] Granted this line of development in the heated argument, namely, that Jesus is raising the question of *their* legitimate birth and that he is discussing their legitimacy in spiritual rather than physical terms (he admits that physically they are sons of Abraham), to see a hidden reference to Jesus' physical illegitimacy in vv 39–41 is, in my opinion, highly imaginative.

After all, when the verbal battle becomes even fiercer in v 48, when for the first time the Jews stop defending themselves and start attacking Jesus with slurs, their first accusation is that he is a Samaritan. This is hardly intended in a physical, biological sense. Rather, by questioning the Jerusalemite Jews' status as the true children of Abraham, Jesus, in their minds, is aligning himself with the "heterodox and schismatic" Samaritans, who question the Jews' status as the only children of Abraham and Jerusalem's status as the one true place of temple worship (cf.

John 4:20).[112] The slur is not meant on a literal, biological level, but on a spiritual one. True, spiritual descent and legitimacy have been the thrust of the entire debate, and presumably that is the sense of vv 39 + 41 as well. Indeed, whether Jesus is a target at all in those defensive verses is unclear.

In short, only if one had already determined on other grounds that a tradition of Jesus' illegitimate birth was known among both Christians and Jews in the 1st century A.D. and was a source of debate between them would a reading of John 8:39 + 41 in terms of Jesus' illegitimacy enjoy any probability. Since there is no clear attestation of such a polemic before the middle of the 2d century (and then it seems to be a reaction to the Infancy Narratives),[113] the theme of illegitimacy in John 8—as in Mark 6:3—must be judged a classic case of retrojecting later theological debates into an earlier text that shows no signs of such disputes.[114]

F. CONCLUSIONS

I began this consideration of the birth and lineage of Jesus by observing that little or nothing can be said with certitude or high probability about the birth, infancy, and early years of the vast majority of the historical figures in the ancient Mediterranean world. Jesus turns out to be ahead of many such figures in that at least some facts can be affirmed with fair certainty or at least high probability.

During the reign of King Herod the Great (and if Matthew is to be believed, toward the end of his reign, therefore somewhere around 7–4 B.C.),[115] a Jew named Yēshûaʿ (=Jesus) was born, perhaps in Bethlehem of Judea but more likely in Nazareth of Galilee—at any rate, in a small town somewhere within the confines of Herod's kingdom. Jesus' mother was named Miryam (=Mary),[116] his (putative) father Yôsēf (=Joseph). While the claim in the Infancy Narratives that Jesus was born at Bethlehem may be simply a *theologoumenon* symbolizing his status as the royal Davidic Messiah, the many diverse traditions in the NT about his Davidic descent argue well for his being known during his lifetime as a descendant of King David, whatever the biological truth may have been —a truth probably not accessible even to Jesus' contemporaries. Whatever the precise place of his birth, Jesus grew up in Nazareth and was so identified with that town that "Nazorean," "Nazarene," or "of Nazareth" became almost a second name.

The tradition that Jesus was virginally conceived by the power of the Holy Spirit is also affirmed in both Infancy Narratives. The truth of the claim, which was hardly verifiable even when Jesus appeared on the public stage as an adult, is a fortiori not open to verification today. Decisions on this tradition, limited within the NT to the Infancy Narratives, will largely be made on the basis of one's philosophical views about the miraculous and the weight one gives to later Church teaching. In any case, the precise origins of the virginal conception tradition remain obscure from a historical point of view. A countertradition that Jesus was illegitimate is not clearly attested until close to the middle of the 2d century A.D.; it is most likely a mocking, polemical reaction to the claims of the Infancy Narratives, perhaps as filtered through popular disputes.

By now, just about everything that could be said with fair certitude about the birth and infancy of Jesus has been said. The next question we must face is whether we should leap over some thirty years to Jordan's banks and the Baptist's cry, or whether something can be known, at least in general terms, about the so-called "hidden years" of Jesus' childhood, adolescence, and adulthood in Nazareth.

NOTES TO CHAPTER 8

¹ I say "more correct" because the shorter form, *Yēšû*, comes from the loss in popular pronunciation of the final Hebrew letter *ʿayin*. The rabbinic literature, which deplores the loss of the pronunciation of the *ʿayin*, associates it with the dialect of Galilee (see, e.g., *b. Ber.* 32a; *b. ʿErub.* 53a; *b. Meg.* 24b). David Noel Freedman has suggested to me (letter of Nov. 26, 1990) that in the 1st century Jesus of Nazareth would have been called *Yēšû* by his Galilean neighbors, and only in more formal situations, or perhaps in Jerusalem, would the fuller form *Yēšûaʿ* or even *Yĕhôšûaʿ* have been used. The peculiarities of Galilean pronunciation probably lie behind the caustic remark to Peter in the story of his denial of Jesus in the Passion Narrative (Matt 26:73: "Truly you also are one of them, for even your speech betrays you"). I say "probably" because only Matthew focuses on the speech of Peter. Both Mark 14:70 and Luke 22:59 say simply: "for you are [Luke: he is] a Galilean." As usual, with his learned scribal tendencies Matthew draws what is probably a correct conclusion from his Marcan source; on all this, see Donald P. Senior, *The Passion Narrative According to Matthew* (BETL 39; Leuven: Leuven University, 1975) 205 n. 2.

It should be noted that the *a* found in the vocalized form of *Yēšûaʿ* is a creation of the Masoretes to aid pronunciation of the final *ʿayin*. Its technical name is the *pataḥ furtivum;* it has no grammatical or etymological significance.

² Some have suggested that the shortening of the name involved an intermediate contraction of *Yĕhôšûaʿ* to *Yôšûaʿ* and then to *Yēšûaʿ;* so Ludwig Koehler and Walter Baumgartner, *Lexicon in Veteris Testamenti Libros* (Leiden: Brill, 1958) 410; Joseph A. Fitzmyer, *The Gospel According to Luke* (AB 28 and 28A; Garden City, NY: Doubleday, 1981, 1985) 1. 347. However, David Noel Freedman has pointed out to me by letter (Nov. 26, 1990) that the passage from *ô* to *ē* is difficult to explain on any account. He suggests that ultimately the two names *Yĕhôšûaʿ* and *Yēšûaʿ* may have had different roots or derivations and became equated because they sounded alike and probably had the same meaning.

Yĕhôšûaʿ is the fuller *(plene scriptum)* spelling of the Hebrew name, with the Hebrew letter *wāw* written to represent the vowel *šûreq*. In reality, this fuller spelling occurs only at Deut 3:21 and Judg 2:7 in the Masoretic text of the Hebrew Bible. Otherwise the shorter *(defective scriptum)* spelling, without the *wāw*, is used; it occurs, e.g., in the first two instances of the name of Moses' successor (Exod 17:9–10), in the title of the Book of Joshua, and then throughout the book. To avoid unnecessary complication in an already complicated topic, I will always use the fuller *(plene scriptum)* Hebrew spelling when referring to the name "Joshua" in the Hebrew Bible, since it helps emphasize the relation of *Yĕhôšûaʿ* (Joshua) to *Yēšûaʿ* and *Yēšû* (Jesus).

³ Significantly, all occurrences of *Yēšûaʿ* are found in the postexilic books of Ezra, Nehemiah, and Chronicles: Ezra 2:6,36,40; 3:9; 8:33; Neh 3:19; 7:11,39,43; 8:7; 9:4–5; 10:10; 12:8,24; 1 Chr 24:11; 2 Chr 31:15. In all these texts, *Yēšûaʿ*, not the shorter form *Yēšû*, is used. Joshua the successor of Moses continues to have his name spelled *Yĕhôšûaʿ* in 1 Chr 7:27 (in a genealogy) and Sir 46:1, but is referred to as *Yēšûaʿ* in Neh 8:17. The high priest Joshua, who returned to Jerusalem with

Zerubbabel after the exile, is always called *Yĕbôšûaʿ* in the prophets Haggai and Zechariah and always *Yēšûaʿ* in Ezra and Nehemiah. From these data Werner Foerster deduces that *Yĕbôšûaʿ* was the predominant form before 500 B.C. and *Yēšûaʿ* the predominant form after 500 B.C. For further details, see his article "*Iēsous*," *TDNT* 3 (1964) 284–93. Of special interest is his reference (p. 286 n. 23) to the necropolis inscription from Jaffa that bears the form *Yĕbôšûaʿ*, showing that "Joshua" had not completely died out around the turn of the era.

⁴ See, e.g., the twenty-one rabbinic Joshuas listed in Str-B, 5–6. 169–73. Significantly, there is no entry for any *Yēšûaʿ* or *Yēšû*.

⁵ Interestingly, rabbinic writings almost always use the shorter form of "Jesus," *Yēšû*, for Jesus of Nazareth, and the Talmud employs this form only for Jesus of Nazareth; see Foerster, "*Iēsous*," 286–87. He notes that "with the 2nd century A.D. *Yēšûaʿ* or *Iēsous* disappears as a proper name. In rabbinic literature *yšwʿ* is found only as the name of the 9th priestly class. . . ." Foerster goes on to note a few scattered exceptions, but they only confirm the rule.

⁶ It is a somewhat shocking experience for Christians of, e.g., Irish or German background when, for the first time, they hear males called "Jesus" in Spain or Latin America. This Spanish/Latino tradition brings us as close as possible to what the name "Jesus" would have "felt like" as an ordinary name in Palestine of the 1st century A.D.

⁷ Some count nineteen or twenty-one. The exact number remains uncertain since we are not always sure whether, in a given passage of Josephus, the author means a different Jesus or a Jesus also referred to in another work or passage. For other occurrences of the name Jesus around the turn of the era, see Martin Hengel, *Between Jesus and Paul* (London: SCM, 1983) 187 n. 79 and the literature cited there. Both the Hebrew *Yēšûaʿ* (possibly *Yēšû* as well) and the Greek *Iēsous* are witnessed by Palestinian grave inscriptions from the 1st centuries B.C. and A.D. Indeed, the name Jesus is among the names most frequently found on ossuaries of that period.

Often debated is the precise meaning of two occurrences of the Greek form *Iēsous* on the ossuaries at Talpioth, a suburb of Jerusalem. They seem to date from around the 1st century B.C. or A.D. One graffito, in charcoal, reads *Iēsous iou* ("Jesus woe"? or "Jesus, help"?); the other, incised, reads *Iēsous aloth* ("Jesus, alas"? or "Jesus, [let him] rise"?). Speculation on the exact meaning has been wide-ranging and sometimes bizarre. E. L. Sukenik suggested soon after the graffiti were discovered in 1945 that they represented a bewailing of the crucifixion of Jesus by some of his disciples This view has generally been rejected in subsequent literature. Others (e.g., Gustafsson) have suggested that both graffiti are Jewish-Christian laments for the dead and prayers to Jesus Christ (the latter being interpreted as "Jesus, [let the one who rests here] rise"). Others have suggested that *iou* and *aloth* are forms of Yahweh and Sabaoth (so Fishwick). We have similar examples of such deformations of divine names in the great Magical Papyrus of Paris (ca. A.D. 300), in which Jesus is also invoked as the God of the Hebrews. But such wild syncretism dates from the late Roman period, when eclectic magic was rife. At the early date of the Talpioth inscriptions, the most likely interpretation of the two inscriptions is "Jesus son of X" (perhaps "son of Judas [or Jehu?]" and "son of Aloth"). Hence the Talpioth ossuaries would be further proof of the commonness of the name Jesus in 1st-century Palestine. In one family tomb, we have a Jesus son of Judas and a Jesus son of Aloth, perhaps grandfather and grandson or (less likely) father and son. On all this, see E. L. Sukenik, "The Earliest Records of Christianity," *AJA* 51 (1947) 351–65; Berndt Gustafsson, "The Oldest Graffiti in the History of the Church," *NTS* 3 (1956–57) 65–69; Duncan Fishwick, "The Talpioth Ossuaries Again," *NTS* 10 (1963–64) 49–61; Erich Dinkler, "Comments on the History of the Symbol of the Cross," *JTC* 1 (1965) 124–46; J. P. Kane, "The Ossuary Inscriptions of Jerusalem," *JSS* 23 (1978) 268–82; C. K. Barrett, *The New Testament Background: Selected Documents* (rev. ed.; San Francisco: Harper & Row, 1987) 57; Everett Ferguson, *Backgrounds of Early Christianity* (Grand Rapids: Eerdmans, 1987) 470–71.

[8] The Greek language simply took over the shorter form *Yēšû*, substituted an *s* sound (the Greek *sigma*) for the *sh* sound (which did not exist in Greek) and added a final *s* *(sigma)* to make the Hebrew name declinable in Greek: *Iēsous*. It is from this Greek form *Iēsous* that Latin derives its *Iesus* or *Jesus;* hence the English "Jesus." The fact that the Greek form *Iēsous* could stand for both "Joshua" and "Jesus" would in time lead Greek-speaking Christians to draw typological comparisons between Joshua son of Nun and Jesus of Nazareth. Interestingly, though, such typology does not get started in earnest until Justin Martyr in the mid-2d century. The NT is surprisingly free of such typology. A possible exception is Jude 5, if one reads *Iēsous* instead of *kyrios;* see Bruce M. Metzger, *A Textual Commentary on the Greek New Testament* (United Bible Societies, 1971) 725–26.

[9] For discussion of the relevant texts from Tacitus and Suetonius, see Chapter 4 above. The use of "Christ" as a proper name for Jesus among pagans may have been accelerated by the confusion between *Christos* and *Chrēstos,* a common name at the time; a similar confusion arose between *Christiani and Chrestiani.* See, e.g., Raymond E. Brown (with John P. Meier), *Antioch and Rome* (New York/ Ramsey: Paulist, 1983) 100–1; Peter Lampe, *Die stadtrömischen Christen in den ersten beiden Jahrhunderten. Untersuchungen zur Sozialgeschichte* (WUNT 2/18; Tübingen: Mohr [Siebeck] 1987) 6.

[10] Besides an abbreviated form of the divine name Yahweh *(yahu),* the name is formed from the Hebrew root *šwʿ,* which may mean "to help," though that is not certain.

[11] Besides an abbreviated form of the divine name Yahweh *(yahu),* the name is imagined to be formed from the Hebrew root *yšʿ,* "to save." On all this, see Raymond E. Brown, *The Birth of the Messiah* (Garden City, NY: Doubleday, 1977) 131; Fitzmyer, *The Gospel According to Luke,* 1. 347 and the literature cited there.

[12] Philo, *De mutatione nominum (On the Change of Names)* 21 §121: . . . *Iēsous de sōtēria kyriou* (". . . but 'Jesus' [means] 'salvation of the Lord' "). Philo at this point is commenting on Num 13:16 and the meaning of the name of Joshua son of Nun. For the text, see F. H. Colson and G. H. Whitaker, *Philo. Volume V* (LCL;

London: Heinemann; Cambridge, MA: Harvard University, 1934) 204–5. David Noel Freedman observes (letter, Nov. 26, 1990): "While the etymology doubtless was derived by unscientific means, the connection with 'salvation' may not be so farfetched, especially in the postexilic form of the name."

[13] Jesus was not the only Jew of his time to structure a group around the patriarchal and tribal number twelve; that number served the same role at Qumran. The council of the community seems to have been made up of twelve (lay)men and three priests (1QS 8:1–4), though the text could also be taken to mean twelve men in all, three of whom had to be priests. Twelve chief priests and twelve chief levites were to minister in the temple of the end time (1QM 2:1–3). Living in the wilderness of Judea, the Qumranites perhaps looked back especially to Moses and the twelve heads of the twelve tribes during the wilderness sojourn.

[14] See, e.g., Plutarch's presentation of the wonders surrounding the conception, birth, and youth of Alexander the Great in the *Parallel Lives. Alexander,* 1–2, 6–7: Olympias, wife of Philip of Macedon and mother of Alexander, dreams that her womb is struck by a thunderbolt; a serpent is seen stretched out at Olympias' side as she sleeps; this cools Philip's ardor for her, perhaps because he thinks that she is the consort of some higher being; Philip is told by the oracle of Delphi to sacrifice to Zeus Ammon (who, later on in Alexander's life, will be thought to be the true father of Alexander); Alexander shows remarkable skills in his youth and is initiated by Aristotle into secret lore. Suetonius recounts similar stories of the birth and youth of Augustus in his *Lives of the Caesars. Augustus,* 94: omens occur around the time of Augustus' birth; again, a serpent glides by his mother; Augustus is considered the son of Apollo; dreams and portents show that Augustus will rule the world; he shows miraculous power even as a youth.

[15] See *Ant.* 2.9.2–3 §205–16: an Egyptian scribe foretells to Pharaoh the birth of an Israelite liberator; and God appears to the father of Moses, Amaram, in his sleep and reveals to him the future career of Moses before his birth.

[16] See the *Life of Moses,* 1.2–4 §5–17.

[17] The whole question of miracles will be taken up later, in the context of Jesus' public ministry. Only a few brief considerations, aimed mostly at the particular nature of the Infancy Narratives, are offered here.

[18] This hardly novel insight has become a traditional rule of exegesis among Catholics as well as Protestants. For Catholics, see the epoch-making acceptance of form criticism in the great biblical encyclical of Pope Pius XII, *Divino Afflante Spiritu,* issued on Sept. 30, 1943; the key passages are available in Henricus Denziger-Adolfus Schönmetzer, *Enchiridion Symbolorum* (Freiburg: Herder, 1963) 756 (nos. 3829–30). For an English translation, see James J. Megivern, ed., *Official Catholic Teachings. Bible Interpretation* (Wilmington, NC: McGrath, 1978) 331–33. Even more explicit is the exhortation to exegetes given by the Second Vatican Council in the dogmatic constitution *Dei Verbum,* no. 12: God speaks to human beings in a human way; the exegete must investigate what the human author

intended to communicate; to do this, he or she must be attentive to various literary forms, since truth is expressed in different ways in historical, prophetic, and poetic texts. For the original Latin text, see *Constitutio Dogmatica De Divina Revelatione* (Rome: Vatican Polygot Press, 1965) 9–10.

[19] On this whole matter, see Raymond E. Brown, *The Birth of the Messiah*, 26–37. Brown's book is *the* magisterial treatment of our generation; an update of his bibliography and his comments on more recent research can be found in his two articles, "Gospel Infancy Narrative Research from 1976 to 1986: Part I (Matthew)" and "Gospel Infancy Narrative Research from 1976 to 1986: Part II (Luke)," *CBQ* 48 (1986) 468–83 and 660–80 respectively.

[20] See, e.g., C. H. Dodd, *The Apostolic Preaching and Its Developments* (London: Hodder & Stoughton, 1936).

[21] Even if one held that the presence of Mary at both of these events was the result of the evangelists' redactional theology, at the very least we have two independent streams of tradition holding the general view that Mary survived into the early days of the Church. Granted that a young Jewish girl would be espoused around the age of twelve or thirteen, there is nothing unlikely in this. If Jesus was around thirty-five when he was crucified, Mary would be around forty-eight.

[22] So, e.g., Rainer Riesner, *Jesus als Lehrer* (WUNT 2d series, 7; Tübingen: Mohr [Siebeck], 1981) 210, ignoring for the most part the objections considered below.

[23] The same point could be made about "things Roman" with which Mary was supposedly directly involved, notably the worldwide census ordered by Caesar Augustus when Quirinius was governor of Syria (Luke 2:1). See the detailed study in Brown, *Birth of the Messiah*, 547–56. His conclusion is clear: "When all is evaluated, the weight of the evidence is strongly against the possibility of reconciling the information in Luke 1 and Luke 2. . . . Luke seems to be inaccurate in associating that birth [of Jesus] with the one and only census of Judea (not of Galilee) conducted in A.D. 6–7 under Quirinius" (p. 554).

[24] For overall treatments, see Brown, *Birth of the Messiah*, 435–70; Fitzmyer, *The Gospel According to Luke*, 1. 418–33.

[25] See Brown, *Birth of the Messiah*, 436, 447–51; Metzger, *Textual Commentary*, 134.

[26] See Fitzmyer *(Gospel According to Luke*, 1. 424), who states that Luke's confusion over "their" purification is an indication that Luke's information "is not derived from Mary's recollections or memoirs—which might be presumed to have got the matter correct."

[27] Note that the Greek text of the Magi's question in Matt 2:2 is *pou estin ho techtheis basileus tōn Ioudaiōn.* The proper translation is simply "Where is he [who has been] born king of the Jews." There is no "newborn" in the Greek, though it has often been supplied by translators who unconsciously conflate Matthew's

story with Luke's and so must fit the Magi's visit into the relatively short time that Joseph and Mary stay in Bethlehem.

[28] It is important to remember that this is the first mention of Nazareth in the Gospel, and the evangelist obviously feels that it has to be "introduced," explained, and almost apologized for.

[29] Compare the two accounts in the Greek: *kai elthōn katōkēsen eis polin legomenēn Nazaret* (Matt 2:23); *kai . . . elthōn katōkēsen eis Kapharnaoum* (4:13).

[30] See Brown, *Birth of the Messiah*, 547–56.

[31] The *peri autou* in 2:38 is obviously the infant Jesus, not *theō* from v 38a (see Alfred Plummer, *The Gospel According to S. Luke* [ICC; 5th ed.; Edinburgh: Clark, 1922] 73). Fitzmyer translates v 38b as: ". . . she spoke about the child to all who were waiting for the deliverance of Jerusalem" *(The Gospel According to Luke*, 1. 419). Fitzmyer comments that the Greek literally means " 'she kept speaking,' since the verb is in the [imperfect]. . . . It does not mean on that occasion alone, but rather that she spread abroad the word about the child" (p. 431).

[32] Whether this should be called "midrash" is debated among scholars and largely depends on how wide or narrow a definition of midrash one allows; for various views, see Myles M. Bourke, "The Literary Genus of Matthew 1–2," *CBQ* 22 (1960) 160–75; A. Wright, *The Literary Genre Midrash* (Staten Island, NY: Alba, 1967); Brown, *Birth of the Messiah*, 557–63.

[33] In their origins, the Infancy Narratives do not seem to have had any contact with traditions of preexistence and incarnation; see, e.g., Luke 1:35 as compared to John 1:1–18. The first writer to draw together in his thought Christ's preexistence and his virginal conception was Ignatius of Antioch.

[34] See Brown, *Birth of the Messiah*, 29–32, 311–16.

[35] See, e.g., how quickly the Infancy Narratives are dismissed by Herbert Braun, *Jesus of Nazareth. The Man and His Time* (Philadelphia: Fortress, 1979) 24–25; similarly, Bornkamm, *Jesus of Nazareth*, 52. The silence of Sanders on the Infancy Narratives in his *Jesus and Judaism* no doubt indicates the same general attitude.

[36] At the return from Egypt after Herod's death (Matt 2:19–20), Jesus is still referred to with the same diminutive form *(paidion,* "little child") that was applied to him before the flight (2:8,11,13,14).

[37] Questions of chronology will be taken up in Chapter 11. For a brief survey of the chronology of Jesus' life, see Joseph A. Fitzmyer in the composite article, "A History of Israel," *NJBC*, 1247–50. For more detailed studies of the dates of Jesus' birth and death—all learned, but some not very critical—see Jerry Vardaman and Edwin M. Yamauchi, eds., *Chronos, Kairos, Christos* (Jack Finegan Festschrift; Winona Lake, IN: Eisenbrauns, 1989).

[38] Interestingly, Joseph is never mentioned in Mark directly or even indirectly (unless one reads "son of the carpenter" in Mark 6:3 along with p[45] and a

few other manuscripts; but this is almost certainly an assimilation to Matt 13:55, as Metzger points out in *Textual Commentary*, 88–89). If one were to claim that the references to this Joseph in the rest of Luke-Acts are simply echoes of Luke's Infancy Narrative, we would still have, at the very least, the joint witness of two very different streams of tradition: (1) the primitive tradition lying behind the Infancy Narratives of both Matthew and Luke, and (2) the tradition behind John's Gospel.

[39] One is struck by how infrequently the mother of Jesus is explicitly *named* outside the Infancy Narratives. John's Gospel, while using her as a symbol, never mentions the name of "the mother of Jesus" (John 2:1,3,5,12; 6:42; 19:25–27). If we were to decide that Luke knew Mary's name only from his Infancy Narrative and from Mark, once again we would still have at the very least the joint witness of two notably different streams of tradition: (1) the primitive tradition behind the Infancy Narratives in Matthew and Luke, and (2) Mark, confirmed by Matthew and Luke.

[40] Brown *(The Gospel According to John*, 1. 330) prefers the view that the evangelist did know the tradition of Jesus' birth at Bethlehem, but he concludes his treatment by stressing that certainty is not to be had in this matter. He is still more tentative in his approach in *Birth of the Messiah*, 516 n. 6; similarly, Rudolf Schnackenburg, *Das Johannesevangelium. II. Teil* (HTKNT 4/2; Freiburg/Basel/Vienna: Herder, 1971) 220. In favor of the evangelist's ignorance or intentional neglect of the Bethlehem tradition, see Rudolf Bultmann, *Das Evangelium des Johannes* (MeyerK 2; 19th ed.; Göttingen: Vandenhoeck & Ruprecht, 1968) 231 n. 2. Christoph Burger *(Jesus als Davidssohn* [FRLANT 98; Göttingen: Vandenhoeck & Ruprecht, 1970] 153–58) suggests the possibility that John the evangelist had heard that in other Christian circles a narrative had arisen claiming that Jesus was a descendant of David and had been born in Bethlehem. According to Burger's hypothesis, John pointedly rejected such an idea by placing it in the mouths of the Jewish adversaries of Jesus. In reply to Burger, one must wonder whether, if John's point had been so polemical, he would have left the matter so murky and ambiguous.

[41] *Theologoumenon* is a tricky concept. In itself, the word need not necessarily mean that the affirmation of faith presented as a historical narrative lacks all historical basis; a *theologoumenon* could be a historical event loaded with a heavy amount of theological symbolism and interpretation. As a matter of fact, though, the term is usually employed to signify a theological narrative that does not represent a historical event.

[42] See Brown, *Birth of the Messiah*, 513–16.

[43] In Ignatius, Mary's Davidic descent is more implied than explicitly affirmed; see *Ephesians* 18:2: "For our God Jesus the Messiah was conceived by Mary according to the plan of God: on the one hand of the seed of David [cf. Rom 1:3], on the other hand of the holy spirit [cf. Matt 1:18,20]. . . ." See also *Smyrneans* 1:1 and *Trallians* 9:1. Notice in Ignatius the typical blending of elements from the Johannine tradition (Jesus is God), Matthew (conceived by [the

virgin] Mary by the power of the Holy Spirit), and the pre-Pauline tradition (of the seed of David). The concept of Mary's descent from David becomes more explicit in Justin; see, e.g., *Dialogue with Trypho* 45: ". . . the Son of God . . . submitted to becoming incarnate and being born of this virgin who was of the line of David." See also the *Protevangelium Jacobi* 10:1. As Brown notes *(Birth of the Messiah,* 287–88), even the patristic writers fluctuated somewhat in their description of Mary's lineage; similarly, Raymond E. Brown, Karl P. Donfried et al., *Mary in the New Testament* (Philadelphia: Fortress; New York: Paulist, 1978) 260–61.

[44] Riesner, who suffers from an uncritical view of the Lucan Infancy Narrative, suggests that, while Jesus was of Davidic origin, Mary may have been of priestly origin *(Jesus als Lehrer,* 214).

[45] See, e.g., Fitzmyer, *The Gospel According to Luke,* 1. 357.

[46] A fortiori, one should not rest any interpretation of the beginning of Jesus' ministry on the idea that the Baptist and Jesus were some sort of cousins—a logical conclusion of the Lucan narrative that Luke himself never draws. When the adult Baptist and Jesus appear on the scene in Luke 3, there is a strange silence—granted Luke's Infancy Narrative—about the Baptist and Jesus being relatives. Needless to say, no other passage in the NT—to say nothing of Josephus!—intimates such an idea.

[47] Any attempt to use one of the two genealogies of Jesus (Matt 1:1–17; Luke 3:23–38) to establish Mary's lineage is doomed to failure because (1) both genealogies explicitly trace Jesus' genealogy through Joseph and (2) both genealogies are theological constructs and should not be taken as biological records. On all this, see Brown, *Birth of the Messiah,* 57–94. With minor exceptions, the two genealogies contradict each other from the time of David to the time of Joseph, legal father of Jesus. In theory, one of the two genealogies might possibly contain some historical information, but it is impossible for us today to know which that might be; and one must confess that such data would not make the slightest difference to the sum total of relevant knowledge about the historical Jesus.

[48] This is especially true of Matt 1:18–25, where the whole point of the passage is that Joseph's key function in the theological drama is to accept the virginally conceived child as his own son and thus insert him into the Davidic genealogy that Matthew has detailed in 1:1–17. Notice the emphasis of the angel's address in v 20: "Joseph, *son of David.* . . ." The same point is made more indirectly in Luke 1:27; 2:4; 3:23–31.

[49] This is basically the position of Burger, *Jesus als Davidssohn.* See, e.g., his conclusion on p. 178: ". . . Jesus became a descendant of David not by his birth but by Easter and the confession of faith of the church." Besides the particular arguments I offer in what follows, Brown *(The Virginal Conception and Bodily Resurrection of Jesus* [New York: Paulist, 1973] 55 n. 87) offers a general argument against Burger's position: "James, the brother of Jesus, was known widely in the Christian world and lived into the 60s. . . . Can we posit James' acquiescence in such a fictional affirmation about the family ancestry?" Moreover, Paul, who

knew James precisely in his quality as "the brother of the Lord [Gal 1:19]," quotes a creedal formula that proclaims that Jesus was "of the seed of David" (Rom 1:3). Hence belief that Jesus was of Davidic descent cannot be pushed away from early Palestinian Christianity during the first Christian generation, as Burger would like to do.

⁵⁰ *tou genomenou ek spermatos Dauid kata sarka.* On the theology of the confessional formula and the reasons for thinking that it is pre-Pauline, see, besides the standard commentaries on Romans, M.-E. Boismard, "Constitué Fils de Dieu (Rom. I, 4)," *RB* 60 (1953) 5–17; R. Bultmann, *Theology of the New Testament* (London: SCM, 1965) 49–50; O. Cullmann, *Christology of the New Testament* (Philadelphia: Westminster, 1959) 235, 291–92; N. Dahl, "Die Messianität Jesu bei Paulus," *Studia Paulina* (Haarlem: Bohn, 1953) 83–95, esp. 90–91; D. Duling, "The Promises to David and Their Entrance into Christianity—Nailing Down a Likely Hypothesis," *NTS* 20 (1973–74) 55–77; R. Fuller, *The Foundations of New Testament Christology* (New York: Scribner's, 1965) 165–67, 187; F. Hahn, *The Titles of Jesus in Christology* (London: Lutterworth, 1969) 246–51; W. Kramer, *Christ, Lord, Son of God* (SBT 1/50; London: SCM, 1966) 108–11; E. Linnemann, "Tradition und Interpretation in Röm 1, 3f.," *EvT* 31 (1971) 264–75 (with a response by E. Schweizer on pp. 275–76); R. Longenecker, *The Christology of Early Jewish Christianity* (SBT 2/17; London: SCM, 1970) 80, 96–98, 111; E. Schweizer, "Röm 1, 3f und der Gegensatz von Fleisch und Geist vor und bei Paulus," *Neotestamentica* (Zurich/Stuttgart: Zwingli, 1963) 180–89; D. M. Stanley, *Christ's Resurrection in Pauline Soteriology* (Rome: Biblical Institute, 1961) 160–66; P. Stuhlmacher, "Theologische Probleme des Römerbriefpräskripts," *EvT* 27 (1967) 374–89; K. Wegenast, *Das Verständnis der Tradition bei Paulus und in den Deuteropaulinen* (WMANT 8; Neukirchen: Neukirchener Verlag, 1962) 70–76; H. Zimmermann, *Neutestamentliche Methodenlehre* (3d ed.; Stuttgart: KBW, 1970) 192–202.

⁵¹ Notice the deft way in which Paul moves from the definition of the gospel common to all Christians (Rom 1:3–4) to his specific understanding of the gospel in terms of justification by faith (1:16–17).

⁵² See Brown (with Meier), *Antioch and Rome*, 89–127; Lampe, *Die stadtrömischen Christen.*

⁵³ Rom 1:3 is the only passage in the undisputed Pauline epistles that mentions Jesus' descent from David, and there Paul seems to be quoting a traditional creedal formula. Paul is willing to mention Davidic descent at this point because he is trying to win over the Roman Christians, whose theological viewpoint was still strongly Jewish in coloration. When Paul states, at the end of a list of Israel's privileges in salvation history, that Jesus was "the Messiah according to the flesh" (Rom 9:5), he may have in the back of his mind Davidic descent. If so, it is all the more significant that in this sentence that recalls Israel's adoption, glory, covenants, law, cult, promises, and patriarchs, David is never mentioned by name (Rom 9:4–5). It is Abraham, not David, who in Paul's theology symbolizes the opening to the Gentiles; perhaps King David may have struck Paul as too particularistic (not to say political) a figure to serve his theological program.

[54] See, e.g., Norbert Brox, *Die Pastoralbriefe* (RNT 7/2; Regensburg: Pustet, 1969) 242; Martin Dibelius and Hans Conzelmann, *The Pastoral Epistles* (Hermeneia; Philadelphia: Fortress, 1972) 108; A. T. Hanson, *The Pastoral Epistles* (NCB; Grand Rapids: Eerdmans, 1982) 130–31; J. N. D. Kelly, *The Pastoral Epistles* (Black's New Testament Commentaries; London: Black, 1963) 177; Walter Lock, *The Pastoral Epistles* (ICC; Edinburgh: Clark, 1924) 95; C. Spicq, *Les épitres pastorales* (EBib; 4th ed.; Paris: Gabalda, 1969) 746.

[55] Mark certainly takes the cry of Bartimaeus in 10:47 ("Son of David, Jesus, have mercy on me") in a positive sense, and so he probably does not mean 12:35–37 (the question about whether the Messiah is the Son of David) to be a rejection of Jesus' Davidic sonship, but rather simply an indication that it is of less importance than Jesus' status as Lord and Son of God. The meaning of this story in the pre-Marcan tradition is more open to question, but it is by no means axiomatic—as some commentators seem to think—that the pre-Marcan form intended a rejection of Davidic sonship. For the position favoring rejection, see Burger, *Jesus als Davidssohn,* 52–59, 64–70, 166. As Brown observes *(The Virginal Conception,* 55 n. 87), Mark 12:35–37 "need not be interpreted as a rhetorical question implying a negation of Davidic sonship. Rather it may be a rabbinic *haggada*-type question requiring that two seemingly contradictory scriptural positions be reconciled—the Messiah is both David's Son and David's Lord, but in different ways." In my view, both 10:47 and 12:35–37 probably represent pre-Marcan traditions and so witness to another stream of Son-of-David christology in first-generation Christianity.

[56] A great deal of the Son-of-David inflation in Matthew's Gospel may be due to Matthean redaction. But since I think Matthew is basically in continuity with rather than opposed to his Church's special tradition, some Son-of-David theology probably existed in the pre-Matthean tradition called "M." On Matthew's use of the M tradition, see Meier (with Brown), *Antioch and Rome,* 53–57. The existence of a "Davidic" motif in M material before Matthew's redaction is especially likely in the Matthean genealogy and Infancy Narrative, granted the use of "David traditions" in Luke's very different genealogy and Infancy Narrative. On the royal Davidic motifs in Matthew, see Brian M. Nolan, *The Royal Son of God* (OBO 23; Fribourg: Editions universitaires; Göttingen: Vandenhoeck & Ruprecht, 1979).

[57] Luke never directly calls Jesus "Son of David" in Acts, but he says the equivalent through Peter in Acts 2:30: "Being therefore a prophet, and knowing that by oath God had sworn to him that the fruit of his loins would sit upon his throne, he [David] prophetically spoke about the resurrection of the Messiah. . . ." See the similar statement by the Lucan Paul in Acts 13:22–23,35–37; cf. E. Schweizer, "The Concept of the Davidic 'Son of God' in Acts and Its Old Testament Background," *Studies in Luke-Acts* (Paul Schubert Festschrift; ed. L. E. Keck and J. L. Martyn; London: SPCK, 1968) 186–93; see also Eric Franklin, *Christ the Lord* (Philadelphia: Fortress, 1975).

[58] This is all the more likely when one considers the application to Jesus the

Son of the royal enthronement Psalms 2 and 110, as well as of Nathan's promise to David (2 Sam 7:14), in Heb 1:5,13.

[59] Note the key words of the LXX in v 12: *anastēsō* and *sperma;* see Duling, "The Promises to David," 55–77.

[60] Most commentators take the description in Isa 61:1–3 to apply to a prophet, either the author (often called Trito-Isaiah) or some other prophetic figure; so Claus Westermann, *Isaiah 40–66* (OTL; Philadelphia: Westminster, 1969) 365–66; R. N. Whybray, *Isaiah 40–66* (NCB; Grand Rapids: Eerdmans; London: Marshall, Morgan & Scott, 1975) 239–40; John L. McKenzie, *Second Isaiah* (AB 20; Garden City, NY: Doubleday, 1968) 181–82; Carroll Stuhlmueller, "Deutero-Isaiah and Trito-Isaiah," *NJBC,* 346. In a letter to me (Nov. 26, 1990), David Noel Freedman suggests instead that the passage comes from Deutero-Isaiah and proclaims the edict that the prophet imagines and hopes King Cyrus will issue when he takes over the Babylonian Empire. In any case, as Westermann points out, the verb "anoint" is used here in a metaphorical sense to designate divine commissioning and sending. It opens the way for "messiah" and "messianic" to be used in a broader sense; it need not mean someone who has been literally, physically anointed with oil, such as the reigning king of Israel.

[61] Some might object that the fact that Jesus was condemned and executed by the Romans on the charge of claiming to be "king of the Jews" (Mark 15:2,26 parr.) was the great historical catalyst leading to the designation of the crucified and risen Jesus as the Messiah by almost all strands of NT proclamation, including the earliest available to us by means of form criticism. This, then, was what gave rise as well to the identification of Jesus as the Son of David; there is no need to appeal to a tradition of Jesus' being a Son of David that supposedly circulated during the public ministry.

In reply, one cannot deny that the crucifixion of Jesus as "king of the Jews" did have a decisive impact on early Christian preaching and on the use of the title Messiah/Christ as almost a second name for Jesus. This is argued well by N. A. Dahl in his famous essay, "Der gekreuzigte Messias," in Ristow and Matthiae, *Der historische Jesus und der kerygmatische Christus,* 149–69; ET: N. A. Dahl, "The Crucified Messiah," *The Crucified Messiah and Other Essays* (Minneapolis: Augsburg, 1974). However, precisely because "Messiah" was a designation open to many different interpretations in 1st-century Judaism (a point acknowledged by Dahl), one cannot move automatically from designations like "Messiah," "king of Israel," and "king of the Jews" to the title "Son of David." Jews and Christian Jews had had recent experience of various "kings of the Jews," and none of them had been a Son of David. The Hasmonean rulers from Aristobulus (104–103 B.C.) onward claimed the title of king, and Herod the Great received that designation from Rome in 40 B.C. Herod's grandson, Herod Agrippa I, was also king of a reunited Israel from A.D. 41 to 44.

The Hasmoneans were of levitical, not Davidic lineage; and Herod's father Antipater stemmed from the Idumeans (=Edomites), who had been forcibly converted to Judaism during the Hasmonean period (but see the claim made by

Nicolaus of Damascus that Antipater's family belonged to the leading Jews who came to Judea from Babylon [*Ant.* 14.1.3. §9]; cf. the revised Schürer, *The History of the Jewish People*, 1. 234 n. 3). Herod's Jewishness was somewhat compromised by the fact that his mother was Cypros, a woman from a famous Arabian family (*J.W.* 1.8.9 §181). This was not fatal to Herod's claim to be a Jew, since tracing one's Jewishness through one's mother was not a firmly established principle in pre-A.D. 70 Judaism (see Shaye J. D. Cohen, "Was Timothy Jewish (Acts 16:1–3)? Patristic Exegesis, Rabbinic Law, and Matrilineal Descent," *JBL* 105 [1986] 251–68). Significantly, Josephus traces Herod's Jewishness through his grandfather and father; see *Ant.* 14.1.3 §8–10; 14.7.3 §121 (although the text is confused here); 14.15.2 §403 (where Antigonus tells the Romans that Herod was "an Idumean, that is, a half-Jew," and so unfit to be king of the Jews). Herod tried to secure both the rights of his children as his heirs and the favor of those who supported the Hasmonean dynasty by marrying the Hasmonean princess Mariamme I. Herod might therefore have claimed that both by birth (on his father's side) and by marriage he was properly positioned to be "king of the Jews," but he could hardly be considered a "Son of David." In short, the concrete experience of Jews in the 1st centuries B.C. and A.D. precluded any automatic identification of the title "king of the Jews" with the title "Son of David."

[62] The literature on the subject, from biblical, theological, and historical points of view, is vast. For general orientation on the question and the literature, see Brown, *The Virginal Conception*, 21–68; Joseph A. Fitzmyer, "The Virginal Conception of Jesus in the New Testament," *TS* 34 (1973) 541–75; Brown, *Birth of the Messiah*, 517–33; Brown, Donfried, et al., *Mary in the New Testament*, 289–92.

[63] At times, attempts have been made by some exegetes to see references to the virginal conception elsewhere in the NT: e.g., Gal 4:4–5 ("God sent his son, born of a woman"); Mark 6:3 ("son of Mary"); John 1:13 (a weakly attested variant that would read the plural verb *egennēthēsan* ["they (the believers) were begotten"] in the singular instead ["he (the Word) was begotten"]. On all this, see Brown, Donfried, et al., *Mary in the New Testament*, 62–63, 181–82; Brown, *Birth of the Messiah*, 518–21.

[64] Interestingly, the tradition of Jesus' birth at Bethlehem and the tradition of the virginal conception do not intersect in the two Infancy Narratives. The former is found only in Chapter 2 of each Gospel, the latter only in Chapter 1.

[65] It should be noted that, paradoxically, the Infancy Narrative of Matthew, which focuses less on Mary than on Joseph, is more explicit about the virginal conception (Matt 1:18–25) than is the Infancy Narrative of Luke, which focuses more on Mary (cf. Luke 1:27,34–35). On the allusive nature of the Lucan reference to virginal conception in the annunciation to Mary, see Brown, *Birth of the Messiah*, 298–303; Fitzmyer, "Virginal Conception," 566–67; and Fitzmyer's altered position in his commentary, *The Gospel According to Luke*, 1. 338.

[66]For surveys of suggested origins and "catalysts" of the idea of the virginal conception of Jesus, see Brown, *The Virginal Conception*, 61–66; idem, *Birth of the Messiah*, 521–31; Brown, Donfried, et al., *Mary in the New Testament*, 291–92.

[67] E.g., Mark 3:21,31–34; John 7:5.

[68] Some authors look beyond the immediate field of Greco-Roman myths and invoke birth stories of great religious figures like Krishna, Buddha, and Zoroaster. Two difficulties make such parallels of little use: (1) It is extremely difficult to date with any accuracy the first appearance of such stories. (2) Even if such stories existed in the early 1st century A.D., it is highly unlikely that they were known by—much less acceptable as sources to—the early Christians who were the bearers of the tradition of the virginal conception, prior to its being written down by the evangelists. On all this, see Brown, *Virginal Conception*, 62 (along with n. 104); idem, *Birth of the Messiah*, 523 n. 13.

[69] Martin Hengel may therefore be right in seeking the seedbed for the idea of virginal conception in Jewish apocalyptic. Problematic, however, is his use of *Slavonic Enoch* (also known as *2 Enoch*) to bolster his opinion. Dating this book is notoriously difficult; suggestions range from pre-Christian times to the late Middle Ages (see F. I. Andersen's treatment in *The Old Testament Pseudepigrapha. Volume I* [Garden City, NY: Doubleday, 1983] 94–97). On all this, see Martin Hengel, *The Son of God* (Philadelphia: Fortress, 1976) 82; Brown, *Birth of the Messiah*, 524 n. 21.

[70] One might try to explain the rise of the idea of Jesus' virginal conception in early Christianity by suggesting that Palestinian Jewish Christians first cited Isa 7:14 in Hebrew or Aramaic with a purely christological intent: Jesus was Immanuel, the promised Davidic Messiah. Later, when the text was taken up by Greek-speaking Jewish Christians, the presence of *parthenos* in the Septuagint version was noticed and gave rise to the idea of the virginal conception. Two major difficulties stand in the way of this theory: (1) In the NT, Isa 7:14 is never quoted or clearly alluded to outside of the Infancy Narratives; there is thus no evidence for a purely "christological" use in the early Church divorced from its present use in Matt 1:23. (2) It is not even certain that Isa 7:14 is behind Luke's presentation of the virginal conception. Unlike Matthew, Luke never cites the text, and Fitzmyer argues that the virginity of Mary in the annunciation scene is not derived from Isa 7:14 (*The Gospel According to Luke*, 1. 336). Moreover, many authors argue that, even in Matthew, the evangelist has secondarily added the formula citation of Isa 7:14 to a pre-Matthean story that did not contain it (see Brown, *Birth of the Messiah*, 96–104, 144–45). Hence the use of the citation would not be the origin of the story, but one means of interpreting it.

[71] The word is capable of being used of a woman up until the time she bears her first child. All the text need mean in Isaiah is that a young woman of marriageable age will soon conceive and bear a son. The woman may indeed be a virgin at the moment the prophecy is uttered. But that is not the point of the text, nor is there the slightest idea that she will remain a virgin when she conceives and bears the child.

[72] See G. Delling, "*parthenos,*" *TDNT* 5 (1968) 827. The sense in ancient Greek was often "girl" or "young woman"; such a woman was indeed usually a virgin, but there was no special emphasis on that.

[73] The Greek *parthenos* here represents the Hebrew *na'ărâ*, "young girl."

[74] See, e.g., his *De Cherubim (On the Cherubim)* 12–15; cf. Brown, *Birth of the Messiah*, 524.

[75] Brown has often reiterated this point; see, e.g., *The Virginal Conception*, 66–67; *Birth of the Messiah*, 527; "Gospel Infancy Narrative Research (Luke)," 678. The same conclusion was reached by the Catholic-Protestant task force that authored *Mary in the New Testament*: "The task force agreed that the question of the historicity of the virginal conception could not be settled by historical-critical exegesis . . ." (pp. 291–92). A similar view is held by Johann Michl, "Die Jungfrauengeburt im Neuen Testament," *Jungfrauengeburt gestern und heute* (Mariologische Studien 4; ed. H. Brosch and J. Hasenfuss; Essen: Driewer, 1969) 145–84, esp. 183.

[76] Lest it seem that the reserved position taken here is dictated not by the limitations of historical-critical research but rather by the Catholic faith, attention should be drawn to the work of those Catholic theologians who, after reviewing the evidence, think that the virginal conception is simply a *theologoumenon:* e.g., Otto Knoch, "Die Botschaft des Matthäusevangeliums über Empfängnis und Geburt Jesu vor dem Hintergrund der Christusverkündigung des Neuen Testaments," *Zum Thema Jungfrauengeburt* (Stuttgart: KBW, 1970) 37–59, esp. 57–58. Knoch takes a paradoxically "Catholic" stand: precisely because he affirms the high christology of John and the Chalcedonian "true God, true man," he feels he can view the story of the virginal conception simply as a *theologoumenon.* For Knoch, the virginal conception is the "historical clothing" of the faith-conviction of the church of Matthew and Luke that Jesus is as the Messiah not only true man but also Son of God in the genuine sense. Knoch affirms that today, in Catholic theology, it is generally acknowledged that profession of faith in Jesus Christ, true man and true God, does not necessarily demand the virginal conception and birth of Jesus. A similar view is held by Gisela Lattke, who affirms that Luke's presentation of the virginal conception is a product of theological reflection, not of a historical event; see her "Lukas 1 und die Jungfrauengeburt," *Zum Thema Jungfrauengeburt*, 61–89, esp. 88.

Other Catholic exegetes who label the virginal conception a *theologoumenon* or who do not consider it a necessary part of Christian faith include Gerhard Lohfink, "Gehört die Jungfrauengeburt zur biblischen Heilsbotschaft?" *TQ* 159 (1979) 304–6; John McKenzie, "The Mother of Jesus in the New Testament," *Concilium* 168 (1983) 3–11; and Rudolf Pesch, "Gegen eine doppelte Wahrheit. Karl Rahner und die Bibelwissenschaft," *Vor dem Geheimnis Gottes den Menschen verstehen. Karl Rahner zum 80. Geburtstag* (ed. Karl Lehmann; Freiburg: Katholische Akademie; Munich: Schnell & Steiner, 1984) 10–36, esp. 26–34. While McKenzie is reserved in his formulations ("The Mother," 5), Lohfink speaks in absolute terms: the virginal conception certainly does not belong to the content of early Christian faith and confession and so to the biblical "message of salvation" ("Gehört," 304). Pesch seems to be in full agreement with Lohfink.

As Pesch's remarks indicate, Karl Rahner was not willing to consider the virginal conception purely a *theologoumenon.* For some earlier comments of

Rahner concerning Pesch's position on Mary's virginity, see Karl Rahner, "Jungfräulichkeit Marias," *Schriften zur Theologie. Band XIII. Gott und Offenbarung* (Zurich/Einsiedeln/Cologne: Benziger, 1978) 361–77. A still earlier treatment of Mary's virginity by Rahner can be found in his essay, "Dogmatische Bemerkungen zur Jungfrauengeburt," *Zum Thema Jungfrauengeburt*, 121–58. In this essay, Rahner seems willing to consider as *theologoumena* the later ideas of Mary's virginity in the act of giving birth to Jesus *(virginitas in partu)* and her perpetual virginity after giving birth to Jesus *(virginitas post partum)*. Rahner seems unwilling to go that far in the case of the virginal conception *(virginitas ante partum)*.

I mention the views of these Catholic exegetes such as Pesch not to adopt them, but simply to indicate that my own position is not predetermined by confessional concerns. Rahner's more moderate, mainline Catholic view on the subject is shared by (now Bishop) Walter Kasper in his "Letter on 'the Virgin Birth,'" published in *Communio* 15 (1988) 262–66. Kasper admits that formerly, as a theologian, he had for a while considered the virginal conception an open question. He still holds that historical criticism by itself does cast the traditional interpretation into doubt; "but this criticism, when truly critical, is just as unable to prove anything to the contrary. All that had resulted, then, was a draw" (p. 263). He accepts the doctrine on the combined authority of Scripture, tradition, the magisterium, and theological reflection. Nevertheless, echoing the view of Rahner, he thinks it wise pastoral care not to disturb a sincere believer who cannot accept the doctrine (p. 266). See also Gerhard L. Müller, *Was heisst: Geboren von der Jungfrau Maria? Eine theologische Deutung* (QD 119; Freiburg/Basel/Vienna: Herder, 1989).

[77] These two different possibilities are not always carefully distinguished in the literature on the subject. Strictly speaking, if Mary and Joseph had sexual relations after their betrothal but before the completion of the marriage process (i.e., before Joseph had taken Mary home to his house and they had begun permanent cohabitation), and then completed the marriage process before Jesus' birth, he would not count as illegitimate. That Jesus was conceived in the interim between the formal betrothal *('ērûsîn)* of Joseph and Mary and the official taking of the wife into the husband's home *(nîśû'în)* is affirmed clearly in Matt 1:18–25 and somewhat less clearly in Luke 1:27,34–35; 2:5. Accordingly, some might want to hypothesize that Joseph and Mary had sexual relations during this interim period, a practice allowed later on in Judea but frowned upon in Galilee (though it was not, strictly speaking, either fornication or adultery, since the couple counted as husband and wife once the betrothal took place).

Such a theory would suffer from depending not only on a subordinate point within the virginal conception tradition but also on rabbinic material of a later date that may or may not have been generally recognized as valid at the end of the 1st century B.C. The clear distinction between Judea and Galilee in this matter is enunciated only in the Babylonian Talmud's version of the question *(b. Ketub.* 9b, 12a), not in the earlier Mishna text *(m. Ketub.* 1:5). For an English translation of the talmudic text, see *The Babylonian Talmud. Seder Nashim. Kethuboth* (trans. Samuel Daiches and Israel Slotki; London: Soncino, 1936) 46–

47, 63–64. Significantly, the editor indicates that the custom may have differed in various parts of Judea itself (p. 63). Then, too, Matthew is the Gospel that speaks more clearly of this interim period; yet Matthew sets the events of the conception in Bethlehem of Judea, not Nazareth of Galilee. Hence later rabbinic distinctions about differences of customs in Judea and Galilee are of questionable relevance. On all this, see Brown, *Birth of the Messiah*, 123–24.

In any case, the theory of illegitimacy is usually proposed after the manner of Celsus or the *Toledoth Yeshu:* Jesus was born of the illicit union of Mary and someone other than Joseph. This is the sense of "illegitimacy" that will be pursued in the text.

[78] See, e.g., Jane Schaberg, *The Illegitimacy of Jesus. A Feminist Theological Interpretation of the Infancy Narratives* (San Francisco: Harper & Row, 1987). Morton Smith (*Jesus the Magician* [San Francisco: Harper & Row, 1978] 47) considers illegitimacy "possible, though not likely" (p. 47). For other scholars, see Brown's appendix on "The Charge of Illegitimacy," *Birth of the Messiah*, 534–42.

In what follows, I will be treating the more usual form of the question: Behind and perhaps concealed by the Infancy Narratives can we find a tradition about Jesus' illegitimacy? This approach is notably different from the thesis proposed by Schaberg. She holds that Matthew and Luke, in their Infancy Narratives, knowingly incorporate the tradition of Jesus' illegitimate conception, a conception perhaps due to rape. The tradition, says Schaberg, is most likely historical. Schaberg claims that ". . . the doctrine of the virginal conception is a distortion and a mask . . . behind it lies the illegitimacy tradition" (p. 197). Though Schaberg favors the theory of rape, she does not exclude the possibility of willing fornication on Mary's part (p. 152). The different emphasis of Schaberg consists in her contention that Matthew and Luke intended to pass down the illegitimacy tradition they inherited (p. 1). In other words, both Matthew and Luke understood that the narratives had to do with an illegitimate conception, though their caution and androcentric perspectives make this aspect of the Infancy Narratives difficult to perceive.

In my view, Schaberg's thesis is self-conflicted from the start; the threat of self-contradiction looms larger as the thesis of the book is evolved. She tries to bolster her strange position with a tour de force of exegetical expertise. Unfortunately, to support her views she regularly has to choose a less likely interpretation of a given text. To be sure, all interpreters at times decide that they should choose a less likely interpretation. But Schaberg's long catena of dubious interpretations makes the whole project dubious in the extreme. Repeated affirmations of a theory take the place of detailed arguments, rhetorical questions abound, and counterindicating data are ignored or passed over quickly in footnotes. Increasingly, one gets the impression of exegesis that is going against the "natural grain" of the text for the sake of hermeneutical positions determined before the exegesis ever began. Thus, it is not surprising that, by the end of her exegesis of Luke, Schaberg seems annoyed with the evangelist for being so recalcitrant to her mode of interpretation (p. 144). In short, a great deal of learning is wasted on a quixotic project.

[79] Some individual claims, however, may be treated briefly, as having no

great probative value for the basic thesis of a primordial illegitimacy tradition. For example, Schaberg *(Illegitimacy,* 164–65) adduces logion 105 from the Coptic *Gospel of Thomas:* "He who knows the father and the mother will be called the son of a prostitute [the Greek word *pornē* is used for 'prostitute' in this Coptic saying]." I do not find Schaberg's argument about this text probative. (1) In her argument, Schaberg depends on the position of Koester that the *Gospel of Thomas* contains some sayings that are more primitive than their parallels in the NT. As I have argued above in Chapter 5, this is a very dubious position. (2) Schaberg argues that logion 105 may draw on the pre-Gospel tradition of illegitimacy reflected in John 8:41 and Mark 6:3; I will argue below that neither text reflects such a tradition. (3) As so often happens with the cryptic sayings of the *Gospel of Thomas,* the logion without larger context means anything or nothing. As Brown *(Birth of the Messiah,* 534) rightly observes, this saying "is too obscure to be really helpful." (4) At any rate, the designation of Jesus as the son of a prostitute would represent not the earliest form of the illegitimacy tradition as reported by Celsus, but rather the slightly later form attested by Tertullian in *De spectaculis* 30.6 *(quaestuariae filius,* i.e., "son of a prostitute").

[80] The great variety in spelling is due to the fact that the Semitic consonants of the name *pntyr'* were both vocalized differently and then transliterated in different ways when put into Greek and other languages. Besides Panthera, one runs into Pantira, Pandera, Pantiri, and Panteri.

[81] For a critical edition of the texts involved, see *Origène, Contre Celse. Tome I (Livres I et II)* (SC 132; ed. M. Borret; Paris: Cerf, 1967) 150–53, 162–65. On p. 163 n. 4, Borret still accepts the possibility of Klausner's explanation, namely, that the idea of Jesus' being the son of Panthera developed from the Greek *ho huios tēs parthenou* ("the son of the virgin")—though such a theory is questioned by many scholars today. Borret thinks that the the talmudic tradition about Jesus Ben Pandera may go back to the end of the 1st century A.D.

[82] The next datable reference to the illegitimacy tradition is in Tertullian's *De spectaculis* 30.6, written ca. A.D. 197. For a critical edition, see *Tertullien, Les Spectacles* (SC 332; ed. M. Turcan; Paris: Cerf, 1986). The entire passage in which the passing reference to Jesus as *fabri aut quaestuariae filius* ("the son of a carpenter or a prostitute") occurs is significant: Tertullian is tossing together all sorts of slanders spoken against as well as outrages perpetrated on Jesus. His rhetorical flourish is a mélange of material from the canonical Gospels, especially Matthew and John, spiced with some mocking legendary expansions. "Mocking midrash" on the Gospels might well be the correct category to apply to the illegitimacy tradition in Celsus as well.

[83] Hence I do not bother reviewing here material like the apocryphal *Acts of Pilate,* a document that has a very complicated history. The work as a whole seems to have been composed at the beginning of the 5th century, but various parts date from earlier centuries—how early it is difficult to say. Some of the parts were perhaps written to counteract spurious pagan *Acts of Pilate* in the early 4th century. Justin Martyr mentions an *Acts of Pilate* in the mid-2d century, which enlisted Pilate and the Emperor Tiberius as witnesses to Christ's inno-

cence and divinity. Nothing more can be known with certainty about this primitive form of the *Acts*, but this is enough to make one doubt that it contained any historically reliable information. The earliest form of an *Acts of Pilate* that can be reconstructed with fair certainty dates from the latter part of the 2d century; it mentions in passing Jesus' virginal conception but says nothing of a charge of illegitimacy. For this reconstructed text, see Johannes Quasten, *Patrology. Volume I* (Westminster, MD: Christian Classics, 1983; originally 1950) 117. The charge of illegitimacy is mentioned (and denied) in a later, fuller form of the *Acts*, which is obviously dependent on at least some of the canonical Gospels. Even Schaberg concludes that the *Acts* is not a witness independent of the NT to the tradition of Jesus' illegitimacy *(Illegitimacy,* 159). The claim of F. Scheidweiler that the *Acts* gives a form of the story earlier than that of Celsus' account is not substantiated by any hard evidence; see his introduction to the *Acts* in Edgar Hennecke and Wilhelm Schneemelcher, *Neutestamentliche Apokryphen. I. Band. Evangelien* (Tübingen: Mohr [Siebeck], 1968) 330–33, esp. 330. Scheidweiler seems to presuppose in his line of argument that the charge of illegitimacy began in a relatively mild form (e.g., premarital sex in the *Acts of Pilate)* and then progressed to harsher forms (e.g., adultery with Panthera in the story reported by Celsus). However, the vagaries of the whole illegitimacy tradition make one wary of any argument that presupposes a neat rectilinear development. This does not happen in christology; it should not be presumed in the antichristology of the illegitimacy tradition.

[84] Actually, it is not agreed by all scholars that Celsus is telling the truth here; the possibility remains that he fabricated the story as a reaction to the Infancy Narratives and then placed the story in the mouth of a Jew. Celsus was not overly fond of Judaism either. However, the fact that about two decades later Tertullian *(De spectaculis* 30.6) ascribes the charge of illegitimacy to Jews rather than to pagans argues for a Jewish source of the idea in Celsus.

[85] The exact date of the composition of Justin's *Dialogue with Trypho* is debated; but it was probably written a few years after A.D. 150.

[86] Maier *(Jesus von Nazareth,* 252, 255, 265, 268–70) insists that methodologically one must distinguish between the story in Celsus and early rabbinic traditions about "Ben Pantere," which show no knowledge of the charge of illegitimacy. The illegitimacy tradition may have been added when "Ben Pantere" was identified at a later date with "Ben Stada."

[87] Other elements of the story are present as well in Luke but are more clearly stated by Matthew, e.g., the fact that the conception took place during the time of betrothal.

[88] That the change is due to Matthew's redaction of Mark is generally acknowledged by critics who accept the two-source theory; see, e.g., Walter Grundmann, *Das Evangelium nach Matthäus* (THKNT 1; 3d ed.; Berlin: Evangelische Verlagsanstalt, 1972) 358–59; Rudolf Schnackenburg, *Matthäusevangelium 1,1-16,20* (Die Neue Echter Bible 1/1; Würzburg: Echter, 1985) 131–32. Note that Joseph is never mentioned directly or indirectly in Mark's Gospel.

[89] The Jewish polemicists need not have actually read the text of Matthew's Gospel; knowledge of his Infancy Narrative through disputes with Christians is a sufficient explanation. Schaberg has to admit that Celsus' story drew upon Matthew and also shows polemical embellishments of the NT narratives. Her attempt to argue that, in addition, the account of Celsus drew from "independent, parallel tradition" is not supported by the evidence (*Illegitimacy*, 166).

[90] This does not keep Schaberg from sketching a scenario: see *Illegitimacy*, 153–56.

[91] For an inventory of the various interpretations of the key phrase in Mark 6:3, see Harvey K. McArthur, " 'Son of Mary,' " *NovT* 15 (1973) 38–58.

[92] The reading *ho tou tektonos huios* ("the son of the woodworker") is supported by p[45], family 13, minuscules 33, 472, 543, 565, 579, 700, the Old Latin manuscripts a, b, c, e, i, r², δ, aureus, many manuscripts of the Vulgate, three manuscripts of the bohairic Coptic, the Aethiopic, and implicitly by Origen in *Contra Celsum* 6.36 ("Nowhere in the gospels received by the churches is Jesus himself called a carpenter [*tektōn*]"). For a critical edition of the Greek text of Origen's statement, see *Origène, Contre Celse. Tome III (Livres V et VI)* (SC 147; ed. M. Borret; Paris: Cerf, 1969) 266–69.

[93] Most of the "dissenting" manuscripts add "and of Mary," though p[45] reads only "son of the carpenter."

[94] For example, Vincent Taylor takes the simple *ho tou tektonos huios* (without *kai tēs Marias*) as what Mark originally wrote; see his *The Gospel According to St. Mark*, 300. McArthur (" 'Son of Mary,' " 52) thinks that the alternate reading "the son of the carpenter and of Mary" is the original one; but he readily admits the difficulty of reaching a firm decision.

[95] Riesner (*Jesus als Lehrer*, 218) rejects the two-source hypothesis, holding that the Matthean formulation is more original. Mark, dealing with a non-Jewish, Greek-speaking audience, supposedly wanted to avoid the misconception that Jesus was a physical son of Joseph. This whole approach imports the virginal conception tradition known to Matthew and Luke into Mark, who gives no clear indication of being aware of it.

[96] *ho tektōn, ho huios* receives an "A" rating (="virtually certain") in the *UBSGNT³*. See the commentary in Metzger, *Textual Commentary*, 88–89.

[97] Notably Ethelbert Stauffer, "Jeschu Ben Mirjam," *Neotestamentica et Semitica* (Matthew Black Festschrift; ed. E. Earle Ellis and Max Wilcox; Edinburgh: Clark, 1969) 119–28. Stauffer interprets "son of Mary" as a claim that Jesus was the illegitimate child of Mary; he then proceeds to interpret Matthew 1 as a polemical reply to such a charge. Two basic weaknesses mar the article: (1) Stauffer engages much more in assertions than in arguments and proof. The essential basis of his whole argument is never proved but rather taken for granted: namely, that a phrase like "son of Mary" was understood in the OT and at the time of Jesus as a regular way of referring to an illegitimate child. As we shall see, this was not the case. (2) The evidence he does adduce is a mélange of

rabbinic, Samaritan, and Mandean texts from widely different times and places. Those that explicitly refer to the illegitimacy tradition are all later—and most much later—than the Gospel of Mark and the Infancy Narratives of Matthew and Luke.

[98] Josef Blinzler falls into the trap of making this claim, especially with regard to the only son of a widow, in his *Die Brüder und Schwestern Jesu* (SBS 21; 2d ed.; Stuttgart: KBW, 1967) 72. A better evaluation of the evidence on widows is given by McArthur, " 'Son of Mary,' " 38–58, esp. 44.

[99] See the evidence collected by McArthur, " 'Son of Mary,' " 45, as well as the various reasons he adduces for not using such a solution in Mark 6:3 in particular (pp. 52–53); see also Brown, *Birth of the Messiah*, 540.

[100] See McArthur, " 'Son of Mary,' " 41; McArthur treats the case under remnants of matriarchal family patterns, but he readily admits that such an explanation is by no means certain. See also Detlev Dormeyer, "Die Familie Jesu und der Sohn der Maria im Markusevangelium (3,20 f. 31–35; 6,3)," *Vom Urchristentum zu Jesus* (Joachim Gnilka Festschrift; ed. Hubert Frankemölle and Karl Kertelge; Freiburg/Basel/Vienna: Herder, 1989) 109–35, esp. 127–29.

[101] David Noel Freedman (in a letter dated Nov. 26, 1990) suggests that the reason for the mention of Zeruiah is twofold: (1) she was a sister of David, and (2) the father of her three sons was dead. He goes on to suggest another possibility: the husband of Zeruiah had had more than one wife, and Zeruiah's children are identified by naming the mother, à la Joseph and Benjamin, the sons of Rachel. While Freedman does not think it likely that Joseph had had another, earlier wife, he does think that the possibility is at least worth pondering.

[102] It is symptomatic of her approach that, in her treatment of Mark 6:3, Schaberg *(Illegitimacy,* 160–64) does not discuss this remarkable case of the sons of Zeruiah. She uncritically accepts much of Stauffer, without a careful consideration of all the arguments of McArthur.

[103] Such an idea, totally unprepared for in Mark's presentation, runs up against the fact that the phrase is in the mouths of unbelieving adversaries of Jesus. In keeping with Mark's theme of the "messianic secret," even Jesus' disciples cannot understand his true identity as Son of God before his death and resurrection. Suggesting that Jesus' enemies know of his virginal conception shows a complete failure to accept the theological vision and limits of Mark's Gospel. Moreover, the evangelists who do clearly affirm the virginal conception have no difficulty in calling Jesus "the son of the carpenter" or "the son of Joseph." To argue that Mark, who never clearly mentions the virginal conception, intimates the idea by using instead "the carpenter, the son of Mary" is curious logic. Furthermore, Mark is the evangelist who is most severe in his treatment of Jesus' relatives (cf. Mark 3:21,31–35; 6:4). Understandably, Matthew and Luke, in keeping with the idea of virginal conception, omit or soften these Marcan passages. How does Mark's severity jibe with the idea that his mother, if no other relative, would have had to know about his virginal conception? On all this, see Brown, Donfried, et al., *Mary in the New Testament*, 62–63.

[104] So rightly Brown, Donfried, et al., *Mary in the New Testament*, 64. Their starting point is the supposition, most probably correct, that Joseph is dead.

[105] The townspeople are hardly mentioning Jesus' brothers and sisters in order to intimate that they too are illegitimate!

[106] I stress that this contextual explanation does not claim that "son of Mary" is a set title of Jesus or is due to a set way of referring to sons of widows. Rather, the usage is a popular one occasioned by the rhetorical situation of the moment. An intriguing parallel to this "occasional" usage is found in Luke's story of the raising of the son of the widow of Nain. The dead man is called precisely "the only son of his mother" *(monogenēs huios tē̦ mētri autou,* Luke 7:12). The solution I adopt is basically the one favored by McArthur under the rubric of "informal description" (" 'Son of Mary,' " 54). Besides Luke 7:12, he points to such "informal descriptions" in Acts 23:16 and Gal 4:21–31. McArthur's conclusion bears repeating: "I conclude, therefore, that the ancient scholars were correct in assuming that the phrase had no special connotation beyond the fact explicitly stated, and that modern scholars have been led astray by regarding 'Son of Mary' as a problematic phrase" (p. 58).

[107] See the comments of Brown, *John*, 1. 315, 342. On p. 342 Brown observes: "An analysis of the structure of ch. viii (12 ff.) is perhaps more difficult than that of any other chapter or long discourse in the first part of the Gospel."

[108] Schnackenburg *(Das Johannesevangelium. II. Teil*, 283) is correct when he observes that, at this point in the debate, the Jews press their claim that Abraham is their *spiritual* father, the prototype of faith and good works.

[109] In John's immediate context and argument, the works of Abraham may be, in particular, faith in God and hospitable reception of his divine emissary.

[110] See, e.g., the classic statement of Yahweh to the prophet Hosea in LXX Hosea 1:2: *labe seautō̦ gynaika porneias kai tekna porneias, dioti ekporneuousa ekporneusei hē gē apo opisthen tou kyriou;* "Take to yourself a woman of fornication [or prostitution] and children of fornication [or prostitution], for the land shall commit fornication upon fornication in refusing to follow the Lord." Cf. LXX Hosea 2:6.

[111] This pivotal point is missed in the exegesis of the passage by Schaberg, *Illegitimacy*, 157–58.

[112] See J. H. Bernard, *A Critical and Exegetical Commentary on the Gospel According to St. John* (ICC; 2 vols.; Edinburgh: Clark, 1928) 2. 316. Bultmann, instead, sees in the charge the idea that Jesus is a heretic *(Das Evangelium des Johannes*, 225 n. 6), while Brown prefers to connect it with the subsequent charge of having a demon: Jesus is demented *(John*, 1. 358). Whatever the precise nuance of the accusation, all these commentators agree that "Samaritan" is not to be understood literally and biologically.

[113] It is useful to recall at this point that John in general shows no knowledge

of the virginal conception tradition. It would be quite remarkable if he neverthe-less reflected knowledge of the polemical countertradition of Jesus' illegitimacy.

[114] Schnackenburg *(Das Johannesevangelium. II. Teil*, 285) is firmly against any reference to illegitimacy in John 8:41; Brown is less certain in *John*, 1. 357; *Birth*, 541–42. Likewise against a reference to Jesus' supposed illegitimacy in this pas-sage is M.-J. Lagrange, *Evangile selon saint Jean* (EBib; 5th ed.; Paris: Gabalda, 1936) 246. Both C. H. Dodd and Barnabas Lindars apparently accept the "illegit-imacy interpretation" as a possible, but not the most probable, interpretation; see C. H. Dodd, *The Interpretation of the Fourth Gospel* (Cambridge: Cambridge University, 1965) 260 n. 1; Barnabas Lindars, *The Gospel of John* (NCB; Grand Rapids: Eerdmans, 1972) 328.

[115] The question of the reliability of this chronological indicator will be treated in Chapter 11.

[116] In the LXX, the Hebrew *Miryām* is transliterated as *Mariam*. Josephus, however, regularly uses the declinable form *Mariamē* or *Mariammē*, although he uses *Maria* in *J.W.* 6.3.4 §201. Obviously, Josephus (and some NT authors) sought ways to create a declinable form for the indeclinable *Mariam*. As might be imagined, the Greek NT manuscripts that have come down to us show great variations in the spelling of the name. If we may trust the present-day critical editions of the NT, individual evangelists were capable of calling Mary the mother of Jesus both *Mariam* and *Maria* in the same chapter of their Gospels: so Luke 1 regularly uses *Mariam*, but 1:41 reads *tēs Marias*. The same alteration is found with Mary Magdalene, even within the same pericope; thus John 20:11 has *Maria*, but 20:16 has *Mariam*. There is no basis in seeing in these variations different names, different persons, or different sources. The equivalence of the two forms is underlined by the remarkable coincidence that each form occurs in the NT exactly 27 times *(Maria* in Matthew, Mark, Luke, John, Acts, and Ro-mans; *Mariam* in those same books with the exception of Mark and Romans). For the debate about the etymology of the name, see Manfred Görg, "Mirjam—ein weiterer Versuch," *BZ* 23 (1979) 285–89. Two major candidates are a West Se-mitic form meaning "gift of God" and an Egyptian form meaning "beloved of Amun." While stressing our present uncertainty, Görg leans toward the latter solution.

CHAPTER 9

IN THE INTERIM . . .

Part I: Language, Education, and Socioeconomic Status

1. CAN ANYTHING BE SAID ABOUT THE FORMATIVE YEARS?

The reason why a biography of Jesus—in the modern sense of biography—cannot be written is by now obvious. We are dealing with a man who died in his mid-thirties and whose first thirty-two years or so are almost completely unknown and unknowable. One does not have to be a Freudian of the Strict Observance to realize that, without any data about Jesus' childhood relationships, his adolescent struggles and coming to adulthood, and his activities during his twenties—to say nothing of his specifically intellectual and religious development—nothing certain can be said about the influences that molded the Jesus known to us through the public ministry. The reason why authors of both apocryphal Infancy Gospels (like the *Infancy Gospel of Thomas)* and modern novels have gravitated to the so-called "hidden years" of Jesus' life in Nazareth is that they can give free rein to their imaginations (pious or impious), with no facts to restrain them. It all makes for great fiction and specious history.

Granted our nescience, one might ask why not one but two chapters about the "in-between years" of Jesus' life should even exist in this book. Why not just leap from the slight data about Jesus' birth to the beginning of his public ministry? To a great extent, that is indeed what we have to do. Yet a certain interplay between salient aspects of his public ministry and well-known facts about Judea, Galilee, and Judaism during the time of Jesus' "hidden years" allows us to make a few educated guesses about some of the circumstances surrounding his childhood, adolescence, and early adulthood.

As one attempts such educated guesses, one must carefully distinguish between certain basic facts that can be taken for granted—"facts" that are actually sweeping generalizations—and more detailed information that could concretize those basic facts—information, though, that is usually lacking. For example, that Jesus as a boy and adolescent experienced physical, sexual, intellectual, and religious development is to be presupposed from the laws of nature and historical analogy. Not only is there nothing in the NT to contradict such a presupposition; there are a number of texts which imply precisely such normal maturation: "the boy grew and gained strength . . ." (Luke 2:40); "Jesus advanced in wisdom and age [or stature] and favor in the eyes of God and humans" (Luke 2:52); "it was necessary that he [Jesus] become like the brethren [=his fellow human beings] in every way" (Heb 2:17; cf. 4:15). Although later theology has tried at times to restrict the scope of this last sweeping statement, Christian theology itself affirms in its saner moments that, sin excepted, every basic experience a human being undergoes during his or her physical and psychological development Jesus underwent. There is thus no conflict here between the general use of historical analogy and the perspectives of Christian theology.

At the same time, the vague generalizations of historical analogy do not bring us very far. To take an example dear to the heart of our post-Freudian society, that Jesus experienced sexual maturation like any other Jewish boy of his day is obvious; what that experience meant to him personally as an individual, or what special aspects that experience may have held for him, is completely hidden from us. Likewise, that Jesus underwent considerable intellectual and psychological development as he passed from childhood to adulthood is to be taken for granted. That he, like every human being, struggled toward some definition of self within, in relation to, and perhaps in opposition to, larger social units is equally clear. But what exactly such development entailed in his case, what stages his journey toward self-knowledge involved, we cannot say. It is hopeless, over the chasm of twenty centuries, to attempt to put Jesus on the psychiatrist's couch.[1] Here is where the scholar is silent and the novelist has a field day. With practically no data to control speculation, no particular scenario can be disproved any more than it can be proved. All one can do is repeat the old philosophical dictum: what is gratuitously asserted may be gratuitously denied.

With sober awareness of the limitations on what we can say, we shall take a look in this chapter at various "external" circumstances that would naturally mold the life and thought of Jesus as he grew up in Nazareth: the language(s) he learned, the education he received, the occupation he plied, and the socioeconomic status he thus attained. In the following chapter, we shall try to discern the influences on his life that would be more "internal," i.e., his family relations and marital status.

2. WHAT LANGUAGE DID JESUS SPEAK?

One of the first questions we would want to ask about Jesus' formation is what education, if any, he received and what languages, if any, he could read. These questions, however, presuppose a prior question: What language or languages did Jesus speak, especially when he taught?

In one sense, we can answer this question very simply, though very vaguely. Since the adult Jesus became an itinerant teacher traversing both Galilee and Judea, and since as a teacher he obviously wished to be understood by his audience, which was largely made up of ordinary Palestinian Jews, Jesus would have spoken whatever was the language commonly used by ordinary Jews in their daily lives in Palestine. The real question, then, is obvious: What language was that? The answer is simple: We cannot be absolutely sure. The reason for our puzzlement is likewise simple: We have no tape recordings from 1st-century Palestine. Failing such tapes, we are thrown back on literary and epigraphic (i.e., inscriptional) evidence. Unfortunately, both are mute in the sense that neither translates directly into unambiguous evidence about the most commonly spoken language of ordinary Jews in 1st-century Palestine. The ambiguity of the data explains why scholars can be so divided on whether Jesus regularly spoke Greek (so R. O. P. Taylor and, more cautiously, A. W. Argyle[2]), Aramaic (so Joseph A. Fitzmyer[3]), or Hebrew (so Harris Birkeland[4]).

A number of factors contribute to the ambiguity of the data. First, the two major sources of knowledge, literary works and inscriptions, both have built-in limitations. As we shall see in the next section, which deals with Jesus' literacy, William V. Harris has shown that the ability to read, and even more the ability to write, lengthy works in any language was a relatively rare skill in the Greco-Roman world, a skill restricted largely to scribes and an intellectual elite.[5] To take a concrete example from Palestine: the sectarian literature produced at and for Qumran (e.g., *The Manual of Discipline, The Thanksgiving Hymns, The Pesher on Habakkuk*) is written mostly in "postbiblical" Hebrew.[6] That tells us something about the linguistic abilities of the special type of learned and esoteric Jew resident at Qumran, and also shows that at least at Qumran Hebrew was a "living" language.[7] Whether it indicates that Jews in general throughout Palestine spoke Hebrew as their ordinary language is quite another question. One would need further evidence to draw that conclusion.

Inscriptions likewise have their inherent limitations as sources of information about the colloquial language of Palestine.[8] Ancient inscriptions of a public nature were usually provided by elite groups for elite groups (the rulers, the rich, the cultured few). Inscriptions were addressed to the larger populace in the sense that the inscriptions, along with the buildings or other structures they adorned, spoke a wordless message of political domination, military or economic achievement, or cultural superiority. In the Greco-Roman world, where the vast majority of ordinary people were functionally illiterate, we must beware of presuming that inscriptions were meant to be read word by word by the general populace.

In this regard, it is useful to recall the famous "Pontius Pilate inscription" discovered at Caesarea Maritima in 1961. The inscription proclaims that a particular building in Caesarea (the city that was the capital of the Roman province of Judea) was dedicated to the Emperor Tiberius by the perfect Pontius Pilate (A.D. 26–36). The inscription is in Latin. One may rightly doubt whether the vast majority of Gentiles and the large minority of Jews who lived in Caesarea at the time could have understood what the Latin text said—to say nothing of their ability to speak Latin as their common language. Probably Pilate was not the least bit interested in communicating a precise verbal message to the masses. He was speaking to and for "his own kind," the relatively few elites in the service of the Roman Empire, elites who could not only speak but also read Latin. To the masses, Pilate, by his inscription and his building, simply spoke the language of power. I would suggest that any time an argument about the most commonly spoken language in Palestine appeals to a public inscription, we should remember the Caesarea Maritima inscription and ask: What does this inscription really prove? Funerary inscriptions are another matter, and there at least one might expect the common language of the deceased or the mourners to be used. Yet even there one must reckon with the possibility of special factors: nostalgia for the "good old-time religion" or a desire to create an impression of high culture.[9] One could not deduce the common language spoken by American Catholics of the early 20th century from the *Requiescat in pace* on their tombstones, just as one could not deduce the various languages spoken by modern Europeans by the many modern Latin inscriptions that dot the Continent.

A second problem with the evidence is the way it is often treated. At times scholars will toss together Palestinian inscriptions from different centuries.[10] This is an illegitimate procedure, especially since we are asking a very specific question about the languages spoken in Palestine in the 1st century A.D. Palestine, according to some scholars, experienced an eclipse of the Aramaic language during the Hellenization program of the Seleucid monarchs of Syria in the 3d and 2d centuries B.C.[11] Moreover, Aramaic definitely seems to have receded in favor of Greek as a result of the two Jewish Wars in the 1st and 2d centuries A.D. Consequently, it is a questionable procedure to compile epigraphic evidence from Palestine without due regard for the particular century from which a given inscription comes. Inscriptions from the 2d century B.C. or from the latter part of the 2d century A.D. do not necessarily tell us what was the language of the ordinary Jew in the early 1st century A.D.

With these caveats in mind, we can now summarize what the evidence appears to show about the four languages used in 1st-century A.D. Palestine: Latin, Greek, Hebrew, and Aramaic.[12]

(1) Almost everyone agrees that Latin, the most recent language on the Palestinian scene,[13] was also the least used. It was employed almost exclusively by, for, and among Roman officials. As we saw in the case of the Pontius Pilate inscription, the Romans gladly used Latin in inscriptions placed on public buildings and on public works like aqueducts. They were blissfully unconcerned that the vast majority of Jews in Palestine could neither read nor understand the stately Latin phrases. The very presence of a Latin text in Palestine proclaimed domination; that— and not the particular words of the text—was the message understood by the Jews. We also find some Latin funerary inscriptions on tombstones of Roman legionnaires who died in Palestine. Such inscriptions remind us of another difficulty with funerary texts: they may say something about the language of the person who has died without necessarily indicating anything about the language of the vast majority of persons who might later see the inscriptions.[14] All in all, it is hardly an accident that the most significant Latin inscriptions known to us from archaeol-

ogy or descriptions in literary works were situated in and around Caesarea Maritima and Jerusalem. Latin was at home in the seats of power, not in a Galilean village. There is no reason to think that Jesus ever spoke, much less read, Latin.[15]

(2) Greek was another matter altogether. It served the Roman Empire as the lingua franca from Rome itself eastward around the Mediterranean through Greece and Asia Minor, the main cities of Syria and Palestine, and down into Egypt. From the time of Alexander the Great (356–323 B.C.) onward, and especially under the Seleucid emperors, notably Antiochus IV Epiphanes (reigned 175–165/4 B.C.), as well as during the reign of Herod the Great (37–4 B.C.), Greek culture and language made increasing inroads in Palestine. In that sense, the Palestinian Judaism of Jesus' day was Hellenistic Judaism.[16] The question debated among scholars today is simply the precise degree of Hellenization in any given time or locality. During most of the last three centuries B.C. it certainly was massive. The Seleucid kings of Syria had founded new Greek cities in Palestine, and some earlier Jewish settlements were transformed into cities that were Greek both politically and culturally (poleis). From these centers Greek language and culture radiated out to the countryside.

Despite the nationalist uprising under the Maccabees, the Hasmonean rulers who followed them were to a great degree Hellenistic monarchs.[17] Toward the end of the 1st century B.C., Herod the Great continued this policy of Hellenization with his massive building projects, such as the splendid harbor at Caesarea Maritima on the coast, the city of Sebaste in Samaria, and massive construction in Jerusalem—all in the Greco-Roman style.[18] Greek inscriptions were to be found in Jerusalem, including the inscription forbidding non-Jews to enter the inner courts of the temple and a synagogue inscription set up by the priest Theodotos Vettenus. Many Greek inscriptions on tombs and ossuaries have also been found. Martin Hengel claims that a good third of the epitaphs from Jerusalem from the Second Temple period were written in Greek, and he proceeds to estimate that, of the 80,000 to 100,000 persons resident in greater Jerusalem, between 8,000 and 16,000 would have spoken Greek.[19] But Greek culture and language touched Jews not only in Jerusalem.[20] A good number of Jews lived in the Hellenized cities of the coastal plain, from Gaza in the south to Dor or Ptolemais-Acco in the north.[21] Caesarea, the Roman capital of Judea, had almost as many Jews as Gentiles.[22] The caves of Murabbaʿat have yielded Greek papyri from everyday life and even copies of Greek letters from—ironically!—the time of the Bar Kochba revolt, precisely when nationalists were fighting and dying to free themselves from foreign rule and cultural domination.[23]

However, the cultural invasion of the Greek language did not go unresisted. The Maccabean revolt signaled not only a military counterattack against the armies of Antiochus IV but also, in a sense—at least among certain segments of the Jewish population—a linguistic counterattack. This counterattack was marked by an emphasis on "the language of the forefathers" (which, in the Book of Daniel, turns out to be a mixture of Hebrew and Aramaic).[24] It is probably from the time of the Maccabees and their successors that a revitalization of interest in Hebrew and Aramaic spreads in Palestine, a revitalization reflected in the literary works produced or preserved by Qumran.[25] While the Hasmonean and Herodian ruling class and the urban intelligentsia in Jerusalem would continue to use and be immersed in Greek language and culture, a definite reaction set in among devout Jews dedicated to their national and religious identity. It is symbolic of the situation that the Greek fragments found at Qumran are far fewer in number than the lengthy Hebrew and Aramaic documents. Just as striking is the type of Hebrew and Aramaic we find. In the Hebrew of the Qumran documents, with the exception of the *Copper Scroll,* practically no Greek loanwords appear.[26] The same is basically true of the Aramaic documents from Qumran. This contrasts notably with Palestinian Hebrew and Aramaic of a few centuries later; there we find abundant examples of Greek and Latin loanwords.

Hence one may wonder whether or to what degree the tidal wave of the Greek language was still engulfing Palestinian Jews in the early 1st century A.D.[27] The answer may have varied from area to area and from social class to social class. In my view, a number of passages in Josephus warn us not to presuppose that Greek was everywhere well known by Jews in 1st-century Palestine or was the most commonly spoken language. A priestly aristocrat from Jerusalem, Josephus boasts of his fine education, which was helped along—he is careful to note—by his excellent memory and intellectual ability *(Life* 2 §8). When he was about fourteen years old (ca. A.D. 51–52), he was already famous—he does not blush to tell us—among the chief priests and Jerusalem leaders. After spending much of his teenage years exploring the various Jewish "schools" of thought, he became a Pharisee (or so he claims at a later date). About A.D. 61 he visited Rome to intercede with Poppaea, Nero's mistress and later empress, for certain Jewish priests who had been arrested and sent to Rome. Obviously, even after making allowances for Josephus' boasting, he belonged to a small elite of cultured men of international experience, capable of reading and writing a number of languages. Yet some statements in Josephus' works make us wonder about the supposed widespread knowledge of Greek in Palestine at his time, which is just slightly after the time of Jesus.

At the end of his *Jewish Antiquities*, Josephus begins to praise himself in the most shameless fashion imaginable *(Ant.* 20.12.1 §262–66). Not only has he surpassed all his fellow Jews in knowledge of the Law;[28] he has also labored mightily to learn Greek prose and poetry, after having studied Greek grammar. He must then immediately defend himself—with more than a little awkwardness in the Greek text—against the apparently well-known fact that his pronunciation of Greek, even after so many years in Rome (a city where much Greek was spoken), still left something to be desired.[29]

It seems, however, that it was not simply Josephus' pronunciation of Greek that was not masterful; his control of the written language was not exactly perfect either. At the beginning of the *Jewish Antiquities,* Josephus relates how, after finishing the *Jewish War,* he had intended to write a larger work on the whole history of the Jewish people from creation to the eve of the revolt (the *Jewish Antiquities).* He then excuses himself for putting off this new, vaster project by emphasizing the difficulty of writing such a huge work in Greek. Greek, he confesses—even after the composition of the *Jewish War* and decades spent in Rome!—still represents for him linguistic usage that is foreign and strange.[30] We are not surprised, therefore, to learn that Josephus had originally composed the *Jewish War* in his native tongue (probably Aramaic) and then employed "collaborators" *(synergois)* to translate the work into Greek *(Ag.Ap.* 1.9 §50).[31] The need for coworkers to help him with the Greek is all the more striking in this passage, since Josephus stresses that he now had abundant leisure time in Rome, granted by his patron Vespasian, with all his source materials laid out before him.

It seems fair to infer that, in the 1st century A.D., even an intellectually gifted and well-educated Jewish aristocrat of Jerusalem did not necessarily have a firm grasp of all the niceties of written as well as spoken Greek.[32] On the other hand, Josephus did at least know how to understand and speak Greek while he was still in Palestine. One incident in the Jewish War, however, leaves us wondering how much Greek the majority of Jews in Jerusalem could understand, let alone speak. While Titus was pressing the siege of Jerusalem, we are told that he *both* personally exhorted the Jewish defenders to save themselves by surrendering the city *and* sent Josephus to speak with them "in the language of their forefathers" (probably Aramaic, possibly Hebrew).[33]

The distinction Josephus implies here is intriguing. Titus, of course, had no choice. Knowing neither Aramaic nor Hebrew, he could address the Jerusalemites only in Greek. Josephus, being able to speak to his fellow Jews of Jerusalem in either Greek or Aramaic, used the latter. Employing a Semitic language could have been just a *captatio benevolentiae*, an appeal to blood ties; but it might also have been a necessity if some Jews simply could not understand Greek and hence Titus' appeals.[34] Especially after rebels from the countryside had poured into Jerusalem, Josephus may have had to speak in Aramaic to make sure that everyone understood him. But even if the use of Aramaic instead of Greek was simply a diplomatic gesture to emphasize kinship,[35] that very fact tells us something about what language these Palestinian Jews gathered in Jerusalem felt more comfortable with when it came to critical, life-or-death negotiations. They were more comfortable with Aramaic, not Greek. The natural deduction is that it was the language they knew best and regularly used.[36]

Significantly, this passage does not stand alone. There are a number of other statements in Josephus' works that support the impression that, as a rule, an interpreter was needed when the Roman leaders tried to deal with Palestinian Jews.[37] Apparently, Greek could not be used on such occasions as a common language. Since Suetonius goes out of his way to assure us that Titus enjoyed an excellent command of Greek, the lack must have been on the side of the Palestinian Jews.

Admittedly, all this sheds at most a very indirect light on our main question, the language Jesus knew and used best. But if even the gifted Jerusalemite intellectual Josephus was not totally at home in Greek after years of writing in it while living in Rome, and if in A.D. 70 he had found it necessary or at least advisable to address his fellow Jews in Jerusalem in Aramaic rather than Greek, the chances of a Galilean peasant knowing enough Greek to become a successful teacher and preacher who regularly delivered his discourses in Greek seem slim. Especially if scholars like Sean Freyne are correct about the basic conservative nature of the Judaism of Galilean peasants,[38] the citizens of Nazareth and other villages of the Galilean countryside may have consciously avoided the use of Greek whenever they could.

None of this, however, proves that Jesus knew and used absolutely no Greek. Probably the demands of business and trade, as well as the

general need to communicate with the larger world, made some use of
Greek necessary at times, even for conservative Galilean peasants.[39] But
exactly how much Greek would have been employed by the average
peasant remains difficult to estimate. In his woodworking establishment
Jesus may have had occasion to pick up enough Greek to strike bargains
and write receipts. Regular pilgrimages by his family to the holy yet
Hellenized city of Jerusalem would have exposed the youthful Jesus to
steady doses of Greek culture and Greek spoken on street corners.[40]
Naturally, such catch-as-catch-can exposure might help one gain enough
Greek to get through some everyday business transactions ("tradesman's
literacy") such as bargaining or writing receipts. It might even be that
Jesus was able to speak enough Greek to communicate directly with
Pilate at his trial.[41] But, without formal education in Greek, it is highly
unlikely that Jesus ever attained "scribal literacy"—or even enough
command of and fluency in Greek to teach at length in it with his striking verbal artistry. Hence, along with Fitzmyer, I remain doubtful that
any body of Jesus' sayings existed from the very beginning in Greek,
needing no translation as it passed into our Greek Gospels.[42]

(3) Hebrew, the ancient and sacred language of Israel, suffered a
great decline in popular use after the Babylonian exile and the return of
the Jews to Palestine. Increasingly Aramaic, the lingua franca of the
ancient Near East from the neo-Assyrian and Persian periods onward,
made inroads among ordinary Jews resettled in Israel.[43] The books of
the Hebrew Bible written after the exile (e.g., Qoheleth) show at times
marked influence from Aramaic on the type of Hebrew used.[44] Indeed,
the books of Ezra and Daniel contain whole chapters written in Aramaic, Daniel having about six of its twelve chapters in Aramaic.[45] Contrary to popular opinion, however, Hebrew never died out in Israel as a
written (and probably spoken) language. Even before the Maccabean
revolt against Antiochus Epiphanes, the composition of the Wisdom of
Ben Sira in Jerusalem (ca. 180 B.C.) shows that late classical Hebrew was
alive and well in the spiritual capital of Israel.

This impression has been reinforced by the discoveries at Qumran,
which have revealed a large number of Hebrew works, many previously
unknown. Some of these writings were composed in and for the
Qumran community itself—hence from the 2d century B.C. through
most of the 1st century A.D. In fact, Hebrew is the language most represented at Qumran, with Aramaic second and Greek a distant third. Most
of the Hebrew works are written in a kind of postbiblical, "neoclassical"
Hebrew that betrays elements of later developments in the language.

The *Copper Scroll,* however, seems to point ahead to the Hebrew of the Mishna and hence is said to be written in a "proto-Mishnaic" Hebrew.[46] The Qumran scrolls compass such varied genres as community rules *(The Manual of Discipline),* apocalyptic prophecy *(The War Scroll),* psalmody *(The Thanksgiving Hymns),* and eschatological interpretations of Scripture in the light of Qumran's history *(The Pesher on Habakkuk).* The amount and variety of such compositions argue strongly for a lively and living tradition of the Hebrew language.

At the same time, one must be careful in making claims. These works are theological and literary compositions stemming from a very special, esoteric, and marginal group. They do not necessarily prove that Hebrew was widely spoken at the time in Palestine, and they might not directly reflect the type of Hebrew that was in fact spoken.[47] Still, these sectarian works, along with other material from Qumran (e.g., the *Copper Scroll*) do seem, in the view of scholars like Fitzmyer, to prove a living link between biblical Hebrew and that of the rabbis who produced the Mishna. Given the quantity and variety of the Hebrew works witnessed to at Qumran (not all of which were composed at Qumran), these writings probably reflect, at least indirectly, a type of Hebrew spoken by some pockets of Jews fiercely dedicated to religious and/or nationalist ideals. Thus, not only in the temple liturgy and the scholars' debates, but also in groups of zealous and pious Jews, both at Qumran[48] and elsewhere in Israel, Hebrew continued to be used both in writing and most probably in speaking.

Nevertheless, the claim of scholars like J. T. Milik[49] that this proto-Mishnaic or "neoclassical" Hebrew was the normal language of people in Judea during the Roman period simply lacks verification. The rise of the Aramaic targums (translations of Hebrew Scriptures), witnessed already in a Qumran community that was so devoted to compositions in Hebrew, is a primary objection to seeing Hebrew as *the* language of the common people. Interestingly, targums of Job have been found at Qumran (4QtgJob, 11QtgJob). Although the fragments we have of 11QtgJob comprise only about fifteen percent of the whole book, enough has been preserved to show that the targum does not engage very much in freewheeling paraphrase and long, midrashic expansions of the Hebrew text, as do some of the later, "classical" targums. Rather, this Qumran targum, for the most part, attempts a fairly literal translation of the Hebrew text into Aramaic.[50] This indicates that such targums had as their primary purpose not extensive commentary and homiletic application but simply the translation of a sacred Hebrew text that was no longer intelligible to some Jews, even pious Jews devoted to the Scriptures.[51]

As far as Jesus is concerned, we shall see in the next section that source and redaction criticism should make us wary of appealing to the Lucan scene in which Jesus reads from the Book of Isaiah in the Nazareth synagogue (Luke 4:16–20), as though this were clear proof of his knowledge of Hebrew.[52] Still, Jesus' habit of preaching in synagogues and debating both scribes and Pharisees on points of Scripture during his public ministry does make it likely that he had some knowledge of biblical Hebrew. There is, however, no firm proof that he spoke Hebrew regularly in its colloquial, proto-Mishnaic form.

(4) From the time of Gustaf Dalman onward,[53] the work of Aramaic specialists like Matthew Black and Joseph Fitzmyer has convinced most researchers that Aramaic was the ordinary, everyday language spoken by the average Jew in Israel in the 1st century A.D. Even Martin Hengel, the proponent of massive Hellenistic influence in Palestine during the Greco-Roman era, concedes this point.[54] As I have already noted, the Hellenizing policy of the Seleucid monarchs in Syria probably caused Aramaic to go into eclipse in Palestine during the 3d and 2d centuries B.C. The forced-Hellenization policy of Antiochus IV went too far, however, and provoked a reaction. It is in the crucible of conflict with Antiochus that the "Hebrew" Book of Daniel was redacted (ca. 165 B.C.), with almost six of its present twelve chapters in Aramaic. From about the middle of the 1st century B.C., Jewish Aramaic inscriptions begin to appear and become more numerous under Herod the Great. Indeed, present-day archaeology has supplied us with a large number of ossuary and sepulchral inscriptions in Aramaic.

The discoveries at Qumran have greatly increased our knowledge of Jewish-Palestinian Aramaic from the 1st centuries B.C. and A.D. The finds include previously unknown Aramaic works like the *Genesis Apocryphon* (1QapGen) and the *Prayer of Nabonidus* (4QprNab), as well as several Aramaic copies of the deuterocanonical/apocryphal Book of Tobit, targums of Job, and a targum of Leviticus (4QtgLev). As I have already stressed in my treatment of the Hebrew language, the existence of Aramaic targums of sacred books written in Hebrew is especially probative for establishing Aramaic as the regular language of ordinary Jews during this period. After all, Leviticus and Job were hardly books restricted to the esoteric community at Qumran; hence the targums on them may well have originated outside of Qumran and then been incorporated into the sectarians' library.[55] Likewise, the Aramaic *Genesis*

Apocryphon, though found at Qumran, displays no special signs of Essene theology and may well have been composed outside the community.[56] A type of haggadic midrash, it retells in Aramaic stories from the Hebrew Bible (Genesis 1–15) with admixture of folklore. It could thus be another witness to the use of Aramaic among pious Palestinian Jews of the "mainstream."

Alongside these literary works, Aramaic is also represented by scraps of writing from everyday life in Palestine: e.g., an IOU from the year A.D. 56, which was found in one of the Murabba'at caves,[57] as well as a letter on an ostracon from Masada. Significantly, the Palestinian Aramaic that comes from around the 1st century A.D. (e.g., Qumran) displays surprisingly little Greek influence on its vocabulary.[58] In contrast, after A.D. 200 the influence of the Greek language on Palestinian Aramaic becomes marked.[59] For instance, many borrowed Greek words appear in the later, "classical" targums, as well as in inscriptions from Palestinian synagogues from the 3d to the 6th centuries. The contrast should make us wary of exaggerating the dominance of Greek in the everyday speech of ordinary Jews in the Palestine of the 1st century A.D.

It has long been acknowledged that this Aramaic-speaking milieu is reflected in the Four Gospels of the NT. From Gustaf Dalman through C. F. Burney[60] and C. C. Torrey[61] to Joachim Jeremias, Matthew Black,[62] and Joseph A. Fitzmyer, Aramaic scholars have shown how the sayings of Jesus preserved in Greek often take on new poetic force and even greater clarity of meaning when they are retroverted into Aramaic.[63] Some sayings of Jesus contain expressions that are idiomatic in Aramaic but alien to both Hebrew and Greek (Aramaisms); there may even be Greek versions of sayings of Jesus that are the result of mistakes in translating the Aramaic original.[64] One famous example of an Aramaism is found in Matthew's version of the Our Father (6:12): "Forgive us our debts *[opheilēmata].*" "Debt" is not a usual image for sin or guilt in Hebrew or Greek, but the Aramaic noun for "debt," *ḥôbā*, is often used metaphorically in this sense.[65] Decisions on individual sayings are debatable, but a rough consensus has emerged that a good deal of the sayings tradition in the Gospels rests on an Aramaic substratum.

In a few cases, the substratum emerges into plain view when some of the Aramaic words Jesus used are preserved in our Greek Gospels. A prime example is the famous *talitha koum* ("young girl, arise") that Jesus addresses to the daughter of Jairus in Mark 5:41.[66] Mark, while writing in Greek, thus witnesses to Jesus' use of Aramaic not in solemn prayer or in formal literary composition but rather in his interaction with

other Palestinian Jews in daily life. Even if the incident of the raising of
Jairus' daughter should be judged to be not historical, the fact remains
that early pre-Marcan tradition, stemming most likely from Palestine,
represents Jesus as speaking Aramaic. In my view, however, Mark 5:41
and the *abbā* prayer of Jesus (14:36) are the best candidates for Aramaic
words that go back to the historical Jesus. The command *ephphatha* ("Be
opened!"), addressed to a deaf man in 7:34, is probably also Aramaic,
though Rabinowitz's argument that it is Hebrew instead has created
some (though not insuperable) difficulties.[67] The Marcan version (15:34)
of the cry of dereliction on the cross, "My God, my God, why have you
forsaken me?" *(elōi, elōi, lema sabachthani)*, is certainly Aramaic. The question is whether it really goes back to the historical Jesus or—as I would
maintain—reflects the early theological interpretation of Jesus' death as
the death of the suffering just man of the Psalms.[68] In any case, we
would still have in Mark 15:34 the theologizing of the early Palestinian
Church, which put Aramaic in the mouth of Jesus. Who would know
better than the first Palestinian Christians what language Jesus spoke—
even when it came to intense, personal prayer?[69]

Joachim Jeremias has made numerous studies of all the occurrences
of Aramaic in the sayings of Jesus. Apart from proper nouns and adjectives, he counts 26 Aramaic words attributed to Jesus by the Gospels or
rabbinic sources.[70] Not all the examples he appeals to are probative, but
some are especially useful for establishing that Jesus did instruct his
disciples in Aramaic. For example, if Jesus regularly spoke in Greek, one
is hard pressed to explain the tenacious survival of the Aramaic address
to God, *abbā*, even among Paul's Greek-speaking Gentile converts in
Asia Minor (Gal 4:6)—to say nothing of Gentile Christians in Rome who
had never met Paul (Rom 8:15). The most reasonable explanation is that
abbā represents a striking usage of the Aramaic-speaking Jesus, a usage
that so impressed itself on and embedded itself in the minds of his first
disciples that it was handed on as a fixed prayer-formula even to the first
Gentile believers.[71] Interestingly, this clear presence of an Aramaic substratum in many of Jesus' sayings stands in stark contrast to the relative
absence of Hebrew words and constructions (Hebraisms).[72]

In summary, the question of the language(s) Jesus spoke is a complex
one, mirroring the complex situation of 1st-century Palestine as a "quadrilingual" country. There is no reason to believe that Jesus knew or used
Latin, the language employed almost exclusively by the Roman con-
querors. It is likely that he knew and used some Greek for business
purposes or general communication with Gentiles, including perhaps

Pilate at his trial. But neither his occupation as a woodworker in Nazareth nor his Galilean itinerary, restricted to strongly Jewish towns and villages, would demand fluency in and regular use of Greek. There is thus no reason to think that Jesus regularly taught the crowds who flocked to him in Greek. As for Hebrew, Jesus would have learned it in the Nazareth synagogue or a nearby school, and he probably used it at times when debating Scripture with Pharisees or scribes. Yet, as a teacher who directed himself to the mass of ordinary Jewish peasants, whose everyday language was Aramaic, Jesus almost necessarily spoke to and taught his coreligionists in Aramaic, some traces of which remain embedded in the text of our Greek Gospels. To be more precise, Jeremias identifies Jesus' Aramaic as a Galilean version of western Aramaic, distinct in some words and usages from the Aramaic spoken in Judea. Matthew's version of Peter's denial may be alluding to such differences when the bystanders say to Peter: "Truly you also belong to them [the followers of Jesus *the Galilean*], for even your speech betrays you" (Matt 26:73).[73]

The general picture is thus clear enough. Special problems remain and perhaps are insoluble in our present state of knowledge. If, as John's Gospel indicates, Jesus regularly went to Jerusalem for the great feasts, what language did he use for teaching there? As we have seen, by the 1st century A.D. Jerusalem had become heavily Hellenized. Not only the Hasmonean princes, the priestly aristocrats, and the intellectual elite would have known Greek, but so would a sizable number of Diaspora Jews who had come to study or settle down in Jerusalem. One thinks, for example, of Stephen and the other "Hellenists" (Acts 6:1–15), Greek-speaking Diaspora Jews living in Jerusalem who are present in the Christian Church from its earliest days—probably because at least some of them were attracted to Jesus and his teachings during his visits to Jerusalem.

In what language did they listen to him? Probably some of these Diaspora Jews were bilingual, but others (e.g., recent émigrés from the Diaspora) may have spoken nothing but Greek.[74] Did Jesus sometimes address this special audience in Greek? Did he know enough Greek to do so effectively? We have seen reasons for doubting that he did. Instead, did someone—for example, a disciple with a Greek name and possible Greek background like Andrew or Philip[75]—act as interpreter? In that case, we would have the phenomenon of some Aramaic words of Jesus being translated into Greek during his lifetime. An intriguing surmise —but nothing more than that.[76] Scholarship must rather proceed with the most probable opinion, viz., that Jesus regularly and perhaps exclusively taught in Aramaic, his Greek being of a practical, business type, and perhaps rudimentary to boot. In a quadrilingual country, Jesus may indeed have been a trilingual Jew; but he was probably not a trilingual teacher.

3. WAS JESUS ILLITERATE?

If Jesus had been raised as an aristocratic intellectual in Rome or Athens, or even in Jerusalem, it would be easier to speculate on the nature of his education and the level of literacy he achieved. However, he grew up in Nazareth, an insignificant village in the hills of Lower Galilee, a village so obscure that it is never mentioned in the OT, Josephus, Philo, or the early literature of the rabbis or the OT pseudepigrapha.[77] Hence it is hard to decide what, if any, formal education would have been available to Jesus in such an environment. To put the question more bluntly: Could Jesus read or write? That he was an effective teacher is clear. But in an oral culture, one could theoretically be an effective teacher, especially of ordinary peasants, without engaging in reading or writing. So the question remains: Was Jesus literate or illiterate?

A. THREE KEY NT TEXTS

Some would say that the question is ridiculous, since three NT passages prove that Jesus could read and/or write: John 8:6; John 7:15; and Luke 4:16–30. Actually, even if that claim should prove true, we should still notice a surprising fact: at best, *only* three NT texts have any bearing on the question. Our surprise turns to chagrin when we realize that all three passages are beset with problems of interpretation and historicity.

Indeed, of the three texts put forward as proof, John 8:6 is for all practical purposes useless. It occurs in the curious pericope of the woman caught in adultery (John 7:55–8:11), a passage that "was originally no part of the Fourth Gospel."[78] As a matter of fact, this pericope is not present in the best and earliest manuscripts of John's Gospel, it appears in a few manuscripts of Luke's Gospel, it receives almost no commentary from Greek exegetes during the first millennium,[79] and it is judged by some experts to be a creation of a 2d-century Church locked in controversy over how mercifully sinners should be treated.[80] Still, the possibility remains that the story may preserve a reliable tradition about Jesus.[81]

But even if that is the case, we are not terribly enlightened by the statement that "Jesus bent over and wrote on the ground with his finger" (8:6) as the Pharisees asked him what was to be done with the woman caught in adultery. The compound verb *katagraphō* (literally, "write down") is used of Jesus' action in v 6, the simple verb *graphō* ("write") in v 8. Endless speculation has been devoted to what Jesus supposedly wrote: the sins of the accusers, the judicial decision he would deliver in v 7, or relevant biblical texts like Jer 17:13 or Exod 23:1b. As Raymond E. Brown observes, the "much simpler possibility" is that Jesus was just drawing lines on the ground to show his lack of interest in or his disgust with the excessive zeal of the accusers.[82] The very fact that the evangelist stresses the action of writing and omits its content argues for this last interpretation. In any case, even the scratching of a few words into the ground would not tell us much about Jesus' level of literacy.

The second text proposed as proof of Jesus' literacy is at least an original part of John's Gospel. It presents "the Jews" who are gathered in Jerusalem for the feast of tabernacles marveling at Jesus and asking: "How does this fellow know Scripture when he has not studied?" (John 7:15). Actually, the phrase translated here as "know Scripture" could simply mean "know how to read" *(grammata oiden)*. But the general context of the Jews' question—Jesus' disputing with the Jewish authorities (e.g., Chapters 5 and 10)—involves not his basic literacy but rather his use of Scripture in theological argumentation.[83] Hence the demeaning reference in 7:15 is not to Jesus' failure to learn his ABCs but to his lack of formal education in Scripture under the guidance of some noted scholar—no doubt in Jerusalem! Interestingly, the comment, though hostile in the context of John 7, does reflect the general state of affairs presented throughout the Four Gospels: although Jesus never studied formally under any great rabbi, he was adept in the use of Scripture— which would seem to argue for more than a beginner's knowledge of reading. Of the three NT texts proposed, this one at least provides some indirect basis for supposing that Jesus could read and comment on the Hebrew Scriptures.

A dramatic depiction of such ability is given by our third text, Luke's presentation of the inaugural homily of Jesus at Nazareth (Luke 4:16–

30). Upon entering the synagogue in his hometown, Jesus is given the scroll of the prophet Isaiah,[84] finds and reads Isa 61:1–2,[85] rolls up the scroll, gives it back to the synagogue attendant, and sits down. When all expectantly fix their attention on him, he begins to tell them that the Isaiah text is being fulfilled even as they listen to it.[86] If only we could take Luke 4:16–30 as a faithful report of a historical event, we would have unquestionable proof of Jesus' ability to read and expound the Hebrew Scriptures.

However, the sources and the historicity of the narrative in this pericope are disputed. Some exegetes consider Luke's scene a tradition from his special "L" source and hence an independent verification of what the other Gospel traditions tell us about Jesus' return to and preaching in Nazareth.[87] However, it is also possible that Luke 4:16–30 simply represents Luke's imaginative and colorful reworking of Jesus' preaching and rejection at Nazareth as recounted in Mark 6:1–6a. A middle ground is also possible: the pericope shows Luke's acquaintance with Mark, but some important elements come from Luke's special source.[88] Certainly the Lucan pericope is loaded with Lucan motifs; the highly symbolic scene functions as a programmatic preview of the course of Jesus' ministry, death, and resurrection, resulting in the proclamation of the good news to the Gentiles.[89] The clear presence of Luke's redactional hand makes one wary.

Granted these different possibilities, a decision is not easy; and so, not surprisingly, the scholars are divided. On the one hand, the substance of Luke 4:16,22,24 could come from Mark 6:1,3–4, though the wording is often different. While Bultmann thinks that the Lucan pericope as a whole represents a further development of the Marcan story, he does allow that Luke 4:25–27 (the homily on Elijah and Elisha) may come from a special tradition. In Bultmann's view, Luke has connected the homily—not entirely smoothly—with the Marcan story.[90] Other exegetes, including Heinz Schürmann, suggest that the entire Lucan story came to the evangelist from a non-Marcan source.[91] Of course, even if the whole Lucan pericope could be shown to be non-Marcan, that would still not prove that it faithfully represents a particular incident in Jesus' ministry. Fitzmyer prefers the view that the Lucan story is a reworking of the Marcan source with some pieces of Lucan tradition.[92] What is more significant for us is that even Schürmann, who argues for a non-Marcan source, admits that the description of Jesus reading from Isaiah (vv 17–21) is a later addition to the early form of the tradition. Hence the very part of the pericope that is relevant to the question of Jesus' literacy is probably secondary and cannot help us answer the question.[93]

The result of our survey of the three supposedly probative texts has not been encouraging. John 8:6 drops out of consideration for a number of reasons. John 7:15 indirectly intimates a reading knowledge of the Hebrew Scriptures; this indirect witness is the firmest we have. The usefulness of Luke 4:16–30 remains questionable because the reference to Jesus' reading may not be part of the original story. Obviously, we must broaden the scope of our considerations if we hope to gain more clarity on this question of Jesus' literacy.

B. Jewish Education and Literacy at the Time of Jesus

The natural place to begin a broader consideration of the issue would be the state of Jewish education and literacy at the time of Jesus. Scholars have often been optimistic about solving the question in this way, but two problems raised by recent research make this optimism appear dubious.

The first problem, put simply, is this: To what extent can later rabbinic descriptions of a widespread system of Jewish education be applied to the Palestine of the 1st century A.D.—and to a place like Nazareth in particular? Some authors are quite confident about the picture of education they create by mixing together rabbinic texts from different centuries and then retrojecting the results into the 1st century. With varying degrees of caution they cite rabbinic material from the 2d to the 5th centuries A.D. to produce a "homogenized" picture of Jewish education around the turn of the era.[94]

S. Safrai is a prime example of this approach. According to Safrai, as early as the 1st century A.D., and perhaps even earlier, the majority of Jewish children received education at schools; the education involved almost exclusively the reading of the Hebrew Bible. Such schools counted among the institutions that a town was obliged to maintain. An "elementary" school of this type, devoted to the reading of the Bible, was called a *bet ha-sēfer*, a "school of the book."[95] Indeed, in the 1st century, such schools existed in all Jewish towns in Palestine, even in the smallest settlements, thanks to the work of two great figures, Simeon ben Shetah (active ca. 103–76 B.C.) and the high priest Joshua ben Gamala (active ca. A.D. 63–65).[96] Simeon, according to the Palestinian Talmud,[97] ordered that children go to school, while the Babylonian Talmud[98] relates that Joshua ordered that teachers be appointed in each district and town and that children should go to school at the age of six or seven.[99] Writing was a professional skill and was not necessarily learned along with reading. Yet, says Safrai, "writing was fairly widespread," though less so than the ability to read, *"which everyone possessed."*[100] The early tractate *m. Abot* 5:21 fixes the age for school attendance at five for studying the Scriptures and at ten for the study of Mishna, though other sources mention six or seven as the suitable age for starting one's studies.[101]

At twelve or thirteen a boy finished his studies at school. If he was especially bright, he might frequent the more "advanced" type of education, the *bet ha-midrash*, where he would study Torah at the feet of teachers of the Law. But this was a privilege of relatively few. A formal, continuous educational system after the age of twelve or thirteen was unknown in Israel at this time.[102] The school was connected with the synagogue; instruction took place in the synagogue itself or, if space allowed, in an adjoining room or building. However, classes in some cases were also held in the courtyard of the teacher's house. In smaller towns, the *ḥazzān* (a type of sacristan) also acted as teacher.[103] The Talmud laid down rules for the financial support of teachers, so that even children from poor families were not deprived of schooling.[104]

The problem with this homogenized picture, presented by Safrai and others, is that the earliest source for this description, the Mishna, was written down about two hundred years after Jesus' boyhood. Some traditions in the Mishna are no doubt quite old, but deciding which go back centuries and which may be of more recent vintage is no easy task. The tacking on of a revered rabbi's name to a saying hardly guarantees its authenticity. Moreover, the sayings of the rabbis may at times represent the ideal the rabbis urged rather than a sober sociological description of what was actually going on in the average Jewish town. If all this be true of the relatively early Mishna, the use of the Talmuds to describe what the education of Jesus might have been like is even more problematic.

Even so sympathetic a writer as George Foot Moore has his doubts about such reconstructions. He observes that the reforms of Joshua ben Gamala, decreed on the eve of the First Jewish Revolt, would have to have been reinstituted from the start after the revolt was over, and perhaps once again after the revolt against Hadrian (A.D. 132–35). It was after the Second Revolt, says Moore, that we can speak of the elementary and advanced schools as a normal thing for each community. Still, while admitting that the Jewish school became more universal and regular only after the revolt against Hadrian, Moore thinks that nothing really novel was introduced into Jewish schooling, compared to its previous form.[105] William Barclay, despite some caveats, is even more trusting of the later rabbinic traditions.[106] He is therefore surprised at the "paradox" that the word "school" never occurs in the NT except for the pagan "school of Tyrannus" *(scholę Tyrannou)* used by Paul in Ephesus (Acts 19:9).[107]

Emil Schürer is very cautious about the tradition about Simeon ben Shetah, since this shadowy figure became the subject of many stories in later rabbinic literature. Hence Schürer rejects the educational program of Simeon as a "later legend."[108] He does, however, accept the tradition about the educational reforms of Joshua ben Gamala. Still, in itself, such a reform, instituted in the sixties of the 1st century A.D., would have nothing to say about the boyhood of Jesus. Nevertheless, Schürer claims that the enactments of Joshua presuppose that schools for boys had already existed for some time. It would therefore be reasonable to suggest that they were operating at the time of Jesus, "though perhaps not yet as a general and well-established institution."[109] This proviso once again leaves us in doubt about any schooling available to Jesus at Nazareth.

Much more skeptical in his approach to these rabbinic accounts is Shaye Cohen. He thinks that it is not likely that the traditions about Simeon ben Shetah and Joshua ben Gamala have historical value.[110] There is no clear indication that the Jewish community in either Palestine or the Diaspora supported "public schools" (in the American sense) in the 1st century B.C. or A.D. The references of Philo and Josephus to Jewish children's knowledge of the Law reflects the public reading of the Torah in the synagogue. Neither Philo nor Josephus claims that Jews had set up a formal, institutionalized system of schools for children. What elementary education did exist was carried out within the family, and most often it simply involved instruction in a given craft by the father. This could, of course, include a rudimentary "craftsman's literacy," sufficient for writing up bills and signing agreements. But any sort of "higher education" was the prerogative of the rich and leisured class. For example, the pupils in Ben Sira's school ("my house of study," Sir 51:23)[111] probably came from the aristocratic and well-to-do families of Jerusalem. While none of this is cheering to the quester of the historical boy Jesus, Cohen's sober conclusions seem to reflect most honestly the meager data we have. We are left wondering whether Jesus had any education beyond paternal directions in woodworking. Was the historical Jesus the illiterate Jesus?[112]

This question conjures up a second, and allied, problem: we cannot take for granted a high degree of literacy in the Roman Empire during this period. As William V. Harris has pointed out, too many scholars have presupposed a relatively high literacy rate in Greco-Roman societies on very flimsy evidence. Barclay maintains, for instance, that in NT times literacy was more widespread than it would be for the next eighteen hundred years.[113] According to Barclay, literacy was especially common among Jews at the turn of the era; in the elementary school all Jewish boys learned to read.[114] After a detailed study of all the available evidence, Harris himself comes to much more reserved conclusions: even in classical Attica the literacy rate probably ranged between five and ten percent.[115] Moreover, literacy deteriorated in the eastern Mediterranean basin once Rome came on the scene. Neither social expectations, government programs, nor demands of the marketplace created the conditions necessary for a high degree of literacy in the general population. That Nazareth was a happy exception to this generally dismal picture is something to be proved, not presumed.

Nevertheless, even apart from appeals to rabbinic literature, we have reasons to think that, especially among pious Jews, there existed counterinfluences that would have favored literacy. By the 1st century A.D., the Jewish people had created a unique body of sacred literature, at the heart of which stood the "five books of Moses," the so-called Pentateuch, *the* Torah par excellence. So central was this literature that it had generated literature about itself, e.g., the *Genesis Apocryphon* found at Qumran and the *Book of Jubilees,* not to mention (later on) Philo's *Life of Moses* and the early parts of Josephus' *Jewish Antiquities.* While we must not think anachronistically of a closed canon of Scripture during Jesus' lifetime, the Pentateuch, along with the continuation of its sagas in Joshua, Judges, Samuel, and Kings, created the national consciousness of all religiously aware Jews, whatever their particular theological bent. In addition, the prophetic books both directed the ongoing interpretation of the Torah in new situations and held out to an oppressed nation the hope of future glory. For all the differences among various groups of Jews, the narratives, laws, and prophecies of their sacred texts gave them a corporate memory and a common ethos.[116] The very identity and continued existence of the people Israel were tied to a corpus of written and regularly read works in a way that simply was not true of other peoples in the Mediterranean world of the 1st century. In this sense we can

speak of a canon of sacred Scripture among Jews of the early 1st century
A.D., though it must be understood as an "open" rather than a "closed"
canon.

With such pivotal importance attributed to these Scriptures by devout Jews, it is no wonder that the pious would hold the ability to read
and expound the sacred texts in high esteem. The praise of the professional scribe (Sir 39:1–11), penned by Ben Sira in such lofty religious
terms in the 2d century B.C., had lost none of its cogency for the devout
of the 1st century A.D.[117] To be able to read and explain the Scriptures
was a revered goal for religiously minded Jews. Hence literacy held
special importance for the Jewish community.

Riesner argues that both archaeological and literary indications
point to a fairly wide diffusion of literacy among Palestinian Jews in the
1st centuries B.C. and A.D.[118] Inscriptions are commonly found on ordinary vessels and instruments, e.g., pitchers and arrows. In recounting
the persecution unleashed by Antiochus Epiphanes, Macc 1:56–57 presupposes that some devout Jews possessed private copies of the Torah.
In his admittedly apologetic work, *Against Apion,* Josephus states that the
Law orders children to be taught to read and learn the laws and deeds of
their forebears.[119] In the caves of Murabbaʿat, the last refuge of the Bar
Kochba rebels during the Second Jewish Revolt (A.D. 132–35), ABC exercises have been found, at least one of them from the hand of a beginner.
Similar exercises have been found in the citadel called the Herodium
(just southeast of Bethlehem), to which Bar Kochba withdrew for a
while. Of course, none of this proves that there was widespread "scribal
literacy." In many cases the literacy that did exist probably remained
minimal, restricted to commercial and social necessities. But plainly
there were special factors in Jewish life that fostered respect for and
pursuit of literacy, and archaeology provides at least some relics of this
pursuit.

Naturally, some groups were better positioned than others for putting the Jewish desire for literacy into practice. Besides intellectuals
from the Jerusalem aristocracy (e.g., Josephus) and professional scribes,
Pharisees, who probably came mostly from the town "bourgeoisie,"[120]
would be both zealous and financially equipped to spread the ability to
read the Scriptures among their comrades and offspring.[121] Peasants in
villages in the hills did not enjoy the same luxury of time and resources.

Hence, despite inflated claims from some modern authors,[122] we are
not to imagine that every Jewish male in Palestine learned to read—and
women were rarely given the opportunity.[123] Literacy, while greatly

desirable, was not an absolute necessity for the ordinary life of the ordinary Jew. Indeed, the very existence of Aramaic targums (translations) of the Hebrew Scriptures argues that a good number of ordinary Jews present in the synagogue could not understand Hebrew even when it was spoken, to say nothing of an ability to read or write it. Jewish peasants who never learned to read or write could still assimilate and practice their religion through family traditions in the home, the reading of the Scriptures in the synagogue (with accompanying Aramaic translations), and the homily that preceded or followed the reading. These living traditions of the community would have been the matrix of Jesus' religious life and thought, as they were for most Palestinian Jews at the time. Taken by themselves, therefore, such influences as reverence for the Torah and respect for literacy do not prove that Jesus was counted among those Jews who could read and study the Scriptures; they simply show that he might have been.

Fortunately, though, we are not left solely with such general considerations. If we glance ahead to Jesus' activities during his public ministry, activities witnessed to by almost all of the various Gospel traditions, we can make some reasonable extrapolations about the boyhood that produced such an adult. If we take into account that Jesus' adult life became fiercely focused on the Jewish religion, that he is presented by almost all the Gospel traditions as engaging in learned disputes over Scripture and halaka with students of the Law,[124] that he was accorded the respectful—but at that time vague—title of rabbi or teacher,[125] that more than one Gospel tradition presents him preaching or teaching in the synagogues (presumably after and on the Scripture readings),[126] and that, even apart from formal disputes, his teaching was strongly imbued with the outlook and language of the sacred texts of Israel,[127] it is reasonable to suppose that Jesus' religious formation in his family was intense and profound, and included instruction in reading biblical Hebrew.[128]

Being the firstborn son,[129] Jesus would have been the special object of Joseph's attention, not only in the practical matter of teaching the son the father's trade[130] but also in teaching the son the religious traditions and texts of Judaism.[131] To be sure, in a strongly oral culture,[132] a great deal could have been conveyed by word-of-mouth catechesis and memorization. Yet Jesus' reported skill in debating interpretations of Scripture and halaka with pious Pharisees, professional scribes, and Jerusalem authorities in both synagogue and temple would argue for some reading knowledge of the sacred texts, a reading knowledge imparted either directly by Joseph or by some more learned Jew procured for the purpose. Apart from Joseph, the most likely conduit of an education would be the synagogue at Nazareth, which could also have served as a sort of religious "elementary school."[133] If indeed Jesus did receive his first scriptural formation in the Nazareth synagogue, one can well understand the emotionally charged atmosphere surrounding the return of the adult Jesus to that same synagogue to teach his peers and elders (Mark 6:1-6a parr.). The reaction of "Who does he think *he* is?" becomes quite understandable.[134]

While the very idea that this hill-town boy from Lower Galilee could have obtained any formal education might at first glance seem unlikely, this would not be the only time in history that poor but pious parents secured some elementary learning for their oldest son so that he could be well versed in their religious traditions. As Riesner observes, whether a Jewish youngster from the lower social strata of Palestine received an "elementary" education depended especially on two conditions: the piety of the father and the existence of a local synagogue. As far as we can tell, both conditions seem to have been verified in the case of Jesus.[135] The circumstantial evidence from archaeology points to a Nazareth that was a thoroughly Jewish settlement.[136] Granted, then, that Nazareth was a village of close to 2,000 people, practically all of whom were Jews, the existence of a synagogue with some educational program for Jewish boys is a likely hypothesis. Especially if Jesus' family shared in a resurgence of religious and national sentiment among Galilean Jewish peasants, this hypothesis of some formal education in the local synagogue is well grounded.[137]

Of course, we are not to imagine Jesus' family or the Nazareth synagogue devoted to a Judaism of Pharisaic niceties, developed by way of oral tradition. The Judaism of Galilean peasants, while fiercely loyal to basics like the Mosaic Torah, circumcision, and the Jerusalem temple, had a strong conservative streak that would not be attracted to what they considered the novelties of the Pharisees, especially if the latter were viewed by the former as refined townspeople.[138] Hence we need not be surprised if, in the early days of the Church, James "the brother of the Lord" was associated with Christian Jews of a conservative bent who were intent on preserving the observance of circumcision and food laws, at least by Christian *Jews* (Gal 2:11–14; cf. Acts 15:13-29).[139] James had not suddenly become an urban Pharisee; he had rather remained very much a Galilean peasant.

To sum up: individual texts from the Gospels prove very little about the literacy of Jesus. Instead, it is an indirect argument from converging lines of probability that inclines us to think that Jesus was in fact literate. As we have seen, general considerations about 1st-century Palestinian Judaism, plus the consistent witness of many different streams of Gospel tradition about Jesus' teaching activity, plus the indirect evidence from John 7:15 make it likely that Jesus could both read the Hebrew Scriptures and engage in disputes about their meaning. He therefore enjoyed a fair degree of literacy in Hebrew and—a fortiori—Aramaic, the language he usually spoke.[140] Thus, even if Luke 4:16–30 were totally a redactional reworking of Mark 6:1–6a, it would still be "true" in the sense that it depicts accurately the "sort of thing" Jesus did during his public ministry. It is sobering to realize, though, how here, as so often in Jesus research, we reach our conclusions not by direct, clear-cut, indisputable texts, but rather by indirect arguments, inference, and converging lines of probability.

The natural conclusion from all this is that, sometime during his childhood or early adulthood, Jesus was taught how to read and expound the Hebrew Scriptures. This most likely happened—or at least began—in the synagogue at Nazareth. Yet there is no indication of higher studies at some urban center such as Jerusalem, and indeed this seems explicitly denied in John 7:15. One therefore has to allow for a high degree of natural talent—perhaps even genius—that more than compensated for the low level of Jesus' formal education.[141]

At any rate, in at least one aspect Jesus was atypical of most men and women of the Greco-Roman world in the 1st century A.D.: he was literate, and his literacy probably extended beyond the mere ability to sign one's name or to conduct basic business transactions ("tradesman's literacy") to the ability to read sophisticated theological and literary works and comment on them ("scribal literacy"). Jesus comes out of a peasant background, but he is not an ordinary peasant.

4. WAS JESUS A POOR CARPENTER?

That Jesus was a Palestinian peasant is a commonplace, though it can be a misleading one. The word "peasant" allows of a range of meanings, and anthropologists debate the fine points of the definition.[142] Eric R. Wolf maintains that, in essence, peasants are "rural cultivators; . . . they raise crops and livestock in the countryside."[143] The peasant is not the same type of person as the modern American farmer, who may be simply an agricultural entrepreneur engaged in a particular kind of business to make a profit in the market. The peasant does not run an enterprise in the modern economic sense, but rather a household.

At the same time, peasants differ from so-called primitive peoples who also live in the countryside and raise crops and livestock. In "primitive" societies the producers control the means of production, including their own labor. They directly exchange their own labor and its products for the equivalent goods and services of others. However, as culture develops, the means of production pass from the hands of the primary producers into the hands of groups who do not engage in the productive process themselves. Rather, this new group, the rulers of the state or the city, assumes special executive administrative functions, backed up by force. The flow of goods and services is centralized in a state or city whose dominant members absorb the surplus produced by the peasants, both to support themselves and to distribute the remainder to nonfarming groups in society. In other words, it is the rise of the state or the city that calls forth the precise social group we call peasants.

As a result, the peasants live in a curious condition of tension vis-à-vis the state or the city, a condition of dependence and mutual benefit, and yet a condition of suspicion and distrust, if not outright hatred. The controlling, centralizing power is both a source of economic stability and yet a burden. In normal times the "symbiosis" is basically positive,[144] and the burden is grudgingly borne. But if the system is disrupted or if the central power's demands become too crushing, the peasants may resort to banditry, a protest movement, or even open rebellion.

This thumbnail sketch of peasant society fits Galilee quite well. The question not often asked is whether it really fits Jesus. The problem, in a nutshell, is that "peasant" denotes someone tilling the soil and raising livestock; and in the Gospels, Jesus is nowhere portrayed as a farmer. To be sure, Jesus and the rest of his family may have been engaged in part-time farming of some plot of land.[145] The size of the family (Joseph, Mary, Jesus, four brothers of Jesus, and an undetermined number of sisters) would argue for both the need and the ability of his family unit to provide at least some of its food from farming—as one would expect anyway in the case of villagers close to the fertile slopes and fields of Lower Galilee.[146] This may help explain—though only in part—why a good deal of the imagery in Jesus' parables and metaphorical language is taken from agriculture rather than from the workshop.[147]

In what sense, then, was Jesus a peasant? At the very least, Jesus lived in, was economically connected with, and in some sense was supported by an agrarian society. He may have even participated, part time, in agriculture. To that extent, he may be considered a peasant, however atypical. In any event, he certainly was a member of a peasant society.

Still, Jesus did not live as a worker on a great estate, nor was he a freeholder of some isolated farm. He lived in a village of between roughly 1,600 and 2,000 people, and most of his income probably came from plying a trade among them. I say "probably" because, although even religiously illiterate people today will readily identify Jesus as a "carpenter," that universally accepted "fact" rests on one slim half verse in the NT: Mark 6:3a, where the astonished Jews of Nazareth pose a rhetorical question about Jesus, the former hometown boy who now presumes to teach them in their own synagogue: "Is this fellow not the woodworker [tektōn]?"[148] Nowhere else in the entire NT is the precise trade Jesus plied in Nazareth identified. Perhaps out of his reverence for the Son of God who is derided with this question, Matthew, while obviously dependent on Mark for this story, changes the question to "Is this fellow not the son of the woodworker?" (Matt 13:55), thus transferring the designation to the unnamed Joseph.[149] Luke, apparently also finding the jibe offensive, likewise changed Mark's text, though Luke's solution was simply to drop the mention of Jesus' trade entirely: "Is this fellow not the son of Joseph?" (Luke 4:22).

In short, in the whole of the NT, "woodworker" (tektōn) is used only in Mark 6:3 and Matt 13:55, in the former text of Jesus and in the latter of Joseph. Hence the universally known "fact" that Jesus was a carpenter hangs by the thread of a half verse. Yet there is no cause for us to think that Mark 6:3 is inaccurate, especially since there was no reason why Mark or Christian preachers before him should have gone out of their way to attribute to Jesus a calling that enjoyed no special prominence in his society, is never referred to in Jesus' own teaching, and has absolutely no echo elsewhere in the doctrine of the NT.[150] With no countertradition to challenge it, the universally known "fact" may be allowed to continue to hang by its thread.

I prefer to translate tektōn as "woodworker" rather than as the popular "carpenter" because the latter term has acquired a somewhat restricted sense in the contemporary American workplace, with its ever increasing specialization. A common definition of "carpenter" today is "a workman who builds or repairs wooden structures or their structural parts."[151] We tend to think of carpenters in terms of building houses or crafting the major wooden parts thereof. These days, most of us do not go to a carpenter for a piece of furniture, let alone for plows or yokes to use on oxen. Yet the ancient Greek word *tektōn* encompassed that and much more. The term *tektōn* could be applied to any worker who plied his trade "with a hard material that retains its hardness throughout the operation, e.g., wood and stone or even horn or ivory."[152] More specifically, the term was often applied to a woodworker. That is likely the sense in Mark and Matthew since (1) that is the ordinary meaning in classical Greek; (2) the ancient versions of the Gospels (Syriac, Coptic, etc.) translate *tektōn* with words that mean "woodworker"; and (3) the word was understood in this way by the Greek Fathers.[153]

Some of Jesus' work would have been carpentry in the narrow sense of the word, i.e., woodwork in constructing parts of houses.[154] But in Nazareth the ordinary house would have had walls of stone or mud brick. Wood would be used mostly for the beams in the roof, the space between beams being filled in with branches along with clay, mud, and compacted earth. The people of Nazareth could not have afforded the use of wood to build whole houses, or even the floors in them. However, doors, door frames, and locks or bolts were often made of wood, as at times were the lattices in the (few and small) windows. Beyond carpentry in this sense, Jesus would have made various pieces of furniture, such as beds, tables, stools, and lampstands (cf. 2 Kgs 4:10), as well as boxes, cabinets, and chests for storage. Justin Martyr claims that Jesus also made "plows and yokes."[155] While this is probably an inference by Justin rather than a relic of oral tradition, it does tell us what work a person from Palestine—which Justin was—would attribute to a *tektōn*.

It was a calling involving a broad range of skills and tools. Indeed, archaeology, as well as written sources, tells us that a large number of tools were used in ancient woodworking, tools—as well as techniques—not too different from those employed as late as colonial America.[156] Thus, while Jesus was in one sense a common Palestinian workman, he plied a trade that involved, for the ancient world, a fair level of technical skill. It also involved no little sweat and muscle power. The airy weakling often presented to us in pious paintings and Hollywood movies would hardly have survived the rigors of being Nazareth's *tektōn* from his youth to his early thirties.[157]

In one sense, therefore, Jesus certainly belonged to the poor who had to work hard for their living. And yet our imagination, rhetoric, and desire for instant social relevance can get carried away in depicting the grinding poverty Jesus supposedly endured: "Jesus, the poorest of the poor!" The problem with us modern Americans speaking of the "poor

Jesus" or the poor anybody in the ancient Mediterranean world is that poverty is always a relative concept. As Ramsay MacMullen points out, in the Roman Empire of Tacitus' day the senatorial class would have been something like two-thousandth of one percent of the total population, while the next highest class, the "knights" *(equites)*, was less than one percent.[158] In a petty, dependent princedom like Galilee, the truly "rich" were a very small group that would have included Herod Antipas, his powerful court officials (cf. Mark 6:21), the owners of large estates (at times absentee landlords), highly successful merchants, and a few overseers of the collection of taxes and tolls (cf. Zacchaeus in Luke 19:2, though the city involved is Jericho in Judea).

Many people fell into a vague middle group *(not* our American "middle class"), including business people and craftsmen in cities, towns, and villages, as well as freehold farmers with fair-sized plots of land.[159] In speaking of this middle group, we must not be deluded into thinking that belonging to this group meant the economic security known to middle-class Americans today. Small farmers in particular led a precarious existence, sometimes at subsistence level,[160] subject as they were to the vagaries of weather, market prices, inflation, grasping rulers, wars, and heavy taxes (both civil and religious). Further down the ladder were day laborers, hired servants, traveling craftsmen, and dispossessed farmers forced into banditry—what Sean Freyne calls the "rural proletariat."[161] At the bottom of the ladder stood the slaves,[162] the worst lot falling to slaves engaged in agricultural labor on large estates—though this was not the most common pattern for Galilean agriculture.[163]

On this rough scale, Jesus the woodworker in Nazareth would have ranked somewhere at the lower end of the vague middle, perhaps equivalent—if we may use a hazy analogy—to a blue-collar worker in lower-middle-class America.[164] He was indeed in one sense poor, and a comfortable, middle-class urban American would find living conditions in ancient Nazareth appalling. But Jesus was probably no poorer or less respectable than almost anyone else in Nazareth, or for that matter in most of Galilee.[165] His was not the grinding, degrading poverty of the day laborer or the rural slave.

Indeed, for all the inequities of life, the reign of Herod Antipas (4 B.C.–A.D. 39) in Galilee was relatively prosperous and peaceful, free of the severe social strife that preceded and followed it. While modern Americans used to democracy would find Antipas intolerable, he was no worse than most despots of the ancient Near East and probably better than most. Milder than his father Herod the Great, he was an able ruler who managed to live at peace with his people. It was no accident that he ruled longer than any other Herodian king or prince, with the exception of Agrippa II.[166]

The picture some writers paint of a Galilee seething with revolt results from an acritical projection of the revolutionary sentiment erupting after the death of Herod the Great—or an acritical retrojection of the turmoil from A.D. 52 to 70—onto the comparatively quiet reign of Antipas. Despite the burden of supporting Antipas "the fox" (Luke 13:32), the ordinary people judged the advantages of peace and a modest standard of living to outweigh the perilous promise of revolt.[167] Subsequent events proved them right. It was, among other things, this relatively peaceful state of society that enabled Jesus to undertake a multiyear itinerant mission around Galilee and beyond.

In fairness, it should be noted that some scholars suggest an alternate description of Jesus' socioeconomic status. According to them, both Joseph and Jesus were master builders who traveled extensively, worked sometimes in cities like Sepphoris and Jerusalem, and were relatively well to do.[168] If such were the case, the renunciation of wealth by Jesus as he began his public ministry would have been all the more radical. Such scenarios, however, usually rest on an acritical meshing of various texts, dubious exegesis, and more than a little imagination.[169] Nothing in the Gospels speaks positively for such a hypothesis.

Sometimes, to bolster this suggestion, appeal is made to the Aramaic word supposedly behind the *tektōn* of our Greek Gospels, namely *naggārā*.[170] But *naggārā*, like *tektōn*, has a wide range of meanings: carpenter, turner, artisan, and, in a metaphorical sense, master or artist.[171] Even if we were sure that this is the precise Aramaic word behind *tektōn* in our Greek text, it would prove nothing. Riesner, however, pushes the significance of this hypothetical Aramaic source even further by appealing to some later talmudic passages, where *naggārā* seems to mean "scholar," while *bar naggārā* ("son of the carpenter") means "student, disciple."[172] From this Riesner concludes that people in the "carpenter" trade were known for their knowledge of Scripture. Since all the talmudic passages of this sort are of proverbial nature and hence of venerable age, Riesner argues that the connection between a carpenter and special knowledge of Scripture could reach back to Jesus' day. One can only comment that such reasoning leans heavily on very slight and late evidence. Talmudic proverbs could preserve material two or three hundred years old and still not bring us back to the lifetime of Jesus. What is perhaps most telling here is that Riesner can supply no examples of this usage from the earliest rabbinic compilation, the Mishna.

One suggestion about Jesus' trade that is not so divorced from his own time is that he possibly found employment for a while in Sepphoris, a major city of Galilee that was only 3.7 miles north-north-west of Nazareth and just about an hour's walk. Sepphoris had been destroyed during a revolt against Rome in 4 B.C. After his confirmation by Rome as tetrarch, Herod Antipas chose Sepphoris as his capital and began rebuilding it in grand Hellenistic style. While initial, intensive efforts tapered off, some building continued until Antipas moved his capital to the new city of Tiberias ca. A.D. 26. If Jesus had been employed in Sepphoris during the period of its magnificent reconstruction, he would have been brought into contact with urban culture in a strongly Hellenistic city.[173] The experience might have helped loosen the natural provincialism adhering to conservative Jewish peasants from the countryside.[174]

While intriguing, this suggestion remains a pure possibility with no real footing in any Gospel text.[175] More to the point, the Gospels never present Jesus preaching in or even talking about the strongly Hellenistic urban centers of Galilee. As far as we know, within Galilee his ministry (as well as verbal references) was restricted to traditional Jewish villages and towns: Nazareth, Capernaum, Cana, Nain, and Chorazin. Within Galilee proper, the Hellenistic cities of Sepphoris and Tiberias are notable by their absence on Jesus' itinerary.[176] This general picture of Jesus' activity in Galilee, consistent throughout the Four Gospels, does not favor early and influential contact with Hellenistic centers like Sepphoris. Such a theory, of course, cannot be positively disproved. But there is no solid evidence to support it, and the Gospels indirectly supply some indications against it. In the end, we must conclude that the sparse evidence we have about the "interim" years of Jesus points in one direction: Jesus spent those years almost entirely as a citizen of Nazareth in Galilee, plying the trade of a woodworker. Special experiences in the area of education or employment that would have taken him out of Nazareth for a lengthy period of time must remain pure hypotheses, unsupported by the NT text.

Throughout this chapter we have been able to rely on generalizations about the culture, politics, society, and economics of 1st-century Palestine to help us decipher the meager and indirect references in various Gospel texts. A rough, general picture of the conditions surrounding Jesus' youth and adulthood in Nazareth does emerge from the interaction of text and context. Much more difficult, though, is the descent from the general to the particular that will concern us in the next chapter. There we shall try to say something about the particular family relationships that molded Jesus' individual experience. At that point, general observations about overall culture and society give little aid; we are largely thrown back on a few ambiguous texts. But then family relationships are often ambiguous.

[1] Of course, this has not prevented psychiatrists and popularizers alike from penning sketches of Jesus' psychological development or treatises on Jesus as a Jungian archetype. Such authors should not all be lumped together, since some consciously prescind from the question of the historical Jesus, others simply ignore the question, and still others do claim to be speaking of the historical Jesus as extricated from the Gospel records. Examples of the first type of author include Françoise Dolto and Gérard Sévérin, who pointedly refuse to take a position with regard to the historicity of Gospel texts (*The Jesus of Psychoanalysis. A Freudian Interpretation of the Gospels* [Garden City, NY: Doubleday, 1979] prefatory note). Obviously, they are not concerned with the historical Jesus (or with his individual psyche) as I have defined him.

Also unconcerned with historical questions as treated here are those who approach the story of Jesus as an archetype open to Jungian analysis. For instance, G. H. Slusser (*From Jung to Jesus. Myth and Consciousness in the New Testament* [Atlanta: John Knox, 1986]) uses the "hero archetype" developed by Joseph Campbell to analyze the "mythic hero story" of Jesus. Similarly, Edward F. Edinger (*The Christian Archetype. A Jungian Commentary on the Life of Christ* [Toronto: Inner City Books, 1987]) seeks to study the mythic life of Christ (including the assumption and coronation of the Virgin Mary), understood psychologically to represent the vicissitudes of the self.

Different from these attempts, which consciously prescind from the question of the historical Jesus, is Elizabeth Boyden Howes, *Jesus' Answer to God* (San Francisco: Guild for Psychological Studies, 1984). Operating in the Jungian tradition, Howes tries to separate the myth Jesus lived from the myth of Jesus the Christ that stimulated the faith of the early Church. However, despite the author's claims to sift the Gospel material critically according to various criteria of historicity, the treatment is often naive, with patently redactional creations of the evangelists being accepted as the words and deeds of the historical Jesus. Judgments about historicity are often introduced by phrases like "my feeling is . . ." and "I feel that . . ." with little or no concrete argumentation to ground these feelings. Another and more serious attempt to work within the constraints of historical-critical research is Hanna Wolff, *Jesus der Mann. Die Gestalt Jesu in tiefenpsychologischer Sicht* (4th ed.; Stuttgart: Radius, 1979); and her companion work, *Jesus als Psychotherapeut. Jesu Menschenbehandlung als Modell moderner Psychotherapie* (4th ed.; Stuttgart: Radius, 1981). Although the first book promises to take into account modern Jesus research, the focus is usually on such topics as "the image of Jesus in the constellation of the mother-archetype" and "the androgynous image of Jesus." What historical-critical considerations do appear are mainly borrowed from a small group of German post-Bultmannian scholars (e.g., Bornkamm, Käsemann). Wolff herself does not engage in any extensive evaluation of Gospel material according to criteria of historicity.

Finally, there are the blatantly popular presentations, which can range from an orthodox Christian perspective to a New Age vision. For example, Andrew G. Hodges (*Jesus. An Interview Across Time. A Psychiatrist Looks at His Humanity* [Birmingham, AL: Village House, 1986]) pretends to interview Jesus face to face and presumes to fashion Jesus' answers. In all this, the Gospels are taken at face value, with no critical sifting. The author, while seeking to give due consideration to Jesus' human development, accepts the Chalcedonian formulation of Jesus as "true God and true man." Truly creative and completely uncritical is Frank Jakubowsky's *The Psychological Patterns of Jesus Christ* (Oakland, CA: Frank Jakubowsky, 1982); the treatment of Jesus is tied to that of astrological signs. One is not surprised to be told that this book is the sequel to the author's earlier *Jesus Was a Leo.* Some perceptive observations on the whole psychological approach to Jesus are made by Ulrich Ruh, "Die Schwierigkeiten mit dem 'wirklichen' Jesus," *Herder Korrespondenz* 44 (1990) 287–91: the supposedly "real" Jesus turns out to be the projection onto Jesus of the wishes, needs, and interests of each author. Needless to say, such books are usually quite successful in the marketplace, if not in the academy.

² A "strong" position, that the majority of Israelites "had Greek for their familiar tongue," is represented by R. O. P. Taylor, "Did Jesus Speak Aramaic?" *ExpTim* 56 (1944–45) 95–97; Taylor thinks that Jesus might have spoken Aramaic in secluded places, but that he regularly taught the crowds in Greek. A more moderate position is espoused by A. W. Argyle, who holds that Jesus taught at times in Aramaic and at times in Greek; see his "Did Jesus Speak Greek?" *ExpTim* 67 (1955–56) 92–93, which began a mini-debate in the *ExpTim:* J. K. Russell (same title), ibid., 246; H. Mudie Draper (same title), ibid., 317; A. W. Argyle (same title), ibid., 383; R. M. Wilson (same title), *ExpTim* 68 (1956–57) 121–22. Unfortunately, a good deal of the argument is guided either by acritical presuppositions or by a desire to have direct access to the original sayings of Jesus (in Greek).

³ Almost all the articles in Joseph A. Fitzmyer's volume of collected essays on biblical Aramaic, *A Wandering Aramean. Collected Aramaic Essays* (SBLMS 25; Missoula, MT: Scholars, 1979), bear directly or indirectly on the question. Those that bear most directly are "The Study of the Aramaic Background of the New Testament," pp. 1–27; "The Languages of Palestine in the First Century A.D.," pp. 29–56; "The Phases of the Aramaic Language," pp. 57–84; and "The Contribution of Qumran Aramaic to the Study of the New Testament," pp. 85–113. Much of what is presented in this section is dependent on Fitzmyer's work, even when this is not explicitly stated in individual notes.

⁴ H. Birkeland, *The Language of Jesus* (Oslo: Dybwad, 1954). See also Isaac Rabinowitz, " 'Be Opened'=*Ephphatha* (Mark 7,34): Did Jesus Speak Hebrew?" *ZNW* 53 (1962) 229–38; idem, "Ephphatha (Mark VII. 34): Certainly Hebrew, not Aramaic," *JSS* 16 (1971) 151–56; J. Cantineau, "Quelle langue parlait le peuple en Palestine au Iᵉʳ siècle de notre ère?" *Sem* 5 (1955) 99–101; J. A. Emerton, "The Problem of Vernacular Hebrew in the First Century A.D. and the Language of Jesus," *JTS* n.s. 24 (1973) 1–23; P. Lapide, "Insights from Qumran into the Languages of Jesus," *RevQ* 8 (1972–75) 483–501; Chaim Rabin, "Hebrew and Aramaic in the First Century," *The Jewish People in the First Century* (CRINT 1/2; ed. S. Safrai and M. Stern; Philadelphia: Fortress, 1976) 1007–39.

As with the champions of Greek, there is a spectrum of positions. For exam-

ple, the "strong" position is held by Birkeland, who claims that a dialectical
form of what would become Mishnaic Hebrew was the language of the common
people; therefore Jesus normally spoke Hebrew when teaching them, though he
at times probably used Aramaic and Greek as well. It is curious that this monograph of Birkeland is regularly referred to—and even praised—by scholars
maintaining the "Hebrew hypothesis." In fact, Birkeland's work is almost an
embarrassment to read today. It is not just that his views, especially on Aramaic,
have become outdated. More astounding are the self-contradictions, contorted
arguments, and uncritical use of sources (especially the NT); his position is
rightly rejected by J. N. Sevenster, *Do You Know Greek? How Much Greek Could the
First Jewish Christians Have Known?* (NovTSup 19; Leiden: Brill, 1968) 34–36. It is
not surprising that writers who appeal to Birkeland in more recent times quietly
alter or forsake many of his arguments—indeed, sometimes his whole position
on lower-class Jews speaking a dialect of Mishnaic Hebrew while the upper
classes spoke Aramaic.

For example, Rabin restricts Birkeland's thesis by claiming that Mishnaic
Hebrew was the dominant spoken language of the Judean, but not the Galilean,
population. Like Birkeland, however, he must struggle to explain the presence
and function of Aramaic targums. His answer is that Aramaic-speaking Jews
from outside Judea settled in Judea, making it necessary for priests and Pharisaic
teachers to be completely bilingual and to supply targums for those who were
not. Hence, in Judea Hebrew was dominant and Aramaic in second place. In
Galilee, the reverse was true. When Jesus took part in discussions in the synagogue, temple, or a group of scribes, he would use Mishnaic Hebrew. A somewhat similar view is held by Cantineau. J. T. Milik *(Ten Years of Discovery in the
Wilderness of Judaea* [SBT 26; Naperville, IL: Allenson, 1959] 130) also holds that
Mishnaic Hebrew "was the normal language of the Judaean population in the
Roman period."

Like Rabin, Lapide applies to the problem the sociolinguistic distinction of
high language (the language of culture, literature, religion) and low language
(the language of the home and everyday affairs) within the same speech community, a situation called diglossia. Mishnaic Hebrew was the high language Jesus
used in formal religious situations; he used Aramaic in everyday life (here Birkeland's thesis is turned upside down). Lapide must struggle (unsuccessfully, in
my view) against Jesus' use of Ps 22:2 in Aramaic on the cross. Rabinowitz,
besides arguing that *ephphatha* cannot be an Aramaic verb form and so must be
Hebrew, draws the wide-ranging conclusion that both Hebrew and Aramaic
texts narrating the story of Jesus were translated into Greek and were drawn
upon for the Greek Gospel of Mark. This awkward solution is typical of sustainers of the "Hebrew hypothesis": their position forces them to adopt very unlikely source and tradition histories for the Gospels.

Perhaps the most nuanced view is taken by Emerton, who tries to do justice
to the complicated linguistic situation: Aramaic was the common language of
the ordinary people of Galilee, and so there Jesus regularly spoke Aramaic. In
Judea, both Aramaic and Hebrew were spoken by the people, and there Jesus
spoke both at various times.

[5] See William V. Harris, *Ancient Literacy* (Cambridge, MA/London: Harvard University, 1989).

[6] By "postbiblical" Hebrew is meant a type of Hebrew that seeks to imitate the style of the classical Hebrew found in the books of the OT, yet which betrays traces of influence from Aramaic and also points forward to the different type of Hebrew found in the Mishna.

[7] As a number of authors point out, a "living" language is not necessarily the opposite of an "artificial" language. It could be that recently arrived members of the Qumran community underwent intensive training in the special type of Hebrew spoken at Qumran and then began to use it as the regular, "living" language of the community, even though it was "artificial" in the eyes of Palestinian society as a whole.

[8] This is admitted in theory by Sevenster *(Do You Know Greek?*, 180–81), but in practice he tends to brush the methodological difficulty aside in his eagerness to use inscriptions to establish the wide diffusion of Greek in Palestine in the 1st century A.D.

[9] Gerard Mussies ("Greek in Palestine and the Diaspora," *The Jewish People in the First Century* [CRINT 1/2; ed. S. Safrai and M. Stern; Philadelphia: Fortress, 1976] 1040–64) remarks (p. 1041): ". . . in the case of many inscriptions, if not all, we do not know whether the Greek is that of the deceased person's relatives or that of the stone-mason, who may or may not have been Jewish."

[10] This problem is recognized in the laudable work of Sevenster, *Do You Know Greek?*; see, e.g., pp. 126–49. Sevenster also shrewdly observes that the ossuaries of the poor may well have been made of wood and therefore have largely disappeared, while the stone ossuaries of the well to do are more likely to have survived (p. 138). Hence the data are weighted in favor of the upper classes, who might well be expected to know Greek, or at least affect it on their ossuaries. Moreover, almost all of the funerary inscriptions Sevenster considers are from the 2d century A.D. or later (pp. 139–40). Yet, despite all Sevenster's agonizing over the difficulty of dating material and then of drawing conclusions from material of the 2d to 4th centuries for the 1st century A.D., at times he does just that. Still, Sevenster is more careful than many other writers on the subject. It is symptomatic of the scholarly scene that Mussies ("Greek in Palestine and the Diaspora," 1042) lists in one sentence Jewish inscriptions in Greek from Joppa (2d–3d cent. A.D.), Beth-Shearim (1st–4th cent. A.D.), and Jerusalem (2d cent B.C.– 2d cent. A.D.).

[11] See the statement of the problem in William F. Albright, *The Archaeology of Palestine* (5th ed.; Pelican A 199; Baltimore: Penguin, 1960) 201–2.

[12] One can safely prescind from other languages which had at best a meager existence in Palestine at the time: e.g., early Arabic dialects in marginal areas of Palestine and possible remnants of Phoenician; see Rabin, "Hebrew and Aramaic," 1010–11.

[13] Fitzmyer states that, as far as he knows, the earliest Latin texts from Pales-

tine are all dated to the 1st century A.D.; see his "The Languages of Palestine," 47 n. 7. This makes perfect sense, since Judea, Samaria, and Idumea did not become a province under a Roman prefect until the ethnarch Archelaus, a son of Herod the Great, was deposed in A.D. 6.

[14] Mussies ("Greek in Palestine and the Diaspora," 1057) suggests that "many if not most" of the Jewish ossuaries found in Palestine with Greek inscriptions contained the bones of deceased Diaspora Jews who had returned to Palestine, of their descendants, or of Jews who had assimilated in one of the Hellenistic towns.

[15] John 19:20 states that the *titulus crucis* ("Jesus the Nazorean, the King of the Jews") was written in Hebrew (probably Aramaic is meant), Latin *(rhōmaisti)*, and Greek. As Fitzmyer points out, this detail could be historical, since Josephus mentions occasions when decrees or inscriptions were displayed in Palestine in both Latin and Greek (Fitzmyer, "The Languages of Palestine," 31). For examples from Josephus, see, e.g., *J.W.* 5.5.2 §193–94; *Ant.* 14.10.2 §191. Brown *(The Gospel According to John,* 2. 902) observes that "Jewish tombstones in Rome were sometimes inscribed in these three languages." However, one must reckon with the possibility that this detail, recorded only in John, simply symbolizes the public proclamation of the universal kingship and salvific impact that Jesus achieved by "being lifted up on" or "ascending" the throne of the cross. Notice how this theme is developed in John 11:47–53; 12:13–15,19,20–24,31–32. Schnackenburg *(Das Johannesevangelium,* 3. 315) tends toward the purely symbolic interpretation: ". . . it is less likely that a Roman made such a fuss over a crucified person."

[16] The classic expression of this insight in recent research is Martin Hengel's *Judaism and Hellenism. Studies in Their Encounter in Palestine during the Early Hellenistic Period* (Philadelphia: Fortress, 1974). For an update that focuses more directly on Judea and the 1st century, see Martin Hengel, *The "Hellenization" of Judaea in the First Century after Christ* (London: SCM; Philadelphia: Trinity Press International, 1989); on the linguistic question in particular, see pp. 7–18. Hengel's view, however, has not gone without challenge; for one expression of a more cautious approach, see Tessa Rajak, *Josephus. The Historian and His Society* (Philadelphia: Fortress, 1984) 53.

[17] Hengel *(The "Hellenization" of Judaea,* 8) gives as an example the first bilingual Jewish coins, in Hebrew and Greek, issued by the Hasmonean high priest and king Alexander Jannaeus (103–76 B.C.); see also pp. 31–32.

[18] Hengel *(The "Hellenization" of Judaea,* 33) remarks: "Herod's Jerusalem was a Hellenistic city through and through, which had been decked in a splendour as a result of the king's ambition. . . . It contained a theatre and a hippodrome, as did the winter residence of Jericho." Symptomatically, in contrast to Alexander Jannaeus, Herod the Great used purely Greek inscriptions on Jewish coins and weights.

[19] Needless to say, such rough estimates must be received with caution, especially since (1) Hengel includes Jericho in "greater Jerusalem," and (2) the epi-

taphs are not restricted to the narrow period within the 1st century A.D. that we are interested in.

[20] Hengel *(The "Hellenization" of Judaea,* 21, 28–29) suggests that much of what we consider the literature of Greek-speaking Diaspora Judaism, including a good deal of the apocryphal/deuterocanonical books of the Bible, originated in Palestine.

[21] Yet Mussies ("Greek in Palestine and the Diaspora," 1059) cautions against supposing that everyone in these Hellenistic towns spoke Greek as their first language; even some of the non-Jews may have spoken Aramaic as their native language.

[22] See Hengel, *The "Hellenization" of Judaea,* 14.

[23] On the various letters and papyri fragments found in caves and dating from around the time of Bar Kochba, see Sevenster, *Do You Know Greek?,* 153–74.

[24] There is a certain irony here: the Hebrew-Aramaic Book of Daniel turns out to be the only book of the Hebrew canon that contains undeniably Greek words. Thus the book is a linguistic microcosm reflecting the Palestine of its day.

[25] Hebrew works produced by Qumran include the *Manual of Discipline* (alias *Rule of the Community),* the *War Scroll,* and the *Hymns of Thanksgiving* (alias *Hodayot Psalms).* Hebrew works not produced at Qumran but used and preserved by the community include the deuterocanonical/apocryphal Book of Ben Sira (alias Sirach or Ecclesiasticus).

[26] See Mussies, "Greek in Palestine and the Diaspora," 1050. The same is true of the Hebrew text of the earlier Book of Ben Sira.

[27] Obviously, the destruction of Jerusalem and the defeat of the Jewish rebellion in A.D. 70 created a situation in which Greek would become notably more dominant in Palestinian life. Sevenster *(Do You Know Greek?,* 178–79) tries to argue against the idea of A.D. 70 as a linguistic watershed, but the adversaries he cites seem to have the better of the argument. Hence I think it is perilous to read the linguistic situation of Palestine in the 2d century A.D. (especially after the Bar Kochba revolt!) back into the early 1st century A.D.

[28] One is struck by the similar boast of Paul in Gal 1:14: "And I was making progress in Judaism superior to [that of] many contemporaries among my own people, since I was even more zealous [than they were] for the traditions of my forefathers." Similar autobiographical statements can be found in 2 Cor 11:22; Phil 3:5–6; Rom 11:1. Unlike Josephus, Paul proclaims his rejection of rhetorical skills in 1 Corinthians 1–3, only to proceed to write in 1 Corinthians 13 (the praise of love) and 1 Corinthians 15 (the resurrection) some of the most stirring Greek since Plato. More of Paul than of Josephus will be found in world-literature textbooks because, while Josephus was the better "technician" of Greek literature, he was basically an imitator of Greek historians like Thucydides and Polybius, while Paul, for all the Greco-Roman parallels, was "an original." If we

were to draw a sliding scale of technical literary skill among Jews in the 1st century A.D., with zero on the left side and one hundred on the right, Jesus would probably stand close to the left end, Paul somewhere in the middle, Luke and the author of the Epistle to the Hebrews past the center moving to the right, and Josephus and Philo close to the far right end.

²⁹ The Greek of this passage suffers from textual difficulties and differing interpretations of phrases; but the basic sense is clear enough. For various ways of translating some of the troublesome phrases, see the footnotes of Louis H. Feldman in Vol. 10 of the Loeb Library edition of Josephus (no. 456), pp. 139–40. Some scholars (e.g., Sevenster, *Do You Know Greek?*, 70) make much of the fact that in this passage Josephus blithely dismisses mastery of foreign languages as the sort of skill common not only to ordinary free men but also to household slaves who wish to acquire it. Instead, says Josephus, "our people" (i.e., Palestinian Jews) esteem those who have an exact knowledge of the laws. All this tells us not what was the common language of ordinary people in Palestine but rather how nervous Josephus was about his poor pronunciation of Greek and how desperate he was to deprecate an ability he did not possess. Sevenster misses the boastful-yet-apologetic thrust of the passage.

³⁰ (*Ant.* Proem 2 §7): *oknos moi kai mellēsis egineto tēlikautēn metenegkein hypothesin eis allodapēn kai xenēn dialektou synētheian.*

³¹ Even Sevenster (*Do You Know Greek?*, 75), for all his emphasis on the use of Greek in 1st-century Palestine, says of Josephus: ". . . this use of assistants makes it difficult to deduce accurately from the Greek of those works how much knowledge a painstaking Jew of the first century could assimilate of the Greek language and literature." It is questionable whether assistants should also be posited for the writing of the *Antiquities.* Against Thackeray's theory of a "Thucydidean Hack" and a "Sophoclean Assistant" visible in parts of the *Antiquities,* see Rajak, *Josephus,* 233–36.

³² To be fair to Josephus, we should note that he is speaking primarily of elegant literary Greek that imitates the classical histories. Yet his comment about his failure to pronounce Greek correctly does take us into the realm of spoken Greek. Rajak (*Josephus,* 62) summarizes her investigation of Josephus' knowledge of Greek as follows: ". . . there is no reason to believe that Josephus was inclined, in his Jerusalem days, to gravitate towards those restricted circles in which Greek literature might be admired. We should, I think, consider it probable that he had not read any of the Classical Greek authors before he went to Rome. There would have been plenty of time to do this during the second part of his life." In the view of H. St. J. Thackeray (*Josephus. Volume II. The Jewish War, Books I–III* [LCL; Cambridge, MA: Harvard University; London: Heinemann, 1927] xiii–xix), Josephus' *Jewish War* has great merits as a literary work, the style being "an excellent specimen of the Atticistic Greek fashionable in the first century" (xiii). As we have seen, this was not accomplished without the help of assistants (xv). Josephus' *Life* is not as polished in its Greek style, but that may be partly due to the fiery, polemical nature of the work.

[33] *J.W.* 5.9.2 §361: *Iōsēpon kathiei tȩ patriǫ glōssȩ dialegesthai.* On the question of whether *tȩ patriǫ glōssȩ* means Aramaic or Hebrew in such contexts, see Fitzmyer, "The Languages of Palestine," 34 and 51 n. 36. Birkeland, naturally, rejects the idea that "the language of the forefathers" could ever mean Aramaic in Josephus *(The Language of Jesus,* 13). It is true, to be sure, that at times Josephus carefully distinguishes between Hebrew and Aramaic (which he calls "Syrian," *syristi,* Syriōn); see *Ant.* 10.1.2 §8; 12.2.1. §15. But this is a prime example of context controlling usage. In the two passages from the *Jewish Antiquities* just cited, the whole point of the narrative is the difference between Hebrew and Aramaic. Despite his knowledge of this difference, Josephus in other contexts will blithely identify Aramaic as well as Hebrew words as Hebrew. Thus, in *Ant.* 1.1.1 §33 he identifies the Aramaic form *sabbata* as Hebrew *(tēn Hebraiōn dialekton),* as he does the Hebrew *Adamos* in 1.1.2 §34; in *Ant.* 3.10.6 §252 he identifies the Aramaic word *asartha* as the Hebrew name for the feast of weeks *(bēn Hebraioi asartha kalousi),* when in fact the Hebrew form (which no doubt Josephus knew full well) was *'ăṣeret.* Hence, the distinction Josephus knows in theory he ignores in practice, especially when the context does not demand a neat distinction between Hebrew and Aramaic. And that is just the case in passages like *J.W.* 5.9.2 §361: the linguistic distinction being made is between the Greek Titus speaks and the Aramaic Josephus speaks. That a 1st-century author who had some knowledge of the topography and customs of Palestine and Jerusalem could consistently identify Aramaic words as Hebrew is proven in the case of John the evangelist. He pointedly uses *hebraisti* ("in Hebrew") with the Aramaic words *Bēthzatha* (5:2; on the complicated textual problem, see Metzger, *Textual Commentary,* 208), *Gabbatha* (19:13), *Golgotha* (19:17), and *Rabbouni* (20:16). On all this, especially *rabbouni* as an Aramaic form, see Gustaf Dalman, *Die Worte Jesu* (Leipzig: Hinrichs, 1898) 5–10; idem, *Grammatik des jüdisch-palästinischen Aramäisch* (Darmstadt: Wissenschaftliche Buchgesellschaft, 1960; original, 1905) 176 n. 1; idem, *Jesus-Jeshua* (New York: Ktav, 1971; original, 1929) 13. For the difficulties of deciding whether in Jerusalem Josephus habitually spoke Hebrew, or Aramaic, or both languages to an equal extent, see Rajak, *Josephus,* 230–32; she thinks that he was totally at home in both.

[34] Sevenster *(Do You Know Greek?,* 63–65) tries to blunt this line of argumentation by observing that we do not know how well Titus himself could speak Greek; hence Josephus' mission does not necessarily mean that little Greek was actually understood by the Jerusalemites. But the fact is that we do know that Titus could speak Greek well, if we may trust one of the best sources available, namely, Suetonius. In his *Lives of the Twelve Caesars,* Suetonius states that the talented, intelligent, and well-educated Titus could deliver orations and compose poems in both Latin and Greek quickly and easily, indeed even extemporaneously *(Latine Graeceque vel in orando vel in fingendis poematibus promptus et facilis ad extemporalitatem usque);* see Suetonius, *Divus Titus* 3 §2. (In developing his argument, it is odd that Sevenster appeals to Suetonius' statements concerning other emperors' knowledge of Greek—e.g., Caesar Augustus could not speak Greek fluently—but totally ignores what Suetonius says about Titus.) Moreover, Titus had to operate in the East from A.D. 67 to 71. With the exception of his

immediate Roman entourage and other Roman officials he would meet on his journeys, he would have had to communicate with most people in Greek, the lingua franca of the eastern part of the Empire.

[35] This is implied by the final phrase of the sentence, "thinking that perhaps they might give in to a person of the same race" *(tach' an endounai pros homophylon dokōn autous)*. However, the participle *dokōn* refers back to Titus, not Josephus, and seems to explain the reason why Titus sends Josephus to speak to the defenders rather than the reason why Josephus speaks in Aramaic.

[36] The attempt of Taylor ("Did Jesus Speak Aramaic?" 96) to avoid this conclusion is unconvincing.

[37] Other passages that indicate a regular need for an interpreter in such dealings include *Ag. Ap.* 1.9 §49 (Vespasian and Titus needed to have Josephus in constant attendance, since he alone was able to understand what the deserters reported); *J.W.* 6.2.1 §96 (Josephus reports to the rebels in Jerusalem the message of Caesar [=Titus], putting it into "Hebrew" [=Aramaic]); 6.6.2 §327 (Titus addresses the rebel leaders in Jerusalem, having first placed an interpreter at his side).

[38] See Sean Freyne, *Galilee from Alexander the Great to Hadrian 323 B.C.E. to 135 C.E.* (University of Notre Dame Center for the Study of Judaism and Christianity in Antiquity 5; Wilmington, DE: Glazier; Notre Dame: University of Notre Dame, 1980). This position is examined at length in the subsequent sections of the present chapter.

[39] Hengel *(The "Hellenization" of Judaea,* 14–15) makes strong claims for the Hellenization of Galilee as well as Judea: "Galilee, completely encircled by the territories of the Hellenized cities of Ptolemais, Tyre and Sidon in the west and north-west, by Panias-Caesarea Philippi, Hippos and Gadara in the north-east, east and south-east, and finally by Scythopolis and Gaba, a military settlement founded by Herod, in the south, will similarly have been largely bilingual." I would suggest that perhaps more of a distinction should be made between the small villages in the countryside and the cities and towns around the Sea of Galilee. In any case, Draper ("Did Jesus Speak Greek?" 317) makes a good point: a bilingual situation often cuts both ways. If some or many Galilean Jewish peasants knew Greek as well as Aramaic, presumably at least some Galilean Gentiles and urbanized, Hellenized Galilean Jews knew some Aramaic.

[40] Despite the tendency to identify the Galilean capital of Sepphoris as the main locus of Jesus' contact with Greek culture, we have no firm proof that Jesus ever set foot inside Sepphoris. In contrast, we are certain that he visited Jerusalem and—if John's Gospel is correct on this point—visited it often. The whole of Martin Hengel's *The "Hellenization" of Judaea* bears testimony to the heavy presence of Hellenistic culture in the spiritual capital of Judaism.

[41] It is possible, though, that, even if Pilate knew Greek, he would have preferred to conduct trials in Latin with the help of an interpreter. Granted the compressed and schematic nature of the narratives we have in the Gospels, the

evangelists need not have felt obliged to mention the presence of an interpreter, especially if they could assume general knowledge that in such circumstances an interpreter was usually employed.

As for other occasions when Jesus might have spoken Greek, authors sometimes point to the healing of the centurion's servant (Matt 8:5–13 || Luke 7:1–10) and the exorcism of the daughter of the Syrophoenician woman (Mark 7:24–30; Matt 14:21–28 makes the woman a Canaanite instead); so Hengel, *The "Helleniza-tion" of Judaea,* 17; cf. Sevenster, *Do You Know Greek?,* 190. That is possible, but by no means certain. The Lucan form of the story of the centurion's servant tells us that the centurion used the Jewish elders of the town as intercessors who bore his petition to Jesus. Even if the simpler Matthean form of the story is more original—something that is not to be taken for granted, since Matthew usually shortens miracle stories he receives from the tradition—we have no way of knowing how long this particular centurion had been resident in Israel and whether he might have picked up some Aramaic. As for the Syrophoenician woman, she is first of all called a *Hellēnis.* This word could mean "Greek-speaking," but such a meaning seems to play no role in a story where the whole point is the tension between Jesus' mission to Israel (the children) and the needs of the Gentiles (the dogs, v 27). Hence Walter Bauer is probably correct when he assigns the meaning of "Gentile woman" to this text; see his *Griechisch-deutsches Wörterbuch zu den Schriften des Neuen Testaments und der frühchristlichen Literatur* (6th ed.; ed. Kurt and Barbara Aland; Berlin/New York: de Gruyter, 1988) col. 508. She represents a theological problem and paradigm for Mark not because she is Greek-speaking but because she is Gentile. Taylor *(The Gospel According to St. Mark,* 349) sums up the view of many commentators when he remarks: "Mark . . . describes the woman by her religion and her nationality." Furthermore, the Marcan scene is set vaguely in "the region of Tyre," not the city of Tyre. If the woman is thought of as coming from the countryside and is of mixed Syrian and Phoenician ancestry, she would probably have spoken some form of a Semitic language, either Aramaic or Phoenician. This last point is conceded by Hengel, who admits that even in the late Roman period citizens in Gaza with a Greek upbringing could speak the Aramaic vernacular (p. 74 n. 88).

[42] Fitzmyer, "The Study of the Aramaic Background," 10.

[43] The need to translate Hebrew into Aramaic may be reflected as early as Neh 8:8 and Ezra 4:7. Rabin ("Hebrew and Aramaic," 1013) notes that this view, espoused by many scholars, is already reflected in the Babylonian Talmud. But these passages in Nehemiah and Ezra allow of other interpretations.

[44] To take only one example: R. B. Y. Scott *(Proverbs. Ecclesiastes* [AB 18; Garden City, NY: Doubleday, 1965] 192) remarks on the Hebrew of Qoheleth: "It has features which resemble the Hebrew of the Mishnah (A.D. 200) . . . apparently this was a dialect developed in certain circles under Aramaic influence shortly before the beginning of the Christian era." For a similar view, see Robert Gordis, *Koheleth—The Man and His World* (3d ed.; New York: Schocken, 1968) 59–62. However, David Noel Freedman questions this view (letter dated Nov. 26, 1990); he thinks that "Mishnaic Hebrew, and its exemplars in earlier times, as in

Ecclesiastes and some Qumran documents, is indigenous, and not influenced particularly by Aramaic, although there are similarities."

⁴⁵ The reference here is, of course, to the Masoretic text of Daniel; the deuterocanonical/apocryphal form of the book contains additional chapters preserved in Greek. It is probable, though not certain, that the entire Masoretic version of the book was originally written in Aramaic; see Louis F. Hartman and Alexander A. Di Lella, "Daniel," *NJBC*, 408.

⁴⁶ For these designations, see Fitzmyer, "The Languages of Palestine," 44–45. For a detailed study of tense and verb usage in the *Manual of Discipline* and the *Damascus Document*, see John C. Kesterson, *Tense Usage and Verbal Syntax in Selected Qumran Documents* (Ph.D. dissertation; Washington, DC: The Catholic University of America, 1984). Kesterson sees the Qumran Hebrew of these documents as standing between biblical Hebrew and the significantly different Hebrew of the Mishna.

⁴⁷ Some scholars consider inscriptions on tombs and ossuaries better indicators of colloquial language. Unfortunately, apart from Qumran, such inscriptions from the 1st century A.D.—written in what is clearly Hebrew—are extremely scarce; see Fitzmyer, "The Languages of Palestine," 44.

⁴⁸ Certainly the Essene movement extended beyond the confines of Qumran, and groups of Essenes located in various parts of Palestine would probably be dedicated to preserving a living Hebrew tradition.

⁴⁹ Milik, *Ten Years of Discovery*, 130; similarly, Rabin, "Hebrew and Aramaic," 1015; Cantineau, "Quelle langue," 100.

⁵⁰ On this, see Fitzmyer, "The First-Century Targum of Job from Qumran Cave XI," *A Wandering Aramean*, 161–82, esp. pp. 174 and 178 n. 29. As Fitzmyer observes, we must allow for the possibility that the targumist was working from a Hebrew text slightly different from the canonized Masoretic text.

⁵¹ Rabin ("Hebrew and Aramaic," 1029–36) realizes that the existence of Aramaic targums in and before the early 1st century A.D. poses a major problem to his view that in Judea the major spoken language among Jews was a type of Mishnaic Hebrew. He struggles to answer the objection with various, perhaps even contradictory, proposals (Aramaic-speaking Jews from elsewhere had migrated to Judea; the targum was more of a guide for those who already understood the Hebrew words), but he never really finds a solution to the problem posed by the relatively literal *Targum of Job* from Qumran.

⁵² Lapide ("Insights from Qumran," 497) lacks a sense of the problems that redaction criticism raises with regard to this pericope.

⁵³ See, e.g., his *Die Worte Jesu, Grammatik des jüdisch-palästinischen Aramäisch*, and *Jesus-Jeshua*.

⁵⁴ See, e.g., his *The "Hellenization" of Judaea*, 8: "While Aramaic was the vernacular of ordinary people, and Hebrew the sacred language of religious worship and of scribal discussion, Greek had largely become established as the lin-

guistic medium for trade, commerce and administration." In a similar vein, after reviewing the evidence for the use of Greek in Palestine during the 1st century A.D., Mussies ("Greek in Palestine and the Diaspora," 1058) cautions: "On the other hand, we must take care not to exaggerate: Greek remained a second language to the people at large." Sevenster, another great champion of the wide diffusion of Greek in 1st-century Palestine, likewise remarks: ". . . Aramaic was certainly spoken and written in Palestine at that time and . . . it was and remained the naturally current language of communication in many circles. In actual fact this is seldom denied" *(Do You Know Greek?,* 176).

[55] See the discussion in Fitzmyer, "The First-Century Targum of Job," 166.

[56] For a discussion of opinions on Essene or non-Essene origin, see Joseph A. Fitzmyer, *The Genesis Apocryphon of Qumran Cave I. A Commentary* (BibOr 18A; 2d ed.; Rome: Biblical Institute, 1971) 11–14. Fitzmyer states: ". . . there is nothing in the *Genesis Apocryphon* which forces us to affirm the Essene authorship of the text. Nor does anything exclude it."

[57] The four caves of Wadi Murabba'at are about 12 miles south of Qumran and about 2 miles inland from the Dead Sea.

[58] The relatively few exceptions include the names of Greek musical instruments in Dan 3:5,10,15; the references to drachmas in Ezra 2:69 and Neh 7:69–71; and a few Greek words in the *Copper Scroll.*

[59] See Fitzmyer, "The Languages of Palestine," 40–42.

[60] C. F. Burney, *The Aramaic Origin of the Fourth Gospel* (Oxford: Clarendon, 1922).

[61] See, e.g., C. C. Torrey, *Our Translated Gospels: Some of the Evidence* (New York: Harper, 1936); idem, "Studies on the Aramaic of the First Century A.D. (New Testament Writings)," *ZAW* 65 (1953) 228–47; idem, "The Aramaic Period of the Nascent Christian Church," *ZNW* 44 (1952–53) 205–23.

[62] Matthew Black, *An Aramaic Approach to the Gospels and Acts* (3d ed.; Oxford: Clarendon, 1967).

[63] Needless to say, this brief list of great Aramaic scholars of the 20th century does not imply that they all held the same views or employed the exact same methods. Various positions of, e.g., Burney and Torrey would not be defended by scholars today.

[64] For various examples, see Joachim Jeremias, *New Testament Theology. Part One. The Proclamation of Jesus* (London: SCM, 1971) 6–7.

[65] See Jeremias, *New Testament Theology,* 6 n. 15.

[66] The precise Aramaic here that the Greek tries to represent would probably be *ṭalyĕtā' qûm.* An intriguing philological point is that one would have expected the feminine form of the second person singular imperative of the verb, viz., *qûmî* (a form that is indeed supplied by way of correction in some later Greek manuscripts and versions of Mark). Has Mark or his Greek tradition made a

mistake in transliteration, or do the words of Jesus represent a "pop" form of spoken Aramaic in 1st-century Palestine that ignored the separate feminine form of the imperative? On this, see Jeremias, *New Testament Theology*, 4 n. 9.

[67] Rabinowitz, " 'Be Opened,' " 229–38. Rabinowitz admits that there are a few rare forms that might, by analogy, make possible the classification of *ephphatha* as an Aramaic instead of a Hebrew imperative. Moreover, the present state of our knowledge should make us wary of stating absolutely what forms were or were not possible in Galilean or Judean Aramaic of the early 1st century A.D. On the argument, see Jeremias, *Theology*, 7 n. 4.

[68] On this point, see my treatment under the criterion of embarrassment in Chapter 6.

[69] The presence of this Aramaic sentence in Mark is the rock on which Lapide's distinction between Jesus' high language (Hebrew), which he spoke on formal and religious occasions, and his low language (Aramaic), which he spoke in everyday life, founders ("Insights from Qumran," 496–97). Like other embarrassed critics, Lapide points to the confused state of the text in both Mark and Matthew. Yet there is no serious doubt that the Aramaic text in today's critical editions of the NT represents the original reading of Mark 15:34; see Metzger, *Textual Commentary*, 119–20; cf. 70. Moreover, for anyone who holds the two-source theory, Matt 27:46 simply represents a redactional alteration of the initial invocation of *elōi* to *ēli* to make the misunderstanding of the word as addressed to Elijah *(ēlias)* more intelligible to the reader. The change is thus on the redactional level of the Greek text of Matthew. The objection to Lapide's basic distinction thus remains, especially since he seems to accept the cry of dereliction as actually coming from Jesus.

Arguments for Aramaic as the common languages of ordinary Palestinian Jews, including Jerusalemites, can also be found in the Acts of the Apostles. For example, before the choice of Matthias to fill the place of Judas, Peter delivers a speech in which he recalls the death of Judas. We are told that the death of Judas on the field he had bought "became known *to all the inhabitants of Jerusalem*, so that that field is called *in their language* 'Hakeldama,' that is, 'Field of Blood' " (1:19). A few points should be noted: (1) Hakeldama is certainly an Aramaic name: *ḥăqēl dĕmāʾ*. (2) Luke implicitly represents the name as being given to the field by "all the inhabitants of Jerusalem," to whom the story became known. (3) This Aramaic name, given by all the inhabitants of Jerusalem, is said by Luke to be "in their own language," i.e., Aramaic. (The explanation "in their own language" obviously comes from Luke or his Greek tradition; it makes no sense in the mouth of Peter.) Therefore, at the very least, Luke, writing toward the end of the 1st century A.D., represents the language of the inhabitants of Jerusalem to be Aramaic. Moreover, while Peter's speech as it stands is a Lucan composition, the story of the death of Judas, the connection with the field, and the name "Field of Blood" all go back to earlier oral tradition, as the very different handling of the same motifs in Matt 27:3–10 shows; see Gerhard Schneider, *Die Apostelgeschichte* (HTKNT 5; 2 vols.; Freiburg/Basel/Vienna: Herder, 1980, 1982) 1. 214. Even so skeptical a critic as Ernst Haenchen sees Palestinian tradition in the theme of the divine punishment of Judas; see his *Die Apostelgeschichte* (MeyerK 3; 15th ed.; Göttingen: Vandenhoeck & Ruprecht, 1968) 128. The attempt of R. O. P. Taylor ("Did Jesus Speak Aramaic?" 96) to reject the argument from Acts 1:19 is weak.

[70] Jeremias, *New Testament Theology*, 5–6. As I indicated when treating the possible rabbinic sources for our knowledge of Jesus in Chapter 4, I do not think (contrary to the opinion of Jeremias) that the tradition in *b. Šabb.* 116b represents an original form of Matt 5:17; it is rather a later garbling of the Gospel text.

[71] For the classic treatment, see Joachim Jeremias, "Abba," *Abba. Studien zur neutestamentlichen Theologie und Zeitgeschichte* (Göttingen: Vandenhoeck & Ruprecht, 1966) 15–67. As Jeremias himself notes, *'abbā'* had by NT times replaced the possessive form *'ābî* in both Aramaic and Hebrew (pp. 26, 60–61). Indeed, I think one must allow for the fact that, with the great similarity between Hebrew and Aramaic, there was a considerable overlap and blending of the two languages, especially in the area of religion. It is not surprising that *'abbā'* entered into Hebrew as a regular word and continues to be used in modern Hebrew. Yet, looking at the other Aramaic words on the lips of Jesus in the NT tradition, Jeremias continues to count *'abbā'* as an Aramaic word (pp. 65–66; see also his *New Testament Theology*, 5, 62, 64).

[72] So Jeremias, *New Testament Theology*, 7–8.

[73] Jeremias *(New Testament Theology*, 4) is on shakier ground when he uses as his main source of this Galilean Aramaic of Jesus "the popular Aramaic passages of the Palestinian Talmud and Midrashim which have their home in Galilee." A fair amount of time separates the Jesus tradition and this later rabbinic material. Jesus' Aramaic would belong to Fitzmyer's category of "Middle Aramaic," as do the Aramaic documents from Qumran. See Fitzmyer, "The Study of the Aramaic Background," 8.

[74] Some authors think that the Hellenists knew nothing but Greek. This is the opinion of Joseph A. Fitzmyer, "Jewish Christianity in Acts in Light of the Qumran Scrolls," *Studies in Luke-Acts* (Paul Schubert Festschrift; London: SPCK, 1968) 233–57; in this he follows the view of C. F. D. Moule. A different view, similar to my own, is espoused by Sevenster *(Do You Know Greek?*, 31): "They [the Hellenists] were people who spoke Greek in their daily life at home, even though they would not always have lost their knowledge of Hebrew or Aramaic and would perhaps still have understood both. But they no longer spoke those languages regularly and sometimes they would have forgotten them entirely."
The basic problem here is that the word *Hellēnistai* does not occur before Luke and may be his own invention. In that case, appealing to Paul's use of *Hebraios* is beside the point. One must divine Luke's meaning from Luke's presentation. For instance, if the group of seven Hellenist leaders were to interact with the Twelve to keep peace between the "Hebrews" and the "Hellenists" in the Jerusalem church (Acts 6:1–6), presumably some of them could handle Aramaic. Indeed, at least in the way he paints his (obviously redactional) scene, Luke seems to presuppose that the Twelve are addressing the whole assembly of

Christians (including the Hellenists), who then choose the seven Hellenist leaders, on whom the Twelve impose hands. Note the phrases *proskalesamenoi de hoi dōdeka to plēthos tōn mathētōn* (v 2) . . . *episkepsasthe de, adelphoi, andras ex hymōn* (v 3) . . . *kai ēresen ho logos enōpion pantos tou plēthous* (v 5). Cf. the disagreement between Raymond E. Brown and John P. Meier on the definition of *Hellēnistai* in their *Antioch and Rome* (New York/Ramsey, NJ: Paulist, 1983) 34 n. 79.

⁷⁵ Andrew and Philip are the only two members of the Twelve to bear Greek names. Thus, in John 12:20–22, it is probably not by accident that, in Jerusalem, some *Hellēnes* (most probably Greek-speaking Gentiles) approach Philip with a request to see Jesus; Philip then asks Andrew to help him convey the request. Of course, the scene as it stands is a piece of Johannine theology: the very fact that Gentiles are being drawn toward Jesus is the sign for him that the hour has struck for him to be lifted high on the cross so as to draw all human beings to himself (12:23,32). But does the concatenation of Jerusalem—*Hellēnes*—Philip and Andrew lie further back in the tradition? On the question of "Hellenized" disciples of Jesus, see Hengel, *The "Hellenization" of Judaea*, 16–18. Hengel notes in addition that two other disciples of Jesus had names that were Greek in origin, but Aramaized in their present form: Thaddaeus is probably a short form of Theodotus (or something similar), and Bartholomew comes from *(bar) Ptolemaios*. Hengel also affirms that Simon Peter "must have been bilingual" on the basis of his successful missionary work outside Judea, from Antioch via Corinth to Rome. Actually, it would not have been impossible for Peter to have employed interpreters; one is reminded of Papias' description of Mark as the "interpreter of Peter" *(hermēneutēs Petrou)* in Eusebius' *Ecclesiastical History*, 3.39.15. Perhaps a better reason for thinking that Peter knew at least some Greek was his active participation in the "fishing industry" on the Sea of Galilee.

⁷⁶ Hengel *(The "Hellenization" of Judaea,* 1–6, 18) is certainly correct on one point: from the very earliest days of the Church in Jerusalem, there were Greek-speaking Christian Jews who *from the beginning* were formulating their faith in Jesus in Greek just as the Aramaic-speaking Christian Jews were doing in Aramaic. The idea that "Hellenistic-Jewish" Christianity was a later stage of development on the linguistic and theological level is an academic myth that still appears in many textbooks on NT christology; it should be put to rest once and for all.

⁷⁷ Despite Nazareth's obscurity (which had led some critics to suggest that it was a relatively recent foundation), archaeology indicates that the village has been occupied since the 7th century B.C., though it may have experienced a "refounding" in the 2d century B.C. For the problem of the various spellings of the name *(Nazaret[h], Nazara, Naṣrat[h])*, see Raymond E. Brown, *The Birth of the Messiah* (Garden City, NY; Doubleday, 1977) 207–8; also Freyne, *Galilee from Alexander the Great to Hadrian*, 382–83 n. 21. In the Four Gospels, two different adjectival forms of the town's name are applied to Jesus: "Nazarene" *(Nazarēnos)* occurs in Mark (4×) and Luke (2×); "Nazorean" *(Nazōraios)* occurs in Luke/Acts (8×), John (3×), Matthew (2×). Some scholars have raised the possibility that at least the *Nazōraios* form originally referred to a pre-Christian sect to

which Jesus belonged. However, along with W. F. Albright and other noted Semitists, Brown holds that the derivation of *Nazōraios* from the name Nazareth is defensible on purely philological grounds *(Birth of the Messiah,* 209–10). The modern town of Nazareth most probably preserves the location of ancient Nazareth. As Robert North has observed ("Biblical Archaeology," *NJBC,* 1216), in a Holy Land where various sites fight over the honor of being the biblical Capernaum or Cana, a good argument for Nazareth's claim is that it has virtually no rival. Nazareth is located roughly 15 miles from the Sea of Galilee and some 20 miles from the Mediterranean. It is situated to the north of the Plain of Esdraelon. At an elevation of about 1,300 feet above sea level, it is within the hills of Lower Galilee, more precisely on the side of a hill that faces to the south and southeast, in a sort of basin opening to the south. Nazareth was not a totally isolated village; it was close to the city of Sepphoris to the north, a district capital that in turn was just south of the key road from Tiberias on the Sea of Galilee to Ptolemais on the Mediterranean coast. The north–south road between Jerusalem and Sepphoris also ran close to Nazareth. The ancient village probably occupied about 40,000 square meters and at the time of Jesus the population would have numbered somewhere between 1,600 and 2,000. Most of the houses in the village were probably made up of small groups of rooms located around a central courtyard, though some houses seem to have had two stories. For all this, see Eric M. Meyers and James F. Strange, *Archaeology, the Rabbis, and Early Christianity* (Nashville: Abingdon, 1981) 56–57.

[78] Metzger, *Textual Commentary,* 221 (reporting the unanimous opinion of the editorial committee of the *UBSGNT*).

[79] For the complicated text history of the pericope, see Brown, *The Gospel According to John,* 1. 335–36 (while Brown allows for the possibility that the stray narrative may have been composed in Johannine circles, he points out that stylistically the story is more Lucan than Johannine); cf. Metzger, *A Textual Commentary,* 219–22. At least one patristic reference is now known from the recently discovered OT commentaries of Didymus of Alexandria. For a discussion of the text and the history of the pericope, see Bart D. Ehrman, "Jesus and the Adulteress," *NTS* 32 (1988) 24–44; Ehrman's theory of the existence of three different versions of the pericope by the 4th century remains highly speculative.

[80] The composition of the pericope is dated ca. A.D. 100–50 by Hans F. von Campenhausen, "Zur Perikope von der Ehebrecherin (Joh 7:53–8:11)," *ZNW* 68 (1977) 164–75. Hence for von Campenhausen the pericope does not relate a historical event in the life of Jesus.

[81] Ehrman ("Jesus and the Adulteress," 35–36) thinks that one of the two hypothetical sources of the pericope (i.e., the form of the story close to that of Synoptic dispute stories) has a good claim to authenticity.

[82] Brown, *The Gospel According to John,* 1. 333–34. Ehrman ("Jesus and the Adulteress," 36) suggests that, in the second hypothetical story Ehrman isolates, Jesus sees the trap his enemies have laid for him and so stoops over to draw in the dust while he considers his options.

[83] So Schnackenburg, *Das Johannesevangelium. II Teil,* 184–85.

[84] We are probably meant to understand that Jesus himself chooses the passage. It is anachronistic to think of a universally observed lectionary for synagogue services in the early 1st century A.D. Riesner *(Jesus als Lehrer,* 145) states that up until the 2d century the choice of the prophetic reading (the *haftara)* was quite free.

[85] Actually, as we shall see, the text is conflated.

[86] The Lucan account presupposes the placement of the homily after the reading from the prophets. Even in the later rabbinic period, this was not the only order observed. S. Safrai ("Education and the Study of the Torah," *The Jewish People in the First Century* [CRINT 1/2; ed. S. Safrai and M. Stern; Philadelphia: Fortress, 1976] 967) notes that "some sages gave their public sermons immediately after the prayer or the reading from the Torah or even as an introduction to the lesson, while others gave it only later in the day." Presumably things were just as flexible, if not more so, earlier on.

[87] A somewhat different view is expressed by Asher Finkel, "Jesus' Sermon at Nazareth," *Abraham unser Vater. Juden und Christen im Gespräch über die Bibel* (Otto Michel Festschrift; ed. O. Betz, M. Hengel, and P. Schmidt; Leiden/Cologne: Brill, 1963) 106–15. He suggests, without much probing by way of source and redaction criticism, that the Lucan pericope (and John 4:44) represents the earlier narrative of rejection and astonishment at Jesus' hometown at the beginning of his ministry, while Mark and Matthew record a narrative of rejection at a later date.

[88] So Walter Grundmann, *Das Evangelium nach Lukas* (THKNT 3; 7th ed.; Berlin: Evangelische Verlagsanstalt, 1974) 119. At the same time, Grundmann stresses the programmatic function of the pericope for the whole of Luke-Acts.

[89] The theme of the initial offer of the gospel to the Jews, rejection by them, and turning to the Gentiles is sounded here for the first time; it will return often in Acts. On the similarities yet differences between the programmatic discourses of Acts and the "sermon" in Luke 4, see J. Dupont, "Les discours de Pierre dans les Actes et le chapitre XXIV de l'évangile de Luc," *L'évangile de Luc. Problèmes littéraires et théologiques* (Lucien Cerfaux Memorial; BETL 32; ed. F. Neirynck; Gembloux: Duculot, 1973) 329–74, esp. pp. 349–50. As I. Howard Marshall *(The Gospel of Luke* [New International Greek Testament Commentary; Grand Rapids: Eerdmans, 1978] 177–78) says, "The narrative is placed here . . . for its programmatic significance, and it contains many of the main themes of Lk.-Acts *in nuce."* His subsequent conservative decision in favor of the historicity of Luke's narrative (p. 180) does not jibe well with this insight. But Marshall does observe correctly (p. 179) that it is unlikely that the Marcan and Lucan versions stem from two different visits of Jesus to Nazareth. The basic outline of the two stories is too similar. Moreover, it is not irrelevant to note that the vast majority of pericopes in Luke 3–4 result from Luke's creative redaction of Mark and Q; this seems to hold true as well at least for the redactional summary and transition in 4:14–16a. On this last point, see J. Delobel, "La rédaction de Lc., IV, 14–

16a et le 'Bericht vom Anfang,' " *L'évangile de Luc*, 203–23. Hence it is not surprising that W. C. van Unnik reaches the lapidary conclusion about 4:16–30: "Il est clair que le récit est une composition de Luc . . ." ("Eléments artistiques dans l'évangile de Luc," *L'évangile de Luc*, 129–40, on p. 138).

[90] See Bultmann, *Geschichte*, 31.

[91] See Schürmann, *Das Lukasevangelium. Erster Teil*, 227–28 and 241–44; he suggests that Luke may have taken the pericope from Q.

[92] Fitzmyer, *Luke*, 1. 527; pp. 526–27 give a good overview of the various theories of sources. Similarly, Josef Ernst *(Das Evangelium nach Lukas* [RNT; Regensburg: Pustet, 1977] 169) concludes that the Lucan pericope is a not entirely unified reworking of the Marcan narrative.

[93] Anyone who would wish to defend Luke's depiction of the Isaiah reading as historically reliable even in its details would have to explain (1) how Jesus managed to read from an Isaiah scroll a passage made up of Isa 61:1a,b,d; 58:6d; 61:2a, with the omission of 61:1c,2b; (2) why it is that Jesus read a text of Isaiah that is basically that of the Greek Septuagint, even when at times the Septuagint diverges from the Masoretic text. With regard to the first point, Ernst *(Lukas*, 170) remarks that the citation is a conflated text "that was not to be found in this form in any scroll of the prophets."—The ending of Luke's story likewise suffers from a historical difficulty. Luke says that the angry Nazarenes dragged Jesus "to the edge of the cliff [literally, the brow of the mountain] on which the city was built, to throw him down the precipice" (Luke 4:29). Actually, Nazareth lies in a sloping basin on the side of a hill; there are a number of higher elevations around it.

[94] Examples of this "homogenized" approach can be found in S. Safrai, "Education," 945–70; George Foot Moore, *Judaism in the First Centuries of the Christian Era* (2 vols.; New York: Schocken, 1971; originally 1927) 1. 308–22; H. I. Marrou, *A History of Education in Antiquity* (New York: Sheed and Ward, 1956) 317; William Barclay, *Train Up a Child. Educational Ideals in the Ancient World* (Philadelphia: Westminster, 1959) 11–42; Schürer, *History of the Jewish People*, 2. 415–20. Many of the authors using the "homogenized" approach issue a general warning not to ignore the idealized and later nature of the rabbinic texts; yet some of them proceed promptly to forget their own warning.

[95] Or *bet ha-sōfēr*, the house of the scribe.

[96] Safrai, "Education," 948.

[97] *y. Ketub.* 8.32c.

[98] *b. B.Bat.* 21a.

[99] The historicity of these two traditions is also defended by Barclay, *Train Up a Child*, 32–33.

[100] Safrai, "Education," 952; emphasis mine. Barclay *(Train Up a Child*, 42) is

even more confident: many, though not all, Jewish boys learned to write in elementary school.

[101] See the various later rabbinic texts cited by Safrai, "Education," 952.

[102] Safrai, "Education," 953.

[103] See *m. Šabbat* 1:3.

[104] Safrai, "Education," 957.

[105] Moore, *Judaism*, 1. 316–21, along with n. 92 on p. 104 of the notes.

[106] Hence he readily accepts as historical the stories about Simeon ben Shetah and Joshua ben Gamala *(Train Up a Child,* 32–33).

[107] Ibid., 31.

[108] Schürer, *History of the Jewish People*, 2. 418.

[109] Ibid., 419.

[110] Shaye J. D. Cohen, *From the Maccabees to the Mishnah* (Library of Early Christianity 7; Philadelphia: Westminster, 1987) 120–23, esp. 120.

[111] The Hebrew fragment of manuscript B of Ben Sira reads at this point *bet midraší* ("my house of instruction" or literally, "the house of my instruction"; the LXX has *oikǭ paideias*, without any possessive pronoun. In the light of all the evidence from the versions, Alexander Di Lella (in collaboration with Patrick W. Skehan) prefers the translation without the "my"; see his *The Wisdom of Ben Sira* (AB 39; New York: Doubleday, 1987) 575.

[112] David Noel Freedman (in a letter dated Nov. 26, 1990) points out to me that a similar question has been posed about Mohammed. The majority opinion seems to be that Mohammed was illiterate, though obviously a man of eloquence and rare judgment.

[113] Barclay, *Train Up a Child*, 14. Views similar to Barclay's can be found in many surveys of culture at the time of Christ; see, e.g., Everett Ferguson, *Backgrounds of Early Christianity* (Grand Rapids: Eerdmans, 1987) 85–86.

[114] Barclay, *Train Up a Child*, 42; while Barclay issues a general warning about the ideal nature of regulations in rabbinic literature, his statements quickly take on the air of affirmations of historical fact. Ferguson *(Backgrounds*, 86) is more guarded, but holds that "most Jewish boys would have studied until age thirteen so that there was probably a higher degree of learning among a larger number of Jews than among any other people of the ancient world."

[115] Harris, *Ancient Literacy*, 114.

[116] Today scholars stress—and rightly so—the great diversity in pre-A.D. 70 Judaism. Like any valid insight, this can be pushed to an extreme. The common sacred texts, along with basic observances (circumcision, Sabbath, food laws) and devotion to the Jerusalem temple (in its actual or ideal state), did help form a "mainstream" Judaism that nevertheless contained within itself strikingly differ-

ent views. On the whole question, see the various essays in Jacob Neusner, William S. Green, and Ernest S. Frerichs, eds., *Judaisms and Their Messiahs at the Turn of the Christian Era* (Cambridge: Cambridge University, 1987).

[117] After speaking of various artisans, Ben Sira exclaims: "How different the man who devotes himself to the study of the law of the Most High! He explores the wisdom of the men of old and occupies himself with the prophecies . . . his care is to seek the LORD, his Maker. . . . Many will praise his understanding; his fame can never be effaced . . ." (Sir 39:1,6,9, *NAB*). This high esteem in which study of the Scriptures (and hence literacy) was held continued into the Mishnaic period, as the quotations from the Mishna cited by Schürer *(History of the Jewish People*, 2. 415–16) indicate. Examples include *m. Abot* 1:15, "Shammai said: Make thy [study of the] Law a fixed habit . . ."; 2:7, ". . . the more study of the Law the more life; the more schooling the more wisdom . . ." (Danby translation).

[118] Riesner, *Jesus als Lehrer*, 112–15.

[119] *Ag. Ap.* 2.25 §204; notice the explicit mention of *grammata paideuein ekeleusen . . . epistasthai.* The text therefore speaks of something more than knowledge of the Torah, which could be gained through oral instruction in the family and the synagogue.

[120] Riesner *(Jesus als Lehrer*, 208–9) holds that, to the extent that the Pharisees were present in Galilee in the early 1st century A.D., they would have lived more in Hellenized towns and cities west and north of the Sea of Galilee. Naturally, phrases like "bourgeoisie" and "middle class" must be taken with more than a grain of salt in a 1st-century Palestinian context; the terms can be used at best only in an analogous sense. On the complicated question of the social status of the Pharisees, see Anthony J. Saldarini, *Pharisees, Scribes and Sadducees in Palestinian Society. A Sociological Approach* (Wilmington, DE: Glazier, 1988).

[121] Riesner *(Jesus als Lehrer*, 173) thinks that the initiative for popular education came from two partially overlapping groups: "proto-rabbis" and Pharisees. He stresses that, at the time of Jesus, many scribes may not have belonged to the Pharisaic movement, and Pharisees themselves were by no means uniform in their outlook and practice (pp. 174–75).

[122] Harris *(Ancient Literacy*, 281–82) rightly complains of the sweeping, often unfounded claims of authors like C. H. Roberts, who states that "the world into which Christianity was born was, if not literary, literate to a remarkable degree; in the Near East in the first century of our era writing was an essential accompaniment of life at almost all levels to an extent without parallel in living memory. In the New Testament reading is not an unusual accomplishment . . ." "Books in the Graeco-Roman World and in the New Testament," *The Cambridge History of the Bible. Volume 1. From the Beginnings to Jerome* (ed. P. R. Ackroyd and C. F. Evans; Cambridge: Cambridge University, 1970) 48. Unfortunately, Roberts proceeds to try to prove his claim by quoting Jesus' rhetorical question "Have you not read . . . ?" (Matt 12:3). He fails to note that Jesus is speaking not to the ordinary Jew in the street but to the Pharisees.

[123] For the few exceptions known to us from rabbinic literature, see Safrai, "Education," 955.

[124] See, e.g., Mark 2:23–28; 3:16 parr.; 3:22–30, with the Q parallel of Matt 12:22–37||Luke 11:14–23; Mark 7:1–23 par.; 10:2–12; 12:13–17,18–27,28–34 parr.; both the Q and M material in Matthew 23; Luke 13:10–17; 14:1–6; and John 3:1–14; 5:16–47; 8:13–20; 9:40–10:39. The point here is not that all the texts cited preserve sayings of the historical Jesus; the examples from John in particular betray heavy redactional concerns. The point is rather that all the different streams of Gospel tradition (Mark, Q, M, L, and John) insist on the same basic point: that Jesus engaged Pharisees, scribes, and/or Jerusalem authorities in debates or dialogues on disputed questions arising from Scripture, halaka, or Jewish theological views in general. In short, this is a case of the criterion of multiple attestation, which is also supported by other criteria (discontinuity in the case of the teaching on divorce, the final fate of Jesus, etc.).

[125] For "rabbi" addressed to Jesus, see Mark 9:5; 11:21; 14:45; Matt 26:25; John 1:38,49; 3:2; 4:31; 6:25; 9:2; 11:8. Besides *rabbi*, its Greek equivalent *didaskalos* ("teacher") is found as an address to or description of Jesus in, e.g., Mark 4:38; 9:17,38; 10:17,20,35; 12:14,19,32; 13:1; Matt 8:19; 23:8; Luke 7:40; 11:45; 12:13; 19:39; John 13:13. The variant *epistatēs*, unique to Luke in the Gospels, is found in 5:5; 8:24,45; 9:33,49; 17:13. Again, the point here is not to affirm the historicity of all the passages, but simply to indicate the wide spread of attestation this title possesses (Mark, M, L, and John). The large amount of teaching material in the Gospels makes the use of the title natural (criterion of coherence). Granted the widespread presence of the title in the Gospel traditions, it is noteworthy that no christology built on the title rabbi/teacher develops in the early Church; christologies are built on other titles (criterion of discontinuity).

Notice that the title of rabbi or teacher occurs at various times on the lips of the Twelve, other disciples, well-disposed outsiders, and not so well disposed outsiders. The fact that, in John's Gospel (3:26), it is also addressed to John the Baptist by his disciples reminds us that, in the early 1st century, the title had a very wide and vague range and was not tied to formal study or "ordination" to the rabbinate. On all this, see Riesner, *Jesus als Lehrer*, 239.

[126] See, e.g., Mark 1:21,39; 6:2; Matt 4:23; 9:35; 12:9; Luke 4:15,16,20,28,33,44; 6:6; 13:10; John 6:59; 18:20. To these might be added the passages where he is presented teaching or disputing publicly in the Jerusalem temple (e.g., Mark 12; John 7–8).

[127] See Riesner, *Jesus als Lehrer*, 225.

[128] Riesner (*Jesus als Lehrer*, 227) is probably correct in claiming that Jesus regularly read his Bible in Hebrew and translated it into Aramaic, but once again Riesner is somewhat uncritical in his use of texts. It is especially unfortunate that he spends so much time defending the historicity of Luke 2:46–47 (the twelve-year-old Jesus in the temple); for a more critical treatment, see Brown, *Birth of the Messiah*, 472–95.

[129] See the *prōtotokon* of Luke 2:7 and the equivalent statement in Matt 1:25.

[130] See Safrai, "Education," 958, though the texts he cites are from the Talmuds. Riesner appeals to the general practice of the ancient Near East, as well as to some OT texts (Gen 4:20–22; Neh 3:8), which are not as probative as Riesner might wish. But cf. the parable-like statement in John 5:19: "The son cannot do anything by himself, but only what he sees the father doing; for whatever he [the father] does, that the son does likewise." It is possible that in its original form, as a simple metaphor, the saying intended the definite articles generically: "a son, a father." This suggestion is offered by Jeremias, *New Testament Theology*, 58. Jeremias, in turn, is relying here on C. H. Dodd; cf. Dodd's *Historical Tradition in the Fourth Gospel* (Cambridge: Cambridge University, 1963) 386 n. 2. See also the similar metaphor behind the logion on revelation in Matt 11:27||Luke 10:22.

[131] Riesner (*Jesus als Lehrer*, 103) thinks that the Jewish father would have taken over the task of teaching his son from the mother after the child's third birthday. As sometimes happens in Riesner's book, such precise claims rest on later rabbinic literature. The OT texts he cites (Lev 19:3; 2 Macc 7:27) do not support his claim. Besides the Greek Chrysippus and the Latin Quintilian, all the other authorities for the statement come from rabbinic material later than the early 1st century A.D. Riesner, however, does have a good deal of support from the OT for the claim that the Jewish father had responsibility for teaching the Jewish faith to his son (pp. 105–8); see, e.g., Deut 6:1–7,20; 32:7; Ps 78:3–4; Tobit 4:3–21; Sir 3:1; 8:9; 30:1–13. Beyond individual texts, one need only think of all the "my son" lectures in the wisdom literature, in which the wisdom teacher dons the mantle of the father teaching his son. As Riesner points out, addressing one's teacher as "father" was common throughout the ancient Mediterranean world (pp. 108–10, though note the difficulty of documenting the use of "father" as second-person address—as opposed to a third-person title—for the early rabbis).

[132] On the question of oral and literary cultures, see Werner H. Kelber, *The Oral and the Written Gospel* (Philadelphia: Fortress, 1983); and as an important corrective, Paul J. Achtemeier, "*Omne verbum sonat:* The New Testament and the Oral Environment of Late Western Antiquity," *JBL* 109 (1990) 3–27. Achtemeier has a better sense of the ongoing influence of oral culture even after an oral composition has been consigned to writing. Both authors rely to varying degrees on the many works of Walter J. Ong; see, e.g., *Orality and Literacy* (New York/London: Methuen, 1982).

[133] This is not to return to the anachronistic (and perhaps idealized) picture of a uniform system of public education throughout Palestine. Nor are we to think of "the Nazareth synagogue" as necessarily a special building set apart for purely religious and educational purposes. A devout householder owning one of the larger buildings in Nazareth might have made his house available as the local synagogue. Things were obviously different in Jerusalem and probably even in Capernaum, where excavations have uncovered the ruins of a basalt synagogue (*not* the later limestone structure built over it) whose origins may go back to the early 2d century, or even the 1st century A.D. For the dispute on dating, see

Jerome Murphy-O'Connor, *The Holy Land* (2d ed.; Oxford/New York: Oxford University, 1986) 192; Charles H. Miller, "Capernaum," *Harper's Bible Dictionary* ed. Paul J. Achtemeier (San Francisco: Harper & Row, 1985) 154–55.

[134] Riesner (*Jesus als Lehrer*, 240–41) invokes Mark 6:2 rather than 1:22 to conclude that Jesus had no formal schooling as a scribe, i.e., no advanced education beyond the basics that were taught in the local synagogue. He also relies on Luke 4:16 and John 7:15.

[135] Riesner, *Jesus als Lehrer*, 199, 222–23, 232. The synagogue of Jesus' day would have been a very modest affair; indeed, it could have been situated in the house of one of the more "well-to-do" citizens of Nazareth (wealth being always a relative matter), rather than in a self-standing building dedicated to religious and educational purposes. One and the same person might have served as servant of the synagogue, scribe, and elementary school teacher (pp. 184–85).

Needless to say, the present "synagogue of Nazareth" that is shown to pilgrims is not the one from the time of Jesus; there is no way of knowing where the 1st-century A.D. synagogue might have been located, though a number of sites are suggested by Jack Finegan, *The Archeology of the New Testament. The Life of Jesus and the Beginning of the Early Church* (Princeton: Princeton University, 1969) 33. See also Murphy-O'Connor, *The Holy Land*, 310, 313–14. B. Bagatti holds that the bases of pillars that have been found northeast of the Church of St. Joseph in Nazareth are remains of the synagogue that the anonymous pilgrim from Piacenza mentions in A.D. 570. Bagatti hypothesizes that the synagogue of the 1st century A.D. would also have stood at this location. On all this see Riesner (*Jesus als Lehrer*, 222–23), who is rightly skeptical.

[136] Meyers and Strange, *Archaeology, the Rabbis, and Early Christianity*, 57.

[137] A Hebrew inscription found at Caesarea in 1962 and dating from about the 4th century A.D. lists Nazareth as one of the villages in which the priestly divisions were resident after the Jewish revolt. Some have speculated that this honor accorded Nazareth might point to a reputation for solid Jewish piety. It may be no accident that archaeology at Nazareth has so far produced no remains with pagan symbolism; see Pheme Perkins, "Nazareth," *Harper's Bible Dictionary*, ed. Paul J. Achtemeier (San Francisco: Harper & Row, 1985) 689; Finegan, *Archeology*, 29. Riesner (*Jesus als Lehrer*, 215–17) tries to bolster the view of Jesus' family as especially pious by appealing to the picture of Joseph and Mary in the Infancy Narratives; as I have indicated in Chapter 8, this is a precarious argument. In general, Riesner is too uncritical in his use of the Infancy Narrative material. The conservative Jewish piety of James "the brother of the Lord," so influential in the early Church, is a better argument.

[138] For the whole question of the conservative, non-Pharisaic Judaism of Galilean peasants, see Freyne, *Galilee from Alexander the Great to Hadrian*, 259–343; idem, *Galilee, Jesus and the Gospels* (Philadelphia: Fortress, 1988) 176–218. In agreement with him is Riesner, *Jesus als Lehrer*, 208–9.

[139] Notice that, while James is presented as concerned about basic "border markers" that preserve Jewish identity in a Gentile milieu (circumcision, food

laws), he is not associated with the punctilious observances of the Pharisees. In a sense, James probably transferred the effective border markers of his Jewish life in Galilee of the Gentiles into the problems of a Jewish church beginning to admit Gentile members. He thought the border markers were still necessary and effective. If James the Galilean Jew had no use for the urban Pharisees, perhaps James the Christian Jew had an added reason for not liking the urban ex-Pharisee, Paul. We might even add to this speculative "mix" the difference between an illiterate peasant and a literate tradesman.

[140] Since Hebrew and Aramaic are closely related Semitic languages, and since by the time of Jesus Hebrew was commonly (though not always) written in the so-called "square" script of Aramaic, a reading knowledge of classical biblical Hebrew would almost necessarily entail a reading knowledge of the Aramaic the reader ordinarily spoke.

[141] For the first time in this work I raise a question that will return: the historical phenomenon of the "Jewish genius." The fact is that human history—especially the history of the Western world—has been marked and substantially altered by great Jews, both religious and secular, whose massive impact seems out of proportion to their early origins. One could multiply examples from Moses through King David, Johannan ben Zakkai, and Maimonides, to Spinoza, Marx, Freud, and Einstein. Amid all the categories used to understand Jesus of Nazareth, perhaps we might consider the category supplied by historical analogy, the category of the Jewish genius.

[142] See George M. Foster, "What Is a Peasant?" in *Peasant Society: A Reader*, ed. Jack M. Potter, Mary N. Diaz, and George M. Foster (Boston: Little, Brown, and Co., 1967) 2–14. Foster points out that the average person often thinks of peasants in terms of medieval European agricultural serfs and marginal farmers. Yet anthropologists today understand the term more widely; some would include, e.g., Malay fishermen. See also Paul J. Magnarella, *The Peasant Venture* (Cambridge, MA: Schenkman, 1979) 4–5.

[143] Eric R. Wolf, *Peasants* (Foundations of Modern Anthropology Series; Englewood Cliffs, NJ: Prentice-Hall, 1966) 2. What follows is heavily indebted to his presentation.

[144] On the image of symbiosis, see Bruce J. Malina, *The New Testament World. Insights from Cultural Anthropology* (Atlanta: John Knox, 1981) 72: "To borrow an expression from biology, this sort of relationship among communities in the Mediterranean world (and peasant societies in general) can be called symbiotic, that is, the living together in more or less close union of two or more dissimilar organisms in a mutually beneficial relationship."

[145] This possibility would be strengthened if we could take as historical the account that Hegesippus (2d century) relates through Eusebius *(Ecclesiastical History* 3.20.1–3). Suspicious of anyone claiming to be descended from King David, the Emperor Domitian interrogated the grandsons of Judas, a brother of Jesus. They assured him that all they owned was a small amount of land, which they tilled with their own hands. While the story as it stands is probably a piece of

Christian legend, it may preserve an authentic memory of some descendants of Jesus' family continuing to live as Palestinian peasants. At the very least, it is interesting that later Palestinian Christians (of whom Hegesippus was probably one) portrayed these descendants of Jesus' family not as woodworkers or artisans in the image of Jesus but rather as farmers. Even apart from this anecdote, the supposition that a family in a Galilean village would own and till a plot of land is a natural one, since even city dwellers in the ancient world often owned plots of various sizes (see Shimon Applebaum, "Economic Life in Palestine," *The Jewish People in the First Century* [CRINT 1/2; ed. S. Safrai and M. Stern; Phildelphia: Fortress, 1976] 631–700, esp. p. 659 n. 4).

146 Freyne *(Galilee from Alexander the Great to Hadrian,* 11) comments on the fertility of the land around Nazareth: the rock formations are semipervious chalk, "therefore providing adequate soil coverage and plenty of springs which make agriculture possible even on the top of the range."

147 I say "only in part," since a major factor in determining the imagery that a good teacher uses is the audience he or she is addressing. Hence the heavy use of agricultural imagery may reflect the peasant audience Jesus is addressing rather than the specific occupation he formerly pursued. Strange to say, George Wesley Buchanan ("Jesus and the Upper Class," *NovT* 7 [1964–65] 195–209) emphasizes the point of determination of imagery by the audience being addressed (p. 204), yet proceeds to use it in an odd way in his desire to create his portrait of Jesus the wealthy businessman.

148 As I noted when dealing with the accusation of Jesus' illegitimacy in Chapter 8, the Greek text of Mark 6:3 is plagued with variant readings. As I argued there—in agreement with most modern critical texts of the Greek NT— the most probable reading is *ouch houtos estin ho tektōn, ho huios tēs Marias.*

149 Perhaps there is also an echo of Matthew's virgin-birth tradition in the alteration. Joseph is mentioned obliquely in a question separate from the question in which Mary and Jesus' brothers are mentioned together by name.

150 Some might even want to invoke the principle of embarrassment here, insofar as Matthew shifts *tektōn* to Joseph, while Luke, the evangelist with the greatest literary (and social?) ambitions, suppresses the designation entirely. From a methodological point of view, we have an interesting example of something in the gospel tradition being generally accepted by scholars as historical without multiple attestation in the sources. The lack of any theological reason for inventing the tradition of Jesus as woodworker, along with the possible embarrassment of the later Gospel tradition, seems sufficient reason for acceptance.

151 Webster's Ninth Collegiate Dictionary (Springfield, MA: Merriam-Webster, 1983) s.v.

152 Richard A. Batey, " 'Is Not This the Carpenter?' " *NTS* 30 (1984) 249–58, esp. 257 n. 2. Batey goes on to note that soft materials such as clay or wax would

therefore be excluded—as would, strictly speaking, metals softened by heat, though *tektōn* was sometimes applied to a smith.

[153] Paul Hanly Furfey, "Christ as *Tektôn,*" *CBQ* 17 (1955) 204–15, esp. 204.

[154] What follows is dependent on Furfey, "Christ as *Tektôn,*" 205–10.

[155] *Dialogue with Trypho* 88 (written around A.D. 155–60). Justin remarks that Jesus was thought to be a *tektōn,* for he made those products of a *tektōn,* namely, plows and yokes *(kai tektonos nomizomenou tauta gar ta tektonika erga eirgazeto en anthrōpois ōn, arotra kai zyga).*

[156] Furfey ("Christ as *Tektôn,*" 209) lists the hammer, mallet, chisel, saw, hatchet, ax, adz, gimlet, drill, knife, plane, rasp, lathe, the square, straightedge and ruler, chalk line, plumb line, level, and compasses. Furfey notes that most of these instruments appeared very early in the ancient Near East and were widespread throughout the ancient Mediterranean world. One poignant detail: nails were expensive and so less freely used than today.

[157] As Furfey points out ("Christ as *Tektôn,*" 213), it is unlikely that a village like Nazareth could have supported more than one woodworking establishment.

[158] *Roman Social Relations 50 B.C. to A.D. 284* (New Haven/London: Yale University, 1974) 88–89.

[159] Freyne observes *(Galilee from Alexander the Great to Hadrian,* 166) that the picture we can derive from Josephus is one of Galileans usually living in villages and being mostly "free landowners, however small their plots." As Freyne warns, one must distinguish between this relatively healthy socioeconomic situation and the much worse one that arose subsequent to the two Jewish Revolts.

[160] James C. Scott *(The Moral Economy of the Peasant. Rebellion and Subsistence in Southeast Asia* [New Haven/London: Yale University, 1976] 1) quotes a famous remark of R. H. Tawney: "There are districts in which the position of the rural population is that of a man standing permanently up to the neck in water, so that even a ripple is sufficient to drown him." Tawney was speaking of China in 1931, but the remark fits at least some of the Galilean peasants remarkably well.

[161] Freyne, *Galilee from Alexander the Great to Hadrian,* 196–97. Cf. the description of the 1st-century Jewish peasant by Applebaum, "Economic Life in Palestine," 691: ". . . the overpopulation reduced the Jewish peasant unit of cultivation and endangered the cultivator's margin of livelihood. This was further curtailed by climatic instability and taxation, leading to chronic indebtedness, and the growth of a landless tenantry and labouring class, whose ranks were also enlarged by political developments—Rome's reduction of Jewish territory and Herod's policy of confiscation—and whose existence is indirectly evidenced by the vast increase of 'bandits,' more particularly in the years between 40 and 66 C.E."

[162] This statement is basically true, since slavery in its essence means that a human being is considered in law to be a piece of property, a thing totally subject to another human being who owns the slave. In practice, however, slav-

ery was a very complex reality, and different types of slaves might be placed on different rungs of the socioeconomic ladder. The trusted slaves of rulers and rich merchants might rise to the heights of power and wealth themselves and might eventually buy their freedom. They enjoyed greater economic security and a more comfortable life than day laborers. Yet as long as they remained slaves, their servile status meant that all power and possessions could be swept away from them at any time. Slaves born in a household and used as domestic servants were often treated more humanely than slaves bought for work on the land. Among Jews, Hebrew slaves were guaranteed a limited time of slavery, depending upon their particular circumstances; see Exod 21:2–4; Deut 15:12; Lev 25:39–43,47–55; Exod 21:7–11; Exod 21:26–27. On the question of slavery in NT times, see S. Scott Bartchy, *First-Century Slavery and the Interpretation of 1 Corinthians 7:21* (SBLDS 11; Atlanta: Scholars, 1973).

[163] As Freyne notes *(Galilee from Alexander the Great to Hadrian,* 166), agricultural slavery (i.e., the large *latifundia* manned by slaves working under the supervision of a slave manager) was not widely practiced in the Roman Empire outside of Italy and Sicily. Yet, despite apologetic presentations, slavery did exist among Jews in Palestine in the 1st century A.D. Applebaum ("Economic Life in Palestine," 677) notes: "Piracy and the slave trade were inseparable, and in the Hellenistic period instances are found of slaves named after Joppa port. Clearly, for the Gentile towns, a considerable import of slaves may be assumed, and Gentile slaves were certainly not absent from Jewish society." He goes on to state in n. 5 on the same page: "The extent of the survival of Jewish slavery in Judaea in this period is highly controversial. To judge from Jos. *War* IV, 508, 510, their number may have been considerable on the eve of the Destruction."

[164] It cannot be stressed too much that this is only a crude approximation, the class structures and economic conditions of the Roman Empire and contemporary America being vastly different. Hence Hengel's description of Jesus as "a building craftsman [who] belonged to the middle class" *(The "Hellenization" of Judaea,* 17) could be misleading.

[165] It is important to remember that alongside wealth or poverty stood another important determinant of one's place in society: honor or shame, the ancient Mediterranean world being basically a "shame culture." On this concept, see Malina, *The New Testament World,* especially Chapter 2, "Honor and Shame: Pivotal Values of the First-Century Mediterranean World," 25–50. When Jesus forsook his clearly defined social role as the woodworker of Nazareth to assume the ambiguous role of itinerant teacher and wonderworker, he left an assured position of honor—however modest—to enter a position that meant high honor in the eyes of believers and great shame in the eyes of opponents.

[166] For this balanced, revisionist view of Antipas, see Harold W. Hoehner, *Herod Antipas* (SNTSMS 17; Cambridge: Cambridge University, 1972) 264–65. By way of comparison: Antipas reigned from 4 B.C. to A.D. 39; Herod the Great from 37 B.C. (in Jerusalem) to 4 B.C.; Archelaus from 4 B.C. to A.D. 6; Philip from 4 B.C. to A.D. 34; Agrippa I from A.D. 37 to 44; Agrippa II from A.D. 48 to 52 in Chalcis and from 52 to ca. 93 in Iturea.

[167] See Freyne, *Galilee from Alexander the Great to Hadrian,* 192. Commenting on the innate conservatism of peasants with regard to farming techniques, Scott *(The Moral Economy of the Peasant,* 35) states: ". . . the narrowness of the peasant's economic margin leads him to choose techniques that are safe even if they give away something in average yield." In a grudging sort of way, Galilean peasants may have viewed Antipas as safe too.

[168] Variations on these basic themes can be found in W. F. Albright and C. S. Mann, *Matthew* (AB 26; Garden City, NY: Doubleday, 1971) 21–22, 172–73; C. S. Mann, *Mark* (AB 27; Garden City, NY: Doubleday, 1986) 289; Batey, " 'Is Not This the Carpenter?' " 249–58; Riesner, *Jesus als Lehrer,* 219. Perhaps the most extreme and uncritical treatment of this type is by Buchanan, "Jesus and the Upper Class," 195–209. Buchanan concludes that Jesus' teachings were largely directed to the upper economic class, with whom Jesus associated; Jesus himself may have been reared in an upper-class society. He was a business administrator who supervised craftsmen. This conclusion is reached by a remarkably uncritical use of gospel texts that usually ignores the formulations contributed by the post-Easter tradition and the redaction of the evangelists. Worse still, texts are often made to say what they do not say: e.g., the miracles done for the centurion's servant, Jairus' daughter, and the Syro-Phoenician's daughter show that Jesus directed his teachings [!] to the upper classes (p. 205).

[169] Notice, e.g., how Albright and Mann *(Matthew,* 21–22), without further ado, mesh various texts from the Infancy Narratives along with Matt 13:55; Mark 6:3; Luke 4:22; and John 6:42. Their claim that Matt 13:53–58 parr. and John 6:42 show that the people of Nazareth did not know Jesus by sight when he first came back after the beginning of his ministry and that therefore he had spent little time in Nazareth during the "hidden years" is not borne out by the exegesis of the various verses in the context of their respective pericopes. In particular, the mocking rhetorical questions introduced by *ouch* (e.g., Matt 13:55; Mark 6:3) should not be taken in a literalistic fashion. Presumably the townspeople did know that the sisters of Jesus lived among them; yet they also ask that question, introduced in Matthew by *ouchi* and in Mark by *ouk.* Moreover, in Luke 4:16–17 it seems unlikely that Jesus would have been invited to read the lesson from the prophets on the Sabbath if the Nazarenes considered him an unknown stranger. The statement of Jesus in 4:23 presumes that they already knew something about him and his ministry. As for John 6:42, it simply does not belong in this discussion at all, since the rhetorical *ouch* question is posed by the Jews in the synagogue of Capernaum, not Nazareth.

[170] So Riesner, *Jesus als Lehrer,* 219; he points to the forms of this word found in the Peshitta and the Curetonian Syriac.

[171] See Marcus Jastrow, *A Dictionary of the Targumim, the Talmud Babli and Yerushalmi, and the Midrashic Literature* (2 vols.; New York: Pardes, 1950) 2. 876. The postbiblical Hebrew *naggār* also has a broad range of meanings. Neither the Hebrew nor the Aramaic word occurs in the canonical Hebrew-Aramaic Scriptures.

[172] Riesner, *Jesus als Lehrer*, 219; he is dependent on Geza Vermes, *Jesus the Jew* (Philadelphia: Fortress, 1973) 21–22. For the passages, see *y. Yebam.* 9b; *y. Qidd.* 66a; *b. Abod. Zar.* 50b. A. Cohen (*'Abodah Zarah* in *The Babylonian Talmud* [ed. I. Epstein; London: Soncino, 1935] 252) translates the two phrases as "a scholar" and "a scholar's son," and then comments that the two phrases mean "an ordained Rabbi" and "a rabbinical student."

[173] This is a major thesis in Batey's " 'Is This Not the Carpenter?' " 249–58. Curiously, Hengel (*The "Hellenization" of Judaea*, 17) seems to embrace this position in his text, only to back off from it in his accompanying note (p. 74 n. 90): "As Jesus came from a pious Jewish craftsman's family, with country origins, there are reasons which tell *against* too close a connection with the largely Hellenistic city in the vicinity after its reconstruction. . . . It is at any rate striking that the Gospel tradition does not mention Sepphoris at all."

[174] Some writers, however, are dubious about Sepphoris' effectiveness in Hellenizing the Galilean countryside. For instance, Bernard J. Lee (*The Galilean Jewishness of Jesus. Retrieving the Jewish Origins of Christianity* [New York/Mahwah: Paulist, 1988] 63) claims that "it is certainly the case that Sepphoris does not inculturate Galilee."

[175] Batey pursues and develops his point in Richard A. Batey, "Jesus and the Theatre," *NTS* 30 (1984) 563–74. From the presence of *hypokritēs* in all the Synoptic sources, Batey draws wide-ranging conclusions: e.g., Jesus understood and spoke Greek (apparently understanding the classical poetic Greek used in the theater), attended Greek plays in the theater at Sepphoris, used the word *hypokritēs* in his teaching on the basis of his "firsthand knowledge . . . of the dramatic actor" (p. 563), and delivered at least some of his teaching in Greek. A great deal is being built here on very little. (1) The majority of occurrences of *hypokritēs* in the Synoptics may well be due to Matthew's redaction or the special vocabulary of the M tradition he inherited. Out of the 17 occurrences of *hypokritēs*, 1 is in Mark and 3 are in Luke; the rest are all in Matthew. (2) There is indeed one clear occurrence in Mark and one in the Q tradition. The usage could therefore go back to Jesus. Yet the fact that some cases of *hypokritēs* in the Synoptics are clearly redactional and that the allied words *hypokrinomai* and *hypokrisis* can occur in the narrative comments of Luke reminds us of the possibility that the vocabulary could come from the early bearers of the tradition rather than from Jesus himself. (3) More to the point, Batey jumps too quickly from Jesus' metaphorical use of *hypokritēs* to his supposed firsthand experience of seeing an actor on a stage, specifically the theater at Sepphoris. One must take into account the intervening tradition of a metaphorical use of the word in popular Greek philosophy, in both positive and negative senses. More importantly, there is the tradition of its use as a religious metaphor, in the negative sense, in Hellenistic Judaism of the Diaspora. See, e.g., 2 Macc 5:25; 6:21; Sir 1:28–30; LXX Job 36:13. The passages from 2 Maccabees have the more precise sense of intentional dissembling in a religious context, while in Job 36:13 the sense is rather the general one of ungodliness or impiety, not especially hypocrisy in the sense of intentional dissembling. Various nuances of the term are also

found in Josephus and Philo, who both use the *hypokrinomai/hypokrisis/hypokritēs* word-field at times to express the idea of hypocrisy. It is not hard to see how the basic deceit or deception of sin, which involves some sort of contradiction, easily "slides over" into the more specific idea of deceitful sin that intentionally disguises itself as virtue. The more general sense is found in such sayings of Jesus as Luke 12:54–56; 13:15–16; the more specific idea of playacting or hypocrisy is especially typical of Matthew. The upshot of all this is that the use of *hypokritēs* to express the specific religious metaphor of playacting could be due to early Jewish Christians translating Jesus' sayings into Greek in an urban Hellenistic Jewish-Christian context. That Jesus did use the metaphor of playacting in some form is not impossible, but even in that case the tradition of the term as a moral or religious metaphor in both pagan and Jewish culture weakens any deduction about Jesus' firsthand experience of the Greek theater. Batey's broad conclusions need much more argumentation than he provides. For an analysis of the philological data, see Ulrich Wilckens, *"hypokrinomai,* etc.," *TDNT* 8 (1972) 559–71. Similar ungrounded exuberance about the influence of Sepphoris on Jesus can be found in Hengel, *The "Hellenization" of Judaea,* 44: "Why should not the craftsman Jesus, who grew up in the neighbourhood of Sepphoris, have made contact with Cynic itinerant preachers, especially as he himself spoke some Greek?"

[176] Tiberias is mentioned in passing in John 6:23, which is the only reference to the city itself in the NT. The "Sea of Tiberias," an alternate designation of the "Sea of Galilee," is found in John 6:1; 21:1. Lee (*The Galilean Jewishness of Jesus,* 66) comments: "The mystery, if there is one, is why Sepphoris is not a recipient of the teaching and preaching of Jesus. . . . It does not seem unreasonable that Jesus' reasons for avoiding Sepphoris would have been inherited from his own rural culture in Nazareth. . . ." One should remember that, for all the talk of Hellenistic urban culture in 1st-century Palestine, "the Jews of Palestine were less urbanized than the population of other equally developed Roman provinces" (Applebaum, "Economic Life in Palestine," 631).

CHAPTER 10

IN THE INTERIM . . .

Part II: Family, Marital Status, and Status as a Layman

In the previous chapter we investigated some of those "external" influences that helped mold Jesus during his formative years in Nazareth: language, education, occupation, and socioeconomic conditions. In the present chapter we will ask questions about the immediate personal context of Jesus' life, the "internal" influences that contributed to his formation: family ties, marital status, and status as a layman. The next chapter will conclude Part Two with a survey of the time frame of Jesus' life, thus providing a bridge from Jesus' "hidden years" to the beginning of his public ministry.

1. THE IMMEDIATE FAMILY OF JESUS

"Family" meant something very different in ancient Palestine than it does in contemporary middle-class society in the United States today. Indeed, not only in Jewish Palestine but also throughout the ancient Mediterranean world the large extended family was the major social "safety net" for the individual. Correspondingly, an "individual" understood himself or herself differently in the ancient world. The individual was not an isolated, completely autonomous person—as some Americans foolishly think they are today—but rather a part of a larger, sprawling social unit. The extended family, and then the village or town as a whole, imposed identity and social function on the individual in exchange for the communal security and defense the individual received from the family.[1] The break Jesus made with these ties to his extended family and village, after so many years of an uneventful life in their midst, and his concomitant attempt to define a new identity and social role for himself, no doubt left deep scars that can still be seen in the Gospel narratives (see Mark 3:21,31–35 parr.; 6:1–6 parr.; John 7:3–9).

A. The Parents of Jesus

In a village like Nazareth, with some 1,600 people, the extended family of Jesus probably made up a sizable proportion of a population where many people would be distantly related to one another by blood or marriage. Later apocryphal traditions and patristic writers try to bring various Gospel figures into the family circle of Jesus,[2] but the canonical Gospels are more sober and sparse in their identifications. As we saw when treating the Infancy Narratives, the identification of Mary and Joseph as mother and putative father is secure, though the multiple attestation is not as broad as one might a priori imagine.[3] As was pointed out in the previous chapter, Joseph's designation as a carpenter is due to Matthew's reworking of Mark's description of Jesus (Matt 13:55; cf. Mark 6:3), but in any event it is likely that the firstborn son followed the trade of his father.[4]

Unlike Jesus' mother, brothers, and sisters, Joseph is not present on the narrative stage once the ministry begins. In various Gospel passages Jesus interacts with his mother alone (John 2:3–5), his brothers alone (John 7:3–10), and his mother and brothers together (Mark 3:31–35 parr.), along with passing references to his sisters (Mark 3:35; 6:3). In light of these multiple relations, the total silence about Joseph is significant. Theoretically, a number of different reasons might be suggested for Joseph's absence: e.g., Joseph had abandoned the family, or he maintained a completely neutral stance toward Jesus' ministry and hence was of no symbolic use to the evangelists.[5] But the traditional solution, already known in the patristic period,[6] remains the most likely: Joseph had died by the time Jesus began his public ministry.[7] Granted that we do not know how old Joseph was when Jesus was born, and granted that life expectancy was much lower in the ancient world than in the United States today, there is nothing intrinsically improbable about Joseph's death before Jesus reached the age of roughly thirty to thirty-five.[8]

In contrast, Mary lived through the public ministry (Mark 3:31; John 2:1–12) and on into at least the early days of the Church (John 19:25; Acts 1:14). If it be granted that she would have been about fourteen years old when Jesus was born, and if it be granted that she was robust enough to bear at least six other children,[9] there is nothing improbable about Mary's surviving Jesus. She would have been roughly forty-eight to fifty years old at the time of his crucifixion.

B. Brothers and Sisters: History of Interpretation

It is neither Joseph nor Mary but rather the "brothers" and "sisters" of Jesus who create the greatest problem for both historians and theologians. Ordinary Americans today, if they know anything about the problem, have a vague notion that Catholics hold that Jesus' "brothers" and "sisters" were really cousins, while Protestants maintain that they were true siblings having the same two parents. Actually, the theological battle lines down through the centuries have been much more complex. In the first four centuries of the Church, different views on this question were held by various Christians, who were not formally excommunicated by the Church of their day for their differing positions.

In the 2d century, for example, Hegesippus,[10] a convert from Judaism probably hailing from Palestine, seems to have considered the brothers and sister of Jesus to be true siblings, distinct from the cousins and uncles Hegesippus also mentions. Strictly speaking, since Hegesippus presumably accepted the virginal conception of Jesus, the brothers and sisters would be half brothers and half sisters (i.e., with only one common biological parent, Mary). Yet the *Protevangelium Jacobi* (also from the 2d century) seems to imply that Mary remained perpetually a virgin, the brothers and sisters of Jesus being the children of Joseph by a previous marriage. In this case, the brothers and sisters would be stepbrothers and stepsisters of Jesus (i.e., with no common biological parent, but with a legal link by way of a second marriage).[11]

What is often considered the common teaching of the Roman Catholic Church, namely that the brothers and sisters were really cousins, and that not only Mary but also Joseph were perpetual virgins, was first championed by Jerome in his tract *Against Helvidius* in the late 4th century (ca. 383). This became the predominant position of Christianity in the West during the Middle Ages, while the view that the brothers and sisters were children of Joseph by a previous marriage remained dominant in the East. It sometimes surfaced in the West as well, thanks to the popularity of the stories in the *Protevangelium Jacobi.*

A startling fact that many present-day Catholics and Protestants do not know is that the great figures of the Protestant Reformation, e.g., Martin Luther and John Calvin, held to Mary's perpetual virginity and therefore did not consider the brothers and sisters of Jesus to be true siblings. It was only with the rise of the Enlightenment that the idea that the brothers and sisters were biological children of Mary and Joseph gained acceptance among "mainline" Protestants. With the exception of a few "high-church" Protestants, this is the common view in Protestant churches today.[12]

That the brothers and sisters were really cousins or some other distant relations is still the common teaching of the Roman Catholic Church, although some Catholic theologians and exegetes have, in recent decades, espoused the view that the brothers and sisters were true siblings. Notable among Catholic exegetes is the German scholar Rudolf Pesch, who championed the "true siblings" position in his massive two-volume commentary on Mark.[13] Although his claims raised a fire storm of controversy among German Catholics, he has never been officially censured or condemned by Rome for his views.[14]

This all too brief sketch of the history of interpretation at least warns us that intelligent, well-educated, and sincere Christians have differed and can differ on this question because (1) the data are sparse and ambiguous and (2) the doctrinal positions of various churches have naturally influenced scholars, however objective they try to be. As we try to sift the data to reach what is the most probable conclusion, we must remember the severe limits of this book: for methodological reasons, it prescinds from what is known from faith or later Church teaching and asks simply and solely what can reasonably be deduced from the raw data of the NT and a few noncanonical passages, viewed purely as potential historical sources.[15] Granted this limited scope, we must expect results that are also quite limited and tentative. If the quest for the "historical Jesus" is difficult, the quest for the "historical relatives of Jesus" is nigh impossible. The best we can do is examine honestly and in their own contexts the various NT and early patristic texts that bear on this question. For convenience' sake, we will start with the striking way the problem is posed by particular texts in the Gospel of Matthew, and then proceed to broaden out our inquiry with an investigation of the use of the word "brother(s)" in the rest of the NT.

C. Relevant Texts in Matthew: 1:25; 13:55; 12:46–50

Present-day readers of the Bible are confronted with the problem almost as soon as they open their copies of the NT. Chapter 1 of Matthew deals with the genealogy of Jesus through Joseph (1:1–17), the virginal conception of Jesus by Mary, and Joseph's role in acknowledging Jesus as his legal son ("giving the name"), thus inserting Jesus into Joseph's Davidic genealogy and making Jesus a "Son of David" and candidate for Davidic messiahship (1:18–25). In fact, it is the role of Joseph in the face of the mystery of the virginal conception that is the major concern of the pericope about the "dream of Joseph" or the "annunciation to Joseph" (1:18–25). Since Matthew apparently does not consider Mary to be of Davidic lineage (which would be irrelevant anyway to Jews who traced a son's lineage through his legal father), it is vital that Joseph accept Jesus as his own child so that Jesus will have a Davidic genealogy.

Granted this major theological concern, the tradition of the virginal conception almost gets in the way; it is a tradition in Matthew's church that must be carefully balanced over against Matthew's major concern, Jesus' Davidic sonship through Joseph. We might almost sum up the message of 1:18–25 with a paradox: although Jesus is virginally conceived, nevertheless he is the Son of David through Joseph, his legal father.

This double concern of the pericope, and indeed of the whole chapter, is neatly summed up in the two halves of the chapter's final verse (v 25): "And he [Joseph] did not have sexual relations[16] with her [Mary] until she bore a son (v 25a); and he called his name Jesus (v 25b)." While our modern theological concerns might focus on the first half of the verse, the emphasis for Matthew falls on the second half: Joseph fulfilled his role as legal father, inserted Jesus into his Davidic lineage, and thus opened up the way for the fulfillment of all prophecy by the Son of David who is also Son of God by virginal conception. In this context, the first half of the verse (25a) simply intends to stress the other truth inculcated by the pericope, the virginal conception. Verse 25a explicitly affirms that Joseph had no sexual relations with Mary during the whole time[17] of her conceiving and bearing Jesus; any participation of Joseph in the child's conception is carefully ruled out. To use later theological vocabulary, Matthew is teaching here *virginitas ante partum*, Mary's virginity before the birth of Jesus.[18]

Thus, any question of Mary's continued virginity after the birth of Jesus, *virginitas post partum*, is really outside of Matthew's major concern. It arises only because of the temporal clause he uses to stress Joseph's abstinence during the period of the conception and gestation of Jesus: "He did not know her *until [beōs hou] she bore a son* (v 25a)." To a 20th-century person reading this statement in English translation, the natural inference would be that the couple had relations after the birth of Jesus. Yet the meaning of the Greek (and any underlying Hebrew or Aramaic) text is not so clear-cut. At times, in both Hebrew *('ad)* and Greek *(beōs hou)*, the conjunction we translate as "until" may not imply that any change takes place after the event mentioned in the "until" clause occurs.

A prime example is the famous beginning of Psalm 110: "The Lord said to my Lord: 'Sit at my right hand until [Hebrew: *'ad*; Greek: *beōs an*] I make your enemies your footstool' " (v 1). The sense of the psalm is hardly that God ("the Lord") will withdraw from the king ("my Lord") the favored position at his right hand *after* the king's enemies are subdued. The position of favor at God's right hand is obviously meant to perdure; no change is implied by "until." A similar case arises in the Pastoral Epistles when the author exhorts Timothy in 1 Tim 4:13: "Be attentive to reading, to exhortation, and to teaching *until [beōs] I* come." Certainly the author does not mean that Timothy should become lax in these activities after Paul arrives. Here again, the emphasis is on what is to happen before the event contained in the "until" clause occurs; nothing is implied about a change after the event occurs.

The whole question becomes more difficult when the main clause contains a negative, yet there are examples in Matthew where the word "until" does not indicate a change even then. For example, Matthew's citation of Isa 42:1–4 in Matt 12:20 contains the sentence "the bruised reed he shall not break and the smoldering flax he shall not quench *until [beōs an]* he brings judgment to victory." Matthew applies Isaiah's prophecy about the gentle ministry of the servant to Jesus the gentle Messiah. Matthew certainly does not think that Jesus the gentle servant will turn harsh and cruel toward the weak and crushed after he makes God's saving justice victorious. Hence, looking at Matt 1:25a in isolation, we can say that we are not forced to take it to mean that Joseph and Mary did have sexual relations after Jesus' birth. At the same time, none of these texts proves that we *should* take 1:25a to mean that Joseph and

Mary did not have relations after Jesus' birth.[19] For Matthew is also capable of using "until" when the context clearly shows that a change is indicated. For instance, in the story of the flight into Egypt, the angel instructs Joseph in 2:13: "Stay there [in Egypt] *until* I tell you [to return to the land of Israel]."

Therefore, to solve the problem of the meaning of 1:25a, we must look to the larger context. Whether we are oriented more to redaction criticism or to modern narrative criticism, we realize that we cannot take Matt 1:25a in splendid isolation. It is a very small part of a large literary and theological work with a surprising amount of coherence and "cross-referencing."[20] Matthew often points forward and backward in his text to foreshadow and recapitulate. Such is the case here. The author who tells us in 1:25a that Joseph did not have relations with Mary until she bore a son is the same author who tells us in 13:55 that Jesus' mother is called Mary and his brothers James, Joseph, Simon, and Jude. Putting aside for the moment the special question of the meaning(s) of "brother" *(adelphos)* in NT Greek, we must admit that, at first glance, the combination of the "until" statement in Matt 1:25a with the naming of Jesus' mother and brothers all in the same verse (13:55) creates the natural impression that Matthew understood 1:25a to mean that Joseph and Mary did have children after the birth of Jesus.

This initial impression of the redactional intention of Matthew is strengthened when we examine the way Matt 13:55 recasts Mark's version of the question hurled at Jesus by the unbelieving townspeople of Nazareth. In Mark 6:3, the citizens of Nazareth ask: "Is this not the woodworker, the son of Mary and brother of James and Joses[21] and Jude and Simon? And are not his sisters here with us?" Notice the structure of Mark's questions: there is no mention of Jesus' father; the designation "woodworker" (applied to Jesus), the name of the mother, and the name of the four brothers are all placed in one question; and the (unnamed) sisters are referred to in a separate question.

In Matthew, things are sorted out differently. First, perhaps in deference to Jesus' dignity, Matthew shifts the slur about being a mere woodworker to Jesus' father. But, since Matthew has made clear in the Infancy Narrative that Joseph is merely Jesus' putative father, the reference to the (unnamed) father is cordoned off in a separate question: "Is this not the son of the woodworker?" (13:55). Then, beginning a separate question, Matthew puts together and names—apart from the putative father—the mother and brothers of Jesus: "Is not his mother called Mary and his brothers James and Joseph and Simon and Jude?"

The one mother and the four brothers, treated separately from Jesus' merely legal father, are all the subject of the one verb, "is called." Then, as in Mark, the unnamed sisters are mentioned by the androcentric audience as an afterthought: "And are not all his sisters with us?" Thus, simply on the level of Matthew's redaction, it is difficult to maintain that the brothers are thought of only as stepbrothers or cousins of Jesus, when Matthew is at pains to separate the legal but not biological father of Jesus from Jesus' real, biological mother. Faced with this great divide that he himself creates, Matthew chooses to place Jesus' brothers with his biological mother, not his legal father.

The mother and brothers of Jesus are also mentioned in a pericope that Matthew takes over from Mark with only a few redactional changes, namely, the story of the mother and brothers seeking to speak with Jesus while he is surrounded by a crowd (Matt 12:46–50=Mark 3:31–35). The way "the mother and brothers" are introduced as a unit and are treated as a unit throughout the story, set over against Jesus and his audience, reinforces the impression that the mother and brothers naturally belong together as blood relations. Even minor redactional traits of Matthew support this impression. While Mark speaks of "his mother and his brothers" in 3:31, Matthew pulls the two nouns even closer together by writing "his mother and brothers" (12:46, *hē mētēr kai hoi adelphoi autou*, the possessive pronoun coming at the end of the whole phrase and modifying both nouns—one would think—equally).

Moreover, in both Mark's and Matthew's versions of the story, the final "punch line" of Jesus carries full weight only if the mother, brothers, and sisters all have a close, natural relationship to Jesus: "Whoever does the will of my Father in heaven is my brother and sister and mother" (Matt 12:50). The whole thrust of the metaphor is weakened if we must interpret the natural point of comparison to mean: "Whoever does the will of my Father in heaven is my male cousin, my female cousin, and my mother."[22] The full force of the aphorism is retained only if the natural relationships mentioned are all equally close and blood-related, at least in the eyes of the redactors of the Gospels.[23]

Thus, the Catholic and Protestant scholars who authored the ecumenical study *Mary in the New Testament* seem justified in their final assessment of the problem in Matt 1:25a: "It is only when this verse is combined with Matthew's reference to Mary and the brothers of Jesus (12:46), along with the sisters (13:55–56), that a likelihood arises that (according to Matthew's understanding) Joseph did come to know Mary after Jesus' birth and that they begot children."[24] Of course, we are only on the level of Matthew's redactional intention, not of historical events in the life of Jesus. Matthew, like Luke, may simply have followed and developed the natural or "surface" sense of "brothers" that they found in Mark. Hence we must move back to the sense of "brother(s)" in the earlier Christian tradition, as witnessed not only in Mark but also in statements that are earlier than Mark (Paul).[25] To these we can add the usage of Josephus, which is independent of the writings of the NT.

D. The Texts Concerning Jesus' Brothers

Our treatment of Mary and Joseph in Matthew's Infancy Narrative and during the public ministry has already introduced us to texts that speak of the "brothers"[26] of Jesus. As we have seen, the immediate, natural, "surface" sense of the passages favors the idea of "blood brothers." Hence, the so-called "Epiphanian solution,"[27] whereby these brothers are seen as sons of Joseph by a previous marriage, strikes one from the start as arbitrary and gratuitous. The Infancy Narrative of Matthew, like that of Luke, lends no support to such an idea. The natural impression gained from the two narratives is that the marriage is the first for Joseph, as it clearly is for Mary. More importantly, as we shall see below, there is no case in the NT where the word *adelphos* ("brother") clearly carries the sense of "stepbrother"—the meaning demanded by the Epiphanian solution. This solution probably traces its roots to the presentation of Joseph in the *Protevangelium Jacobi*, a wildly imaginative folk narrative that is outrageously inaccurate about things Jewish. It may well be that we are dealing with a solution thought up after the fact to support the emerging idea of Mary's perpetual virginity, which did not become common teaching until the latter half of the 4th century.

1. The Position of Jerome

What can be said instead for the solution of Jerome, who seems to be the first Father of the Church to have suggested that the brothers of Jesus were actually cousins and that both Joseph and Mary were perpetual virgins? Once again, we must observe that the solution seems thought up to defend the perpetual virginity of Mary. The idea that Joseph was a perpetual virgin was a novelty in the 4th century and has no basis in Scripture. Indeed, later on in life, Jerome himself did not always explain his position in the same way. But what of the heart of Jerome's claim, namely, that the Greek word for "brother," *adelphos*, actually means "cousin" in the Gospel texts that speak of the brothers of Jesus? A number of philological arguments can be brought forward to support Jerome's theory; but close examination shows that they are not as probative as might at first appear.[28]

Jerome's most important claim is that there are a number of passages in the OT where the Hebrew word for brother *('āḥ)* plainly means not blood brother but cousin or nephew, as can be seen from the wider context (e.g., LXX Gen 29:12; 24:48). Indeed, neither biblical Hebrew nor Aramaic had a single word for "cousin." The Hebrew *'aḥ* and the Aramaic equivalent *'aḥā'* were often used to express the relationship. In these passages, the Greek OT, if translating literally, would naturally translate *'āḥ* as *adelphos* ("brother"). While all this is perfectly correct, the number of OT passages where in fact *'āḥ* indisputably means cousin is very small—perhaps only one![29] It is simply not true that *adelphos* is used regularly in the Greek OT to mean cousin, and the equivalence cannot be taken for granted.

Moreover, one should remember that the very reason why we know that *'āḥ* or *adelphos* can mean cousin is that the immediate context regularly makes the exact relation clear by some sort of periphrasis. For example, we know that in 1 Chr 23:22, when the daughters of Eleazar marry the sons of Kish, "their brothers," the sons of Kish are really their cousins, for v 21 makes it clear Kish was the brother of Eleazar. Given the ambiguity of *'āḥ* in Hebrew, such further clarification would be necessary to avoid confusion in the narrative. No such clarification is given in the NT texts concerning the brothers of Jesus. Rather, the regularity with which they are yoked with Jesus' mother gives the exact opposite impression.

2. The New Testament Is Not Translation Greek

Actually, the whole analogy between the Greek OT and the NT documents with regard to the use of *adelphos* for "cousin" is questionable because these two collections of writings are so different in origin.[30] In the case of the Greek OT, we are dealing with "translation Greek," a Greek that sometimes woodenly or mechanically renders a traditional sacred Hebrew text word for word. Hence it is not surprising that at times *adelphos* would be used to render *'āḥ* when the Hebrew word meant not "brother" but some other type of relative. But in the case of the NT writers, whatever written Aramaic sources—if any—lay before them, the authors certainly did not feel that they were dealing with a fixed sacred text that had to be translated woodenly word for word. The improvements both Matthew and Luke make on Mark's relatively poor Greek make that clear.

A more glaring case is that of Paul, who, in writing the cannon blast of Galatians (ca. A.D. 54) and the pastoral "question-and-answer" tract of 1 Corinthians (around the same time), is speaking very much in his own person, in his own style, and on his own authority. In Gal 1:19 he speaks of "James, the brother of the Lord," and in 1 Cor 9:5 he speaks globally of "the brothers of the Lord"—hardly because he is woodenly translating some document previously composed in Hebrew or Aramaic! Unlike the evangelists, he is not passing on and reshaping revered stories of past events in the life of Jesus. In Gal 1:19 and 1 Cor 9:5 he is referring to people who are personally known to him and who are living and active in the Church even as he writes. Writing on his own, without the pressure of a set tradition or formula, Paul refers to these people as brothers, not cousins. Now, there was a perfectly good word for cousin in NT Greek, *anepsios,* and presumably it was known to the Pauline churches, since it occurs in Col 4:10. If Paul had meant "cousin" and not "brother," most likely he would have written *anepsios* in Galatians and 1 Corinthians, and not *adelphos.*

Even apart from Paul, it is highly questionable whether one can appeal to some supposed long-standing, sacred tradition in Christian Aramaic (e.g., *'aḥā' dî mārĕyā'*), which later on, at a second stage of Christian development, would have been woodenly translated into Greek as *ho adelphos tou kyriou* ("the brother of the Lord"). As we have seen already, the whole theory of early Christian development that claims that an earlier Aramaic-speaking Christianity was followed later on by a Greek-speaking Christianity ignores the existence of Greek-speaking Christian Jews in Jerusalem from the very beginning of the Church (the Hellenists in Acts 6). Presumably, these Christian Jews of Jerusalem, who no doubt knew James and other "brothers of the Lord" personally, called them *hoi adelphoi tou kyriou* ("brothers of the Lord") and not *hoi anepsioi tou kyriou* ("cousins of the Lord") from the very beginning. Their usage did not arise after some supposed revered Aramaic way of speaking had become fixed and traditional.

There is another indication that "brothers of the Lord" as a designation for Jesus had not become such a fixed, unchangeable locution among 1st-century Greek-speaking Jews and Christians that any other way of speaking about these relatives of Jesus was precluded. When referring to James of Jerusalem in *The Jewish Antiquities* (20.9.1 §200), Josephus speaks simply and directly of "the brother of *Jesus,*" not "the brother of the *Lord.*" This passage shows that, contrary to claims made at times by certain exegetes, "brothers of the Lord" was not an invariable title that precluded some more exact designation, such as "the cousins of Jesus."

While not all would be convinced by such an argument, this passage from Josephus has a still greater importance. As we saw in Chapter 3, Josephus was not dependent on any of the NT writings for his assertions about Jesus and James. Speaking independently, Josephus, who knows full well the distinction between "brother" and "cousin"[31] in Greek and who even corrects the Hebrew usage in the Bible in favor of Greek precision on this point,[32] clearly calls James the brother, not the cousin, of Jesus. The import of the NT usage thus receives independent confirmation from a Greek-speaking Jew who knows full well when and how to avoid "brother" and write "cousin" when that is the precise relationship under discussion.

3. The Meanings of "Brother" in the NT

Even within the NT, if we prescind from the disputed case of "the brothers of the Lord," there is no clear use of the Greek word *adelphos* ("brother") to mean precisely "cousin." The various meanings of *adelphos* in the NT can be boiled down to two basic senses: literal and metaphorical.

(1) First and foremost, *adelphos* is used literally to mean a blood brother, either a full brother or a half brother (i.e., with one common biological parent). (a) The clear cases of "full brother" are so manifest that there is no need to belabor the point. Suffice it to note that when Mark, in 1:29–30, introduces us to James, his brother *(adelphon)* John, and their father Zebedee, it never crosses the mind of any exegete or theologian to claim that James and John are really cousins and Zebedee is really their stepfather or uncle. Why an exegete, operating purely on philological and historical grounds, should judge differently in Mark 6:3, where we hear that Jesus is the son of Mary and the brother *(adelphos)* of James, Joses, Jude, and Simon, is not clear.

(b) Interestingly, Mark also knows the use of *adelphos* to mean "half brother," as seen in 6:17, where Philip is called the brother of Herod Antipas. Actually, exegetes dispute whether "Philip" in this text refers to Philip, Herod the Great's son by Cleopatra of Jerusalem, or Herod "Philip," Herod the Great's son by Mariamme II.[33] But the debate makes no difference to our point: "brother" in this text has to mean half brother, since Herod Antipas was the son of Herod the Great by still another wife, Malthace the Samaritan. Hence the blood bond was only through the common biological father, and so Philip (whoever he was) was the *adelphos* of Antipas in the sense of being a half brother.

(c) With "full brother" and "half brother" we exhaust the literal meaning of *adelphos* found in the NT—which is all the more surprising when we realize that the "literal" sense of "brother" could be fairly broad in the extended families of the ancient world. For example, koine Greek outside the NT knows of wider uses of *adelphos* to signify various relationships of blood and law: e.g., the stylized use of "brother" applied to one's husband, sometimes in an incestuous relationship, or the use of "brother" by a father writing to his son.[34] In addition, koine Greek knows the various metaphorical uses we shall examine below.

Still, one cannot avoid asking what is for us the pivotal question: What is the constant usage of the NT in this matter? The answer is clear: in the NT, *adelphos*, when used not merely figuratively or metaphorically but rather to designate some sort of physical or legal relationship, means only full or half brother, and nothing else. Outside of our disputed case, it never means stepbrother (the solution of Epiphanius), cousin (the solution of Jerome), or nephew. When one considers that *adelphos* (in either the literal or the metaphorical sense) is used a total of 343 times in the NT, the consistency of this "literal" usage is amazing. To ignore the strikingly constant usage of the NT in this regard, as well as the natural redactional sense of the Gospel passages we have already examined, and to appeal instead to the usage of koine Greek in various Jewish and pagan texts cannot help but look like special pleading.[35]

(2) Every other use of *adelphos* in the NT falls under the general rubric of a figurative or metaphorical sense. This covers all those cases where "brother" refers to some broad relationship that cannot be equated with the bond forged by direct blood relationship or marriage. Under this metaphorical sense come all those texts referring to followers of Jesus (e.g., Mark 3:35), fellow Christians in the early Church (e.g., 1 Cor 1:1; 5:11), fellow Jews (Acts 2:29 [more in a religious sense]; Rom 9:3 [more in an ethnic or national sense]), any neighbor (without a particular stress on a common religious or racial bond; e.g., Matt 7:3–5), and potentially any human being (Heb 2:11,17). Obviously, the Gospel references to the brothers of Jesus do not fall into this category.

In short, the "cousin" approach of Jerome, like the "stepbrother" approach of Epiphanius, simply lacks sufficient philological basis in the usage of the NT.[36] It is significant that, when contemporary exegetes such as Josef Blinzler and John McHugh[37] have tried to defend something similar to Jerome's position, but in updated versions, they have been constrained to adopt convoluted theories of relationships within the families of Joseph and Mary that simply cannot be verified. As with the Epiphanian solution, so with the cousin theory: what is gratuitously asserted may be gratuitously denied.

4. "Real Brothers" in the Early Fathers of the Church

Those who wish to sustain the cousin approach must face the further difficulty that it is a relatively late, post-Nicene solution.[38] By contrast, both the Epiphanian solution and the view that the "brothers of Jesus" were real brothers can find supporters in the 2d and 3d centuries. The antiquity and spread of the opinion that the brothers of Jesus were real brothers are often overlooked by supporters of the cousin approach.

For example, one of the earliest witnesses to the "real brother" approach is Hegesippus, whose testimony about the teachings of bishops in the great cities of the Roman Empire is highly esteemed by defenders of traditional Catholic ecclesiology. Yet such defenders are usually silent when it comes to Hegesippus' testimony about the brothers of Jesus. Granted, we have this testimony only in fragments, preserved mostly in Eusebius,[39] and the testimony is not without its problems and possible self-contradictions. But at least it is clear that Hegesippus knew how to distinguish among various precise terms for the relatives of Jesus. This is the point I wish to stress; I do not necessarily accept all of what Hegesippus says as historically true.[40] My interest is rather in what a 2d-century Father of the Church *thought* was true about the relatives of Jesus, and what terminology he used to express his ideas.

In Eusebius' *Ecclesiastical History*, 2.23 §4, Hegesippus refers to "the brother of the Lord *[ho adelphos tou kyriou]*, James, who was called by all 'the Just.' " While recounting the martyrdom of this "James the Just" (i.e., the James called by both Paul and Hegesippus "the brother of the Lord"), Hegesippus also mentions an "uncle" and a "cousin" *(anepsion!)* of Jesus (4.22 §4).[41] Hegesippus is thus capable of distinguishing carefully between the brother, the uncle, and the cousin of Jesus. Therefore, when he calls James the brother of Jesus, there is no valid reason for not taking him at his word. As though he were at pains to confirm this point, Hegesippus also speaks in another passage (3.19 and 3.20 §1) of Jude the brother of the Savior (or the Lord) "according to the flesh." Since Hegesippus knows perfectly well how to apply the words "cousin" and "uncle" to specific relatives of Jesus, it becomes extremely difficult to claim that a precise phrase like "brother of the Lord according to the flesh" really means "cousin," or simply refers to spiritual as opposed to physical brotherhood.[42]

Hegesippus was not the only pre-Nicene Father to lean toward a "real brother" approach. The only pre-Nicene Father of the Latin-speaking Church to take up the issue, Tertullian (ca. A.D. 160–220), considered the brothers of Jesus true brothers. Interestingly, he argues especially from the passage in Mark 3:31–35 (paralleled in Luke 8:19–21), where the mother and brothers are yoked together in an uncomplimentary light. This interpretation of Jesus' brothers as real brothers is all the more remarkable because Tertullian tended toward rigorist, ascetic views and had a high esteem for virginity. However, his fierce opposition to Marcion and the Marcionites, with their docetic view of Christ's humanity, caused Tertullian to assert emphatically that Jesus' mother and brothers were *truly (vere)* his mother and brothers. For Tertullian, this was an irrefutable way to prove the full humanity of Christ.[43]

The last texts from a pre-Nicene Father of the Church that may betray an inclination to the "real brother" approach come from the *Adversus Haereses* of Irenaeus (ca. A.D. 130–200). However, the implication of these texts is less clear than those of Hegesippus and Tertullian. In Book 3 of the *Adversus Haereses*, Irenaeus engages in a complicated analogy between the story of the creation and fall of Adam and Eve in Paradise and the virginal conception and birth of Jesus by Mary. Twice during this analogy he makes statements that could be construed as implying that Mary had other children after the birth of Jesus *(Adv. Haer.* 3.21.10; 3.22.4).

In 3.21.10 he writes: "And just as that first-formed man, Adam, received his make-up from the untilled and up-to-that-time *[adhuc]* virgin earth (for God had not yet sent rain and man had not yet worked the earth) and was formed by the hand of God, that is, the Word of God . . . so too the Word, recapitulating Adam in himself and existing from Mary, who was up-to-that-time *[adhuc]* a virgin, correctly received the kind of generation that recapitulated Adam's." Similarly, in 3.22.4, Irenaeus draws an analogy between Eve and Mary. Eve was disobedient when she was still *[adhuc]* a virgin, though she already had a husband.

Mary was obedient when she had an already chosen husband and never-theless was still *[adhuc]* a virgin.

Since every analogy limps, it is difficult to say how far Irenaeus' analogy should be pressed. But one must at least leave open the possibil-ity that Irenaeus presupposed that Mary did not remain a virgin after the birth of Jesus. Needless to say, Blinzler is not willing to allow for this option.[44] At any rate, we can see that when Helvidius in the 4th century supported the interpretation of the brothers of Jesus as real brothers, he was not inventing something out of thin air. There does seem to have been such a tradition of interpretation in the pre-Nicene period, witnessed to at least by Hegesippus and Tertullian, and perhaps by Irenaeus as well—to say nothing of the independent witness of Josephus.

E. CONCLUSION

Needless to say, all of these arguments, even when taken together, cannot produce absolute certitude in a matter for which there is so little evidence. Nevertheless, if—prescinding from faith and later Church teaching—the historian or exegete is asked to render a judgment on the NT and patristic texts we have examined, viewed simply as historical sources, the most probable opinion is that the brothers and sisters of Jesus were true siblings.

This judgment arises first of all from the criterion of multiple attesta-tion: Paul, Mark, John, Josephus, and perhaps Luke in Acts 1:14 speak independently of the "brother(s) of Jesus" (or the Lord). Most of their statements yoke the brothers (and at times sisters) directly with Mary the mother of Jesus in phrases like "his mother and (his) brothers."

To this initial fact of multiple attestation of sources must then be added the natural sense of "brother(s)" in all these passages, as judged by the regular usage of Josephus and the NT. The Greek usage of Josephus distinguishes between "brother" and "cousin," most notably when he is rewriting a biblical story to replace "brother" with the more exact "cousin." Thus it is especially significant that Josephus, an independent 1st-century Jewish writer, calls James of Jerusalem, without further ado, "the brother of Jesus."

In the NT there is not a single clear case where "brother" means "cousin" or even "stepbrother," while there are abundant cases of its meaning "physical brother" (full or half). This is the natural sense of *adelphos* in Paul, Mark, and John; Matthew and Luke apparently followed and developed this sense. Paul's usage is particularly important because, unlike Josephus or the evangelists, he is not simply writing about past events transmitted to him through stories in oral or written sources. He speaks of the brother(s) of the Lord as people he has known and met, people who are living even as he is writing. His use of "brother" is obviously not determined by revered, decades-long Gospel tradition whose set formulas he would be loath to change. And Paul, or a close disciple, shows that the Pauline tradition knew perfectly well the word for "cousin" (anepsios in Col 4:10). Hence, from a purely philological and historical point of view, the most probable opinion is that the brothers and sisters of Jesus were his siblings.[45] This interpretation of the NT texts was kept alive by at least some Church writers up until the late 4th century.

2. WAS JESUS MARRIED?

As with the question of the possible illegitimacy of Jesus, the mere act of asking whether Jesus was ever married will strike some readers as imprudent, others as vulgar, and still others as blasphemous. Actually, there is no justification for putting Jesus' marital status on the same level or in the same category as the question of his illegitimacy. In many cultures, even those that claim to be enlightened, illegitimacy carries a certain social stigma, however innocent and good the illegitimate person may be. The stigma seems all the more disturbing to the devout when it is imputed to a great religious leader, and a fortiori to a person acknowledged by many as their Lord and Savior.

Obviously, in itself being married carries no such stigma. While many patristic and medieval theologians considered consecrated celibacy a higher state of life than marriage, they did not—at least in their better moments—see marriage as something shameful. From Moses to Simon Peter to Thomas More, great saints have been married, without that status being felt an impediment to their holiness or leadership. The case of Jesus is, of course, unique in that orthodox Christianity confesses him to be the eternal Word of God made man, the Son of God in mortal flesh. Granted this commitment to Christ's divinity (as well as the view traditional among Catholics that celibacy is superior to marriage as a state of life), the almost universal belief of mainstream Christians that

Jesus remained unmarried is understandable from the vantage point of orthodox Christian faith.

However, the quest for the historical Jesus undertaken by this book operates by different and more restrictive rules, as Part One stressed. Since the Jesus of history is by definition the Jesus open to investigation by any and all scholars using accepted historical sources and criteria, the insights of faith, while by no means denied, cannot be employed in the arguments of modern questers. Hence, we must ask: Simply from the historical sources at our disposal, can we tell whether or not Jesus was married?

It is intriguing to notice that, even among nonbelievers, this question is often not raised, perhaps because the traditional view that Jesus remained celibate continues to have a subliminal influence. In recent years, however, the question of Jesus' marital status has been explicitly raised by William E. Phipps in his book, *Was Jesus Married? The Distortion of Sexuality in the Christian Tradition.*[46] The subtitle alerts the reader that a perfectly legitimate historical inquiry into the marital status of Jesus has become entangled in a fiery polemic against traditional Christian views on sexuality, especially those of the Roman Catholic Church. To be fair, Phipps has some valid points to make about negative views of sexuality in traditional Christian theology. However, even his overview of that history is tilted in the direction of the worst tendencies of theologians and Church leaders. Christian pronouncements on the sanctity of marriage—indeed, its status in Catholicism as a sacrament—have produced better and brighter moments, which are not given their due. The same could be said of the remarkable progress made by Roman Catholic moral theology on the subject of sexuality in the 20th century.[47]

One must therefore disentangle the historical question of Jesus' marital status from the contemporary concerns that are the driving engine of Phipps's book. Once that is done, we can appreciate the honest question Phipps raises and evaluate his arguments in favor of the position that Jesus had indeed, at some time in his life, been married.

The basic argument that underlies many of Phipps's individual arguments is fairly simple: granted the positive Jewish ethos regarding sex and marriage at the time of Jesus, the silence of the NT concerning a wife of Jesus should be interpreted as meaning that Jesus did in fact, at least at some point in his life, have a wife. To unpack this a bit: Phipps ranges through the whole of the OT, intertestamental, and rabbinic literature to emphasize that Jews saw sexuality and marriage as blessings given to humanity by a gracious Creator. Celibacy as a life style for the ordinary religious Jew, and especially for a teacher or rabbi, would have been unthinkable at the time of Jesus. The picture of Jesus as a perpetual celibate is the product of later Christian theology, which traditionally suffered from a skewed view of sex and marriage. In short, silence must be interpreted according to a given context. This means that the silence in the NT about Jesus' marital status must be interpreted according to the context of a Judaism for which marriage was the norm. The silence of the NT on the subject arises from the fact that the earliest traditions about Jesus simply took for granted that Jesus was married.

It is to Phipps's credit that he focuses on a question that is often ignored or treated in passing. He also makes us face the fact that, no matter what our final decision about the marital status of Jesus, the NT is simply silent on the question. Hence any position will have to be based on indirect arguments that seek to solve the riddle of a largely unnoticed sphinx. This complex situation is compounded for those who argue that Jesus was not married, for they are put in the notoriously difficult position of trying to prove a negative in ancient history. Despite this difficulty, I nevertheless think that there are solid reasons for holding that Jesus was celibate.

(1) First of all, there is the argument about context. To be sure, the silence of the NT can be meaningful only when interpreted in a given context. But which context should be looked at first and given prominence? Phipps appeals to a curiously homogenized Judaism as the primary context for interpreting the NT's silence about Jesus' wife and children. Methodologically, though, the immediate context of the NT's silence must be the NT's statements, i.e., what the NT *does* say about Jesus and his familial relations. After all, the NT is far from silent about Jesus' other family ties, as we have seen in Chapter 8 (dealing with the Infancy Narratives) and earlier in this chapter (dealing with the brothers and sisters of Jesus). Indeed, from the various testimonies of Mark, Matthew, Luke, John, Paul, and Acts, we learn about Jesus' mother, named Mary, about his putative father, named Joseph, about his four brothers, named James, Joses, Jude, and Simon, and about his unnamed sisters. Moreover, the 2d-century Jewish Christian writer Hegesippus tells us about Clopas, an uncle of Jesus, and Symeon, a cousin. We also hear from the NT a good deal about the various women who followed Jesus during his public ministry: Mary Magdalene, Joanna the wife of Chuza, the steward of Herod, Susanna (Luke 8:2–3), Mary, the mother of

James the Less and Joses, Salome (Mark 14:20), and the mother of the sons of Zebedee (Matt 20:20; 27:56).

Granted this surprising loquacity of the NT and the early Church about both the family of Jesus and the women who were close to him, the silence of the NT about a supposed wife of Jesus (to say nothing of children) does take on significance—but hardly the significance Phipps wants. In face of the multiple relationships of blood and belief, both male and female, that the NT and Hegesippus report, the total silence about a wife or children of Jesus, named or unnamed, has an easy and obvious explanation: none existed. In my opinion, it is not by accident the Gospels at times say or intimate that some of Jesus' disciples left their wives and/or children (at least temporarily), while never speaking of that precise sacrifice in his own case.[48] He had made an earlier and more radical sacrifice.

Phipps objects that, in early rabbinic literature, we hear nothing about the wives of Hillel and Shammai, yet no one doubts that these two great Jewish teachers were married. From what we have just seen, though, the case of Jesus, simply from the viewpoint of literary evidence, is not the same as that of Hillel and Shammai. We do not have lengthy narrative works purporting to describe a year or more in the active ministry of Hillel or Shammai. The early references to Hillel and Shammai do not name all sorts of relatives and female friends while remaining strangely silent about their wives. The very different context and content of the Gospel narratives do make the silence about Jesus' wife and children telling. And what it seems to tell us is that there was no wife and no children.[49]

Strictly speaking, of course, this judgment derives from and refers to Jesus' life during his public ministry. However, the clashes that occur with regard to his hometown roots bring him (directly or indirectly, personally or simply by name) into contact with his putative father, his mother, his brothers, and his sisters, not to mention the townspeople of Nazareth. In this context, the absence of any reference to wife or children probably indicates that there was no wife or child in his past life in Nazareth.

(2) But what of the larger context of Judaism to which Phipps appeals? First, we should remember what we saw when we considered the criterion of continuity in Chapter 6. Just as it would be wrong to portray Jesus as someone totally "discontinuous" from the Judaism of his day, so it is questionable, in the light of authentic material from the

Gospels, to portray him as always in agreement with his Jewish milieu. He did not wind up crucified for being so agreeable.

More to the point, one must always ask: With what sect, branch, stream, or tendency of 1st-century Judaism was Jesus "continuous" or "discontinuous"—and under what aspect? The Judaism of the early 1st century A.D. was remarkably rich and complex in the variety of its thought and expression. One wonders whether Phipps appreciates this wide diversity sufficiently as he constructs a fairly monochromatic Judaism by putting together material from the OT, Philo, Josephus, the Essenes, and the rabbis.[50] This is a critical point, since it may well be that the stream within 1st-century Judaism that emerged triumphant in later rabbinic Judaism may not have been representative of all the wings of Judaism when it came to sex and marriage. We cannot be sure a priori that, for example, Pharisaic Judaism had the same view of celibacy and marriage as did various esoteric, prophetic, apocalyptic, or mystical currents within the Judaism of Jesus' day.

It is not by accident that Phipps has to struggle mightily to bring the Essene movement within his construct of a monochromatic Judaism, especially when it comes to marriage. If we simply apply to 1st-century Jewish and pagan material the same criterion of multiple attestation that we apply to the Gospels, we have good grounds for thinking that some Essenes, at least for some period in the movement's history, did practice celibacy. Just as a matter of fact, a Jew from 1st-century Palestine (Josephus), a Jew from the 1st-century Diaspora (Philo), and a highly educated 1st-century pagan (Pliny the Elder) all claimed, in one way or another, that most, if not all, Essenes were celibates.[51]

Josephus has an intriguingly complicated explanation of Essene celibacy in *The Jewish War* (*J.W.* 2.8.2 §120–21). He tells us that the main group of Essenes, spread throughout various cities of Palestine, formed communities of ascetics. While they did not condemn marriage for humanity in general, since it was necessary for the propagation of the race, they felt contempt (*hyperopsia*) for it in their own lives. They did, however, adopt young children, apparently as one way of replenishing their own numbers. Josephus presents the Essenes' abstinence from marriage as arising from a virtuous control of all passions and a suspicion about a woman's ability to be faithful to one husband.

Nevertheless, at the end of his treatment of the Essenes, Josephus admits that there is another "order" (*tagma*) of Essenes, who observe the same customs as other Essenes except in the case of marriage. They view abstinence from marriage as contrary to the main function of biological life, namely, its prolongation by procreation. Hence, these Essenes do marry, although their wives must undergo a probationary period of three years, and both sexes practice restraint within marriage.

Josephus also gives a shorter description of the Essenes in *The Jewish Antiquities (Ant.* 18.1.5 §18–22). In passing he mentions that the Essenes bring neither wives nor slaves into their community; the reason for not having wives is that they would create dissensions (§21). No mention is made of a group of Essenes that allows marriage.

Philo speaks of the Essenes in two major passages. In a fragment of his *Hypothetica* (preserved in Eusebius' *Praeparatio Evangelica* 8.11.1–18, especially 14),[52] he states that the Essenes banned marriage altogether, thus agreeing with Josephus' shorter notice in the *Antiquities.* However, Philo stresses that Essenes are men of middle to old age, people who are "no longer" under the sway of bodily passions. These older men are said to avoid marriage because they are set on practicing self-control. No one among the Essenes takes a wife because a wife is selfish, jealous, and demanding. All this would threaten the common life of the brotherhood. In this fragment, one gets the impression that most of the Essenes would have been widowers, separated, or divorced individuals. But were all of them older men who had been previously married?

In the second relevant passage, from *Every Good Man Is Free (Quod Omnis Probus Liber* 12–13 §75–91), Philo does speak of various ages in the brotherhood, "the young men placed below the older men in rank" (§81). Rejection of marriage is not explicitly mentioned, but the emphasis on both close communal living and perfect purity seems to presuppose it.

However, the Essenes are not the only celibates of whom Philo has knowledge. He dedicates a whole work *(On the Contemplative Life [De Vita Contemplativa])* to another ascetic group, the Therapeutae, who are at home in Egypt.[53] The Therapeutae bear various resemblances to the Essenes of Palestine, and it is not clear whether they are a branch of the Essenes or simply a similar Jewish movement. The Therapeutae practice abstinence and self-control; Philo intimates that some of them have left behind their family and friends, including their children and wives (2 §18). Yet he also states that some of the Therapeutae have from an early age pursued this contemplative branch of philosophy (8 §67), and he speaks elsewhere of the young men in the group (10 §77). According to Philo, there is also a female branch of the Therapeutae that shares Sabbath worship with the males, though with a partition between them

(3 §32–33). Most of the women are specifically said to be elderly virgins (8 §68), who have voluntarily preserved their chastity.

Pliny the Elder (ca. A.D. 23–79) mentions the Essenes in his *Natural History* (5.73.1–3). He describes them as "a people living apart . . . without any woman, having renounced all sexual love . . . an eternal race in which no one is born."[54] Unlike Josephus and Philo, Pliny pointedly places the Essenes near the western shore of the Dead Sea. Therefore, in all probability he is referring to the Qumran community in particular.

Thus, for all their differences, the Palestinian Jew, the Diaspora Jew, and the pagan Roman, all writing in the 1st century A.D., agree that some sort of celibacy was practiced at least by some Essenes. It may well be that the practice of celibacy was more pronounced at certain periods of the movement than at others. Josephus may indicate that, while most groups of Essenes living in community were celibate males, at least some Essenes, at least at certain periods, accepted marriage. Then, too, the celibate males may well have been a mixed group of widowers, divorced men, men who had abandoned their families, and young men who had started their spiritual ascetic journey quite early in life (like Josephus) and who persevered in it (unlike Josephus).

Qumran, the "monastery" at the northwest corner of the Dead Sea in the Judean wilderness, was one concrete expression of the larger Essene movement. It poses special problems because of the various community documents discovered in its monastery; some are fragmentary, and all must be read with an eye to heterogeneous sources that may have been incorporated into the works we possess.[55] Like the Essene movement of which it was a part—indeed, perhaps the "motherhouse"— Qumran may have known different practices with regard to marriage and celibacy at different stages of its existence. Possibly even during the same period, some Qumranites practiced celibacy while others did not.[56] All in all, the basically harmonious testimony of Josephus, Philo, and Pliny has convinced many scholars who otherwise differ widely in their views on Qumran that some kind of celibacy was practiced among at least some members of the Qumran community.[57]

The precise reason for the practice of celibacy at Qumran (or among the Essenes in general) is still debated: a Sinai-covenant theology that demanded sexual abstinence in preparation for encounter with God (cf. Exod 19:15); the extension of the rules for priestly cultic purity to the whole community, which was a living temple worshiping God in the company of the angels; or the belief that the group was or would be engaged in a holy war in the company of the angels against the powers of evil at the end of time.[58] Although the misogynistic reasons mentioned by Josephus and Philo have been discounted by some authors as merely an adaptation of Jewish views to the mentality of a Greco-Roman audience, misogynistic passages can be found in the OT, the intertestamental literature, and the rabbis; it is not impossible that misogyny played a role at Qumran as well. In general, it is safe to say that, during a time of crisis in Israel's social and religious institutions, a number of these factors converged to create an atmosphere conducive to the practice of celibacy among certain marginal Jewish groups.

All in all, then, it is more probable that at least some Essenes in the 1st centuries B.C. and A.D. did practice celibacy. We can certainly say without fear of contradiction that two prominent Jewish authors of the 1st century A.D., Josephus and Philo, spoke of celibacy among some marginal Jewish groups (Essenes and Therapeutae) as a fact. More to the point, far from being shocked or disgusted by the idea of celibacy, both Jews include it in their highly laudatory description of the Essenes—as in fact does Pliny. Thus, not only does the silence of the NT about a supposed wife or child of Jesus point in the opposite direction from what Phipps suggests; the full range of 1st-century Judaism does not supply, as Phipps would have it, a milieu totally opposed to religious celibacy. Needless to say, celibacy was a most unusual life style, practiced by only a few, including one or two marginal groups. But we should not be totally incredulous if the marginal Jew we pursue, a Jew so unusual in so many ways, should manifest his marginality by celibacy as well.

(3) But the Essenes, Qumran, and the Therapeutae were not the only examples of Jewish religious celibates who were considered in a reverent light around the time of Jesus. The OT was not lacking in at least one celibate religious figure, and later interpretation of the OT added some others. The one case from the OT is the tragic prophet Jeremiah. Far from being some positive religious commitment, celibacy was for Jeremiah a tragic personal sign, a lived-out prophetic symbol of the destruction of life that awaited the sinful people of Judah (Jer 16:1–4).[59] We have, then, at least one example of an OT prophet for whom celibacy was not a minor matter, an optional life style. It was, by the order of Yahweh, a very literal and painful "embodiment" of Jeremiah's prophetic message of judgment, pronouncing imminent doom as punishment for the apostasy of God's people.[60]

We should not be completely surprised that another fiery prophet of judgment around the time of Jesus also seems to have been celibate, namely, John the Baptist. Granted, our sources do not speak explicitly of John's celibacy; as usual, we are left with arguments from indirection and inference. But, even apart from Luke's picture of the boy John being raised in the wilderness until the time he began his ministry (at Qumran?),[61] the mere fact that this ascetic prophet feeding on locusts and wild honey roamed up and down the Jordan Valley and the Judean wilderness, apparently with no fixed abode as he proclaimed a radical message of imminent judgment on Israel, makes it probable that John was a celibate (Mark 1:4-8).

It is fitting that such a figure should stress that Jews should not trust in blood ties and descent from Abraham (see the Q saying in Matt 3:7-10 || Luke 3:7-9). This Q tradition would certainly fit in with the picture Luke implicitly presents: the young John had in effect turned his back on his duty to succeed his father Zechariah as priest and to continue the priestly line by marriage and progeny (Luke 1:80; 3:2). It may be no accident that Mark closes the story of John's execution by Antipas with the words: ". . . his [John's] disciples came and took his corpse and laid it in a tomb" (6:29). Without intending to reflect on the fact directly, Mark may be in effect seconding what Luke implies: there was no wife, children, or other family around John to see to one of the most sacred obligations incumbent on family members in Judaism: arranging for and participating in the obsequies of a husband or parent. In his radical itinerant prophetic ministry, John may have consciously been imitating Elijah, an OT itinerant prophet of judgment, who not only was interpreted as an eschatological figure in later Judaism (as early as Malachi and Ben Sira) but was also interpreted as a celibate by various patristic writers (e.g., Ambrose and Jerome).

Judaism saw nothing wrong in portraying as celibate the great primordial prophet, seer, and lawgiver Moses (though only after the Lord had begun to speak to him). We see this interpretation already beginning to develop in Philo in the 1st century A.D.[62] What is more surprising is that this idea is also reflected in various rabbinic passages. The gist of the tradition is an a fortiori argument. If the Israelites at Sinai had to abstain from women temporarily to prepare for God's brief, once-and-for-all address to them, how much more should Moses be permanently chaste, since God spoke regularly to him (see, e.g., *b. Šabb.* 87a).[63] The same tradition, but from the viewpoint of the deprived wife, is related in the *Sipre on Numbers 12.1* (99).[64] Since the rabbis in general were unsympathetic—not to say hostile—to religious celibacy, the survival of this

Moses tradition even in later rabbinic writings argues that the tradition was long-lived and widespread by the time of the rabbis. We should note once again the typology seen in Jeremiah, John the Baptist, and the recycled Moses figure: the prophet who directly receives divine revelation that is to be communicated to his beloved yet sinful people Israel finds his whole life radically altered by his prophetic vocation. This alteration, this being set apart by and for God's Word, is embodied graphically in the rare, awesome, and—for many Jews—terrible vocation of celibacy.

While accepting the idea of an ancient figure like Moses as celibate (at least during his ministry to Israel), the rabbis did not as a general rule allow celibacy among their rabbinic colleagues and disciples. Rabbi Eliezer ben Hyrcanus (end of 1st century A.D.) is said to have equated a man's refusal to procreate offspring with murder. One rare exception, according to the same rabbinic passage, was Rabbi Simeon ben Azzai (a younger contemporary of Eliezer ben Hyrcanus), who paradoxically recommended marriage and procreation, though he himself remained unmarried. When accused of not practicing what he preached, he replied: "My soul is in love with the Torah. The world can be carried on by others" (*b. Yebam.* 63b).[65]

That such a "deviant" tradition could be enshrined in the Babylonian Talmud may suggest that celibacy, though frowned upon by the rabbis, was not totally stamped out in Judaism during the centuries immediately following the Baptist and Jesus. More to the point, though ben Azzai is hardly a Jeremiah or a Baptist, his rationale for celibacy is at root similar to that of the more overtly prophetic figures: an all-consuming commitment to God's word in one's whole life precludes the usual path of marriage and child-rearing. In view of this "marginal" tradition in early Judaism, it is hardly surprising that the Jewish scholar Geza Vermes has no difficulty in seeing Jesus as celibate and explaining his unusual state by his prophetic call and the reception of the Spirit.[66]

(4) As long as we are reviewing the narrower and broader contexts of Jesus' celibacy in Judaism, we might do well to note, simply in passing, that "vocational celibacy" was not entirely unknown in the pagan Greco-Roman world of the 1st century A.D. Philosophical and religious figures might, for various reasons, remain unmarried. The Stoic philosopher Epictetus[67] and the mystic Pythagorean and itinerant teacher Apollonius of Tyana[68] come readily to mind, not to mention the ideal Cynic philosopher whom Epictetus extols.[69] When we correlate all these tendencies, we notice that the 1st century A.D. was populated by some

striking celibate individuals and groups: some Essenes and Qumranites, the Therapeutae, John the Baptist, Jesus, Paul,[70] Epictetus, Apollonius, and various wandering Cynics. Celibacy was always a rare and sometimes offensive choice in the 1st century A.D. But it was a viable choice.[71]

We cannot be sure why Jesus of Nazareth chose a celibate life. Some of the motives we have seen (the incorporation of the ideal of priestly cultic purity into lay spirituality, a holy-war ideology, misogyny) do not square with his basic message and conduct. Jesus did not share the Pharisees' zeal for extensive purity rules, to say nothing of the extremism of the superobservant Essenes. His message of peace hardly jibed with a theological mind set or policy laden with war imagery. Finally, he stood out in his day because of his easy association with female disciples and other women. If Jesus' celibacy is something of a question mark for us, perhaps Jesus intended it to be just that for his contemporaries. Mirroring his parabolic speech, and like his easy fellowship with the socially and spiritually marginalized in Palestine, his celibacy was a parable in action, an embodiment of a riddle-like message meant to disturb people and provoke them to thought—both about Jesus and about themselves.

To find any more precise explanation of what Jesus intended by his celibacy forces us to anticipate a little of what we shall see in Part Three of this quest. A number of scholars have suggested that ideas about the renewal of the Sinai covenant, the reconstitution of the true Israel, and fierce eschatological expectation helped fuel not only the general theological outlook of the Essenes but also their practice of celibacy in particular. While Jesus did not share all the theological views of the Essenes, we do find in his teaching and action an eschatological concern centered on the people Israel. Whatever else Jesus intended, he was intent on gathering together an Israel that had been fragmented by sin and on preparing it by repentance for the final coming of God's kingdom. Jesus' sense of having a unique prophetic call to give himself totally to this mission to Israel in the final, critical moment of its history may explain, at least in part, his celibacy.

Furthermore, it is possible that Jesus refers to his total, all-consuming commitment to proclaiming and realizing the kingdom of God in the puzzling saying of Matt 19:12: "There are eunuchs such as were born so from [their] mother's womb, and there are eunuchs such as were made eunuchs by men, and there are eunuchs such as make themselves eunuchs [literally: 'who eunuchize themselves'] because of [or: with a view to] the kingdom of heaven."[72] Granted, it is possible that this saying was created by the early Church to justify a state of voluntary religious celibacy among some of its members.[73] Indeed, whether or not it originated in such a context, it no doubt functioned as a justification for voluntary celibacy in Matthew's church and is so understood in his Gospel.

Yet, at the very least, the present position of Matt 19:12, connected as it is with a dispute over divorce, is a redactional creation of Matthew. In Matt 19:3–9, Matthew takes over and reformulates the dispute over divorce that he found in Mark 10:1–12. At the end of the Marcan story, which concludes with Jesus' saying equating divorce and remarriage with adultery (vv 11–12), Mark proceeds immediately to the story of Jesus blessing the children (Mark 10:13–16). As so often happens in the second half of the Matthean Gospel, Matthew basically follows Mark's order; but in between the dispute on divorce and the blessing of the children, Matthew inserts the eunuch saying with its introductory verses (Matt 19:10–12). This connection of the eunuch saying to Jesus' teaching on divorce occurs nowhere else in the many varied forms of the NT teaching on divorce. The connection is thus clearly of Matthew's own making. The saying about eunuchs originally had nothing to do with the saying about divorce.

Moreover, the eunuch logion in v 12 has its own distinctive form and vocabulary, not to mention thought-content, that mark it off from the preceding discussion of marriage and divorce, and even from the immediately preceding vv 10–11. As Stephenson H. Brooks points out in his careful analysis of the M tradition in Matthew's Gospel, vv 10–11, which connect the eunuch saying with the Marcan dispute on divorce, are most likely Matthew's redactional creation, acting as a bridge between the divorce question and the very different matter of voluntary celibacy.[74] Brooks correctly notes that "Matthew nowhere else shows any knowledge of, or concern with, the subject of eunuchs, or the possibility of celibacy as a means of expressing dedication to the Kingdom of Heaven."[75] The noun "eunuch" and the verb "to castrate" (literally, "to eunuchize") occur only here in Matthew's Gospel. Indeed, "eunuch" occurs nowhere else in the NT with the exception of the story of the Ethiopian eunuch (Acts 8:27–39, where the noun may not have its literal sense but may rather signify a royal official); the verb "to castrate" *(eunouchizō)* occurs absolutely nowhere else in the NT.[76] All signs therefore point to v 12 being not Matthean redaction[77] but rather a saying that Matthew has inherited from the special oral tradition of his community and has attached, as best he can, to a context dealing with the opposite theme of marriage.[78]

In fact, so striking, indeed shocking and violent—and so unparalleled in 1st-century Judaism or Christianity—is the imagery of a religious celibate as someone who "eunuchizes" himself for the kingdom of heaven that one might argue, by the criteria of embarrassment and discontinuity, that this offensively graphic metaphor for celibacy goes back to the unconventional and shocking Jesus.[79]

On the Jewish side, neither Josephus nor Philo, who extol the celibate life of the Essenes and/or Therapeutae, nor the later rabbis, who generally speak against religious celibacy, use this metaphor, and understandably so. When the later rabbis do give reasons for rejecting celibacy, the rationale usually portrays failure to procreate as equivalent to shedding blood or diminishing the divine image (so, e.g., *b. Yebam.* 63b).

On the Christian side, it is first of all remarkable how relatively infrequent an explicit treatment of voluntary religious celibacy or virginity is in the NT. The only lengthy exposition in the whole of the NT is found in 1 Cor 7:7–8,25–40, and not all exegetes are agreed on which verses actually deal with virgins (male or female) and/or widows and widowers.[80] The only other NT passage that may speak of voluntary virginity (and only for males) is Rev 14:4 ("These are those [men] who were not defiled with women, for they are virgins *[parthenoi].*" But whether this text refers literally to a special group of virgins in the Church or rather symbolically either to martyrs or to the whole Church as the virgin bride of Christ is open to debate.[81] In any case, neither Paul nor the Book of Revelation seeks to explain, defend, or extol the celibate state with the strange praise that celibates are people who, metaphorically speaking, have castrated themselves.[82]

To go one step further: this violent imagery could possibly derive from the fact that the logion echoes slurs and jibes aimed at the celibate Jesus—or possibly some of his disciples—as he hobnobbed with the religious low life of Palestine and traveled around the countryside with a strangely mixed entourage of men and women "on leave" from their spouses. At any rate, Matt 19:12 certainly coheres perfectly with the probability that Jesus was celibate, a probability that we have established on other grounds. In my opinion, then, the life of the celibate Jesus provides the most likely context for the original *Sitz im Leben* of the eunuch logion, however useful it may have proved later for celibates in Matthew's church.[83] It is the only echo of Jesus' celibate life style in his recorded sayings. On the whole, then, the criteria of embarrassment, discontinuity, and coherence argue impressively for the position that the eunuch saying, in some form or other, derives ultimately from Jesus himself.[84]

To sum up: we cannot be absolutely sure whether or not Jesus was married. But the various proximate and remote contexts, in both the NT and Judaism, make the position that Jesus remained celibate on religious grounds the more probable hypothesis. If we may anticipate what we shall see later, Jesus probably interpreted his celibacy as the result of an all-consuming prophetic mission to Israel, seeking to regather the fragmented, sinful people of God into a purified whole in preparation for God's final coming as king. It is therefore possible that Jesus—perhaps with an ironic tone in his voice—counts himself among those "who make themselves eunuchs for the kingdom of heaven." The total silence about wife and children in contexts where his various relatives figure may well indicate that he had never married. But the place and meaning of celibacy in his life before the beginning of the public ministry are questions that go beyond what our sources allow us to know. Any further speculation crosses the border from historical hypothesis into novel writing.[85]

3. JESUS' STATUS AS A LAYMAN

One aspect of Jesus' family background was so obvious to his Jewish contemporaries that, as far as we know, neither he nor they ever commented on it during his lifetime. Yet this aspect has been so overlooked or misunderstood by later Christians that it needs to be emphasized. It is the simple fact that Jesus was born a Jewish layman, conducted his ministry as a Jewish layman, and died a Jewish layman. There is no reliable historical tradition that he was of levitical or priestly descent.[86] In fact, as we saw in Chapter 8, there is good reason for thinking that, even during his lifetime, Jesus was believed to be of Davidic descent. While that might have heightened some Jews' evaluation of him, at the same time it meant that he belonged to the category of "laity" at a time in Israel's history when, whether in Jerusalem or at Qumran, priests, and not the laity, controlled the levers of power. Simply by being a layman from an obscure town in the countryside of Lower Galilee, Jesus was already marginal to the holders of religious power when he set foot in Jerusalem.

It is probably not just a coincidence that, while the Synoptic Gospels present Jesus in frequent conflict with scribes, Pharisees, and local "rulers of synagogues," at least he speaks to these groups on a regular basis. The lines of communication are open, even if they are often red hot. Moreover, in a few instances the rulers, scribes, or Pharisees appear in a neutral or positive light (e.g., Jairus in Mark 5:22–43; the scribe in Mark 12:28–34; the Pharisee in Luke 7:36; and possibly the Pharisees in Luke 13:31). Even Matthew, who makes "scribes and Pharisees" a stock phrase designating the "united front" of Judaism opposed to Jesus, is willing to use the image of "scribe" to describe any follower of Jesus who learns the mysteries of the kingdom of heaven (Matt 13:52).

In contrast, the Synoptic Jesus engages in debate with the Sadducees (made up mostly of the priests and lay aristocracy in Jerusalem) only once, namely, in the dispute over belief in the resurrection of the dead on the last day (Mark 12:18–27 parr.). The encounter is marked by hostility on both sides. The Sadducees seek to make Jesus look ridiculous by proposing a ludicrous question about which of seven brothers at the resurrection will have as wife a woman whom all seven married in this life. Before Jesus replies to their question in detail, he goes out of his way to attack the Sadducees personally: "Is this not the reason why you are in error, namely, that you are ignorant both of the Scripture and of the power of God?" This is a remarkably pointed barb aimed at the priestly guardians of divine revelation and divine power, supposedly centered in the Jerusalem temple.

One need not argue for the historicity of all the details of the material just cited. What is telling is rather the general pattern that emerges. With the Pharisees, the scribes, and the rulers of the synagogues, Jesus engages in regular debate, and sometimes relations can even be friendly. The Synoptics depict Jesus in only one exchange with the priestly party by itself, and it is markedly hostile.[87]

Since John's Gospel places Jesus in Jerusalem more often than the Synoptics do, it is not surprising that Jesus encounters priests more frequently in the Fourth Gospel than in the Synoptics. In John's redactional activity, the "united front" of Judaism at times becomes simply the high priests plus the Pharisees (e.g., 7:45; 11:47). Yet the Pharisee Nicodemus seeks a respectful, if not cordial, exchange of views (John 3:1–15). Nicodemus later defends Jesus before the Jerusalem authorities (7:50–52) and finally helps Joseph of Arimathea in providing Jesus with an honorable burial (19:39–40). No such good intentions or gestures (however benighted or ambivalent) are forthcoming from anyone specifically designated a priest. In John's view, the high priests as a group are totally, irrevocably in the other camp, and no comparatively "irenic" discussion of the Nicodemus type is possible.

Again, we are not concerned at this point with the historicity of particular details or even of whole pericopes. What stands out is the overall pattern that provides a neat correlation between the Synoptics and John on this one point. While Jesus can at times engage in civilized debate or even friendly dialogue with Pharisees, scribes, or "rulers," the priests are never presented in such a positive light. Their hostility is unrelieved; and both the Synoptics and John present the priests, specifically the high priest Caiaphas, as instigating the plot to have Jesus put to death (Mark 14:1-2; Matt 26:57-66; John 11:49-50).

When we consider that the priests as a central power in Judaism had disappeared by the time the Gospels were written[88] and that the Pharisees or their spiritual heirs became the major opponents of Christianity in the last quarter of the 1st century (and appear so especially in Matthew and John), this tendency to allow some "good" Pharisees but no "good" priests may be rooted in the pattern of Jesus' own ministry. The pious laity known as Pharisees and the lay scholars/lawyers/theologians known as scribes[89] were at least acceptable debating partners and sometimes sympathetic listeners. But between Jesus the Galilean peasant layman, who claimed charismatic religious authority outside the recognized channels, and the high priestly families of Jerusalem, whose power depended on controlling the sacred center of Judaism, the temple, there was only unrelieved hostility.

No doubt many aspects of Jesus' background converged to put him on a collision course with Caiaphas and the Jerusalem priesthood: he was a no-account Galilean in conflict with Jerusalem aristocrats; he was (relative to his opponents) a poor peasant in conflict with the urban rich; he was a charismatic wonderworker in conflict with priests very much concerned about preserving the central institutions of their religion and their smooth operation; he was an eschatological prophet promising the coming of God's kingdom in conflict with Sadducean politicians having a vested interest in the status quo. But underneath many of these conflicts lay another conflict: he was a religiously committed layman who seemed to be threatening the power of an entrenched group of priests. That, as well as the other facets of his background, contributed to the final clash in Jerusalem. In short, that Jesus was a layman was not a neutral datum; it played a role in the development and denouement of his drama.

I have purposely emphasized Jesus' status as a layman because Christians are so accustomed to the imagery of Jesus the priest or the "great high priest." We owe this theological vision of Jesus the priest to a highly educated 1st-century Christian, otherwise unknown, who penned the NT Epistle to the Hebrews. Here, and here alone within the NT, Jesus is called a priest and a high priest.[90]

But even our learned author does not try to base his claim that Jesus is a priest on levitical lineage. Instead, Jesus is specifically said to be of the tribe of Judah, not Levi; and our author readily admits that the Jewish priesthood had nothing to do with the lineage of Judah (Heb 7:11–14). Hence the author of Hebrews must engage in a somewhat contorted hermeneutic to explain how Jesus obtained a priestly office superior to the levitical one, namely, a priesthood like that of Melchizedek (7:15–28).

Yet no sooner does our author finish his exposition of Christ's priesthood according to the order of Melchizedek than he makes an observation often forgotten by Christian theologians, but in perfect harmony with what we have seen in the Gospels. Having just referred to Jesus as a priest seated at the right hand of God (in virtue of Jesus' exaltation to heaven after his death), the author explains: "For if he [Jesus] were on earth, he would not be a priest." This is obvious to our author, since in his theology Jesus becomes a priest only by undergoing a sacrificial death on the cross and then entering the heavenly sanctuary. In other words, in the Epistle to the Hebrews, Jesus' atoning sacrifice is also his ordination sacrifice.

Thus, for all the theology of Christ the high priest in Hebrews, the epistle in no way contradicts the Gospel presentation of Jesus as a Jewish layman. Rather, Hebrews confirms that picture: from a Jewish point of view, Jesus could not count as a priest (7:14). Indeed, Hebrews goes on to say that, even from a *Christian* point of view, Jesus was not a priest during his earthly ministry (8:4). He achieved that status in Christian eyes only by his death and exaltation. This point must be stressed because, in some Christian quarters, the Epistle to the Hebrews has been misinterpreted to mean that Jesus was a priest during his earthly life. That is to misunderstand the author's teaching that Jesus' incarnation as a true human being, sharing all our human sufferings and even our death, equipped him with that total solidarity with humanity—and, concretely, with a true human body—that made possible his death and exaltation (Heb 2:5–18; 4:14–5:10; 9:23–10:18). His human life on earth was thus the necessary precondition, but not the constitutive factor, of his becoming a priest. Therefore, even for the Epistle to the Hebrews, while Jesus was on earth, he was a Jewish layman, not a priest.

Thus, as we read through the Gospels, we must remember that Jesus, the layman who confronts the various authorities of Judaism, had no formal or official basis for his own authority. All the more astounding did that authority seem, and all the more did it become a source of contention (e.g., Mark 1:21–28; 11:27–33; John 2:18), especially for the priests in Jerusalem. But apart from certain clashes in Jerusalem, priests were not Jesus' usual dialogue partners. When they did talk with him, the tone was harsh on both sides.

It is perhaps in this atmosphere of mutual hostility that we should hear the parable of the Good Samaritan (Luke 10:30–37), with its slighting references to the Jerusalem priest and Levite who pass by their fellow Jew—presumably a layman—in need (vv 31–32). If we visualize Jesus the Galilean layman telling this story to other Galilean lay people, the parable takes on an anticlerical tone.[91]

None of these remarks should be taken as falling back into the old stereotype of Galileans as obstreperous rebels who were unconcerned about worship in the Jerusalem temple. As Sean Freyne has shown, Galilean Jews were faithful to the duty of pilgrimage to the Jerusalem temple.[92] It was there, more than anywhere else, that they might be carried away with nationalistic and religious fervor. But reverence toward the central place of worship and its cult by no means dictated an uncritical stance toward the rich and worldly priestly families in Jerusalem. A pious laity, dedicated to the ideals of a holy priesthood conducting pure worship, can for that very reason be all the more critical of the flesh-and-blood priests before their eyes. Christianity can certainly supply parallel phenomena of a devout laity criticizing a corrupt clergy, as can also the Talmud. We should think of Jesus as belonging to a pious Jewish laity that regularly went up to Jerusalem to worship even as it bewailed the failings of at least the upper-level priests who officiated there. The fact that his ministry made Jesus stand out from the run-of-the-mill laity made his criticism much more dangerous—for the priests and for himself.

4. A SUMMARY OF THE ORIGINS AND "HIDDEN YEARS" OF JESUS

It is time to summarize what we have been able to distill from our sources in the last three chapters.

During the reign of Herod the Great, and probably toward its end (ca. 7–4 B.C.), Jesus was born in the hill town of Nazareth in Lower Galilee. His mother was Mary, his putative father, Joseph. We hear of four brothers of Jesus (James, Joses, Jude, and Simon) and at least two unnamed sisters. It may be significant that all the names in the family hark back to the glorious days of the patriarchs, the exodus, and the conquest of the Promised Land. Jesus' family may have shared in the reawakening of Jewish national and religious identity that looked forward to the restoration of Israel in its full glory. That is all the more likely if Joseph claimed to be a descendant of King David. At any rate, judging by the fiercely religious focus of Jesus' life once it becomes visible to us, we may reasonably suppose that his family had been deeply devout Jews of a peasant Galilean type: firmly committed to the basic practices of the Mosaic Law (especially its "boundary symbols" of circumcision, Sabbath, and pilgrimage to the Jerusalem temple), but not given to the niceties of Pharisaic observance.

As the firstborn son, Jesus would have been the object of Joseph's special attention, both in training him for a trade and in seeing to his religious education. The fact that Joseph is notably absent during the public ministry is best explained by the traditional idea that he had already died. Jesus' mother, brothers, and sisters survived into the period of the ministry, though not without some tension between themselves and Jesus. We are specifically told by various evangelists that the family thought Jesus mad (Mark 3:21), or that his brothers did not believe in him (John 7:5), or that Jesus refused a request of his family to see him (Mark 3:31–35 parr.).[93] It is therefore all the more startling, when we glance ahead to the history of the early Church, to find Jesus' brother James prominent in an early creedal formula listing witnesses to the resurrection (1 Cor 15:7) and in the leadership of the Jerusalem church (Gal 1:19; 2:9,12; Acts 15:13–21; 21:18)—with other family members following in his steps. In the face of all this information about members of

Jesus' family, the total silence about a wife or children is best taken as indicating that Jesus chose the highly unusual—but not unknown—path of celibacy.

Growing up in Nazareth, Jesus would have spoken Aramaic as his everyday tongue, while also learning some Hebrew from the local synagogue services and perhaps more Hebrew from formal instruction provided by his father. As he started to learn the trade of woodworker from Joseph, he would have found it useful or even necessary to acquire some Greek phrases for business purposes. Frequent visits by his family to Jerusalem for the great feasts would have exposed him to more Greek in that polyglot city. Although he might have used Greek when dealing with Gentiles, and Hebrew when debating the meaning of Scripture with professional scribes, the bulk of his teaching, directed as it was to ordinary Palestinian Jews, would have been delivered in Aramaic.

Jesus' teaching was delivered orally, and oral teaching could in theory have been the sole conduit of Jesus' own education in the Scriptures and Jewish traditions. In the oral popular culture in which he grew up and later taught, literacy was not an absolute necessity for common people. Yet the matrix of a devout Jewish family, Jesus' own preoccupation with the Jewish religion, and the debates over Scripture that Jesus held with professional scribes and pious Pharisees during his ministry all make his ability to read the sacred text a likely hypothesis.

Jesus the woodworker of Nazareth was poor by our modern American standards, though relative to his own society he was no poorer than the vast majority of Galileans. Actually, not knowing the grinding destitution of the dispossessed farmer, the city beggar, the rural day laborer, or the rural slave, he was not at the bottom of the socioeconomic ladder. While we would find the economic and political realities of Antipas' Galilee unbearable, they were on the whole preferable to the chaotic last days of Herod the Great, the chaotic first days of the Jewish War in the late sixties, or the sense of oppression by foreigners that the presence of the Roman prefect aroused in Judea. Strange though it may seem, Jesus grew up and conducted much of his ministry in an uncommonly peaceful oasis sheltered from the desert whirlwind that was most of Palestinian history. Despite intriguing hypotheses about Jesus the master builder traveling far and wide or imbibing Greek drama at the theater in Sepphoris, all signs point to an uneventful adolescence and adulthood spent at woodworking in Nazareth. However galling the Gospels' silence about Jesus' "hidden years" may be, the silence may have a simple explanation: nothing much happened. The shoot out of the stump of David was sprouting slowly and silently.

Jesus in Nazareth was insufferably ordinary, and his ordinariness included the ordinary status of a layman, without any special religious credentials or "power base." As a Galilean layman, he would have appeared at first negligible to the high priestly families in Jerusalem—until he began to appear dangerous. Jesus' frequent visits to Jerusalem during his ministry may have fueled a rapidly increasing, mutual hostility between the Jerusalem priests and the Galilean layman.

As we glance back over this summary, one deficiency should be glaring to any reader with a historical sense. Our overview wanders in a historical twilight zone in the sense that almost no chronological markers light the path Jesus trod. History is more than chronicle, to be sure; but there can be no history without chronology serving as one of its bases. To round off our survey of the origins and background of Jesus, and to open up the way to our study of the public ministry, we will conclude Part Two with an attempt to fix some key dates in the life of Jesus.

[1] On this social dynamic, called technically "dyadic personality," see Bruce J. Malina, *The New Testament World* (Atlanta: John Knox, 1981) 51–60.

[2] For example, Jerome (at times) identified "Mary of Clopas" (John 19:25) as daughter of Clopas and sister of Mary the mother of Jesus (see Brown et al., *Mary in the New Testament*, 67 n. 125). Thomas the Apostle is identified as the twin brother of Jesus in more than one gnosticizing work (e.g., in the Greek version of *The Acts of Thomas* and in the Nag Hammadi work, *The Book of Thomas the Contender*). Further "identifications" in Christian literature are discussed by Josef Blinzler, *Die Brüder und Schwestern Jesu* (SBS 21; 2d ed.; Stuttgart: KBW, 1967) 31–35.

[3] See Chapter 8, under section 2A.

[4] See Chapter 9, under section 4.

[5] Any such explanation would still have to face the curious formulation of Jesus' saying in Mark 3:35: "Whoever does the will of God, he is my brother and sister and mother." The presence of the word "sister" is unmotivated by the immediate context; the preceding story has spoken only of Jesus' mother and brothers. The addition of sister in the concluding statement of Jesus (the "punch line" of this apophthegm) probably intends to underline the general truth of what Jesus says by including all of Jesus' immediate earthly relatives. Granted such a thrust to the saying, the absence of any mention of Jesus' father is most naturally explained by Joseph's having already died.

[6] It is already hinted at in the *Protevangelium Jacobi*, where Joseph is presented as very old at the time of his espousal to the virgin Mary. It is clearly affirmed in the 4th-century *History of Joseph the Carpenter* and by Epiphanius, who claims in his *Panarion* 3.78.10 (completed ca. A.D. 377) that Joseph died soon after the visit of the twelve-year-old Jesus to Jerusalem narrated in Luke 2. For a collection and analysis of patristic texts dealing with Joseph, see F.-G. Bertrand and G. Ponton, "Textes patristiques sur saint Joseph," *Cahiers de Joséphologie* 3 (1955) 141–74; 4 (1956) 325–57; 5 (1957) 125–67, 289–320; 6 (1958) 139–79, 265–321; 7 (1959) 151–72, 275–333; 8 (1960) 171–86, 347–74; 9 (1961) 333–57; 10 (1962) 149–82. Speculation on the time of the death of Joseph among traditional Catholic authors is summarized in the (largely uncritical) book of Adelmo Marrani, *S. Giuseppe nella scrittura e nella vita della chiesa* (Francavilla a Mare: Edizioni Paoline, 1967) 172–75.

[7] Complete skepticism on the question of the time of Joseph's death is expressed by Lorenz Oberlinner, *Historische Überlieferung und christologische Aussage* (FB 19; Stuttgart: KBW, 1975) 73–78. Oberlinner does well to stress the great distance that lies between redactional statements (or silences) in our Gospels and the historical events in the life of Jesus. However, (1) in Oberlinner's presentation the distance threatens at times to become an unbridgeable gulf; (2) he does not take seriously the converging evidence of the notable silences found in the Four Gospels and Acts, all of which have references to the mother and brothers (and sometimes the sisters).

[8] In John's Gospel, "the Jews" ask rhetorically: "Is this fellow not Jesus the son of Joseph, whose father and mother we know?" (John 6:42). At first glance, this might seem to imply that, in the evangelist's mind, both parents were still living during the public ministry. But the evangelist himself seems to think otherwise. Near the beginning of the public ministry, he presents Jesus descending from Cana to Capernaum with an "entourage" made up of "his mother, his brothers, and his disciples." The absence of any mention of Joseph in such an all-inclusive group is striking. Confirming the impression that John considers Joseph dead is Jesus' commendation of his mother to the beloved disciple at the cross: "From that hour the [beloved] disciple took her [the mother of Jesus] into his care [or home]" (John 19:27). That makes no sense if Joseph, according to the evangelist, is still living. Hence the question of "the Jews" in 6:42 must be understood as a very general objection, intended to counter Jesus' implicit claim to preexistence and incarnation in the bread-of-life discourse by appealing to his well-known human origins.

[9] Counting the four named brothers and at least two female siblings among the unnamed but plural "sisters" in Mark 6:3. As we shall see, though, the exact nature of these "brothers" and "sisters" has been disputed down through the centuries; hence my formulation "if it be granted that . . . ."

[10] The patristic witness of Hegesippus, Tertullian, and Irenaeus in favor of the idea of true siblings will be given more detailed consideration below.

[11] I stress the distinction between "half brother" and "stepbrother" because the otherwise fine treatment of this question in *Mary in the New Testament* confuses the two terms; see, e.g., pp. 65 and 67 n. 125; similarly, Brown, *The Birth of the Messiah*, 132; Fitzmyer, *The Gospel According to Luke*, 1. 724.

[12] However, those Protestants who hold to a literal interpretation of the virginal conception of Jesus by Mary (e.g., many low-church evangelicals) would seem committed to the logical conclusion that the brothers and sisters of Jesus were only half brothers and half sisters (i.e., with only one common biological parent).

[13] Pesch, *Das Markusevangelium*, 1. 322–25.

[14] See the remark in *Mary in the New Testament*, 72 n. 139.

[15] It cannot be stressed too often that, for reasons of method, this book *prescinds* from faith and Church teaching as sources of knowledge, but by no means *denies* them.

[16] Literally, "he did not know her." As many commentators note, this is a typically Semitic expression for sexual intercourse. Hebrew regularly uses the verb *yāda^c* ("know") for this idea. See the obvious parallel in Gen 4:1: "And the man [Adam] knew *[yāda^c]* Eve his wife and she conceived and bore Cain." However, ancient Greek also used "know" as a euphemism for sexual intercourse; see Heraclides, *Peri Politeias Athēnaiōn* 64: *tas te koras pro tou gamiskesthai autas eginōsken* ("he used to know [=have sex with] the young girls before they were married"). A critical edition of the text may be found in Valentine Rose, *Aristote-*

lis qui ferebantur librorum fragmenta (Leipzig: Teubner, 1886) 383. W. Bauer's Greek dictionary adds references to Menander and Plutarch *(s.v. ginōskō)*.

[17] The use of the imperfect verb (literally, "he was not knowing her") may be meant to emphasize that Joseph had absolutely no sexual relations with Mary during the entire period of conception and gestation.

[18] This text, like the rest of the NT, never takes up the later theological concept of *virginitas in partu*, the miraculous preservation of Mary's physical virginity in the very act of giving birth to Jesus. Like many other mariological developments, *virginitas in partu* is first hinted at in the *Protevangelium Jacobi*, 19:3–20:4. On this text and its possible docetic implications, see Brown et al., *Mary in the New Testament*, 275–78. Although the idea is never explicitly treated in the NT, the fact that Luke 2:23 cites Exod 13:2,12,15 in reference to Jesus' birth ("every male that *opens the womb* shall be called holy to the Lord") seems to indicate that Luke was not concerned with such a position.

[19] In the life of Plato (Book 3 of his *Lives of the Philosophers*), Diogenes Laertius (3.1.2) makes a similar statement about the father of Plato in his sexual relations with Plato's mother (and Plato was not an only child): *hothen katharan gamou phylaxai heōs tēs apokyēseōs* ("hence he observed chastity with her in the marriage [literally: kept her clean of marriage] until the birth [of Plato]," 3.1.2). For a critical text, see *Diogenis Laertii. Vitae Philosophorum. Tomus Prior*, ed. H. S. Long (Oxford: Clarendon, 1964) 121.

[20] This point is well made throughout the commentary by Robert H. Gundry, *Matthew. A Commentary on His Literary and Theological Art* (Grand Rapids: Eerdmans, 1982).

[21] Traditionally, much has been made of the appearance of a "Mary the mother of James the Younger [or Smaller] and Joses" at a distance from the cross of Jesus in Mark 15:40. Two questions in particular arise: (1) Is this Mary the mother of Jesus, referred to now in an oblique way? (2) If this Mary is not the mother of Jesus, are the James and Joses mentioned in 15:40 the same James and Joses whom Mark lists among the "brothers" in 6:3? If the answer to the latter question be "yes," then the "brothers" of 6:3 would not be true siblings of Jesus, since they would have a different mother, also called Mary.

The great problem with all of this is that the identification of the women and men mentioned in Mark 15:40,47; 16:1 (and parallels) is fraught with difficulty. It is no wonder that the committee in charge of writing *Mary in the New Testament*, after treating the problem on pp. 68–72, could reach no consensus on a solution: "We were not even agreed on which solution might be called the more likely" (p. 72). To try to make Mark 15:40 a key to the solution of the brothers of Jesus in the NT is to attempt to explain the obscure by the still more obscure.

As for the two questions about "Mary the mother of James . . . and Joses" in Mark 15:40, my opinion is as follows. (1) This Mary is not to be identified with Mary the mother of Jesus. Elsewhere Mark clearly speaks of Mary as "his [Jesus'] mother" (3:31) and of Jesus as "the son of Mary" (6:3). To refer to her as Mary the mother of James and Joses would be unparalleled both in Mark and in the rest of the NT. How could Mark's readers be expected to make the identification? Even if we suppose that Mark wished to make some theological point by this unusual designation (e.g., Mary no longer counts as the mother of Jesus, who has just been declared Son of God [15:39]), he would have had to mention all four sons to make the connection with 6:3 clear. Probably the identification of the Mary in 15:40 with the mother of Jesus would not have been seriously considered by critics if it were not for the parallel scene in John 19:25, where the mother of Jesus does appear by the cross. But her presence at the cross in John's Gospel, as well as that of the beloved disciple, may be due to John's own theology. Be that as it may, John's depiction of the women at the cross should not be read into the very different presentation of Mark.

(2) Most likely, James the Younger (or Smaller) and Joses in Mark 15:40 should not be identified with the James and Joses listed as brothers of Jesus in 6:3. Granted the insights of modern redaction criticism and narrative criticism, both of which stress the importance of the final work of the creative author, seen as a coherent whole, Mark's specification of the James in 15:40 as *ho mikros* (literally, "James the Small") actually tells against such an identification. Nothing in the preceding narrative has prepared us for or explains to us the use of this "title" for the James of 15:40. If it were meant to differentiate James "the brother of Jesus" from James the son of Zebedee and one of the Twelve, it should have been used by Mark in 6:3, where James "the brother of Jesus" first appears, just a few chapters after the other James has been listed as one of the Twelve (3:17) and just before the Twelve (including James) are sent out on mission (6:7–13). If *ho mikros* is meant to distinguish James "the brother of the Lord" from James the son of Zebedee, it comes nonsensically late in the narrative. Rather, the absence of any such designation after the name of James the brother of Jesus in 6:3 naturally tends to create a distinction between him and the James pointedly called *ho mikros* in 15:40; on all this, see Oberlinner, *Historische Überlieferung*, 112–17. As Oberlinner admits (p. 113), the occurrence of the Greek form *Iōsēs* for "Joseph" only in Mark 6:3 and 15:40 within the NT is striking. But granted that the Hebrew *Yôsēf* is transliterated in koine Greek in a number of different ways (e.g., *Iōsēph*, *Iōsēphos*, *Iōsēpos*), including cases of *Iōsēs* outside the NT, the same form in the two Marcan passages is not very probative. Moreover, James (=Jacob) and Joses (=Joseph) were common Jewish names in the 1st centuries B.C. and A.D. We may have in 15:40 a situation similar to the identification of Simon of Cyrene as "the father of Alexander and Rufus" (15:21). The identification made perfect sense to Mark and his first readers, who apparently knew the people involved; the reference is totally lost on us, as perhaps it was already lost on Matthew and Luke. Matthew omits "the Small" after "James" in 27:56, and Luke omits the entire list of female names in 23:49, just as both omit "the father of Alexander and Rufus" when they mention Simon of Cyrene (Matt 27:32; Luke 23:26).

In short, in my opinion, Mark 15:40 is a red herring across the trail leading to the brothers of Jesus.

For the sake of completeness, it should be noted that some authors use the presence of the name Joses (Joseph) in the list of Jesus' brothers to fashion an argument against the view that the brothers are true siblings. For instance,

W. F. Albright and C. S. Mann *(Matthew* [AB 26; Garden City, NY: Doubleday, 1971] 9) claim that, while it was "not unknown for sons to be named after their fathers, it was at the same time uncommon." Hence one could argue from the presence of a Joseph among Jesus' brothers that the brothers are not true physical sons of Joseph. However, granted the fragmentary state of our evidence for the practices of the common people in Palestine in the 1st century A.D., talk about what was more or less common is not subject to rigorous controls.

What NT authors themselves might expect by way of the custom of naming a son after his father is seen in Luke 1:59–63, where the friends and relatives of Zechariah and Elizabeth naturally expect that the newborn child will be named after his father. Both Elizabeth and Zechariah must intervene to convince them that the child should be called John instead. Brown *(Birth of the Messiah,* 369) comments: "The custom of naming a child after his father is attested in the second-century A.D. Wadi Murabbaʿat legal documents (Eleazar son of Eleazar, Judah son of Judah). But naming the child after the grandfather (papponymy) seems to have been more common in priestly circles." Needless to say, Jesus of Nazareth and his brothers did not belong to priestly circles. Perhaps even more interesting an example for "questers" exists in one of the documents pertaining to a woman named Babata, found in the "Cave of Letters" at Naḥal Ḥever (about 3 miles south of En-gedi and 7 miles north of Masada). The documents indicate that Babata had married a Jew named Yeshua ben Joseph and that their son was also named Yeshua; on this, see J. N. Sevenster, *Do You Know Greek? How Much Greek Could the First Jewish Christians Have Known?* (NovT Sup 19; Leiden: Brill, 1968) 160.

[22] See the similar remarks about Mark's redactional stance in Oberlinner, *Historische Überlieferung,* 238–40. On p. 239, Oberlinner states: ". . . we can affirm with fair certitude that Mark, in his narrative in 3:31–35 . . . hardly had in mind anyone else than the physical brothers of Jesus."

As Oberlinner (p. 248) notes, there is no reason to go into a special consideration of the parallel in the Coptic *Gospel of Thomas,* saying 99. It is clearly dependent on the Synoptics, especially Luke. Notice the reduction to brothers and mother—omitting all reference to sisters—in the "punch line" of Jesus. As can be readily seen in any synopsis, this is a redactional omission that Luke, but not Matthew, makes in Mark's text. As in a number of other logia, the *Gospel of Thomas* follows the Lucan version.

[23] What is said here about the natural rhetorical thrust of Mark 3:35∥Matt 12:50 could also be applied to John 7:1–10, in which Jesus' brothers urge him to go to Jerusalem and Judea, so that his disciples there may also see his works. The evangelist then turns to his audience and sadly informs them that this exhortation by the brothers was not the positive sign of trust in Jesus that it seemed to be: "For not even his brothers believed in him" (v 5, *oude gar hoi adelphoi autou episteuon eis auton).* The bitter sadness of this aside loses a great deal of its rhetorical force if it means instead "for not even his cousins believed in him."

[24] Brown et al., *Mary in the New Testament,* 86–87. Strange to say, although Oberlinner emphasizes the evangelists' redactional theology as opposed to his-

torical fact throughout his *Historische Überlieferung* (see, e.g., pp. 78–85), on pp. 352–54 he fails to consider how Matthew's redactional theology in his Infancy Narrative might have affected his treatment of the mother and brothers of Jesus in 13:55.

What has been said with regard to Matt 1:25 could be applied, *mutatis mutandis*, to Luke's statement in his Infancy Narrative that Jesus was Mary's "firstborn" (*prōtotokon*, 2:7). In itself, the word need not indicate that Mary had further children; "firstborn" was a legal designation that the OT (Exod 13:2; Num 3:12–13; 18:15–16) applied to the first child a mother bore even when no siblings were born later. Indeed, a tombstone of a Jewish woman from 5 B.C. describes how she died while giving birth "to a firstborn child"; see Brown, *Birth of the Messiah*, 398. However, since the author who writes Luke 2:7 also speaks of Jesus' mother and brothers in Luke 8:19–21 and Acts 1:14, the title "firstborn" takes on a more precise meaning in light of the larger context.

[25] With reference to the pre-Marcan tradition present in Mark 6:1–6, Oberlinner judges, after a detailed analysis, that "the fact of the existence of physical brothers of Jesus was clearly and firmly anchored in the early Christian tradition and was also passed down in the tradition without any second thoughts" (p. 355). But once again, Oberlinner warns about overhasty conclusions concerning the original historical events. However, when one combines Oberlinner's findings about Mark and the pre-Marcan tradition with the independent affirmations in Paul, John, and Josephus, a strong argument from converging lines of probability emerges concerning the historical facts of the case.

[26] For the sake of brevity of expression, I shall speak from here on simply of the "brothers" of Jesus. This is not done to slight his sisters. It just acknowledges certain realities in the texts: (1) The brothers are spoken of more often than the sisters. (2) The brothers are named, while the sisters are not. (3) The fact that the first brother is named James enables us to link the brother passages of the Gospels with Paul's references to James in Gal 1:19 (cf. the brothers of the Lord in 1 Cor 9:5). (4) It is the brothers, not the sisters, who are usually mentioned in relevant patristic texts. Nevertheless, the conclusion we shall reach applies equally to Jesus' brothers and sisters and hence I will resume the fuller expression at the end of this section. For later legends about the number and names of Jesus' sisters, see Blinzler, *Die Brüder*, 35–38.

[27] So-called because one of its great sponsors in the 4th century was the Bishop of Salamis on Cyprus, Epiphanius (315–402/3 A.D.); see his exposition in his *Panarion*, 1.29.3–4; 2.66.19; 3.78.7,9,13. For a critical edition of the Greek text of the *Panarion*, see *Epiphanius* (3 vols.; Vol. 1, GCS 25; ed. Karl Holl; Leipzig: Hinrich, 1915; Vol. 2, GCS 31; ed. Karl Holl and Jürgen Dummer; Berlin: Akademie, 1980; Vol. 3, GCS 37; ed. Karl Holl; Leipzig: Hinrich, 1933). For an English translation of parts 1–46, see Frank Williams, trans., *The Panarion of Epiphanius of Salamis. Book I (Sects 1–46)* (NHS 35; ed. James M. Robinson; Leiden: Brill, 1987). For an English translation of all the passages describing the 80 sects, see Philip R. Amidon, trans., *The* Panarion *of St. Epiphanius, Bishop of Salamis.*

Selected Passages (New York/Oxford: Oxford University, 1990); relevant passages on the brothers and sisters of Jesus can be found on pp. 90–91, 229, 348–51.

[28] I speak in general terms of the "cousin approach" of Jerome, for the fact is that Jerome did not always hold to exactly the same interpretation of the relevant texts as he tried to defend the perpetual virginity of Mary in his various writings. For the variations in his interpretation of "Mary the mother of James and Joses" and "James the brother of the Lord," see Blinzler, *Die Brüder*, 142–44. A lengthy exposition of Jerome's theory, its further development by other Church writers, and the telling criticism of it by J. B. Lightfoot are given by John McHugh, *The Mother of Jesus in the New Testament* (Garden City, NY: Doubleday, 1975) 223–33.

[29] In fact, Oberlinner (*Historische Überlieferung*, 29) suggests that there is only one clear case, 1 Chr 23:22, where the daughters of Eleazar marry the sons of Kish, "their brothers," who, according to 23:21, are actually their cousins. Other examples of *'āḥ* for a close relation seem to refer to nephews or to a large group of more remote, undefined relations.

[30] On this, see Oberlinner, *Historische Überlieferung*, 22–41.

[31] In all his works, Josephus uses the Greek word for "cousin" *(anepsios)* 12 times.

[32] Notice in particular Josephus' expansion and rewording of Jacob's speech to Rachel to make the terminology more precise in the Greek as opposed to the Hebrew. In the Hebrew of Gen 29:12, Jacob tells Rachel that he is a "brother" *('āḥ*, which simply means here a relative, and as the context shows, nephew) of her father Laban because he is the son of Rebekah, the sister of Laban. Hence the word *'āḥ* in this Hebrew text obviously means "nephew." In his reworking of this speech, Josephus has Jacob explain his relationship to Rachel at greater length and with greater precision: "For Rebekah my mother is the sister of Laban your father. They had the same father and mother, and so we, you and I, are cousins *[anepsioi]*" *(Ant. 1.19.4 §290)*. The avoidance of a literal translation of *'āḥ* as *adelphos* and the introduction of *anepsioi* to clarify the relationship is striking. Therefore, when Josephus calls James "the brother of Jesus," there is no reason to think that he means anything but "brother."

[33] Exegetes are divided on which Philip is meant. See, e.g., Robert A. Guelich *(Mark 1–8:26* [Word Biblical Commentary 34A; Dallas: Word, 1989] 331), who favors "Herod Philip"; so too Ernst Haenchen, *Der Weg Jesu* (2d ed.; Berlin: de Gruyter, 1968) 238 n. 1. Surprisingly, the conservative Taylor *(The Gospel According to St. Mark,* 312) inclines to the view that Mark has simply made a mistake here; similarly, Daniel J. Harrington, "Mark," *NJBC,* ed. Raymond E. Brown, Joseph A. Fitzmyer, and Roland E. Murphy (Englewood Cliffs, NJ: Prentice Hall, 1990) 609 (§41). Taylor seems to have the better of the argument since (1) there is no firm proof that Herod the son of Mariamme II was also known as Philip, and (2) the attempt to have this Herod bear the name of Philip looks like a desperate ploy to harmonize Mark and Josephus (cf. *Ant.* 18.5.4 §136–37).

Whichever choice is made, the main point remains: *adelphos* in Mark 6:17 means "half brother."

[34] Brown et al., *Mary in the New Testament*, 66 n. 122. One should note that, even in these cases, the relationship is usually a very close one, and the actual precise relationship is made clear by the larger context. Oberlinner *(Historische Überlieferung*, 41–48) observes that "sister" enjoyed similar use as a Hellenistic title, either given to one's wife (sometimes related by blood to the husband) or used in court etiquette. Yet Oberlinner states that he has found no exact, clearcut parallel to the supposed use of *adelphoi* to mean "cousins" in the unique case of the brothers of Jesus.—In general, as Oberlinner stresses, it is simplistic to appeal purely to "semitic" usage when analyzing the many various meanings "brother" can have in koine Greek. Such variety of usage is witnessed in many languages, and is by no means restricted to Hebrew or Aramaic.

[35] As Oberlinner and many other exegetes have pointed out, no amount of parallels from outside the NT can tell us a priori what the NT texts mean; only a detailed exegesis of the NT texts *in their own context* can tell us that.

[36] It is significant that Joseph A. Fitzmyer, who discusses with care the many possible meanings of *adelphos* in the *Gospel According to Luke*, 1. 723–24, nevertheless states apodictically on p. 724: "Jerome thought that *adelphos* could mean 'cousin,' but this is almost certainly to be ruled out as the NT meaning. . . ."

[37] Blinzler, *Die Brüder*, passim, summarized on pp. 145–46; and McHugh, *The Mother of Jesus*, 200–54. Both authors hold that the "brothers" of Jesus were some sort of cousins, though their theories differ in details.

Blinzler (p. 145) thinks that Simon and Jude were sons of Clopas, a brother of Joseph. Clopas was thus of Davidic descent, but his wife is unknown. The mother of James and Joses was a Mary. Either she or her husband was somehow related to Jesus' family; perhaps her husband was of priestly or levitical descent and was a brother of Mary.

McHugh, rejecting the precise theory of Jerome (which Jerome himself did not attach too much importance to later in life), depends partly on Blinzler but develops his own convoluted and highly hypothetical theory (pp. 234–54). A Mary who was a sister of Joseph married an unknown man and gave birth to James and Joses. Clopas, a brother of Joseph, married a Mary who gave birth to Simon. Hence all the "brothers" were legally first cousins of Jesus. McHugh is too honest to claim that "brother" in Mark 6:3 really means "cousin" or close relative à la Jerome. To explain the use of the term "brother," McHugh suggests that Joseph undertook the charge of his brother-in-law's children after their father's death. So "brother" really means "foster brother"; James and Joses were thus brought up with Jesus in the same family. How Simon and Jude wind up under the same familial umbrella remains unclear in McHugh's reconstruction —a tour de force that dazzles because of its intricacy even as it fails to convince because of its arbitrariness.

McHugh's gratuitous hypothesis is interesting in that it indicates that even McHugh is uncomfortable with "brother" simply meaning "cousin," without any further reason for the strange equation. His touching story of the brother-in-law's death and Joseph's reception of his nephews into his house would help supply the missing link, but it is nothing more than pure imagination. One cannot avoid the impression that every escape hatch imaginable is being pried open because a highly unlikely position has been adopted a priori on other grounds. The same basic criticism can be made of the various permutations of the cousin theory espoused by many authors, both ancient and modern.

[38] "Pre-Nicene" and "post-Nicene" refer to that watershed in Church history, the first ecumenical council, held at Nicea in Asia Minor in 325 A.D. to deal with the Arian heresy.

[39] Hegesippus' own work was entitled the *Hypomnēmata* ("Memoirs").

[40] The naive acceptance of Hegesippus' testimony as historically true weakens greatly the treatment of Blinzler, *Die Brüder*, 94–108. That Blinzler accepts Hegesippus' legendary picture of James the Just as a super-ascetic Nazirite who also had access to that part of the Jerusalem sanctuary forbidden to the laity makes one doubtful about Blinzler's overall critical ability. Blinzler then goes on to use this datum to confirm his theory that James was of priestly or levitical lineage. For a more critical study of this James legend in Hegesippus, one that suggests that James is being presented here as the true high priest, see Ernst Zuckschwerdt, "Das Naziräat des Herrenbruders Jakobus nach Hegesipp (Euseb, h. e. II 23, 5–6)," *ZNW* 68 (1977) 276–87.

[41] Interestingly, Hegesippus' testimony is cited by Pesch, Blinzler, and McHugh as supporting each author's position—an indication that the fragments of Hegesippus that we have are not without their ambiguity. The translation of 4.22 §4 is especially fraught with difficulty; see Blinzler *(Die Brüder,* 105–8) for various suggestions; also McHugh, *The Mother of Jesus,* 245 n. 21; cf. 212–16. (McHugh's treatment is remarkable in that it ignores the pivotal point that Hegesippus shows that he knows how to use "brother," "uncle," and "cousin" exactly when speaking of Jesus' relatives.) Since I am merely interested in Hegesippus' care in distinguishing different types of Jesus' relatives, a precise translation of the entire passage in 4.22 §4 is not vital to my argument, as it is to Blinzler's. On pp. 94–105, Blinzler is uncritical in his mixing of texts from the NT and Church Fathers to extract his own interpretation of the Hegesippus passages. On the danger of conflating statements in the NT and Hegesippus without respecting the different nature of the works involved, see Oberlinner, *Historische Überlieferung,* 141–43.

The text of 4.22 §4 does seem to say that the Simon under discussion was the son of Clopas, the uncle of Jesus (or of James?—the text is ambiguous at this point). Given the ambiguity and fragmentary state of this passage from Hegesippus, as well as the wide use of Simon/Symeon for Jews in the 1st centuries B.C. and A.D., we cannot be sure that Hegesippus means the Simon identified as the brother of Jesus in Mark and Matthew, or, for that matter, that Hegesippus was always consistent in his statements and identifications. For the opposite view, see Blinzler, *Die Brüder,* 98–99.

[42] So, in desperation, Blinzler, *Die Brüder,* 101, 108–10. His treatment of "ac-

cording to the flesh" is a prime example of his interpretation of words in isolation, apart from the context that gives them their obvious meaning.

[43] The major texts giving Tertullian's views are *Adversus Marcionem* 4.19 (see *Tertullian, Adversus Marcionem* [ed. and trans. Ernest Evans; Oxford: Clarendon, 1972] 360–63); *De carne Christi* 7 (see *Tertullien. Le chair du Christ. Tome I* [SC 216; ed. Jean-Pierre Mahé; Paris: Cerf, 1975] 240; *De monogamia* 8.1–2 and *De virginibus velandis* 6.6 (see *Tertulliani Opera. Pars Quarta* [CSEL 76; ed. V. Bulhart and P. Borleffs; Vienna: Hoelder-Pichler-Tempsky, 1967] 58, 88).

It is sad to see so fine a scholar as Blinzler *(Die Brüder,* 139–41) strain to water down or make ambiguous what Tertullian clearly says, especially when all these texts are taken together. Faced with this embarrassing patristic evidence, Blinzler (1) discusses individual phrases in individual texts atomistically instead of viewing all the relevant texts together to grasp Tertullian's overall position; (2) stresses that Tertullian was developing his view while engaged in polemic against heretics, as though this were not true of most of the creative theology of the Church Fathers.

At times, Blinzler ignores key phrases that run against his policy of "damage control." For example, in *Adversus Marcionem* 4.19, while discussing the scene in Mark 3:31–35, Tertullian notes how Jesus transfers the "names" of "blood relatives" [i.e., "mother" and "brothers"] to others, namely to those inside the house, whom Jesus judges to be closer to himself because of their faith *(transtulit sanguinis nomina in alios, quos magis proximos prae fide iudicaret . . .).* Tertullian then sums up his whole argument with another use of *sanguis* for "blood relation": "It is not surprising that he [Jesus] preferred faith [in those sitting around him in the house] to blood-relationship [in his mother and brothers] *(nihil magnum si fidem sanguini praeposuit).* " Blinzler also ignores the obvious sense of Tertullian's rhetorical question about Jesus' brothers: "Tell me, does everyone who is born have brothers who are born in addition to him as well?"

Blinzler likewise ignores the logical thrust of Tertullian's comparison in *De monogamia* 8.1–2. There are two kinds of Christian sanctity, says Tertullian: John the Baptist represents total continence, while his father Zechariah represents modest monogamy (a monogamy that obviously includes intercourse, witness his son John). Insofar as Mary bore Christ when she was a virgin and then married once, she embodies both kinds of sanctity. The implication here is that, as virgin mother of Christ, Mary embodied total chastity, and as spouse of Joseph she later embodied modest monogamy. The parallel with Zechariah naturally suggests normal intercourse and childbearing. Unfortunately, McHugh's attempt at damage control *(The Mother of Jesus,* 448–50) is even weaker than Blinzler's. All McHugh can do is run quickly past the strongest evidence, that of the *Adversus Marcionem,* and keep insisting that Tertullian never calls the brothers of Jesus "the sons of Mary." McHugh fails to realize that the viewpoint of the NT and of Tertullian, unlike his own, is strongly christological, not mariological. Hence all the relationships are defined from the vantage point of Jesus, not Mary. After insisting that Jesus' mother and brothers were *truly* his mother and brothers, and after insisting on their "blood" relationship, Tertullian would have probably replied in his most biting fashion to anyone asking him whether Jesus' brothers were sons of Mary.

⁴⁴ Blinzler, *Die Brüder*, 141.

⁴⁵ I purposely speak of "the most probable opinion." That is all, in my view, that a philological and historical investigation into the question can hope to reach. Hence I am not opposed to the view of Joseph A. Fitzmyer, who, after reviewing the problems of *adelphos* in the NT, concludes that the idea that the brothers of Jesus were kinsmen or relatives in the broad sense "is certainly not ruled out" *(A Christological Catechism. New Testament Answers* (New York/Ramsey, NJ: Paulist, 1981) 73. But to say that an opinion cannot be ruled out is not to say that it is the most probable solution on purely linguistic and historical grounds.

⁴⁶ New York: Harper & Row, 1970. See also his reiteration and expansion of his views in *The Sexuality of Jesus* (New York: Harper & Row, 1973).

⁴⁷ In this ecumenical age, the fierce animus Phipps displays against the Roman Catholic Church strikes a strange, not to say embarrassing, note. It reminds one of an older and sadder period of theological discourse.

⁴⁸ See Mark 10:29 parr. for children; the Lucan parallel (18:29) adds "wife." The literal following of Jesus around Galilee and beyond meant that Simon Peter had to leave, at least temporarily, his mother-in-law (Mark 1:30) and presumably his wife (1 Cor 9:5). Nothing similar is intimated about the man he followed.

⁴⁹ Apart from the question of his handling of the NT's silence, Phipps's presentation must be faulted for his citation of various sayings of Jesus without sufficient critical probing of their claim to historicity. Any saying that aids his argument is called upon without further ado.

⁵⁰ Even within the rabbinic material, sayings are not always referred to according to their natural sense within their context. Moreover, some arguments are clearly anachronistic: e.g., using later rules incumbent on rabbis as applying to "Rabbi" Jesus. The structured institution of an ordained rabbinate probably did not exist in Jesus' time, and Jesus in any case did not belong to such a formal institution.

⁵¹ The case of the Essenes and Qumran is, of course, in many ways special, since it was limited to a relatively small group of extremists and survived for only a little over two hundred years. Yet since the movement was active and Qumran was standing precisely during the ministry of Jesus, it deserves special consideration.

⁵² For the Greek text, see Karl Mras, ed., *Eusebius Werke. Achter Band. Die Praeparatio Evangelica. Erster Teil* (GCS 43/1; Berlin: Akademie, 1954) 455–57.

⁵³ While some scholars in the 19th century thought the Therapeutae were the invention of Philo, most 20th-century commentators accept their existence as a fact. For an affirmation of the historicity of the Therapeutae and the basic reliability of Philo's description of them, see Jean Riaud, "Les Thérapeutes d'Alexan-

drie dans la tradition et dans la recherche critique jusqu'aux découvertes de Qumran," *Aufstieg und Niedergang der römischen Welt* II/20.2, 1189–1295. On p. 1288 Riaud supports the view that the Essenes and the Therapeutae were two autonomous entities that must be held completely separate.

[54] The Latin text can be found in *Pliny. Natural History* (LCL; 10 vols.; ed. H. Rackham, W. H. S. Jones, and D. E. Eichholz; London: Heinemann; Cambridge, MA: Harvard University, 1938–62) 2. 276: *Ab occidente litora* [of the Dead Sea] *Esseni fugiunt usque qua nocent, gens sola et in toto orbe praeter ceteras mira, sine ulla femina, omni venere abdicata* . . . *ita per seculorum milia (incredibile dictu) gens aeterna est in qua nemo nascitur.* . . .

[55] On this point, see the remarks by Jerome Murphy-O'Connor, "The Judean Desert," *Early Judaism and Its Modern Interpreters*, ed. Robert A. Kraft and George W. E. Nickelsburg (Atlanta: Scholars, 1986) 119–56, including the extensive bibliography.

[56] A number of the documents that were found at Qumran and that apparently refer to the life either of the monastery or of the wider Essene movement speak of or presuppose marriage and offspring. The *Damascus Document* (CD) thinks in terms of a community of married men. The *Rule of the Congregation* (1QSa) speaks of men who reach the age of twenty as having sexual relations. What is therefore surprising, by way of contrast, is that what seems to be the most basic rule of life at Qumran, the *Manual of Discipline* (1QS), never mentions marriage or wives. Many—though not all—interpret the *Manual's* silence to mean that it assumes an all-male community.

[57] Those who support some kind of celibacy at least for some period of Qumran's history include (obviously, with variations) William R. Farmer ("Essenes," *IDB*, 2. 147); Helmer Ringgren *(The Faith of Qumran* [Philadelphia: Fortress, 1963] 139–40); Matthew Black *(The Scrolls and Christian Origins* [Brown Judaic Studies 48; Chico, CA: Scholars, 1961, reprint 1983] 30–32, 165—but suggesting that celibacy may have been more the exception than the rule); John Allegro *(The Dead Sea Scrolls. A Reappraisal* [2d ed.; London: Penguin, 1964] 116–18); Geza Vermes *(The Dead Sea Scrolls. Qumran in Perspective* [Philadelphia: Fortress, 1977] 106, 181–82); Emil Schürer *(The History of the Jewish People* [rev. ed.], 2. 578); Hans Hübner ("Zölibat in Qumran?" *NTS* 17 [1970–71] 153–67); Anton Steiner ("Warum lebten die Essener asketisch?" *BZ* 15 [1971] 1–28); A. Marx ("Les racines du célibat essénien," *RevQ* 7 [1969–71] 323–42); Anthony J. Saldarini ("Essenes," *Harper's Bible Dictionary*, 279–80); Philip R. Davies *(Behind the Essenes. History and Ideology in the Dead Sea Scrolls* [Brown Judaic Studies 94; Atlanta: Scholars, 1987] 83–85); Everett Ferguson *(Backgrounds of Early Christianity*, 414); James H. Charlesworth *(Jesus within Judaism*, 72), and Raymond E. Brown *(NJBC*, 1075 [#108]).

[58] For discussions of the various reasons proposed, see Marx ("Les racines"), Hübner ("Zölibat in Qumran?"), and Steiner ("Warum lebten die Essener asketisch?").

[59] The vast majority of commentators on Jeremiah take 16:1–4 to refer to

celibacy; the only significant dispute among them is whether this text gives us historically reliable information about Jeremiah or is rather the interpretation of a later generation. John Bright considers 16:1–4 to be historical *(Jeremiah* [AB 21; 2d ed.; Garden City, NY: Doubleday, 1981] 112); similarly, Ernest W. Nicholson, *The Book of the Prophet Jeremiah. Chapters 1–25* (Cambridge: Cambridge University, 1973) 142; William L. Holladay, *Jeremiah 1* (Hermeneia; Philadelphia: Fortress, 1986) 467–72. In favor of the text as an interpretation of or midrash on Jeremiah's life and message by a later writer is William McKane, *Jeremiah* (ICC; 2 vols; Edinburgh: Clark, 1986 [Vol. 1]) 1. 367; cf. Kathleen M. O'Connor, *The Confessions of Jeremiah: Their Interpretation and Role in Chapters 1–25* (SBLDS 94; Atlanta: Scholars, 1988) 138. In fairness, it should be noted that Robert P. Carroll *(Jeremiah* [OTL; Philadelphia: Westminster, 1986] 338–42) interprets the text as presenting a hyperbolic description of the destruction of the community and land of Israel. However, Carroll achieves this unusual interpretation by focusing on hypothetical traditions behind the present text. He admits that most commentators do favor the view that Jeremiah was celibate. One may add that this is certainly the natural sense of the MT as it stands. Phipps claims that Jeremiah intended to marry after the war with Babylon was over *(Was Jesus Married?,* 29); needless to say, this is an untestable assumption. For the opposite view, that 16:1–4 speaks a command never to marry, see Holladay, *Jeremiah 1,* 467–68.

[60] It is not impossible that two other OT prophets were celibate, namely, Elijah and Elisha. The mysterious figure of Elijah appears throughout the biblical narrative without any family connections; his only "family" or "support group" seems to be the "sons of the prophets" or prophetic guild. In the case of Elisha, it is significant that when Elijah calls him to the prophetic office (1 Kings 19:19–21) Elisha asks leave to bid farewell to his father and mother; nothing is said of wife or children. Moreover, when Elisha slaughters his oxen and uses the plowing equipment for fuel to boil their flesh as a feast for his people, he seems to be signifying a total break with his former life and livelihood, a literal burning of all bridges to the past (see John Gray, *I & II Kings* [OTL; Philadelphia: Westminster, 1963] 368). Thus, while celibacy was certainly rare even among Israel's prophets, it was perhaps more frequent among them than in other walks of life. Some might want to draw a connection between the supposed celibacy of Elijah and that of John the Baptist; but, as we shall see in Chapter 12, I remain uncertain about any intention on the part of the historical Baptist to imitate Elijah.

[61] One is reminded both of Josephus' personal experience in the wilderness with the ascetic Bannus *(Life* 2 §11) and of his report that the Essenes adopt and raise abandoned boys in their communities.

[62] See *Moses [De Vita Mosis]* 2.14 §68–69 [LCL 6. 482–83]: ". . . purifying himself from all things that pertained to mortal nature: food and drink and [sexual] relations with women. But for a long time he disdained such relations with women, indeed almost from the time that he first began to prophesy. . . ."

[63] The English translation can be found in *The Babylonian Talmud. Seder Mo'ed. Shabbath II,* ed. I. Epstein; trans. H. Freedman (London: Soncino, 1938) 411–12.

[64] See the discussion in Geza Vermes, *Jesus the Jew* (Philadelphia: Fortress, 1973) 100–1.

[65] See the English translation in *The Babylonian Talmud. Seder Nashim I. Yebamoth I,* ed. I. Epstein; trans. I. Slotki (London: Soncino, 1936) 426–27. George Foot Moore remarks cautiously that cases like that of ben Azzai "were evidently infrequent" (*Judaism in the First Centuries of the Christian Era* [2 vols.; New York: Schocken, 1971, originally 1927, 1930] 2. 120. Phipps (*Was Jesus Married?,* 32) argues that other sources indicate that ben Azzai had married. Whatever be the case of the historical ben Azzai, at the very least there was a rabbinic tradition about his being celibate.

[66] Vermes, *Jesus the Jew,* 99–102. Vermes carefully notes that he speaks only of Jesus' state during his public ministry. Historical research, he feels, cannot speak of Jesus' situation before his baptism by John simply because of "a total lack of evidence" (p. 101).

[67] Epictetus did marry in old age in order to have someone to aid him in bringing up a little child whose parents were about to expose it; see W. A. Oldfather, *Epictetus* (LCL; 2 vols; Cambridge, MA: Harvard; London: Heinemann, 1925, 1928) 1. x); cf. Iason Xenakis, *Epictetus. Philosopher—Therapist* (The Hague: Nijhoff, 1969) 4; also the article on "Epictète" in the *Dictionnaire des philosophes* (2 vols; ed. Denis Huisman; Paris: Presses Universitaires de France, 1984) 1. 860.

[68] So at least according to Philostratus, *The Life of Apollonius of Tyana* 1. 13; see the LCL edition by F. C. Conybeare (2 vols.; London: Heinemann; Cambridge, MA: Harvard, 1969) 1. 34–35.

[69] *Discourses* 3.22 §67–82; see Oldfather, *Epictetus,* 2. 152–59. On Stoicism and celibacy, see David Balch, "1 Cor 7:32–35 and Stoic Debates about Marriage, Anxiety, and Distraction," *JBL* 102 (1983) 429–39.

[70] The exact marital status of Paul would demand a treatise in itself. Suffice it to say that Paul presents himself in 1 Corinthians as a celibate for religious reasons (7:1–7; 9:5). It has been suggested at times that Paul was actually a widower. Like any good rabbinic student, it is claimed, he married by the time of early adulthood. His Christian status as a celibate indicates that his wife had died (or, much less likely, been divorced). We again seem on the verge of writing a novel. If Paul had been a widower or a divorced man, I wonder whether he would have written to the married people with problems in 1 Cor 7:7: "But I wish that all people were as I myself am." If Paul were a widower or divorced, his wish might have an unintended comic effect on his audience. For a brief consideration of the various ways in which this passage has been interpreted, see William F. Orr and James Arthur Walther, *I Corinthians* (AB 32; Garden City, NY: Doubleday, 1976) 209. I think it more probable that Paul, like Jesus, the Baptist, and some Essenes, belonged to a very small group of lifelong Jewish celibates. What in Paul's religious background had led him to such a strange commitment while still a Jew is an intriguing but unanswerable question. We

are reminded once again that Judaism in the early 1st century A.D. was a much more multifaceted phenomenon than we once supposed.

[71] Historians, sociologists, and psychologists might investigate whether and why the 1st century A.D. in particular was marked by this *relatively* remarkable number of celibates influential in religious and philosophical movements.

[72] For a survey of opinions and further bibliography, see Alexander Sand, *Reich Gottes und Eheverzicht im Evangelium nach Matthäus* (SBS 109; Stuttgart: KBW, 1983). See also Giuseppe G. Gamba, "La 'eunuchia' per il regno dei cieli. Annotazioni in margine a Matteo 19, 10–12," *Salesianum* 42 (1980) 243–87; W. A. Heth, "Unmarried 'for the Sake of the Kingdom' (Matthew 19:12) in the Early Church," *Grace Theological Journal* 8 (1987) 55–88. For the highly unlikely view that Jesus, in this saying, shows direct influence from the Neo-Pythagoreanism of the 1st century A.D., see Johannes Schattenmann, "Jesus und Pythagoras," *Kairos* 21 (1979) 215–20. To establish his view, Schattenmann has to call upon a text from Iamblichus, who wrote in the late 3d century A.D. Even then, Schattenmann has to engage in some contorted reasoning to advance his theory.

[73] Sand, for instance, thinks the saying functioned in the Matthean community to justify and protect those Christians who practiced voluntary celibacy and who therefore experienced suspicion or mockery from some other members of the community *(Reich Gottes,* 74–77). As we shall see, though, Sand also thinks it probable that the core of the saying goes back to the celibate Jesus. Matt 19:12 is therefore instructive for the methodology of form criticism: the fact that we can suggest a likely *Sitz im Leben* for a saying in an early Christian community does not mean—even if our suggestion is perfectly correct—that the saying was necessarily invented by the community. A saying that has its original *Sitz im Leben* in the ministry of the historical Jesus may find a new *Sitz im Leben* in the needs of the early Church.

[74] Stephenson H. Brooks, *Matthew's Community. The Evidence of His Special Sayings Material* (JSNTSup 16; Sheffield: JSOT, 1987) 107–9; similarly, Sand, *Reich Gottes,* 51–55. Once one reaches this conclusion, the whole argument as to whether 19:12, in its Matthean redactional context, refers to voluntary celibates or to disciples who have been divorced (the context supplied by Matt 19:1–9) and who therefore cannot remarry is beside the point, since the context of the dispute on divorce and remarriage is secondary. If one asks about the meaning of Matt 19:12 in the pre-Matthean tradition or in the mouth of Jesus, the sense of the isolated logion can only be voluntary celibacy; nothing in the saying itself conjures up the idea of divorce. For the interpretation that Matthew understands 19:12 to refer to an innocent husband who must put away his wife because of her *porneia* and who therefore cannot marry again, see Quentin Quesnell, " 'Made Themselves Eunuchs for the Kingdom of Heaven' (Mt 19, 12)," *CBQ* 30 (1968) 335–58; similarly, Pierre-René Côté, "Les Eunuques pour le Royaume (Mt 19, 12)," *Eglise et Théologie* 17 (1986) 321–34. For the view that, even in its redactional context, v 12 refers to voluntary celibates, see John P. Meier, *Matthew* (New Testament Message 3; Wilmington, DE: Glazier, 1980) 216–17.

[75] Brooks, *Matthew's Community*, 107–8.

[76] In Gal 5:12 Paul uses the more general verb *apokoptō* ("to cut off") in the middle voice when he refers with biting sarcasm to the circumcising group in Galatia: "Would that those who are disturbing you would [not just circumcise but also] castrate themselves!"

[77] One might also note the construction of *dia* with the accusative *basileian*, which occurs nowhere else in Matthew; see Sand, *Reich Gottes*, 56–57.

[78] However, I remain dubious about Brooks's attempt to discern three distinct stages and types of material in the M tradition; see his summary on pp. 188–91 of *Matthew's Community*. An argument for pre-Matthean tradition in 19:12 that takes a different tack can be found in Francisco Marín, "Un recurso obligado a la tradición presinóptica," *EstBib* 36 (1977) 205–16.

[79] For Sand *(Reich Gottes,* 66–68) the offensive nature of v 12abc lies not in the use of the word "eunuch" but in Jesus' positive view of voluntary celibacy in a milieu that generally rejected it. Sand interprets the first two clauses ("born so . . . made so by men") in the same metaphorical sense that the third clause has, claiming that the point at issue is not physical inability to have sex or be married but simply the state of being unmarried or being unsuited for marriage. While this is possible, one must admit that this is not the most natural sense of v 12a: "There are eunuchs such as were born so from their mother's womb. . . ." Obviously, everyone is born unmarried or celibate, and for a good number of years everyone usually remains unmarried or at least unsuited for marriage and sex. Sand never makes clear in what sense some men are *born* unsuited for marriage. The most natural sense of v 12a is "unsuited because of some physical defect."

[80] See the standard commentaries, e.g., E.-B. Allo, *Première épitre aux Corinthiens* (EBib; Paris: Gabalda, 1935) 152–94; Hans Conzelmann, *Der erste Brief an die Korinther* (MeyerK 5; Göttingen: Vandenhoeck & Ruprecht, 1969) 138–61; Gordon D. Fee, *The First Epistle to the Corinthians* (NICNT; Grand Rapids: Eerdmans, 1987) 266–357. Strictly speaking, 1 Tim 3:2,12; 5:9; Tit 1:6 do not belong in this discussion of voluntary virginity or celibacy, since they issue a prohibition of remarriage for certain special Church figures (the bishop, the deacon, the widow) after the death of the first spouse. In the mind of the author of the Pastoral Epistles, remaining unmarried after the death of the first spouse is not voluntary but obligatory for those assuming or holding such "offices."

[81] See the standard commentaries on Revelation, e.g., E.-B. Allo, *Saint Jean. L'apocalypse* (EBib; Paris: Gabalda, 1921) 196–97. He rejects the idea that "virgins" is simply a metaphor for the pure of heart or for those who have not let themselves be defiled by idolatry or pagan uncleanness. Nor does it refer first of all to martyrs; the natural sense refers to those who are virgins within the Christian community. Robert H. Mounce *(The Book of Revelation* [NICNT; Grand Rapids: Eerdmans, 1977] 269–71) prefers to take the phrase symbolically as referring to the Church, the virgin bride of Christ, who keeps herself pure from the defiling relationships of the pagan world. A similar view is held by

J. P. M. Sweet, *Revelation* (Pelican Commentaries; Philadelphia: Westminster, 1979) 222. The emphasis on males who are not defiled with women and the general context that suggests that a special group within the wider circle of the redeemed is being presented make this otherwise attractive interpretation difficult.

While Elisabeth Schüssler Fiorenza warns against too narrow an understanding of symbolic-poetic language, her interpretation is basically along the lines of Mounce and Sweet (i.e., symbolic rather than literal virginity); see her *The Book of Revelation. Justice and Judgment* (Philadelphia: Fortress, 1985) 181–92. Her concern, however, is more with the social and political context of the imagery. Taking a different approach, Adela Yarbro Collins *(Crisis and Catharsis: The Power of the Apocalypse* [Philadelphia: Westminster, 1984] 129) thinks that the concreteness and specificity of the language argue for a literal understanding, though she would restrict its application to older men who had been married. My own opinion is that the primary reference is to a special group of virgins within the Church; however, for the author, in a very concrete way they "embody" the reality of the virgin bride of Christ.

[82] Unease or embarrassment with regard to the metaphor of eunuchs may partially explain why Matt 19:12 is not cited all that frequently in the patristic literature of the first four centuries; see Sand, *Reich Gottes,* 23–27. According to Eusebius *(Ecclesiastical History* 6.8 §1–3—note the very circumspect terminology of the passage!), Origen in his youth took the saying quite literally and castrated himself. In later years, Origen rejected such a literal interpretation and indeed moved to an allegorical interpretation that did not even acknowledge a reference to voluntary celibacy in the last part of the saying. See his *Commentary on Matthew's Gospel* 15.1–5 in Erich Klostermann (ed.), *Origenes Werke. Zehnter Band. Origenes Matthäuserklärung* (GCS 40; Leipzig: Hinrichs, 1935), especially the summation on p. 361.

[83] Sand *(Reich Gottes,* 50, 74) thinks that 19:12abc may be an authentic saying of Jesus. He notes that Walter Grundmann and Herbert Braun favor this view, while Ethelbert Stauffer opposes it. Sand is also probably right in claiming that 19:12d ("let him who can accept it accept it"), while pre-Matthean tradition, was attached to the eunuch logion secondarily by Matthew.

[84] Note the proviso "in some form or other." As with many sayings of Jesus, we are not in a position to fix the exact wording of the original statement— which, indeed, might have been said a number of times in a number of ways. The arguments of embarrassment, discontinuity, and coherence concern the substance of the statement, especially the key idea of making oneself a eunuch for the sake of the kingdom. The exact wording need not be a major issue here.

[85] Unfortunately, Phipps does precisely that, spinning out one conjecture after another. One of the most imaginative is that Jesus had married Mary Magdalene during the second decade of his life. She became an adulteress, but Jesus' love for her was unwavering. He pursued a course of reconciliation rather than of divorce, thus bringing her to repentance. His experience with his wife led Jesus to believe that divorce should be opposed *(Was Jesus Married?,* 66–67).

Phipps seems to be working under the influence of later Western Church tradition, which in its preaching and liturgy tended to conflate Mary Magdalene with the unnamed sinful woman of Luke 7:36–50. The Eastern Church was on the whole more sober in distinguishing—quite correctly—between Mary Magdalene, Mary of Bethany, and the unnamed sinful woman. Need it be pointed out that male exegetes are all too ready to take for granted, with no basis in the text of Luke 7, that the sin of the sinful woman was prostitution or adultery?

[86] As I have argued in Chapter 8, the indirect link Luke forges between Mary and priestly descent (via Elizabeth, 1:5,36) is part of Luke's redactional work, as he welds together Baptist and Jesus traditions in his Infancy Narrative.

[87] Matthew does add the Sadducees to scenes in which they did not originally figure, notably Matt 16:1–12. This is a prime example of his united-front-of-Judaism approach, and perhaps also of his ignorance of who exactly the Sadducees were (note the strange yoking of the Pharisees and Sadducees under the rubric of a supposedly common doctrine in 16:12).

[88] Unless one prefers to date Mark before A.D. 70.

[89] It was by no means impossible that an individual priest might adhere to the Pharisaic school of thought or learn the technical skills of a scribe. But, on the whole, Pharisaism was a lay spiritual movement, and the profession of scribe tended to be a lay profession.

[90] Some other passages in the NT refer to Jesus' voluntary self-offering in terms that conjure up the idea of priesthood. But the term "priest" is never explicitly applied to Jesus in these passages (e.g., Eph 5:2; 1 Tim 2:5–6). When sacrificial terminology is used in the NT of Jesus' death, Jesus is more often presented as the willing victim than the priest of the sacrifice.

[91] On this, see John D. Crossan, "The Good Samaritan. Towards a Generic Definition of Parable," *Semeia* 2 (1974) 82–112.

[92] Sean Freyne, *Galilee from Alexander the Great to Hadrian 323* B.C.E. *to 135* C.E. (University of Notre Dame Center for the Study of Judaism and Christianity in Antiquity 5; Wilmington, DE: Glazier; Notre Dame: University of Notre Dame, 1980) 259–97.

[93] With regard to the disputed meaning of Mark 3:21, I accept what seems to be the common view today, namely, that the *hoi par' autou* are the family of Jesus, that they are the subject of the verb *elegon* as well as the verb *exēlthon*, and that Jesus is the understood subject of *exestē*. (1) This is first of all the most natural meaning of the words in view of their order within the two sentences. No other plural subject intervenes between *exēlthon* and *elegon*, and *auton* (referring to Jesus) is the word immediately preceding *elegon gar hoti exestē*. Note also that the *elegon gar hoti* of v 21 is paralleled by the *elegon hoti* of v 22, where the other accusers, the scribes, are clearly the speakers. (2) Especially with regard to the ambiguous *hoi par' autou*, the sense I propose is the only likely meaning within the larger context of Mark's composition in 3:20–35. As often happens in Mark, we have duality (two similar accusations from two groups, *hoi par' autou*

and the scribes) and also a chiastically ordered section (A: accusation by *hoi par'
autou,* who set out to seize him [vv 20–21]; B: accusation by the scribes [v 22]; B':
Jesus' brusque rejection of the scribes [vv 23–30]; A': Jesus' brusque rejection of
his mother and brothers, who in the meantime have arrived outside the house
where Jesus is teaching [vv 31–35]). The neat correspondence of A and A' identifies the *hoi par' autou* concretely as *hē mētēr autou kai hoi adelphoi autou* (v 31). On
all this see Taylor, *The Gospel According to St. Mark,* 236–37; Cranfield, *Mark,* 133–
35; Pesch, *Markusevangelium,* 1. 212–13; Mann, *Mark,* 251–52 (although he takes
the *elegon* to mean "people were saying"). Needless to say, one must not take the
exact configuration and details of Mark 3:20–35 and naively retroject all of it
back to the historical scene of A.D. 28.

CHAPTER 11

"IN THE FIFTEENTH YEAR . . ."

A Chronology of Jesus' Life

The reader may be somewhat surprised that a treatment of the chronology of Jesus' life[1] is placed at this point in the book, just as we leave the "hidden years" of Jesus and are poised to investigate his public ministry. There are, however, good reasons for locating a treatment of chronology at this point. Basically, there are three places in a book on the historical Jesus where a treatment of chronology might reasonably be located. These three locations correspond roughly to the three places in the Gospels where significant chronological information about Jesus' life seems to be directly or indirectly supplied: the Infancy Narratives, the beginning of the public ministry (especially in Luke), and the Passion Narratives. As we shall see, however, the data in the Infancy Narratives are of little use for fixing the main dates in the life of Jesus. On the other hand, postponing the question of chronology till the Passion Narratives would leave most of the book floating in a time vacuum. Hence it seems best to follow Luke's lead in 3:1–2 by placing a formal treatment of chronology just before the beginning of the public ministry.

It should disturb no one acquainted with ancient history that the main dates in the life of Jesus must remain approximate. With the exception of outstanding rulers, authors, and thinkers, the same holds true for most of the important historical figures of the Greco-Roman period. Indeed, the birth dates of even some of the Roman emperors are not certain,[2] and we are totally ignorant of the birth and death dates of Herod Antipas and Pontius Pilate. Perhaps we can gain perspective by remembering that the birth and death dates of Jerome, a prolific writer and one of the greatest Fathers of the Western Church, are still debated by scholars.[3] Thus, what should surprise us is that the dates of Jesus' birth, ministry, and death can be known with even fair approximation.

1. AN INITIAL SURVEY TO SET LIMITS

Five key pieces of data help impose initial, though rough, limits on our speculation about Jesus' dates. Once these general limits are set, we can attempt to be more precise.

A. THE BASIC TIME FRAME: A.D. 26–36

The Four Gospels (and various streams of earlier tradition within them[4]), the Acts of the Apostles, Josephus, and Tacitus all agree that Jesus was put to death during the rule of Pontius Pilate, the governor of Judea. There is absolutely no competing tradition on this matter in Jewish, Christian, or pagan sources from this period. Thanks to Josephus, with supplementary information supplied by Philo, Tacitus, Suetonius, Cassius Dio, and Eusebius, we can calculate that Pilate held his office from A.D. 26 to 36 (or very early in 37).[5]

Moreover, we can be fairly certain that Jesus was not executed at the very end of Pilate's tenure. Data from Paul's epistles and the Acts of the Apostles, plus such extrabiblical evidence as the Delphi inscription mentioning Gallio as proconsul of Achaia (cf. Acts 18:12–17), help determine that Paul's arrival in Corinth on his second missionary journey (Acts 18:1) must have occurred around A.D. 49–51.[6] When we consider all the events that had to take place in early Church history between the death of Jesus and Paul's arrival in Corinth ca. A.D. 50 (e.g., the spread of Christianity in Palestine, the persecution and scattering of the Hellenists, the founding of the church at Antioch, the conversion of Paul and his years of seclusion and activity before he joined the church at Antioch, his first missionary journey and the so-called "Council of Jerusalem"), it is almost impossible to place Jesus' execution as late as A.D. 36.[7] It must be pushed back at least a few years in Pilate's governorship.

Jesus therefore died sometime in the late twenties or early thirties of the 1st century A.D. In addition, Josephus tends to confirm an idea often taken for granted but made explicit in Luke 3:1, namely, that Jesus' entire ministry occurred during Pilate's rule.[8] Hence the whole ministry of Jesus lasted somewhere between A.D. 26 and the early 30s. This last point brings us to the next key text, Luke 3:1–2.

B. NARROWING THE TIME FRAME: JESUS DIED BETWEEN A.D. 28 and 33

The impression that Jesus was active sometime around the late twenties is reinforced by the "synchronism" in Luke 3:1–2,[9] where the evangelist coordinates the reigns of various rulers with the beginning of the ministry of John the Baptist: "Now in the fifteenth year of the reign of Tiberius Caesar [who reigned as sole emperor A.D. 14–37], when Pontius Pilate was governor of Judea [A.D. 26–36] and Herod [Antipas] was tetrarch of Galilee [ruled 4 B.C.–A.D. 39],[10] and his brother Philip was tetrarch of the region of Iturea and Trachonitis [ruled 4 B.C.–A.D. 33/34], when Lysanias was tetrarch of Abilene [dates unknown], and during the high-priesthood of Annas and Caiaphas [Caiaphas was high priest A.D. 18–36], the word of the Lord came to John the son of Zechariah in the desert." The mention of Pilate places the beginning of John's ministry within the decade of A.D. 26–36 and indicates that Jesus' ministry began after Pilate had already taken up his office as governor of Judea. The mention of Philip, who died in A.D. 33 or 34,[11] again suggests that Jesus did not begin his ministry at the very end of Pilate's tenure. This much confirms what we saw under our first point, but does not bring us much further.

We could be more precise if we could be sure what year corresponded to the fifteenth year of the reign of Tiberius. Unfortunately, there are different ways of calculating the years of Tiberius' reign.[12] Tiberius was associated with Augustus (i.e., Octavian) in Augustus' rule of the provinces of the Roman Empire from around A.D. 12 and then became emperor in his own right in A.D. 14, when Augustus died. Given the different calendars (Julian, Syro-Macedonian, Egyptian, or Jewish) that Luke might be using, Tiberius' fifteenth year could be fixed in any year between A.D. 26 and 29.[13]

Still, the information in Luke 3:1–2 does give us some help in establishing the chronological limits of Jesus' ministry. We do at least have a clear succession of events: Tiberius' entering upon his fifteenth year, the Baptist's beginning of his ministry, and then Jesus' beginning of his ministry (probably not too long after the Baptist had begun his ministry).[14] Moreover, even on a minimalistic reading of the picture presented in the Synoptics, Jesus' ministry lasted about a year, and even Mark may contain some slight hints of a ministry of more than one year.[15] If John's Gospel is taken into account for chronological purposes —and I think it should be—Jesus' ministry could have lasted about two to three years, if not more.[16]

In any case, the succession of the events just listed—Tiberius' entrance upon his fifteenth year (at the earliest, A.D. 26), the Baptist's commencement of his public activity, and then Jesus' beginning of a ministry that lasted at least one year—makes it impossible that Jesus could have been executed as early as A.D. 26. Hence, just as one cannot place Jesus' execution at the very end of Pilate's tenure (A.D. 36), so one cannot place it at its very beginning (A.D. 26). Therefore, even from a very superficial, initial survey of the data, a time somewhere between 28 and 33 seems the most likely date for Jesus' death, with a ministry of roughly one to three years preceding it.

C. AT THE OTHER END: JESUS WAS BORN NOT LONG BEFORE THE DEATH OF HEROD THE GREAT (4 B.C.)

Our study of the Infancy Narratives in Chapter 8 indicated why the statements in that block of Gospel tradition must be used with extreme caution. Lacking the direct testimony of eyewitnesses, the evangelists and the traditions they used had to expand meager memories with the help of OT prophecies, Christian creedal formulas, and foreshadowings of Christ's death and resurrection. Since, however, the Infancy Narratives of Matthew and Luke are independent of each other, often run in opposite directions, and sometimes contradict each other, the occasional agreement on a concrete fact may be of significance. Such is the case when they agree (Matt 2:1; Luke 1:5) that Jesus was born during the reign of King Herod the Great (37–4 B.C.).[17] This helps set vague limits for Jesus' life as a whole: he was not born after 4 B.C.,[18] his ministry took place around the late twenties or early thirties A.D., and he was crucified somewhere between A.D. 28 and 33.

Beyond this, can one fix more precisely the year of Jesus' birth? After all, to say that he was not born after 4 B.C. is not to say much. In other words, can one venture a reasonable guess about the length of Jesus' life?

If Matthew's story of the Magi (Matt 2:1–12), as well as the flight into

and return from Egypt (2:13–23), could be accepted as basically historical, we would have grounds for supposing that Jesus was born only a
few years before Herod's death in 4 B.C. According to Matthew's account, King Herod carefully inquired about the time of the star's appearance in order to be able to calculate the age of the Christ child.
Later, when he discovered that the Magi had gone back to their own
country without returning to report to him, he sought to catch the
Christ child in a murderous "dragnet" by killing all the boys in and
around Bethlehem *"two* years of age and under" (2:16). No doubt Herod
wanted to leave no room for error; "two years" probably represents the
oldest the Christ child could possibly be.

The approximate age calculated by Herod jibes with the often overlooked fact that Matthew never presents the Christ child of the Magi
story as the *newborn* king of the Jews (2:2), despite some translations to
that effect.[19] The impression that Chapter 2 of Matthew's Gospel thus
gives is of a child one to two years old at the time of the flight into
Egypt.[20] Matthew never directly tells us how long the Christ child was
kept in Egypt before Herod's death, but the evangelist creates the general impression that it was not a great number of years. He uses the
same diminutive word *paidion* ("little child") to describe Jesus during
the visit of the Magi (2:11), the flight into Egypt (2:13), and the return
from Egypt after Herod's death (2:20). The last verse of Matthew's Infancy Narrative (2:23) might be taken to imply that so short was Jesus'
residence in both Bethlehem and Egypt and so long was his residence in
Nazareth that he was naturally known as "the Nazorean" throughout
his adult life. In brief, the overall impression created by these stories is
that Jesus was born a few years—but not a great many years—before
Herod died.

The problem with all these observations, which are perfectly true
from a literary point of view, is that, as we have already seen, the historicity of the stories of the Magi and of the flight into and return from
Egypt are highly questionable.[21] Still, just as the vague memory of Jesus'
birth during Herod's reign was preserved independently in Matthew's
and Luke's infancy traditions, one can at least ask whether the idea that
Jesus was born neither at the beginning nor in the middle but toward
the end of Herod's reign is a historical reminiscence preserved in Matthew's Infancy Narrative.

D. Confirmation from Luke 3:23

An indirect but independent indicator that Matthew's placing of Jesus' birth toward the end of Herod's reign may be historical is found in Luke's statement that, when Jesus began his public ministry,[22] he was "about thirty years old" (hōsei etōn triakonta, Luke 3:23). This statement is obviously independent of Matthew's Infancy Narrative and is also clearly a passing remark that plays no great part in Luke's theological program.[23] Hence it is intriguing that this "aside" basically supports the impression created by Matthew that Jesus was born toward the end of King Herod's life. No doubt, in weighing Luke's statement, one should take seriously his careful qualifier "about." Granted the nature of Gospel traditions, "thirty" is only a "ballpark figure." Yet, if we should decide that Jesus' ministry began somewhere around A.D. 27–29, Luke's "about thirty years" would be of some help in calculating the date of Jesus' birth.

If, for example, we should arbitrarily take A.D. 28 as the beginning of Jesus' ministry, he would have been at least thirty-one years old—and that would demand placing his birth very soon before Herod's death. If, instead, Matthew is at all correct in intimating that Jesus was born a few years before Herod died, it is more likely that Jesus was about thirty-four years old when he began his ministry. On the other hand, a birth a good number of years before Herod's demise would place Jesus in his forties or fifties at the beginning of his ministry and would make Luke's assertion in 3:23 wildly inaccurate. The correlation of Matthew 2 and Luke 3:23 does make it likely—though not certain—that Jesus was born a few, but only a few, years before 4 B.C.[24]

E. Confirmation of the General Outline from John 8:57 and 2:20

If it is legitimate to draw conclusions from the convergence of independent traditions in Matthew and Luke, we may also rightly inquire whether the independent tradition in John can shed further light on Jesus' chronology. Actually, although the Johannine tradition, outside of the Passion Narrative (which we shall study below), has nothing new to tell us about the exact dates and age of Jesus during his ministry, it does

offer modest confirmation of the general results of our survey so far.
Two texts from the public ministry (John 8:57 and 2:20), both mocking
rhetorical questions put in the mouths of Jesus' adversaries in Jerusalem,
do coincide with some of the chronological data gleaned from the
Synoptics. Naturally, the rapid-fire dialogue between Jesus and his enemies is not to be taken as a videotape replay of what exactly occurred
during a visit of the historical Jesus to Jerusalem. But, as happens a
number of times in the Johannine tradition, a nugget of historical information may be embedded within a dialogue or discourse that, in its final
form, clearly comes from the evangelist.

1. John 8:57

In John 8:57, "the Jews" (i.e., the opponents of Jesus in Jerusalem) respond to Jesus' claim that Abraham saw the "day" of Jesus and rejoiced
(v 56). The "Jews" object: "You are not yet fifty years old, and you have
seen Abraham?" Obviously, the claim that Abraham saw the day of
Jesus is a reflection of the evangelist's preexistence christology and can
hardly be attributed to the historical Jesus. But what of the objection
that Jesus is not yet fifty? At the very least, it tells us what the evangelist, and presumably his tradition, thought about the age of Jesus during
his public ministry.

At first glance, the Jews' objection seems to imply that Jesus is in his
forties, indeed perhaps in his late forties. One would not ordinarily be
disposed to say to a man in his thirties, "You are not yet fifty years old."
The time limit simply would not fit; one would naturally refer instead
to the next decade that the person had not yet reached. In fact, Irenaeus
used this kind of reasoning to argue that, while Jesus was just under
thirty when he was baptized, he was already in his forties when John
8:57 was spoken (*Adv. Haer.* 2.22.6).[25] Hence, for Irenaeus, Jesus' ministry lasted over ten years.

But this is a prime example of interpreting a verse outside its rhetorical context. John 8:57 comes just before the theological and dramatic
climax toward which the whole of Chapters 7 and 8 (the disputes during
the feast of tabernacles) has been heading: "Before Abraham came to be,
I am" (8:58). Increasingly in the latter part of Chapter 8, Jesus has at-
tacked "the Jews' " claim to be true (spiritual) children of Abraham and
true children of God. Instead, God is declared to be the Father not of the
Jews but of Jesus; therefore, if anyone keeps the word of Jesus, he or she
will never die (v 51).

The Jews object that both Abraham and the prophets suffered death (v 52). Does Jesus make himself greater than *their* father Abraham (v 53)? The question that has been simmering since the beginning of Chapter 7 thus comes to full boil: "Whom do you make yourself?" Jesus first insists that he is not "making himself" anybody or seeking his own glory; rather, God *his* Father is the one who gives him glory (v 54). Jesus then returns to the Jews' question about Abraham and claims that Abraham did see the "day" of Jesus and rejoice. When the Jews object that Jesus is not yet fifty, Jesus replies with the solemn formula of self-revelation that sums up the opposition between being and becoming first sounded in the Prologue of the Gospel: "Before Abraham came to be *(genesthai)*, I am *(egō eimi)*." Faced with this blatant claim to divinity and eternal, unchanging existence in contrast to Abraham's short span of earthly life, the Jews seek to stone Jesus for blasphemy (v 59).

In the light of this dramatic climax, the function of v 57, sandwiched between vv 56 and 58, becomes clearer. The Jews, exasperated in the extreme and on the verge of trying to execute Jesus for blasphemy, are hardly concerned with attempting to fix the exact decade of life in which Jesus belongs. Caught between the vast, sweeping chronology of v 56, which looks back to Abraham, who somehow saw in advance the Incarnation of the Word in Jesus, and the solemn statement "I am," placing Jesus above all time and history, including the salvation history of Abraham and Israel, the Jews counter in mocking tones that this teacher who speaks of himself in terms of countless centuries has not reached even a half century of age.[26] The number fifty seems chosen precisely as a round number, long enough in the context of human life, but incredibly short and insignificant (a *mere* half century!) vis-à-vis Jesus' vast claims concerning Abraham and himself.[27]

Granted the line of argument and counterargument in John 7–8, as well as the red-hot polemics exploding at the end of Chapter 8, "fifty years old" in 8:57 is best taken as a round yet modest number roundly rejecting Jesus' huge, mind-boggling claims. The number does agree with everything we have seen, insofar as all other chronological texts would place Jesus below fifty during his public ministry. But to use John 8:57 to fix exactly how much below fifty Jesus was would be to overlook the rhetoric and polemic of the wider context.[28]

2. John 2:20

What seems to be a more promising text, at least at first reading, is John 2:20, where, during the feast of Passover, "the Jews" have just heard Jesus' challenge, "Destroy this temple and in three days I will raise it" (v 19). They object in v 20: "This temple has been [or: "was," *oikodomēthē*] forty-six years in the building. And you will raise it in three days?" At first glance, this precise reference, datable from the first Passover of Jesus' ministry, gives us a firm basis for calculation. However, a number of problems arise as soon as we probe this text more carefully.

First, what is the exact force of the aorist verb *oikodomēthē* ("was built," "has been built," or "has been in the process of being built")? Is it a "complexive aorist," which views an event that in fact extended over a good deal of time in the past as though it were a single past act?[29] Or do we have here an aorist with a perfect or present sense, leaving open the possibility that the speakers conceive of the activity of building the temple as recently completed or as still going on?[30]

Naturally, as we try to answer the question of what sort of aorist *oikodomēthē* is, an important consideration is the actual date of Herod's rebuilding of the temple. Unfortunately, the question of this date is complicated by apparent contradictions in the writings of Josephus. Josephus says in his *Jewish Antiquities* (15.11.1 §380) that the temple was rebuilt in Herod's eighteenth year (i.e., 20–19 B.C.). Yet he claims in his *Jewish War* (1.21.1 §401) that the temple was restored in Herod's fifteenth year (i.e., 23–22 B.C.). Schürer argues effectively for the correctness of the date in the *Antiquities* (20–19 B.C.), and both Finegan and Brown follow his solution.[31] A further complication, as Finegan points out, is that one must also decide in which passages Josephus distinguishes *hieron* (the whole temple precincts) from *naos* (the temple edifice proper, the inner temple accessible only to the priests) and in which passages he uses *naos* loosely for the entire temple precincts.[32] The same question must be asked about *naos* in John 2:20.

With all these confusing variables, a number of interpretations of John 2:20 are possible. To name just three: (1) The aorist could be taken in the sense that the process of building the temple is continuing in Jesus' day. This is the interpretation of Brown, and has in its favor the fact that some subsidiary building activity continued in the temple precincts into the sixties of the 1st century A.D.[33] Brown thus calculates the date of the scene in John 2:20 as A.D. 27–28, or more exactly, the Passover of 28.[34]

(2) While Finegan acknowledges that the idea of an ongoing process of building is a possible meaning of the verb, he prefers to stress the strict aorist meaning of *oikodomēthē:* the act of building was completed long ago. The sense of the chronological statement is rather: "This temple has stood for forty-six years."[35] Finegan goes on to stress that John's Gospel does observe the distinction between *naos* (temple in the narrow sense) and *hieron* (temple precincts in the wide sense). Indeed, John 2:19–21 is the only passage in the Fourth Gospel where *naos* is used. Elsewhere John always speaks of the *hieron* and clearly means by it the entire temple complex. Hence John 2:20, in its unusual use of *naos,* seems intent on specifying the temple proper.[36] This is a pivotal point for Finegan; for he calculates that, while the priests began to build the *naos* at the same time that Herod began the construction of the entire *hieron* (ca. 19 B.C.), the priests completed their work in 17 B.C.[37] If the forty-six years are counted inclusively from that date, the scene in John 2 would be laid in A.D. 29.

(3) Finegan also points to another possibility: if instead the forty-six years are computed as calendar years subsequent to the completion of the *naos,* the date of the scene would be A.D. 30. In any case, we see that, even with careful attention to the Greek text and calendrical calculations, the scene in John 2 could be situated anywhere from A.D. 28 to A.D. 30.

Even beyond all these considerations, there is another major obstacle to using John 2:20 to fix a precise date in the life of Jesus. From the viewpoint of source and redaction criticism, the story of the "cleansing" of the temple in John 2:13–22 is a shaky basis on which to compute the exact year in which the historical Jesus actually "cleansed" the temple. As is well known, the Synoptics place the cleansing of the temple just before the Passover at the end of the public ministry (e.g., Mark 11), while John places it at the Passover close to the beginning of the ministry (John 2). While older authors sought to reconcile these accounts by supposing that there were two cleansings, and while some scholars favor the chronology of John,[38] most critics hold that John or his tradition has purposely moved the cleansing back to the beginning of the ministry for theological and literary purposes (e.g., to place the whole ministry under the shadow of Jesus' death and resurrection, or to make room for the raising of Lazarus as the immediate cause of the plot to execute Jesus).[39]

If it be true that the cleansing of the temple is displaced in John, and if, moreover, we should accept John's indication that Jesus' ministry lasted for two to three years, we are left asking: To what date does the phrase "forty-six years" refer? Should we calculate it according to what may have been its original place in the Johannine tradition, i.e., at the end of Jesus' ministry, or has the evangelist changed the key number in v 20 ("forty-six") to compensate for his moving the cleansing back a few years to the beginning of the ministry?[40]

Granted all the question marks that a study of John 2:20 unearths, my opinion is that we cannot use John 2:20 to fix an exact date for the first Passover of Jesus' ministry. At best, we can say that John 2:20 fits in well with a ministry of Jesus that occurred somewhere around the years A.D. 27–30.

At the very least, therefore, the two Johannine passages give independent support to the general picture in the Synoptics. John 8:57 agrees with them that Jesus was below fifty years of age during his ministry; and, given the larger context, the verse need not indicate that he was close to fifty. John 2:20, while plagued with too many problems to give us an exact date, does confirm the years around A.D. 27–30 as the general time span of Jesus' ministry.

F. PRELIMINARY CONCLUSIONS

In sum, a brief initial survey of the main chronological indicators in the NT confers a high degree of probability on the following hypotheses: (1) Jesus exercised his entire ministry and then suffered crucifixion while Pontius Pilate was prefect of Judea (A.D. 26–36). (2) His ministry began somewhere between A.D. 26 and 29, extended over at least a year and perhaps as long as three years and some months, and ended with his execution somewhere between 28 and 33. (3) Jesus was born during the reign of Herod the Great (37–4 B.C.), and slight indications make it likely that he was born toward the end of Herod's reign rather than toward its beginning or during its middle years. Hence Jesus was probably in his early to mid-thirties at the beginning of his ministry and in his mid- to late thirties at its conclusion.

For a marginal figure in Greco-Roman history, these chronological limits are remarkably good, and perhaps they are the best we can hope for. Nevertheless, a closer inspection of some of the passages we have already surveyed, in addition to other chronological references, may help us to sharpen this picture.

2. AN ATTEMPT TO BE MORE EXACT

If we wish to be more precise about the "corridor" of A.D. 27–33, within which the ministry and death of Jesus transpired, we have only two sources of information that might prove useful: (1) the synchronism in Luke 3:1–2 (specifically, the fifteenth year of Tiberius' reign) and (2) the various time indicators within the Passion Narratives of the Four Gospels.

A. The Fifteenth Year of Tiberius

As we take a closer look at the synchronism in Luke 3:1–2, we should first appreciate its theological and literary function. Theologically, Luke wishes to impress on his Greco-Roman readers that the seemingly paltry events of Jesus' public ministry belong to the sweep and indeed the pivotal moment of history, a history which in Christ has reached out to embrace the Gentiles as well as the Jews. Hence Luke brings the solemn beginning of John's and Jesus' ministries[41] into contact with both the one emperor of the whole Roman world and the many minor rulers closer to or in Palestine. From a literary point of view, Luke marks the beginning of a major part of his work with a lengthy periodic sentence (cf. Luke 1:1–4; Acts 1:1–5). Using the style and forms of Greco-Roman historiography to address his cultured audience, Luke employs a synchronism that has literary parallels in the writings of Thucydides *(History of the Peloponnesian War* 2.2.1), Polybius *(Histories* 1.3.1–2),[42] and Josephus *(Ant.* 18.4.6 §106), while at the same time maintaining links with the conventions of OT narrative and prophecy (e.g., Isa 1:1; Jer 1:1–3; cf. 1 Macc 1:10).[43]

These theological and literary concerns are interwoven and should not be played off against each other. It is his theological concern about Jesus' place in history that moves Luke to designate the precise year in which the Baptist's ministry commenced. That Luke wants to be as specific as possible is clear from his naming one particular year in the reign of Tiberius. He could have referred vaguely to the reign of Tiberius as he does here to the rule of Pilate and Antipas, and as he does elsewhere to "the days of Herod the king" (1:5) or to the days when Caesar Augustus issued a decree while Quirinius was ruling Syria (2:1–2). Luke instead goes out of his way to specify the fifteenth year of Tiberius. Of course, Luke may be right or wrong in his calculations, but his intention to be precise in his chronological information is clear.[44] Since all the other references to tenure in office yield only general time spans (e.g., Pilate's governorship from 26 to 36), any exact information Luke might give us is reduced to his clearly intended focus on the *fifteenth* year of Tiberius.[45]

As mentioned above, there are a number of reasons why "the fifteenth year of Tiberius" is an ambiguous marker, capable of referring to any year between A.D. 26 and 29. Fortunately, not all the causes of ambiguity are equally weighty, and some can safely be put aside.

(1) As we have seen, Tiberius held a "coregency" with Augustus for a few years before the latter's death. While the beginning of this joint reign over the provinces of the Roman Empire has at times been dated to A.D. 11 or 13, the most likely year is 12. A number of older scholars, following the lead of Archbishop James Ussher of Armagh (1581–1656), calculated the fifteenth year of Tiberius from the time of this coregency and so arrived at a date of 26 or 27.[46] As I. H. Marshall and Harold W. Hoehner both note, this approach is largely abandoned today, since such a method of calculating the years of Tiberius' reign has no basis in either ancient historical documents or coins, whereas there is abundant evidence that Tiberius did reckon the first year of his reign from the death of Augustus.[47] As a matter of fact, all the major Roman historians who calculate the years of Tiberius' rule—namely, Tacitus, Suetonius, and Cassius Dio—count from A.D. 14, the year of Augustus' death. While all these authors wrote—in my opinion—after Luke, their agreement in this mode of calculation bespeaks a set convention. Presumably, Luke, who is intent on trying to follow the conventions of Greco-Roman historiography, would not have chosen an unheard-of means of reckoning Tiberius' years over a generally accepted one.[48]

(2) Hence it is probable that Luke is reckoning the fifteenth year from A.D. 14 and—as was common in the ancient world—using inclusive counting (i.e., including the years at both ends of the series in the count). This narrows down the possibilities, but a number of variables still come into play.

For instance, Augustus died on August 19, 14, but Tiberius was not elected to be his successor by the Senate until September 17, 14. From which date should the years of Tiberius be counted? Then, too, Luke could have counted the time from August/September to the next New Year's Day as the first regnal year ("nonaccession-year system"), or he could have left that partial year out of his count of the regnal years ("accession-year system"). But then, when did New Year's Day occur in Luke's "mental calendar"? A number of calendars were still in use in the Mediterranean world of the 1st century A.D. The relatively new Julian calendar placed New Year's Day on January 1, but the Jewish lunar calendar began with the 1st of Nisan (occurring somewhere in March or April), while the Syrian-Macedonian calendar began on October 1 and the Egyptian calendar on August 29.

In the face of all these variables, it is helpful for us to recall that, whatever be the sources of the information in Luke 3:1–2, the synchronism as it stands is a product of Lucan creative redaction.[49] In my opinion, Luke, an educated Gentile Christian, composed his two-volume work probably in Greece or Asia Minor, or possibly in Rome, where his evangelical epic concludes.[50] At any rate, he is certainly aiming his ambitious literary creation at a cultured Greco-Roman audience, embodied in the "excellent Theophilus" of Luke 1:3 and Acts 1:1.[51] Hence it seems improbable that, at the beginning of this solemn synchronism meant to tie the Christ-event into Greco-Roman history, he would use a Jewish or Egyptian calendar.[52] The more likely possibilities are as follows:

(a) Luke simply counted the *de facto* regnal years of Tiberius: i.e., the first year was August 19, 14, to August 18, 15, and so on. The fifteenth year would have run from August 19, 28, to August 18, 29.

(b) Luke used the Julian calendar, counting the time from August 29, 14, to December 31, 14, as the first year of Tiberius' reign ("nonaccession-year system"). The second year would have run from January 1 to December 31, 15, and so on. The fifteenth year would have run from January 1 to December 31, 28.

(c) Luke used the Julian calendar but did not count the time before January 1, 15, as a separate year of Tiberius' reign ("accession-year system"). In this case, the fifteenth year would have run from January 1 to December 31, 29.[53]

(d) Luke could also have used the Syro-Macedonian calendar. In the nonaccession-year system, the fifteenth year would run from October 1, 27, to September 30, 28; in the accession-year system, from October 1, 28, to September 30, 29.[54]

There is no way that we can be certain which of these methods of reckoning was used by Luke. Looking at the main possibilities listed above, we see that the fifteenth year of Tiberius could have included at least parts of A.D. 27, 28, or 29. Interestingly, almost all of the various methods of computation include at least some part, if not the whole, of A.D. 28 as belonging to the fifteenth year. Indeed, if Luke used the Julian calendar and the nonaccession-year system of reckoning, A.D. 28 coincides exactly with Tiberius' fifteenth year. Hence, for convenience' sake and as a preliminary, not definitive, judgment, I will accept A.D. 28 as the year in which John began his ministry and also baptized Jesus.[55] Even if the reckoning be a little off, it is not off by much, since the only other serious candidates are 27 or 29.[56]

Having reached a tentative judgment about the time of John's and Jesus' appearance on the public scene, we must now turn to the other end of Jesus' ministry and ask about the dates of the Last Supper and the crucifixion.

B. The Dates of the Last Supper and of the Crucifixion of Jesus

If we could fix the exact year in which Jesus died, we would have a much firmer basis on which to reckon the length of his ministry. Unfortunately, the calculation of the year of Jesus' crucifixion is fraught with difficulties, most of which arise from disagreements between the Synoptics and John on the dates of the Last Supper and the crucifixion. Faced with many confusing questions, we would do well to proceed point by point, from the more clear to the less clear.[57]

1. The Days of the Week

When it comes to passion chronology, the Four Gospels do agree on something: the days of the week on which Jesus celebrated his last meal with his disciples and then was put to death. All the Gospels place the Last Supper on Thursday evening, and the crucifixion, death, and burial on Friday before sunset. Actually, in establishing these days of the week from the Gospel texts, we must move backward, for all of the Gospels state in one way or another that the day after Jesus' crucifixion was the Jewish Sabbath, i.e., Saturday.

Indeed, in a surprisingly detailed fashion, Mark introduces the story of Jesus' burial by specifying in 15:42: "And as it was already evening, since it [i.e., the day of Jesus' death] was the day of preparation [paraskeuē], that is, the day before the Sabbath [prosabbaton] . . . ."[58] Hence, according to Mark, Jesus was crucified on a Friday, and the Last Supper, held on the evening before Jesus' death, took place on a Thursday.[59]

Matthew has the same basic schema, but he expresses it in a more "diffuse" way as a result of his adding the story of the guards placed at the tomb (27:62–66) after the narrative of Jesus' burial (27:57–61). At the beginning of the story of the burial, Matthew takes over only the first time reference present in the Marcan version of the story, "when evening came" (27:57). Then, in the subsequent pericope, the day on which the guards are placed at the tomb is described in a cumbersome way as "the next day, which is [the day] after the day of preparation [paraskeuē]." By this odd phrase Matthew obviously means the Sabbath. One wonders whether he uses such a convoluted way of saying "the Sabbath" because he himself realizes the unlikelihood of all the unseemly business taking place between the high priests, the Pharisees, and Pilate on the solemn Sabbath of Passover week. In any case, Matthew agrees with Mark that Jesus died on Friday and celebrated the Last Supper on Thursday evening.

Luke presents the same basic scenario, though perhaps more by inference. After Jesus is buried, the faithful women prepare spices and ointments and then rest "on the Sabbath according to the commandment" (23:56). "But on the first day of the week they came to the tomb, carrying the spices they had prepared" (24:1). The natural inference is that the women would have proceeded to anoint the body immediately after preparing the spices if the Sabbath had not intervened. The reader almost automatically concludes that the events surrounding the burial— and, indeed, all the occurrences narrated since Luke 22:66 ("and when day came," kai hōs egeneto hēmera)—are to be placed on Friday. Counting backward, we see that the women came to the tomb on Sunday, rested on Saturday, and saw Jesus executed and buried on Friday. Accordingly, the Last Supper on the previous evening took place on Thursday.

Interestingly, although both Matthew and Luke have Mark as the basic source of their Passion Narratives,[60] they express the time relationships among the days in different ways and place them at different points in the narrative. One wonders whether stray oral traditions may at times be reflected in these differences. At any rate, despite the different ways of indicating the succession of days, the end result in all three Synoptics is the same when it comes to identifying the days of the week in the passion chronology.

John is especially important in this regard, since he represents an independent passion tradition.[61] Just as he begins to narrate the story of the piercing of Jesus' side after his death, John explains why the Jews do not want the corpses to remain on the crosses overnight. Since the day of the crucifixion was the day of preparation (*paraskeuē,* the same word as in Mark and Matthew), there was a need to hurry, lest the bodies remain on the crosses on the Sabbath (19:31). The same point is made with reference to the hasty burial in a nearby garden: "Therefore, because of the preparation day (*paraskeuēn*) of the Jews, they placed Jesus there [in the new tomb in the garden], because the tomb was nearby" (19:42).[62] In the next verse we are told that "on the first day of the week" Mary Magdalene came to the tomb (20:1). John thus indicates indirectly that the day of Jesus' death was Friday, with the farewell meal the night before occurring on Thursday. Thus, for all their many chronological differences, the Marcan and Johannine passion traditions agree that Jesus held the Last Supper with the disciples on a Thursday night and died on a Friday. These results may seem so ordinary as to need no discussion; but, as we shall soon see, some dispute them in order to bridge the apparent contradictions between Synoptic and Johannine chronologies of the passion.

2. The Dates in the Month of Nisan According to the Jewish Calendar

It is when we try to specify the dates of the fateful Thursday and Friday according to the Jewish calendar that we run into the sharp difference between the Synoptic and Johannine chronology.

To understand the difference, we must first look at the Jewish calendar for Passover. According to the rules of Exodus 12 as interpreted by "mainstream" Jews[63] at the time of Jesus, the Passover lambs were slain in the Jerusalem temple on the fourteenth day of the month of Nisan (March/April). Exodus 12:6 directs that the killing of the lambs is to take place "between the two evenings," which perhaps originally meant "during the evening twilight." In the 1st century A.D., however, the sacrifice took place between 3 and 5 P.M., according to Josephus (*J.W.* 6.9.3 §423), though the hour may have been moved up some when the fourteenth of Nisan fell on a Friday.[64] Exodus 12:8 goes on to direct that the Passover lambs be eaten "on that night," which, in the context, must mean after sundown on the day the lambs were slain. Now, according to the Jewish way of calculating liturgical days at the time of Jesus, sundown would mark the beginning of a new day, the fifteenth of Nisan, Passover Day proper. This type of calculation for liturgical days is already witnessed in the OT (e.g., for the Day of Atonement in Lev 23:27,32)[65] and is explicitly applied to Passover in the *Book of Jubilees* 49:1 (written in the 2d century B.C.): "Remember the commandment that the Lord commanded you concerning Passover, that you observe it in its time, on the fourteenth of the first month [Nisan], so that you might sacrifice it before it becomes evening and so that you might eat it during the night on the evening of the fifteenth from the time of sunset."[66]

Now we are in a position to appreciate the difference between the Synoptic and Johannine chronologies. The Synoptics portray the Last Supper on Thursday evening as a Passover meal (specifically in the story of the preparation of the meal, Mark 14:12–17 parr.; also Luke 22:15). Hence the story of the preparation of the meal must take place on Thursday in the daytime, which is the fourteenth of Nisan, when the Passover lambs were being slaughtered (so Mark 14:12; Luke 22:7). The Passover meal (Mark 14:20–30 parr.), held in the evening after sundown, would take place as the fifteenth of Nisan, Passover Day proper, began. Therefore, according to the Synoptics, the arrest, trial, crucifixion, death, and burial of Jesus took place on a Friday which was (until sunset) the fifteenth of Nisan, Passover Day. The Sabbath which followed was the sixteenth of Nisan.

John presents us with a different chronology. Nothing in John's narrative designates the Last Supper as a Passover meal, though the meal is quite obviously taking place on the evening between Thursday and Friday. Indeed, what John says subsequently seems to make it impossible that the Last Supper, in his eyes, was a Passover meal. Early on Friday morning *(prōi,* John 18:28) the Jewish authorities bring Jesus from Caiaphas to the praetorium, the residence of Pilate in Jerusalem. Verse 28 continues: "And they themselves [i.e., the Jewish authorities] did not enter the praetorium, lest they be rendered unclean; rather [they remained outside and remained legally clean] so that they might eat the Passover." The phrase used here, *phagein to pascha* ("to eat the Passover"), is the very one used by the Synoptics to describe what was to be done at the Last Supper (Mark 14:12; Matt 26:17; Luke 22:8,15). Clearly, in John's reckoning, the Passover meal has not yet been celebrated.

John makes his position explicit at the climax of the trial before Pilate. Just as Pilate takes his seat on the tribunal to render his verdict, John tells his audience in an aside: "Now it was the Day of Preparation for Passover *[paraskeuē tou pascha]*" (19:14).[67] In John's reckoning, therefore, Thursday was the thirteenth of Nisan up until sunset; the Last Supper was held as the fourteenth of Nisan began and so was not a

Passover meal; Jesus was crucified, died, and was buried on a Friday that was the fourteenth of Nisan up until sunset; and Passover Day began with the Passover meal at sunset on Friday, as the fifteenth of Nisan began. As can readily be seen, according to John, in that fateful year of Jesus' death, Passover Day coincided with the Sabbath. This may be why John stresses the special concern of the Jews to remove the corpses from the crosses before the Sabbath began, "for great was the day of that Sabbath" (19:31),[68] i.e., that Sabbath was an especially solemn day.[69]

On a first reading, therefore, there seems to be a hopeless contradiction between the Synoptic and Johannine chronologies. Despite the fact that both place the Last Supper on Thursday evening and the death of Jesus on a Friday before sunset, they disagree on the dating of these two days. For the Synoptics, the Last Supper on Thursday was a Passover meal and so Jesus died on a Friday that was Passover Day (the fifteenth of Nisan). For John, the Last Supper was not a Passover meal. Jesus died on a Friday that was the fourteenth of Nisan, which in that year was the Preparation Day *both* for Passover *and* for the Sabbath. In that year, the two observances coincided on a Saturday that was the fifteenth of Nisan.

How are these chronologies to be reconciled—or should they be reconciled?

3. Attempts to Reconcile the Synoptic and Johannine Chronologies

Various scholars have tried to harmonize the Synoptic and Johannine chronologies for various reasons. Some theologians naively equate divine inspiration with inerrancy in the smallest historical and geographical details. Others, with a more historical bent, are concerned to show that the Gospels are as reliable as other ancient historical documents. Whatever the precise reasons, the attempts at reconciliation usually boil down to some theory that shows that both the Synoptics and John are right—in different ways. They are simply calculating the date of Passover according to different Jewish calendars or modes of reckoning.

(a) Among the older solutions, the best known was the one enshrined in the massive "rabbinic" commentary on the NT produced by Hermann L. Strack and Paul Billerbeck. In a lengthy excursus, Billerbeck adopted the theory that, in the year of Jesus' death, the Sadducees and Pharisees disagreed on when the month of Nisan had begun and therefore on what day Passover (the fifteenth of Nisan) began.[70] Since neither party could prevail against the other, they compromised by having Passover lambs slaughtered on both Thursday and Friday. The Pharisees (and Jesus with them) counted Thursday as the fourteenth of Nisan and so celebrated the Passover meal Thursday evening. The Sadducees instead counted Friday as the fourteenth of Nisan, and so celebrated the Passover meal as the Sabbath was beginning. Besides various problems that affect almost all such harmonizing solutions, the greatest objection to Billerbeck's proposal is the simple philosophical dictum: what is gratuitously asserted may be gratuitously denied. For all his learned disquisitions about disagreements between the Pharisees and the Sadducean group called the Boethuseans[71] on the proper day for offering sheaves during Passover week, Billerbeck cannot prove that any two-day slaughtering of Passover lambs ever took place in the Jerusalem temple during the time of Jesus.[72]

(b) It is strange that, after refuting Billerbeck's theory, S. Dockx gives simply a different version of the same basic distinction: some Jews present for the Passover in Jerusalem computed Passover one way, while other Jews also present in Jerusalem computed it another way. Dockx suggests that, in the year Jesus died, a disagreement arose between Galileans and Judeans concerning the day on which the fourteenth of Nisan fell.[73] If anything, Dockx's theory seems even more gratuitous than that of Billerbeck; it lacks any basis in the historical records of the period.[74]

(c) Thus, a major weakness of the approaches of both Billerbeck and Dockx is that they are not anchored in the concrete history of Judaism at the time of Jesus. Annie Jaubert seeks to overcome this weakness by appealing to a concrete historical reality of that period: the solar calendar evinced in the *Book of Jubilees* and at Qumran.[75] Jaubert suggests that this calendar represents an archaic priestly calendar that placed major feasts permanently on specific days of the week. For instance, Passover always fell on a Wednesday.[76] Jaubert then attempts to establish a link between this calendar and the calendar reflected in early Christian liturgy. She stresses in particular a tradition in the 3d-century *Didascalia apostolorum*, which presents the Last Supper as being held on a Tuesday evening.[77]

From all this Jaubert draws the radical conclusion that Jesus celebrated the Passover meal on Tuesday evening, with Passover falling on Wednesday according to the old priestly calendar. Jesus was arrested during the night between Tuesday and Wednesday. After various hearings and trials on Tuesday night, Wednesday, Thursday, and Friday morning, he was put to death on Friday, which was the fourteenth of Nisan, the eve of Passover, according to the official lunar calendar of the

Jerusalem temple.[78] Thus, the Synoptics preserved a primitive tradition that reflected the old priestly calendar. John, with his interest in Jesus' replacement of the Jewish feasts as celebrated in the Jerusalem temple, portrays the final meal and death of Jesus according to the official calendar.[79] In Jaubert's view, placing Jesus' arrest on Tuesday evening has the added advantage of creating more time for all the hearings and/or trials described in both the Synoptics and John to take place.

Jaubert's theory displays great learning and seeks to base itself on the concrete realities of 1st-century Palestine. And yet it too suffers from insuperable difficulties.

(1) We never receive an adequate explanation of why Jesus should have been observing a sectarian or specifically a Qumranite calendar for the major feasts of Judaism.[80] As we shall see later in this book, there is no solid reason for thinking that Jesus had ever been a member of the Qumran community or the wider group of Essenes. His freewheeling attitude toward the fine points of the Law stands diametrically opposed to all that was most dear to the legal extremists at Qumran.[81]

(2) More specifically, when the Gospels present Jesus in interaction with the official leaders of Judaism, it is always with the Jerusalem authorities or their representatives, never with the counterauthorities of Qumran. Whether we accept as historical the one journey of Jesus to the Jerusalem temple presented in Mark or the many journeys to the Jerusalem temple presented in John, it is to Jerusalem, not Qumran, that Jesus goes to celebrate the major Jewish feasts. Be it during the days immediately preceding the feast (so for Passover in the Synoptics) or during the feast itself (so for Tabernacles in John 7–8), Jesus is active in the Jerusalem temple.

Granted this general context, it is difficult to read the story of the preparation of the Last Supper in the Synoptics as indicating anything other than the celebration of the Passover on the day when other Jews in general and the temple authorities in particular would also be celebrating it. What, after all, is the natural meaning of Mark 14:12, coming as it does after days of public activity in the temple area by Jesus: "And on the first day of the unleavened bread, when *they were accustomed to sacrifice [ethyon] the Passover lamb*"? Notice the imperfect tense of the verb *ethyon*, for customary action, plus the unexpressed subject contained in the verb, "they." Who exactly are these "they" who are so taken for granted that they are not even mentioned by name, and where did they perform as a matter of custom the ritual sacrifice of the Passover lambs? Given the whole literary context of the previous chapters, set in and around the temple, it is extremely arbitrary suddenly to introduce otherwise unmentioned Qumranites into the Gospel and into this particular text— to say nothing of making Jesus and his disciples the sacrificing priests! The natural sense of the clause is "when the temple priests [and the Jews with them in the temple] were accustomed to sacrifice the Passover lamb." Jaubert realizes how damaging this clause is to her theory, but all she can do is gratuitously suppose that it comes from some "glossator" (otherwise unexplained, undated, and unidentified).[82] She is reduced to suggesting that Jesus held a *Passover* meal that dispensed with the *Passover* lamb but included unleavened bread![83]

Apparently Jaubert would have to multiply glosses, since we meet the same objection to her theory in Luke's redactional form of Mark 14:12: "Now there arrived the day of the unleavened bread, in which it was necessary that the Passover lamb be sacrificed" (Luke 22:7). From his Infancy Narrative onward, Luke has stressed a Jewish piety that is centered on the Jerusalem temple and fulfills the Mosaic Law as practiced by the priestly authorities ruling there (e.g., Luke 1:5–23; 2:22–24). In 22:7 he again takes up this theme of what *must* be done *(edei)* according to the Law.[84] To introduce suddenly at this point the necessity of obeying anti-temple Qumranite liturgical law flies in the face of Luke's whole presentation throughout his Gospel.

Jesus' connection with the Jerusalem temple and its liturgy, which is clear to a certain degree even in the Synoptics, becomes superabundantly clear in the Fourth Gospel. To take the most glaring example: John presents Jesus as going up to the Feast of Tabernacles just after everyone else has gone up to the feast (John 7:1–10). After apparently "lying low" at the beginning of the feast, Jesus proceeds to preach and dispute in the temple at *midpoint* during the festival week (7:14) and again on the last day of the feast (7:37), when crowds of Jews are present as they celebrate Tabernacles—obviously according to the lunar calendar used in the temple.

Jaubert, however, sweeps away the whole of the Johannine tradition with a wave of the hand, but with no detailed discussion. One can see why. If, early on in the Fourth Gospel, Jesus' observance of Jewish feasts in the Jerusalem temple *at the same time that other Jews observe them* is allowed to stand as basically historical, there is no good reason to think that his observance of his last Passover in Jerusalem would diverge from his set custom.

Hence it is no accident that, although John's Gospel (in its final form) spends five chapters on the Last Supper—chapters filled with variant forms of Gospel material coming from different strata of the tradition—there is no clear indication anywhere that the supper is or was ever thought to be a Passover meal. It is not simply the evangelist's redactional intervention that has transformed the Last Supper into a non-Passover meal. It never was a Passover meal at any stage in the Johannine tradition.[85]

To return to the main point: for all their differences, neither the Synoptic nor the Johannine presentation of the days preceding and including Jesus' last Passover creates the slightest impression that, during the final days of his life, Jesus was observing any other calendar than that of the Jerusalem temple, the only liturgical center of Judaism with which he ever interacted.

(3) A great weakness in Jaubert's approach is that, while she seeks to vindicate the Synoptics' presentation of the Last Supper as a Passover meal, she must claim at the same time that the Synoptics are in error with regard to their chronology of the days of the week: the meal occurred historically not on Thursday but on Tuesday evening, and Jesus was arrested on Tuesday night. Hence Mark must also be wrong when he places the meeting of the Jewish authorities to plot Jesus' arrest "two days before the Passover" (14:1). Since Mark places Passover on Friday, the meeting of the authorities takes place, in Mark's mind, on Wednesday (or possibly, by inclusive reckoning, on Thursday). Judas' offer to betray Jesus, which follows upon this meeting, presumably occurs either later on Wednesday or early on Thursday. Yet, according to Jaubert, Jesus was arrested on Tuesday night. Thus, Mark's errors include much more than simply the day on which the Supper was held.

In sum, in her effort to explain the divergences of the Synoptics and John on the dating of the Last Supper and the crucifixion, Jaubert ends up with an extremely strange position on the historical reliability of the Gospels. In effect, (1) the Synoptics and John are *both right* when they *disagree:* thanks to the different calendars, the Last Supper was a Passover meal (Synoptics), but the Passover was going to be celebrated the day after Jesus died (John). Yet (2) the Synoptics and John are *both wrong* when they *agree* that the Last Supper and Jesus' arrest took place on Thursday evening. All right when they disagree, all wrong when they agree. This is to turn the critical study of the passion chronology on its head and to sacrifice clear data to a befuddled theory.[86]

Sadder but wiser after this survey of typical attempts to harmonize or reconcile the differing passion chronologies of the Synoptics and John, we conclude that such harmonizations are well-meaning but contrived maneuvers to avoid one obvious fact: the Synoptics and John are in direct disagreement over the nature of the Last Supper as a Passover meal and over the date (fourteenth or fifteenth of Nisan?) of Jesus' death. As the existentialists constantly proclaim, to try not to choose is already to have made the wrong choice. Now we must choose.

4. Choosing Between the Passion Chronologies of the Synoptics and John

It would be foolish to claim that the choice between the two chronologies is a clear or easy one. Great scholars have defended and continue to defend both positions. For example, Joachim Jeremias was a passionate champion of the Last Supper as a Passover meal, while Joseph Blinzler and Raymond Brown brought forward weighty arguments for accepting the Johannine chronology of the passion.[87] Sometimes the arguments on both sides tend to cancel each other out; at other times, the balance of probability must be very finely weighed. The reasoning of some critics appears circular; but circularity in such arguments may be to a certain degree inescapable, granted the paucity of our data. The best one can hope to do is to ask which of the possible scenarios seems the most probable. In the end, a number of considerations lead me to favor the basic outline of the Johannine chronology as the most likely.

(1) While Jeremias shows great skill and voluminous knowledge of rabbinic traditions, one cannot avoid a certain sense of unease in his overall approach. The OT, Qumran, Philo, and Josephus are freely mixed together with rabbinic material both early and late. At times rabbinic material seems to be declared applicable or nonapplicable to the time of Jesus on the basis of whether or not it supports Jeremias's position. When Gospel texts do not lend themselves to Jeremias's desired interpretation, we are told that the Greek (which makes perfect sense as Greek) is a mistranslation of some unknowable and uncontrollable Aramaic original—a common escape hatch in Jeremias's approach to the Gospels. At times the Gospels are simply not treated as autonomous works to be read and interpreted on their own terms.

(2) With his great knowledge of rabbinic material and matters Jewish, Jeremias is able to show that, in the Synoptic presentation, certain events that at first glance seem unlikely could indeed occur on Passover Day. For instance, he points out that it was not impossible for a criminal to be executed on a feast day;[88] and, of course, in the case of Jesus, it was the Romans, not the Jewish authorities, who carried out the execution.

However, some events simply cannot be explained away so easily. Despite Jeremias' deft command of the material, he cannot really establish the likelihood that, at the time of Jesus, the supreme Jewish authorities in Jerusalem would arrest a person suspected of a capital crime, immediately convene a meeting of the Sanhedrin to hear the case (a case involving the death penalty), hold a formal trial with witnesses, reach a decision that the criminal deserved to die,[89] and hand over the criminal to the Gentile authorities with a request for execution on the same day —all within the night and early day hours of Passover Day, the fifteenth of Nisan! Yet this is what the Synoptic passion chronology and presentation of the Jewish "process" basically demand. In contrast, John's dating of Jesus' arrest at the beginning of the fourteenth of Nisan and his presentation of a more informal "hearing" before some Jewish officials during the night hours—while not without its own problems—does not labor under the same immense weight of historical improbability.[90]

(3) This general judgment is supported by the insights of form and redaction criticism. The intriguing fact is that, if Mark's Passion Narrative is shorn of two passages that probably come from either a secondary level of the tradition or from Mark's own redactional activity, the remaining Passion Narrative contains no clear indication that the Last Supper was a Passover meal or that Jesus died on Passover Day.

The two passages in question, both bearers of Marcan passion chronology, are the half verse that introduces the whole Passion Narrative (Mark 14:1a) and the story of the preparation of the Last Supper (14:12–16). In the case of 14:1a, many a critic would be inclined to think, a priori, that the introductory verse of a major section of a Gospel probably stems from its author. More specifically in our case, the wording of 14:1a favors the theory of composition by Mark. The phrasing, "It was the Passover and the [feast of the] unleavened bread after two days," fits in nicely with the style of "Marcan duality," i.e., the tendency of Mark to say things twice, the second phrase giving greater specificity to the first. Frans Neirynck has pointed out that Mark's love of duality is seen especially in temporal expressions, and he includes Mark 14:1 (as well as 14:12) among his examples.[91] Of course, it is also possible that the introductory clause was composed when various blocks of passion tradition were first put together to form a pre-Marcan passion narrative. Either way, 14:1a comes from a secondary or redactional stage of the tradition.[92]

More to the point, Mark 14:1a by itself is a vague time indicator at best. "Now it was the Passover and [the feast] of the unleavened bread after two days" could indicate a time one or two days before the Passover, depending on whether or not inclusive reckoning was being used. It is only when Mark 14:1a is connected with the more precise time indicator of Mark 14:12 that the sense becomes clearer, though still somewhat muddled: "And on the first day of the unleavened bread, when they were accustomed to sacrifice the Passover lamb, his disciples say to him . . . ." Mark 14:12 clearly places us on the fourteenth of Nisan, the day when the priests sacrificed the lambs in the temple. This makes perfect sense with what follows: a story in which Jesus directs two disciples to a Jerusalemite householder, who makes available an upstairs room suitable for the Passover meal (vv 12–16). The remarkable point, then, is that, since even 14:1a is somewhat ambiguous, it is only 14:12–16 that explicitly makes the Last Supper a Passover meal. Once the narrative of the meal begins, none of its three pericopes (the prophecy of betrayal, vv 17–21; the institution of the eucharist, vv 22–26; and the transitional pericope on the way to Gethsemane, with the prophecy of Peter's denial, vv 26–31) contains any element that demands that we consider the Last Supper a Passover meal. Indeed, without 14:1 + 12–16, it would never cross the mind of the reader that this meal was supposed to be taken as a Passover meal.

It is highly significant, then, that *even* Joachim Jeremias, the staunchest champion of the Passover nature of the meal, thinks that Mark's story of the preparation of the meal (14:12–16) belongs to the latest of the four stages of the Passion Narrative that Jeremias posits.[93] In effect, then, Jeremias himself admits that the only pericope that clearly makes the Last Supper a Passover meal is a late development in the Gospel tradition. Moreover, even critics who do not necessarily follow all of Jeremias' reasoning think that 14:12–16 is a later development inserted into the earlier passion traditions. Eduard Schweizer in particular gives solid reasons for this position.[94]

Likewise late or redactional, in my opinion, is Luke 22:15–16, spoken by Jesus at the beginning of the meal: "With desire I have desired to eat this Passover meal with you before I suffer. For I tell you that I will not eat it until it is fulfilled in the kingdom of God." Taken in its strict sense, this saying (according to the best critical text)[95] would mean that Jesus will *not* eat the Passover meal in front of him before he suffers and dies. Actually, its sense is more likely, "I will not eat it again until . . . ," presupposing that Jesus has already begun eating the meal before him.[96]

More to the point, I think it likely that we have here a reworking, expansion, and inversion of the Marcan eucharistic narrative rather than an independent, early Lucan tradition.[97] Mark has his two eucharistic formulas (14:22–24) followed by a lone word that speaks of drinking no longer *(ouketi)* of the fruit of the vine until he drinks it new in the kingdom of God (14:25). Luke has revised and given greater balance to this series of sayings by moving the statement about not drinking up toward the beginning of the pericope (Luke 22:17–18) and by balancing it with a parallel word about eating the Passover meal (22:15–16).[98] The reworked material contains sufficient indications of Lucan vocabulary, style, and theology to justify this conclusion.

The result of all this Lucan redaction is a neat pattern of two words about not eating and not drinking any ordinary food, followed by the two words of institution over the bread and the wine.[99] But even if one prefers the opinion of those exegetes who see in vv 15–16 special Lucan tradition, one must make a long and hardly justified leap to arrive at the position that these verses reflect the exact words of Jesus at the Last Supper rather than early Christian reflection on the Last Supper.

(4) Once the Synoptic Passion Narratives are deprived of their late or redactional references to Passover, we realize that the Last Supper in the underlying Synoptic tradition is no more a Passover meal than is the Last Supper in John's Gospel. Actually, when one stops to think about it, the witness of John's Gospel is quite remarkable when taken by itself. As almost all redaction critics will agree, John 13–17, enshrining the narrative and lengthy farewell discourses of the Johannine Last Supper, preserves many different layers of the Johannine tradition, from primitive material that parallels Synoptic pericopes (the prediction of the betrayal, the prediction of Peter's denial, the exhortation to service), to the form of the farewell discourse that comes from the evangelist (basically John 14), to the forms of the farewell discourses that come from the final redactor (John 15–17). What is noteworthy is that, throughout all this many-layered, lengthy material, there is no trace of a tradition about the Last Supper as a Passover meal.[100] The entire Johannine tradition, from early to late, agrees perfectly with the primitive Synoptic tradition on the non-Passover character of the meal.

(5) Jeremias goes on at great length to show that various details of both the Synoptic and Johannine Passion Narratives make sense only if the Last Supper was a Passover meal and that apparent objections to the meal's Passover nature are not valid.[101] Indeed, he even claims that aspects of John's narrative argue for a Passover meal in the Fourth Gospel.[102] At the root of many of his arguments, however, there lies one

fundamental weakness. Jeremias basically poses an either-or proposition: either (1) a solemn Jewish ritual meal of some sort (especially the Passover meal),[103] with all its religious trappings, or (2) an ordinary, everyday meal, which would not be marked by great formality, elaborate religious formulas and hymns, drinking wine, reclining at table, an evening setting, and a Jerusalem venue. The problem is that Jeremias is proposing a false dichotomy.[104]

There is another possible scenario, one that is quite plausible on any reading of the Gospel tradition: sensing or suspecting that his enemies were closing in for an imminent, final attack, and therefore taking into account that he might not be able to celebrate the coming Passover meal with his disciples, Jesus instead arranged a solemn farewell meal with his inner circle of disciples just before Passover. Wanting privacy, and having his days taken up with teaching in the Jerusalem temple, Jesus chose to have an evening meal with his closest followers in the house of some affluent Jerusalem supporter on a Thursday around sunset, as the fourteenth of Nisan was beginning. The supper, though not a Passover meal and not celebrated as a substitute Passover meal, was nevertheless anything but an ordinary meal. With Jesus bidding farewell to his closest disciples as he prepared himself for the possibility of an imminent and violent death, the tone of the meal would naturally be both solemn and religious, accompanied by all the formalities (reclining at table, drinking wine, singing hymns, etc.) that Jeremias uses to prove the Passover nature of the supper.

Moreover, if we should allow the basic historicity of the eucharistic narrative (Mark 14:22–25 parr.), we would have to admit that Jesus did and said some astounding and unprecedented things at the Last Supper, things that cannot be explained simply by positing the context of some Jewish ritual meal, Passover or otherwise.[105] Given the unique circumstances of this unusual person, it is not surprising that what he did at his last meal with his inner circle of disciples does not fit neatly under any conventional religious rubric of the time. Trying to make it fit under such a rubric is what has caused so much of the problem about passion chronology. In a sense, the Synoptics were the first to take that route, by making an "extraordinary" meal fit under the rubric of Passover. Both the pre-Synoptic and Johannine traditions are much better explained by a special farewell meal, planned and executed by Jesus according to his own desires and peculiar circumstances.

(6) By way of corollary, I might note two advantages to the solution I propose, as opposed to the Synoptic chronology.

First, the Johannine chronology explains the Barabbas incident (Mark 15:6–14; John 18:39–40) much more easily than does the Synoptic chronology.[106] This is not the place to argue whether or not the Barabbas incident is actually historical. Suffice it to say that, being present in both the Marcan and Johannine traditions, it belonged to one of the earlier strata of the primitive Passion Narrative. Yet the obvious premise of the Barabbas narrative—an amnesty or pardon granted to some Jewish prisoner at Passover—is that the amnesty or pardon was given precisely so that the Jew, upon release, could take part in the Passover meal. What would be the point of granting release to a Jewish prisoner on Passover Day after the Passover meal, the central ritual of Passover Day, had already taken place? In other words, if the Barabbas incident, historical or not, was in an early form of the Passion Narrative, then that form of the Passion Narrative would naturally give the impression that the Barabbas incident took place on the morning of the fourteenth of Nisan, when there was still time for Barabbas to take part in the Passover meal, and not on the morning of the fifteenth of Nisan, when the meal was already over. The presence of the Barabbas incident in some early form of the Passion Narrative agrees, at least implicitly, with the Johannine, not the Synoptic, chronology.

Second, both the Marcan and Johannine Passion Narratives place the Last Supper in some Jerusalem home in the evening or night hours.[107] Yet, in both Mark and John, the Last Supper is presented as a special meal that Jesus holds with his innermost circle of disciples; it is not a large, indiscriminate gathering around a table. If, however, the meal is the regular Passover meal, we must suppose that Jesus is eating in the home of an extremely rich patron with an extraordinarily large house, since presumably the patron would have to be holding his own Passover meal with his relatives and friends on the same evening that Jesus would be celebrating his Passover meal with his disciples. The scenario of the Last Supper becomes much more imaginable if Jesus is using his patron's house on the evening that marks the beginning of the fourteenth of Nisan, the day of preparation. On that evening, the patron would be in a much better position to offer privacy as well as dining facilities for Jesus' special group.

Both of these points are admittedly minor and therefore have been mentioned only after the major arguments.[108] Yet they do fit in perfectly with the Johannine chronology and do not seem to square with Mark's. As so often in our quest, it is the converging lines of probability that lead us to decide which, among many options, is the most likely scenario.[109]

C. The Year of Jesus' Death and the Length of His Ministry

1. The Year of Jesus' Death

If we decide that John's chronology of the passion is more likely to be historically accurate, does that decision give any indication of the exact year in which Jesus died? It may—within a certain range of probability. On the one hand, we have already seen that, within the ten-year span of Pilate's rule as prefect (A.D. 26–36), Jesus' ministry may well have begun in A.D. 28, with 27 and 29 also being serious candidates. That means we can safely ignore every year up to 28 as a candidate for the year of Jesus' death. Furthermore, given a date around A.D. 28 as the beginning of Jesus' ministry, his execution in the very last years of Pilate's tenure also seems unlikely, since anything like a five-to-eight-year ministry would be in glaring disagreement with both the Synoptic and the Johannine chronologies. Nor, as a practical matter, is such a lengthy ministry usually defended by exegetes or historians.

In brief, then, the year of Jesus' death, in the opinion of most commentators, must lie within the range of A.D. 29–34—and even then we are casting the net as widely as possible. As we shall see, the net is more often cast within the range of A.D. 30–33. In the light of our frequent ignorance of the exact year of the death of many notables in the ancient world, we should be happy that we can be even this precise about the year of Jesus' crucifixion.

Yet there are those who wish to be more precise still. To narrow down the candidates even further, some exegetes call upon the insights of astronomy to calculate in which years—within the range of A.D. 29–34 —the fourteenth of Nisan fell on a Friday. At first glance, the use of science to solve this problem of biblical chronology looks very promising; but there is more than one obstacle to a clear scientific solution.

(1) In the official lunar calendar, the new month (e.g., Nisan) was declared on the evening of the twenty-ninth day of the old month *if* two trustworthy witnesses could attest to the calendar commission in Jerusalem that they had seen the new light of the new moon after sunset.[110] The declaration therefore depended not on whether the new light actually existed, but on whether human beings had seen it. Clouds, rain,

dust, and other atmospheric disturbances of which we cannot now be sure could have delayed the sighting of the new light. This difficulty was mitigated somewhat by the rule that months could be neither shorter than twenty-nine days nor longer than thirty. Hence the delay was only one day at most.

(2) To adjust the lunar calendar to the actual solar year, every now and then a leap year would have to be added to the Jewish calendar. There was probably no regular cycle of leap years in the early 1st century A.D.; they were added whenever the authorities decided from concrete observation (especially of agriculture) that they were needed.[111] We cannot be sure whether a leap year fell between A.D. 29 and 34.

Any calculations must therefore remain tentative. That is why I did not introduce the question of astronomy until this relatively late point in the discussion. At least our major conclusions can stand apart from an appeal to astronomical calculations and the special problems they entail. At any rate, according to the tables drawn up by Jeremias, within our designated range of A.D. 29–34, the only years in which the fourteenth of Nisan probably fell on a Friday are A.D. 30 (Friday, April 7) and A.D. 33 (Friday, April 3).[112] Put negatively, A.D. 29 and 32 seem to be excluded no matter whether the Synoptic or the Johannine chronology is preferred,[113] and A.D. 31 is not a viable candidate if we opt for the Johannine chronology. For all practical purposes, then, we are left with a choice between A.D. 30 and 33.

In my opinion, A.D. 30 is the more likely date. To begin Jesus' ministry in A.D. 28 (which seems to me the most probable year) but to put off his death until A.D. 33 would result in a ministry of some four to five years. While this is not impossible, it goes beyond what either the Synoptics or John indicate. As a tentative conclusion, then, I suggest that Jesus began his ministry soon after that of John the Baptist in A.D. 28 and that he was executed on the cross on April 7, 30.[114] This conclusion naturally implies a further one concerning the length of Jesus' ministry, a topic that up till now I have discussed only tangentially. As the last step in our treatment of the chronology of Jesus' life, we will take up a direct consideration of the duration of the ministry. We are in a much better position to discuss this question now, and it may also provide some indirect confirmation of the positions we have already adopted.

2. The Length of Jesus' Ministry

It is customary to start out the debate on the duration of Jesus' ministry by underscoring the different, not to say contradictory, presentations of the Synoptics and John. We might well begin by asking just how different or contradictory the stories in the Synoptics and John really are. I stress that at this point I am simply addressing the *stories* that the Synoptics and John tell the reader in their literary works; I am not yet drawing any conclusions as to history.

It is often said that Mark's story comprises less than a year or a year at most. But one should be very careful with one's formulation of the problem. Mark's story—unlike John's—*does not demand* more than a year for the events narrated, simply because only one Jewish feast is ever explicitly mentioned in Mark, namely, the Passover of Jesus' death. In other words, we *could* compress all the events narrated in Mark into a year or less. But let us turn the question around: Does Mark's story *demand* that all the events transpire within one year? No. The exact same absence of chronological indications that allows a ministry of a year or less also allows a ministry of more than one year.

Moreover, purely on the level of the Gospel story—again, therefore, prior to drawing any historical conclusions—various details in the stories told by the Synoptics might lead the reader to think in terms of a ministry of more than one year. For instance, we have already noted that Chapters 3 and 6 of Mark have the appearance of taking place during springtime in Galilee (plucking the heads of ripe grain, 2:23; five thousand people sitting on the green grass in a desert area, 6:39). An indication of springtime does not occur again in Mark until the direct reference to Passover in 14:1. While theoretically all these passages could be referring to the same spring, the large amount of narrative material, including lengthy travels, in between Chapters 2 and 6 on the one hand and Chapter 12 on the other could easily lead the reader to think in terms of at least two springtimes within the ministry of Jesus. Again I emphasize that I am merely speaking of what the story might suggest, not what it demands or what it indicates about history.

Furthermore, other scattered details in the Synoptic Gospels imply what John makes explicit: that, during his public ministry, Jesus went to Jerusalem more often and was more active there than one would gather from a hasty reading of Mark. In a Q logion that Luke places on Jesus' lips while he is on his way up to Jerusalem for his final Passover, but which Matthew situates in Jesus' last days in Jerusalem, Jesus rhetorically addresses the holy city: "Jerusalem, Jerusalem, you who kill the prophets and stone those sent to you, how often I wanted to gather your children just as a bird gathers her young under her wings, but you refused" (Matt 23:37 || Luke 13:34). Whether we picture Jesus saying this on the road up to Jerusalem (so Luke) or after a few days in Jerusalem (so Matthew), it seems odd, not to say churlish, for the Synoptic Jesus to issue such a complaint against Jerusalem—unless the reader is being invited to suppose that Jesus engaged in repeated ("how often!") attempts to win over Jerusalem during numerous visits and that Jerusalem repeatedly refused. Once again, I am not drawing historical conclusions here, but simply remarking on the natural impression made on the reader by the story in the Synoptics.[115]

Indeed, Luke may be preparing the reader for such an impression when he states globally quite early in the public ministry: "And he [Jesus] was preaching in the synagogues of Judea."[116] Since Luke is closely following Mark at this point (Mark 1:35–39 || Luke 4:42–44), it seems that Luke has quite consciously broadened out Mark's geographical indication, "in all of Galilee," to the more inclusive "of Judea," understood as the whole land of the Jews, all of Palestine.[117] Luke continues this theme in 7:17: "And this report about him [Jesus] went throughout the whole of Judea and the surrounding region." Similarly, during the trial before Pilate, the high priests sum up Jesus' whole ministry by depicting him as "teaching throughout the whole of Judea, beginning from Galilee unto here" (23:5). Once more, I stress that at this point we are dealing not with historical judgments but with the impression the texts make on the reader. Jesus' cry of rebuke to Jerusalem, made while Jesus is still journeying up to the holy city for his last Passover, may not seem so strange to the reader who notices the various references to Jesus' ministry and fame "throughout the whole of Judea."

Once the Synoptic Jesus reaches Jerusalem for his last Passover, there may be one final hint of a previous, more extended ministry in the holy city. Mark's story of the preparation of the Passover meal (14:12–16), taken over by Matthew and Luke, has Jesus commanding two disciples to say in a rather peremptory manner to some Jerusalem householder: "Where is *my* guest room where I may eat the Passover meal with *my* disciples?" (v 14). Notice that Jesus is not asking to join the householder in the latter's Passover meal. Jesus requests or rather implicitly commands that a room that he pointedly calls his own be prepared for him and his inner circle of disciples (in v 17, the Twelve). Jesus goes on to prophesy to the two disciples that the householder will show them a large upstairs room "prepared with couches" (v 15). Naturally, the disciples find everything just as Jesus has foretold (v 16). Once more I emphasize that my point here is not whether this event actually happened in A.D. 30 but rather that such a story creates in the reader the impression that Jesus may have been previously active in Jerusalem and so could count on a loyal and affluent Jerusalemite disciple to supply for his needs on short order.

Throughout this brief review of Synoptic passages I have been at pains to emphasize that I am not at this point trying to prove that these passages are all historical, therefore allowing further conclusions about the historical Jesus to be drawn. Instead, I am simply pointing out that, for all the differences between the Synoptic and Johannine depictions of Jesus' public ministry, they do not, strictly speaking, pose a formal contradiction as to the length of his ministry and the number of visits he paid to Jerusalem. The Synoptic presentation of the public ministry could be compressed into a year or less, but need not be. Indeed, there are a few fleeting hints that Jesus' ministry took more than one year and involved more than one visit to Jerusalem.

We turn now to John's Gospel and ask how many years the ministry lasted according to the story narrated in the Fourth Gospel. Again, we must distinguish. If we ask what *minimum* length of time the Gospel narrative *demands*, the answer must be two years plus a month or two.[118] After some initial activity that need not demand more than a few weeks (John 1:35–2:12), Jesus goes up to Jerusalem for the first Passover of his public ministry (2:13). At the time of the feeding of the five thousand we are told that the (second) Passover was near (6:4). And of course Jesus goes to Jerusalem in preparation for the (third) Passover, which, according to John, he does not live to celebrate (11:55; 12:1,12; 13:1; 18:28). At a minimum, therefore, the Fourth Gospel demands a ministry of two years plus a month or so. As with the Synoptics, so with John, this absolute minimum does not mean that the Fourth Gospel forbids us to suppose that the ministry actually took longer. In fact, both the Fourth Evangelist and the final redactor emphasize that they are not presenting a complete record of Jesus' deeds (John 20:30–31; 21:25).

If, however, we stay close to the minimum duration of the ministry that John narrates, we see that, for all their many differences, there is not a vast, unbridgeable gap between the Synoptic and Johannine presentations of the duration of the ministry. The Synoptics depict a ministry that *could* have taken only a year; yet the reader is given various hints that might point to a longer ministry and more frequent visits to Jerusalem. This "extended" reading of the Synoptic story is not all that far off from John's depiction of a ministry of two years and a few months. Purely from the viewpoint of the story presented in the Gospels, therefore, when it comes to the question of the duration of the ministry, the Synoptics and John are not so diametrically opposed to each other as is sometimes supposed.

We come now to a correlation of all these literary observations with the results of our chronological investigations. We have seen that it is likely that Jesus began his ministry in A.D. 28 and died on Friday, April 7, 30. If we hypothesize that Jesus began his ministry very early in A.D. 28, at least a few weeks before Passover of that year, and that he then died the day before Passover in A.D. 30, we have a "snug" fit with the Johannine outline: two years plus a month or two.[119] Our survey of Synoptic passages has indicated that, while such a chronology does not directly flow from the Synoptic presentation, the Synoptics do not directly contradict or exclude it and may even contain a few passages that point in its direction.

At the same time, I think it wise not to extend gratuitously the ministry of Jesus much beyond the two years and some months that John demands as a minimum. On the one hand, the alternative Gospel chronology to that of John, namely, the Synoptics', is a chronology that, at first glance, points to a shorter, not longer period. On the other hand, the close correlation between the minimum time demanded by John's presentation and the span of A.D. 28 to 30 that I established on other grounds counsels reserve rather than expansive speculation. Once we move beyond the limits that our correlation makes likely, unbridled imagination rather than any historical controls would set the outer limits.

3. A FINAL SUMMARY AND A FINAL CAUTION

I began this chapter by emphasizing that the main dates in the life of Jesus must remain approximate. Now that the reader has wandered down the labyrinthine paths of NT chronology, he or she is in a better position to understand why that is so. Yet the reader can also feel relieved that our meanderings have not been completely in vain. The marginal Jew we are pursuing has left some footprints in the sands of time. Fortunately those chronological sands also bear the larger imprint of the death of Herod the Great, the fifteenth year of Tiberius, the prefecture of Pontius Pilate, and the annual feast of Passover, which in the year of Jesus' death happened to coincide with a Sabbath. It is largely because this marginal Jew brushed up against what were considered the great men and religious institutions of the day that we can hazard a guess about some key dates in his life.

To summarize the chronology we have seen—as well as to begin to understand how it fits into the larger picture of Jesus' ministry—let us draw up a skeletal outline of Jesus' life according to chronology and geography.

Jesus of Nazareth was born—most likely in Nazareth, not Bethlehem —ca. 7 or 6 B.C., a few years before the death of King Herod the Great (4 B.C.). After an unexceptional upbringing in a pious family of Jewish peasants in Lower Galilee, he was attracted to the movement of John the Baptist, who began his ministry in the region of the Jordan Valley around the end of A.D. 27 or the beginning of 28. Baptized by John, Jesus soon struck out on his own, beginning his public ministry early in 28, when he was around thirty-three or thirty-four years old. He regularly alternated his activity between his home area of Galilee and Jerusalem (including the surrounding area of Judea), going up to the holy city for the great feasts, when the large crowds of pilgrims would guarantee an audience he might otherwise not reach. This ministry perdured for two years and a few months.

In A.D. 30, while Jesus was in Jerusalem for the approaching feast of Passover, he apparently sensed that the increasing hostility between the Jerusalem temple authorities and himself was about to reach a climax. He celebrated a solemn farewell meal with his inner circle of disciples on Thursday evening, April 6 by our modern reckoning, and the beginning of the fourteenth of Nisan, the Day of Preparation for Passover, according to Jewish liturgical reckoning. Arrested in Gethsemane on the night of April 6–7, he was first examined by some Jewish officials (less likely by the whole Sanhedrin) and then handed over to Pilate early in the morning of Friday, April 7. Pilate quickly condemned him to death by crucifixion. After being scourged and mocked, Jesus was crucified outside Jerusalem on the same day. He was dead by the evening of Friday, April 7, 30. He was about thirty-six years old.

It is against the background of this sparse chronological grid that we will now seek to understand what Jesus of Nazareth said and did during those two short but world-changing years that led up to his death. One thing should strike the reader almost immediately upon reading this summary. Almost all the dates—even the approximate ones—are bunched together at the beginning and the end of Jesus' life and/or ministry. Once the two years of ministry begin, we are largely in the dark, chronologically speaking.

I stress this negative point because all too often those exegetes who arrive at some vague chronological outline such as the one above proceed to fill in the gaping hole of the public ministry with a table of neatly arranged events from John and the Synoptics—the events being meshed together according to some homogenized order and decked out with hypothetical dates. Sometimes the outline of John's Gospel provides the overarching pattern, sometimes that of the Synoptics, and sometimes a potpourri of both. It is, of course, very satisfying intellectually to be able to pinpoint where Jesus is during any part of any given year, but there is simply no firm basis for such detailed reconstruction of the chronology of the public ministry.

The basic objection to all such endeavors is that they ignore the fundamental insights of form and redaction criticism. As William Wrede and Karl Ludwig Schmidt[120] both showed early on in the 20th century, the present succession of events, the framework of time and place surrounding pericopes and chapters, the narrative flow and "plot"—all are largely the work of the individual evangelist or of some collector of Gospel traditions on whom the evangelist depended. Outside of the special case of the Passion Narrative, in which many individual events would make sense only as parts of an ordered whole, most stories and sayings from Jesus' public ministry probably circulated at first without any overarching chronological sequence, in fact without any precise anchoring in time or place.

As I have made clear in this chapter, I do think that embedded in John's Gospel we have the historical recollection that Jesus regularly went to Jerusalem for the great feasts and that he was there for a number of Passovers. Actually, John's presentation is only what common sense would expect anyway. It would be strange indeed if, in the early 1st century A.D., a Palestinian Jew with strong religious interests did not go regularly to Jerusalem for the pilgrimage feasts.

But beyond the vague and hardly surprising datum of Jesus' regular pilgrimages to Jerusalem, John's ordering of events and sayings is just as theologically motivated as that of the Synoptics—indeed, many would say more so. To use either John or the Synoptics as a chronologically reliable grid for the discrete events of the public ministry is to confuse theological artistry with historical fact.[121] For instance, we have no way of knowing whether the beginning of Jesus' ministry was actually marked by a wedding feast at Cana (John 2:1–11), or by a sermon and exorcism in the Capernaum synagogue (Mark 1:23–28), or by a sermon in the Nazareth synagogue (Luke 4:16–30), or by the Sermon on the Mount (Matthew 5–7), or by all of these, or by none of these. The placement of these programmatic events and sermons at the beginning of the public ministry in each Gospel is probably due to the conscious decision of each evangelist. We have here one of the prime reasons why a "life of Jesus" (in the sense of a modern biography) cannot be written—even if we restricted that "life" to his public ministry and death. How can one write a biography, even a partial one covering only the significant years of a person's life, if one cannot discover what came before what, if the historical flow of before and after, cause and effect, remains unknowable?

I have just enunciated in a nutshell the reason why most of the subsequent chapters in Volume Two of this work will be ordered not according to a chronological framework but by major topics, e.g., proclamation of the kingdom of God, parables, Jesus' stance toward the Mosaic Law, healings, and so forth. Once we leave the initial events surrounding John the Baptist and the baptism of Jesus, and until we reach the events that move toward the final clash in Jerusalem in A.D. 30, we cannot properly speak of before and after, except in a few rare cases. We are back to our image of the pieces of a mosaic that we must put together as best we can. Still, in another sense, there is a certain dynamism of cause and effect, before and after, pervading our whole project. Whatever the exact order of Jesus' events and sayings, as a whole they precede and somehow precipitate the final confrontation with his enemies in Jerusalem, resulting in his crucifixion. The criterion of Jesus' violent death, while not solving individual problems of chronology or authenticity, does provide a thread that runs true to the end. In the next chapter, which will open Volume Two, we shall begin to trace that thread with the help of John the Baptist.

¹ For general surveys and special problems, see Urbanus Holzmeister, *Chronologia Vitae Christi* (Scripta Pontificii Instituti Biblici; Rome: Biblical Institute, 1933); George Ogg, *The Chronology of the Public Ministry of Jesus* (Cambridge: Cambridge University, 1940); J. Lebreton, "Jésus-Christ. II. Chronologie de la vie de Jésus," *DBSup* 4, cols. 970–75; Jack Finegan, *Handbook of Biblical Chronology* (Princeton: Princeton University, 1964); S. Dockx, *Chronologies néotestamentaires et vie de l'église primitive. Recherches exégétiques* (Paris/Gembloux: Duculot, 1976); Harold W. Hoehner, *Chronological Aspects of the Life of Christ* (Grand Rapids: Zondervan, 1977); Ormond Edwards, *The Time of Christ. A Chronology of the Incarnation* (Edinburgh: Floris, 1986); *Chronos, Kairos, Christos. Nativity and Chronological Studies Presented to Jack Finegan,* ed. Jerry Vardaman and Edwin M. Yamauchi (Winona Lake, IN: Eisenbrauns, 1989). Also useful—and often more critical—are Hans Conzelmann, *Jesus* (Philadelphia: Fortress, 1973) 20–25; Brown, *The Birth of the Messiah,* 547–56; Robert Jewett, *A Chronology of Paul's Life* (Philadelphia: Fortress, 1979) 25–29; J. A. Fitzmyer, "A History of Israel," *NJBC,* 1246–50.

For an introduction to the problems connected with the chronology of the Passion Narrative, see Annie Jaubert, *La date de la cène* (EBib; Paris: Gabalda, 1957), and its English translation, *The Date of the Last Supper* (Staten Island, NY: Alba House, 1965); Eugen Ruckstuhl, *Chronology of the Last Days of Jesus. A Critical Study* (New York: Desclée, 1965); Joachim Jeremias, *The Eucharistic Words of Jesus* (London: SCM, 1966) 15–88; Josef Blinzler, *Der Prozess Jesu* (4th ed.; Regensburg: Pustet, 1969) 101–26; Paul Winter, *On the Trial of Jesus* (Studia Judaica 1; 2d ed.; ed. T. A. Burkill and Geza Vermes; Berlin/New York: de Gruyter, 1974); Brown, *The Gospel According to John,* 1. 555–56.

The volume by Finegan *(Handbook of Biblical Chronology)* is still in common use today, and it is a mine of valuable information. But it suffers from two weaknesses: (1) It lacks a thorough application of historical criticism, especially form and redaction criticism, to the Gospel texts, notably the Infancy Narratives, which are too often treated as modern historical records. (2) There is too ready a use of later patristic and rabbinic literature, without sufficient questioning of the sources and reliability of the claims made. The same sort of criticism holds for a number of essays in the *Chronos* volume dedicated to Finegan; at times the treatment of the NT text approaches fundamentalism. Dockx's *Chronologies* suffers even more from a naive, uncritical, harmonizing use of sources. While Hoehner's presentation in *Chronological Aspects* could not be accused of fundamentalism, a conservative evangelical theology is the driving engine of his whole project, as Chapter 6, on Daniel's prophecy of the seventy weeks, reveals (see, e.g., p. 139). Standing somewhat apart, Edwards' *The Time of Christ* is a strange mixture of chronology, theology, and philosophical speculation on human evolution and psychology. Insofar as its chronology seems dictated at times by theological presuppositions and goals, it may stand for many other popular presentations that I do not bother to list.

² It need not surprise us that Grant *(The Roman Emperors,* 69, 71) expresses some doubt about the exact birth dates of the last two emperors of the 1st

century A.D. He writes that Nerva was born "probably in 30" and that Trajan was born "probably in about 53." Later on (p. 115), we are told that Coldius Albinus (reigned 195–97) "was probably born between 140 and 150."

³ See J. N. D. Kelly, *Jerome. His Life, Writings, and Controversies* (Westminster, MD: Christian Classics, 1975) 1, 331, 337. Kelly prefers A.D. 331 as the date of Jerome's birth, though he admits that some biographers place his birth in the middle forties of the 4th century. Jerome's death took place in either 419 (so Quasten) or 420 (so Kelly). In contrast, the dates of Augustine of Hippo are fairly secure. He was born on November 13, 354, and died on August 28, 430; see Agostino Trapè, "Saint Augustine," in Angelo di Berardino, ed., *Patrology. Vol. IV. The Golden Age of Latin Patristic Literature* (Westminster, MD: Christian Classics, 1986) 345–50.

⁴ The presence of Pilate in the story of Jesus' ministry and/or death is supported most strongly by the passion traditions behind Mark and John, and secondarily by special M and L material.

⁵ The data in favor of this dating, which is almost universally accepted, can be found in Jean-Pierre Lémonon, *Pilate et le gouvernement de la Judée. Textes et monuments* (EBib; Paris: Gabalda, 1981). On pp. 15 and 126–27, Lémonon defends A.D. 26 as the date of arrival; on pp. 241–44, he suggests the time between December 15, A.D. 36 and the end of February in A.D. 37 as the period during which Pilate must have left Palestine for Rome. For earlier disputes on whether Pilate was dismissed from his office in A.D. 35, 36, or 37, see Blinzler, *Der Prozess Jesu*, 271–73. For a convenient list of the prefects and procurators of Judea, see Fitzmyer, "A History of Israel," 1248. In order to sustain his highly unusual theory that Jesus was born in 12 B.C. and died ca. A.D. 21, Jerry Vardaman ("Jesus' Life: A New Chronology," *Chronos, Kairos, Christos*, 55–82) tries to date Pilate's rule in Judea from A.D. 14–15 to ca. 25–26 (pp. 77–82). Not only must Vardaman give various passages in Josephus' *Antiquities* forced interpretations, he must even rewrite Luke 3:1 to make it say "in the second [instead of the fifteenth] year of Tiberius." This is pure fantasy.

⁶ See the treatment of the date of Paul's arrival in Corinth in Jerome Murphy-O'Connor, *St. Paul's Corinth* (Wilmington, DE: Glazier, 1983) 129–40; Murphy-O'Connor favors A.D. 49. However, Joseph A. Fitzmyer ("Paul," *NJBC*, 1332) while arguing from the same basic data that Murphy-O'Connor uses (the statements of Acts and the Corinthian correspondence, the Gallio inscription, Claudius' expulsion of Jews from Rome), prefers to place the arrival in early A.D. 51. Jewett (*A Chronology of Paul's Life*, 100) fits right in between, with A.D. 50. The attempt by Gerd Luedemann (*Paul, Apostle to the Gentiles. Studies in Chronology* [Philadelphia: Fortress, 1984] 157–77, 262) to place Paul's arrival notably earlier (ca. A.D. 41) has not met with general acceptance.

⁷ See the standard works on the chronology of Paul's life, e.g., John Knox, *Chapters in a Life of Paul* (New York/Nashville: Abingdon, 1950) 74–88; Jewett, *A Chronology of Paul's Life*, 95–104; Luedemann, *Paul, Apostle to the Gentiles*, 262–63; Fitzmyer, "Paul," 1330–32. The positions of Jewett and Fitzmyer are more

"mainstream" than those of Luedemann, whose dates many would consider too early.

[8] Josephus' introductory phrase in the *Testimonium Flavianum* (*Ant.* 18.3.3 §63), *kata touton ton chronon* ("during this time," "about this time," "at this time"), refers to the rule of Pontius Pilate, whose difficulties with the Jews Josephus has been narrating since 18.3.1 §55. The phrase in §63 directly introduces not a reference to Jesus' execution, but rather a short account of his ministry. At the end of that account Josephus repeats Pilate's name as he states that "Pilate, because of an accusation made by the leading men among us, condemned him to the cross. . . ." The fact that Josephus feels no need to use the fuller form of identification, "Pilate, the governor of Judea" (as in §55), confirms that the *Testimonium Flavianum* in §63–64 is considered by Josephus to be simply a continuation of the Pilate stories starting in §55 and extending through §62. Thus, Josephus indicates that the whole of Jesus' ministry, from its beginning to its conclusion on the cross, took place during Pilate's rule of Judea. Curiously, only Luke among the evangelists states this point explicitly.

[9] For standard treatments of these key verses, see Schürmann, *Das Lukasevangelium*, 1. 149–53; Fitzmyer, *The Gospel According to Luke*, 1. 455–58. Luedemann (*Paul, Apostle to the Gentiles*, 9) is too cavalier in his dismissal of the synchronism. To be sure, Luke makes chronological errors at times (the census under Quirinius in Luke 2:1–2, which really took place in A.D. 6–7, instead of at the birth of Jesus as Luke thinks; the revolt of Theudas, mentioned by Gamaliel in Acts 5:36—though the revolt actually took place ca. A.D. 44, years after the time when Gamaliel supposedly gave this speech). The difference here is that Luke's dating .is basically in line with what we know from other traditions. Moreover, Luke goes out of his way to name an exact year, which is not his usual manner in chronological references. Hence it is not amiss to ask whether his statements can make our general knowledge of the time frame of Jesus' ministry more precise.

[10] For the dates of Antipas, see Harold W. Hoehner, *Herod Antipas* (SNTSMS 17; Cambridge: Cambridge University, 1972) 10, 262–64. On p. 262 n. 4 (continued on p. 263), Hoehner discusses the slight evidence for Antipas' reign extending into A.D. 40; but Hoehner himself thinks that Antipas' deposition by Caligula most likely took place in the summer of 39.

[11] See Stewart Perowne, *The Later Herods. The Political Background of the New Testament* (London: Hodder and Stoughton, 1958) 56.

[12] See the explanations and tables in Finegan, *Handbook of Biblical Chronology*, 259–73.

[13] Actually, the first few months of the year 30 would have to be included if Luke, using the "accession-year system," were calculating the regnal years of Tiberius from the death of Augustus according to the calendar years of the Jewish calendar (beginning with the 1st of Nisan); on this point, see Finegan, *Handbook*, 269. As shall be seen below, it is highly unlikely that Luke was composing his synchronism according to the Jewish calendar.

[14] Mark 1:14—and then the other Synoptics following him—creates the impression that Jesus' ministry began only after John's ended with imprisonment. The presentation of the Fourth Gospel (notably Chapter 1 and 3:22–30) suggests that things were much more complicated: Jesus remained for a while in the entourage and shadow of the Baptist, drew some of the Baptist's followers to himself, and finally struck out on his own, though Jesus continued the Baptist's practice of baptizing followers, at least for the initial period of his own separate ministry—all this while the Baptist was still active. As we shall see later, this picture may well come closer to the historical truth than Mark's schematization. On this point, see Jerome Murphy-O'Connor, "John the Baptist and Jesus: History and Hypotheses," *NTS* 36 (1990) 359–74.

[15] If Mark 2:23 (the disciples pluck the ears of grain, which are ripe enough to eat) and 6:39 (the large crowd at the multiplication of loaves sits on the green grass) may be taken to indicate that a significant part of Jesus' ministry took place *according to Mark's redactional presentation* in and around Galilee over the course of a springtime, there may be an underlying idea *on the redactional level of Mark* of a ministry of over a year and perhaps about two years.

On differing views as to whether Mark 2:23 has any value as a chronological indication, see, in favor, M.-J. Lagrange, *Evangile selon Saint Marc* (EBib; 4th ed.; Paris: Gabalda, 1928; reprint 1966) 52; Karl Ludwig Schmidt, *Der Rahmen der Geschichte Jesu* (Darmstadt: Wissenschaftliche Buchgesellschaft, 1969; reprint of 2d ed. of 1919) 89–92 [only for the pericope taken in isolation, not as a means of constructing a chronology of Jesus' ministry]; Taylor, *The Gospel According to St. Mark*, 216; against, Morton Smith, "Comments on Taylor's Commentary on Mark," *HTR* 48 (1955) 21–64, esp. p. 28; William L. Lane, *The Gospel According to Mark* (NICNT; Grand Rapids: Eerdmans, 1974) 114 n. 79; C. S. Mann, *Mark* (AB 27; Garden City, NY: Doubleday, 1986) 237. The debate revolves around whether the plucking of the grain really took place during an extended tour of Galilee in springtime, perhaps after the feast of Passover (so, e.g., Lagrange) or whether we must give great weight to two opposing considerations: (1) Palestinian grain can at times ripen early in spring (hence before Passover), especially in the Jordan Valley; (2) there is no reason why this incident could not have taken place historically on the way up to Jerusalem for Passover. However, if we are asking simply about the impression that *Mark* creates in his presentation of the ministry (a distinction many of the older authors do not make), the mention of springtime circumstances early in the Galilean ministry does give one the impression, within Mark's literary work, of a ministry that extends over more than one year.

The mention of green grass in 6:39 is likewise ambiguous as a time indicator: (1) while green grass would usually denote springtime, some green grass could remain in sheltered areas or along the lakeside into summer, or sprout up as early as November (though Mark states that the area was "desert" [6:31,35]); (2) the green grass could be merely a symbolic touch. However, in the same basic story, John 6:4,10 independently notes that "Passover was near" and that "there was much grass in the place." Hence the detail may indeed be meant to indicate a springtime ministry in Galilee, reinforcing, *at least on the literary level of Mark's redaction,* i.e., on the level of Mark's story read in order and as a whole, the impression of 2:23.

In sum, it is one thing to say that Mark's presentation of the ministry *can* be fitted into one year and does not demand more than one year; that is true. It is quite another thing to say that Mark's presentation *demands* that Jesus' ministry last only one year and therefore excludes a multiyear ministry; that is not true. Obviously, it is still quite another thing to move from Mark's literary presentation to a decision about historicity.

[16] See the cautious statement of Brown *(The Gospel According to John,* 1. XLIX–LI), who notes that, since John's Gospel explicitly denies that it is giving a full account of all Jesus did during his ministry (John 20:30), there "is no real reason why one cannot postulate a four- or five-year ministry."

[17] Herod was appointed king by Mark Antony and Octavian (the future Caesar Augustus) in 40 B.C. However, he did not effectively begin his reign as king of the Jews until he captured Jerusalem in 37 B.C. Strictly speaking, Luke 1:5 tells us only that the parents of the Baptist lived during Herod's reign. But obviously the chronological note intends to date not their lives as a whole (if they were so advanced in years, they must have lived part of their lives before Herod's reign) but rather the birth of the Baptist, which occurred, according to Luke, some six months before the birth of Jesus. While these last details are questionable, the main point remains: Luke does intend to date the birth of Jesus during the reign of King Herod, and this agrees with the statement of Matthew, who explicitly places Jesus' birth during Herod's reign. The agreement of Luke's oblique reference and Matthew's direct dating is itself significant.

[18] The attempts by a few historians to prove that Herod the Great died in some other year have not met with general acceptance. For example, W. E. Filmer ("The Chronology of the Reign of Herod the Great," *JTS* 17 [1966] 283–98) uses contorted arguments in an attempt to establish that Herod died instead in 1 B.C. As Timothy D. Barnes points out very well ("The Date of Herod's Death," *JTS* 19 [1968] 204–9), Filmer's thesis collides with two major pieces of evidence: (1) Herod's successors all reckoned their reigns as beginning in 5–4 B.C. (2) The synchronisms with events datable in the wider context of the history of the Roman Empire—synchronisms made possible by Josephus' narrative of the circumstances attending Herod's death—make 1 B.C. almost impossible to sustain. Barnes goes on to suggest that perhaps December of 5 B.C. may be a better candidate for the date of Herod's death than March/April of 4 B.C. As is the case with other alternatives, this innovation has not met with general approval.

The question of Herod's death is taken up once more in a number of essays in the *Chronos, Kairos, Christos* volume edited by Vardaman and Yamauchi. Ernest L. Martin ("The Nativity and Herod's Death," 85–92) revives the theory that Herod died in 1 B.C., with Jesus' birth placed in 3 or 2 B.C. This does not receive support from the other contributors to the volume who address the same issue. Douglas Johnson (" 'And They Went Eight Stades Toward Herodeion,' " 93–99) defends the traditional date of 4 B.C. for Herod's death, pointing out that Martin has mistranslated a key text concerning Herod's funeral in *Ant.* 17.8.3 §199.

Harold W. Hoehner ("The Date of the Death of Herod the Great," 101–11) likewise champions 4 B.C. Paul L. Maier ("The Date of the Nativity and the Chronology of Jesus' Life," 113–30) adds still another voice in favor of 4 B.C., though his further thoughts on the exact year of Jesus' birth betray an uncritical use of the Infancy Narratives. (Indeed, most of the authors never face the critical questions addressed in Brown's *Birth of the Messiah.*) All in all, the scattered attempts to undermine 4 B.C. as the year of Herod's death must be pronounced a failure.

[19] "Newborn king of the Jews" or similar phrases are found in Luther's German translation, the NAB, the Revised NAB, and Brown, *Birth of the Messiah*, 165, 170. The RSV correctly translates: "Where is he who has been born king of the Jews?" (Matt 2:2). The New Revised Standard Version of 1989 follows this tradition by translating: "Where is the child who has been born king of the Jews?" For Herod to inquire about the exact time that the star had appeared (in order to be able to calculate the child's age) and then to fix the upper limit of the children to be killed at two full years of age implies that, at least in the mind of the storyteller, Jesus had not just recently been born.

[20] This makes perfect sense in Matthew's overall view of things in his Infancy Narrative: Joseph and Mary are permanent residents of Bethlehem and have no intention in the beginning of the story of going to Nazareth.

[21] If this be the case, the interminable arguments about which astronomical phenomenon should be identified with the "star of Bethlehem" are beside the point. Of course, as Brown notes *(Birth of the Messiah,* 171), some historical phenomenon remembered by Christians could have served as a catalyst for the present Matthean story. But that is another matter, and the vague memory of some celestial phenomenon would not aid us in deciding when Jesus was actually born or how old he was when Herod died. The "star of Bethlehem" would help us in our calculations only if the Magi story were taken quite literally as precise history.

[22] As Fitzmyer *(The Gospel According to Luke,* 1. 499) notes, Luke's use of the participle *archomenos* here is "cryptic." But from the parallel uses of the verb *archesthai* (or its cognates) elsewhere in Luke-Acts to denote the beginning of Jesus' ministry (Luke 23:5; Acts 1:1,22; 10:37), it is clear that *archomenos* is being used here absolutely to mean "as he began his public ministry." It therefore does not mean "Jesus began to be about thirty years of age" (so the KJV). As is clear even in the English translation, the very precise "was beginning to be thirty years old" clashes hopelessly with the vague "about." See also Maier, "The Date of the Nativity," 121. Hence Vardaman's attempt ("Jesus' Life: A New Chronology," 57) to bolster his strange theory that Jesus was born in 12 B.C. and died ca. A.D. 21 by translating Luke 3:23 as the KJV does goes contrary both to Lucan usage and to the natural sense of the verse taken in itself. Finegan *(Handbook of Biblical Chronology,* 273–75) at first treats both the KJV translation and the translation espoused here equally; but in the end he inclines toward the KJV (see his conclusion on p. 300). It is symptomatic of his whole book that he never investigates the use of *archesthai* in Luke-Acts as does Fitzmyer.

[23] How Luke knew or calculated the number thirty is not clear. Schürmann (*Lukasevangelium*, 1. 199) suggests that Luke may have deduced the number from 2:2 and 3:1. Yet, granted that Luke is most probably mistaken about the census under Quirinius, what year 2:2 represented in Luke's mind is far from clear; nor are we completely sure what year Luke understood by the "fifteenth year of Tiberius." Schürmann also suggests that the number thirty refers to the age of King David when he assumed the throne (2 Sam 5:4 [2 Kgdms 5:4] *huios triakonta etōn*). That is possible, and yet 3:23 is used to introduce a genealogy that plays down the theme of "royal son of David" in favor of the theme of "the new Adam" who comes directly as son from God (3:38). Note that, while Matt 1:1–17 traces Jesus' descent through the sons of David who actually reigned on the throne of Judah, Luke pointedly traces Jesus' lineage through sons of David who did not reign. One might also wonder why, if Luke was not constrained by some tradition, he did not make Jesus' age exactly thirty so that it would coincide perfectly with David's at the time of his accession. Fitzmyer (*The Gospel According to Luke*, 1. 499) rightly rejects Davidic and other possible OT allusions (e.g., Joseph's age in Gen 41:46 or the adult age at which Levites begin to serve in the tent in Num 4:3); such allusions would be farfetched in this context. Still more esoteric would be the idea that Joshua (=Jesus) son of Nun was thirty years old at the time of the exodus. The weakness of this supposed allusion is that the OT never says expressly that Joshua was thirty at the exodus. Rather, one must count back from Joshua's age at the time of his death (a hundred and ten, as stated in Josh 24:29) through the generation of the settlement in Canaan (traditionally reckoned as forty years) and the generation of the wandering in the wilderness (likewise traditionally reckoned as forty years) to arrive at thirty. Another weakness of this suggestion is that Luke refers the word *exodos* not to the beginning of Jesus' ministry but to the entire event of his death, resurrection, and ascension (see Fitzmyer, *The Gospel According to Luke*, 2. 800).

[24] The paradox that Jesus was born sometime before 4 B.C. is due to the fact that our present system of designating years B.C. ("before Christ") and A.D. ("anno Domini," "in the year of the Lord [Jesus]") comes from the monk Dionysius Exiguus. In the first half of the 6th century A.D., Dionysius suggested that Christians should count years from the birth of Christ, and not from the reign of the Emperor Diocletian (a notorious persecutor of Christians)—to say nothing of counting from the traditional date of the founding of the city of Rome (A.U.C. [*ab urbe condita*, from the founding of the city], which would be 753 B.C. in our system of reckoning). Unfortunately, Dionysius' piety was better than his arithmetic. He miscalculated the year of Herod's death (thus foreshadowing the views of some 20th-century exegetes) and hence the year of Jesus' birth. Dionysius thought that A.D. 1 was equivalent to 754 A.U.C.; he was off by at least four years, since Herod died in 750 A.U.C.

[25] See the Latin text in *Irénée de Lyon. Contre Les Hérésies. Livre II. Tome II. Texte et Traduction* (SC 166; ed. A Rousseau and L. Doutreleau; Paris: Cerf, 1982) 224–27.

[26] Cf. the similar interpretation in Schnackenburg, *Das Johannesevangelium. II.*

Teil, 299. Barnabas Lindars (*The Gospel of John* [NCB; Grand Rapids: Eerdmans, 1972] 335) is quite right in taking fifty as a "round number" that is not to be pressed. Contrary to Ernst Haenchen (*John* [Hermeneia; 2 vols.; Philadelphia: Fortress, 1984] 2. 29 and 1. 184–85), he is also right in thinking that the number fifty has nothing to do with the number forty-six in 2:20.

[27] Similarly Hoehner, *Chronological Aspects*, 23.

[28] Finegan (*Handbook*, 275) is disappointing here. All he can do is weakly suggest that perhaps "even more latitude must be allowed in the interpretation of 'not yet fifty' than in the case of 'about thirty.' " Yet he never explains why this is so.

[29] See Max Zerwick, *Graecitas Biblica* (5th ed.; Rome: Biblical Institute, 1966) 84 (#253). C. F. D. Moule (*An Idiom-Book of New Testament Greek* [2d ed.; Cambridge: Cambridge University, 1960] 11) calls this phenomenon the "constative" or "summary" aorist.

[30] Brown (*John*, 1. 116) combines these two possibilities under the rubric of the complexive aorist, ". . . summing up the whole process of building which is not yet completed." Brown finds a "perfect parallel" in the LXX of Ezra 5:16: "And from that time on until now [the Jerusalem temple] has been in the process of being built [N.B., *ǭkodomēthē*, the aorist of *oikodomeō!*] and has not [yet] been finished."

[31] Schürer, *The History of the Jewish People*, 1. 292 n. 12; Finegan, *Handbook*, 277–78; Brown, *John*, 1. 116. Making matters still more murky, however, Finegan understands the temporal reference in the *Antiquities* in a pluperfect sense and so thinks that Herod had actually entered upon his nineteenth year.

[32] Finegan, *Handbook*, 278–79.

[33] Hoehner (*Chronological Aspects*, 41) points out that work continued on the temple until the procuratorship of Albinus (A.D. 62–64); cf. Josephus' statement in *Ant.* 20.9.7 §219.

[34] Brown, *John*, 1. 116; Schürer (*The History of the Jewish People*, 1. 292 n. 12) allows the Passover of either 27 or 28; Finegan (*Handbook*, 279) prefers the Passover of 27, *if* one accepts the interpretation that the act of building is still continuing. Such differences in calculation can easily occur in these chronological discussions, since it is not always clear, either in Josephus or in the Gospels, at what time of year an event is occurring, what calendar is being referred to, whether parts of years are being counted as whole years, and whether years are being counted inclusively (i.e., with both ends of the series being counted).

[35] For all that follows in the second and third solutions, see Finegan, *Handbook*, 279–80. Notice, though, that, for all the talk of the literal sense of the aorist, in effect this interpretation of the aorist makes it equivalent to a perfect tense: the act of building is over, but the effect of the action perdures into the present. Hence Hoehner (*Chronological Aspects*, 42) speaks of an "effective or perfective" aorist.

[36] Finegan argues this point in *Handbook*, 279–80. By examining various Johannine passages, he provides a more convincing argument than does Otto Michel, who simply affirms that "quite plainly . . . neither Jn. nor the NT takes *naos* in the strict sense for the temple proper" (*"naos,"* *TDNT* 4 [1967] 884 n. 19). Michel goes on in the same note to observe that often Josephus uses *naos* and *hieron* without distinction (*J.W.* 6.2.1 §97 and §110), though at times he does distinguish between the two (*J.W.* 6.2.3 §121). Curiously, while Gottlob Schrenk admits that the NT at times observes the distinction, he flatly denies this in the case of John 2:19—though without any argumentation to support his point (*"hieron,"* *TDNT* 3 [1965] 235).

[37] While all this is perfectly true, we may wonder whether the evangelist, writing toward the end of the 1st century A.D., was aware of such chronological niceties.

[38] See, e.g., J. A. T. Robinson, *The Priority of John* (Oak Park, IL: Meyer-Stone Books, 1987) 185.

[39] See, e.g., Brown, *John*, 1. 118.

[40] This problem is not addressed by Hoehner (*Chronological Aspects*, 42), who confidently uses John 2:20 to fix Jesus' first Passover in A.D. 30. But if the original cleansing took place just before Jesus' arrest and crucifixion, then John 2:20 argues for A.D. 30 as Jesus' last Passover (which for Hoehner is rather A.D. 33).

[41] Adhering to the strict letter of the text of Luke 3:1–2, we must admit that the synchronism "dates" only the beginning of the ministry of the Baptist. However, I think Blinzler is quite correct when he says (*Der Prozess Jesu*, 102): "In 3,1f. Luke obviously wants to date not only the appearance of the forerunner but also at the same time the appearance of Jesus himself. Indeed, he gives no further exact date for the beginning of the public ministry of Jesus; rather he restricts himself to a remark about the approximate age of Jesus (3, 13)" (translation mine).

[42] For the texts, see *Thucydides. History of the Peloponnesian War* (LCL; 4 vols.; ed. C. F. Smith; Cambridge, MA: Harvard; London: Heinemann, 1962–65) 1. 258–59; *Polybius. The Histories* (LCL; 6 vols.; ed. W. R. Paton; Cambridge, MA: Harvard; London: Heinemann, 1922–27) 1. 6–7. Luke's synchronism is closer to Thucydides' than to Polybius'.

[43] The text of 1 Macc 1:10 may not at first look like much of a parallel. But the author has an introductory biographical narrative precede a date that fixes events in Israel by the reign of a pagan monarch ruling outside Israel, and the date makes a glancing reference to Rome. There is therefore a vague resemblance in structure and content to Luke 1–2 preceding Luke 3:1–2.

[44] It is with such texts that a purely modern literary-critical approach to the Gospels, intent on avoiding the "referential fallacy," runs into trouble. Luke is here simply making explicit what all the Gospels are implicitly doing: namely, putting forth truth claims about certain events that occurred (from the perspective of the evangelists) in recent human history. These truth claims may or may

not, in actual fact, be true. But a critical method that cannot come to grips with the basic claims inherent in the Gospel literature is missing a good deal of what the Gospels as 1st-century Greco-Roman religious propaganda were all about.

[45] The very positioning of *pentekaidekatǭ* as the first significant word in 3:1 highlights its importance: *en etei de pentekaidekatǭ.* . . .

[46] For our purposes, we may safely leave aside the possibility of part of the year 25 coming into play, since the synchronism with Pilate's rule does not allow a date earlier than 26 for the appearance of the Baptist.

[47] I. H. Marshall, *Luke,* 133; Hoehner, *Chronological Aspects,* 31–32.

[48] This tells against Finegan's preference for the fifteenth year of Tiberius equaling A.D. 26, based on a computation from Tiberius' coregency *(Handbook,* 300–1). Curiously, Finegan (p. 272) nevertheless notes that Josephus uses *hēgemonia* (the very word Luke 3:1 uses of Tiberius' rule) to refer to the passing of imperial rule to Tiberius upon Augustus' death *(J.W.* 2.9.1 §168). While hardly probative in itself, this detail joins other data in pointing in the direction of computation from Augustus' death in Luke 3:1.

[49] This is rightly stressed by both Marshall *(Luke,* 132) and Fitzmyer *(The Gospel According to Luke,* 1. 450, 452).

[50] For a quick survey of views, see Fitzmyer *(Luke,* 1. 57), who also mentions Caesarea and the Decapolis. I would agree with Fitzmyer that the Gospel was certainly not written in Palestine.

[51] The address *kratiste* in Luke 1:4 is an indication that Theophilus—be he real or fictional—is to be conceived of as socially respected and probably well off, and possibly even a Roman official (see Fitzmyer, *Luke,* 1. 300).

[52] Finegan, however, does consider the use of the Jewish calendar a serious possibility in his *Handbook,* 272–73. Hoehner *(Chronological Aspects,* 34) rightly rejects the likelihood of its use.

[53] Finegan notes cases in which Tacitus and Suetonius use the accession-year system for Tiberius *(Handbook,* 273).

[54] These and other possibilities are spelled out at great length with the help of tables in Finegan, *Handbook,* 259–73.

[55] It is interesting to note that many authors, despite the great differences in the arguments employed, gravitate toward A.D. 28 as the most likely year for the beginning of John's ministry; so, e.g., Holzmeister, *Chronologia,* 82; and apparently Ogg, *Chronology,* 276–77.

[56] The year 29 is preferred by Hoehner *(Chronological Aspects,* 37). Following the Syrian calendar, Blinzler *(Der Prozess Jesu,* 102) suggests that Jesus began his ministry probably at the beginning of 28, or at the latest the beginning of 29.

[57] Hoehner *(Chronological Aspects,* 95–96) gives a brief overview of all the theories proposed in modern times, from the serious to the silly (Eisler proposed A.D.

21 as the year of Jesus' death, while Theodor Keim, Kirsopp Lake, and Hugh J. Schonfield pushed it to the spring of 35 or 36). The very late dating results from undue stress being given to the fact that Josephus mentions the Baptist's death in relation to Antipas' defeat by King Aretas IV in A.D. 36 or 37 *(Ant.* 18.5.1 §116). But Josephus simply states that "it seemed to some of the Jews" that Antipas' defeat was divine punishment for his execution of the Baptist. Granted Josephus' sloppy ordering of events in the latter part of the *Antiquities,* no chronological conclusion can be drawn concerning the date of the death of the Baptist (which the Gospels place before the death of Jesus). This point is missed by Nikos Kokkinos, "Crucifixion in A.D. 36: The Keystone for Dating the Birth of Jesus," *Chronos, Kairos, Christos,* 133–63. In a more serious vein, the years 27, 28, 29, 30, 32, and 33 have all had noted champions.

[58] The use of *paraskeuē,* which occurs in pagan literature in the general sense of preparation, to mean the day of preparation for a feast, and specifically for the Sabbath, is found in Josephus *(Ant.* 16.6.2 §163). Note that, since *paraskeuē* could be the preparation day for some special annual feast (e.g., John 19:42, *paraskeuē tou pascha),* Mark strives to be precise by specifying that the *paraskeuē* he is referring to is the day before the Sabbath, the *prosabbaton.* We have here a typical example of the stylistic trait known as "Marcan duality."

[59] Note the succession of time indications in Mark: *kai opsias genomenēs* for the beginning of the Last Supper (14:17), the first and second cockcrow in the scene of Peter's denial (14:68,72), the decision to hand Jesus over to Pilate *prōi* (15:1), crucifixion at the third hour (15:25), darkness from the sixth to the ninth hour (15:33), and Jesus' cry at the ninth hour, followed soon by his death (15:34–37); finally there is the burial when it was evening on the *paraskeuē,* that is, the *prosabbaton* (15:42).

[60] For Matthew's dependence on Mark, see the exhaustive study by Donald P. Senior, *The Passion Narrative According to Matthew* (BETL 39; Leuven: Leuven University, 1975). For Luke, see Fitzmyer, *Luke,* 2. 1365–66. Fitzmyer allows that Luke also evinces a heavy use of special L material. My own opinion on these matters is slightly different. On the one hand, contrary to Senior's view, I would hold that Matthew at times uses special M traditions in his Passion Narrative, though he stays closer to Mark than does Luke. On the other hand, I think the work of Marion L. Soards and Frank J. Matera should make one cautious about positing large amounts of pre-Lucan oral or written traditions in Luke 22–23. Much of what is not found in Mark may come from Luke's creative redaction. See Marion L. Soards, *The Passion According to Luke. The Special Material of Luke 22* (JSNTSup 14; Sheffield: JSOT, 1987); and Frank J. Matera, "The Death of Jesus According to Luke: A Question of Sources," *CBQ* 47 (1985) 469–85. Obviously, therefore, I would not accept the theory that there was a non-Marcan, pre-Lucan Passion Narrative that Luke drew upon in addition to Mark. For such a theory (usually propounded as part of a larger Proto-Lucan theory), see Vincent Taylor, *The Passion Narrative of St Luke. A Critical and Historical Investigation* (SNTSMS 19; ed. Owen E. Evans; Cambridge: Cambridge University, 1972); cf.

Joachim Jeremias, "Perikopen-Umstellungen bei Lukcas?" *Abba*, 93–97. For reasons for rejecting the Proto-Luke hypothesis, see Fitzmyer, *Luke*, 1. 89–91.

⁶¹ On this point, see Dodd, *Historical Tradition*, 21–151; and Brown, *John*, 2. 787–91. Two attempts to reconstruct what the Johannine passion source would have looked like can be found in Robert Tomson Fortna, *The Fourth Gospel and Its Predecessor* (Philadelphia: Fortress, 1988) 149–86; and Urban C. von Wahlde, *The Earliest Version of John's Gospel* (Wilmington, DE: Glazier, 1989) 133–50.

⁶² We should note an intriguing difference: while Mark uses the word *paraskeuē* to introduce his story of the burial of Jesus, John employs it one pericope earlier, to introduce the reason why Jesus' body was pierced rather than broken. In a sort of inclusion, John then repeats *paraskeuē* at the end of the story of the burial.

⁶³ Qumranites and perhaps certain other Jewish sectarians used a solar calendar that differed from the lunar calendar then in use in the Jerusalem temple; they differed from "mainstream" Judaism in various liturgical matters. See Geza Vermes, *The Dead Sea Scrolls. Qumran in Perspective* (Philadelphia: Fortress, 1977) 175–77.

⁶⁴ Literally, "from the ninth to the eleventh hour." Finegan *(Handbook,* 13–14) lists the various prescriptions for the time of the Passover sacrifice in both the Mishna and Josephus. As one would expect, the Mishna makes various detailed distinctions. Interestingly, it considers the special case of the eve of Passover falling on a Friday. In that case the Passover lambs were to be slaughtered after the daily evening offering was made at 1:30 P.M.; see *Pesaḥ.* 5:1. Philo, on the other hand, speaks in more general terms of the slaughtering of the lambs "from noon until evening" *(De Specialibus Legibus [The Special Laws]* 2.27.145); this idea is echoed in later rabbinic discussions. In my opinion, Finegan reasonably concludes that Josephus represents the standard practice of the Jerusalem temple in the 1st century A.D. Yet the specifications in *Pesaḥ.* 5:1 retain an importance for those who favor the Johannine chronology.

⁶⁵ This reckoning of the day from evening to evening apparently replaced an older method of reckoning from morning to morning. The change seems to have occurred sometime between the end of the Israelite monarchy and the age of Nehemiah; see Roland de Vaux, *Ancient Israel. Its Life and Institutions* (2d ed.; London: Darton, Longman & Todd, 1965) 182. Finegan *(Handbook,* 290–91) tries to solve the differences between the Synoptic and Johannine passion chronologies by suggesting that the Galilean Jesus reckoned the festival days according to the older method of counting from morning to morning, while the temple authorities counted from evening to evening. Besides being a gratuitous assumption, this theory does not explain how Jesus obtained a Passover lamb for a Passover meal in Jerusalem by Thursday evening (according to the Synoptics), if John is correct in telling us that the Passover lambs were being slain in the temple on Friday.

⁶⁶ Translation by O. S. Wintermute in *The Old Testament Pseudepigrapha* (2 vols.; ed. James H. Charlesworth; Garden City, NY: Doubleday, 1983, 1985) 2.

140. Wintermute dates *Jubilees* around 161–140 B.C. (p. 44) and considers its prove-
nance to be Hasidic or Essene (p. 45). Although the book may display Essene
tendencies, it seems to have been written before the definitive split between the
Essenes and the Jerusalem authorities (pp. 48–49). While the solar calendar of
Jubilees differed from the lunar calendar used in the Jerusalem temple of Jesus'
day, there is no indication that the custom of reckoning the beginning of liturgical days from sundown was a point of dispute.

[67] The phrase probably reflects the Hebrew *'ereb pesaḥ*, "the vigil [i.e., the day
before] Passover"; see Brown, *John*, 2. 882.

[68] Note, by the way, that, alone among NT authors, John displays two different liturgical applications of the word *paraskeuē*: (1) used absolutely, it means
Friday as the preparation for the Sabbath (19:31); (2) used with *tou pascha*, it
means the fourteenth of Nisan, the day of preparation for Passover (19:14). In
this, John correctly reflects the flexibility of the Hebrew *'ereb*.

[69] However, the adjective "great" could also be applied to the Sabbath that
fell during Passover week since, in Pharisaic tradition, it was the day for offering sheaves; see Brown, *John*, 2. 933; Str-B, 2. 847–48; cf. Lev 23:9–14.

[70] The entire excursus on the day of Jesus' death is found in Str-B, 2. 812–53;
Billerbeck's own solution is found on pp. 847–53. His reasoning, besides being
talmudic in more than one sense, proceeds from the naive supposition that the
Synoptic tradition is to be identified wholly with the tradition of that will-o'-
the-wisp, the *Urgemeinde*. There is a painful lack of any sense of the diversity
present in the earliest streams of NT tradition.

[71] On the Boethuseans, see Joachim Jeremias, *Jerusalem in the Time of Jesus*
(London: SCM, 1969) 194–95.

[72] This is likewise the gist of the criticism of Billerbeck's theory by Jeremias,
Eucharistic Words of Jesus, 23–24. Dockx (*Chronologies*, 25) develops a subtle argument against Billerbeck: Mark 14:1 presents "the high priests and the scribes"
(representing the whole Sanhedrin) as hatching a plot to arrest Jesus. This whole
scene is put under the introductory rubric: "Now it was the Passover and the
[feast of] unleavened bread after two days." Mark thus places the Passover on
Friday and this meeting on Wednesday (or, less likely, Thursday), and all the
Jewish authorities in this scene—and throughout the Passion Narrative—seem
to march together according to the calendrical indications given here. Yet the
"scribes" in the Sanhedrin certainly included at least some, if not many, Pharisees. Hence, not only does Mark give no indication of a difference between
Sadducees and Pharisees in computing the date of Passover; what Mark does say
leaves the natural impression that both groups are counting the days in the same
way.

[73] Dockx, *Chronologies*, 26–28.

[74] Of the drawing of arbitrary and unsubstantiated distinctions among Jewish groups in reference to Passover observance there is no end. Jeremias (*Eucharistic Words of Jesus*, 24) mentions another version of the Galilean-Judean distinc-

tion, which he attributes to J. Pickl. Still another version can be found in Fritz Chenderlin, "Distributed Observance of the Passover—A Hypothesis," *Bib* 56 (1975) 369–93; and "Distributed Observance of the Passover. A Preliminary Test of the Hypothesis," *Bib* 57 (1976) 1–24. Hoehner *(Chronological Aspects,* 87) creates the dubious distinction between Galileans and Pharisees on the one hand and Judeans and Sadducees on the other. In a somewhat different vein, Massey H. Shepherd, Jr. ("Are Both the Synoptics and John Correct about the Date of Jesus' Death?" *JBL* 80 [1961] 123–32) suggests that John was following the Palestinian mode of reckoning, while Mark, reflecting the tradition of his church in Rome, followed the reckoning customary in the Diaspora. Massey gives the best refutation of his own theory when he asks rhetorically (p. 131): "What do we know, however, about Jewish calendar systems in the Dispersion? Very little. . . . Of the synagogal usage at Rome, we know nothing."

[75] Jaubert, *La date de la cène.* For the convenience of the reader, I will give citations according to the English translation, *The Date of the Last Supper.* Jeremias *(Eucharistic Words of Jesus,* 24–25) issues a salutary warning about our ignorance of many details of this solar calendar.

[76] Jaubert, *The Date of the Last Supper,* 48.

[77] Jaubert, *The Date of the Last Supper,* 69–76. Jeremias *(The Eucharistic Words of Jesus,* 25) dismisses her use of the *Didascalia* by arguing that "the strange passion week chronology first found in the Didascalia is a secondary development out of the fasting practice of the Church. . . ."

[78] Jaubert, *The Date of the Last Supper,* 111–12.

[79] Jaubert, *The Date of the Last Supper,* 97–98.

[80] Actually, as she develops her thesis, Jaubert feels the need to posit an intermediate kind of calendar, a solar calendar that had been somewhat assimilated to the lunar calendar. Only thus will her hypothesis work smoothly. One of course becomes wary when hypothetical entities have to be multiplied to explain the data adequately.

[81] For a critique of Jaubert's picture of Jesus using an Essene calendar, as well as for more general criticism of Jaubert's theory, see Raymond E. Brown, "The Problem of Historicity in John," *New Testament Essays* (Garden City, NY: Image Books, Doubleday, 1968; originally 1965) 187–217, esp. 207–17. Brown, it should be noted, has done detailed research on the Qumran documents and has not been loath to see certain parallels between Qumranite and Johannine theology.

Eugen Ruckstuhl has attempted to support Jaubert's hypothesis by stressing Jesus' connections with the Essenes and suggesting that in Jesus' time the Essenes had their own separate part of the Jerusalem temple in which they could observe the liturgy and offer sacrifice through their own priests and according to their own calendar. According to Ruckstuhl, Jesus, who opposed the Pharisees and the Sadducees but who felt a certain affinity to the Essenes, followed their calendar for the Last Supper. For this theory, which has no solid basis in the literature of the time and has not found wide support among scholars, see his

Chronology of the Last Days of Jesus. A Critical Study, esp. 97–101, 117–24. Jaubert herself does not accept the idea that, at the time of Jesus, the Sadducean priests in the Jerusalem temple would have allowed the Essenes to immolate their own lambs in the temple on a different date of Passover. She proposes instead a "secret" celebration of Passover in a private house; see her article, "Jésus et la calendrier de Qumrân," *NTS* 7 (1960–61) 1–30, esp. 25.

A careful consideration and rejection of the theories of both Jaubert and Ruckstuhl can be found in Blinzler, *Der Prozess Jesu,* 109–26.

[82] Jaubert, *The Date of the Last Supper,* 97–98. She bases her theory of a gloss on the fact that the difficult clause does not appear in Matthew. Her whole defense thus rests on an unlikely reading of the Synoptic relationships. The weakness of the gloss theory is noted by Dockx, *Chronologies,* 24–25. He goes on to observe that the various references in the Synoptics to eating the *pascha* can only mean eating the Passover lamb.

[83] Jaubert, *The Date of the Last Supper,* 163 n. 4: ". . . it may be questioned whether, in many cases, a ritual of unleavened bread was not sufficient for the celebration of the Pasch. This solution appears the most likely for the Supper of Jesus."

[84] Walter Bauer places the use of the impersonal verb *dei* in Luke 22:7 under the rubric of necessity "from the force of Law or custom"; see Walter Bauer, *Griechisch-deutsches Wörterbuch zu den Schriften des Neuen Testaments und der frühchristlichen Literatur* (6th ed.; ed. Kurt and Barbara Aland; Berlin/New York: de Gruyter, 1988) col. 343.

[85] Here I obviously disagree with the claims of Jeremias, *Eucharistic Words of Jesus,* 79–81; and even to a certain degree with Brown, *John,* 2. 556. My reasons for disagreeing with Jeremias will be given below.

[86] Jaubert sought to refine her thesis and defend it against attacks in "Jésus et la calendrier de Qumrân"; "Les séances du sanhédrin et les récits de la passion," *RHR* 166 (1964) 143–69 and 167 (1965) 1–33; and "Le Mercredi où Jésus fut livré," *NTS* 14 (1967–68) 145–64. She made no substantive change in her thesis in these articles; and, in my opinion, she never adequately answered the basic objections raised against her hypothesis.

[87] Jeremias, *Eucharistic Words of Jesus,* 15–84; Blinzler, *Der Prozess Jesu,* 102–3; Brown, *John,* 2. 555–58, 787–802. One reason why Jeremias is such a passionate champion of the Passover nature of the meal is that otherwise his whole approach to the eucharistic words of Jesus is undermined.

[88] Jeremias, *Eucharistic Words of Jesus,* 76–79.

[89] I purposely use this vague phraseology to avoid becoming entangled in the vexed question of whether, at the time of Jesus, the Jerusalem Sanhedrin enjoyed the right to impose and/or inflict the death penalty in the general run of capital cases. We shall have to investigate this question when we come to the treatment of the Passion Narratives in Volume Two of this work.

[90] Jeremias *(Eucharistic Words of Jesus,* 78) tries to defend himself by claiming that the Mishna, while forbidding the Sanhedrin to sit in judgment on a feast day *(m. Beṣa* 5:2; cf. Philo *De migratione Abrahami* [*On the Migration of Abraham*] 16.91), also forbade criminal processes on the day of preparation for a feast *(m. Sanh.* 4:1). But there is a basic weakness in his argument. Many of those who prefer the Johannine chronology also interpret John as narrating not a formal session of the Sanhedrin in John 18:13–14,19–24,28, but only an informal hearing before Annas and/or Caiaphas before he/they handed Jesus over to Pilate. All Jeremias can say at that point is, "I am sure that John 18.24, is intended to describe an official hearing at which . . . the High Council [=Sanhedrin] is present" (p. 78 n. 4). His being sure is not enough; the text indicates otherwise. Moreover, it is not simply a question of whether this event or that event could have happened on Passover Day. One must face the larger question of whether it is likely that a whole chain of events (the arrest of Jesus, the convening of the Sanhedrin, the hearing of a capital case, the verdict that Jesus deserved to die, and the handing of Jesus over to Pilate with the request that he be put to death on the same day) could or did actually occur in the night and early morning hours of one Passover Day. When the question is posed in that way, I think that John presents the more historically probable scenario.

[91] Frans Neirynck, *Duality in Mark. Contributions to the Study of the Markan Redaction* (BETL 31; Leuven: Leuven University, 1972) 45–46,49; and see 14:1 and 12 in the Greek text of Mark, set in outline form, that concludes the book. (*Duality in Mark* is made up of three essays that first appeared in the 1971 and 1972 volumes of *ETL.*) Neirynck remarks on duality in temporal expressions in Mark: ". . . we are faced here with one of Mark's most characteristic features of style."

[92] In favor of the origin of 14:1a in a secondary or redactional stage of the tradition, see Bultmann, *Geschichte,* 300; Dibelius, *Formgeschichte,* 181; Taylor, *St. Mark,* 527; Eduard Schweizer, *Das Evangelium nach Markus* (NTD 1; 2d ed.; Göttingen: Vandenhoeck & Ruprecht, 1968) 163–65; Walter Grundmann, *Das Evangelium nach Markus* (THKNT 2; 6th ed.; Berlin: Evangelische Verlagsanstalt, 1973) 275; Mann, *Mark,* 552. Pesch *(Das Markusevangelium,* 2. 319) is almost alone in thinking that everything from Mark 14:1 onward is a complete pre-Marcan Passion Narrative into which Mark has inserted nothing of his own.

[93] Jeremias, *Eucharistic Words of Jesus,* 92–93, 95–96.

[94] See Schweizer *(Markus,* 169–70), who lists the following reasons for seeing 14:12–16 as a late addition to the Passion Narrative: (1) Four times in the one pericope (vv 12,13,14,16) the phrase "the disciples" is used to describe the inner circle of Jesus. In the surrounding context, the descriptive phrase is rather "the Twelve" (so vv 10,17,20,43; "disciples" appears again only at v 32). (2) Despite attempts at saving its accuracy, the introductory time indicator in v 12, "on the first day of the unleavened bread, when they were accustomed to sacrifice the Passover lamb," most likely betrays an author not completely at home with things Jewish. Strictly speaking, the day on which the lambs were sacrificed was the fourteenth of Nisan (which is what Mark means); the first day of the feast of

the unleavened bread is rather the fifteenth of Nisan, which coincides with Passover Day proper. The examples of the loose application of "the first day of unleavened bread" to mean the fourteenth of Nisan are all much later (the two Talmuds; see Jeremias, *Eucharistic Words of Jesus*, 17 n. 2) and occur in learned rabbinic discussions; they can hardly be presupposed in the popular parlance of a 1st-century Christian, be he of Jewish or Gentile origin. If we do not accept Jeremias's escape hatch of a mistranslation (the words make perfect sense in Greek and simply display an inaccurate knowledge of things Jewish), the only conclusion to be made is that whoever composed 14:12a not only was not an eyewitness to the original events but also cannot be trusted to give us exact detailed chronological information about the Last Supper. Indeed, even Jeremias, who prefers the solution of a mistranslation, admits the possibility of a "faulty expression of a non-Jewish author" *(Eucharistic Words of Jesus*, 93). (3) The whole episode is lacking in John's Passion Narrative; this is another point that leads even Jeremias to see Mark 14:12–16 as a later addition. (4) The general structure of the story and whole parts of verses (14:13a,16) echo the story of the finding of the donkey for Jesus' triumphal ride into Jerusalem in Mark 11:1–7, and the whole of Mark 14:12–16 may have been constructed on that model. Since Schweizer is quite aware that only Mark 14:12–16 explicitly depicts the Last Supper as a Passover meal, these considerations lead him to decide that the Johannine chronology is to be preferred. Other exegetes who think 14:12–16 is a later addition to the primitive passion tradition include D. E. Nineham, *Saint Mark* (Pelican NT Commentaries; Harmondsworth: Penguin, 1963) 376; and Shepherd ("Are Both the Synoptics and John Correct," 130), who lists other commentators who share this view.

[95] See the discussion in Metzger, *Textual Commentary*, 173. Although the reading without "again" *(ouketi)* receives only a "C" rating ("considerable degree of doubt"), nevertheless Metzger is right in declaring: "If the word *[ouketi]* were present originally, there is no satisfactory explanation to account for its absence" from a large number of early and good manuscripts.

[96] Hence the addition of *ouketi* in later manuscripts does not distort but simply clarifies the meaning.

[97] In favor of Lucan redaction ("a new redactional arrangement by Luke") is Pesch *(Markusevangelium*, 2. 365–66), who considers the so-called Semitisms in Luke 22:15–16 to be taken over from Mark and who also points out clear Lucanisms in the text. Other proponents of Lucan redaction of Marcan tradition include Gerhard Schneider *(Das Evangelium nach Lukas* [Ökumenischer Taschenbuchkommentar zum Neuen Testament, 3/1–2; Gütersloh: Mohn; Würzburg: Echter, 1977] 2. 444) and A. R. C. Leaney *(The Gospel According to St. Luke* [Black's NT Commentaries; 2d ed.; London: Black, 1966] 267). An earlier proponent of this view was Emmanuel Hirsch, *Frühgeschichte des Evangeliums* (2 vols.; Tübingen: Mohr [Siebeck], 1941) 2. 255–57; while I agree with his basic point, I would not follow his theories on Marcan sources and Lucan redactional intent.

In seeing Luke 22:15–16 as Lucan redaction, I differ from Fitzmyer *(Luke*, 2. 1386–87), who follows the opinion of Heinz Schürmann. Schürmann has dealt with the Lucan version of the Last Supper in a number of writings. Perhaps his most influential work on the subject is found in the two volumes, *Der Pascha-mahlbericht. Lk 22, (7–14.) 15–18* (NTAbh 19/5; 2d ed.; Münster: Aschendorff, 1968, originally 1952); and *Der Einsetzungsbericht. Lk 22, 19–20* (NTAbh 20/4; Münster: Aschendorff, 1955). The point at issue here is treated in *Der Pascha-mahlbericht*, 1–74. He gives a list of scholars opposing and favoring Luke's dependence on Mark on p. 1 nn. 1 and 2. On p. 74, Schürmann summarizes his position: ". . . Luke 22:15–18 presents a piece of tradition that is literarily independent of Mark 14:25 and is slightly redacted by Luke; Mark 14:25 and its parallel in Matthew witness only in fragmentary fashion to this piece of tradition" (translation mine).

One should note, however, that Schürmann's judgment on 22:15 by itself is more reserved (pp. 3–14). While he argues for pre-Lucan tradition redacted by Luke, it is telling that he waives any attempt to reconstruct the wording of the tradition; that, he says, would be a step backward into hypotheses that cannot be tested (p. 14). Actually, if one looks at Schürmann's data, it seems that there are very few if any elements in v 15 that could not be assigned to redaction. Schürmann's argument relies to a heavy degree on the general belief that Luke is conservative in handing on the words of the Lord and that examples of Luke's creation of such words are rare. It is this general thesis—in addition to the more specific views of Schürmann—that has come under greater scrutiny in recent years. In my opinion, Schürmann's conclusions on 22:15 are made highly questionable by the careful analysis of Soards, *The Passion According to Luke;* see esp. 45, 50, 116. On p. 50 Soards states: "Luke created a new setting for the Markan material in 17a–18c by composing 15a–16c on the model of the dislocated Markan material."

[98] Commentators debate whether *touto to pascha* in Luke 22:15 means the Passover lamb or the Passover meal, but this argument does not affect the question at hand.

[99] I here take for granted the originality of the "longer text" of Luke 22:17–20; for a discussion, see Metzger, *Textual Commentary*, 173–77. The eucharistic traditions will be discussed in Volume Two. I may note here, though, that Luke's artistic reworking of Mark in terms of two groups of two words was apparently misunderstood by the scribe of Codex Bezae (D), who proceeded to omit all reference to the cup in the second group of words since he understood the cup word in the first group to be the eucharistic "consecration" of the cup. In my opinion, it was this scribal misunderstanding that led to the "shorter text." It is sobering to remember that Codex Bezae is the only manuscript in the entire NT Greek manuscript tradition to omit the longer text. It should also be noted that Fitzmyer *(Luke,* 2. 1388) feels confident enough about the longer reading to suggest that the *UBSGNT³*'s rating of "C" for the longer text be raised to a "B."

[100] At times commentators will speak of a Passover tone, mood, or character visible in John's portrayal of the Last Supper. Insofar as John pointedly places the meal just before Passover (13:1), the Passover "tone," which indeed perme-

ates the whole Gospel, is indisputable. But I deny that in John the meal itself has any characteristics that necessarily refer to Passover. I maintain that such an idea would not have crossed the minds of exegetes if they did not also know the Synoptic Last Supper in its present Marcan form.

[101] Jeremias, *Eucharistic Words of Jesus*, 41–84.

[102] See especially pp. 79–84 of his *Eucharistic Words of Jesus*.

[103] Besides Passover, the options Jeremias considers are the *kidduš* (sanctification) meal for Sabbath and feasts, the *ḥăbûrâ* (fellowship) meals to fulfill a religious duty, and the ceremonial meals of the Essenes.

[104] This is pointed out by Xavier Léon-Dufour, *Sharing the Eucharistic Bread. The Witness of the New Testament* (New York/Mahwah, NJ: Paulist, 1987) 307–8.

[105] Since we will not be examining the historicity of the eucharistic narratives until much later on in this book, this argument must remain for now an *ad hominem* argument against Jeremias's approach. Jeremias wants the Last Supper to be a Passover meal because that will provide an explanatory framework for his interpretation of the eucharistic words and actions of Jesus. But if those words and actions are historical in some form or other, they burst any Jewish *Sitz im Leben* that might be proposed for them, be it *kidduš*, or *ḥăbûrâ*, or Essene meal, or Passover.

[106] I stress that the argument I make here has nothing to do with the interpretation of *m. Pesaḥ.* 8:6, which Jeremias discusses in his *Eucharistic Words of Jesus*, 73. In a sense, it is a shame that the discussion of this Mishna passage obscures the fact that Jeremias never does come to grips with the problem of the Barabbas incident.

[107] While this is explicitly stated in the Marcan pericope of the preparation of the Last Supper (Mark 14:12–16 + the transitional v 17), it must be inferred—correctly, in my opinion—from various statements in John (John 13:2,4–5,12, 30; 18:1). It is intriguing to note that, shorn of the all-decisive 14:12–16, the pre-Marcan Passion Narrative, very much like the Johannine, would intimate rather than specify the location of the Last Supper.

[108] Other minor arguments could be adduced; but their value is more confirmatory, and so they should be considered only after we have made our decision on the basis of the main arguments. For example, proponents of both the Synoptic and the Johannine chronologies appeal to the relatively early statement of Paul in 1 Cor 5:7, where he exhorts the Corinthians to purge the sinful elements from their community, just as Jews would purge their houses of leaven before Passover: "Purge out the old leaven, that you may be a fresh batch [of dough], since you are [in fact] unleavened loaves. For indeed our Passover lamb has been sacrificed—namely, Christ!" Commentators sometimes suggest that Paul was writing this passage around the time of Passover/Easter, but that is pure speculation; for a detailed exegesis of 5:7, see Gordon D. Fee, *The First Epistle to the Corinthians* (NICNT; Grand Rapids: Eerdmans, 1987) 216–18.

What is of interest is that, as early as the mid-fifties, Paul, who does not in his own theology exploit the idea of Christ's death as a Passover sacrifice, mentions the idea in passing in a parenetic context. He apparently can presuppose that his Gentile converts understand the metaphor without any explanation. This implies that as early as the mid-fifties of the 1st century the idea of Christ's death as a Passover sacrifice was common Christian tradition. What is of greater importance to us is that the immediate context in 1 Corinthians 5 has nothing to do with the eucharist or the Last Supper, and so the natural reference of "our Passover lamb has been sacrificed—namely, Christ" is to the physical death of Christ on the cross. This comes close to the Johannine imagery of Christ's passion and death (e.g., John 18:28; 19:14,29,36) and to a chronology that puts Christ's physical death on the fourteenth of Nisan, when the Passover lambs were sacrificed in the temple. I repeat, however, that this argument is at best confirmatory.

[109] I have spent a great amount of time choosing between the Synoptic and Johannine chronologies simply because these are the two presented in the Gospels and the two most scholars argue over. In theory, of course, it is possible that *both* Mark *and* John are wrong; we have already seen one version of this possibility in the position of Annie Jaubert—as well as the difficulties such an approach entails. Let us, though, for the sake of argument, spin out another scenario: The reason both Mark and John agree about a general Passover milieu is that Jesus did die during Passover week. The reason Mark and John disagree is that all either had was a vague memory about Passover, which each one developed according to his own theology. In fact, Jesus was put to death during Passover week, but a day or two after the fifteenth of Nisan.

Viewed in the abstract, such a theory is by no means impossible. But once we examine it more closely, it runs into some serious problems of both method and content. (1) As to method, we should consider a rough analogy from text criticism. Given a number of different readings in different manuscripts of the same text, text critics must use various criteria to decide which text is original. Sometimes elements of a number of different readings will be brought together to reconstitute what seems most likely to have been the original reading. Only in the rarest of cases, though, will all the extant readings be rejected in favor of a hypothetical reconstruction that is witnessed in none of the manuscripts or versions. That is allowable only when none of the extant readings enjoys solid arguments in favor of its being the original reading. By analogy, to create a scenario for the date of Jesus' death that is supported by none of the Gospel traditions and to prefer it over Gospel traditions that are by no means impossible brings us close once again to writing a novel. All controls are abandoned in favor of a fertile imagination.

(2) To pursue this methodological objection further: such an approach flies in the face of the criterion of multiple attestation. Precisely because Mark and John disagree so sharply on the dating of the Last Supper and Jesus' death, all the more striking is their agreement on the days of the week: the Last Supper was on Thursday evening and Jesus died on the next day, Friday. 1 Cor 11:23 gives very early independent confirmation of a "tight" succession of events, while 1 Cor 5:7 presupposes that first-generation Christians who knew neither

the Gospel of Mark nor the Gospel of John would naturally understand Jesus' death as *the* Passover sacrifice—a metaphor that follows immediately after Paul's allusion in the same verse to the removal of leaven from Jewish houses prior to the Passover meal. In short, multiple attestation points to the historical truth of some key points of the Passion Narrative chronology that Mark and John do have in common. To dismiss them in favor of a scenario that is simply unattested in all the NT traditions is to forsake any scholarly investigation controlled by the criteria of historicity examined in Chapter 6. (These first two arguments of mine are equally valid against a theory that would want to push Jesus' death back a few days before the Friday designated independently by both the Johannine and the Synoptic tradition.)

(3) As to content, the hypothetical scenario sketched above may appear attractive at first glance. But in the long run it must face some of the same difficulties that confront the Marcan chronology. To take but one example: we have seen that the Barabbas incident, whether historical or not, goes back to an early pre-Marcan and pre-Johannine stage of the passion tradition. Two things should be noted about this tradition: (a) in all the Gospels it occurs in the narrative of Jesus' trial before Pilate, soon before Pilate condemns Jesus to execution; indeed, it would make sense nowhere else; (b) the Barabbas story makes sense only if the amnesty or pardon is being given so that an imprisoned Jew may take part in the Passover meal upon his release. Hence, early on, in both the pre-Marcan and pre-Johannine passion tradition there stood a story that makes perfect sense given the Johannine chronology and that creates difficulties for the Marcan chronology and likewise for a hypothetical scenario that places Jesus' execution sometime later in Passover week. Since this hypothetical scenario runs up against a number of the difficulties that render Mark's chronology unlikely, the Johannine chronology, in my view, remains preferable.

I readily admit that one must remain suspicious of a chronology that fits so neatly into John's theology (e.g., Jesus the true Passover lamb is condemned to death as the Passover lambs are about to be sacrificed in the temple). Yet, if we pushed this objection to the extreme, we should likewise reject the larger assertion that Jesus was put to a bloody death in Jerusalem on or just about Passover. It is this larger historical fact (which few would contest) that gave rise to much of the theologizing in all the various forms of the Passion Narrative. Such subsequent theologizing does not render doubtful the basic historical event that gave rise to the evangelists' reflections. The underlying problem is that the influence of history on theology and theology on history is a two-way street. My conclusion from all the arguments we have seen is that most likely certain historical events in the Passion Narrative either gave rise to or happened to coincide with specific theological concerns of the Fourth Evangelist.

[110] See the discussion in Jeremias, *Eucharistic Words of Jesus,* 36–37.

[111] See the sobering warning of Blinzler *(Der Prozess Jesu,* 108) against depending too much on arguments from astronomical calculations. Yet even he allows them a certain confirmatory role, after we have reached our position on other grounds. Similar warnings are issued by Roger T. Beckwith in his article, "Cautionary Notes on the Use of Calendars and Astronomy to Determine the Chro-

nology of the Passion," *Chronos, Kairos, Christos,* 183–205. It is unfortunate that Beckwith proves to be so uncritical in his use of Gospel material in the last part of his article (pp. 198–205). Regrettably, this uncritical use of NT texts is even more evident in the article by Colin J. Humphreys and W. G. Waddington, "Astronomy and the Date of the Crucifixion," *Chronos, Kairos, Christos,* 165–81; note the bizarre use of Acts 2:14–21 to show that there was a lunar eclipse following the crucifixion. Perhaps the strangest article of all in this collection is the one that mixes a misreading of Josephus and astronomy to arrive at A.D. 36 as the year of the crucifixion; see Kokkinos, "Crucifixion in A.D. 36," *Chronos, Kairos, Christos,* 133–63.

[112] One must be extremely cautious here, since different authors will quote different results from the calculations of different astronomers. Indeed, both astronomers and exegetes have at times modified their positions. For example, Jeremias went out of his way to emphasize that he employed a more cautious formulation of his views concerning possible years for Jesus' death when he revised the *Eucharistic Words of Jesus* for the third German edition (reflected in the English edition, pp. 39–40). The tentative nature of all these calculations must therefore be stressed.

[113] Jeremias, *Eucharistic Words of Jesus,* 41.

[114] April 7, 30, as the date of Jesus' death is supported by a wide range of scholars who take differing views on many other questions; see, e.g., Holzmeister, *Chronologia,* 205–15; Blinzler, *Der Prozess Jesu,* 101–8; Ruckstuhl, *Chronology,* 1–9; Dockx, *Chronologies,* 9–10, 28–29. Blinzler gives a lengthy list of authors who opt for various years; he himself claims that by far the majority of scholars choose A.D. 30. It should be noted that Jeremias *(Eucharistic Words of Jesus,* 41), who of course prefers the Marcan chronology and who earlier upheld A.D. 30, remains—in the third German edition of his book—undecided between 30 and 33, and does not exclude the possibility of 31. Finegan *(Handbook,* 298–301) allows for three possible schemas, the first two of which would place Jesus' death on Friday, April 7, 30, while the third would place it on April 3, 33. The first schema, which locates the beginning of Jesus' ministry in late A.D. 26, is the one that Finegan considers most probable.

[115] Alfred Plummer *(The Gospel According to S. Luke* [ICC; 5th ed.; Edinburgh: Clark, 1922] 352) does draw the historical conclusion that this verse is evidence in the Synoptics for John's portrayal of Jesus' many visits to Jerusalem; similarly, though with various emphases, M.-J. Lagrange, *Evangile selon Saint Luc,* 395; Marshall, *Luke,* 575; Ellis, *Luke,* 190–91. Fitzmyer *(Luke,* 2. 1036) refers the rhetorical cry "how often!" simply to Jesus' "untold desires"; but Fitzmyer does not explain how Jesus could rightly complain that Jerusalem refused these ardent and frequent desires if there were no previous visits.

[116] The *UBSGNT³* rightly reads *Ioudaias* and gives it a "B" rating ("some degree of doubt," but fairly certain), since it has excellent early witnesses (p^{75}, Sinaiticus, Vaticanus) and the other candidates ("synagogues of the Jews," "their synagogues," "synagogues of Galilee") are all obvious attempts to correct what

is the more difficult reading, granted that Luke basically follows the Marcan outline of the public ministry and that he specifically presents Jesus returning "to Galilee" in 4:14. See Metzger, *Textual Commentary*, 137–38.

[117] This is the interpretation given *Ioudaias* by Schürmann, *Lukasevangelium*, 1. 256 n. 268.

[118]Hoehner *(Chronological Aspects*, 48–49) objects that, to find a two-year ministry in John, one must invert the order of Chapters 5 and 6. While it is true that some exegetes do invert the two chapters because of their own presuppositions, such an inversion is not necessarily tied to the idea of a two-year ministry, which is the natural impression the Fourth Gospel gives on any reading. As Hoehner himself admits (p. 55), the three-year ministry he champions demands that one read an extra Passover into John's Gospel where none is mentioned. To take the unnamed "feast of the Jews" in John 5:1 as Passover is arbitrary for a number of reasons: (1) The best critical reading (supported by p^{66}, p^{75}, Alexandrinus, Vaticanus, Bezae, and many other manuscripts) is "a feast of the Jews," not "*the* feast of the Jews." (2) Even if the reading were "*the* feast of the Jews," the feast could easily be tabernacles (cf. John's usage in 7:2,10,14,37). (3) John is obviously at pains throughout his Gospel to emphasize the Passovers of Jesus' public ministry. That he would present Jesus working a major sign and delivering a weighty discourse in Jerusalem during a feast and yet not mention that the feast involved was Passover seems very unlikely. The vague "a feast of the Jews" would rather point to a minor observance, such as Purim. But obviously for the evangelist, whichever minor observance it may be, it is—unlike the major feasts —of no great importance to his theology.

To import another Passover into the Fourth Gospel, Finegan *(Handbook*, 283) appeals to Jesus' words in 4:35: "Do you not say: 'Four more months and then the harvest comes'?" Finegan reasons that, since the harvest referred to would come in April or May of the year, this saying should be situated in the preceding January or February. Hence another Passover, which is not otherwise mentioned in the Fourth Gospel, occurred after the one in Chapter 2 and before the one of Chapter 6. But this is to take part of a single verse out of context and press it beyond its proper intent. (1) The initial "Do you not say" implies that Jesus is quoting a proverb that the disciples might use to express the need for patience while waiting for a desired event that is still in the future but certain to happen within a relatively short time. For a similar introduction to a proverbial saying, see Matt 16:2 (though the reading of the Greek text is dubious here; see Metzger, *Textual Commentary*, 41). In defense of the idea that a proverb is being cited in John 4:35, see Lagrange, *Saint Jean*, 118–19; Bultmann, *Das Evangelium des Johannes*, 144–45; Dodd, *Historical Tradition in the Fourth Gospel*, 394–95; Brown, *John*, 1. 173–74; Lindars, *John*, 195. While rejecting the idea of a proverb, Barrett *(The Gospel According to St. John*, 202) likewise rejects the use of the verse for chronological computations. He rather takes the "Do you not say . . . ?" to mean "On the common reckoning, there is a four month interval between sowing and harvest." (2) If Finegan is engaged in the reconstruction of historical events in John 4, he has to explain why Jesus and his disciples are undertaking a difficult journey through hostile (Samaritan) territory precisely during the miserable rainy season of the Palestinian winter (January/February), when many roads would be nigh impassable—to say nothing of Jesus' needing to find a drink of water at a time when one would likely be inundated by torrents. Schnackenburg's comment is apropos: "The text cannot be used as a firm pointer for the chronology of Jesus's ministry" *(The Gospel According to St John,* 449).

[119]This is essentially the position of Blinzler *(Der Prozess Jesu,* 103), though he leaves open the possibility of a ministry of three years and some months. It should be noted that the basic chronology I propose could be adopted by those who place the beginning of the Baptist's and Jesus' ministries somewhere in the latter part of A.D. 27. The only difference would be that more time could be allowed for the Baptist's ministry prior to his baptism of Jesus and for Jesus' early activity before the Passover of John 2.

[120] William Wrede, *Das Messiasgeheimnis in den Evangelien* (4th ed.; Göttingen: Vandenhoeck & Ruprecht, 1969, originally 1901); Schmidt, *Der Rahmen der Geschichte Jesu.*

[121] That, I think, is the basic flaw in such erudite works as John A. T. Robinson's *The Priority of John;* cf. Heinz Kruse, "Jesu Seefahrten und die Stellung von Joh. 6," *NTS* 30 (1984) 508–30.

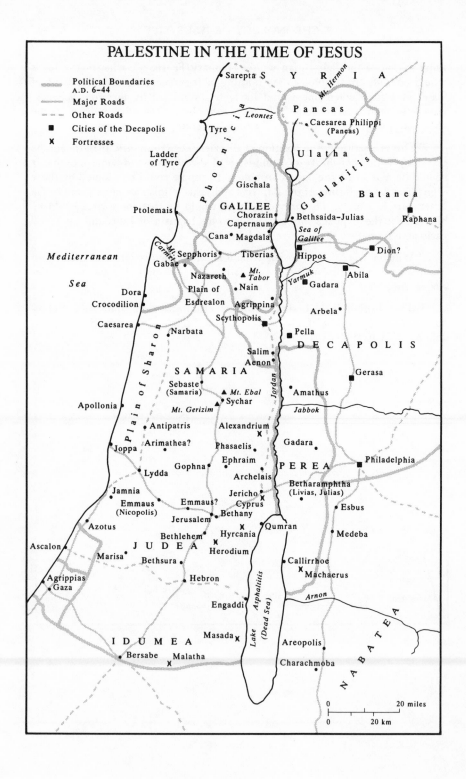

PALESTINE IN THE TIME OF JESUS

Political Boundaries A.D. 6-44
Major Roads
Other Roads
■ Cities of the Decapolis
✗ Fortresses

Sarepta S Y R I A
Mt. Hermon
Leontes
P a n e a s
Caesarea Philippi (Paneas)
Tyre
Phoenicia
Ladder of Tyre
U l a t h a
Gischala
GALILEE
G a u l a n i t i s
Chorazin
Capernaum Bethsaida-Julias
B a t a n e a
Raphana
Ptolemais
Cana Magdala
Sea of Galilee
Sepphoris Tiberias Hippos ■ Dion?
Mt. Carmel
Gabae
Nazareth Mt. Tabor
Yarmuk Abila
Mediterranean
Plain of Esdrealon Nain Gadara
Sea
Dora
Crocodilion
Agrippina
Arbela
Scythopolis
Caesarea
Narbata Pella
D E C A P O L I S
Salim
Aenon
S A M A R I A
Plain of Sharon
Sebaste (Samaria) ▲ Mt. Ebal Sychar
Gerasa
Amathus
Apollonia
Mt. Gerizim Jabbok
Antipatris Alexandrium ✗
Jordan
Joppa Arimathea? Phasaelis Gadara
Lydda Gophna Ephraim P E R E A Philadelphia
Archelais
Jamnia Emmaus? Jericho Betharamphtha
Emmaus Cyprus (Livias, Julias)
(Nicopolis) Bethany Esbus
Jerusalem
Azotus Bethlehem Hyrcania ✗ Qumran
J U D E A Herodium ✗ Medeba
Ascalon Marisa Bethsura
Agrippias Hebron Callirrhoe
Gaza Machaerus ✗
Engaddi Arnon
I D U M E A Masada ✗ Areopolis
Bersabe Malatha ✗ Charachmoba
N A B A T E A
Lake Asphaltitis (Dead Sea)

0 _____ 20 miles
0 _____ 20 km

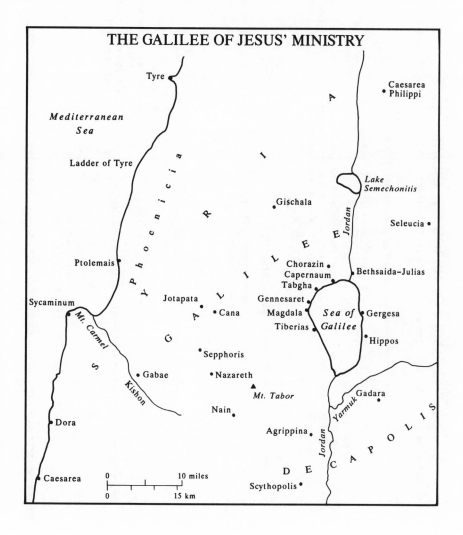

THE GALILEE OF JESUS' MINISTRY

Tyre

Caesarea
Philippi

*Mediterranean
Sea*

Ladder of Tyre

Gischala

Lake
Semechonitis

P h o e n i c i a

Seleucia

Jordan

Ptolemais

Chorazin
Capernaum
Tabgha

Bethsaida–Julias

Sycaminum

Jotapata

Gennesaret

G A L I L E E

Cana

Magdala

*Sea of
Galilee*

Gergesa

Tiberias

Hippos

Mt. Carmel

Sepphoris

Gabae

Nazareth

Kishon

Mt. Tabor

Gadara

Nain

Yarmuk

Dora

Agrippina

Jordan

D E C A P O L I S

Caesarea

0   10 miles

0   15 km

Scythopolis

THE FAMILY OF HEROD THE GREAT

Herod the Great had ten wives. Only the wives and descendants of direct interest to students of the NT are listed here.

b. = born
d. = died
r. = reigned
m. = married
K. = King
E. = Ethnarch
T. = Tetrarch

King Herod the Great
b. ca. 73 B.C.
d. 4 B.C.

m.

MARIAMME I (Hasmonean) d. 29 B.C.

Aristobulus IV d. 7 B.C.; m. Bernice I

Herod (of Chalcis)
m. Bernice II
r. Chalcis A.D. 41–48 (K.)
d. A.D. 48

Herod Agrippa I
r. tetrarchies of Philip and Lysanias as K. from A.D. 37—tetrarchy of Antipas added A.D. 40—Judea and Samaria added A.D. 41–44
d. A.D. 44

Herodias
m. (1) Herod (misnamed Philip)*
(2) Herod Antipas

MARIAMME II

Herod (misnamed Philip)
m. Herodias
Salome III
m. Philip

MALTHACE (Samaritan)

Archelaus
r. 4 B.C.–A.D. 6 (E.)

Herod Antipas
m. (1) Daughter of Aretas IV (Nabatean K.)
(2) Herodias
r. 4 B.C.–A.D. 39 (T.)

CLEOPATRA (of Jerusalem)

Philip
m. Salome III
r. 4 B.C.–A.D. 34 (T.)
d. A.D. 34

*Mark's Gospel confuses Herod, the son of Mariamme II, with Philip; this has led some NT scholars to speak (wrongly) of "Herod Philip" as Herodias' first husband.

THE REGNAL YEARS OF THE
ROMAN *PRINCIPES* (EMPERORS)

Compared with the dates of the Prefects/Procurators of Judea, Samaria, and Idumea

OCTAVIAN (AUGUSTUS)

[Prefects]

31 B.C. (battle of Actium)

27 B.C. (assumes title of Augustus)

A.D. 14 (dies)

Coponius	A.D. 6–9
M. Ambivius	9–12 (?)
Annius Rufus	12–15 (?)

TIBERIUS

14–37

Valerius Gratus	15–26
Pontius Pilate	26–36
Marcellus	36–37

GAIUS (CALIGULA)

37–41

Marullus   37–41 (?)

CLAUDIUS

41–54

[Reign of Agrippa I over the restored kingdom of the Jews, 41–44]

[Procurators]

C. Cuspius Fadus	44–46
Tiberius Julius Alexander	46–48
Ventidius Cumanus	48–52

NERO

54–68

M. Antonius Felix	52–60 (?)
Porcius Festus	60–62 (?)
Lucceius Albinus	62–64
Gessius Florus	64–66

GALBA, OTHO, VITELLIUS

(all in 69)

Jewish Revolt   66–70

VESPASIAN

69–79

List of Abbreviations

1. Abbreviations of the Names of Biblical Books (with the Apocrypha)

Gen	Nah	1-2-3-4 Kgdms	John
Exod	Hab	Add Esth	Acts
Lev	Zeph	Bar	Rom
Num	Hag	Bel	1-2 Cor
Deut	Zech	1-2 Esdr	Gal
Josh	Mal	4 Ezra	Eph
Judg	Ps *(pl.:* Pss)	Jdt	Phil
1-2 Sam	Job	Ep Jer	Col
1-2 Kgs	Prov	1-2-3-4 Macc	1-2 Thess
Isa	Ruth	Pr Azar	1-2 Tim
Jer	Cant	Pr Man	Titus
Ezek	Eccl *(or* Qoh)	Sir	Phlm
Hos	Lam	Sus	Heb
Joel	Esth	Tob	Jas
Amos	Dan	Wis	1-2 Pet
Obad	Ezra	Matt	1-2-3 John
Jonah	Neh	Mark	Jude
Mic	1-2 Chr	Luke	Rev

2. Abbreviations of the Names of Pseudepigraphical and Early Patristic Books

Adam and Eve	Books of Adam and Eve	*Sib. Or.*	Sibylline Oracles
2-3 Apoc. Bar.	Syriac, Greek Apocalypse of Baruch	*T. 12 Patr.*	Testaments of the Twelve Patriarchs
Apoc. Mos.	Apocalypse of Moses	*T. Levi*	Testament of Levi
As. Mos.	Assumption of Moses	*T. Benj.*	Testament of Benjamin, etc.
1-2-3 Enoch	Ethiopic, Slavonic, Hebrew Enoch	*Acts Pil.*	Acts of Pilate
		Apoc. Pet.	Apocalypse of Peter
Ep. Arist.	Epistle of Aristeas	*Gos. Eb.*	Gospel of the Ebionites
Jub.	Jubilees	*Gos. Eg.*	Gospel of the Egyptians
Mart. Isa.	Martyrdom of Isaiah	*Gos. Heb.*	Gospel of the Hebrews
Odes Sol.	Odes of Solomon	*Gos. Naass.*	Gospel of the Naassenes
Pss. Sol.	Psalms of Solomon	*Gos. Pet.*	Gospel of Peter

Gos. Thom.	Gospel of Thomas	*Pol.*	Ignatius, Letter to Polycarp
Prot. Jas.	Protevangelium of James	*Rom.*	Ignatius, Letter to the Romans
Barn.	Barnabas		
1-2 Clem.	1-2 Clement		
Did.	Didache	*Smyrn.*	Ignatius, Letter to the Smyrnaeans
Diogn.	Diognetus		
Herm.	Hermas,		
Man.	Mandate	*Trall.*	Ignatius, Letter to the Trallians
Sim.	Similitude		
Vis.	Vision		
Ign. *Eph.*	Ignatius, Letter to the Ephesians	*Mart. Pol.*	Martyrdom of Polycarp
Magn.	Ignatius, Letter to the Magnesians	Pol. *Phil.*	Polycarp to the Philippians
Phld.	Ignatius, Letter to the Philadelphians	*Bib. Ant.*	Ps.-Philo, Biblical Antiquities

3. Abbreviations of Names of Dead Sea Scrolls and Related Texts

CD	Cairo (Genizah text of the) Damascus (Document)		yielding written material; followed by abbreviation of biblical or apocryphal book
Ḥev	Naḥal Ḥever texts		
Mas	Masada texts		
Mird	Khirbet Mird texts	QL	Qumran literature
Mur	Wadi Murabbaʿat texts	1QapGen	*Genesis Apocryphon* of Qumran Cave 1
p	Pesher (commentary)	1QH	*Hôdāyôt (Thanksgiving Hymns)* from Qumran Cave 1
Q	Qumran		
1Q, 2Q, 3Q, etc.	Numbered caves of Qumran,		

1QIsa[a,b]	First or second copy of Isaiah from Qumran Cave 1		from Qumran Cave 4
1QpHab	*Pesher on Habakkuk* from Qumran Cave 1	4QMess ar	Aramaic "Messianic" text from Qumran Cave 4
1QM	*Milḥāmāh (War Scroll)*	4QPrNab	Prayer of Nabonidus from Qumran Cave 4
1QS	*Serek hayyaḥad (Rule of the Community, Manual of Discipline)*	4QTestim	*Testimonia* text from Qumran Cave 4
1QSa	Appendix A *(Rule of the Congregation)* to 1QS	4QTLevi	*Testament of Levi* from Qumran Cave 4
1QSb	Appendix B *(Blessings)* to 1QS	4QPhyl	Phylacteries from Qumran Cave 4
3Q15	Copper Scroll from Qumran Cave 3	11QMelch	*Melchizedek* text from Qumran Cave 11
4QFlor	*Florilegium* (or *Eschatological Midrashim)*	11QtgJob	*Targum of Job* from Qumran Cave 11

4. Targums

Tg. Onq.	*Targum Onqelos*	Tg. Neof.	*Targum Neofiti 1*
Tg. Neb.	*Targum of the Prophets*	Tg. Ps.-J.	*Targum Pseudo-Jonathan*
Tg. Ket.	*Targum of the Writings*	Tg. Yer. I	*Targum Yerušalmi I**
Frg. Tg.	*Fragmentary Targum*	Tg. Yer. II	*Targum Yerušalmi II**
Sam. Tg.	*Samaritan Targum*	Yem. Tg.	*Yemenite Targum*
Tg. Isa.	*Targum of Isaiah*	Tg. Esth I, II	*First or Second Targum of Esther*
Pal. Tgs.	*Palestinian Targums*	*optional title	

5. Abbreviations of Orders and Tractates in Mishnaic and Related Literature.

To distinguish the same-named tractates in the Mishna, Tosepta, Babylonian Talmud, and Jerusalem Talmud, we use (italicized) *m.*, *t.*, *b.*, or *y.* before the title of the tractate. Thus *m. Pe'a* 8:2; *b. Šabb.* 31a; *y. Mak.* 2.31d; *t. Pe'a* 1.4 (Zuck. 18 [=page number of Zuckermandel's edition of the Tosepta]).

'Abot	'Abot	Nazir	Nazir
'Arak.	'Arakin	Ned.	Nedarim
'Abod. Zar.	'Aboda Zara	Neg.	Nega'im
B. Bat.	Baba Batra	Nez.	Neziqin
Bek.	Bekorot	Nid.	Niddah
Ber.	Berakot	Obol.	Obolot
Beṣa	Beṣa (= Yom Ṭob)	'Or.	'Orla
Bik.	Bikkurim	Para	Para
B. Meṣ.	Baba Meṣi'a	Pe'a	Pe'a
B. Qam.	Baba Qamma	Pesaḥ.	Pesaḥim
Dem.	Demai	Qinnim	Qinnim
'Erub.	'Erubin	Qidd.	Qiddušin
'Ed.	'Eduyyot	Qod.	Qodašin
Giṭ.	Giṭṭin	Roš. Haš.	Roš Haššana
Ḥag.	Ḥagiga	Sanh.	Sanhedrin
Ḥal.	Ḥalla	Šabb.	Šabbat
Hor.	Horayot	Šeb.	Šebi'it
Ḥul.	Ḥullin	Šebu.	Šebu'ot
Kelim	Kelim	Šeqal.	Šeqalim
Ker.	Keritot	Soṭa	Soṭa
Ketub.	Ketubot	Sukk.	Sukka
Kil.	Kil'ayim	Ta'an.	Ta'anit
Ma'aś.	Ma'aśerot	Tamid	Tamid
Mak.	Makkot	Tem.	Temura
Makš.	Makširin (= Mašqin)	Ter.	Terumot
Meg.	Megilla	Ṭohar.	Ṭoharot
Me'il.	Me'ila	Ṭ. Yom	Ṭebul Yom
Menaḥ.	Menaḥot	'Uq.	'Uqṣin
Mid.	Middot	Yad.	Yadayim
Miqw.	Miqwa'ot	Yebam.	Yebamot
Mo'ed	Mo'ed	Yoma	Yoma (= Kippurim)
Mo'ed Qat.	Mo'ed Qatan	Zabim	Zabim
Ma'as. Š.	Ma'aśer Šeni	Zebaḥ	Zebaḥim
Našim	Našim	Zer.	Zera'im

6. Abbreviations of Other Rabbinic Works

'Abot R. Nat.	'Abot de Rabbi Nathan	Pesiq. Rab Kah.	Pesiqta de Rab Kahana
'Ag. Ber.	'Aggadat Berešit	Pirqe R. El.	Pirqe Rabbi Eliezer
Bab.	Babylonian		
Bar.	Baraita	Rab.	Rabbah
Der. Er. Rab.	Derek Ereṣ Rabba		(following
Der. Er. Zuṭ.	Derek Ereṣ Zuṭa		abbreviation for
Gem.	Gemara		biblical book:
Kalla	Kalla		Gen. Rab. [with
Mek.	Mekilta		periods] =
Midr.	Midraš; cited		Genesis Rabbah)
	with usual	Ṣem.	Ṣemaḥot
	abbreviation for	Sipra	Sipra
	biblical book;	Sipre	Sipre
	but Midr.	Sop.	Soperim
	Qoh. = Midraš	S. 'Olam Rab.	Seder 'Olam
	Qobelet		Rabbah
Pal.	Palestinian	Talm.	Talmud
Pesiq. R.	Pesiqta Rabbati	Yal.	Yalquṭ

7. Abbreviations of Nag Hammadi Tractates

Acts Pet. 12 Apost.	Acts of Peter and the Twelve Apostles	Disc. 8–9	Discourse on the Eighth and Ninth
Allogenes	Allogenes	Ep. Pet. Phil.	Letter of Peter to Philip
Ap. Jas.	Apocryphon of James	Eugnostos	Eugnostos the Blessed
Ap. John	Apocryphon of John		
Apoc. Adam	Apocalypse of Adam	Exeg. Soul	Exegesis on the Soul
1 Apoc. Jas.	First Apocalypse of James	Gos. Eg.	Gospel of the Egyptians
2 Apoc. Jas.	Second Apocalypse of James	Gos. Phil.	Gospel of Philip
		Gos. Thom.	Gospel of Thomas
Apoc. Paul	Apocalypse of Paul	Gos. Truth	Gospel of Truth
Apoc. Pet.	Apocalypse of Peter	Great Pow.	Concept of our Great Power
Asclepius	Asclepius 21–29		
Auth. Teach.	Authoritative Teaching	Hyp. Arch.	Hypostasis of the Archons
Dial. Sav.	Dialogue of the Savior	Hypsiph.	Hypsiphrone
		Interp. Know.	Interpretation of Knowledge

Marsanes	*Marsanes*	*Steles Seth*	*Three Steles of Seth*
Melch.	*Melchizedek*	*Teach. Silv.*	*Teachings of*
Norea	*Thought of Norea*		*Silvanus*
On Bap. A	*On Baptism A*	*Testim. Truth*	*Testimony of Truth*
On Bap. B	*On Baptism B*	*Thom. Cont.*	*Book of Thomas the*
On Bap. C	*On Baptism C*		*Contender*
On Euch. A	*On the Eucharist A*	*Thund.*	*Thunder, Perfect*
On Euch. B	*On the Eucharist B*		*Mind*
Orig. World	*On the Origin of*	*Treat. Res.*	*Treatise on*
	the World		*Resurrection*
Paraph. Shem	*Paraphrase of Shem*	*Treat. Seth*	*Second Treatise of*
Pr. Paul	*Prayer of the*		*the Great Seth*
	Apostle Paul	*Tri. Trac.*	*Tripartite Tractate*
Pr. Thanks.	*Prayer of*	*Trim. Prot.*	*Trimorphic*
	Thanksgiving		*Protennoia*
Sent. Sextus	*Sentences of Sextus*	*Val. Exp.*	*A Valentinian*
Soph. Jes. Chr.	*Sophia of Jesus*		*Exposition*
	Christ	*Zost.*	*Zostrianos*

8. Abbreviations of Commonly Used Periodicals, Reference Works, and Serials

(Titles not found in this list are written out in full. Titles of periodicals and books are italicized, but titles of series are set in roman characters, as are acronyms of authors' names when they are used as sigla.) Short, one-word titles not on this list are not abbreviated.

AAS	*Acta apostolicae sedis*	*AH*	F. Rosenthal, *An*
AASOR	Annual of the		*Aramaic Handbook*
	American Schools	*AJA*	*American Journal of*
	of Oriental		*Archaeology*
	Research	*AJBA*	*Australian Journal of*
AB	Anchor Bible		*Biblical Archaeology*
AcOr	*Acta orientalia*	*AJP*	*American Journal of*
ACW	Ancient Christian		*Philology*
	Writers	*AJSL*	*American Journal of*
AfO	*Archiv für*		*Semitic Languages and*
	Orientforschung		*Literature*
AGJU	Arbeiten zur	*AJT*	*American Journal of*
	Geschichte des		*Theology*
	antiken Judentums	ALBO	Analecta lovaniensia
	und des		biblica et orientalia
	Urchristentums		

ALGHJ	Arbeiten zur Literatur und Geschichte des hellenistischen Judentums	**ASOR**	American Schools of Oriental Research
AnBib	Analecta biblica	*ASS*	*Acta sanctae sedis*
ANEP	J. B. Pritchard (ed.), *Ancient Near East in Pictures*	*AsSeign*	*Assemblées du Seigneur*
		ASSR	*Archives des sciences sociales des religions*
ANESTP	J. B. Pritchard (ed.), *Ancient Near East Supplementary Texts and Pictures*	*ASTI*	*Annual of the Swedish Theological Institute*
		ATAbh	Alttestamentliche Abhandlungen
ANET	J. B. Pritchard (ed.), *Ancient Near Eastern Texts*	**ATANT**	Abhandlungen zur Theologie des Alten und Neuen Testaments
Ang	*Angelicum*	*AtBib*	H. Grollenberg, *Atlas of the Bible*
AnOr	Analecta orientalia		
ANQ	*Andover Newton Quarterly*	**ATD**	Das Alte Testament Deutsch
ANTF	Arbeiten zur neutestamentlichen Textforschung	*ATR*	*Anglican Theological Review*
ANRW	*Aufstieg und Niedergang der römischen Welt*	*Aug*	*Augustinianum*
		AusBR	*Australian Biblical Review*
AOAT	Alter Orient und Altes Testament	*AUSS*	*Andrews University Seminary Studies*
AOS	American Oriental Series	*BA*	*Biblical Archaeologist*
AP	J. Marouzeau (ed.), *L'Année philologique*	**BAC**	Biblioteca de autores cristianos
APOT	R. H. Charles (ed.), *Apocrypha and Pseudepigrapha of the Old Testament*	**BAGD**	W. Bauer, W. F. Arndt, F. W. Gingrich, and F. W. Danker, *Greek-English Lexicon of the NT*
Arch	*Archaeology*		
ARW	*Archiv für Religionswissenschaft*	*BAR*	*Biblical Archaeologist Reader*
ASNU	Acta seminarii neotestamentici upsaliensis	*BARev*	*Biblical Archaeology Review*

BASOR	*Bulletin of the American Schools of Oriental Research*	*BHH*	B. Reicke and L. Rost (eds.), *Biblisch-Historisches Handwörterbuch*
BBB	Bonner biblische Beiträge		
BBET	Beiträge zur biblischen Exegese und Theologie	*BHK*	R. Kittel, *Biblia Hebraica*
		BHS	*Biblia hebraica stuttgartensia*
BCSR	*Bulletin of the Council on the Study of Religion*	*BHT*	Beiträge zur historischen Theologie
BDB	F. Brown, S. R. Driver, and C. A. Briggs, *Hebrew and English Lexicon of the Old Testament*	*Bib*	*Biblica*
		BibB	Biblische Beiträge
		BibBh	*Bible Bhashyam*
		BibLeb	*Bibel und Leben*
BDF	F. Blass, A. Debrunner, and R. W. Funk, *A Greek Grammar of the NT*	BibOr	Biblica et orientalia
		BibS(F)	Biblische Studien (Freiburg, 1895-)
BDR	F. Blass, A. Debrunner, and F. Rehkopf, *Grammatik des neutestamentlichen Griechisch*	BibS(N)	Biblische Studien (Neukirchen, 1951-)
		BIES	*Bulletin of the Israel Exploration Society (= Yediot)*
BeO	*Bibbia e oriente*		
BETL	Bibliotheca ephemeridum theologicarum lovaniensium	*BIFAO*	*Bulletin de l'institut français d'archéologie orientale*
		Bijdr	*Bijdragen*
BEvT	Beiträge zur evangelischen Theologie	*BIOSCS*	*Bulletin of the International Organization for Septuagint and Cognate Studies*
BFCT	Beiträge zur Förderung christlicher Theologie		
		BJPES	*Bulletin of the Jewish Palestine Exploration Society*
BGBE	Beiträge zur Geschichte der biblischen Exegese	*BJRL*	*Bulletin of the John Rylands University Library of Manchester*
BHEAT	Bulletin d'histoire et d'exégèse de l'Ancien Testament	*BK*	*Bibel und Kirche*

BKAT	Biblischer Kommentar: Altes Testament	CCath	Corpus catholicorum
BLit	*Bibel und Liturgie*	*CH*	*Church History*
BN	*Biblische Notizen*	*CHR*	*Catholic Historical Review*
BO	*Bibliotheca orientalis*	*CIG*	*Corpus inscriptionum graecarum*
BR	*Biblical Research*		
BSac	*Bibliotheca Sacra*	*CII*	*Corpus inscriptionum iudaicarum*
BSOAS	*Bulletin of the School of Oriental (and African) Studies*	*CIL*	*Corpus inscriptionum latinarum*
BT	*The Bible Translator*	*CIS*	*Corpus inscriptionum semiticarum*
BTB	*Biblical Theology Bulletin*		
BTS	*Bible et terre sainte*	*CJ*	*Classical Journal*
BurH	*Buried History*	*CJT*	*Canadian Journal of Theology*
BVC	*Bible et vie chrétienne*	CNT	Commentaire du Nouveau Testament
BWANT	Beiträge zur Wissenschaft vom Alten und Neuen Testament	ConB	Coniectanea biblica
		ConBNT	Coniectanea biblica, New Testament
ByF	*Biblia y fe*	ConBOT	Coniectanea biblica, Old Testament
BZ	*Biblische Zeitschrift*		
BZAW	Beihefte zur *ZAW*	*ConNT*	*Coniectanea neotestamentica*
BZNW	Beihefte zur *ZNW*		
BZRGG	Beihefte zur *ZRGG*	*CP*	*Classical Philology*
CAH	*Cambridge Ancient History*	*CQ*	*Church Quarterly*
		CQR	*Church Quarterly Review*
CabEv	*Cahiers évangile*		
CahRB	Cahiers de la Revue biblique	*CRAIBL*	*Comptes rendus de l'académie des inscriptions et belles-lettres*
CahThéol	Cahiers théologiques		
CAT	Commentaire de l'Ancien Testament	CRINT	Compendia rerum iudaicarum ad Novum Testamentum
CB	*Cultura bíblica*		
CBQ	*Catholic Biblical Quarterly*	CSCO	Corpus scriptorum christianorum orientalium
CBQMS	Catholic Biblical Quarterly— Monograph Series		
CC	Corpus christianorum	CSEL	Corpus scriptorum ecclesiasticorum latinorum

CTJ	*Calvin Theological Journal*	*EnchBib*	*Enchiridion biblicum*
		ErIsr	Eretz Israel
CTM	*Concordia Theological Monthly (or CTM)*	*ErJb*	*Eranos Jahrbuch*
		EstBib	*Estudios bíblicos*
CTQ	*Concordia Theological Quarterly*	*EstEcl*	*Estudios eclesiásticos*
		EstTeol	*Estudios teológicos*
CurTM	*Currents in Theology and Mission*	*ETL*	*Ephemerides theologicae lovanienses*
DACL	*Dictionnaire d'archéologie chrétienne et de liturgie*	*ETR*	*Études théologiques et religieuses*
		EvK	*Evangelische Kommentare*
DBSup	*Dictionnaire de la Bible, Supplément*	*EvQ*	*Evangelical Quarterly*
		EvT	*Evangelische Theologie*
DJD	Discoveries in the Judaean Desert	*EWNT*	H. Balz and G. Schneider (eds.), *Exegetisches Wörterbuch zum Neuen Testament*
DRev	*Downside Review*		
DS	Denzinger-Schönmetzer, *Enchiridion symbolorum*		
		ExpTim	*Expository Times*
		FB	Forschung zur Bibel
DTC	*Dictionnaire de théologie catholique*	FBBS	Facet Books, Biblical Series
EBib	Études bibliques	FC	Fathers of the Church
EDB	L. F. Hartman (ed.), *Encyclopedic Dictionary of the Bible*		
		FRLANT	Forschungen zur Religion und Literatur des Alten und Neuen Testaments
EHAT	Exegetisches Handbuch zum Alten Testament		
		GAT	Grundrisse zum Alten Testament
EKKNT	Evangelisch-katholischer Kommentar zum Neuen Testament	GCS	Griechische christliche Schriftsteller
EKL	*Evangelisches Kirchenlexikon*	GKB	Gesenius-Kautzsch-Bergsträsser, *Hebräische Grammatik*
EncJud	*Encyclopedia Judaica* (1971)		

GKC	*Gesenius' Hebrew Grammar*, ed. E. Kautzsch, tr. A. E. Cowley
GNT	Grundrisse zum Neuen Testament
GRBS	*Greek, Roman, and Byzantine Studies*
Greg	*Gregorianum*
GTA	Göttinger theologische Arbeiten
GTJ	*Grace Theological Journal*
HALAT	W. Baumgartner et al., *Hebräisches und aramäisches Lexikon zum Alten Testament*
HAT	Handbuch zum Alten Testament
HDR	Harvard Dissertations in Religion
HeyJ	*Heythrop Journal*
HibJ	*Hibbert Journal*
HKAT	Handkommentar zum Alten Testament
HKNT	Handkommentar zum Neuen Testament
HNT	Handbuch zum Neuen Testament
HNTC	Harper's NT Commentaries
HR	*History of Religions*
HSM	Harvard Semitic Monographs
HSS	Harvard Semitic Studies
HTKNT	Herders theologischer Kommentar zum Neuen Testament
HTR	*Harvard Theological Review*
HTS	Harvard Theological Studies
HUCA	*Hebrew Union College Annual*
HUT	Hermeneutische Untersuchungen zur Theologie
IB	*Interpreter's Bible*
IBS	*Irish Biblical Studies*
ICC	International Critical Commentary
IDB	G. A. Buttrick (ed.), *Interpreter's Dictionary of the Bible*
IDBSup	Supplementary volume to *IDB*
IEJ	*Israel Exploration Journal*
Int	*Interpretation*
IOS	*Israel Oriental Society*
ITQ	*Irish Theological Quarterly*
JA	*Journal asiatique*
JAAR	*Journal of the American Academy of Religion*
JAC	Jahrbuch für Antike und Christentum
JAL	Jewish Apocryphal Literature
JANESCU	*Journal of the Ancient Near Eastern Society of Columbia University*

JAOS	*Journal of the American Oriental Society*	JQRMS	Jewish Quarterly Review Monograph Series
JAS	*Journal of Asian Studies*	*JR*	*Journal of Religion*
JB	A. Jones (ed.), *Jerusalem Bible*	*JRelS*	*Journal of Religious Studies*
JBC	R. E. Brown et al. (eds.), *The Jerome Biblical Commentary*	*JRH*	*Journal of Religious History*
JBL	*Journal of Biblical Literature*	*JRS*	*Journal of Roman Studies*
JBR	*Journal of Bible and Religion*	*JRT*	*Journal of Religious Thought*
JDS	Judean Desert Studies	JSHRZ	Jüdische Schriften aus hellenistisch-römischer Zeit
JEH	*Journal of Ecclesiastical History*	*JSJ*	*Journal for the Study of Judaism in the Persian, Hellenistic and Roman Periods*
JEOL	*Jaarbericht . . . ex oriente lux*		
JES	*Journal of Ecumenical Studies*	*JSNT*	*Journal for the Study of the New Testament*
JETS	*Journal of the Evangelical Theological Society*	JSNTSup	Journal for the Study of the New Testament—Supplement Series
JHNES	Johns Hopkins Near Eastern Studies	*JSOT*	*Journal for the Study of the Old Testament*
JHS	*Journal of Hellenic Studies*	JSOTSup	Journal for the Study of the Old Testament-Supplement Series
JJS	*Journal of Jewish Studies*		
JMES	*Journal of Middle Eastern Studies*	*JSS*	*Journal of Semitic Studies*
JNES	*Journal of Near Eastern Studies*	*JSSR*	*Journal for the Scientific Study of Religion*
JPOS	*Journal of the Palestine Oriental Society*	*JTC*	*Journal for Theology and the Church*
JPSV	*Jewish Publication Society Version*	*JTS*	*Journal of Theological Studies*
JQR	*Jewish Quarterly Review*	*Judaica*	*Judaica: Beiträge zum Verständnis . . .*

KAT	E. Sellin (ed.), Kommentar zum A.T.
KB	L. Koehler and W. Baumgartner, *Lexicon in Veteris Testamenti libros*
KD	*Kerygma und Dogma*
KJV	*King James Version*
KIT	Kleine Texte
LB	*Linguistica biblica*
LCC	Library of Christian Classics
LCL	Loeb Classical Library
LCQ	*Lutheran Church Quarterly*
LD	Lectio divina
LLAVT	E. Vogt, *Lexicon linguae aramaicae Veteris Testamenti*
LPGL	G. W. H. Lampe, *Patristic Greek Lexicon*
LQ	*Lutheran Quarterly*
LR	*Lutherische Rundschau*
LS	*Louvain Studies*
LSJ	Liddell-Scott-Jones, *Greek-English Lexicon*
LTK	*Lexikon für Theologie und Kirche*
LTP	*Laval théologique et philosophique*
LumVie	*Lumière et vie*
LW	*Lutheran World*
McCQ	*McCormick Quarterly*
MDB	*Le monde de la Bible*

MDOG	Mitteilungen der deutschen Orient-Gesellschaft
MeyerK	H. A. W. Meyer, Kritisch-exegetischer Kommentar über das Neue Testament
MGWJ	*Monatsschrift für Geschichte und Wissenschaft des Judentums*
MM	J. H. Moulton and G. Milligan, *The Vocabulary of the Greek Testament*
MNTC	Moffatt NT Commentary
MPAIBL	Mémoires présentés à l'académie des inscriptions et belles-lettres
MScRel	*Mélanges de science religieuse*
MTZ	*Münchener theologische Zeitschrift*
Mus	*Muséon*
MUSJ	*Mélanges de l'université Saint-Joseph*
NAB	*New American Bible*
NCB	New Century Bible
NCCHS	R. D. Fuller et al. (eds.), *New Catholic Commentary on Holy Scripture*
NCE	M. R. P. McGuire et al. (eds.), *New Catholic Encyclopedia*
NEB	*New English Bible*
Neot	*Neotestamentica*
NFT	New Frontiers in Theology

NHS	Nag Hammadi Studies	*OLZ*	*Orientalische Literaturzeitung*
NICNT	New International Commentary on the New Testament	*Or*	*Orientalia* (Rome)
		OrAnt	*Oriens antiquus*
		OrChr	*Oriens christianus*
NICOT	New International Commentary on the Old Testament	*OrSyr*	*L'Orient syrien*
		OTA	*Old Testament Abstracts*
NIV	*New International Version*	OTL	Old Testament Library
NJBC	*New Jerome Biblical Commentary*	*PAAJR*	*Proceedings of the American Academy of Jewish Research*
NJV	*New Jewish Version*		
NKZ	*Neue kirchliche Zeitschrift*	*PCB*	M. Black and H. H. Rowley (eds.), *Peake's Commentary on the Bible*
NovT	*Novum Testamentum*		
NovTSup	Novum Testamentum, Supplements		
		PEFQS	*Palestine Exploration Fund, Quarterly Statement*
NRT	*La nouvelle revue théologique*	*PEQ*	*Palestine Exploration Quarterly*
NTA	*New Testament Abstracts*	PG	J. Migne, Patrologia graeca
NTAbh	Neutestamentliche Abhandlungen	*PGM*	K. Preisedanz (ed.), *Papyri graecae magicae*
NTD	Das Neue Testament Deutsch		
NTF	Neutestamentliche Forschungen	*Phil*	*Philologus*
		PJ	*Palästina-Jahrbuch*
NTS	*New Testament Studies*	PL	J. Migne, Patrologia latina
NTTS	New Testament Tools and Studies	PO	Patrologia orientalis
Numen	*Numen: International Review for the History of Religions*	*PSB*	*Princeton Seminary Bulletin*
		PSTJ	*Perkins School of Theology Journal*
OBO	Orbis biblicus et orientalis	PTMS	Pittsburgh Theological Monograph Series
OIP	Oriental Institute Publications		
OLP	Orientalia lovaniensia periodica	PVTG	Pseudepigrapha Veteris Testamenti graece

PW	Pauly-Wissowa, *Real-Encyclopädie der klassischen Altertumswissenschaft*	RHE	*Revue d'histoire ecclésiastique*
		RHPR	*Revue d'histoire et de philosophie religieuses*
PWSup	Supplement to PW	RHR	*Revue de l'histoire des religions*
QD	Quaestiones disputatae		
QDAP	*Quarterly of the Department of Antiquities in Palestine*	RIDA	*Revue internationale des droits de l'antiquité*
		RivB	*Rivista biblica*
		RNT	Regensburger Neues Testament
RAC	*Reallexikon für Antike und Christentum*		
		RQ	*Römische Quartalschrift für christliche Altertumskunde und Kirchengeschichte*
RANE	Records of the Ancient Near East		
RArch	*Revue archéologique*		
RB	*Revue biblique*	RR	*Review of Religion*
RCB	*Revista de cultura bíblica*	RRef	*La revue reformée*
		RSO	*Rivista degli studi orientali*
RE	*Realencyclopädie für protestantische Theologie und Kirche*	RSPT	*Revue des sciences philosophiques et théologiques*
REA	*Revue des études anciennes*	RSR	*Recherches de science religieuse*
RechBib	Recherches bibliques	RSV	*Revised Standard Version*
REJ	*Revue des études juives*		
RelS	*Religious Studies*	RTL	*Revue théologique de Louvain*
RelSoc	*Religion and Society*		
RelSRev	*Religious Studies Review*	RTP	*Revue de théologie et de philosophie*
RES	*Répertoire d'épigraphie sémitique*	RUO	*Revue de l'université d'Ottawa*
ResQ	*Restoration Quarterly*		
RevExp	*Review and Expositor*	RV	*Revised Version*
RevistB	*Revista bíblica*	SacEr	*Sacris erudiri*
RevQ	*Revue de Qumran*	SANT	Studien zum Alten und Neuen Testament
RevScRel	*Revue des sciences religieuses*		
RevSem	*Revue sémitique*	SB	Sources bibliques
RGG	*Religion in Geschichte und Gegenwart*	SBA	Studies in Biblical Archaeology

SBAW	Sitzungsberichte der bayerischen Akademie der Wissenschaften	SD	Studies and Documents
SBB	Stuttgarter biblische Beiträge	SE	Studia Evangelica I, II, III, etc. (= TU 73 [1959], 87 [1964], 88 [1964], 102 [1968], 103 [1968], 112 [1973])
SBFLA	Studii biblici franciscani liber annuus		
SBJ	La sainte bible de Jérusalem	*Sem*	Semitica
SBLASP	Society of Biblical Literature Abstracts and Seminar Papers	SHT	Studies in Historical Theology
		SJ	Studia judaica
SBLDS	SBL Dissertation Series	SJLA	Studies in Judaism in Late Antiquity
SBLMasS	SBL Masoretic Studies	*SJT*	Scottish Journal of Theology
SBLMS	SBL Monograph Series	*SMSR*	Studi e materiali di storia delle religioni
SBLSBS	SBL Sources for Biblical Study	SNT	Studien zum Neuen Testament
SBLSCS	SBL Septuagint and Cognate Studies	SNTSMS	Society for New Testament Studies Monograph Series
SBLTT	SBL Texts and Translations	SO	Symbolae osloenses
SBM	Stuttgarter biblische Monographien	SOTSMS	Society for Old Testament Study Monograph Series
SBS	Stuttgarter Bibelstudien	*SP*	J. Coppens et al. (eds.), *Sacra pagina*
SBT	Studies in Biblical Theology	*SPap*	Studia papyrologica
SC	Sources chrétiennes	*SPAW*	Sitzungsberichte der preussischen Akademie der Wissenschaften
ScEccl	Sciences ecclésiastiques		
ScEs	Science et esprit	SPB	Studia postbiblica
SCHNT	Studia ad corpus hellenisticum Novi Testamenti	*SPC*	Studiorum paulinorum congressus internationalis catholicus 1961 (2 vols.)
SCR	Studies in Comparative Religion		
Scr	Scripture	*SR*	Studies in Religion/ Sciences religieuses
ScrB	Scripture Bulletin		
ScrHier	Scripta hierosolymitana	SSS	Semitic Study Series

ST	*Studia theologica*	*TDOT*	G. J. Botterweck
STANT	Studien zum Alten		and H. Ringgren
	und Neuen		(eds.), *Theological*
	Testament		*Dictionary of the Old*
STDJ	Studies on the		*Testament*
	Texts of the Desert	TextsS	Texts and Studies
	of Judah	*TF*	*Theologische Forschung*
Str-B	[H. Strack and] P.	*TGI*	*Theologie und Glaube*
	Billerbeck,	THKNT	Theologischer
	Kommentar zum		Handkommentar
	Neuen Testament		zum Neuen
StudNeot	Studia		Testament
	neotestamentica	*ThStud*	*Theologische Studiën*
StudOr	Studia orientalia	*TLZ*	*Theologische*
SUNT	Studien zur		*Literaturzeitung*
	Umwelt des Neuen	*TP*	*Theologie und*
	Testaments		*Philosophie*
SVTP	Studia in Veteris	*TPQ*	*Theologisch-Praktische*
	Testamenti		*Quartalschrift*
	pseudepigrapha	*TQ*	*Theologische*
SymBU	Symbolae biblicae		*Quartalschrift*
	upsalienses	*TRE*	*Theologische Real-*
TAPA	*Transactions of the*		*enzyklopädie*
	American Philological	*TRev*	*Theologische Revue*
	Association	*TRu*	*Theologische*
TBei	*Theologische Beiträge*		*Rundschau*
TBl	*Theologische Blätter*	*TS*	*Theological Studies*
TBü	Theologische	*TSK*	*Theologische Studien*
	Bücherei		*und Kritiken*
TBT	*The Bible Today*	*TToday*	*Theology Today*
TCGNT	B. M. Metzger, *A*	*TTZ*	*Trierer theologische*
	Textual Commentary		*Zeitschrift*
	on the Greek New	TU	Texte und
	Testament		Untersuchungen
TD	*Theology Digest*	*TWAT*	G. J. Botterweck
TDNT	G. Kittel and G.		and H. Ringgren
	Friedrich (eds.),		(eds.), *Theologisches*
	Theological Dictionary		*Wörterbuch zum Alten*
	of the New Testament		*Testament*

TWNT	G. Kittel and G. Friedrich (eds.), *Theologisches Wörterbuch zum Neuen Testament*			Alten und Neuen Testament
			WO	*Die Welt des Orients*
			WTJ	*Westminster Theological Journal*
TynBul	*Tyndale Bulletin*			
TZ	*Theologische Zeitschrift*		WUNT	Wissenschaftliche Untersuchungen zum Neuen Testament
UBSGNT	United Bible Societies *Greek New Testament*			
			WVDOG	Wissenschaftliche Veröffentlichungen der deutschen Orientgesellschaft
UNT	Untersuchungen zum Neuen Testament			
USQR	*Union Seminary Quarterly Review*		*WZKM*	*Wiener Zeitschrift für die Kunde des Morgenlandes*
VC	*Vigiliae christianae*			
VCaro	*Verbum caro*		*WZKSO*	*Wiener Zeitschrift für die Kunde Süd-und Ostasiens*
VD	*Verbum domini*			
VE	*Vox evangelica*			
VF	*Verkündigung und Forschung*		*ZAW*	*Zeitschrift für die alttestamentliche Wissenschaft*
VKGNT	K. Aland (ed.), *Vollständige Konkordanz zum griechischen Neuen Testament*			
			ZDMG	*Zeitschrift der deutschen morgenländischen Gesellschaft*
VP	*Vivre et penser* (= *RB* 1941–44)		*ZDPV*	*Zeitschrift des deutschen Palästina-Vereins*
VS	Verbum salutis			
VSpir	*Vie spirituelle*		*ZHT*	*Zeitschrift für historische Theologie*
VT	*Vetus Testamentum*			
VTSup	Vetus Testamentum, Supplements		*ZKG*	*Zeitschrift für Kirchengeschichte*
WDB	*Westminster Dictionary of the Bible*		*ZKT*	*Zeitschrift für katholische Theologie*
WHAB	*Westminster Historical Atlas of the Bible*		*ZMR*	*Zeitschrift für Missionskunde und Religionswissenschaft*
WHJP	World History of the Jewish People		*ZNW*	*Zeitschrift für die neutestamentliche Wissenschaft*
WMANT	Wissenschaftliche Monographien zum			

ZRGG	*Zeitschrift für*	ZWT	*Zeitschrift für*
	Religions-und		*wissenschaftliche*
	Geistesgeschichte		*Theologie*
ZTK	*Zeitschrift für*		
	Theologie und Kirche		

9. *Miscellaneous Abbreviations*

LXX   The Septuagint
MT   Masoretic Text
NT   New Testament
OT   Old Testament
par(r).   parallel(s) in the Gospels
Vg   The Vulgate
VL   Vetus Latina (Old Latin)
|| two pericopes (often in the Q document) that are basically parallel, though possibly with some differences in wording

INDEX OF SCRIPTURE

OLD TESTAMENT
Genesis, 265
 4:1, 354
 29:12, 359
 34:3, 222
 41:46, 416
Genesis (LXX)
 24:48, 325
 29:12, 325
Exodus
 12:6, 388
 12:8, 388
 13:2,12,15, 355
 13:22, 358
 17:9–10, 231
 19:15, 338
 21:2–4, 312
 21:7–11, 312
 21:26–27, 312
 23:1b, 269
Leviticus
 12:1–8, 210
 19:3, 307
 23:9–14, 422
 23:27,32, 388
 25:39–43,47–55, 312
Numbers
 3:12–13, 358
 4:3, 416
 18:15–16, 358
Deuteronomy
 3:21, 231
 6:1–7,20, 307
 15:12, 312
 21:23, 8

 32:7, 307
Joshua
 24:29, 416
Judges
 2:7, 231
First Samuel
 1:1, 75
 26:6, 226
Second Samuel
 2:13, 226
 5:4, 416
 7:12–14, 218–19
 7:14, 241
Second Samuel (LXX)
 7:12, 241
First Kings, 226
 19:19–21, 365
Second Kings
 4:10, 281
First Chronicles, 226
 7:27, 231
 23:22, 325, 359
 24:11, 231
Second Chronicles
 31:15, 231
Ezra, 262
 2:6,36,40, 231
 2:69, 297
 3:9, 231
 8:33, 231
Ezra (LXX)
 5:16, 417
Nehemiah
 3:19, 231
 7:11,39,43, 231

OLD TESTAMENT, Nehemiah *(cont.)*
  7:69–71, 297
  8:7, 231
  8:17, 231
  9:4–5, 231
  10:10, 231
  12:8,24, 231
Tobit
  4:3–21, 307
First Maccabees
  1:10, 383, 418
  1:56–57, 275
Second Maccabees
  5:25, 314
  6:21, 314
  7:27, 307
Job (LXX)
  36:13, 314
Psalms
  2, 241
  22:1, 170, 171
  22:19, 170
  78:3–4, 307
  110, 241, 321
  118:22, 138
Sirach (Ecclesiasticus), 262
  1:28–30, 314
  3:1, 307
  8:9, 307
  30:1–13, 307
  39:1,6,9, 305
  39:1–11, 275
  46:1, 231
Isaiah
  1:1, 383
  7:14, 221–22, 243
  42:1–4, 321
  58:6d, 303
  61:1, 218
  61:1a,b,d, 2a, 303
  61:1–2, 270
  61:1–3, 241
Isaiah (LXX), 303
Jeremiah
  1:1–3, 383
  16:1–4, 339, 364–65
  17:13, 269
Daniel, 259, 262, 264, 291, 296
  3:5,10,15, 297
Hosea
  2:6, 251
Hosea (LXX)
  1:2, 251

NEW TESTAMENT
Matthew, 41–45, 96, 115–17, 122, 124,
    129, 132–39, 153, 160–62, 191, 224–
    25
  1:1–17, 221, 238, 320, 416
  1:10, 83
  1:18,20, 237
  1:18–2:23, 211
  1:18–20, 224
  1:18–25, 224, 238, 242, 245, 320
  1:21, 207
  1:23, 243
  1:25, 306, 320–23, 358
  1–2, 209–14
  2:1, 211, 214, 375
  2:1–12, 375
  2:2, 235, 376, 414
  2:8,11,13,14, 236
  2:11, 211, 376
  2:13, 83, 322
  2:13–15, 224
  2:15, 224
  2:16, 211, 376
  2:16–18, 212
  2:19–20, 236
  2:23, 212, 236, 376
  2:38, 236
  3:7–10, 340
  3:13–17, 169
  4:13, 212, 236
  4:23, 306
  5:3–12, 43
  5:14, 135
  5:14–17, 109
  5:17, 98, 299
  5:20, 161
  5:32, 46, 132
  5:34,37, 171–72
  5:34–37, 47
  5:38–48, 47
  5–7, 409
  6:1–18, 134
  6:9–13, 43
  6:12, 265
  7:3–5, 328
  7:6, 135
  8:5–13, 64, 295
  8–9, 42
  8:19, 306
  9:27, 218
  9:35, 306
  10:5–6, 64
  10:10, 46
  10:16, 135
  10:37, 164
  10:37–38, 138
  11:27, 307
  11:28–30, 135
  12:3, 305

NEW TESTAMENT, Matthew *(cont.)*

12:9, 306
12:20, 321
12:22–37, 306
12:23, 218
12:46–50, 323
12:50, 357
13:24–30, 135
13:44, 135
13:45–46, 135
13:47–48, 140
13:47–50, 135
13:50, 323
13:52, 346
13:53–58, 313
13:55, 214, 224, 225, 280, 313, 317, 322, 357
13:55–56, 323
14:21–28, 295
14:22–33, 162
15:11, 162, 165
15:12–14, 162
15:13, 135
15:13–14, 162
15:21–28, 64
15:22, 218
16:1–12, 370
16:2, 432
16:9, 83
16:17–19, 189
18:20, 135
19, 83
19:3–9, 342
19:9, 132
19:10–12, 343, 368
19:12, 342–44, 367, 369
19:20,23, 151
20:20, 334
20:30, 218
21:9,15, 218
21:42, 166
21–22, 313
22:42–45, 218
23, 306
23:8, 306
23:13, 135
23:37, 404
24:36, 169
24:43, 47
26:17, 389
26:25, 306
26:26–29, 43
26:57–66, 347
26:73, 231, 267
27:32, 356
27:35, 170
27:46, 170, 298

27:56, 334, 356
27:57–61, 387
27:62–66, 387
27:64b, 117
28:16–20, 64
Mark, 41–44, 116, 121–22, 129, 132–33, 136–39, 192, 193, 250, 306
1:4–8, 340
1:4–11, 168
1:14, 412
1:18–25, 220–21
1:21,39, 306
1:21–28, 348
1:22, 308
1:23–28, 409
1:30, 363
1:35–39, 404
1:40–44, 119
1–8:26, 359
2:1–3:6, 41
2:13–23, 376
2:18–22, 172
2:23, 403, 413, 414
2:23–28, 306
3:13–19b, 181
3:16, 306
3:17, 356
3:20–35, 370–71
3:21, 181, 349, 370–71
3:21,31–34, 243
3:21,31–35, 250, 317
3:22–30, 306
3:31, 318, 355
3:31–35, 317, 323, 330, 350, 357
3:35, 317, 328, 353, 357
4:1–8, 136
4:1–34, 42
4:22, 136
4:22a, 163
4:30–32, 136
4:38, 306
5:22–43, 345
5:41, 265–66
6:1,3–4, 270
6:1–6a, 225, 270, 277, 278
6:2, 306, 308
6:3, 214, 224–26, 229, 236, 242, 247, 310, 313, 317, 322, 355–56, 360
6:3a, 280
6:4, 250
6:6b–8:21, 42
6:7–13, 356
6:17, 359
6:21, 282
6:31,35, 413
6:39, 403, 413
6:45–52, 162

NEW TESTAMENT, Mark *(cont.)*
7:1–23, 135, 306
7:15, 165, 173
7:24–30, 295
7:34, 266
9:5, 306
9:14–19, 190
9:17,38, 306
10:1–12, 132, 343
10:2–12, 172, 306
10:11–12, 46, 132, 175
10:13–16, 343
10:17,20,35, 306
10:26, 164
10:29, 363
10:34, 121
10:38, 161
10:46a, 121
10:47, 218, 240
11, 381
11:21, 306
11:27–33, 348
11:27–12:34, 41
12, 306
12:1–8, 136
12:8, 138
12:13–17, 119
12:13–17,18–27,28–34, 306
12:14,19,32, 306
12:18–37, 346
12:28–34, 345
12:35–37, 218, 240
13:2, 175
13:32, 169
14:1, 394, 403, 425
14:1a, 396–97, 425
14:1–2, 181, 347
14:10–11, 181
14:12, 389, 392, 393, 396, 397
14:12–16, 396, 397, 404, 425–26, 428
14:12–17, 389
14:17, 404, 420, 428
14:17–21, 397
14:20, 334
14:20–30, 389
14:22–24, 398
14:22–25, 43, 175, 399
14:22–26, 397
14:25, 398
14:26–31, 397
14:32–42, 47
14:36, 175, 266
14:51, 151
14:58, 175
14:68,72, 420
14:70, 231
15:1, 420

15:2,26, 241
15:6–14, 400
15:21, 356
15:24, 170
15:25, 420
15:33, 420
15:34, 170, 266, 298
15:34–37, 420
15:39, 356
15:40, 356
15:40,47, 355
15:42, 386, 420
16:1, 355
16:5, 151
Luke, 41–45, 96, 115, 122, 129, 135–39,
      191–92
1:1–4, 383
1:3, 385
1:4, 419
1:5, 214, 216, 375, 383
1:5,36, 370
1:5–23, 393
1:26–27, 212
1:26–38, 220–21
1:27, 238
1:27,34–35, 242, 245
1:31–35, 213
1:35, 236
1:36, 216
1:39–56, 216
1:41, 252
1:56, 212
1:59–63, 357
1:80, 17, 340
1–2, 209–14, 418
2:1, 212–13
2:1–2, 383, 412
2:2, 416
2:5, 245
2:7, 238, 306, 358
2:22, 209
2:22–24, 393
2:22–38, 210
2:23, 355
2:25, 115
2:25–38, 213
2:40, 254
2:46–47, 306
2:52, 254
3:1, 416, 418
3:1–2, 372, 374, 383, 385, 418
3:2, 340
3:7–9, 340
3:19–22, 169
3:23, 214, 377, 416
3:23–31, 238
3:23–38, 238

NEW TESTAMENT, Luke *(cont.)*

3:31, 218
3:38, 416
3–4, 302
4, 302
4:14–16a, 302–3
4:15,16,20,28,33,44, 306
4:16, 308
4:16,22,24, 270
4:16–17, 313
4:16–20, 264
4:16–30, 268–71, 278, 409
4:22, 214, 225, 280, 313
4:23, 313
4:25–27, 270
4:29, 303
4:42–44, 404
5:5, 306
6:6, 306
6:20b–23, 43
6:27–36, 47
6:29, 340
7:1–10, 295
7:12, 251
7:14, 151
7:17, 404
7:36, 345
7:36–50, 370
7:40, 306
8:2–3, 334
8:17, 136, 163
8:19–21, 330, 358
8:24,45, 306
9:8, 83
9:33,49, 306
9:51–19:27, 42
10:7, 46
10:8–9, 137–38
10:22, 307
10:30–37, 349
11:2–4, 43
11:14–23, 306
11:27–28, 136
11:45, 306
11:52, 135
12:13, 306, 322
12:13–14, 150
12:13–15, 135
12:16–21, 135
12:39, 47
12:49, 135
12:54–56, 315
13:10, 306
13:10–17, 306
13:15–16, 315
13:31, 345
13:32, 283

13:34, 404
14:1–6, 306
14:26, 164
14:26–27, 138
16:18, 46, 132, 172, 175
17:13, 306
17:20, 136
18:29, 363
18:38–39, 218
19:2, 282
19:7, 80
19:39, 306
20:17, 166
20:41–44, 218
22:7, 389, 393, 424
22:8,15, 389
22:15, 389, 427
22:15–16, 397, 398, 426–27
22:15–18, 427
22:17–18, 398, 427
22:17–20, 427
22:19–20, 43
22:59, 231
22:66, 387
22–23, 420
23:5, 404, 415
23:26, 356
23:29, 136
23:34, 170
23:35, 60
23:46, 170
23:49, 356
23:56, 387
24:1, 387
24:13–35, 35
24:21, 83
John, 41, 42, 44, 45, 121, 136–39, 169,
    214
1, 412
1:1–18, 209, 236
1:6, 75
1:13, 242
1:29–34, 169
1:35–2:12, 405
1:38,49, 306
1:45–56, 215
1:46, 215
2, 381
2:1,3,5,12, 237
2:1–11, 409
2:1–12, 318
2:3–5, 317
2:13, 405
2:13–22, 381
2:14–22, 175
2:18, 348
2:19, 418

NEW TESTAMENT, John *(cont.)*

2:20, 378, 380–82, 418
3:1–14, 306
3:1–15, 346
3:2, 306
3:5, 161
3:22–30, 412
3:26, 306
4, 432
4:14, 136
4:31, 306
4:35, 432
4:44, 302
4:46–53, 85
5:1, 432
5:6, 169
5:16–47, 306
5:39,45, 119
5–6, 432
6, 42
6:1, 315
6:4, 405
6:4,10, 413
6:6, 169
6:23, 315
6:25, 306
6:42, 214, 225, 237
6:51–58, 175
6:53–56, 161
6:59, 306
6:66–71, 189
7:1–10, 357, 393
7:2,10,14,37, 432
7:3–9, 317
7:3–10, 317
7:5, 243, 350
7:14, 393
7:15, 268, 269, 278, 308
7:26, 60
7:30,32,44, 119
7:37, 393
7:37–38, 136
7:40–44, 214
7:42, 214
7:45, 346
7:50–52, 346
7–8, 227, 306, 379, 392
8:6, 268, 269, 271
8:12, 136
8:13–20, 306
8:14, 169
8:20,59, 119
8:21, 161
8:23, 215
8:31–59, 227–29
8:41, 225, 226, 247
8:51–54, 378–79

8:52, 136
8:56, 378, 379
8:57, 378–79, 382
8:57–58, 227
8:58, 378–79
9:2, 306
9:3, 169
9:29, 119
9:40–10:39, 306
10:30–31, 120
10:31,33,39, 119
11, 122
11:8, 306
11:11–15, 169
11:17, 83
11:47, 346
11:47–53, 290
11:49–50, 347
11:55, 405
12:1,12, 405
12:13–15,19,20–24,31–32, 290
12:20–22, 299
12:20–26, 64
12:23,32, 299
12:27–36a, 47
13:1, 405, 427
13:1–3,11, 169
13:2,4–5,12,30, 428
13:13, 306
13–17, 398
13:33, 161
18:1, 428
18:5,7, 215
18:13–14,19–24,28, 425
18:20, 306
18:24, 425
18:28, 389, 405, 429
18:39–40, 400
19:14,29,36, 429
19:14, 389
19:19, 215
19:20, 290
19:24, 170
19:25, 318, 353, 356
19:25–27, 209, 237
19:27, 354
19:30, 170
19:31, 388, 390
19:39–40, 346
19:42, 388
20:1, 388
20:11, 252
20:16, 252
20:30–31, 405
21, 42
21:1, 315
21:25, 405

Acts of the Apostles, 142
  1:1, 385
  1:1,22, 415
  1:1–5, 35, 383
  1:14, 209, 214, 318, 358
  1:19, 298
  2:14–21, 430
  2:24–36, 218
  2:25–31, 218
  2:29, 328
  2:30, 240
  5:36, 412
  6, 178
  6:1–6, 299, 317, 358
  6:1–15, 267
  8:27–39, 343, 368
  9:22, 60
  10:37, 415
  11:6, 80
  13:22–23, 218
  13:22–23,35–37, 240
  13:22–37, 218
  15:13–21, 350
  15:13–29, 277
  18:12–17, 373
  21:18, 350
  23:16, 251
Romans
  1:3, 46, 237, 239
  1:3–4, 213, 217, 218, 221, 239
  1:16–17, 239
  8:11, 221
  8:15, 266
  9:3, 328
  9:4–5, 239
  9:5, 239
  11:1, 291
  12:14, 47
  15:8, 46
  17–20, 47
First Corinthians, 45–46
  1:1, 328
  1–3, 291
  4:12, 47
  5:7, 428, 429
  5:11, 328
  7:1–7, 366
  7:7–8,25–40, 344
  7:10–11, 46, 54, 173
  7:10–13, 46
  7:21, 312
  9:5, 58, 326, 358, 363, 366
  9:14, 46, 54
  11:23, 429
  11:23–26, 43, 46, 175
  13, 291
  15, 291

  15:3, 46
  15:5, 61, 77
  15:11, 67, 118
  15:17, 350
Second Corinthians
  11:22, 291
Galatians
  1:14, 291
  1:19, 58, 239, 326, 350, 358
  2:9,12, 350
  2:11–14, 277
  4:4–5, 242
  4:6, 266
  4:21–31, 251
  5:12, 368
Ephesians, 156, 157
  5:2, 370
  18:2, 237
Philippians
  2:6–11, 209
  2:7, 222
  3:5–6, 291
Colossians, 156
  4:10, 326, 332
First Thessalonians
  5:2,4, 47
  5:15, 47
First Timothy
  2:5–6, 370
  3:2,12, 368
  4:13, 321
  5:9, 368
Second Timothy
  2:8, 217, 218
Titus
  1:6, 368
Hebrews, 156, 347, 348
  1:5,13, 241
  2:11,17, 328
  2:17, 254
  4:14–5:10, 348
  4:15, 254
  5:7–8, 47
  7, 218
  7:11–14, 348
  7:14, 47, 218
  7:15–28, 348
  8:4, 348
  9:23–10:18, 348
James
  1:1, 81
  5:12, 47, 171–72
First Peter, 47
  3:9, 47
Second Peter
  3:10, 47
First John, 157

Revelation
3:3, 47
3:7, 218
5:5, 218

9:11, 80
14:4, 344
16:15, 47
22:16, 218

Author Index

Achtemeier, Paul J., 307, 308
Ackroyd, P. R., 305
Aland, Barbara, 295, 424
Aland, Kurt, 156, 295, 424
Albright, William F., 289, 301, 313, 357
Allegro, John, 103, 364
Allison, Dale C., Jr., 53, 54
Allo, E.-B., 368
Althaus, Paul, 28, 38, 39
Amidon, Philip R., 358
Andersen, F. I., 243
Anderson, Charles C., 34
Applebaum, Shimon, 310–12, 315
Argyle, A. W., 255, 287
Attridge, Harold W., Jr., 70, 88, 154, 155
Aune, David E., 50, 143
Avi-Yonah, Michael, 75

Bagatti, B., 308
Baillet, M., 105
Balch, David, 366
Baltensweiler, H., 161
Bammel, Ernst, 71, 73, 75, 76, 79, 82, 86, 162
Baras, Zvi, 75, 79, 85
Barclay, William, 273, 274, 302–4
Barnes, Timothy D., 414
Barrett, Anthony A., 32
Barrett, C. K., 52, 148, 233, 432
Bartchy, S. Scott, 312
Barth, G., 161
Barth, Karl, 29
Batey, Richard A., 310, 313, 314
Battifol, P., 74
Bauer, Johannes B., 148

Bauer, Walter, 295, 355, 424
Baumgarten, A. I., 104
Baumgartner, Walter, 231
Beare, Francis W., 162
Becker, J., 53
Beckwith, Roger T., 430–31
Bell, Albert A., Jr., 86
Bellinzoni, Arthur J., Jr., 51
Benoit, P., 51, 105
Berkey, R. F., 75, 187
Bernard, J. H., 251
Bertrand, F.-G., 353
Betz, O., 302
Beyschlag, Willibald, 40
Bietenhard, H., 103
Bilde, Per, 70, 74, 85
Billerbeck, Paul, 390–91, 422
Birdsall, J. Neville, 74, 83–84
Birkeland, Harris, 255, 287, 288, 298
Birley, Anthony, 32
Black, Matthew, 104, 178, 264, 265, 297, 364
Blatt, Franz, 78
Blinzler, Josef, 250, 329, 353, 358–63, 395, 410, 411, 418, 419, 424, 430, 433
Blomberg, Craig L., 154
Boismard, M.-E., 51, 149, 239
Borg, Marcus J., 32, 191, 194
Borgen, P., 103
Boring, M. Eugene, 50, 187–89, 195
Borleffs, P., 362
Bornkamm, Günther, 3, 15, 28, 38, 161, 198, 236
Borret, M., 247
Bosworth, A. B., 32

Bourke, Myles M., 88, 236
Braaten, Carl E., 36, 37
Brandon, S. G. F., 59, 75, 85
Braun, F.-M., 148
Braun, Herbert, 38, 104, 198, 236, 369
Breech, James, 185, 187, 189, 195
Bright, John, 364
Brooks, Stephenson H., 53, 343, 367, 368
Brown, Raymond E., 2, 15, 44, 49, 52,
  53, 99, 102, 118, 122, 136, 148, 152,
  160, 165, 233, 235–40, 242–44, 246, 247,
  251, 252, 269, 290, 300, 301, 306, 355,
  357–60, 364, 380, 395, 410, 414, 415,
  417, 418, 421–24, 432
Brown, Schuyler, 16
Brox, Norbert, 240
Bruce, F. F., 54
Buchanan, George Wesley, 310, 313
Bulhart, V., 362
Bultmann, Rudolf, 5, 25, 27–30, 37–40,
  45, 49, 54, 165, 182, 193, 194, 197, 237,
  239, 251, 270, 303, 425, 432
Burger, Christoph, 237–40
Buri, Fritz, 38
Burkill, T. A., 410
Burkitt, F. C., 74
Burney, C. F., 265, 297
Butts, James R., 33

Cadbury, Henry J., 16
Calvert, D. G. A., 186
Cameron, Ron, 128, 150, 154, 157, 158
Campbell, Joseph, 286
Campenhausen, Hans F. von, 301
Cantineau, J., 287, 288, 296
Carlston, Charles E., 186, 190
Carroll, Robert P., 365
Cazelles, Henri, 77
Cerfaux, Lucien, 149
Charles, R. H., 103
Charlesworth, James H., 32, 59, 70–71,
  75, 103, 105, 364, 421
Chenderlin, Fritz, 423
Chilton, Bruce, 154
Coakley, J. F., 50
Cohen, A., 314
Cohen, Shaye J. D., 70, 72, 85, 86, 88,
  104, 241, 273, 304
Collins, Adela Yarbro, 369
Collins, John J., 103
Colson, F. H., 233
Conybeare, F. C., 366
Conzelmann, Hans, 38, 72, 74, 142, 240,
  368, 410
Cook, Michael J., 75
Corley, Bruce, 151
Cornfeld, G., 70

Côté, Pierre-René, 367
Cothenet, Edouard, 55
Cranfield, Charles E., 371
Cross, F. M., 104
Crossan, John Dominic, 35, 116–18, 120,
  123, 131, 143, 146, 148–50, 152, 155,
  156, 158, 161, 370
Cullmann, O., 239
Culpepper, R. Alan, 105

Dahl, N. A., 36, 239, 241
Dalman, Gustaf, 97, 108, 264, 265, 293
Danby, Herbert, 108
Danielou, Jean, 105
Davids, Peter H., 54–55
Davies, Philip R., 104, 364
Davies, Stevan L., 128, 156–58
Davies, W. D., 53, 54, 109, 158
Dehandschutter, Boudewijn, 129, 154,
  159, 164
de Jonge, Marinus, 16, 52–53
Delling, G., 243
Delobel, Joël, 50, 155, 302
Denker, Jürgen, 146, 147
Dewey, Joanna, 193
Diaz, Mary N., 309
Dibelius, Martin, 49, 240, 425
Di Lella, Alexander A., 296
Dimant, D., 103
Dinkler, Erich, 233
Dockx, S., 391, 410, 422–24, 431
Dodd, C. H., 44, 52, 119–20, 147, 148,
  150, 188, 235, 252, 307, 421, 432
Dolto, Françoise, 286
Donfried, Karl P., 99, 238, 242, 250
Dormeyer, Detlev, 143, 250
Dornseiff, Franz, 73, 87, 101
Douglas, Mary, 11
Doutreleau, L., 416
Draper, H. Mudie, 287, 294
Draper, Jonathan, 160, 161
Dubarle, A.-M., 59–61, 75–81, 87
Duhaime, Jean, 104
Duling, D., 239
Dummer, Jürgen, 358
Dungan, David L., 54
Dunn, James D. G., 15, 50
Dupont, J., 186, 201, 302

Edinger, Edward F., 286
Edwards, Ormond, 410
Edwards, Richard A., 51
Edwards, S. A., 75, 187
Ehrman, Bart D., 301
Eichholz, D. E., 364
Eisler, Robert, 57, 71, 74, 77, 82, 85, 419
Eliade, Mircea, 5

Ellis, E. Earle, 187, 188, 193, 249, 431
Eltester, Walther, 109
Emerton, J. A., 287, 288
Epstein, I., 107, 109, 365, 366
Ernst, Josef, 303
Evans, C. F., 305
Evans, Craig A., 34
Evans, Ernest, 362
Evans, Owen E., 420

Fallon, Francis T., 154
Farmer, William R., 44, 51, 364
Fee, Gordon D., 368, 428
Feldman, Louis H., 59, 67, 70–72, 74–76, 78, 79, 86, 87, 101, 292
Ferguson, Everett, 233, 304, 364
Feuillet, A., 73
Filmer, W. E., 414
Finegan, Jack, 308, 380–81, 410, 412, 415, 417–18, 421, 431–32
Finkel, Asher, 302
Finley, Sir Moses I., 23, 33
Fiorenza, Elisabeth Schüssler, 369
Fishwick, Duncan, 233
Fitzmyer, Joseph A., 15, 51, 53, 103, 105, 149, 157, 163, 164, 178, 186, 187, 191, 192, 231, 233, 235, 236, 238, 242, 255, 262–65, 270, 287, 289, 290, 293, 295–97, 299, 303, 359, 360, 363, 410, 411, 414, 415, 419–21, 426, 431
Flusser, David, 78
Foerster, Werner, 232
Fortna, Robert Tomson, 52, 421
Foster, George M., 309
Fowler, Robert M., 193
Frank, Arthur W., III, 16
Frankemölle, Hubert, 16, 143, 250
Franklin, Eric, 240
Freedman, David Noel, 3, 6, 24, 156, 165, 188, 189, 231, 234, 241, 250, 295, 304
Freedman, H., 109, 365
Frerichs, Ernest S., 104, 305
Freyne, Sean, 263, 282, 300, 308, 310–13, 349, 370
Fuchs, Ernst, 38
Fuchs, Harald, 100
Fuller, Reginald, 187, 239
Funk, Robert W., 33
Furfey, Paul Hanly, 311

Gamba, Giuseppe G., 367
Gardner-Smith, P., 44, 52
Gärtner, Bertil, 129, 159
Gero, Stephen, 143
Ghiberti, Giuseppe, 187
Gnilka, Joachim, 34

Goldstein, Morris, 96, 97, 106, 108, 111
Gooch, Peter, 54
Goodenough, E. R., 104
Goodwin, William, 76
Gordis, Robert, 295
Görg, Manfred, 252
Goulder, M. D., 51
Grant, Michael, 32, 185, 410
Grant, Robert M., 50, 122, 129, 136, 152, 156, 158, 161, 163, 165
Green, Joel B., 117, 147
Green, William S., 104, 305
Gronewald, Michael, 148
Grundmann, Walter, 248, 302, 369, 425
Guelich, Robert A., 359
Guillaumont, A., 154
Gulick, Charles, 76
Gundry, Robert H., 52, 355
Gustafsson, Berndt, 232, 233
Gutschmid, A. von, 82

Haase, W., 70, 103
Haenchen, Ernst, 44, 52, 53, 142, 148, 149, 159, 298, 359, 417
Hagner, Donald A., 160, 161
Hahn, F., 239
Hammond, N. G. L., 32
Hanson, A. T., 240
Hanson, John S., 201
Hanson, Paul D., 103
Hare, Douglas R. A., 72
Harmon, A., 102
Harnak, A. von, 74
Harrington, Daniel J., 188, 359
Harris, Murray J., 99
Harris, William V., 255, 274, 289, 304, 305
Harrisville, Roy A., 36
Hartman, Louis F., 296
Harvey, A. E., 189
Hata, Gohei, 70
Havener, Ivan, 51
Hedrick, C., 157–58
Hedrick, Charles W., 53, 187
Heidegger, Martin, 3, 27
Held, H. J., 161
Hengel, Martin, 193, 232, 243, 264, 290–91, 294, 295, 300, 302, 312, 314, 315
Hennecke, Edgar, 115, 142, 143, 145, 248
Herford, R. Travers, 107–9
Herrmann, Léon, 74, 99, 101
Herrmann, Wilhelm, 36–37
Heth, W. A., 367
Hill, D., 50
Hirsch, Emmanuel, 426
Hodges, Andrew G., 286
Hodgson, R., 157

Hoehner, Harold W., 312, 384, 410, 412, 415, 417–19, 423, 432
Hoffmann, Paul, 50
Holl, Karl, 358
Holladay, William L., 105, 365
Hollenbach, Paul, 5, 16, 29
Holmberg, Bengt, 16, 17
Holzmeister, Urbanus, 410, 419, 431
Hooker, Morna D., 172, 186, 188, 191, 194
Horsely, Richard A., 194, 201
Hoult, Thomas Ford, 16
Howes, Elizabeth Boyden, 286
Hubaut, Michel, 164
Hübner, Hans, 364
Hummel, Richard, 162
Humphreys, Colin J., 431
Hunzinger, C. H., 158

Jackson, F. J. Foakes, 74
Jackson, John, 99
Jakubowsky, Frank, 287
Jastrow, Marcus, 313
Jaubert, Annie, 391–94, 410, 423–24, 429
Jeremias, Joachim, 5, 29, 39, 43, 97, 108, 109, 112–14, 128, 142, 149, 150, 157, 166, 177–79, 192, 198, 265, 266, 297–99, 307, 395–96, 397–99, 410, 421–25, 428, 430, 431
Jewett, Robert, 410, 411
Johnson, Douglas, 414
Jones, W. H. S., 364

Kähler, Martin, 27–30, 35–37, 39, 40, 197
Kane, J. P., 233
Käsemann, Ernst, 38, 186, 187, 201
Kasper, Walter, 245
Kasser, R., 159
Kattenbusch, Ferdinand, 40
Keck, L. E., 240
Kee, Howard Clark, 166
Keim, Theodor, 420
Kelber, Werner H., 49, 52, 160, 193, 307
Kelly, J. N. D., 145, 240, 411
Kennard, J. Spencer, 71–72, 84
Kertelge, Karl, 16, 201, 250
Kesterson, John C., 296
Kingsbury, Jack Dean, 193
Kissinger, Warren S., 34
Klaiber, W., 53
Klausner, Joseph, 77, 95–98, 99, 106–10, 247
Kleinknecht, K., 53
Kloppenborg, John S., 51
Klostermann, Erich, 369
Knoch, Otto, 244
Knox, John, 411

Kobelski, Paul J., 105
Koehler, Ludwig, 231
Koester, Helmut, 54, 122, 123, 128, 142–44, 146–51, 153, 154, 157, 158, 160–62, 247
Köhler, Wolf-Dietrich, 124, 145, 146, 150, 153, 160
Kokkinos, Nikos, 420, 431
Komonchak, Joseph A., 2
Kraft, Robert A., 105, 364
Kramer, W., 239
Krappe, Alexander, 71
Krause, Martin, 157
Kruse, Heinz, 49, 433
Kselman, John S., 34
Kuhn, K. G., 109
Kümmel, W. G., 34
Kundsin, Karl, 193
Küng, Hans, 25, 39

Lagrange, M.-J., 74, 252, 413, 431, 432
Lake, Kirsopp, 420
Lambdin, Thomas O., 156
Lambiasi, Francesco, 147–48, 186, 187, 194
Lampe, G. W. H., 84
Lampe, Peter, 233
Landmann, Isaac, 108
Lane, William L., 193, 413
Lapide, Pinchas E., 110, 287, 288, 296, 298
LaSor, W. S., 105
Latourelle, René, 185, 186, 194
Lattke, Gisella, 244
Laufen, Rudolf, 51
Lauterbach, Jacob Z., 95–96, 106
Layton, Bentley, 125, 155, 156
Leaney, A. R. C., 426
Lebreton, J., 410
Lee, Bernard J., 314
Leipold, Heinrich, 36
Leipoldt, J., 158
Lémonon, Jean-Pierre, 101, 411
Lentzen-Deis, Fritzleo, 186
Léon-Dufour, Xavier, 428
Levick, Barbara, 101
Lightfoot, J. B., 359
Lindars, Barnabas, 52, 148, 252, 417, 432
Lindeskog, Gösta, 108, 111
Linnemann, E., 239
Lock, Walter, 240
Lohfink, Gerhard, 244
Lohse, Eduard, 103
Long, H. S., 355
Longenecker, R., 239
Longstaff, Thomas R. W., 52
Luedemann, Gerd, 411, 412

Lührmann, Dieter, 50, 146, 186, 191
Luther, Martin, 3

McArthur, Harvey K., 50, 159, 175, 186, 190, 193, 195, 249–51
McCant, Jerry W., 117, 146, 147
McCullagh, C. Behan, 33, 194
McEleney, Neil J., 183, 186, 193
McHugh, John, 329, 359–62
Mack, Burton L., 49
McKane, William, 365
McKenzie, John L., 241, 244
Mackey, James P., 34
MacMullen, Ramsay, 282
Macquarrie, John, 201
Magnarella, Paul J., 309
Mahé, Jean-Pierre, 362
Maier, Gerhard, 55
Maier, Johann, 95, 98, 106–9, 248
Maier, P., 70
Maier, Paul L., 415
Malbon, Elizabeth Struthers, 193
Malina, Bruce J., 309, 312, 353
Maloney, Elliott C., 192
Mann, C. S., 44, 313, 357, 371, 413, 425
Manson, T. W., 108, 147
Marcus, Ralph, 70
Marín, Francesco, 368
Marrani, Adelmo, 353
Marrou, H. I., 303
Marsh, John, 85
Marshall, I. Howard, 302, 384, 419, 431
Martin, C., 67, 75–78, 84, 86, 87
Martin, Ernest L., 414, 415
Martini, Carlo M., 59, 74, 75, 100, 101
Martyn, J. L., 240
Marx, A., 364
Marxsen, Willi, 183, 194
Massaux, Edouard, 160
Matera, Frank J., 420
Mathews, K. A., 104
Matthiae, Karl, 36
Maurer, C., 147
Mazar, B., 70
Mealand, David L., 186, 188
Megivern, James J., 234
Meier, John P., 53, 99, 160, 201, 233, 239, 240, 300, 367
Ménard, Jacques E., 128, 156–58, 163–65
Mendelson, Alan, 104
Merkel, Helmut, 49, 122, 152
Metzger, Bruce M., 150, 156, 233, 237, 249, 298, 301, 426, 427, 432
Meyer, Ben F., 33, 168, 183, 185, 186, 194
Meyers, Eric M., 301, 308
Michel, Otto, 36, 418

Miehl, Johann, 244
Milik, J. T., 263, 288, 296
Millar, Fergus, 70, 100
Miller, Charles H., 308
Minear, Paul S., 49
Miranda, José Porfirio, 16
Mischon, A., 108
Montefiore, Hugh, 158
Moore, George Foot, 15, 104, 272–73, 303, 304, 366
Morgenthaler, Robert, 51
Moule, C. F. D., 71, 299, 417
Mounce, Robert H., 368, 369
Mras, Karl, 363
Müller, Gerhard L., 245
Murphy, Roland E., 15, 359
Murphy-O'Connor, Jerome, 105, 308, 364, 411, 413
Mussies, Gerard, 289–91, 297

Neirynck, Frans, 44, 50, 52, 53–54, 122, 149, 151–52, 165, 302, 396, 425
Neusner, Jacob, 15, 16, 104–6, 108, 305
Neyrey, Jerome H., 11, 17
Nicholson, Ernest W., 365
Nickelsburg, George W. E., 103, 105, 364
Nielsen, Helge Kjaer, 187, 188, 191
Niese, Benedict, 70
Nineham, D. E., 165, 426
Nodet, Etienne, 73–74, 78, 85, 101
Nolan, Brian M., 240
Norden, E., 74, 86
Norris, Jenny, 103
North, Robert, 301

Oberlinner, Lorenz, 353, 356–60
O'Callaghan, José, 105
Occam, William of, 168
O'Collins, G. G., 201
O'Connor, Kathleen M., 365
Ogg, George, 410, 413
Oldfather, W. A., 366
Ong, Walter J., 307
Orr, William F., 366
Osborn, Eric, 151

Paton, W. R., 418
Patterson, L., 107
Pearson, L., 32
Pelletier, André, 61, 76, 77, 84, 87
Perkins, Pheme, 308
Perlman, Janice E., 7, 16
Perowne, Stewart, 412
Perrin, Norman, 5, 29–30, 39–40, 52, 172, 188, 190, 193

Pesch, Rudolf, 186, 188, 193, 244–45, 319, 354, 361, 371, 425, 426
Petzke, G., 190
Pharr, Clyde, 75, 85
Phipps, William E., 333–35, 363, 366, 369
Pickl, J., 423
Pines, Shlomo, 78
Piper, John, 54
Pius XII, 234
Plummer, Alfred, 236, 431
Polag, Athanasius, 51
Polkow, Dennis, 187–91, 195
Ponton, G., 353
Pötscher, Walter, 74, 85
Potter, Jack M., 309

Quasten, Johannes, 145, 147, 248
Quesnell, Quentin, 151, 367
Quispel, Gilles, 127, 129, 156–58

Rabin, Chaim, 287–89, 295, 296
Rabinowitz, Isaac, 287, 288, 298
Rackham, H., 364
Radice, Betty, 102
Rahner, Karl, 3, 6, 244–45
Rajak, Tessa, 70, 72, 290, 292, 293
Ranke, Leopold von, 37
Reimarus, Hermann, 25, 29, 34
Rengstorf, Karl A., 75, 80
Reumann, John, 39
Riaud, Jean, 363–64
Richards, G. C., 76, 79
Richardson, Peter, 54
Ricoeur, Paul, 5
Riesner, Rainer, 185, 191, 192, 235, 238, 249, 275, 283–84, 302, 305–9, 313
Ringgren, Helmer, 364
Rist, John M., 51
Ritschl, Otto, 40
Rivkin, Ellis, 72
Robbins, Vernon K., 193
Roberts, C. H., 305
Robinson, J. A. T., 49, 50, 105, 148, 418, 433
Robinson, James M., 34, 36, 38, 51, 123, 128, 152, 155–57, 358
Rolfe, J. C., 102
Rose, Valentine, 354
Rousseau, A., 416
Ruckstuhl, Eugen, 410, 423, 431
Rudolph, Kurt, 129, 159
Ruh, Ulrich, 287
Ruppert, Lothar, 188
Russell, D. S., 103
Russell, J. K., 287

Sabbe, M., 164
Safrai, S., 271–72, 287, 302–4, 306, 307, 310
Saldarini, Anthony J., 305, 364
Sand, Alexander, 367–69
Sanders, E. P., 3, 5, 15, 16, 23, 35, 70, 104, 161, 173, 182, 187, 189, 191, 193, 198, 236
Sandmel, Samuel, 96, 104, 106, 110
Sanford, Eva Matthews, 70, 85
Sato, Migaku, 51
Sauer, Jürgen, 54
Schaberg, Jane, 246–51
Schalit, Abraham, 72, 80
Schattenmann, Johannes, 367
Scheidweiler, Felix, 73, 248
Schenke, Hans-Martin, 122, 151
Schiffman, Lawrence H., 104
Schillebeeckx, Edward, 32, 34, 35, 168, 186, 191
Schippers, R., 159
Schlichting, Günter, 110
Schmidt, Karl Ludwig, 49, 408, 413, 433
Schmidt, P., 302
Schnackenburg, Rudolf, 44, 52, 201, 237, 251, 252, 290, 302, 416, 433
Schneemelcher, Wilhelm, 115, 142, 143, 145, 248
Schneider, Gerhard, 298, 426
Scholem, Gershom G., 104
Schonfeld, Hugh J., 420
Schrage, Wolfgang, 129–30, 159, 164–68
Schreckenberg, Heinz, 70, 81
Schrenk, Gottlob, 418
Schulz, Siegfried, 50
Schürer, Emil, 70–72, 100, 103, 104, 242, 273, 303–5, 364
Schürmann, Heinz, 270, 303, 412, 416, 426–27, 432
Schweitzer, Albert, 28, 32, 34, 36, 39, 194, 198, 200, 201
Schweizer, Eduard, 188, 198, 239, 240, 397, 425, 426
Scott, Bernard Brandon, 33
Scott, James C., 311, 313
Scott, R. B. Y., 295
Seiler, Christoph, 36
Senior, Donald P., 231, 420
Sevenster, J. N., 288, 289, 291–93, 295, 297, 299, 357
Sévérin, Gérard, 286
Sevrin, Jean-Marie, 129, 134, 155, 159, 162, 163, 166
Sheehan, Thomas, 16
Shepherd, Massey H., Jr., 423, 426
Shuler, Philip L., 143

Sieber, John H., 158
Silberman, L., 50
Skehan, Patrick W., 151, 152, 304
Slenczka, Reinhard, 36
Slotki, I., 365
Slusser, G. H., 286
Smallwood, E. M., 71
Smith, C. F., 418
Smith, D. Moody, 52
Smith, Morton, 59, 75, 85, 107, 110, 120–22, 151, 152, 187, 194, 246, 413
Snodgrass, K. R., 165
Soards, Marion L., 420, 427
Spicq, C., 240
Stanley, David M., 54, 239
Stauffer, Ethelbert, 249, 369
Stein, Robert H., 187, 189–91
Steiner, Anton, 364
Stendahl, Krister, 104
Stern, M., 287, 302, 310
Stoker, William D., 112, 142
Stoldt, Hans-Herbert, 51
Stone, Michael E., 103
Strack, Hermann L., 390
Strange, James F., 301, 308
Strecker, Georg, 162
Strugnell, J., 72
Stuhlmacher, P., 187, 239
Stuhlmueller, Carroll, 241
Sukenik, E. L., 232, 233
Sweet, J. P. M., 369

Talbert, Charles H., 143
Talmon, S., 104
Tawney, R. H., 311
Taylor, R. O. P., 255, 294, 297, 299
Taylor, Vincent, 180–81, 192, 249, 295, 359, 371, 413, 420, 425
Temporini, H., 70, 103
Thackeray, H. St. J., 67, 70, 72, 74, 77, 80–82, 85–87, 292
Thiede, C. P., 105
Thiering, Barbara E., 105
Thomas, Page A., 52
Tillich, Paul, 36
Torrey, C. C., 265, 297
Trapé, Agostino, 411
Trilling, Wolfgang, 59, 75, 101
Tuckett, Christopher, 124, 130, 136, 152, 153–54, 157, 159, 161–64
Turcan, M., M., 247
Turner, H. E. W., 129, 158

Ulrich, Eugene, 104
Ussher, James, 384

Vaganay, Léon, 117, 146, 147
Vanhoye, A., 54
Van Segbroeck, Frans, 50, 52
Van Unnik, W. C., 158
Vardaman, Jerry, 100, 410, 411, 414, 415
Vassiliadis, Petros, 51
Vaux, Roland de, 421
Vermes, Geza, 15, 70, 100, 103, 178, 314, 364–66, 410, 421
Visotzky, Burton L., 109

Waddington, W. G., 431
Wahlde, Urban C. von, 421
Walker, William O., 186, 187, 189, 191, 192, 195
Walter, N., 54
Walther, James Arthur, 366
Wegenast, K., 239
Weirich, F., 49
Weiss, Johannes, 101
Wells, G. A., 87
Wenham, David, 54, 55, 145
Werner, Martin, 38
Westermann, Claus, 241
Whiston, William, 7
Whitaker, G. H., 233
White, Leland Jennings, 34
Whybray, R. N., 241
Wiefel, Wolfgang, 99
Wilckens, Ulrich, 315
Wilcox, Max, 249
Wilder, Amos N., 39
Wilken, Robert L., 102
Williams, Frank, 358
Williamson, G. A., 57, 70, 71, 76–77
Williamson, Ronald, 104
Wilson, R. M., 143, 287
Winter, Paul, 59, 66, 71, 72, 75, 410
Wintermute, O. S., 421–22
Wirsching, Johannes, 36
Wobbermin, G., 25, 39
Wolf, Eric R., 278, 309
Wolff, Hannah, 286
Wrede, William, 34, 408, 433
Wright, A., 236
Wright, David F., 144, 146, 149

Xenakis, Iason, 366

Yamauchi, Edwin M., 236, 410, 414
Yelnitsky, L. A., 101

Zahn, Theodor, 151
Zeitlin, Solomon, 71–72, 84, 85
Zerwick, Max, 417
Zimmermann, H., 239
Zuckschwerdt, Ernst, 361

INDEX OF SUBJECTS

'abbā', Jesus' use of, 174, 175, 266
Abraham, 378–79
  children of, 228–29, 340
accession-year system, 385
Achaia, 373
Acts of Pilate, the, 122
Adversus Haereses, 330, 378
Against Apion, 275
Against Helvidius, 318
agrapha, the, 112–15, 130, 139, 140
Agrippa II, 283
Albinus, 57
Alexander the Great, 23, 208, 258
Alexandria, 121
Ananus the Younger, 57, 58–59
Andrew, 267
Anna, 209
Annals, the, 89–91
Annas, 65, 374
Antioch, 373
Antiochus IV Epiphanes, 207, 258, 259,
    262, 264, 275
aphorism, 135, 174, 175
apocalyptic literature, Jewish, 93
apocryphal gospels, *see* gospels, apocryphal
Apocryphon of John, the, 125
Apollonius of Tyana, 24, 340, 341
Aramaic *(see also* targums), 43, 94, 98, 116,
    128, 175, 178–79, 182, 184, 260,
    265–67, 276, 325
  Aramaic-speaking Christians, 113, 178–
    79, 326
  as the language of Jesus, 255, 266–68,
    349–50

as the language of Jesus' teaching, 266,
    268, 350–51
  as the language of Palestine, 257, 258,
    261, 262–65, 267
  Galilean/Judean dialects of, 267
  in targums, 263, 276
  Jesus literate in, 278
  resurgence in Palestine of, 259, 264–65
Archelaus, son of Herod the Great, 212
archetype, 28, 199
aristocracy, Jerusalem *(see also* priests;
    Sadducees), 9, 65, 177, 199, 206,
    219, 259–61, 267, 268, 273, 275,
    276, 345–47, 348–49, 393, 407
arrest of Jesus, 97, 407
Asia Minor, 258, 385
astronomy, 401–2
Augustine, Saint, 29
Augustus, Emperor (Octavian), 23, 25, 208,
    212, 374, 384
authority
  Jesus' clashes with, 199, 345–47
  Jesus' own, 8, 347, 348

banditry, 281, 282
baptism of Jesus by John, 13, 42, 168–70,
    386, 409
Barabbas, 400
Bar Kochba *(see also* Revolt, Second
    Jewish), 258, 275
bastard, 97
beatitude, 43, 175
Ben Pandera, 96, 223
Ben Sira, Jesus, 262, 273, 275, 340
Ben Stada, 96

Bethlehem, 209, 376
  as Jesus' birthplace, 211–17, 229, 407
betrayal by Judas, 170, 181
biography, modern (see also historical-
      critical method), 41, 253, 254, 409
birth legends, 207, 208–9, 221
birth of Jesus, 13, 205, 212, 213, 229
Book of Jubilees, 274, 389, 391
Bothuseans, 391
brother in the NT, 327–28
brothers of Jesus [see also James; Joses
      (Joseph); Jude (Judas); Simon],
      57–58, 62, 210, 221, 279, 317, 322–
      32
burial of Jesus, 13, 46, 116, 387–88

Caesarea Maritima, 256, 258
Caiaphas, 65, 180, 347, 374, 389
calendar
  Egyptian, 374, 385
  Jewish, 374, 385, 388–90
  Julian, 374, 385–86
  lunar, 385, 391, 393, 401–2
  solar, 391
  Syrian-Macedonian, 374, 385
Calvin, John, 319
Cana, 284
Capernaum, 212, 284
carpenter/woodworker, Jesus as, 223–27,
      255, 262, 267, 280, 284, 317, 350
  abandoning his job, 8, 9
  father's trade, 124, 283, 317
  instruction in trade, 273–75, 276, 350
  masterbuilder, Jesus as, 283–84, 351
  tektōn, meaning of, 281
  trade as embarrassing, 225–26, 280, 322
Carpocratians, 121, 122
celibacy
  Christian attitudes toward, 332, 343–44
  Essene practice of, 336–40
  in Greco-Roman world, 341
  in OT, 338, 339, 341
  Jesus of, 8, 9, 333–35, 341–45, 350
  and prophetic call, 341–42, 344–45
Celsus, 96, 223–24
census, 212–13
certitude (see also historical-critical
      method), 30, 130, 167–68, 184, 208,
      216, 230, 331
Chenoboskia (Chenoboskion), 123
children of Jesus, 335, 350
Chorazin, 284
Christ, 5, 7, 27–28, 56, 60–61, 89–92, 96,
      197–98, 206, 213
  Christ of faith, 2, 28–30, 197
Christianity, first-century, 172–73

Christians, 56, 60–61, 66–68, 119, 179, 197–
      98, 207, 222
  Aramaic-speaking, 113, 178–79, 326
  Bithynian, 92
  first Christian generation, 45–47, 118,
      127, 170, 175, 178, 180, 226
  Gnostic, 118, 139, 140
  Gentile, 65, 266
  Jewish, 67–68, 97–98, 113, 116, 171, 179,
      180, 277
  Palestinian, 67–68, 113, 178–80, 266
  Roman, 46, 89–92, 217, 266
  second-century, 115, 118, 121, 127, 130–
      31, 269
christology, 5, 14, 63–64, 198, 200, 215, 378
chronology of Jesus' life, 10, 42, 214, 382
  as approximate, 372–73, 406
  cleansing of the temple, 175, 381, 382
  date of birth, 214, 228, 349, 375–77, 382
  date of death, 90, 373–74, 382, 386–402
  "hidden years," 10, 22, 230, 253, 254,
      316, 351
  Last Supper, 386–401
  length of ministry, 42, 374–75, 382, 383,
      386, 401–6, 408–9
  order of events uncertain, 13, 41–42
  passion chronology, 45, 96, 390–401
church teaching (see also faith), 1, 222, 230
Cicero, 23–25
circumcision, 277, 350
Claudius, Emperor, 91–92
Clement of Alexandria, 58, 120, 121
coherence, criterion of, 175–77, 183, 344
community rules, 124, 180
Contra Celsum, 223–24
Copper Scroll, the, 259, 263
Coptic, see: *Gospel of Thomas*; Nag
      Hammadi, literature at
coregency, 119, 374, 384
Corinth, 45, 373
Corinthians, 45–46
cousins of Jesus, 58, 318, 319, 323, 324–29
craftsmen, 282
criteria of historicity (see also historical-
      critical method), 4, 23, 30, 113,
      141, 167–84, 196, 200
  application of criteria, 6, 113, 167, 170,
      171, 173, 175–77, 180–83
  primary criteria, 168–77, 183
    coherence, criterion of, 175–77, 183,
      344
    discontinuity, criterion of, 47, 171–74,
      183, 344
    embarrassment, criterion of, 168–71,
      183, 199, 226, 280, 322, 344
    multiple attestation, criterion of, 118,

174–75, 183, 214, 218, 219–21, 317,
331, 375, 377
rejection and execution, criterion of,
177, 183, 336
secondary (dubious) criteria, 178–83
historical presumption, criterion of,
183
Palestinian environment, criterion of,
113, 180, 184, 344
tendencies of the developing Synoptic
tradition, criterion of, 132–33,
182, 184
traces of Aramaic, criterion of, 113,
128, 178–79, 184
poetic style, detection of, 113–14,
179
vividness of narration, criterion of,
180–82, 184
Cross Gospel, the, 116–17
crucifixion of Jesus, *see* death of Jesus
cry of dereliction, 170–71
Cynics, the, 341

Daniel, 63, 259, 262, 264
David, King, 24, 208, 214, 217, 226, 229
Davidic descent of Jesus, 46, 216–18, 229,
345, 350, 351
Day of Preparation, 386–89, 407
death (crucifixion) of Jesus, 5, 8, 9, 13, 27,
45, 46, 60–63, 66, 68, 90–92, 96,
97, 118, 124, 126, 134, 138, 140,
170–71, 177, 198, 209, 213, 217,
219, 222–23, 270, 381, 409
date, 45, 90, 373–75, 382, 386–402
day of week, 386–88
Delphi, 373
denial by Peter, 170
Dialogue with Trypho, 224
Diaspora Jews, *see* Hellenistic Jews
Didascalia apostolorum, 391
Dio, Cassius, 61, 373, 384
discontinuity, criterion of, 47, 171–74, 183,
344
dispute story, 174, 176, 181, 276–77
divorce, Jesus' prohibition of, 8, 9, 45–46,
132, 172, 175, 342–43
Domitian, Emperor, 56

earthly Jesus (*see also* historic Jesus;
historical Jesus; real Jesus), 25–26,
45, 48, 196
Ebionites, the, 116
Ecclesiastical History, the, 57, 58, 329
education, Jewish, at the time of Jesus,
271–78
education of Jesus, 8, 255, 350
adept use of Scripture, 269

knowledge of Hebrew, 255, 264, 266,
267, 276–78, 350
literate, 255–56, 267–78, 351
not student of scholar or rabbi, 8, 269,
278
training as carpenter, 273–75, 276, 350
Egerton Papyrus 2, 118–19, 130
Egypt, 23, 123, 207, 212, 213, 223, 224, 258,
376
calendar of, 374, 385
Eliade, Mircea, 5
Eliezer ben Hyrcanus, Rabbi, 97, 341
Elijah, 270, 340
Elisha, 63, 270
Elizabeth, 209, 212, 216
embarrassment, criterion of, 168–71, 183,
199, 226, 280, 322
Enlightenment, the, 25, 26, 198, 319
Epictetus, 341, 342
Epiphanius, 116, 121, 328
the "Epiphanian solution," 324, 329
eschatological discourse, 47–48
eschatology, 126, 134, 138, 221, 263
Essenes, the (*see also* Qumran), 265, 336–
39, 341–42, 344, 392–93
Ethiopian eunuch, the, 343
eucharist
narrative of, 396–97
words of, 43, 45, 175, 397–98
eunuchs, 342–44
Eusebius, 57, 58, 62, 68, 116, 329, 373
evangelists, the, 167, 182, 214, 221
Every Good Man Is Free, 337
existentialism, 27, 31, 199
extracanonical sayings of Jesus (*see also:*
agrapha; gospels, apocryphal), 112,
114
extracanonical gospels, *see* gospels,
apocryphal
Ezra, 262

faith (*see also* church teaching), 1, 2, 6, 13,
27–31, 41, 61, 141, 167, 196–200,
220, 222, 223, 319
family in ancient Mediterranean world,
316–17
family of Jesus, 205, 277
active in early Church, 350
children of Jesus, 335, 350
clashes with family, 181, 317, 335, 350
cousins of, 58, 318, 319, 323–29
extended family, 317
father of Jesus, *see* Joseph
firstborn son, Jesus as, 276, 277, 317, 350
Hegesippus on family of Jesus, 318,
329–30, 331, 334, 335
large size of, 279

mother of Jesus, *see* Mary
national restoration, interest in, 207, 277, 350
named after Jewish heroes, 207, 349–50
siblings of Jesus
  brothers of Jesus [*see also* James; Joses (Joseph); Jude(Judas); Simon], 57–58, 62, 210, 221, 279, 317, 322–32
  Epiphanian solution, 324, 329
  siblings, full, 318–19
  siblings, half, 318, 323–24
  siblings, step, 318, 323, 324
  sisters of Jesus, 279, 317, 322, 323, 334, 349
wife of Jesus, 332–35, 350
farewell discourses of John's Gospel, 136–37
farmers (*see also* peasants), 282, 351
fasting, Jesus' rejection of voluntary, 8, 9, 172
father of Jesus, *see* Joseph
Fathers of the Church, the (patristic Church), 65, 113, 121, 123, 198, 211, 281, 317
  apocryphal gospels, use of, 115–16
  citation of canonical gospels, 129, 131
  independent knowledge of Jesus, 94, 113
  on family of Jesus, 58, 318, 319
  Testimonium Flavianum, 60–62, 68
Festus, 57
fifteenth year of Tiberius Caesar, 374–75, 383–86, 407
flight into Egypt, 212, 213, 224, 376
form criticism (*see also* historical-critical method), 41, 132, 170, 220, 408
Four Gospels, the, *see* Gospels, canonical
Freud, Sigmund (Freudian), 29, 253, 254
fundamentalists, 196–97

Galilee, 8–10, 66, 174, 205, 207–8, 212–14, 224, 229, 253, 255, 268, 277, 279, 282–84, 345, 349–51, 391, 404
  as locus of Jesus' ministry, 41, 42, 267, 284, 407
  economics of, 279, 282
  fidelity to temple worship, 277, 349, 350
  languages spoken in, 257, 260–62, 267–68
  nationalism in, 207–8, 277, 349
Gallio, 373
Genesis Apocryphon, 264–65, 274
Gentiles, 62, 64–65, 180, 266, 270, 350, 383, 396
Gethsemane, 47, 407
gnosticism, 93, 116, 123, 125–30, 133, 134, 138, 139
gnostic literature (*see also: Gospel of Thomas, the Coptic*), 113, 123

Christian, 115, 123, 125–27, 130, 211
gnostic myth, 28, 125–27
Gospel of Peter, the, 116–18, 130, 141
Gospel of Philip, the, 123–24
Gospel of the Ebionites, the, 115–16
Gospel of the Egyptians, the, 122, 130
Gospel of the Hebrews, the, 115–16, 127
Gospel of the Nazarenes, the, 115–16
Gospel of Thomas, the Coptic (*see also* Oxyrhyncus Papyri), 118, 124–39
  and Oxyrhyncus Papyri, 125
  and synoptic order, 128, 129, 131–32, 137–38
  and the historical Jesus, 127, 140–41
  gnostic character, 125–30, 133–34, 138, 139
  gnostic myth implied, 125–26
Gospel of Truth, the, 123
gospels, apocryphal (*see also: Gospel of Peter; Gospel of Philip; Gospel of the Ebionites; Gospel of the Egyptians; Gospel of the Hebrews; Gospel of the Nazarenes; Gospel of Thomas; Gospel of Truth*), 22, 57, 113, 114–23, 130, 139, 140, 196, 253, 317
Gospels, canonical (the Four Gospels; *see also* Synoptic Gospels), 10, 12, 25–26, 41–45, 48, 64, 65, 67, 96, 112, 114, 116, 117, 122, 123, 128–31, 133, 134, 137, 139–41, 167–69, 175, 183, 196, 197, 209, 265–66, 284, 317, 373, 386
  as source for the historical Jesus, 42–43, 139–40, 167–84, 197
  harmonization/conflation of, 42, 115, 129–31, 137, 139, 197, 211, 408
Greece, 258, 385
Greek (*see also* Hellenization), 62, 116, 120, 125, 169, 178–79, 225, 265, 325–26
  as the language of Jesus, 255, 261–62, 266–68, 350
  as the language of Jesus' teaching, 261, 262, 267
  as the language of Palestine, 257–62, 264, 265

Hadrian, Emperor, 272, 273
harmonization/conflation, 42, 115, 129–31, 137, 139, 197, 211, 408
Hasmoneans, 258, 259, 267
Hebrew, 93, 179, 205, 265
  as the language of Jesus, 255, 264, 266, 267, 276–78, 350
  as the language of Palestine, 257, 261, 262–64
  at Qumran, 256, 262–63
  Hebrew names, 205, 206–7

Jesus literate in, 267, 276–78
resurgence in Palestine of, 258, 262–63
Hegesippus
　on the death of James, 58, 97
　on the family of Jesus, 318, 329–30, 331, 334, 335
Heidegger, Martin, 3, 5, 27
Hellenistic Jews (Diaspora Jews), 68, 93, 116, 267, 273
　and illegitimacy of Jesus, 223–24
　and virginal conception, 221–22
Hellenization, 207, 257, 258, 262, 264, 266, 284
　use of Greek in Jerusalem, 262, 267
　use of Greek in Palestine, 257, 258–62, 264
Helvidius, 331
Heraclitus, 28
Herod Antipas the Tetrarch, 66, 169, 180, 212, 282–84, 327–28, 340, 351, 372, 374, 383
Herod the Great, King, 115, 209, 211–13, 229, 258, 264, 282–83, 327–28, 349, 351, 375–77, 380–84, 407
　slaughter of the innocents by, 211
"hidden years," 10, 22, 230, 253, 254, 316, 351
high priest (*see also* priests), 97, 114
Hillel, 23, 335
historic (*geschichtlich*), 26–31, 196
historic Jesus (*see also* earthly Jesus; historical Jesus; real Jesus), 26–31, 196
historical (*historisch*), 26–31, 196
historical Jesus/Jesus of history (*see also* earthly Jesus, historic Jesus, real Jesus), 1, 2, 6, 21, 22, 24–31, 41, 42–43, 46–48, 92, 94, 96, 113, 115, 122–25, 126, 128, 139–40, 167–84, 175–77, 196–200, 205, 213, 223, 266, 274, 319
historical-critical method/historical research/scientific history, 2, 4–6, 9–11, 13, 21, 25, 27, 28, 30–31, 67, 116, 172, 197, 198, 220, 222, 254, 278
　limitations of ancient history, 23–24, 167, 208, 216, 220, 229, 395, 400
　objectivity in the quest for the historical Jesus, 3, 4–6
　presuppositions in the quest for the historical Jesus (*see also* biography, modern; certitude; criteria of historicity; form criticism; historical analogy; laws of nature; probability; redaction

criticism; sociology in NT exegesis), 5–6, 30–31
historical presumption, criterion of, 183
Hymn of the Pearl, 125
Hypothetica, 337

Ignatius of Antioch, 216
illegitimacy of Jesus, 96, 97, 222–30, 332
　Jesus as "Son of Mary," 225–27
Infancy Gospel of Thomas, 115, 254
Infancy Narratives, 41, 96, 115, 205–30, 317, 324, 372, 375, 393
　historical reliability of, 209–14, 221
Irenaeus, 139, 330–31, 378

Jairus, 345
James, 116
　as brother of Jesus, 322, 326–27, 334, 349
　death of, 56–57, 68, 97
　in Hegesippus, 58, 97, 329
　in Josephus, 57–59, 62, 68, 326–27
　in Paul, 58, 326
　patriarchal name, 207, 350
James, son of Zebedee, 327
Jeremiah, 339, 341
Jerome (*see also: Against Helvidius*), 60, 116, 121, 324, 328–29, 340, 372
Jerusalem (*see also* aristocracy; temple of Jerusalem), 9, 178, 212, 213, 218, 228, 259–62, 268, 278, 282, 345, 373, 396, 409
　as locus of Jesus' ministry, 41, 42, 350, 351, 392, 403–7, 408
　Hellenized, 258, 262, 267
　languages of, 258, 260–62, 267
Jesus
　as a Jew, 5, 8–9, 30, 96
　"un-Jewish" Jesus, 3, 10
　as alien to the 20th century, 200
　as Cynic philosopher, 5
　as embarrassing, 199
　as eschatological prophet, 3, 47, 176, 198, 214
　as historical/dehistoricized, 118, 134, 199
　as human, 10, 199, 254
　as layman, 9, 345–49, 351
　　hostility to priests/religious authority, 199, 346–47
　as magician/sorcerer, 3, 96, 198, 223, 224
　as marginal Jew, 6–9, 25, 56, 68, 339, 345, 382, 406, 407
　as rabbi, 276
　as revolutionary, 3, 177, 198, 199
　as unique, 172–74
　as wise man/wisdom teacher, 3, 47, 60–63, 68, 92, 176, 198

authority of, 8, 347, 348
birthplace of *(see* Bethlehem; Nazareth)
carpenter/woodworker, Jesus as *(see*
carpenter/woodworker)
chronology of *(see* chronology of Jesus'
life)
conception of *(see also* illegitimacy of
Jesus; virginal conception of
Jesus), 213
development of, 15, 22, 42, 253–54
education of *(see* education of Jesus)
events of the life of Jesus *(see specific
events)*
ministry of *(see* ministry of Jesus;
passion of Jesus; resurrection of
Jesus)
existence of, proving, 67, 96
family of *(see* family of Jesus)
languages spoken by *(see* languages
spoken by Jesus)
literacy of, 255–56, 267–78, 351
name of *(see* name of Jesus)
origins of, 227
Davidic descent of Jesus, 46, 216–18,
229, 345, 350, 351
not of priestly/levitical descent, 47,
218, 345, 348
of the tribe of Judah, 47, 218, 347–48
Qumran, contact with, 94
sayings of *(see* sayings of Jesus)
socioeconomic status of, 9, 255, 281–83,
347, 351
teachings of, 43, 62, 68, 225, 255, 262,
267, 268, 276, 278
divorce, prohibition of, 8, 9, 45–46,
132, 172, 175, 342–43
fasting, rejection of voluntary, 8, 9,
172
kingdom of God, 121, 125–27, 174–77
love of enemies, 47
missionaries, support of, 46
oaths, prohibition of, 47, 171–72
payment of tribute, on, 119, 120
religious observance, critique of
external, 199
temple, destruction of, 175
titles of *(see* Christ; King of the Jews;
Messiah; Son)
Jewish Antiquities, the, 56, 57–69, 208, 260,
274, 326, 336, 380, 383
Testimonium Flavianum, 59–69, 91, 139
Jewish War, *see* Revolt, First Jewish
Jewish War, the, 56–57, 59, 260, 336, 380,
388
Slavonic *Jewish War,* 57, 62
Jews *(see also* Hellenistic Jews; Palestinian

Jews), 60, 64–65, 66, 179, 227–28,
274–75
Joanna, 334
Job, targums on, 263–64
John, son of Zebedee, 327
John the Baptist, 7, 42, 93–94, 115, 168–69,
186, 209, 212, 216, 230, 374–75,
383, 386, 402, 407, 409
celibacy of, 339–41
in Josephus, 66, 69
Jordan River, 93, 120, 230, 339
Joseph, 58, 96, 124, 207, 209–11, 213, 224,
276, 277, 279, 280, 283, 317, 318
as putative father of Jesus, 214, 229, 317,
320, 322, 334, 349
giving Jesus descent from the house of
David, 216, 217, 320, 350
not mentioned during Jesus' ministry,
317, 350
patriarchal name, 207, 349–50
perpetual virgin, 318, 324
previous marriage, 324
Joseph of Arimathea, 346
Josephus *(see also: Against Apion; Jewish
Antiquities; Jewish War),* 7, 56–69,
91–93, 98, 139–40, 172, 177, 196,
206, 208, 220, 226, 259–61, 268,
273–75, 326–27, 331–32, 336–38,
344, 373–74, 380, 383, 388, 395
Joses (Joseph), brother of Jesus, 322, 327,
334, 349
patriarchal name, 207, 349–50
Joshua ben Ananias, 205
Joshua ben Gamala, 271–73
Joshua son of Nun, 205–6
Judah, Jesus of the tribe of, 47, 218, 348
Judaism at the time of Jesus, 93, 171–73,
218, 253–54, 278, 391
Judas, 170, 181
Jude (Judas), brother of Jesus, 322, 327,
330, 334, 349–50
patriarchal name, 207, 349–50
Judea, 66, 90, 93, 211–13, 229, 253, 255,
263, 267, 339, 351, 373, 391, 404
Julius Caesar, 23, 24
Justin Martyr, 216, 223, 224, 281

King, Martin Luther, Jr., 26
King of the Jews *(see also* Messiah), 65, 177
kingdom of God/Heaven, 121, 125–27,
174–77

languages spoken by Jesus *(see also* Greek;
Hebrew; Latin), 255–68
Aramaic, 255, 266–68, 349–50
as language of Jesus' teaching, 266,
268, 350–51

languages spoken in Palestine at the time of Jesus *(see also* Aramaic, Greek, Hebrew, Latin), 255–67
Last Supper, the *(see also* eucharist), 43, 46, 386–400
    character of the meal, 45, 389–94, 404
    date/day of week, 386–401
Latin, 62, 259
    as the language of Jesus, 258, 266
    as the language of Palestine, 256–58
Law of Moses, 94, 176, 177, 210, 221, 260, 275, 276, 350, 393, 409
laws of nature *(see also* historical-critical method), 254
Lazarus, 121, 122, 381
leper, healing of, 119, 120
Levites, 345, 349
Life of Moses, 208, 274
literacy
    in Palestine, 256, 274–76
    in the Greco-Roman world, 255–56, 274, 278
    Jesus as literate, 255–56, 267–78, 351
literary criticism in NT exegesis, 12, 181
liturgy, 113, 263, 391, 393, 394
L material, 43–44, 134–37, 175, 270
Lord's Prayer, the, 43
love of enemies, 47
Lucian of Samosata, 91, 92, 140, 177
Luther, Martin, 3, 11, 173, 319
Lysanias the Tetrarch, 374

Maccabees, 207, 258, 259
    Maccabean Revolt, the, 207, 258, 259, 262
Magi, the, 209, 211, 223, 375–76
Manual of Discipline, the, 256, 263
Marcus Aurelius, Emperor, 23
marginality, 6–9
    Jesus as a marginal Jew, 6–9, 25, 56, 68, 339, 345, 382, 406, 407
marriage, Jewish attitudes toward, 333–36
Mary, mother of Jesus, 96, 204, 209–30, 279, 317, 322–24, 334, 349
    as eyewitness source, 209–11, 221
    Jesus named "Son of Mary," 225–27
    legends about, 115
    name derived from Hebrew Miriam, 207, 229
    of priestly family, 216–17
    of the house of David, 216, 320
    other children, 318, 322–32
    perpetual virgin, 318, 319, 324
    purification in temple, 210
    surviving Jesus, 318, 350
    virginitas ante partum, 320
    virginitas post partum, 321–25

Mary, mother of James and Joses, 334–35
Mary Magdalene, 334, 388
Melchizedek, 218, 348
Messiah, 60, 64, 169, 206, 214, 216, 218–19, 229
    Jesus-who-is-called-Messiah, 57–59, 62, 68, 206
    messianic figures, 61
midrashim, 94, 96, 131, 208, 265
ministry of Jesus, 13, 22, 134, 183, 205, 211, 219, 220, 253, 264, 270, 276
    as prophetic mission, 9, 199, 344–45
    break with family, 181, 317, 335, 350
    debates with opponents, 264, 267, 276, 346–47, 351
    directed to Jews only, 46, 64, 345
    entourage of men and women, 344
    fellowship with outcasts, 13, 199, 342, 344
    Galilee as place of ministry, 41, 42, 267, 284, 407
    itinerant ministry, 8, 9, 43, 255, 267, 283
    Jerusalem and Judea, visits by Jesus to, 41, 42, 262, 267, 350, 351, 392, 403–8
    length of ministry, 42, 372, 374–75, 382, 383, 386, 401, 403–6, 409
    miracles *(see* miracles)
    order of events, 13, 41–42
    Nazareth, return to, 8, 225, 269–71
    temple, cleansing of, 175, 381, 382
    Twelve, choice of the, 181, 208
miracle story, 175, 181
miracles, 13, 41, 61–63, 67, 96, 119–21, 132, 170, 174, 181, 220, 225
Miriam, 207, 229
Mishna, the, 94–95, 97, 263, 272, 284
missionaries, Jesus and support of, 46
M material, 43–44, 134–37, 175
More, Thomas, 29, 332
Moses *(see also: Life of Moses),* 208
    celibacy of, 340–41
Moses, Books of, *see* Torah, the
mother of Jesus, *see* Mary, mother of Jesus
multiple attestation, criterion of, 118, 174–75, 183, 214, 218, 219–21, 317, 331, 375, 377
Murabba'at, 258, 265, 275
myth *(see also* gnostic myth), 128, 199, 208

Nag Hammadi, 123, 124
    literature at, 118, 123–39, 140
Nain, 284
name of Jesus, 205–7, 229
    as common, 206
    further identified as Christ, 206

"of Nazareth," 214, 229
named after Jewish hero, 207
nationalism, 180, 207–8, 277, 349, 350
Natural History, 337
Nazareth, 206, 212–16, 255, 261, 267, 277, 278, 281, 282, 284
   as Jesus' birthplace, 215–16, 228, 349, 407
   as obscure village, 224, 268
   economy of, 280, 282
   Jesus identified "of Nazareth," 214, 229
   Jesus raised in Nazareth, 212, 229, 230, 253, 255, 268, 350, 376
   Jesus' return to Nazareth, 8, 225, 269–71
   schooling at, 267, 271, 273, 274, 277
   size of, 277, 280, 282, 317
   synagogue at, 225–26, 267, 269, 277, 278, 351
Nero, Emperor, 21, 66, 89–91, 259
Nicodemus, 346–47
Nisan, month of, 385, 388–90, 394, 396, 397, 401–2, 407
Nixon, Richard, 21–22
nonaccession-year system, 385

oaths, prohibition of, 47, 171–72
objectivity, *see* historical-critical method
On the Contemplative Life, 337
oral tradition, 94, 119, 131, 137, 169–70, 181, 182, 211, 220, 281
Origen, 68, 96, 223–24
Oxyrhyncus Papyri *(see also: Gospel of Thomas*, the Coptic), 125, 131–32, 136

Palestine, 8, 11, 92, 178–80, 183, 199, 205, 207, 255–62, 264, 271, 277, 281, 316
Palestinian environment, criterion of, 113, 180, 184, 344
Palestinian Jews, 8, 9, 351
   and illegitimacy of Jesus, 223–24
   languages of, 255–67
   literacy of, 275–76
parables, 42, 124, 128, 129, 134–36, 138, 174, 175, 342, 349
paradox, 176
parenesis, 47
parousia, 134, 138, 169, 180
Passion Narratives, 66, 116, 171, 215, 372, 377, 383, 387, 396–401, 408
passion of Jesus, 64, 211
   arrest, 97, 407
   betrayal by Judas, 170, 181
   burial, 13, 46, 116, 387–88
   cry of dereliction, 170–71
   death [*see* death (crucifixion) of Jesus]

denial by Peter, 170
Gethsemane, prayer in, 47
guard at tomb, 117
Last Supper, the *(see* Last Supper)
Passover, Feast of, 42, 96, 381, 388–401, 403–9
   Passover day, 395, 396
   Passover meal, 390–401, 404–5
Passover lamb, the, 388–89, 392–93, 397
patristic Church/patristics, *see* Fathers of the Church
Paul, 45–47, 58, 118, 206, 217, 266, 326, 341, 373
   parallels to Synoptics, 46, 174, 175
   use of Jesus traditions, 45–47, 139
payment of tribute, Jesus on, 119, 120
peasants *(see also* farmers), 261, 262, 267, 268, 278–79, 280
   Jesus as peasant, 261, 278–80, 347, 350, 407
Peloponnesian War, History of the, 383
Peregrinus, 92
Pesher on Habakkuk, the, 256, 263
Peter, 23, 121, 170, 180, 181, 332
Pharisees, 9, 58, 59, 93, 114, 135, 259, 264, 266, 268, 275–77, 336, 342, 345–47, 350, 351, 387, 390
Philip the disciple, 207
Philip the Tetrarch, 327–28, 374
Philo of Alexandria *(see also: Every Good Man Is Free; Hypothetica; Life of Moses; On the Contemplative Life)*, 93, 172, 207, 208, 222, 268, 273, 274, 336–40, 343, 373, 395
Pilate, Pontius, 9, 25, 60–62, 65–66, 68, 90, 91, 140, 177, 180, 256, 257, 262, 267, 372–74, 382–84, 387, 389, 401, 407
Plato, 123
Pliny the Elder, 336–38
Pliny the Younger, 91, 92, 140
poetic style, 113–14, 128, 179, 262
Polybius, 383
poor, the, 282
Poppaea, 259
poverty of Jesus *(see* socioeconomic status of Jesus)
praetorium, 389
prayer, 43, 175
Prayer of Nabonidus, 264
presuppositions, *see* historical-critical method
priests *(see also* aristocracy, Jerusalem; Sadducees), 9, 58, 115, 181, 199, 216–17, 219, 259, 267, 345–49, 352, 387, 393

Jesus not of priestly/levitical descent, 47, 218, 345, 348

probability *(see also* historical-critical method), 130, 167–68, 183, 208, 229, 278, 395, 400

pronouncement story, 181

prophecy, 124, 169, 174

prophets
Christian, 43, 48, 169–70, 175
OT, 134, 199

Protevangelium Jacobi, 114, 130, 318, 319, 324

proverb, 124

Pseudepigrapha, 93, 268

purification in temple, 210

Pythagoras, 23

Q document, the, 43–44, 46, 119, 124, 129, 132, 134–37, 174, 175, 182, 340, 403

Qoheleth, 262

Quirinius, governor of Syria, 212–13, 384

Qumran *(see also* Essenes), 93–94, 172, 218, 345, 395
and Jesus, 94
and John the Baptist, 92–93, 339–40
calendar at, 391–93
resurgence of Hebrew and Aramaic at, 256, 259, 262–65

rabbinic literature, 93–98, 139, 140, 223, 225, 266, 268, 271–74, 340–41, 395

rabbis (rabbinic Judaism), 93, 95–96, 140, 206, 336

real Jesus *(see also* earthly Jesus; historic Jesus; historical Jesus), 21–26, 31, 196–98

redaction criticism *(see also* historical-critical method), 181, 220, 408

regnal years, 284–85

rejection and execution, criterion of, 177, 183, 336

religious observance, Jesus' critique of external, 199

resurrection of Jesus, 13, 26, 45, 61, 62, 66, 116, 118, 122, 126, 134, 197, 198, 213, 218–19, 221, 270
general resurrection, 346
parousia, 134, 138, 169, 180

Revolt, First Jewish (Jewish War), 58, 67, 257, 260–61, 272, 351

Revolt, Second Jewish *(see also* Bar Kochba), 257, 258, 272, 275

rich, the, 282, 347

Ricoeur, Paul, 5

ritual, 210

Romans, 8, 65, 170, 177, 217, 257, 261, 265, 266, 395
See also Latin

Rome, 46, 67, 89–92, 121, 177, 258–60, 268, 385

Sabbath, the, 350, 386–88, 407

sacrifice, 210

Sadducees *(see also* aristocracy, Jerusalem; priests), 57, 58, 346, 390–91

Salome, witness of the crucifixion, 334

salvation history, 134

Samaria, 258

Samaritan, parable of the Good, 349

Samaritans, 226, 228

Sanhedrin, the, 57, 65, 396, 407

sayings of Jesus, 42–43, 45–46, 112–13, 124–39, 174, 262
'abba', use of, 174, 175, 266
"amen, I say to you," use of, 174

schools, Jewish, *see* education, Jewish, at the time of Jesus

scribes, 58, 135, 256, 264, 267, 275, 276, 345–46, 350

Sebaste, 258

Second-Temple period of Judaism, 93, 95, 258

Secret Gospel of Mark, the, 118, 120–22, 130

Seleucid monarchs, 257, 258, 264

self-understanding of the individual in the ancient world, 316

Sepphoris, 283, 284, 351

Shammai, 23, 335

Simeon, 115, 209

Simeon ben Azzai, Rabbi, 97, 341

Simeon ben Shetah, 271–73

Simon, brother of Jesus, 322, 327, 334, 349
patriarchal name, 207, 349–50

sisters of Jesus, 279, 317, 322, 323, 334, 349

slaughter of the innocents by Herod the Great, 211

slaves, 227, 282, 336, 351

Slavonic *Jewish War,* 57, 62

socioeconomic status of Jesus, 9, 255, 281–83, 347, 351

sociology in NT exegesis, 9–11

Socrates, 23, 29

Solomon, 24, 63

Son (as title of Jesus), 126, 169

Son of David, 5, 213, 215–19, 320

Son of God, 5, 213, 222, 224, 320, 332

Son of Man, 172

Spirit, Holy, 96, 169, 213, 218, 221, 229, 341

Suetonius, 91–92, 140, 206, 261, 373, 384

Susanna, 334

symbol, 28, 199

synagogue, 225, 226, 265, 267, 269, 272, 273, 276–78, 350
synagogue rulers, 346
synchronism, Lucan, 377, 383–86
Synoptic Gospels, the, 43–47, 65, 93, 116–20, 122, 130–34, 138, 139, 174, 175, 182, 184, 346–47, 375, 382, 387, 389–402
use in Nag Hammadi literature, 124–29
Syria, 257, 258, 264

Tabernacles, Feast of, 227, 269, 392, 393
Tacitus, 7, 89–92, 140, 177, 196, 206, 282, 373, 384
Talmud, the, 94–98, 113, 196, 271–72, 283, 349
targums, 94, 131, 263–64, 265, 276
temple of Jerusalem, 58, 115, 175, 210, 213–15, 226, 263, 275, 276, 349, 350, 379–82, 388, 392–94, 400, 407
cleansing of, 175, 381, 382
prediction of destruction of, 175
tendencies of the developing Synoptic tradition, criterion of, 132–33, 182, 184
Tertullian, 330, 331
Testimonium Flavianum, see *Jewish Antiquities,* the
Thanksgiving Hymns, the, 256, 263
theologoumenon, 216–20, 229
Theophilus, 385
Therapeutae, the, 337–39, 341, 344
Thucydides, 383
Tiberias, 284
Tiberius, Emperor, 67, 90, 91, 140, 256
fifteenth year of, 374–75, 383–86, 407

Titus, Emperor, 56, 260–61
Torah, the (Books of Moses), 272–77
Tosefta, 94, 95
traces of Aramaic, criterion of, 113, 128, 178–79, 184
Trajan, Emperor, 92
trial of Jesus, 25, 65, 96–97, 177, 262, 267, 389
True Discourse, 223
Trypho, 223
Twelve, the, 181, 208, 210

usefulness of the quest for the historical Jesus, 3–4, 196, 199–200
as impetus for further research, 2, 13–14, 200
in ecumenism, 2
objections to the quest, 196–97

Vespasian, Emperor, 56, 58, 260
virginal conception of Jesus, 96, 211, 217, 220–22, 223, 229–30
virginitas ante partum, 320
virginitas post partum, 320–25
visitation, 216
vividness of narration, criterion of, 180–82, 184

War Scroll, the, 263
wife of Jesus, 333–35, 350
woodworker, *see* carpenter/woodworker

Zacchaeus, 282
Zechariah, 115, 209, 340, 374
Zeruiah, 226